# Peru

**Rob Rachowiecki**

D0095591

**LONELY PLANET PUBLICATIONS**
Melbourne · Oakland · London · Paris

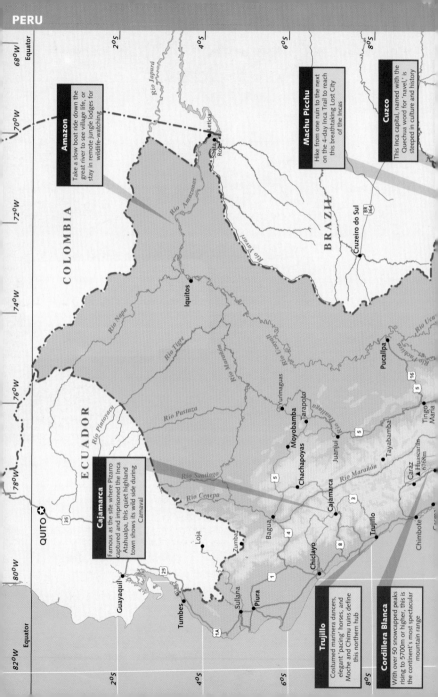

**Amazon**

Take a slow boat ride down the great river to see village life, or stay in remote jungle lodges for wildlife-watching

**Machu Picchu**

Hike from one ruin to the next on the 4-day Inca Trail to reach this breathtaking Lost City of the Incas

**Cuzco**

This Inca capital, named with the Quechua word for 'navel', is steeped in culture and history

**Cajamarca**

Famous as the site where Pizarro captured and imprisoned the Inca Atahualpa, this quiet highland town shows its wild side during Carnaval

**Trujillo**

Costumed marinera dancers, elegant 'pacing' horses, and Moche and Chimú ruins define this northern hub

**Cordillera Blanca**

With over 50 snowcapped peaks rising to 5700m or higher, this is the continent's most spectacular mountain range

Equator

2°S

4°S

6°S

8°S

68°W

70°W

72°W

74°W

76°W

78°W

80°W

82°W

COLOMBIA

ECUADOR

BRAZIL

QUITO

Guayaquil

Loja

Zumba

Tumbes

Sullana

Piura

Bagua

Chiclayo

Trujillo

Chimbote

Caraz

Huascarán
6768m

Cajamarca

Chachapoyas

Moyobamba

Yurimaguas

Tarapoto

Juanjuí

Tayabamba

Tingo
María

Pucallpa

Iquitos

Cruzeiro do Sul

Leticia

Santa
Rosa

Río Japurá

Río Amazonas

Río Napo

Río Tigre

Río Pastaza

Río Santiago

Río Cenepa

Río Pintoyacu

Río Marañón

Río Huallaga

Río Ucayali

Río Urubamba

Río Yavarí

Río Putumayo

35

25

1A

1

4

8

3

5

5

5

5

16

BR
364

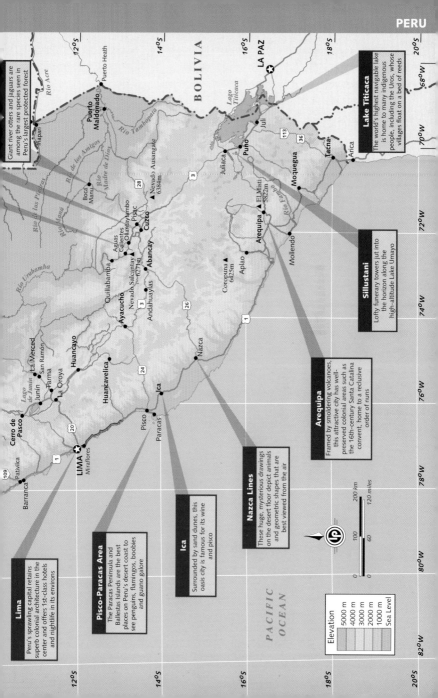

# PERU

**Lima**
Peru's sprawling capital retains superb colonial architecture in the center and offers 1st-class hotels and nightlife in its environs

**Pisco-Paracas Area**
The Paracas Peninsula and Ballestas Islands are the best places on Peru's desert coast to see penguins, flamingos, boobies and guano galore

**Ica**
Surrounded by sand dunes, this oasis city is famous for its wine and pisco

**Nazca Lines**
These huge, mysterious drawings on the desert floor depict animals and geometric shapes that are best viewed from the air

**Arequipa**
Framed by smoldering volcanoes, this attractive city has well-preserved colonial areas such as the 16th-century Santa Catalina convent, home to a reclusive order of nuns

**Sillustani**
Lofty funerary towers jut into the horizon along the high-altitude Lake Umayo

**Lake Titicaca**
The world's highest navigable lake is home to many indigenous people, including the Uros, whose villages float on a bed of reeds

Giant river otters and jaguars are among the rarest species seen in Peru's largest protected forest

PACIFIC OCEAN

BOLIVIA

LA PAZ

Elevation
5000 m
4000 m
3000 m
2000 m
1000 m
Sea Level

**Peru**
**4th edition** – March 2000
**First published** – July 1987

**Published by**
**Lonely Planet Publications Pty Ltd** A.C.N. 005 607 983
192 Burwood Rd, Hawthorn, Victoria 3122, Australia

**Lonely Planet Offices**
**Australia** PO Box 617, Hawthorn, Victoria 3122
**USA** 150 Linden St, Oakland, CA 94607
**UK** 10a Spring Place, London NW5 3BH
**France** 1 rue du Dahomey, 75011 Paris

**Photographs**
Mary Altier, Sandra Bao, Ken Eakin, Victor Englebert, Robert Fried,
Dave G Houser, Richard I'Anson, Craig Lovell, Rob Rachowiecki,
Kevin Schafer, Eric Wheater

**Illustrators**
Mark Butler, Hugh D'Andrade, Hayden Foell, Beth Grundvidg,
Jim Swanson, Wendy Yanagihara

Many of the images in this guide are available for licensing from
Lonely Planet Images.
email: lpi@lonelyplanet.com.au

**Front cover photograph**
Peruvian knitters (Richard I'Anson)

ISBN 0 86442 710 7

text © Rob Rachowiecki 2000
maps © Lonely Planet 2000
photos © photographers as indicated 2000

Printed by The Bookmaker International Ltd
Printed in China

# Contents

# THE SOUTH COAST 154

# THE AREQUIPA AREA 188

# THE LAKE TITICACA AREA 212

# THE CUZCO AREA 234

## THE CENTRAL HIGHLANDS                                    300

## THE NORTH COAST                                          334

## THE HUARAZ AREA                                          388

## ACROSS THE NORTHERN HIGHLANDS                            414

## THE AMAZON BASIN                                           439

## LANGUAGE                                                   491

## ACKNOWLEDGMENTS                                            499

## INDEX                                                      502

## MAP LEGEND                                                 512

# MAP INDEX

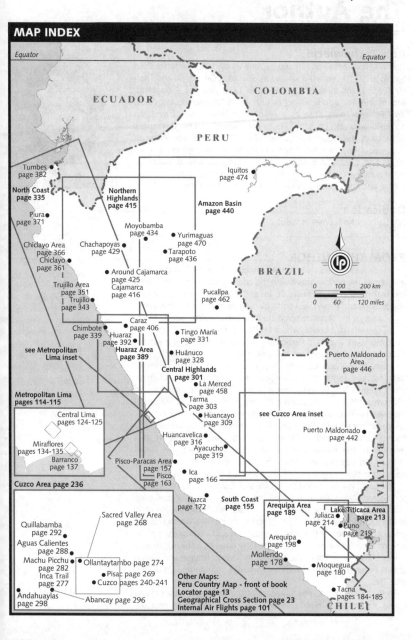

Equator

Equator

ECUADOR

COLOMBIA

PERU

Tumbes
page 382

North Coast
page 335

Piura
page 371

Chiclayo Area
page 366
Chiclayo
page 361

Trujillo Area
page 351
Trujillo
page 343

Chimbote
page 339

Northern
Highlands
page 415

Moyobamba
page 434

Chachapoyas
page 429

Around Cajamarca
page 425
Cajamarca
page 416

Caraz
page 406
Huaraz
page 392

Iquitos
page 474

Amazon Basin
page 440

Yurimaguas
page 470
Tarapoto
page 436

BRAZIL

Pucallpa
page 462

Tingo María
page 331

Huaraz Area
page 389

see Metropolitan
Lima inset

Metropolitan Lima
pages 114-115

Central Lima
pages 124-125

Miraflores
pages 134-135

Barranco
page 137

Cuzco Area page 236

Huánuco
page 328

Central Highlands
page 301

La Merced
page 458
Tarma
page 303

Huancayo
page 309

Huancavelica
page 316
Ayacucho
page 319

Pisco-Paracas Area
page 157
Pisco
page 163

Ica
page 166

Nazca
page 172

South Coast
page 155

0    100    200 km
0    60    120 miles

Puerto Maldonado
Area
page 446

see Cuzco Area inset

Puerto Maldonado
page 442

BOLIVIA

Arequipa Area
page 189

Lake Titicaca Area
page 213

Juliaca
page 214
Puno
page 219

Arequipa
page 198

Mollendo
page 178

Moquegua
page 180

Quillabamba
page 292

Aguas Calientes
page 288

Machu Picchu
page 282
Inca Trail
page 277

Andahuaylas
page 298

Sacred Valley Area
page 268

Ollantaytambo page 274

Pisac page 269
Cuzco pages 240-241

Abancay page 296

Other Maps:
Peru Country Map - front of book
Locator page 13
Geographical Cross Section page 23
Internal Air Flights page 101

Tacna
pages 184-185

CHILE

# The Author

### Rob Rachowiecki

Rob was born near London and became an avid traveler while still a teenager. He has visited countries as diverse as Greenland and Thailand. He spent most of the 1980s in Latin America – traveling, mountaineering and teaching English – and he now works in Peru and Ecuador part time as a leader for Wilderness Travel, an adventure-travel company. He is the author of Lonely Planet's *Ecuador & the Galápagos Islands*, *Costa Rica* and the US guide *Southwest*; he has contributed to LP's *South America on a shoestring* and *Central America on a shoestring*, as well as books by other publishers. When not traveling, he lives in Arizona with his wife, Cathy, and their three school-age children, Julia, Alison and David.

### Dedication

For Cathy, whom I met in Peru.

### FROM THE AUTHOR

Two recent extended visits to Peru enabled me to update this book and renew my enchantment with the country. Many people helped me with their own enthusiasm, insight, hospitality, conversations, suggestions and expertise. I particularly wish to thank the following.

As always, my first stop upon arrival in Lima was the South American Explorers' clubhouse, where I collected a wealth of information from members and staff. Particularly helpful were some of the managers and ex-managers of the club (Tim Currie, Bill Glick, Jane Letham, Rick Vecchio), who provided me with their personal, detailed, and carefully compiled notes on various parts of Peru. Photographer Ken Eakin was most helpful with both the capital and his comments about Ayacucho. Monica and Leo of La Posada del Parque were unfailingly helpful and concerned hosts during my visit, which coincided with the tragically early death of my brother. My friends Fernando and Nellie, of Hostal Iquique, took me in as a member of the family, and Fernando cooked memorably! David Wroughton also was very hospitable, and Rafael Belmonte took me on an impressive nighttime drive around the outskirts of Lima.

In Cuzco, my old friend and guide José Correa drove me all over the Sacred Valley and introduced me to some new places. Carlos and Tecchi Milla, long-term leaders in the local tourism industry, kindly allowed me to be the first guest in their hotel, which was still under construction at the time. (Carlos, José and I also spent a night ensuring the future prosperity of the new hotel by imbibing as only Cuzqueños can, but that's another story.) My colleague and Cuzco expert Peter Frost helped with an up-to-the-minute update on the Inca Trail.

In Puno, Captain Carlos Saavedra of the Yavari permitted me to spend a memorable night on the oldest motorized vessel on Lake

Titicaca. Martha Giraldo Alayza cordially gave me her apartment to house-sit while she was traveling.

Christopher James generously provided his copious knowledge of surfing along the Pacific coast. María Isabel Espinal Tapía of Tourism Information: Sipán, in Chiclayo, was unselfish with both her information and the permanent loan of her useful Auto Club book; Rosa Colmenares in Chiclayo was also helpful. Michael White and Clara Luz Bravo D took me to some interesting new archaeological sites currently under investigation near Trujillo. Jeremy Flanagan of ProAves-Peru was a great source of information about the Sullana area. The Huarmey Tourist Authority continues to be an important resource.

In the Cordillera Blanca area, I thank Julio and Mauricio Olazo of Huaraz, Felipe Díaz of Carhuaz and Alberto Cafferata of Caraz for informational, logistical and practical help. Miguel Chiri Valle also helped with information about various highland areas. Irma Bolster of Cajamarca took me out for a good night and showed me some places I would otherwise have missed. Lucho Hurtado was his usual fun and hospitable self in Huancayo.

In the Amazon Basin, I thank Delta Airlines pilot Jay Taylor, who sent me a fascinating description of his river-boat trip from Pucallpa to Iquitos (over three days in cattle class instead of 30 minutes piloting a jet). Paul Wright of Amazon Tours and Cruises provided hospitality and background information in Iquitos, and Paul Jensen of Explorama was fun to talk to. Al Twiss and Lluis Dalmau of Tarapoto helped me with that region in their own different ways, and Rob Dover was contributive in Chachapoyas. In Puerto Maldonado, Tina Smith of the Bahuaja Lodge was very helpful, and Charlie Munn lent me a mosquito net when I needed one, as well as swiftly answering innumerable emails. Daniella Dowling taught me about giant-otter conservation and other issues while I was at the Sandoval Lake Lodge, and helped me with the giant-otter information in this book. Kurt Holle of Rainforest Expeditions provided much background information about lodges on the Río Tambopata.

I also extend a big thanks to Paul Cripps of Amazonas Explorer, who knows as much about river running in Peru as anyone, but who also keeps me in tune with other important issues, such as beer-drinking and biking. My LP colleague Maria Massolo, whom I serendipitously met in Trujillo, generously shared her information during a relaxing dinner – so nice to talk shop with another author and take a break from the research grind.

Finally, I hug my dear and wonderful children, chess player Julia, soccer player Alison and Lego player David, for understanding that Dad has to work in Peru for weeks on end; and my wife, Cathy, for keeping things on an even keel while I'm on the road. Thank you all.

Readers can contact me with comments, criticisms or updates at robrachow@earthlink.net, but I regret that I am unable to plan your trip for you! I appreciate receiving hotel prices, but please do so in US$ terms, and indicate whether you paid for a single, double or shared room. I do acknowledge all emails I receive.

# This Book

## FROM THE PUBLISHER

The 4th edition of Peru is brought to you by the publishing professionals of Lonely Planet's US office in fashionable Oakland, California. The following people deftly maneuvered a pile of electronic files to the bound beauty before you.

Editing and proofing were done by Wendy Taylor-Hall, China Williams and senior editor Tom Downs. Carolyn Hubbard, Erin Corrigan and Wendy Smith helped create and proof the Language chapter. Ken DellaPenta indexed the book.

The maps were drawn in a curious program called AutoCAD by Kimberly Moses, Darin Jensen and Ivy Feibelman with help from Andy Rebold, Colin Bishop, Connie Lock, Heather Haskell, Guphy, Monica Lepe, Patrick Phelan, Sean Brandt, Timothy Lohnes. Senior cartographers Tracey Croom and Amy Dennis, along with Alex Guilbert, oversaw this technological leap.

Ruth Askevold and Henia Miedzinski tag-teamed layout, Beca Lafore handled colorwraps, and Hayden Foell drew the chapter-end and boxed-text graphics. Rini Keagy designed the cover with production help from Simon Bracken. Senior designer Margaret Livingston and design manager Susan Rimerman supervised the design and production end of the project.

# Foreword

## ABOUT LONELY PLANET GUIDEBOOKS

The story begins with a classic travel adventure: Tony and Maureen Wheeler's 1972 journey across Europe and Asia to Australia. Useful information about the overland trail did not exist at that time, so Tony and Maureen published the first Lonely Planet guidebook to meet a growing need.

From a kitchen table, then from a tiny office in Melbourne (Australia), Lonely Planet has become the largest independent travel publisher in the world, an international company with offices in Melbourne, Oakland (USA), London (UK) and Paris (France).

Today Lonely Planet guidebooks cover the globe. There is an ever-growing list of books, and there's information in a variety of forms and media. Some things haven't changed. The main aim is still to help make it possible for adventurous travelers to get out there – to explore and better understand the world.

At Lonely Planet we believe travelers can make a positive contribution to the countries they visit – if they respect their host communities and spend their money wisely. Since 1986 a percentage of the income from each book has been donated to aid projects and human-rights campaigns.

**Updates** Lonely Planet thoroughly updates each guidebook as often as possible. This usually means there are around two years between editions, although for more unusual or more stable destinations the gap can be longer. Check the imprint page (following the color map at the beginning of the book) for publication dates.

Between editions, up-to-date information is available in two free newsletters – the paper *Planet Talk* and email *Comet* (to subscribe, contact any Lonely Planet office) – and on our website at www.lonelyplanet.com. The *Upgrades* section of the website covers a number of important and volatile destinations and is regularly updated by Lonely Planet authors. *Scoop* covers news and current affairs relevant to travelers. And, lastly, the *Thorn Tree* bulletin board and *Postcards* section of the site carry unverified, but fascinating, reports from travelers.

**Correspondence** The process of creating new editions begins with the letters, postcards and emails received from travelers. This correspondence often includes suggestions, criticisms and comments about the current editions. Interesting excerpts are immediately passed on via newsletters and the website, and everything goes to our authors to be verified when they're researching on the road. We're keen to get more feedback from organizations or individuals who represent communities visited by travelers.

Lonely Planet gathers information for everyone who's curious about the planet – and especially for those who explore it firsthand. Through guidebooks, phrasebooks, activity guides, maps, literature, newsletters, image library, TV series and website, we act as an information exchange for a worldwide community of travelers.

**Research** Authors aim to gather sufficient practical information to enable travelers to make informed choices and to make the mechanics of a journey run smoothly. They also research historical and cultural background to help enrich the travel experience and allow travelers to understand and respond appropriately to cultural and environmental issues.

Authors don't stay in every hotel because that would mean spending a couple of months in each medium-size city and, no, they don't eat at every restaurant because that would mean stretching belts beyond capacity. They do visit hotels and restaurants to check standards and prices, but feedback based on readers' direct experiences can be very helpful.

Many of our authors work undercover; others aren't so secretive. None of them accept freebies in exchange for positive write-ups. And none of our guidebooks contain any advertising.

**Production** Authors submit their raw manuscripts and maps to offices in Australia, the USA, the UK or France. Editors and cartographers – all experienced travelers themselves – then begin the process of assembling the pieces. When the book finally hits the shops, some things are already out of date, we start getting feedback from readers and the process begins again....

---

## WARNING & REQUEST

Things change – prices go up, schedules change, good places go bad and bad places go bankrupt – nothing stays the same. So, if you find things better or worse, recently opened or long since closed, please tell us and help make the next edition even more accurate and useful. We genuinely value all the feedback we receive. Julie Young coordinates a well-traveled team that reads and acknowledges every letter, postcard and email and ensures that every morsel of information finds its way to the appropriate authors, editors and cartographers for verification.

Everyone who writes to us will find their name in the next edition of the appropriate guidebook. They will also receive the latest issue of *Planet Talk*, our quarterly printed newsletter, or *Comet*, our monthly email newsletter. Subscriptions to both newsletters are free. The very best contributions will be rewarded with a free guidebook.

Excerpts from your correspondence may appear in new editions of Lonely Planet guidebooks, the Lonely Planet website, *Planet Talk* or *Comet*, so please let us know if you *don't* want your letter published or your name acknowledged.

Send all correspondence to the Lonely Planet office closest to you:

**Australia:** PO Box 617, Hawthorn, Victoria 3122
**USA:** 150 Linden St, Oakland, CA 94607
**UK:** 10A Spring Place, London NW5 3BH
**France:** 1 rue du Dahomey, 75011 Paris

Or email us at: talk2us@lonelyplanet.com.au

**For news, views and updates, see our website: www.lonelyplanet.com**

## HOW TO USE A LONELY PLANET GUIDEBOOK

The best way to use a Lonely Planet guidebook is any way you choose. At Lonely Planet, we believe the most memorable travel experiences are often those that are unexpected, and the finest discoveries are those you make yourself. Guidebooks are not intended to be used as if they provided a detailed set of infallible instructions!

**Contents** All Lonely Planet guidebooks follow the same format. The Facts about the Country chapters or sections give background information ranging from history to weather. Facts for the Visitor gives practical information on issues like visas and health. Getting There & Away gives a brief starting point for researching travel to and from the destination. Getting Around gives an overview of the transport options available when you arrive.

The peculiar demands of each destination determine how subsequent chapters are broken up, but some things remain constant. We always start with background, then proceed to sights, places to stay, places to eat, entertainment, getting there and away, and getting around information – in that order.

**Heading Hierarchy** Lonely Planet headings are used in a strict hierarchical structure that can be visualized as a set of Russian dolls. Each heading (and its following text) is encompassed by any preceding heading that is higher on the hierarchical ladder.

**Entry Points** We do not assume guidebooks will be read from beginning to end, but that people will dip into them. The traditional entry points are the list of contents and the index. In addition, however, some books have a complete list of maps and an index map illustrating map coverage.

There may also be a color map that shows highlights. These highlights are dealt with in greater detail later in the book, along with planning questions. Each chapter covering a geographical region usually begins with a locator map and another list of highlights. Once you find something of interest in a list of highlights, turn to the index.

**Maps** Maps play a crucial role in Lonely Planet guidebooks and include a huge amount of information. A legend is printed on the back page. We seek to have complete consistency between maps and text, and to have every important place in the text captured on a map. Map key numbers usually start in the top left corner.

Although inclusion in a guidebook usually implies a recommendation, we cannot list every good place. Exclusion does not necessarily imply criticism. In fact, there are a number of reasons why we might exclude a place – sometimes it is simply inappropriate to encourage an influx of travelers.

# Introduction

Peru is a wonderful country! It will fascinate the tourist, the anthropologist and the zoologist equally, for the discerning visitor cannot fail to be impressed by its cultural and geographical variety or be excited by the travel possibilities this country offers.

Peru is frequently referred to as the 'land of the Incas,' yet it could equally be called the 'land of the Moche' (or the Chavín or the Wari). It is true that the Incas formed the greatest empire on the continent and left mysterious cities such as Machu Picchu, the magnificent ruins that can still be visited today. Less well known, but equally true, is that the Incas were the last in a long series of Peruvian civilizations spanning thousands of years, and that the ruins of many of these earlier civilizations can also be visited.

The Peruvian Andean mountains are arguably the most beautiful and accessible on the continent, and the Cordillera Blanca has become world famous among trekkers, hikers and mountaineers. There are several other ranges in Peru that are less visited but no less magnificent. Many of the precipitous glacier-clad mountains have peaks of over 6000m, and the high valleys are the haunts of a host of rarely seen animals.

Visitors may glimpse mammals such as the graceful vicuña or the inquisitive viscacha, and birds ranging from the tiny Andean hummingbird to the giant Andean condor. Soaring effortlessly on a wingspan that can exceed 3m and with a weight of more than 10kg, the condor is the largest flying bird in the world.

But the Peruvian Andes are not just the scene of remote wilderness. They are also home to millions of highland Indians who still speak their ancient tongues of Quechua or Aymara and preserve much of their traditional way of life. Town and village markets are thronged with herds of produce-laden llamas led by Indians wearing distinctive ponchos that protect against the climatic extremes. The larger cities preserve the

legacy of the Spanish conquistadors, and colonial churches and mansions covered with dazzling ornamentation can be visited.

The traveler could easily spend weeks or months in the Peruvian highlands and yet would be visiting only a small portion of the country. More than half of Peru's land area lies in the verdant Amazon Basin, where air or river is often the only means of transportation. Exotic plants and animals amaze and intrigue the observant visitor. The dense tropical rainforest on the eastern edges of the Andes houses the greatest variety of birds on earth – Peru, although less than twice the size of Texas, is home to more than twice the number of bird species in the entire North American continent. It is a naturalist's paradise and, because it has been so little studied, a giant natural laboratory.

The Andes and the Amazon are but two of Peru's three diverse geographical regions. The third is totally different, for the entire coastal strip of Peru is desert. Lima, the capital, is totally surrounded by bare rock and sand. Rivers from the Andes flow through this desert to the Pacific Ocean, creating small oases that have supported a variety of civilizations through the ages. To the north lie the ruins of Chan Chan, the greatest adobe city in the world and capital of the Chimu Empire. To the south are the mysterious Nazca Lines – giant stylized animal shapes etched into the desert many hundreds of years before the Spanish conquest. The etchings, as big as football fields, are visible only from the air. How and why the Nazca Lines were made remains shrouded in mystery – just one of the many fascinating features to encounter on a journey to that most intriguing of all Andean countries – Peru.

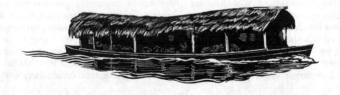

# Facts about Peru

## ARCHAEOLOGY & HISTORY

For many travelers, the first word that comes to mind when thinking of Peruvian history is 'Inca.' Certainly, the Inca civilization is the best known and most studied of all the pre-Columbian cultures of South America and the one that most travelers will experience more than any other. But the Incas are merely the tip of the archaeological iceberg. Peru had many pre-Columbian cultures, some preceding the Incas by many centuries. Peru's pre-Columbian history is the subject of debate and disagreement among scholars, so after reading the outline given here, you may want to do additional research and reach your own conclusions.

The concept that the numerous archaeological sites of Peru date from different eras and belonged to distinct cultures was first seriously proposed by EG Squier, an Englishman who traveled throughout Peru in the 1870s. Since then, archaeologists have slowly pieced together a chronological framework for the cultures of the Peruvian area. But it has been a difficult task – none of the cultures are known to have had any written language, and so their records lie entirely in archaeological excavation. Furthermore, as cultures succeeded one another, they tended to introduce new values and to erode the old, as the Spanish did after defeating the Inca nation. The one difference with the Spanish conquest is that they did produce a written record of their exploits that gives some insight into the Incas.

Peru is unequaled in South America for its archaeological wealth, and many archaeologists find Peru's ancient sites and cultures as exciting as those of Mexico, Egypt or the Mediterranean. For many travelers, learning about and visiting these centuries-old ruins is one of the highlights of their journey, and even visitors with little interest in archaeology usually enjoy visiting one or two of the main sites. With this in mind, this section provides a brief overview of archaeology in Peru.

Without written records, one of the main sources of information for archaeologists has been the realistic and expressive decoration found on the ceramics, textiles and other artifacts of Peru's pre-Columbian inhabitants. These relics often depict everyday life in detail, and so it is well worth your while to inspect many of these artifacts in Peru's museums. One of the best ways to visualize the overall cultural history is to visit the Museo de la Nación in Lima, where exhibits are labeled and displayed chronologically. Archaeologists have found that, with intensive study, they can differentiate between ceramic styles and date them to within the length of about a human lifetime, which is more precise than using radiocarbon dating.

The following names of sites and cultures set in bold type are described in greater detail in the travel sections. The subheadings below refer to periods named by some and recognized by many leading archaeologists. There are many texts, particularly older ones, that have different names for essentially the same time frame.

### Preceramic Period

Humans are relatively recent arrivals in the New World. Not long ago, it was thought that people spread throughout the Americas after migrating across the Bering Strait about 20,000 years ago. However, in 1986 there was a report in the British journal *Nature* claiming the discovery of human fossils in Brazil that dated back 32,000 years – still recent compared to the Old World, but many archaeologists still did not believe this. All human remains found in the Americas belong to *Homo sapiens sapiens*; there is no evidence of the presence of more primitive hominids such as are known from the Old World.

The first inhabitants of Peru were nomadic hunters and gatherers who roamed the country in loose-knit bands. They lived in caves, the oldest known of which is at Piki-machay in the department of Ayacucho. Human remains here date from about 14,000 years ago. They hunted fearsome animals, such as giant sloths, saber-toothed tigers and mastodons, that are long since extinct. The discovery of Paiján projectile points (stone arrowheads) in conjunction with mastodon bones indicates that the species survived as late as about 5000 BC.

From the earliest arrivals until about 4000 BC, cultural development mainly meant improving stone implements for hunting. People made fires, wore animal skins, and crafted simple tools and weapons from stone and bone. As their prey became extinct, they began hunting the animals we know today, such as deer, vicuña, guanaco and llamas. Hunting scenes were recorded in cave paintings at Lauricocha near Huánuco and Toquepala near Tacna. Domestication of the llama, alpaca and guinea pig began by 4000 BC, though some sources claim that Camelid domestication may have begun as early as 7000 BC.

By about 4000 BC (again, some sources claim earlier) people began planting seeds and learning how to improve crops by simple horticultural methods such as weeding. The coastal strip of Peru was then wetter than today's desert, and a number of small settlements were established, thus changing the status of the people from nomadic hunters and gatherers to settled agriculturists and fishermen. Several of these settlements have been excavated, with garbage mounds yielding the best information about life at that time. Although these places can be visited, there are no on-site museums or explanations, so looking at ancient garbage mounds is an activity well-suited for a professional archaeologist.

Some of the best-known sites are Huaca Prieta in the Chicama valley near Trujillo, Chilca and Asia, south of Lima. Chilca was inhabited around 4000 BC and the other two sites around 2000 BC. The inhabitants fished with nets or with bone hooks, sometimes using rafts, and collected food such as crabs and other shellfish, sea urchins, seabird eggs and even sea lions. Various crops were cultivated, including beans and cotton, which appeared early (at least by 3000 BC, though some sources claim earlier), as well as chilis, squashes and, by about 1400 BC, corn. Cotton was used to make clothing, mainly with the simple techniques of twining and later by weaving. Manioc (also called cassava) and sweet potatoes appeared on the coast early on, indicating trade links with the Amazon Basin. The coastal people lived in simple one-room dwellings, lined with stone in Huaca Prieta, or made from branches and reeds in Asia. Ceramics and metalwork were still unknown, although jewelry made of bone and shell has been found.

These early Peruvians built many structures for ceremonial or ritual purposes. One of the oldest – a raised platform facing the ocean and containing human burials – dates from about 4000 BC. It was found in the Supe valley near Barranca on the north central coast. More such temple platforms appeared on the coast in the third millennium BC, indicating a prosperity based on the rich marine life of the coast. Some of these platforms were decorated with painted mud friezes. Trade with Andean and Amazon regions was occurring, as evidenced by the use of the coca leaf for ritual purposes and the introduction of exotic rainforest bird feathers.

Roughly contemporary with the later Preceramic Period coastal settlements was the enigmatic site of Kotosh near Huánuco – one of the earliest ruins in highland Peru. Little is known about the people who lived there, but their buildings were the most developed for that period, and pottery fragments found here predate those found in other parts of Peru by several hundred years. Various forms of the Andean staple, the potato, began to be domesticated around 3000 BC.

## Initial Period

Also called the Lower Formative Period, this extends very roughly from 2000 to 1000 BC and is known originally from remains found in the Virú valley and Guañape area, about 50km south of Trujillo on the north coast. More recently, large ceremonial temples from this period have been discovered in the Rímac valley above Lima and various other coastal sites. Funerary offerings were associated with many of them. During this time, ceramics developed from basic undecorated pots to sculpted, incised and simply colored pots of high quality. Weaving, fishing and horticulture also improved, the latter particularly through the development of irrigation. Toward the end of this time, agricultural terraces appeared in the highlands.

## Early Horizon

Lasting roughly from 1000 to 300 BC (archaeologists' opinions differ by several centuries as to the earlier date), this period has also been called the Chavín Horizon, after the site of Chavín de Huántar, 40km east of Huaraz. It is termed a 'horizon' because artistic and religious phenomena appeared, perhaps independently, within several cultures in different places at about the same time, indicating some kind of interchange of ideas and increasing cultural complexity. This horizon extended throughout much of the northern and central highlands and the northern and southern coast.

The salient feature of the Chavín influence is the repeated representation of a stylized jaguar face with clearly religious overtones, and so the Chavín is often termed a jaguar-worshipping cult. Other animal faces, some mythical, as well as human faces are also found. Most importantly, this period represents the greatest early development in weaving, pottery, agriculture, religion and architecture – in a word, culture. During this time, gold working developed for the first time on the northern coast. Many archaeologists see the Early Horizon as the most important cultural development of pre-Columbian Peru.

## Early Intermediate Period

Around 300 BC, the Chavín style gradually and inexplicably began to lose its unifying influence. Over the next 500 years, several cultures became locally important, but none were individually outstanding or widespread. The best known are the Salinar culture of the Chicama valley area near Trujillo and the Paracas Necropolis south of Lima. Salinar ceramics show advanced firing techniques, while the textiles of the Paracas Necropolis are markedly improved and different from the earlier Paracas Cavernas; these cotton and wool textiles are considered to be the finest pre-Columbian textiles to have been produced in any region in the Americas.

From about 100 AD to 700 AD – formerly known as either the Florescent or Classic Period – pottery, metalwork and weaving reached a pinnacle of technological development in several regions throughout Peru. Two distinct cultures of this period are particularly noted for their exceptional pottery. The Moche from the Trujillo area produced pottery from molds, and the Nazca people from the south coast introduced polychrome techniques. These cultures recorded their ways of life in intricate detail on their ceramics, providing archaeologists with an invaluable reference tool. Many of Peru's main museums have good collections of Nazca and Moche pottery.

These two cultures also left some interesting sites that are worth visiting. The Moche built massive platform mounds (popularly called 'pyramids') such as the Temples of the Sun and Moon near Trujillo and at Sipán near Chiclayo. Sipán contains a series of tombs that have been under excavation since 1987 and are considered the most important archaeological discovery in South America in many decades. The Temple of the Moon is currently under excavation, and amazing friezes have recently been uncovered. The Nazca made enigmatic giant designs in the desert. They are known as the Nazca Lines, and are best appreciated from one of the many overflights in small airplanes available in the town of Nazca.

Other cultures of importance during this period include the Lima culture, with its main site 30km south of Lima at Pachacamac; the Recuay culture, whose ceramics can be seen in the regional museum at Huaraz; and the Cajamarca, Kuélap, Gallinazo and Tiahuanaco cultures.

## Middle Horizon

Most of the latter half of the sixth century was marked by a catastrophic drought along the coast, contributing to the demise of the Moche. From 600 AD to about 1000 AD, the Wari emerged as the first expansionist peoples known in the Andes. The ruin of their capital is the highland city of Wari (also spelled Huari), found about 25km north of Ayacucho. Unlike the earlier Chavín, expansion was not limited to the diffusion of artistic and religious influence. The Wari were vigorous military conquerors who built and maintained important outposts throughout much of Peru. These included Pikillacta near Cuzco, Cajamarquilla near Lima, Wilcahuaín near Huaraz, Wariwillka near Huancayo, Wiracochapampa near Huamachuco and Los Paredones near Cajamarca. The Wari was the first strongly militaristic and urban culture of Peru. Also, it was influenced by the Tiahuanaco religion from the Lake Titicaca region.

The Wari attempted to subdue the cultures they conquered by emphasizing their own values and suppressing local oral traditions and regional self-expression. Thus from about 700 AD to 1100 AD, Wari influence is noted in the art, technology and architecture of most areas in Peru. More significantly, from an archaeologist's point of view, any local oral traditions that may have existed were discouraged by the conquerors and slowly forgotten. With no written language and no oral traditions, archaeologists must rely entirely on the examination of excavated artifacts to gain an idea of what life was like in early Peruvian cultures. The Wari too, in their turn, were replaced by other cultures.

## Late Intermediate Period

Because of their cultural dominance and oppression, it is not surprising that the Wari were generally not welcomed, despite their improvements in urban development and organization. By about 1000 AD, they had been replaced, not by a new conquering force, but by individual groups in their local areas. These separate regional states thrived for the next 400 years, the best known being the Chimu kingdom in the Trujillo area. Its capital was the huge adobe city of Chan Chan, often referred to as the largest adobe city in the world. Chan Chan can easily be visited from Trujillo.

Roughly contemporary with the Chimu was the Chachapoyas culture of the Utcubamba River basin in the department of Amazonas. Its people built Kuélap, one of the most intriguing and significant of the highland ruins, and reasonably accessible to the traveler. Also contemporary with the Chimu were the Chancay people from the Chancay valley just north of Lima. The best collection of Chancay artifacts is at the excellent Museo Amano in Lima. Further south was the Ica-Chincha culture, whose artifacts can be seen in the Ica's Museo Regional. There were also several small altiplano kingdoms that lived near Lake Titicaca and frequently warred with one another. They left impressive *chullpas* (circular funerary towers) dotting the bleak landscape – the best are to be seen at Sillustani. Other groups included the Chanka who lived in the Ayacucho-Apurímac area and, of course, the early Incas, the predecessors of the greatest pre-Columbian empire on the continent.

## The Inca Empire

The Inca Empire, for all its greatness, existed for barely a century. Prior to 1430, the Incas, whose emperor was believed to have descended from the sun, ruled over only the valley of Cuzco. The Cuzqueños and the Chankas were at war for some time, eventually culminating in the 1430s with a major victory for the Cuzqueños. This marked the beginning of a remarkably rapid military expansion. The Inca Empire, known as Tahuantinsuyo (the Land of Four Quarters), conquered and incorporated the cultures mentioned in the preceding section, as well as most of the cultures in the area stretching from southern Colombia to central Chile (including also the Andean regions of Bolivia and northern Argentina). Like the Wari before them, the Incas imposed their way of life on the peoples they conquered. Thus when the Spanish arrived, most of the

Andean area had been politically unified by Inca rule. This unification did not extend completely to many everyday facets of life of the peoples of the Inca Empire, and many of them felt some resentment toward the Inca leaders. This was a significant factor in the success of the Spaniards during their invasion of the New World.

## The Spanish Invasion

After Columbus' first landfall in 1492, the Spanish rapidly invaded and conquered the Caribbean islands and the Aztec and Mayan cultures of Mexico and Central America. By the 1520s, the conquistadors were ready to turn their attentions to the South American continent. In 1522, Pascual de Andagoya sailed as far as the Río San Juan in Colombia. Two years later, Francisco Pizarro headed south, but was unable to reach even the San Juan. In November 1526, Pizarro again headed south, and by 1528, he had explored as far as the Río Santa in Peru. He noted several coastal Inca settlements, became aware of the richness of the Inca Empire, and returned to Spain to raise money and recruit men. Pizarro's third expedition left Panamá late in 1530. He landed on the Ecuadorian coast and began to march overland toward Peru. In September 1532, Pizarro founded the first Spanish town in Peru, naming it San Miguel de Piura. He then marched inland into the heart of the Inca Empire. In November 1532, he reached Cajamarca, captured the Inca emperor, Atahualpa, and effectively put an end to the Inca Empire. (See the Cuzco and Across the Northern Highlands chapter for more details.)

## Colonial Peru

The Inca capital of Cuzco was of little use to the Spaniards, who were a seafaring people and needed a coastal capital to maintain communication with Spain. Accordingly, Pizarro founded Lima in 1535, and this became the capital of the Viceroyship of Peru, as the colony was named.

The next 30 years were a period of turmoil, with the Incas still fighting against their conquerors, and the conquistadors fighting among themselves for control of the rich colony. The conquistador Almagro was assassinated in 1538 and Francisco Pizarro suffered the same fate three years later. Manco Inca tried to regain control of the highlands and was almost successful in 1536, but a year later, he was forced to retreat to Vilcabamba in the jungle, where he was killed in 1544. Succeeding Incas were less defiant until 1572, when the Inca Tupac Amaru organized a rebellion in which he was defeated and executed by the Spaniards.

The next 200 years were relatively peaceful. Lima became the main political, social and commercial center of the Andean nations. Cuzco became a backwater, its main mark on the colonial period being the development of the Cuzco school of art, or the *Escuela Cuzqueña*, which uniquely blended Spanish and highland Indian influences. Escuela Cuzqueña canvases can be admired now in Lima's museums and in the many colonial churches that were built in Lima and the highlands during the 17th and 18th centuries.

The rulers of the colony were the Spanish-born viceroys appointed by the Spanish crown. Immigrants from Spain had the most prestigious positions, while Spaniards born in the colony were generally less important. This is how the Spanish crown was able to control its colonies.

*Mestizos* (people of mixed Indian-Spanish descent) came still further down on the social scale. Lowest of all were the Indians themselves, who were exploited and treated as *peones*, or expendable laborers, under the *encomienda* system. This resulted in the 1780 Indian uprising, led by the self-styled Inca, Tupac Amaru II. The uprising was quelled, and its leaders cruelly executed.

## Independence

By the early 19th century, the inhabitants of Spain's Latin American colonies were dissatisfied with the lack of freedom and high taxation imposed upon them by Spain. All of South America was ripe for revolt and independence. In Peru's case, important factors in the support of independence were the discovery and exploitation of a variety of rich mineral deposits, beginning with the seemingly inauspicious guano (seabird droppings) used for fertilizer.

For Peru, the change came from two directions. José de San Martín liberated Argentina and Chile, and in 1821, he entered Lima. That year, he formally proclaimed independence (in Huacho, a couple of hours' drive north of Lima). Meanwhile, Simón Bolívar had freed Venezuela and Colombia, and in 1822 sent Field Marshall Sucre to defeat the Ecuadorian royalists at the Battle of Pichincha, near Quito, Ecuador. San Martín and Bolívar met privately in Guayaquil, Ecuador. What transpired during that meeting still remains unknown, but as a result, San Martín left Latin America to live in France, and Bolívar and Sucre continued with the liberation of Peru. The two decisive battles for Peruvian independence were fought at Junín on August 6, 1824, and at Ayacucho on December 9. Peru became essentially an independent state, in spite of a few royalists who managed to hold out for more than a year in the Real Felipe fortress near Lima.

## Continued Conflicts

Unfortunately, independence didn't spell the end of warfare for Peru: A brief war

José de San Martín

broke out with Spain in 1866, which Peru won, and was followed shortly by a longer war with Chile from 1879 to 1883, which Chile won. The latter was over the nitrate-rich areas of the northern Atacama Desert and, as a result of the war, Chile annexed a large portion of coastal southern Peru. The area around Tacna was returned in 1929.

## Conflict with Ecuador

Peru went to war with Ecuador over a border dispute in 1941. A treaty drawn up at Rio de Janeiro in 1942 gave Peru jurisdiction over what are now the northern sections of the departments of Amazonas and Loreto, but Ecuador disputed this border, and armed skirmishes occurred between the two countries every few years. The brief war of 1995 was the worst in a couple of decades and cost the lives of several dozen soldiers on both sides, but made no change in the recognized boundaries. Both Peru and Ecuador claimed that the other country had started the conflict. Finally, in 1998, the border issue was resolved, with Peru granting Ecuador access to the Amazon and leaving a tiny area in Ecuador's control. Essentially, the 1942 border remains intact, and the two countries are now at peace, although this could change.

Simón Bolívar

## Recent Events

Peru's turbulence hasn't always been restricted to warfare. The world's worst soccer disaster on record occurred on May 24, 1964, in Lima. Over 300 soccer fans were killed and hundreds more were injured in a riot following a disputed referee call during an international match between Peru and Argentina. On May 31, 1971, a 7.7-magnitude earthquake in northern Peru killed about 70,000 people, the most deadly natural disaster ever to occur in the New World.

Over the last 30 years, Peru's government has been marked by a series of military dictatorships and coups, followed by a period of civilian rule, beginning in 1980 with the election of President Belaúnde Terry. He was replaced in the 1985 elections by Alán García Pérez. After two years of relative economic and political stability under García, the country began experiencing some of its worst economic and guerrilla problems in years.

The biggest economic problems of the late 1980s and early '90s were inflation, which exceeded an astonishing 10,000% at one stage, and the foreign debt, which the García government refused to acknowledge, leaving the country temporarily isolated from the international banking community and the International Monetary Fund. By the end of García's five-year term, the country was in economic and political chaos. García went into exile and is now living in a luxurious apartment in Paris. His return is sought by Peruvian authorities, who accuse him of embezzling millions of dollars.

Recent politics in Peru haven't been affected strictly by government. The Maoist group *Sendero Luminoso* (Shining Path) waged a terrorist campaign against the central government from 1980 until the early '90s, and the struggle claimed over 23,000 lives. The group was linked to drug cartels and was active mainly in the central part of the country, but the effects were often felt in Lima. Another, unrelated, and smaller guerrilla group, the Movimiento Revolucionario Tupac Amaru (MRTA), also waged a war against the government, but this conflict was more localized, beginning mainly in the Department of San Martín.

From the traveler's point of view, the most noteworthy changes from 1996 to 1999 are the bankruptcy and closure, one by one, of four of Peru's major airlines, culminating with AeroPerú shutting down in 1999, leaving Aero Continente as the only major domestic carrier, along with a handful of minor carriers. Also noteworthy is the proliferation of Internet cafés throughout the country.

## The Fujimori Years

The socioeconomic situation began to improve after the 1990 elections, when Alberto Fujimori, a 52-year-old son of Japanese immigrants, was elected president. He defeated the novelist Mario Vargas Llosa, a right-winger who advocated 'shock treatment' for Peru's ailing economy. Fujimori capitalized on fears that such treatment would mean more poverty and increased unemployment, and though his campaign promises of 'honesty and hard work' were vague, he was seen by many disillusioned voters as an alternative to the established parties and policies.

Fujimori took office in 1990, on Peru's Independence Day (July 28), for a five-year term. His immediate program of severe economic austerity resulted in unheard-of rises in the cost of food and other essentials, but it also allowed a liberal reformation of import/export, tax- and foreign-investment regulations, leading to international financial support. He favored gradual reforms, deregulation of government controls on prices and state monopolies, and a new currency pegged to the US dollar. Much of this was, in fact, similar to Vargas Llosa's proposed 'shock treatment.'

Hampered by the disastrous economic situation left by his predecessor, as well as terrorism, drug-trafficking and corruption at most levels of government, Fujimori took dramatic – and for many, alarming – action. In April 1992, he suspended the constitution and dissolved congress in an *auto-golpe* (self-coup). The perceived dictatorial, antidemocratic stance led to a suspension of foreign

Alberto Fujimori

aid, as well as outcry within Peruvian government circles. Nevertheless, Fujimori had the backing of the majority of the population and proceeded to catalyze the greatest improvements Peru had seen in many years.

Fortunately for Fujimori, the primary terrorist leaders were arrested during his presidency. In June 1992, the leader of the MRTA was captured and imprisoned. More importantly, Sendero Luminoso founder and leader Abimael Guzmán and several of his top lieutenants were captured in September 1992. This certainly helped keep Fujimori's huge popular support intact during the difficult months following the auto-golpe. In November 1992, a new, 80-seat unicameral congress was democratically elected (before the auto-golpe, it was a bicameral congress of 60 senators and 180 deputies), and Fujimori's party (Cambio 90/Nueva Mayoría) won a majority of the seats, paving the way to renewed international support and the opportunity to radically change Peru's political, economic and social problems.

In October 1993, a new constitution was approved. Among other things, it changed the law that a president could not run for two successive terms of office, allowing Fujimori to run for reelection. Other changes were the approval of a new, 120-member unicameral congress and the institution of the death penalty for terrorists. In June 1994, the arrest of the new acting head of the Sendero Luminoso, Moises Simón Limaco, was announced. This culminated in a series of arrests of top-level Senderistas, and by 1995, Sendero leaders were calling for an end to hostilities with the government. Certainly, terrorist activity had ceased to be a leading problem soon after Guzmán's arrest in 1992, and only a few remote areas were considered dangerous because of guerrilla warfare.

Meanwhile, inflation dropped from over 10,000% to under 20%, and the Peruvian currency began a period of stability that had not been seen in decades. Previously prohibitive import taxes were restructured, allowing the easy import of items such as buses and cars. Nevertheless, severe socioeconomic problems are still faced by much of the population. A 1996 census indicates that about 70% of the population lives at or below the poverty level.

In 1995, Fujimori ran for an unprecedented second term against former UN Secretary General Javier Pérez de Cuellar. Fujimori won handily, with 64% of the votes, and was reinaugurated on July 28, 1995. In his inauguration speech, Fujimori stated that with stabilization of the economy, his next objective was to combat poverty. He favored birth control and family planning, placing him at odds with the traditional Catholic Church, which wields significant power in the country.

The most memorable incident during Fujimori's second term was the infiltration of a Japanese Embassy reception in December 1996 by 14 Tupac Amaru members. Hundreds of prominent people were taken hostage; most were soon released, although 71 remained under captivity within the embassy until April 1997, when Peruvian commandos stormed the embassy, killing all the Tupac Amarus and releasing the hostages, one of whom died along with two soldiers. This action was criticized in that some of the Tupac Amaru members were repeatedly shot, even though they attempted to surrender.

The next elections are due in 2000, and it is still unclear whether Fujimori will run for a third term. His popularity is at a low ebb, partly because of his austere and authoritarian form of government, and partly because the Peruvian public, like any other, is ready for a change. In 1999, Ketin Vidal, the (now retired) police general who masterminded the 1992 capture of Sendero Luminoso leader Guzmán, formed the United Nation Movement, a new political party. Vidal, considered a hero among many Peruvians, is likely to announce his candidacy for president.

## GEOGRAPHY

Peru covers 1,285,215 sq km, is the third-largest country in South America, and is more than five times the size of Great Britain. Bounded on the north by Ecuador and Colombia, to the east by Brazil and Bolivia, to the south by Chile and to the west by the Pacific Ocean, Peru lies entirely within the tropics. Its northernmost point is only a few kilometers below the equator, and its southernmost point is just over 18° south.

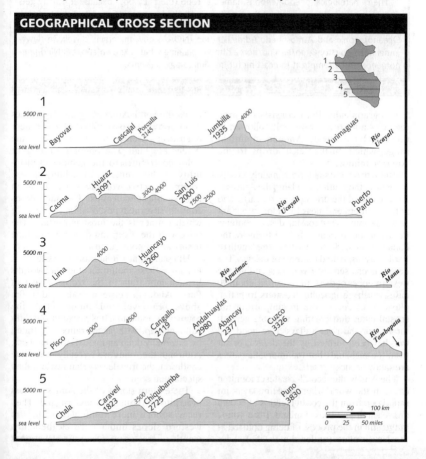

**GEOGRAPHICAL CROSS SECTION**

## El Niño

Every few years or so, the warm January-March ocean of the central Pacific are more pronounced and may flow for a longer period, causing the phenomenon El Niño. This is characterized by abnormally high oceanic temperatures in which much marine life (seaweeds, fishes) is unable to survive. This in turn creates problems for species, ranging from seabirds to human beings, that rely on the marine life. In addition, floods in both the coastal areas and highlands can be devastating, while other areas experience drought.

A particularly intense El Niño in 1982-83 flooded much of Peru's north coast and washed out many kilometers of the Carretera Panamericana. The El Niño of 1997-98 also caused the northern part of the Panamericana to be flooded, and bus journey times from Lima to the Ecuadorian border, normally under 24 hours, grew to four days during the worst months. See the boxed text 'Lago La Niña' in the North Coast chapter.

The climatological phenomenon is named El Niño (the baby boy) because it usually gets under way at year's end, or about the time the Christ child was born. For all its disruptiveness, El Niño is still far from being fully understood by climatologists. However, the US National Oceanographic and Atmospheric Administration (NOAA) now maintains a website (www .pmel.noaa.gov/toga-tao/el-nino/home.html) explaining what is known about El Niño phenomenon and attempts at forecasting future climatological events.

Geographically, Peru consists of three regions – a narrow coastal belt, followed to the east by the wide Andean mountain range, which, further east, drops to the Amazon rainforest.

The narrow coastal strip is mainly desert, merging at the southern end into the Atacama Desert, one of the driest places on earth, and at the northern end, near Ecuador, into mangrove swamps. This coastal desert contains Peru's major cities and its best highway, the Panamericana, which runs the entire length of Peru and is asphalted for most of the way. The desert is crossed by rivers descending the western slopes of the Andes, forming about 40 oases, which are agricultural centers. Irrigation plays an essential role in supporting the coastal cities and creating valuable agricultural land. The river valleys have good soil that has been formed by the deposit of silt from the highlands, but the intervalley areas are sandy or rocky desert.

The Andes, the second-greatest mountain chain in the world after the Himalayas, jut rapidly up from the coast. Heights of 6000m are reached just 100km inland. It's a young range, still in the process of being uplifted as the Nazca plate (under the Pacific) slides

under the South American plate. The Andes don't stop at the coast; 100km offshore there is an ocean trench that is as deep as the Andes are high. The ongoing process of uplift contributes to the geological instability of the range, and earthquakes are common. Active volcanoes are found in Peru's southern Andes. The mountains contain several types of mineral ores, of which copper is the most important. The soils, with the exception of a few montane basins, are of poor quality.

Huascarán, at 6768m above sea level, is Peru's highest mountain and the world's highest mountain in the tropics. Most of Peru's Andes lie between 3000m and 4000m above sea level and support half the country's population. It is a rugged and difficult landscape with jagged ranges separated by extremely deep and vertiginous canyons. Although the roads are typically in terrible condition, the traveler is often rewarded by spectacular scenery.

The eastern slopes of the Andes are less precipitous, though no less rugged. They receive much more rainfall than the dry western slopes and so are clothed in a mantle of green cloudforest. As elevation is lost, the cloudforest becomes the rainforest of the Amazon Basin. This region has been penetrated by few roads, and those that do exist go in for a short distance only. The traveler wishing to continue through the Amazon Basin to Colombia or Brazil must do so by river or air. Comparatively few people live in the Amazon Basin, although it covers well over half of the country's area. Oil is extracted from the rainforests of northeastern Peru. Soil quality is poor.

## CLIMATE

Peru's climate has two seasons – wet and dry – though the weather varies greatly depending on the geographical region. See the climate charts for specifics.

The desert coast is – as you'd expect – arid. During summer (January to March), the sky is often clear, and the weather tends to be hot and sticky. This is the time Peruvians go to the beach. During the rest of the year, *garúa* (a gray coastal mist) moves in and the sun is rarely seen. I find the weather on the coast rather depressing during most of the year. It doesn't feel like the tropics! The garúa is caused by the cold Humboldt current from the south Pacific moving up the coast and causing what little moisture there is to condense into a mist, rather like the condensation on the cold faucet in a warm bathtub. During the summer, warmer central Pacific currents come down from Ecuador and temporarily push back the colder Humboldt current, providing warmer temperatures for swimming and less mist (see the boxed text 'El Niño').

Moving inland, you soon rise above the coastal mist. Nazca, for example, is about 60km inland and 600m above sea level – high enough to avoid the garúa, so it's hot and sunny for most of the year. Generally, the western slopes of the Andes have weather like that of Nazca.

Entering the Andes proper, you begin experiencing the wet and dry seasons. If you're interested in trekking or hiking the Inca Trail to Machu Picchu, you'll probably want to go in the dry season, from May to September. At that altitude, nights can be cold, with occasional freezing temperatures in Cuzco (3326m above sea level), but days are filled with beautiful sunshine in the dry season. Because of this, the dry season in the Andes is known as summer and the warmer wet season is called winter. This leads to general confusion, for when it's summer on the coast, it's winter in the highlands and vice versa. Confused? It gets even worse when you listen to a *Limeño* (inhabitant of Lima)

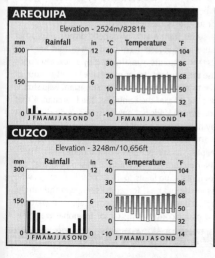

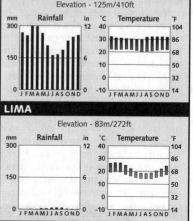

arguing with a *serrano* (sierra or mountain dweller) about whether it's summer or winter. More important is whether it is the wet or dry season. The wet season in the mountains is from October to May, but it usually doesn't get really wet until late January. Still, you can never tell for sure until you go!

Heading down the eastern slopes of the Andes, it gets wetter. The driest months are the same as in the highlands, but the wet season tends to be more pronounced. The wettest months are from January until April,

during which time roads on the eastern slopes of the Andes are often closed due to landslides or flooding. A similar weather pattern exists in the Amazon lowlands.

## ECOLOGY & ENVIRONMENT

The physiographic division of Peru into coastal desert, Andean highlands and the Amazon Basin clearly defines the ecological habitats of the country. The most important are the highland shrub forests and grasslands (called *páramos* in the north and

### Why Conserve the Rainforest?

The loss of tropical forests is a problem that has become acute in recent years. Deforestation is happening at such a rate that most of the world's tropical forests will have disappeared in the 21st century. With this in mind, two important questions arise: Why are habitats such as the tropical rainforests so important, and what can be done to prevent their loss?

Roughly half of the 1.6 million known species on earth live in tropical rainforests such as those found in Amazonia. Scientists predict that millions more species remain to be discovered, principally in the world's remaining rainforests, which have the greatest biodiversity of all the habitats known on the planet. This incredible array of plants and animals cannot exist unless the rainforest is protected; deforestation will result in countless extinctions.

Many medicines – ranging from anesthetics to antibiotics, from contraceptives to cures for illnesses such as heart diseases, malaria and others – have been extracted from rainforest flora. Countless medicinal uses of plants are known only to the indigenous inhabitants of the rainforest. Much of this knowledge is being lost as the various indigenous cultures are assimilated into the western way of life, or when tribal groups are destroyed by disease or genocide. Other pharmaceutical treasures could be locked up in tropical forests, unknown to anybody. They may never be discovered if these forests are destroyed.

Many tropical crops are monocultures that suffer from a lack of genetic diversity. In other words, all the plants are almost identical because agriculturists have bred strains that are high yielding, easy to harvest, taste good, etc. If these monocultures are attacked by a new disease or pest epidemic, they could be wiped out, because the resistant strains may have been bred out of the population. In the event of an epidemic, scientists could look for disease-resistant wild strains to breed into the commercially raised crops. But the smaller the rainforest, the less chance that scientists might find a resistant wild strain. Deforestation leads not only to species extinction, but also to the loss of the genetic diversity that may help species adapt to a changing world.

While biodiversity for aesthetic, medicinal and genetic reasons may be important to us, it is even more important to the indigenous peoples still surviving in tropical rainforests. These peoples rely on the rainforest to maintain their cultural identity and a way of life that has lasted for centuries. The accelerated pace of deforestation leads to a loss of tribal groups who are as unable to survive in a western world as we would be if forced to survive in the jungle.

Rainforests are important on a global scale because they moderate climatic patterns worldwide. The destruction of rainforests is a major contributing factor to global warming, *punas* in the central and south), the various kinds of cloudforests and rainforests in the Amazon Basin and the many rivers that are found flowing down both the Pacific and Atlantic slopes of the Andes.

Major economic activities include farming, grazing and logging, all of which cause serious environmental problems. Deforestation – of the highlands for firewood and of the rainforests for valuable hardwood, and of both to clear land for agricultural use – has led to severe erosion.

The problem of rainforest deforestation has currently caught the attention of the environmentally aware, but deforestation and overgrazing in the highlands, where many people live, is also a severe problem. The soil needs its protective cover of Andean woodlands and puna grasslands. With the ongoing removal of its protective cover, the soil's quality, never very high to begin with, is rapidly deteriorating as soil gets blown off the mountains or washed down the rivers. This has also led to

## Why Conserve the Rainforest?

which, if left unchecked, would lead to disastrous changes to our world. These include the melting of ice caps, causing rising ocean levels and the flooding of major coastal cities – many of which are only a scant few meters above sea level. Global warming would also make many of the world's 'breadbasket' regions unsuitable for crop production.

All these are good reasons why the rainforest and other habitats should be preserved, but the reality of the economic importance of forest exploitation by developing nations that own tropical forests must also be considered. It is undeniably true that the rainforest provides resources in the way of lumber, pastureland and possible mineral wealth, but this is a short-sighted view.

The long-term importance of the rainforest as a resource of biodiversity, genetic variation and pharmaceutical wealth is recognized both by countries that contain forest and by the other nations of the world, which would be affected by destruction of these rainforests. Efforts are now under way to show that the economic value of the standing rainforest is greater than the wealth realized by deforestation.

One way of making the tropical forest an economically productive resource without cutting it down is by protecting it in national parks and reserves and by making it accessible to tourists and travelers. This 'ecotourism' has become increasingly important for the economy of many tropical countries.

People visit the Amazon to see monkeys in the forest rather than cows in a pasture. The visitors spend money on hotels, transportation, tours, food and souvenirs. In addition, many people who spend time in the tropics become more understanding of the natural beauty within the forests and of the importance of preserving them. As a result, visitors return home and become goodwill ambassadors for tropical forests.

Other innovative projects for the sustainable development of tropical forests are being developed. The tagua nut is being harvested sustainably – this South American rainforest product is as hard as ivory and is used to carve ornaments and even to make buttons, which are bought by North American clothing manufacturers. Brazil nuts are also harvested. Debt-for-nature swaps have been initiated by conservation organizations. Iguana farms, orchid plantations, the export of tropical butterfly pupae, wickerwork from aerial roots and the seed harvesting of ornamental plants are some of the other projects that are being explored. Whatever the methods used to preserve the rainforests, it is essential that they are protected.

decreased water quality, particularly in the Amazon Basin, where silt-laden water is unable to support the microorganisms that are the basis of the food chain.

Other water-related problems are pollution from mine tailings in the highlands and from industrial waste and sewage along the coast. Because of sewage contamination, many of the beaches around Lima and other coastal cities have been declared unfit for swimming. Coastal pollution, combined with overfishing, is a serious threat to Peru's rich marine resources.

**Conservation** Protected areas often lack the fundamental infrastructure needed to conserve them fully and are subject to illegal hunting, fishing, logging or mining. The government simply doesn't have the money to hire enough rangers and buy necessary equipment to patrol the parks. Nevertheless, they do receive some measure of protection, and various international agencies – notably, The Nature Conservancy (TNC), Latin American Program, 1815 North Lynn St, Arlington, VA 22209, USA, and the many affiliates of the Worldwide Fund for Nature (called the World Wildlife Fund, WWF, in the USA) – contribute money and resources to help in conservation and local education projects. They work closely with Peruvian organizations such as Fundación Peruana para la Conservación de la Naturaleza, (☎ 241-2269, 446-3801, fax 446-9178, Apartado 18-1393, Lima). Readers who are interested in helping with conservation efforts can donate directly to Fundación Peruana para la Conservación de la Naturaleza, or through TNC or WWF, designating the money specifically for use in Peru.

Several other nonprofit conservation organizations in Peru have a more local approach, including the Asociación de Conservación para la Selva Sur (☎ 24-3408, ☎/fax 22-6392, acss@telser.com.pe, Avenida Sol 582, Cuzco) and Peru Verde (☎ 440-2022, 422-8114, postmaster@peruverde.com.pe, Manuel Bañon 461, San Isidro, Lima 27), both of which are co-owners of InkaNatura (see Organized Tours in the Getting Around chapter). Apart from ecotourism, these organizations also have pure conservation projects such as the one described in the accompanying boxed text 'The Unique Giant River Otter – An Endangered Species.' I visited the Giant River Otter project and was impressed (see Around Puerto Maldonado in the Amazon Basin chapter for more information). If you'd like to contribute to Giant River Otter (or other local conservation efforts), you are encouraged to contact the project coordinator, Daniella Dowling, at Peru Verde.

## FLORA & FAUNA

Peru's flora and fauna are some of the most diverse on earth. The western Amazon uplands (eastern Andean foothills falling into the upper Amazon Basin) is one of the world's most species-rich areas. It has been labeled as one of the world's 10 biodiversity 'hot spots,' where there are an unusually high number of different species combined with a particularly large risk of destruction and extinction. Ecologist Norman Myers estimates that only a third of the western Amazon uplands remain in their original state, and more is disappearing daily. Of Peru's 30,000 known species of vascular plants, over 20,000 have been identified in this region alone, and 25% are endemic. Thousands more species remain to be identified. The incredible variety of plants is correlated with the high biodiversity of the animals that live within the forests.

Terry Erwin of the Smithsonian Institution has spent much time in Amazon rainforests and reports that 3000 species of beetles were found in five different areas of rainforest – but each area was only 12m square! Erwin estimates that each species of tree in the rainforest supports over 400 unique species of animals – given the thousands of known tree species, this means that there are millions of species of animals living in the rainforest, many of them insects, and most unknown to science. Higher animals are also found in great numbers. Peru has about 1700 species of birds, the second-highest number for any country in the world. This is over twice the number found in any one of the continents of

## The Unique Giant River Otter – An Endangered Species

Gold mining, intensive fishing, and mismanaged tourism threaten the survival of one of the four most dominant predators in Latin America – the giant river otter. The international fur trade brought the giant otter to the brink of extinction: between 1950 and 1970, Peru alone exported more than 20,000 otter pelts. Otter carcasses rotted in the Peruvian lowlands while expensive pelts were shipped for sale in Italy, Germany and other countries. Listed in Appendix 1 of the Convention of International Trade of Endangered Species (CITES) as 'vulnerable,' today, both hunting and the international sale of giant-otter fur is prohibited by international law.

KEVIN SCHAFER

New threats to otter survival continue in the Tambopata-Candamo Reserved Zone, a system of rivers and lakes in Madre de Dios Province (see the Amazon Basin chapter). Untrained guides and uninformed tourists get too close to the otters and disturb them with loud, obnoxious behavior. Large groups of visitors drop litter in and around the lakes, fish near otter dens and chase otters in canoes. Canoes and catamarans on the lakes, especially on Lake Sandoval, sometimes trap the otters between two or more boats, distressing the otters, which may harm the development of young cubs.

The otters on the lakes of the Tambopata-Candamo Reserved Zone receive little protection from the threats of extinction. To ensure the survival of the giant otter, these lakes require scientific monitoring, local involvement, and tourism control. Since November 1998, the Otter Project – supported by select nongovernmental organizations, private tourist lodges, and tourist donations – employs local otter-monitoring teams to work on lakes in the Tambopata-Candamo Reserved Zone. The monitoring teams record specific baseline data about otters, otter habitats, and tourism activities on a daily basis.

The Otter Project provides an economic incentive to local communities to conserve and promote the conservation of otters in their natural habitat. Through active participation, the Otter Project educates both local residents and visiting tourists about wildlife conservation. The results of the Otter Project will guide long-term conservation strategies to protect generations of this unique species into the new millennium.

– Daniella Dowling

Europe, North America or Australia. Almost 400 species of mammals, almost 500 species of reptiles and amphibians and about 2000 species of fish have been identified.

Given this incredible diversity, I can no more than give a brief overview here. The flora and fauna are most conveniently described according to Peru's three main physiographic regions.

## Pacific Coastal Area

It's true you won't see much wildlife on the coastal desert compared to the Amazon Basin, but look out to sea and there is a wealth of birds and marine mammals. The single best place to see these is Reserva Nacional de Paracas (see Flora & Fauna in the South Coast chapter), although this wildlife is by no means limited to that particular reserve. A variety of small marine life and fish support huge populations of seabirds, such as pelicans, boobies, cormorants, gulls and frigate birds, as well as small populations of rare Humboldt penguins and Inca terns. Sea lion colonies are also found.

An ascent from the coast through Peru's western Andes takes you through dry and barren slopes. Except in the river valleys, which tend to be cultivated, there is not enough moisture for much wildlife. Occasional forests of cacti are seen, and birds of prey make a living off the lizards found in the dry areas and the rodents and small birds living near the rivers. It is not until the high Andes are reached that there is enough moisture to support much flora and, in turn, fauna.

## Andean Highlands

The páramo and puna are characteristic highland habitats. They are high-altitude shrubland and grasslands that act as the natural 'sponge' of the Andes, catching and gradually releasing much of the water that is eventually used by city dwellers in the highlands. The páramo covers much of Peru's northern highlands, continuing into Ecuador and beyond. It is characterized by a harsh climate, high levels of ultraviolet light and wet peaty soils. In the Huaraz area and on

into southern Peru, the soil and weather tend to be drier, and the highland areas are more grassy – this is the puna.

These highland habitats have a fairly limited flora dominated by hard grasses, cushion plants, small herbaceous plants, shrubs and dwarf trees. These have adapted well to the harsh environment, and consequently, the vegetation looks strange and interesting. Major adaptations include the development of small, thick leaves that are less susceptible to frost and curved leaves with heavy, waxy skins to reflect extreme solar radiation during cloudless days; the growth of a fine, hairy down as insulation on the plant's surface; the arrangement of leaves into a rosette to prevent them from shading one another during photosynthesis and to protect the delicate center of the plant; and the compacting of the plant so it grows close to the ground, where the temperature is more constant and the wind less strong. Thus many highland plants are characteristically small and compact, sometimes resembling a hard, waxy, green carpet, called *laretta*. Beware of the small, compact and hairy Andean cacti. They look like innocuous pads of cotton wool, but have very sharp spines.

Not all highland plants are so compacted, however. The giant *Espeletia*, members of the daisy family, are a weird sight as their loosely arranged stands float into view in a typical páramo mist. Farther south in the drier puna, are the bromeliads called *puyas* – plants with a rosette of spiky leaves growing out of a short trunk (see the Huaraz Area chapter for a description).

There are dense thickets of small trees, often *Polylepis* species, or *quinua* in Spanish, members of the rose family. With the Himalayan pines, they share the altitudinal world record for trees. They were once considerably more extensive, but fire and grazing have pushed them back into small pockets. Instead, spiky, resistant tussock grasses, locally called *ichu*, are commonly encountered. In order to manage the land for cattle, burning is carried out to encourage the growth of succulent young shoots. Burning does not favor older growth and,

Vicuña

Guanaco

combined with erosion caused by overgrazing, poses considerable threats to these fragile habitats.

Animals of the highlands include members of the South American Camelids – the llama, alpaca, guanaco and vicuña. The first two have been domesticated for thousands of years, while the latter two are found only in the wild. The llama is the largest of the four; used as a pack animal, it's capable of carrying up to 25kg. In some areas, it's used for meat (some restaurants in Puno serve it). Also, in remote areas, llamas are sheared for their coarse wool, of which they yield about 4kg every two years. The alpaca, a little smaller, is domesticated almost exclusively for its wool, which is finer than sheep's wool and is used preferentially for clothing in the highlands. An alpaca yields about 5kg

of wool during shearing, which is done every two years. Alpaca wool can be a variety of colors – white, brown, gray or black. The llama and alpaca can interbreed and are sometimes hard to distinguish. Generally, the alpaca has longer hair, and the llama has longer ears and a tail that sticks out. The guanaco looks like a smaller version of the llama but is rarely seen. It is usually an orange-brown color with a whitish belly.

The rare vicuña is the smallest of all, and though it has never been domesticated, it is sometimes caught and sheared for its wool, which is the finest in the world. In Inca times, it was used solely for making the Inca's clothes. In recent years, shearing this endangered animal was illegal, although since 1995, small numbers are again being legally sheared. It produces just 250g of wool

Alpaca

Llama

per shearing, which happens every three or four years, or about five times during the life of the animal. Although vicuña wool is not yet produced commercially, a 1995 report estimated that a coat made of vicuña wool would cost about US$5000. Because of this high value, vicuñas are both endangered and protected.

Other animals of the Peruvian Andean highlands include foxes, pumas, white-tailed deer and viscachas. Viscachas are commonly spotted highland mammals that look like a cross between a large squirrel and a rabbit. They live among boulders on rocky slopes, and even next to the Machu Picchu ruins.

Of the birds, the most well known, but not necessarily frequently sighted, is the Andean condor, often called the largest flying bird in the world. With a wingspan of 3m and a weight of 10kg, it's magnificent. Condors are recognized by their flat, gliding flight with fingered wing tips (formed by spread primary feathers), silvery patches on the upper wing surface (seen when the bird wheels in the sun), a white neck ruff, and unfeathered, flesh-colored head (binoculars help). Otherwise, the bird is black.

Other birds of the highlands include the carunculated caracara, a large member of the falcon family. It has bright orange-red facial skin, yellowish bill and legs, white thighs and underparts, and is otherwise black. The Andean lapwing is common and is unmistakable with its harsh and noisy call; reddish eyes, legs and bill; and brown-white-black striped wing pattern, which is particularly noticeable in flight.

Most towns are host to the ubiquitous rufous-collared sparrow, which has a chestnut collar on the back of the neck and replaces the well-known and similarly sized house sparrow of Europe, Asia, Australia and North America.

Other noteworthy birds in the Andean highlands include the torrent duck, which lives only in the whitewater areas of rivers, swimming submerged with just its head poking out of the water. Three species of flamingo inhabit puna lakes in the south of the country. The Andean flicker is a ground-dwelling puna woodpecker – there aren't

any trees to peck! For the interested observer, there are many other birds in Peru.

## Amazon Lowlands

Descending the eastern Andean slopes into the western Amazon uplands, the scenery is rugged and remote. Here are the little-known tropical cloudforests, so named because they trap (and help create) clouds that drench the forest in a fine mist, allowing some delicate forms of plant life to survive. Cloudforest trees are adapted to steep rocky soils and a harsh climate. They are characterized by low, gnarled growth, dense small-leafed canopies and moss-covered branches supporting a host of plants, such as orchids, ferns, bromeliads and many others. These aerial plants, which gather their moisture and some nutrients without ground roots, are collectively termed epiphytes.

### Hummingbirds

For many visitors to Peru, the diminutive hummingbirds are the most delightful birds to observe. About 120 species have been recorded from Peru, and their exquisite beauty is matched by their extravagant names, such as 'green-tailed goldenthroat,' 'spangled coquette,' 'fawn-breasted brilliant' and 'amethyst-throated sunangel.'

Hummingbirds are capable of beating their wings in a figure-eight pattern up to 80 times a second, thus producing the typical hum for which they are named. This exceptionally rapid wingbeat enables them to hover in place when feeding on nectar, or even to fly backward. These tiny birds must feed frequently to gain the energy needed to keep them flying. Species like the Andean hillstar, living in the páramo, have evolved an amazing strategy to survive a cold night. They go into a state of torpor, which is like a nightly hibernation, by lowering their body temperature by about 25°C, thus lowering their metabolism drastically.

The dense vegetation at all levels of this forest gives it a mysterious and delicate fairy-tale appearance. It is the home of such rare species as the woolly tapir, the Andean spectacled bear and the puma. Many of Peru's endemic birds are found here, and new species of birds are regularly discovered every few years. Who knows what other creatures new to science might dwell here? Apart from being part of a biodiversity hot spot, as discussed earlier in Flora & Fauna, this habitat is important as a source of freshwater and for controlling erosion.

Finally, the Amazon rainforest is reached, with its untold wealth of flora and fauna. A short walk into a tropical forest will reveal that it is very different from the temperate forests that many North Americans and Europeans may be used to. Temperate forests have little variety. It's pines, pines, and more pines, or interminable acres of oak, beech and birch. Tropical forests, on the other hand, have great variety. If you stand in one spot and look around, you see scores of different species of trees, but you often have to walk several hundred meters to find another example of any particular species.

Visitors to the rainforest are often bewildered by the huge variety of plants and animals found there. With the exception of mammals and birds, there are few useful field guides to what you might see there. If you are particularly interested in learning about the fantastic flora and fauna, it is worth investing in a guided tour – not that any guide will be able to answer all your questions!

One thing that often astounds visitors is the sheer immensity of some trees. A good example is the ceiba tree (also called the kapok), which has huge flattened supports, or buttresses, around its base and may easily reach five or more meters across. The smooth gray trunk often grows straight up for 50m before the branches are reached. These spread out into a huge crown with a slightly flattened appearance – the shape is distinctive, and the tree is often the last to be logged in a ranching area. When you see a huge, buttressed, and flattened looking tree in a pasture in the Amazon lowlands, it very often is a ceiba.

Some rainforest trees have strange roots – looking like props or stilts – supporting them. These trees are most frequently found where periodic floods occur – the stilt roots are thought to play a role in keeping the tree upright during the inundation. Rainforest palms, in particular, are among the trees that have these kinds of roots.

In areas that have been cleared (often naturally, as by a flash flood or by a gap created by an ancient forest giant falling during a storm) various fast-growing pioneer species appear. These may grow several meters a year in areas where abundant sunlight is suddenly available. Some of the most common and easily recognized of these are the genus *Cecropia*, found in recently cleared areas, such as riverbanks. Their gray trunks are often circled by ridges at intervals of a few centimeters, but they are otherwise fairly smooth, and their branches form a canopy at the top of, rather than all along, the trunk. The leaves are very large and palmate (like a human hand), with the underside a much lighter green than the top – particularly noticeable when winds make the leaves display alternately light and dark green shades in a chaotic manner.

Visitors to protected areas of the Amazon lowlands may see several species of monkeys, including the howler, spider, woolly, titi, capuchin and squirrel monkeys, as well as tamarins and marmosets. The monkeys of the New World (the Platyrrhini) differ markedly from the monkeys of the Old World (the Catarrhini), which include humans. New World monkeys have been studied comparatively little, and their names are still under constant revision.

## National Parks

Peru has several dozen protected areas called *parques nacionales* (national parks), *reservas nacionales* (national reserves), *santuarios nacionales* (national sanctuaries), *santuarios historicos* (historical sanctuaries), *zonas reservadas* (reserve zones) and *reservas forestales* (forest reserves). Together, these cover roughly a tenth of the country.

## Sloths & Their Toilet Habits

MARY ALTIER

In the Amazon rainforest, the diurnal three-toed sloth is quite often sighted, whereas the two-toed sloth is nocturnal and therefore rarely seen. Sloths are often found hanging motionless from tree limbs, or progressing at a painfully slow speed along a branch toward a particularly succulent bunch of leaves, which are their primary food source. Leaf digestion takes several days, and sloths defecate about once a week.

Sloths are most fastidious with their toilet habits, always climbing down from their tree to deposit their weekly bowel movement on the ground. Biologists do not know why sloths do this; one suggested hypothesis is that by consistently defecating at the base of a particular tree, the sloths provide a natural fertilizer that increases the quality of the leaves of that tree, thus improving the sloth's diet. You are welcome to come up with your own explanation as you travel through this fascinating region.

With a few exceptions, the parks (and other areas) are not geared toward tourism. There are very few information centers, park guards, camping areas or lodges. Those that do exist are often privately run. Many of the parks are very remote and hard to get to, which makes them effectively off-limits to ordinary tourism. Others can be reached, but require a long trip by land and boat, or chartered light aircraft, and are expensive to get to. Some areas are closed to travel in order to fully protect the flora, fauna and people living in them. Large parts of Manu (which include both park and reserved zones) in Peru's southern forests are closed to all travel and are home to several Indian tribes that have had almost no contact with outsiders, although some areas are open to tourism.

Easily and frequently visited parks include the following: Santuario Historico Machu Picchu, with its famed Inca ruins; Parque Nacional Huascarán has wonderful trekking in the Cordillera Blanca; and Reserva Nacional de Paracas is the best place to see coastal and marine wildlife. All three are easily reached by public transport, offer nearby lodging and charge entrance fees. Other places require more time, money and effort to reach. More details are given in the appropriate parts of the text.

## GOVERNMENT & POLITICS

Under the new constitution (see The Fujimori Years under Archaeology & History earlier in this chapter), presidents hold office for five years and are permitted to run for reelection. Peru is a republic, and the current president (since July 28, 1990) is Alberto Fujimori, who is both the head of the government and the chief of state. The next election will be in 2000. The president has two vice presidents and a cabinet of 12 members. The congress is unicameral and consists of 120 members. Voting is compulsory for all citizens between the ages of 18 and 70, and is optional for people older than 70.

Peru is politically divided into 24 departments (states) and the constitutional province of Callao. In 1993, this system was reorganized into 12 regions, Lima and the constitutional province, but the reorganization has met with confusion and nonacceptance. The older departmental system seems to be more adhered to than the new regional system, but that may change. The departments are further divided into provinces, of which there are 155, and the provinces are subdivided into 1586 districts.

## ECONOMY

The domestic economic situation was a disaster at the end of the García administration in 1990. The current government, under the leadership of President Fujimori, has made sweeping economic reforms, beginning with an austerity package that raised prices of food and gasoline manyfold. Tax and import laws were eased, many state-run industries privatized, and monopolies eliminated. This led to renewed international confidence in Peru, significant foreign investment, and the beginning of the repayment of parts of Peru's foreign debt. Inflation, at an annual rate of over 10,000% in the early 1990s, has dropped to the low teens, and in 1994, Peru had the strongest economic growth of any Latin American country. Peru's gross domestic product (GDP) in 1996 was US$92 billion, or about US$3800 per capita, representing considerable growth since the early 1990s.

The economy grew by over 7% in 1997, but only by about 1% in 1998 because of the adverse effects of that year's El Niño, which caused flooding in the coastal areas and decimated the fishing catch, as well as by financial crises in Asia, Brazil and Russia, which caused exports to slow. In January 1999, Brazil suddenly devalued its currency, and the ripple effects will be felt all over Latin America. Growth in 1999 may be the slowest since 1994.

The largest sector of the working population (about 33%) is involved in agriculture and fishing, but this normally produces only 13% of the value of the GDP. Conversely, mining employs only 2.5% of the labor force, yet produces about 10% of the GDP. Agriculture, fishing and mining have been the traditional jobs. In recent decades, however, manufacturing has played an increasing role and now employs over 10% of the labor force, producing about 22% of the GDP. The greatest part of the GDP (over 40%) is raised in the government and service industries, which employ almost 30% of workers. Unemployment looks reasonable at 8%, but the majority of people are underemployed. The minimum monthly wage is officially US$112, but the cost of living for a family of four is estimated at about US$540.

The main food crops are rice, corn and potatoes. The main cash crop is officially coffee, which accounts for almost 6% of the export earnings, though the value of coffee has dropped 44% since 1997 because of the international economic crisis. However, unreported revenue from coca (exported for the production of cocaine) is far higher, and some sources suggest that it is roughly comparable in value to all legal exports combined. In 1999, the value of coca is decreasing as Peru 'voluntarily' complies with US coca-eradication schemes.

In 1997, exports were worth a total of US$6.814 billion, with minerals (US$3.146 billion) being the most important. Copper, in various forms, is by far the largest single mineral export (worth US$1.056 billion in 1997); other significant mineral exports include zinc, gold, petroleum products, lead, silver, iron and tin. Again, since 1997, the value of copper has declined 41%, hurting Peru's economy.

Fishing, particularly for anchoveta and pilchard, yields fishmeal that accounted for US$1.03 billion in exports in 1997 (a very good year), though much less in years affected by recent El Niños (1992 and 1998). Other fishing products, such as frozen fish, shrimp and fish oils accounted for a further US$373 million. In the 1960s, Peru caught more tons of fish than any other country in the world. Overfishing, combined with a disastrous El Niño in 1971-72, caused the fishing industry to collapse in one season. Recovery did not begin until the late 1970s, and today the industry is still well below the levels of the 1960s, partly because of recurring El Niños. There is, however, more effort to manage the overfishing problem.

Nontraditional exports that have become recently important include textiles (US$570.5 million in 1997) and steel products (US$233.9 million).

Imports, which during 1996 exceeded exports by 25%, are mainly basic foodstuffs (particularly cereals), machinery, transportation equipment and manufactured goods. By far the biggest trading partner is the USA (21% of imports and 19% of exports), followed by Japan (9% of exports). Colombia, Chile, Argentina, Brazil, and Germany are also important sources of imports, and Italy and Germany are important export destinations.

## POPULATION & PEOPLE

Peru's population is over 26 million, almost half of which is concentrated in the narrow coastal desert. The population is predicted to double by the 2020s. Lima (including Callao) has a population of almost 8 million, and the second and third cities, Arequipa and Trujillo, also in the coastal region, have populations approaching 1 million.

About half the population is found in the highlands – mostly rural Indians or *mestizos* who practice subsistence agriculture. There are few large cities in the highlands but many small towns. The rural highlanders are called *campesinos* (country people or peasants). Because of the very poor standard of living in the highlands, many campesinos have migrated to the coast but overpopulation problems in the cities mean their lot rarely improves.

More than 60% of Peru lies in the Amazon Basin east of the Andes. This region is slowly becoming colonized, but as yet only 5% of the population lives there.

About 45% of Peru's population is Indian (*indígenas* is an appropriate term; *indios* is insulting). Most are Quechua-speaking and are mainly found in the highlands, although a significant number have been driven down to the coast in recent years following the political unrest caused by the Sendero Luminoso. A few speak Aymara in the Lake Titicaca region, and small Amazon Indians groups speak a plethora of other languages.

About 37% is mestizo, 15% is white and the remaining 3% is black, Asian or other groups.

## EDUCATION

Primary education for 6- to 12-year-olds is compulsory, although this is difficult to enforce in remote rural areas. Nevertheless, primary-school enrollment is about 95% and there are about 30,000 schools with over 4 million students. Secondary school, for ages 12 to 16, is not compulsory, and there is only about 40% enrollment. About 7000 schools provide for about 2 million students. Many schools offer two sessions, morning and afternoon, in order to accommodate more students. Facilities are basic, and the quality of education is low. Parents who can afford it send their children to private schools.

Higher education is carried out in vocational schools, teacher-training schools, pre-universities and universities, of which there are almost 50. Some 40% of these are private, and the rest are state-run. Higher education used to be free in state-run colleges, but since 1993, this is no longer the case. Adult literacy is improving, from only 72.5% in 1972 to 85.1% in 1990 and 89% in 1995.

## ARTS
### Traditional

The heritage of the Andean Indians is best seen in the many folk art forms that are still common today and that serve as much to preserve an ancient culture as to entertain. For the visitor, the most obvious of these art forms will be music, dance and crafts.

Both pre-Columbian and colonial architecture are also of great interest to the visitor.

**Andean Music & Dance** Pre-Columbian Andean music was based on the pentatonic scale of D-F-G-A-C and used wind and percussion instruments. Some of these are found in archaeological museums and date as far back as 5000 BC. The string instruments used today are based on instruments introduced by the Spanish. Traditional Andean music is popularly called *música folklórica* and is frequently heard at fiestas, although it is performed in bars and restaurants as well. Bars that specifically cater to musical entertainment are called *peñas*.

There are many different forms of wind instruments, based on regional differences. The most representative are *quenas* and *zampoñas*. The quena (or kena) is a flute usually made of bamboo of varying lengths, depending on the pitch desired. In the past, it could have been made of bone, clay or wood. A *mohseno* is a large bamboo flute producing the deepest bass notes. The zampoña is the Spanish name for what is referred to as a *siku* in Quechua. It is a set of panpipes with two rows of bamboo canes, seven in one and six in the other. Zampoñas come in sizes ranging from the tiny, high-pitched *chuli* to the meter-long, bass *toyo*. Other forms of panpipes have different names. Also seen are *ocarinas*, small oval clay instruments with up to 12 holes. Occasionally, horns made of animal horns or seashells are heard.

Percussion instruments include the inevitable drum, called a *bombo*, usually made from a hollowed-out segment of cedar, walnut or other tree, and using stretched goatskin for the pounding surface. Rattles, called *shajshas*, are made of polished goat hooves tied together.

Almost all of today's música folklórica groups also use string instruments. The guitar is sometimes seen, but the most typical is the *charango*, which is based on a small, five-string Spanish guitar but modified by the Andean people to the extent that the charango can now be considered an original Andean instrument in its own right. It is a tiny guitar, with the resonance box traditionally made of an armadillo shell, though they are mostly wooden these days. It has five pairs of strings, usually tuned to E-A-E-C-G. The music produced by folklórica groups varies from melancholy and soulful to upbeat and festive. Música folklórica bands have toured North America and Europe in the '80s and '90s, spreading the popularity of their music far beyond the Andes. Perhaps the best known example of Andean music is *El Cóndor Pasa*, adapted by Paul Simon.

*bombo*

*charango*

*quenas*

**Instruments of *música folklórica***

More recent additions to the instruments used in the Andes include harps, violins and a variety of brass instruments. These are most often seen in large outdoor bands strolling around towns and villages on fiesta days, producing a cacophony of sound and surrounded by masked and elaborately costumed dancers.

The many forms of música folklórica change from region to region. The most representative is a *huayno*, which is associated with a dance of the same name. Hundreds of other kinds of dances are known and performed in the highlands. Many have a religious and ceremonial, as well as social, significance. Although dance performances can be seen in theaters and restaurants in the highlands, nowhere are they as colorful and authentic as those that are performed communally during the many fiestas.

**Coastal Music & Dance** On the coast, music and associated dances are quite different. The coastal *música criolla* has its roots in Spain and Africa. The main instrumentation is guitars and a *cajón*, a wooden box on which the player sits and pounds out a rhythm with his hands. The guitar is Spanish, but the cajón is attributed to black slaves brought by the Spanish. The most popular of the coastal dances is the *marinera*, a graceful romantic dance employing much waving of handkerchiefs. This is a performance to be watched rather than a dance with audience participation. Marinera dance competitions are held, with the most important in Trujillo (on the north coast).

In the last few decades, Afro-Peruvian music has enjoyed a comeback, especially in the Chincha area on the south coast. Drawing on Hispanic and Andean influences, Afro-Peruvian music is unique and quite different from Caribbean or Brazilian styles. This music and its accompanying dance has grown increasingly popular on TV shows and as a performance art, though certainly, Peruvians will go to clubs and dance it as well. A popular performance dance is the *alcatraz*, during which one dancer carrying a candle attempts to light a paper flag tucked into the back of the partners waist. This leads to plenty of fast and rhythmic moving of the hips in an attempt to avoid getting burned!

Just as in the highlands, coastal music can be heard at peñas in the main towns.

**Crafts** Handicrafts made in the Andes are based on pre-Columbian necessities, such as weaving (for clothes), pottery and metallurgy. Today, woven cloth is still seen in the traditional ponchos, belts and other clothes worn by Andean Indians. Also, weaving has extended to cover a variety of rugs and tapestries that are popular souvenirs. The traditionally worked alpaca wool is in great demand for sweaters and other items. Pottery, very important and well developed by many pre-Columbian cultures in Peru, is still important today as a popular souvenir item. The best are often based on ancient designs, shapes and motifs. Jewelry, especially the gold and silver pieces that are a direct link back to ancient rituals and heritage, are also in demand as a craft today.

**Architecture** The Inca architecture of Machu Picchu is the greatest attraction in Peru, though there is much more Inca architecture. Various other pre-Columbian cultures have left us with magnificent examples of their architecture – see Visiting Archaeological Sites under Activities in the Facts for the Visitor chapter.

Colonial architecture is especially represented by the many imposing cathedrals, churches, monasteries and convents built during the 16th, 17th and 18th centuries. These are extremely ornate, both outside and inside. Altars are often gold-leafed. The religious statues and paintings found inside churches were often carved or painted by early Indian artists with strong Spanish influence. These gave rise to the Escuela Cuzqueña art form – colonial art blending local Andean and Spanish ideas.

## Modern

**Music & Dance** Traditional music continues to play a major part in Peru's musical scene. Although there is a national symphony orchestra and ballet company, and touring companies from other countries often visit, classical music is enjoyed by relatively few people.

Modern popular music includes rock, pop, blues, reggae and punk, all usually imported, though there are a few Peruvian rock bands. Chilean-style protest songs and jazz also enjoy a limited popularity. Much more popular are other forms of Latin American dance music, such as the omnipresent salsa, and *cumbia* and *chicha*, both from Colombia. *Salsatecas* cram in hundreds of Peruvians for all-night dancefests.

**Film** The film industry is still in its infancy. Few Peruvian films have been produced, and most of them are short documentaries. Going to the movies is a popular pastime, however, and major cities have cinemas screening imported films with Spanish subtitles. In recent years, however, many cinemas have shut down to be replaced by video pubs or video clubs, where you can rent a film and take it home to watch, or watch it right there at the club along with a drink or snack.

**Theater** Drama is quite popular in Lima, less so outside of the capital. It is of little interest to the visitor, however, unless you speak good Spanish. If you do, look for theater bars in the Miraflores and San Isidro districts of Lima, where you can see a play while enjoying a drink and light snack.

**Literature** Peru's most famous novelist is the internationally recognized Mario Vargas Llosa (born 1936), who ran in the Peruvian presidential election of 1990, coming in second. Most of his books have been translated into various languages, including English. As is common among Peruvian authors, his novels often delve deeply into Peruvian society, politics and culture. His first novel, *The Time of the Hero*, was publicly burned because of its detailed exposé of life in a Peruvian military academy. Vargas Llosa's work is very complex, with multiple plots and changing time sequences or flashbacks.

Two Peruvian writers are particularly noted for their portrayals of the difficulties facing Peruvian Indian communities. José María Arguedas (1911-1969) wrote *Deep Rivers* and *Yawar Fiesta* among others. Ciro Alegría (1909-1967) was the author of *The Golden Serpent*, which is about life in a jungle village on the Río Marañón, and *Broad and Alien is the World*, which is about repression among Andean Indians. These have all been translated into English. Other writers who are considered important but await translation include Julio Ramón Ribeyro (born 1929) and Alfredo Bryce Echenique (born 1939).

A recent Peruvian arrival on the literary scene is Sergio Bambarén (born in Lima in 1960) who was educated in the USA and lived in Australia for several years. He wrote *The Dolphin – Story of a Dreamer* in English and self-published it in Australia. It became a best-seller and has been translated into several languages (including Spanish). Bambarén now lives in Lima, where he is working on his third novel.

Women writers can be read in a new anthology, *Fire From the Andes: Short Fiction by Women from Bolivia, Ecuador and Peru*.

**Poetry** César Vallejo (1892-1938) wrote *Trilce*, a book of 77 avant-garde poems touted by some critics as one of the best books of poetry ever written in Spanish. Vallejo is considered Peru's greatest poet. Pablo Neruda, a Chilean poet, describes Machu Picchu as 'Mother of stone and sperm of condors' which is only one of the many powerful images he uses in his epic poem, *The Heights of Machu Picchu*, available in English. Anthologized modern Peruvian poetry is available in English in *Peru: The New Poetry* and *The Newest Peruvian Poetry in Translation*.

## SOCIETY & CONDUCT

Essentially, Peru is a bicultural society. The whites are the rich middle and upper classes, and the Indians are poor peasants, *campesinos*. Indians may also be called 'indígenas' (natives) but never 'indios,' which is considered insulting. What may be acceptable in middle-upper class society might not be acceptable in Indian society, and vice versa. In between, of course, are the mestizo people (of mixed Spanish/Indian heritage), whose customs and attitudes lean either toward white or Indian manners, depending on the individuals and their socioeconomic status. The same comments apply to other very small minority groups.

Generally speaking, Peruvians are more formal than, say, North Americans. Hands are shaken on meeting and leaving a person on most occasions, and verbal greetings are exchanged. *Buenos días* is a good start in a conversation with anyone ranging from a cabdriver to a shop assistant. In more involved situations, this may be followed by a lengthier exchange of pleasantries. Women also kiss one another on the cheek, and men, if they know the woman, may do so as well. Men may use an *abrazo*, a sort of back-slapping hug, between themselves if they are friends. Indians, on the other hand, don't kiss, and their handshakes, when offered, are a light touch rather than a firm grip. In all situations, politeness is a valued habit.

Peruvians are used to less personal space than many North Americans and Europeans may be used to. Conversations tend to take place face to face, streets and public transport are very crowded, and homes have little individual space. Frequent kissing and hugging on a nonsexual basis, such as described earlier, is another example of this. Noise seems part of the way of life. Radios and TVs in hotel rooms are turned on early in the morning and late at night, without thought of whether neighboring rooms can hear. Perhaps this is a way of giving the occupants some privacy. Because of crowded living conditions, decent couples may use budget hotels for a few hours of lovemaking.

If you ask someone if they would like to have a drink or meal with you, you are expected to pay for it. Because of economic constraints, most Peruvians are unable to invite you to their homes or a restaurant for a meal on a casual basis. If you are invited, it is a semiformal occasion, so you should wear nice clothes and bring a small gift (flowers, chocolates, wine). Dinner conversation can run the gamut of sports, religion, politics and the arts, but discussion of personal finances is considered in poor taste.

In poor areas, however, campesinos will often ask you about your lifestyle and how much money you make. They are amazed at your apparently incredible wealth. You can tone this down a bit by talking a little about the higher costs of living in your country and getting onto another subject. A popular topic is the family. Women especially can expect to be asked how many children they have. This can become tiresome for single women who by Peruvian standards appear to be long past the marriageable age. This is, however, less a sexist attitude and more a friendly conversational gambit. Family life is important in Peru. Machismo, however, is also part of the culture. For more information on these attitudes, see Attitudes Toward Women, as well as Gay & Lesbian Travelers, in the next chapter.

Peruvian (indeed, Latin American) attitudes toward time are not very precise. If invited to dinner or to meet someone, being up to an hour late is socially acceptable and expected. However, if you are told *Hora Inglesa* (English time), you are expected to be more or less punctual. In business situations, however, punctuality is more likely to occur than in social settings. In all cases, delays because of anything ranging from a flat tire to a late flight are to be expected, long lines are the norm, and patience is a virtue worth acquiring.

Clothing in the highland regions is fairly sedate. Men don't wear shorts and women don't wear halter tops or shorts. If trekking, shorts are usually viewed as acceptable on the popular tourist hikes, though the locals rarely wear them. Men shouldn't hike bare-chested through villages. In the lowland regions, particularly the jungle, men and women do wear shorts.

Men may be seen urinating and spitting in public. Campesino women also urinate in public by simply squatting down with their voluminous skirts around them. While public urinating and spitting cannot be considered a Peruvian custom, they are not heavily frowned upon. Belching or burping, on the other hand, is considered the height of impoliteness. Spit if you must, but never belch.

When calling someone over to you, don't crook your finger up and beckon, as people may do in North America or Europe. This is considered very rude. A better way to call someone over from a distance is to give a flat, downward swipe of the open hand. Body language using hands and facial expressions is hard to describe, but an important part of interpersonal communications. Watch to see how Peruvians do it.

Andean Indians have used coca leaves for centuries. The most frequent use is by chewing. Leaves are placed in the mouth one by one and moistened with saliva until a wad of wet leaves is produced. A small amount of *llipta* (a mixture of mineral lime and wood ashes – gringos have used baking soda reasonably successfully) is added to the moistened leaves, and the entire mass is kept in the cheek and chewed occasionally. Although this gives some relief from hunger and fatigue, it is by no means equivalent to using cocaine, which Andean people do not do. Cocaine use is illegal, but coca use is legal and normal among Andean Indians. Coca leaves are freely sold at highland markets. Other traditional uses for coca leaf are as offerings to the *apus* (mountain gods), particularly when going on a long trip; as social exchanges between people meeting on a trip; and for medicinal and mystical purposes.

When using alcohol, be it the local *chicha* (a fermented corn drink) or stronger *aguardiente* or other drink, Andean Indians invariably spill a few drops on the ground for *Pachamama* (Mother Earth). This is done both outdoors and inside their houses (which usually have earthen floors).

**Treatment of Animals** Attitudes toward animals are fairly pragmatic – animals are to be used by human beings as needed. Animal-rights activists are generally perceived as lacking cultural sensitivity and have made little headway in Peru.

In common with most Latin American countries, both bullfighting and cockfighting are important and popular parts of the culture.

There are small zoos found in several major towns. By first-world standards, the cages are small, but zookeeping has improved somewhat in recent years, and the animals' conditions are less intolerable than in the past.

In many rural areas, domestic dogs can be a nuisance, charging after passersby and nipping at their heels. Bites are occasionally reported. The locals solve the problem simply by throwing well-aimed rocks at any dog that gets too close. Stooping and flinging a handful of soil (or even a pretend rock) in the direction of a harassing dog works just as well as a rock.

## RELIGION
In common with most Latin American countries, the religion of Peru is predominantly Roman Catholic; over 90% of the population at least nominally professes that faith. Some of the older towns have splendid colonial Catholic churches. The Indians, while outwardly Roman Catholic, tend to blend Catholicism with their traditional beliefs. Thus offerings to the Pachamama or apus, as described in the preceding section, are an essential part of Indian life.

Although Roman Catholicism is the official religion, the constitution allows citizens to practice any religion they choose. Some churches of other faiths can be found, but these form a small minority. In recent years, there has been an increase of small Protestant groups and cults of many kinds.

## LANGUAGE
For the traveler, Spanish is the main language. In the highlands, most Indians are bilingual, with Quechua being the preferred language in most areas, except around Lake Titicaca, where Aymara is spoken. For most Indians, Spanish is a second tongue, and between 1 million and 2 million people do not speak Spanish at all. These people live in very remote areas, so it is rare for the traveler to encounter Indians who speak no Spanish. Although English is understood in the best hotels, airline offices and tourist agencies, it is of little use elsewhere.

If you don't speak Spanish, take heart. It is an easy language to learn. Courses are available in Lima (see the Lima chapter), or you can study books, records and tapes while you are still at home and planning your trip. These study aids are often available free at public libraries – or you might consider taking an evening or college course. Once having learned the basics, you'll be able to talk with people from all over Latin America – apart from Brazilians, who are predominantly Portuguese-speaking.

Spanish is easy to learn for several reasons. Firstly, it uses Roman script. Secondly, with few exceptions, it is spoken as it is written and vice versa. Imagine trying to explain to someone who is learning English that there are seven different ways of pronouncing 'ough.' This isn't a problem in Spanish. Thirdly, many words are so similar to English that you can figure them out – *Instituto Geográfico Nacional* means the National Geographical Institute.

Even if you don't have time to take a Spanish course, at least bring a phrasebook and dictionary. Lonely Planet's *Quechua Phrasebook* and *Latin American Spanish Phrasebook* are recommended. Don't dispense with the dictionary, because the phrasebook won't help you translate the local newspaper.

Although the Spanish alphabet looks like the English one, there are minor differences. 'Ch' is considered a separate letter, so *champú* (which means shampoo) could be listed in a dictionary after all the words beginning with just 'c'. Similarly, 'll' is a separate letter, so a *llama* could be listed after all the words beginning with a single 'l'. The letter 'ñ' is listed after the ordinary 'n'. Bear this in mind also when using telephone directories or other reference works. Vowels with an accent are accented for stress and are not considered separate letters. Recently, however, the Academia Real de la Lengua Española (in Spain) has decided to eliminate 'ch' and 'll' as separate letters, which means that new Spanish dictionaries will always list champú and llama in the same word order that English speakers are used to. Whether this will spread to Latin American Spanish remains to be seen. The 1998 Peruvian telephone directory still adheres to the traditional form.

Pronunciation is generally more straightforward than it is in English. If you say a word the way it looks like it should be said, the chances are that it will be close enough to be understood. You will get better with practice of course. A few notable exceptions are 'll,' which is always pronounced 'y' as in 'yacht,' the 'j,' which is always pronounced 'h' as in 'happy,' and the 'h,' which isn't pronounced at all. Thus the phrase *hojas en la calle* (leaves in the street) would be pronounced 'o-has en la ka-yay.' Finally, the letter 'ñ' is pronounced as the 'ny' sound in 'canyon.'

## Grammar

Word order in Spanish is generally similar to English sentence construction, with one notable exception. Adjectives follow the nouns they qualify instead of preceding them as they do in English. Thus 'the white house' becomes *la casa blanca*.

Articles, adjectives and demonstrative pronouns must agree with the noun in both gender and number. Nouns ending in *a* are generally feminine, and the corresponding articles are *la* (singular) and *las* (plural). Those ending in *o* are usually masculine and require the articles *el* (singular) and *los* (plural). Common exceptions to this rule are *el mapa, el problema, el dentista, el idioma, el día* and *la mano*.

There are hundreds of other exceptions to these guidelines that can only be memorized or deduced by the meaning of the word. Plurals are formed by adding *s* to words ending in a vowel and *es* to those ending in a consonant.

In addition to using all the familiar English tenses, Spanish also uses the imperfect tense and two subjunctive tenses (past and present). Tenses are formed either by adding myriad endings to the root verb or preceding the participle form by some variation of the auxiliary verb *haber* (to have – as in 'I have been').

There are verb endings for first-, second- and third-person singular and plural. Second-person singular and plural are divided into formal and familiar modes. If that's not enough, there are three types of verbs – those ending in 'ar,' 'er' and 'ir' – which are all conjugated differently. There are also a whole slew of stem-changing rules and irregularities.

See the Language chapter at the end of this book for a pronounciation guide, basic grammar tips and a list of useful words and phrases.

# Facts for the Visitor

## HIGHLIGHTS

Peru's most famous attraction is Machu Picchu, an Inca city built in a stunning location on a saddle between two mountains in the southern Peruvian Andes, a few hours from the city of Cuzco. Machu Picchu lives up to its reputation as the most awe-inspiring pre-Columbian site on the continent. Cuzco itself, with its impressive Inca foundations and superb Spanish colonial architecture, has been well preserved and makes a great base from which to visit Machu Picchu and a host of other Inca sites in the area.

Many other archaeological sites predate the Incas by hundreds or even thousands of years. These sites are mainly found along the coast, and the towns of Chiclayo, Trujillo and Nazca give access to ancient pyramids, huge mud-brick cities and intriguing giant petroglyphs.

For travelers interested in outdoor adventures, the Andes – the second-largest mountain chain in the world after the Himalayas – offer unparalleled views and hiking or climbing opportunities. Foremost among Andean mountains is the Cordillera Blanca. This boasts Peru's highest mountain, Huascarán (also the world's highest mountain anywhere in the tropics, as well as being the sixth-highest mountain in the Andes), plus scores of other glacier-clad peaks at over 5000m above sea level. Access to this area is straightforward from the city of Huaraz, which has memorable sunset views of many of the highest peaks.

There is also great trekking from Cuzco and Arequipa. Cuzco is the gateway to the Inca Trail and to hikes around the massive Ausangate, while Arequipa gives access to explorations of the Colca Canyon, which is much deeper than the USA's Grand Canyon.

Rainforest enthusiasts will also find plenty to satisfy their interests. From the northern city of Iquitos, you can visit canopy walkways, stay at jungle lodges or take riverboat journeys on the well-traveled Amazon or one of its many smaller and lesser-known tributaries. In southern Peru, the Manu area offers perhaps the best jungle wildlife-watching opportunities in the country, as well as comfortable lodges and camping opportunities.

Other highlights include Lake Titicaca, which at 3820m is the world's highest navigable lake. Here, you can take a day trip on a motorboat or an overnight cruise on a hydrofoil; visit floating islands inhabited by the Uros people or stay on permanent islands where Aymara-speaking Indians provide simple overnight accommodations devoid of TVs, taxis, telephones or other trappings of the 21st century.

Your itinerary will depend on your interests – do you want to backpack in the chilly Andes, observe wildlife in the steaming Amazon, learn about the many pre-Columbian cultures or step back in time on an island in the middle of Lake Titicaca? The choice is yours.

## PLANNING
### When to Go

Peru's high tourist season is from June to August, which coincides both with the dry season in the highlands and summer vacation in North America and Europe. Certainly, this is the best time to go if you are interested in hiking the Inca Trail to Machu Picchu, or climbing and trekking elsewhere. People can and do visit the highlands year round, though the wettest months of January to April make trekking and backpacking a wet and muddy proposition. If you aren't planning on spending any time in a tent, however, you shouldn't have any major problems in the rainy season. Many of the major fiestas, such as Virgen de la Candelaria, Carnaval and Semana Santa, occur in the wettest months and continue undiminished even during heavy rain.

On the coast, Peruvians visit the beaches during the sunny weather from late December through March, although none of the beaches are particularly enticing. The rest of the year, the coast is cloaked in *garúa* (coastal mist) and, although the beaches don't attract visitors, the coastal cities can be visited at any time.

In the eastern rainforests it rains, of course. The wettest months are December through April, as in the highlands, but tourism continues undiminished for two reasons. One is that it rarely rains for more than a few hours at a time, and so there are plenty of bright sunny periods to enjoy. The second is that it can rain year round, and locals are used to briefly taking cover during the heaviest downpours. It's not a big deal.

## What Kind of Trip?

Whether you take a guided tour or travel independently (or with a friend or family member) is entirely up to you – both guided and independent travel are good options. Independent travelers, however, should rely on public transport rather than renting a car (see Car Rental under Car & Motorcycle in the Getting Around chapter).

## Maps

Road maps of Peru are available in advance from the New York office of the South American Explorers (SAE, see Useful Organizations later in this chapter) or from specialty map stores in major cities in North America and Europe. The SAE and map stores have a limited number of detailed topographical or trekking maps. These are expensive in Peru and more expensive elsewhere. I have also found good selections of topographical maps in the reference departments of some major universities.

In Peru, the Instituto Geográfico Nacional (see Maps under Orientation in the Lima chapter) has the most complete selection of maps. Few city maps are published. Except for perhaps the lack of a detailed map of the whole of Lima, this book is among the best available resources for Peruvian city maps. Road maps can be a little optimistic – some of the roads that are marked, particularly those in the jungle, haven't been built yet or are no more than very rough tracks.

## What to Bring

This is a tough issue. Bring as little as possible…but bring everything you need! You have to make your own decision about bird books and/or binoculars, digital or disposable cameras, telephoto lenses or light tents, shortwave radios or CD players (with CDs!), laptops, and other paraphernalia.

Traveling light is much less of a hassle, so don't bring things you can do without. Traveling on buses and trains is bound to make you slightly grubby, so bring one change of dark clothes that don't show the dirt, rather than seven changes of nice clothes for a four-week trip. Many people go overboard with changes of clothes, but one change to wash and the other to wear is the best idea. Bring clothes that wash and dry easily (jeans take forever to dry).

The highlands are often cold, so bring a windproof jacket and a warm layer to wear beneath, or plan on buying a thick sweater in Cuzco or one of the other Andean towns frequented by tourists. A down jacket (bought at home) is well worth the investment if you get cold easily. A hat is indispensable; it'll keep you warm when it's cold, shade your eyes when it's sunny and keep your head dry when it rains. A great deal! A collapsible umbrella is great protection against sun and rain.

You can buy clothes of almost any size if you need them, but shoes are limited to size 43 Peruvian, which is about 10½ North American. If you are planning on doing a lot of hiking, I suggest you wear your hiking boots on your flight to Peru – of all your luggage, a comfortable, broken-in pair of boots will be one of the hardest things to replace in Peru.

For light traveling, I often divide my trip into segments and take what I need for that segment, leaving my other gear in storage. Most hotels will do this for you, and if you're a member of the South American Explorers (SAE, see Useful Organizations later in this chapter), you can leave your gear in their Lima clubhouse for as long as you want.

The following is a checklist of small, useful items that you will probably need:

- flashlight with spare bulbs and batteries
- travel alarm clock
- Swiss Army-style penknife
- sewing and repairs kit (dental floss makes excellent, strong and colorless emergency thread)
- a few meters of cord (useful as a clothesline or for spare shoelaces)
- sunglasses
- plastic bags (especially sealable ones)
- soap and dish, shampoo, toothbrush and paste, shaving gear, towel
- toilet paper (rarely found in cheaper hotels and restaurants)
- earplugs for sleeping in noisy hotels or buses
- insect repellent
- sunblock
- address book (a copy rather than the original)
- notebook
- pens and pencils
- paperback book (easily exchanged with other travelers when you've finished)
- Spanish-English dictionary
- small padlock
- large folding nylon bag to leave goods in storage
- water bottle
- first-aid kit (see the boxed text 'Medical Kit Checklist' under Health, later in this chapter)

Tampons are available in Peru, but only in larger towns and in regular sizes, so stock up with an adequate supply before visiting smaller towns and villages. If you use contraceptives, these are available in the major cities. However, the choice of contraceptives is limited, and condoms are of poor quality, so if you use a preferred type, bring an adequate supply from home. See Health later in this chapter for suggestions of medical supplies to bring.

A sleeping bag is useful if you plan to travel on a budget (or for camping), because some of the cheaper hotels don't have heating, and it can get cold at night. However, most hotels will give you another blanket if you ask. Overnight Andean buses can also be very cold. If you don't plan on camping, a warm coat will work just as well.

Insect repellent is important; Machu Picchu is known for irritating biting insects, which, though they don't carry diseases, leave itchy welts. If you are planning a trip into the Amazon Basin, you should bring repellent from home, because that sold in Peru is less effective. The most effective brands have a high percentage of DEET (N, N-diethyl-m-toluamide) – look at the label. DEET is toxic to children; instead, try Avon's nontoxic Skin So Soft oil (not the lotion). There are insect repellents without DEET that are available, but they tend to be less effective.

If you wish to go trekking or backpacking, you'll find that Cuzco and Huaraz have gear for rent, including tents, stoves, sleeping pads and bags, and backpacks.

Finally, as you leave your house, make sure that your passport, airline tickets and money are with you and not sitting on your bedside table.

## RESPONSIBLE TOURISM

Peru's tourism industry has been growing in recent years and is now a significant part of the economy. On the surface, international tourists spending money are a positive force. But the impact of tourists and travelers goes beyond just spending their money. In fact, hundreds of thousands of foreign visitors can create a negative impact on the society and environment of Peru.

In rural or wilderness areas where visitation is high, such as the Inca Trail, there are problems with trail erosion, a lack of sanitation and a lack of respect for the local people (see the boxed text 'Inca Trail Tours' in the Cuzco Area chapter). Similar problems exist in other heavily visited areas, such as the Cordillera Blanca and some rivers that provide multiday rafting opportunities. Wildlife may be harassed by large numbers of visitors in the Amazon (see the boxed text 'The Unique Giant River Otter' in the Facts about Peru chapter).

In more urban areas, problems exist with the dichotomy between rich tourists (even the most budget-oriented backpacker is rich by most local standards) and local people who work for substandard wages to provide services for tourists. Demands by groups of non-Spanish-speaking tourists can range from reasonable to rude and obnoxious. Some things that may not seem immediately wrong (taking a person's photograph, demanding toilet paper in a cheap restaurant, expecting the same amenities as you have at home, etc) are not reasonable by local standards.

So what can be done to promote responsible tourism? Here are some suggestions. Start by learning at least enough Spanish to be able to say 'hello,' 'thank you,' 'Peru is a beautiful country' and a few more phrases. Don't be afraid to use them! Read the section on Society & Conduct in Facts about Peru and act in a locally acceptable way. Remember the old proverb 'When in Rome, do as the Romans do' (though not to the point of throwing trash on the street or trail just because some Peruvians do it – use some common sense). Use local services as much as possible to leave your money in the local economy. On outdoor expeditions, don't allow your guides to hunt for food, cut firewood for bonfires, leave litter or harass the wildlife. Try to set a good example, but be sensitive to local customs and beliefs.

## TOURIST OFFICES

Getting reliable, recent, and useful tourist information ahead of your trip is not easy – the SAE, a Peruvian embassy, or this book are your best options. The US Department of State issues travel advisories about every country, including Peru, but their statements tend to be overly cautious.

Once in Peru, you'll find that tourist offices are either travel agencies that can help you plan your trip and sell you services, or small, local offices that have information only about their own area but not the rest of Peru. The best travel agencies and small local offices are detailed in the text where appropriate.

## VISAS & DOCUMENTS
### Passport

Your passport should be valid for at least six months after your arrival date, so check your passport's expiration date if you haven't

done so recently. If you are on an extended trip and your passport comes close to the expiration date, you can normally obtain a new one from your embassy for a fee. This can take several days. If all your pages become full of stamps and visas but your passport is not close to expiring, you can often get extra pages inserted in your passport at your embassy. This is normally cheaper than getting a new passport.

## Visas & Tourist Cards

Currently, citizens of most Western European nations, the USA, Canada, Australia and New Zealand who are entering Peru as tourists do not require visas if they have a valid passport. Some other nationals do require visas, so you should check for the latest changes. Travelers who require visas can normally obtain them from Peruvian embassies or consulates in the capital cities of neighboring countries if they are traveling around South America. Alternatively, you can apply for one at a Peruvian embassy before you leave home.

A tourist card (a sheet of paper in duplicate) is given to everyone upon arrival in Peru. After you fill it out, the immigration official retains one copy and you keep the other. There is no charge for this card, but don't lose it, as you will need it to extend your stay, for passport checks, and to leave the country. If you lose it, another can be obtained at the *migraciones* (immigration office) in Lima and other major cities, or at the exit point from the country. It's best to get a new tourist card in a major city, because the immigration officials hassle you if you try to exit without one, and a bribe is sometimes necessary to obtain one when leaving the country.

On arrival, you are normally given the maximum period of a 90-day stay, but less is sometimes given, so let the official know if you need 90 days. If you have a ticket out of the country, you can usually get enough days to last until you leave, but speak up as soon as you start dealing with the duty officer and before your passport is stamped, as they won't want to change it afterward. You will be given an identical stamp in both your passport and tourist card showing how long you can stay.

**Extensions** To stay in Peru for longer than the 90 days (or whatever) you are given on arrival, you can renew your tourist card. This costs almost US$30 for each 30-day extension and takes a few hours of your time. Three renewals (up to a maximum of 180 days total) are allowed; to stay longer than this, you must leave the country then return to begin the process again. Simply leave the country overland to Ecuador, Chile or Bolivia. The easiest place for tourist-card renewals is migraciones in Lima, where the process can take less than an hour. Read the Lima chapter for details. In other cities, you may have to leave your passport overnight. The addresses of the immigration offices are given under the cities that have them.

## Identification

Always carry identification when you are out of your hotel, as you can be arrested if you don't have identification (though you will rarely be asked). Within a city, it's safest to leave your passport in your hotel's safe and carry a photocopy of the pages with your photo and passport number, which is adequate identification. Another document that is useful for identification is a driver's license (as long as it has a photo) or any official-looking document that has a recent photo of you.

When traveling between towns, always carry your passport, because there are occasional passport controls at the entrance and exit points of main towns, whether you arrive by bus, taxi, air, rail or boat.

## Onward Tickets

In addition to a passport and tourist card, you officially need a ticket out of the country. Evidence of sufficient funds for your stay is not normally required. It's rare to be asked to show an onward ticket, unless you're one of those travelers for whom a visa is required. If you buy an airline ticket for use as an exit ticket, it can normally be refunded if you don't want to use it. Alternatively, buy an MCO (miscellaneous charge order) from an airline belonging to IATA (International Air Transport Association). This can be used for any flight on an IATA airline, or it can be refunded if it hasn't expired. Airline departure desks outside Peru normally don't let you fly to Peru on a one-way ticket and may insist that you buy an onward ticket or an MCO before you can board the aircraft.

At land borders, bus tickets can be bought, but they are not transferable or refundable. If you don't have an exit ticket at a land border, it's best not to worry, as you probably won't be asked to show one anyway.

## Other Documents

International vaccination certificates are not required by law, but vaccinations are advisable. See Health later in this chapter.

I don't recommend renting a car because of poor roads, long distances and inferior rental-car facilities. However, if you want to rent a car, get an International Driver's License from your home country.

Student cards are occasionally useful. These save you money at some of the archaeological sites and museums (entrance fee discounts of up to 50% are possible) but aren't honored everywhere. They must have a photo on them to be honored at all.

Hostel cards are of little use. Discounts for senior citizens are rarely offered.

## Photocopies

The cheapest insurance policy is having copies of your most important documents. I routinely photocopy the pages of my passport with my photograph and passport number. On the back of this, I write the numbers of my traveler's checks, airline tickets, credit-card telephone numbers (in case of loss or theft), health-insurance telephone numbers, and anything else that may be important. Then I photocopy this again and leave a copy at home, and carry my own copy (or two) separate from all my other documents.

## EMBASSIES & CONSULATES

Peru has diplomatic representation in about 60 countries, and about 50 countries have embassies or consulates in Peru. Contact information for embassies and consulates of Peru's most common foreign visitors is listed below. Additional addresses can be obtained from the website (www.rree.gob.pe) of the Ministerio de Relaciones Exteriores (Foreign Ministry).

## Peruvian Embassies & Consulates

Australia
 (☎ 02-6290-0922, fax 02-6290-0924), 43 Culgoa Circuit, O'Malley, ACT 2606; postal address: PO Box 106, Red Hill, ACT 2606
 Also in Sydney

Bolivia
 (☎ 2-35-3550, fax 2-36-7640), Calle Fernando Guachalla, cdra 3, Sopocachi, La Paz
 Also in Santa Cruz

Brazil
 (☎ 61-242-9435, fax 61-244-9344), SES, Avenida das Nações, Lote 43, 70428-900, Brasília, DF
 Also in Rio de Janeiro, Sao Paulo

Canada
 (☎ 613-238-1777, fax 613-232-3062), 130 Albert St, Suite 1901, Ottawa K1P 5G4
 Also in Montreal, Toronto, Vancouver

Chile
 (☎ 2-235-2356, fax 2-235-8139), Av Andrés Bello 1751, Providencia 9, Casilla 16277, Santiago
 (☎ 58-23-1020, fax 58-23-1433), San Martín 220, Arica
 Also in Iquique, Valparaiso

Colombia
 (☎ 1-257-6292, fax 1-623-5102), Carrera 10 bis, No 93-48, Bogotá, DC
 (☎ 98-592-7204, fax 98-592-7402), Calle 13, No 11-48, Leticia

Czech Republic
 (☎ 420-2-24316210, 24318810, 24315741), Muchova 9 Praga 6, 160 00 Dejvica

Ecuador
 (☎ 2-468-410, fax 2-252-560), Avenida República de El Salvador 495 y Irlanda, Quito
 Also in Guayaquil, Loja, Macará, Machala

France
 (☎ 1-53-70-42-00, fax 1-47-55-80-62), 50 ave Kléber, 75116 Paris

Germany
 (☎ 228-373045, fax 228-379475), 53175 Bonn 1, Godesberger Allee 125
 Also in Berlin, Frankfurt, Hamburg

Israel
 (☎ 3-613-5591, fax 3-751-2286), 37 Rehov Ha-Marganit, Shikun Vatikim, 52 584, Ramat Gan

The Netherlands
 (☎ 70-365-3500, fax 70-365-1929), Nassauplein 4, 2585 EA, The Hague
 Also in Amsterdam

New Zealand
 (☎ 4-499-8087, fax 4-499-8057), Level 8, Cigna House, 40 Mercer St, POB 2566, Wellington

Spain
 (☎ 1-431-4242, fax 1-431-2493), Príncipe de Vergara 36, 5D, 28001 Madrid
 Also in Barcelona

UK
 (☎ 020-7235-1917, fax 020-7235-4463), 52 Sloane St, London SW1X 9SP

USA
 (☎ 202-833-9860, fax 202-659-8124), 1700 Massachusetts Ave, NW, Washington DC 20036
 Also in Chicago, Houston, Los Angeles, Miami, New York, Patterson (New Jersey), San Francisco

## Embassies & Consulates in Peru

All the following are in Lima or its suburbs and are open weekdays. There are other embassies or consulates listed under the major cities, particularly Arequipa.

Australia
 Limited services at Honorary Consul (☎ 441-5366, fax 421-6253), Santa Cruz 398, San Isidro

Bolivia
 (☎ 440-2298, fax 422-8231), Los Castaños 235, San Isidro; 9:30 am to 12:30 pm

Brazil
 (☎ 421-5660, fax 445-2421), José Pardo 850, Miraflores; 9 am to 1 pm, 2 to 5 pm

Canada
 (☎ 444-4015, fax 444-4347), Libertad 130, Miraflores; 8 am to 5 pm

Chile
 (☎ 221-2817, 221-2080, 221-4325), Javier Prado Oeste 790, San Isidro; 9 am to 1 pm

Colombia
 (☎ 441-0530, 441-0954, fax 441-9806), Jorge Basadre 1580, San Isidro; 9 am to 1 pm

Ecuador
 (☎ 440-9941, fax 422-0711), Las Palmeras 356, San Isidro; 9 am to 1 pm, 3 to 6 pm

France
 (☎ 221-7837, 221-7598, fax 221-7177), Arequipa 3415, San Isidro; 9 to 11 am

Germany
 (☎ 422-4919, fax 442-6475), Arequipa 4210, Miraflores; 9 am to noon

Israel
(☎/fax 433-4431), Natalio Sánchez 125, 6th floor, Santa Beatriz; 10 am to 1 pm

The Netherlands
(☎ 475-6537, 476-1069, fax 475-6536), Principal 190, Santa Catalina; 9 am to noon

New Zealand
See UK

UK
(☎ 433-4738, fax 433-4735), Natalio Sánchez 125, Lima; 8 am to noon

USA
(☎ 434 3000, fax 434-3037), Avenida Encalada, Cuadra 17, Monterrico; 8 am to 5 pm

## Your Own Embassy

As a tourist, it's important to realize what your own embassy – the embassy of the country of which you are a citizen – can and can't do.

Generally speaking, it won't be much help in emergencies if the trouble you're in is remotely your own fault. Remember that you are bound by the laws of the country you are in. Your embassy will not be sympathetic if you end up in jail after committing a crime locally, even if such actions are legal in your own country.

In genuine emergencies, you might get some assistance, but only if other channels have been exhausted. For example, if you need to get home urgently, a free ticket home is exceedingly unlikely – the embassy would expect you to have insurance. If you have all your money and documents stolen, it should assist in getting a new passport, but a loan for onward travel is out of the question.

Embassies used to keep letters for travelers or have a small reading room with home newspapers, but these days the mail-holding service has been stopped, and newspapers tend to be out of date.

## CUSTOMS

You can bring two liters of alcohol and 400 cigarettes into Peru duty free. You can bring items for personal use but are allowed only US$200 worth of gifts. If bringing in a valuable item for personal use, you may be asked to pay a bond of 25% of the value of the item, which is supposedly refundable when you leave. Unfortunately, it can be problematic to get a refund in the short period of time that you are at the airport leaving the country. It's the usual runaround: 'The officer isn't here; Come back tomorrow; Get your refund at the office downtown,' etc, etc. If asked to pay a bond, resist as much as you can by insisting that the item is for personal use and that you will not be selling it in Peru. Legally, you are allowed to bring in a laptop for personal use, though I wouldn't draw attention to it. You should also be able to bring in cameras, bicycles, kayaks, climbing gear, etc for personal use.

If you absolutely cannot make any headway, undervalue the item as much as you dare in order to minimize your potential loss, and check with customs a day or two before you leave. If you are traveling on a tour, ask your inbound tour operator for assistance.

It is illegal to take any pre-Columbian artifacts out of Peru, and it is illegal to bring them into most countries. Bringing home animal products from endangered species is also illegal. Coca leaves are legal in Peru, but not in most other countries. Coca leaves in the form of tea bags are freely available in Peruvian shops, but these, too, are illegal in most countries (even though it would be impossible to produce any significant amount of cocaine from a box of coca tea bags).

People who have jobs where random urine-testing for drugs occurs should note that (I've been told) drinking coca tea may leave trace amounts of chemical in your urine.

## MONEY
### Currency

Peruvian currency is the nuevo sol (S/). Bills of S/10, S/20, S/50, S/100 and S/200 are currently in circulation. The nuevo sol is divided into 100 céntimos, and there are copper-colored coins of S/0.05, S/0.10 and S/0.20, as well as silver-colored coins worth S/0.50 and S/1. In addition, there are rather odd but not unattractive bimetallic coins that have a copper center surrounded by silver; these are worth S/2 and S/5.

## Exchange Rates

The US dollar is by far the easiest foreign currency to exchange. Other hard currencies (especially German marks) are exchangeable only in the main cities and, often, at a higher commission. Perhaps, the euro will become important in the future, but at this time I would advise travelers to buy US dollars in their home countries, rather than exchanging pounds, francs or other currencies in Peru. In April 1999, the exchange rate was S/3.35 for US$1.

## Exchanging Money

The following information is meant as a guide only. Peruvian currency-exchange regulations can change at any time, and your best source of information when you arrive is probably to ask a fellow traveler who has been in Peru for a while.

Money can be changed in banks, *casas de cambio* (exchange houses) or with street moneychangers. First-class hotels and restaurants will also accept dollars. Exchange rates vary little from place to place (within 1% or 2% of each other for US cash). The exception is your hotel, which may have a high commission. It's best to exchange money in cities; it can be very difficult to do so in the smaller towns and villages.

If you are arriving at the Lima airport, you'll find several banks, some of which are open 24 hours a day. Exchange rates at the airport are almost the same as in Lima, but count your money carefully, as the tellers have been known to shortchange tired travelers arriving late at night. This happened to me, but I counted the money before I left the window and was quickly given the balance when I politely informed the teller of his 'mistake.'

Departing travelers can usually change their remaining Peruvian currency back into US cash, but as this can be unreliable, try not to be left with a huge wad of nuevos soles when you leave. On one occasion in the early 1990s, when leaving Peru through Lima's international airport, I was told that the Peruvian government had suspended trading on Peruvian currency, and I couldn't change my excess back to dollars.

**Cash** It is *most important* to examine US dollars carefully before arriving in Peru. Bills must be in good condition; banks in Peru will not accept dollar bills with even the smallest tears or other damage. Heavily worn or written-on bills aren't accepted either. False dollar bills circulate in Peru occasionally, so examine any that you may obtain there.

**Traveler's Checks** These are exchanged at a lower rate than cash – a commission of several percent (sometimes as much as 10% lower than cash) is often charged, depending on where you change them. People changing traveler's checks should shop around a little bit. The best rates are for receiving nuevos soles rather than US dollars. At this time, I don't recommend traveler's checks because of the low exchange rate. I usually bring traveler's checks with me, as an insurance

---

### The Ups & Downs of the Sol

When I first visited Peru in 1982, I received about 500 soles for US$1. By the end of 1985, the Peruvian currency was valued at 17,300 soles to the US dollar. In 1986, a new currency was introduced by the simple (and, in Latin America, common) expedient of slashing the last three digits. The new currency was called the inti, and was worth I/17.30 to the US dollar when introduced. ('Sol' is the Spanish word for sun, and 'inti' means the same thing in Quechua.)

By 1991, the value of the US dollar had reached about I/1,000,000 and the government introduced yet another currency, the nuevo sol, worth 1,000,000 intis. At this writing, the nuevo sol (written S/) is worth S/3.35 against the US dollar. (Once in a while I figure out how many of the old soles I would get for US$1 if the currency had not been changed. Today it works out at a staggering 3,350,000,000 old soles – quite a wad in the old wallet!)

policy, but I prefer to use ATMs (see ATMs, immediately following).

Banks are good for changing traveler's checks and giving cash advances on credit cards, but can be rather slow and bureaucratic. Casas de cambio are often faster and give about the same rates as the banks for US cash, but rarely take traveler's checks. For changing traveler's checks in smaller towns, the Banco de Crédito is often your only choice. In larger towns, Interbanc has also been recommended. The Banco de Crédito will sometimes change traveler's checks into US dollars at a small commission. This depends on the availability of US cash and so is more likely to occur in larger cities.

If you lose traveler's checks, you have to go to Lima to get new ones. In other cities, you can report the loss but can't get them replaced. American Express is by far the best choice for traveler's checks – other kinds can be problematic to negotiate.

**ATMs** I found ATMs to be the best way to get money on my most recent trip. To avoid getting stung with high interest rates on cash withdrawals from credit cards, you can do one of two things (and not get charged any interest). I used a debit card, which withdraws money from my checking account (this works only if you have money in your checking account). Alternatively, use a credit card by paying your entire credit-card bill and adding enough money to cover your trip. Otherwise, using ATMs will be very expensive.

The best ATM card is definitely Visa, as it is accepted at Banco de Crédito, which has branches in almost every town of any size in Peru. MasterCard can be used at Banco Latino, which is found in all major cities but not many minor ones. Interbanc is also good for Visa transactions, and Banco Wiese often works with MasterCard. Other credit cards (AmEx, Diner's Club) have limited use in ATMs. Most ATMs work with the Plus system for Visa and MasterCard; some work with Star, Interlink, Cirrus or others, but they can be hard to find. Your most useful card, therefore, is a Visa on the Plus system. Make sure that your Personal Identification Number

(PIN) has four digits, as Peruvian ATMs don't recognize longer PINs. If your PIN is a letter code, make sure to find out what the number-code equivalent is before you go, as Peruvian ATMs may not have letters on the PIN pad.

ATMs are often open 24 hours and are usually behind locked doors. To get in, you need a debit card or credit card. This makes withdrawing money safer than doing it on the street, but I suggest trying to avoid withdrawing money late at night. Most ATM screens have a choice of Spanish or English versions, and most allow you to obtain cash in US dollars or nuevos soles. I found that asking for nuevos soles gave me within 1% of the best rate possible, and it saves the hassle of then having to change US dollars into local currency.

Occasionally, ATMs don't work. If this happens, try the next day or try another ATM. I've heard that your card could be retained by the machine if you try three times in succession. During business hours, tellers will give cash against your card. However, I didn't have any major problems with ATMs during a dozen recent transactions.

Peru's economy can go through wild changes in short periods of time. To avoid having problems with ATMs, and to cover yourself should you lose your card, consider carrying traveler's checks and some US cash as emergency backup.

**Credit & Debit Cards** These can be used in stores, restaurants and hotels, but an 8% commission is often added to the bill. The exception is airline tickets, where the price is normally in US dollars. Generally, though, the most economical way to go is to use an ATM for cash and then use cash for your purchases.

For lost or stolen cards, or for local information about cards, the following numbers (all in Lima) are useful:

Visa: lost cards ☎ 441-2112, 428-9898
    information 442-8966

MasterCard: lost cards ☎ 444-1891
    information 422-1290, 422-2499

AmEx: lost cards ☎ 330-4484
    information 424-6410

**Change** Don't expect to be able to pay for inexpensive services with large bills, because change is often not available. Cabdrivers may say they don't have change simply to try to make a bit of extra money. It's worth first asking drivers ¿*Tiene cambio de cinquenta soles?* – Do you have change for fifty soles (or whatever the size of your bill) – to make sure you're not stuck with overpaying later. If traveling to small towns, bring a supply of small-denomination bills.

**International Transfers** If you run out of money, it's easy to have more sent to you, assuming that you have someone at home kind enough to do this. A bank transfer is fastest by fax, although this will take a couple of days to arrange. Ask at a Peruvian bank how to arrange this, what the commission is, and whether you can receive the money in US dollars or Peruvian currency. Only some banks will provide this service (at a small commission). Again, the Banco de Crédito is recommended.

Western Union (☎ 422-0014) has about a dozen branches in greater Lima and many others all over Peru. They provide fast and efficient money-transfer services, but charge a high commission (about 10%, depending on how much is sent).

**Moneychangers** Unofficial moneychangers hang out near the banks and casas de cambio. There is no real advantage to using them – their rates are not significantly better than the best rates in banks or casas de cambio, and travelers have reported being cheated. If you do use street changers, count your money very carefully *before* handing over the dollars, and use your own calculator, as some changers have 'fixed' ones. Street changers are useful at times when you need to change money outside of business hours or at land borders. In this case, your safest bet is to use an 'official' changer, identified by a badge and, often, a bright yellow or blue vest. Refer to Theft under the Dangers & Annoyances section later in this chapter for suggestions about keeping your money safe.

## Costs

Costs in Peru are lower than in most first-world countries, but higher than in neighboring Ecuador and Bolivia, and about the same as in Chile. Costs are higher in Lima and Cuzco than anywhere else on the coast or highlands. If you're on a very tight budget, you can get by on a bare-bones budget of about US$15 per day, but that means staying in the most basic of hotels and traveling very slowly. Most solo budget travelers spend US$20 or more per day, mainly because of the large distances that have to be covered to properly visit Peru. The best ways to save money are to share a hotel room and to eat the standard set-lunch menu in cheap restaurants.

If you can afford to spend a little more, however, you'll probably enjoy yourself more too. The luxury of a simple room with a private hot shower and a table and chair to write letters home can be had for well under US$20 for a double. Saving time and energy by flying back from a remote destination that took you several days of land travel to reach is also recommended.

Due to violent swings in the exchange rate and various political or economic problems, costs in both dollars and nuevos soles has changed rapidly in the past. The costs of many services tripled in dollar terms and went up astronomically in local currency within a few months during 1991, for example. By the same token, prices can fall equally rapidly. Bear this in mind when reading prices in these pages – they are a guideline only. Although dollar costs tend to stay comparatively stable, you can still experience a noticeable change in prices within a month. However, during the economic and political stability of the past few years, prices in dollar have remained fairly stable.

To give you a guideline, some current costs are as follows. Hotel rooms, double occupancy, can be about US$6 in a basic budget place, US$25 for an economy hotel, US$50 to US$80 for a 1st-class hotel and up to US$200 for a luxury hotel in the few cities that have them or in a few places where location is everything (Machu Picchu). Airfares within Peru vary tremendously from year to year, but most one-way tickets are under US$100. Bus fares average about US$1 per hour of travel on the regular buses and US$2 on the luxury buses. A beer will be from US$1 to US$3, depending on where you drink it. A cheap set lunch in a simple restaurant is under US$2; a good meal in a nice restaurant is US$10 to US$20; a superb meal in a fancy restaurant could go over US$50. A local bus ride is US$0.35, an international airmail letter is US$1, and a major newspaper is US$0.60.

## Tipping & Bargaining

The cheapest restaurants do not include a tip in the bill. If you want to tip waiters, make sure you give it directly to them and don't leave it lying on the table. Tipping is not expected in very basic restaurants. In better restaurants, tip the waiter up to 15%. In many better restaurants, a 10% service charge is included, but you should give the waiter an extra 5% if the service is good.

Taxi drivers are not tipped – bargain a fare beforehand and stick to it. Tip bellhops or porters about US$0.50 per bag in the better establishments. When hiring local guides, tip them about US$3 to US$5 per client for each full day's work if they are good, professional, multilingual guides – less if they aren't. If there's a large group of you, tip about US$2 per client per day. These are minimal recommendations; you can, of course, tip more. If going on a trek, it is customary also to tip the cook and porters. Tip them at least as much as the guide, and divide it among them.

Bargaining is accepted and expected in markets when buying crafts, and occasionally in other situations. If you're not sure whether bargaining is appropriate, try to ask for a *descuento*, discount. These are often given in hotels, at tour agencies, in souvenir shops and other places where tourists spend money.

## Taxes

A combination of taxes and service charges is added to bills in the best hotels and restaurants – this can reach as much as 28%, so you should prepare for this. The cheapest

hotels and restaurants don't add a tax. Some better restaurants that do may include it in the prices on the menu (IGV or *Incluye Impuesto*). Ask if you aren't sure. If 28% is added, 10% is for service, so you take this into account when tipping.

## POST & COMMUNICATIONS
### Post

**Sending Mail** The Peruvian postal service (*SerPost*) has recently improved substantially, but letters are more expensive to send than in more-developed countries. Airmail postcards or letters are about US$1 to most foreign destinations. For a few cents more, they can be registered (*certificado*), which gives you peace of mind but isn't really necessary. Letters from Peru to the USA (as an example) can take one to two weeks to arrive, depending where you mail from. Lima is the best place for the fastest service.

The post office in each town is marked on the town maps provided in this book. Opening hours are very convenient. In many towns, the post office is open from 9 am to 8 pm on weekdays, and a half-day on Saturday or Sunday.

Mailing parcels is expensive (more so than almost every country in Latin America) and therefore not recommended. A 5kg parcel reportedly costs over US$100 to North America or Europe. It's best done from the main post office in Lima. Parcels need to be checked by customs, so bring your parcel open and then sew it up in a cloth sack. Small packages weighing less than 1kg (2kg to some destinations) can be sent in an openable (drawstring) bag by *pequeños paquetes* service, which goes by certified airmail. Sealed envelopes will not be accepted, except for normal letters. There is no surface mail outside Lima, meaning there's no alternative to very expensive airmail. Regulations change from year to year.

There are international express services such as DHL, but these are also expensive. If you buy a huge amount of souvenirs, you'll find it cheaper and easier to pay excess luggage charges rather than mailing large parcels home.

**Receiving Mail** The best place to receive mail is at South American Explorers' clubhouses (only for members) or at the main post office of towns you visit.

If you have mail sent to the post office, remember that it is filed alphabetically, so if it's addressed to John Gillis Payson Esq, it could well be filed under G or E instead of the correct P. It should be addressed, for example, to John PAYSON, Lista de Correos, Correos Central, Lima, Peru. Ask your loved ones to clearly print your last name and avoid witticisms such as 'World Traveler Extraordinaire' appended to it.

## Telephone

The country code for Peru is 51. To call a Peruvian number from overseas, dial your international-access code, followed by the country code, followed by the area code *without* the 0, followed by the six- or seven-digit number. When in Peru, don't dial the area code if you are calling locally.

The government-run telephone system was privatized in 1994 and is now the Spanish-owned Telefónica del Peru. In 1999, four more companies (including three US-based ones) were approved to compete with

Telefónica del Peru, so expect changes in the near future. Services have expanded and been modernized since 1994, although the downside is that telephone numbers have been changing too rapidly to keep up with. For directory inquiries call ☎ 103; international inquiries and operators are ☎ 108.

Telefónica offices are marked on all street plans in this book. The bigger towns have fax services there as well; the smaller towns have phone service only. Most towns of any size will have several smaller Telefónica offices in addition to the main one marked on the map. Ask locally about this before going all the way across town to the main office. Many very remote villages can communicate with a major city, which can connect you into an international call.

Since the recent modernization, telephone booths or little green pay phones (available in some stores and restaurants) are becoming widespread in the major cities. To make long-distance or international calls, you can dial direct from coin telephones, if you have a pile of one-nuevo-sol coins (phones don't take two- or five-nuevo-soles coins, but may in the future). Alternatively, go to one of the many Telefónica del Peru

## Telephone Codes

When dialing from abroad, drop the '0' in front of the code; when in Peru, don't dial the area code if you are calling locally. The department capitals and most important towns are listed; telephone directories list smaller towns.

| | | | | | |
|---|---|---|---|---|---|
| Abancay | 084 | Cuzco | 084 | Pisac | 084 |
| Aguas Calientes | 084 | Huancavelica | 064 | Pisco | 034 |
| Aguas Verdes | 074 | Huancayo | 064 | Piura | 074 |
| Andahuaylas | 084 | Huánuco | 064 | Pucallpa | 064 |
| Arequipa | 054 | Huaraz | 044 | Puerto Maldonado | 084 |
| Ayacucho | 064 | Ica | 034 | Puno | 054 |
| Cajamarca | 044 | Iquitos | 094 | Tacna | 054 |
| Caraz | 044 | Juliaca | 054 | Tarapoto | 094 |
| Celendín | 044 | La Merced | 064 | Tarma | 064 |
| Cerro de Pasco | 064 | Lima | 01 | Tingo María | 064 |
| Chachapoyas | 074 | Machu Picchu | 084 | Trujillo | 044 |
| Chiclayo | 074 | Nazca | 034 | Tumbes | 074 |
| Chimbote | 044 | Ollantaytambo | 084 | Urubamba | 084 |

offices and buy a telephone card, which comes in various denominations. These are the cheapest way to call. Telephones accepting credit cards are expected to follow in the future. In some smaller towns, you may have to go through the operator in the Telefónica office until new equipment is installed. Rates are cheaper on Sunday and from 8 pm to 5 am Monday to Saturday.

Telefónica offices are usually open from 8 am to 10 pm or sometimes later in the major cities. The best hotels can connect international calls to your room at almost any time, though these are operator assisted and so more expensive. Collect or reverse-charge phone calls are possible to countries that have reciprocal agreements with Peru.

Telephone numbers are six digits in most of Peru and seven digits in Lima. Area codes are three digits in most towns, always beginning with 0. (The main exception is Lima, with a two-digit code – 01.) To make a long-distance call to a Peruvian number from within Peru, dial the area code first, including the 0. Area codes for Peruvian cities are given in the text under each city.

Cellular phones are becoming increasingly popular. Note that cellular-phone users have to pay for incoming calls, so that if you call someone on their cellular phone, they will often ask if they can call you back (on a cheaper line). Cellular phone numbers are indicated in the text by 'cell.'

### Fax

Fax services are available at many locations, including better hotels and most of the Telefónica del Peru offices. It costs about US$3 to US$7 (rates are higher outside of Lima) to send a page to the USA and a few cents to receive a page. Most will hold faxed replies on request.

Some hotels and other offices have fax machines that double as telephones. Thus you may try to send a fax to a hotel, only to have a Spanish-speaking hotel receptionist come on the line. It can be time-consuming to explain that you need to send a fax. Several tries may be necessary.

### Email & Internet Access

Peru has many public Internet cabins (cabinas). Every town of any size will have one or more, and many are listed in the text under the appropriate town. If they have moved or closed, ask around. Many hotels or stores selling computers will know where to go.

Most public Internet places are as boring as a barn; a few are trying to become cyber-cafés and may sell soft drinks or play background music. At most Internet cabins, you can get online for between US$1.30 and US$3 per hour (the remoter places are more expensive). Most are open long hours, but not all night. You can send email and access your own account if you use a free Internet-based email service like Hotmail (www .hotmail.com) or Yahoo (www.yahoo.com). It's easy and it works. It's cheaper to email your family, friends and workplace than it is to phone, fax or send a postcard. You can also check the Scottish soccer scores or surf the web.

If you are carrying a laptop or handheld computer, it is possible to access email from hotel rooms, though I have had better success with email from public Internet cabins. AOL has a Lima number (☎ 421-1560) that you can access for US$6 per hour plus local phone fees.

Internet access is changing from month to month – ask your Internet service provider for information regarding access from Peru, or get a free Hotmail or Yahoo account.

### INTERNET RESOURCES

The World Wide Web is a rich resource for travelers. You can research your trip, hunt down bargain airfares, book hotels, check on weather conditions or chat with locals and other travelers about the best places to visit (or avoid).

The Lonely Planet Web site (www.lonely planet.com) has summaries on traveling to most places on earth, postcards from other travelers and the Thorn Tree bulletin board, where you can ask questions before you go or dispense advice when you return. You can also find travel news and updates to some of our guidebooks, and the subWWWay section links you to useful travel resources elsewhere on the Web.

Many hotels, tour operators, etc have websites – they are rarely listed in this book unless they are especially interesting. However, email addresses are listed whenever possible; you can email the company to find out if they have a web page.

A good resource for finding links on Peruvian arts, culture, academic research, business and economy (but not much on travel) is lanic.utexas.edu/la/peru/. Another useful Peruvian website, www.rcp.net.pe, can be viewed in Spanish or English.

## BOOKS

There are a few good bookstores in Lima that sell books in English, but they are expensive. The best place for guidebooks is at South American Explorers' clubhouses, but they give preference to members. Outside of Lima, books in English are not easily available, except in Cuzco. It's best to buy the books you want at home.

Some books are published in different editions by different publishers in different countries. As a result, a book might be a hardcover rarity in one country, while it's readily available in paperback in another. Fortunately, bookstores and libraries are able to search by title or author, so your local bookstore or library is the best place to find out about the availability of the following recommendations.

### Lonely Planet

Other guidebooks can supplement or complement this one, especially if you are visiting South American countries other than Peru. Lonely Planet's South America guides include the following titles: *Argentina, Uruguay & Paraguay*; *Bolivia*; *Chile & Easter Island*; *Colombia*; *Brazil*; *Ecuador & the Galápagos Islands* and *Venezuela*. Budget travelers planning to cover a large part of the continent should look for LP's *South America on a shoestring*.

If it's long walks you're interested in, *Trekking in the Patagonian Andes* has detailed descriptions and maps of extensive treks in Chilean national parks and reserves, plus others across the border in Argentina. LP's *Chile & Easter Island Travel Atlas* includes a full depiction of the region's national parks, as well as a legend and travel information in English, French, German, Spanish and Japanese.

LP's *Latin American Spanish Phrasebook* is helpful for travelers without a good grasp of the main language of South America, but if you'd like to attempt communication with the descendants of the Incas in their native tongue, LP's *Quechua Phrasebook* can help you get your point across.

These and other Lonely Planet products can be found in bookstores worldwide, or they can be ordered online via LP's website at www.lonelyplanet.com – click on 'Propaganda' and you're on your way.

### Guidebooks

One of my favorite guidebooks covers only the Cuzco area but does that entertainingly and in some detail. *Exploring Cusco* by Peter Frost (Nuevas Imagenes, Lima) is highly recommended for anyone planning to spend any length of time in the Cuzco area – all the main sites are described. The book is available in Lima and Cuzco; check with the South American Explorers (www .samexplo.org).

### Archaeology & History

A host of books deal with the Incas. Going back to the arrival of the conquistadors, the best book is undoubtedly John Hemming's lucid and well-written *The Conquest of the Incas*. If you read only one book on the Incas and the conquest, make this it.

*The Royal Commentaries of the Incas* was written in the early 17th century by Garcilaso de la Vega. This historian was born in Cuzco in 1539 of an Inca princess and a Spanish soldier. His book is the most widely translated, easily available and readable of the contemporary accounts of Inca life. Although the book is currently out of print, it is a classic and will undoubtedly be reprinted. Check libraries if you have a hard time finding it in stores.

A newer text, particularly recommended for readers more seriously interested in

Peruvian archaeology, is *The Incas and Their Ancestors: The Archaeology of Peru* by Michael E Mosey. Another recommended recent book for serious readers is Richard L Burger's *Chavín and the Origins of Andean Civilizations*.

## Natural History

There are no comprehensive guides to the flora and fauna of Peru.

There are, however, several helpful books about Peruvian and South American birds. A good source for locating the following bird books is the American Birding Association (ABA; ☎ 719-578-0607, 800-634-7736, fax 719-578-9705, abasales@abasales.com, www.americanbirding.org, PO Box 6599, Colorado Springs, CO 80934, USA), speciality birding stores or the SAE.

*An Annotated Checklist of Peruvian Birds*, by Parker III, Parker and Plenge, is a checklist plus information on birdwatching in Peru; it's a bit pricey at US$20. *A Guide to the Birds of Peru: An Annotated Checklist*, by James F Clements, is due in late 1999 and promises to be a comprehensive illustrated field guide.

For the eastern slopes of the Andes and the Amazon lowlands, the best book is *A Guide to the Birds of Colombia*, by SL Hilty and WL Brown. This is a comprehensive guidebook with professional color plates. Because Colombia has a land border with Peru, many of the rainforest species are the same. Dedicated birders often buy the excellent and recommended *Birds of the High Andes*, by Jon Fjeldså and Niels Krabbe. It covers all the Andes (not just Peru) and is very comprehensive, but costs about US$140.

Even more detailed is *The Birds of South America*, by RS Ridgely & G Tudor. This is a new four-volume set for the specialist and is expensive. The first volume, *The Oscine Passerines*, costs US$70. Volume two is *The Suboscine Passerines* and costs US$85. The remaining two volumes will appear in due course.

*Neotropical Rainforest Mammals – A Field Guide*, by Louise H Emmons, describes and illustrates almost 300 species from the rainforests of Peru and other Latin American countries.

For the layperson interested in rainforest biology, try the entertaining and readable *Tropical Nature*, by Adrian Forsyth and Ken Miyata. Other good natural-history books include *A Neotropical Companion*, by John C Kricher. This book is subtitled *An Introduction to the Animals, Plants, and Ecosystems of the New World Tropics*. Another good choice is Catherine Caulfield's *In the Rainforest*, which emphasizes the problems of the loss of the rainforest.

## Hiking & Climbing

The all-around best book on this subject is *Peru & Bolivia: Backpacking & Trekking* by Hilary Bradt, Jane Letham and John Pilkington. It has a wealth of background information, as well as entertaining descriptions and maps of more than a dozen good backpacking trips in Peru and Bolivia. These include classic treks such as the Inca Trail to Machu Picchu and the Llanganuco/Santa Cruz loop in the Cordillera Blanca, as well as some little-known hikes in less-visited areas.

*Yuraq Janka: Guide to the Peruvian Andes – Cordilleras Blanca & Rosko*, by John F Ricker, is the best, if dated, climbing guide to these ranges, and it has useful maps. Several other climbing guides have been written; most are out of print, but may still be available in libraries and some bookstores.

What climbing is *not* normally like is described in *Touching the Void* by Joe Simpson. This is the true story of a deadly climbing accident in the Cordillera Huayhuash – and an accomplished climber who, despite desperate odds, didn't die.

## Travel & Adventure

Of the many good books about Amazon travel, the following are recommended. As with the others, they don't deal with Peru alone, but with the Amazon region as a whole. One is *The Rivers Amazon*, by Alex Shoumatoff; it is currently out of print, so check libraries if you can't find it in stores. It may be reprinted at some point in the future. Peter Matthiessen's *The Cloud Forest* describes his journey from the rivers of Peru to the mountains of Tierra del Fuego; his experience in Peru led to his novel *At Play in the Fields of the Lord*, a superb and believable story of the conflict between the forces of 'development' and indigenous peoples. A more recent, slightly disconcerting and haunting extended essay of an artist's journey to the Peruvian Amazon is Roberta Allen's *Amazon Dream*. Also, *Running the Amazon*, by Joe Kane, is an exciting and insightful personal account of an expedition from the source of the Amazon (high in the Peruvian Andes) to its mouth in Brazil. Much of the action takes place in Peru.

*Journey to Machu Picchu*, by Carol Cumes *et al*, connects New Age travelers to the spiritual and healing powers of Machu Picchu.

## NEWSPAPERS & MAGAZINES

There are dozens of newspapers available in Peru. Most towns of any size publish a local newspaper, which is useful for finding out what's playing in the town cinemas and reading the local gossip, but has little national news and even less international news. Many newspapers are available in Lima, although quite a few of these are sensationalist rags that luridly portray murder victims or women's buttocks on the front page while relegating world affairs to a few columns behind the sports section.

One of the best papers is *El Comercio*, published in Lima. It is a dry, conservative newspaper that comes in several sections and keeps up to date with cultural and artistic events in the capital, as well as with national and international news. It often has interesting travel articles about Peruvian destinations. A shorter version (lacking the events sections) is available in other cities but is more expensive than in Lima. Other decent newspapers are the conservative *Expreso* and the moderate to left-wing *La República*.

The English-language *Lima Times* has been around for decades in many forms. It's currently a magazine that is published every two months (but it used to be a weekly newspaper), and it has well-written and illustrated articles on Peru (about US$3). The new

*Rumbos* (about US$6.50) is a glossy magazine published every two months. The articles that I've read have been very good and are in both Spanish and English. Photographs are superb. *Rumbos* and the *Lima Times* are available by subscription outside of Peru, but the mailing cost makes it more expensive than you'd probably like. These and foreign newspapers and magazines are available at good bookstores and street stands.

The South American Explorers publishes a quarterly magazine called the *South American Explorer*; it has a host of articles about Peru, Ecuador and other parts of the continent.

## RADIO & TV

Peru has seven major television channels plus cable, but the local programming leaves a lot to be desired. Apart from interminable sports programs, the choice is poor: Latin American soap operas or reruns of old North American sitcoms. The evening news broadcasts are quite good, especially for local news. Occasionally, a National Geographic special makes its way to the screen. These types of programs are advertised days ahead in the better newspapers. Many better hotels have cable TV with international programming.

If you carry a portable radio, there are plenty of stations with a better variety of programs to choose from. Programs are in Quechua and Spanish. The BBC World Service and the Voice of America can be picked up in Peru on shortwave radio.

## PHOTOGRAPHY & VIDEO

Definitely bring everything you'll need. Camera gear is expensive in Peru and, off the beaten track, the choice of film is limited, though amateurs will find adequate print film. Rolls may be kept in hot storage cabinets and are sometimes sold outdated, so if you do buy film in Peru, check its expiration date.

The video system is compatible with the US and Canadian video system NTSC, and therefore doesn't work on European and Australian systems.

## Technical Tips

Don't have film developed in Peru if you can help it, as processing is often shoddy (especially for slide film), though print film is adequate if you aren't a professional. However, carrying around exposed film for months if you are on a long trip is also asking for washed-out results. It is best to send film home as soon as possible after it's exposed. The mail service is expensive, so try to send film home with a friend.

Prepaid film developing is a good idea if you're on a budget; this avoids having to find the money to develop a few dozen rolls of film.

The heat and humidity of the tropics can wreak havoc on delicate electronic cameras. If you like to use a 'gee-whiz' camera with electronic auto-iris and atom-splitting viewfinder, you should think about carrying a simple mechanical body as a backup.

Tropical shadows are very strong and come out almost black on photographs. Often a bright but hazy day gives better photographs than a very sunny one. Taking photographs in open shade or using a fill-in flash will help. The best time for shooting is when the sun is low – the first and last two hours of the day. If you are heading into the Amazon lowlands, you will need high-speed film, a flash, a tripod or a combination of these to take photographs in the jungle. The amount of light penetrating the layers of vegetation is surprisingly low.

## Photographing People

The Peruvian people are highly photogenic. From a charmingly grubby Indian child to the handsomely uniformed presidential guard, the possibilities for 'people pictures' are endless. However, most people resent having a camera thrust in their faces and people in markets will often proudly turn their backs on pushy photographers. Ask for permission with a smile or a joke, and if this is refused, don't become offended. Some people believe that bad luck can be brought upon them by the 'evil eye' of the camera.

Sometimes a tip is asked for. This is especially true in the highly visited Cuzco area.

Here, locals will dress up in their traditional finery and pose against Andean backdrops. Some entrepreneurs even bring their llamas into Cuzco's main square. These people consider themselves to be posing for a living and become angry if you try to take their picture without giving them a tip. Be aware of people's feelings – it is not worth upsetting someone just to get a photograph.

## TIME

Peru is five hours behind Greenwich Mean Time. Daylight savings time is not used.

It is appropriate here to mention that punctuality is not one of the things that Latin America is famous for.

## ELECTRICITY

Peru uses 220 volts, 60 cycles AC, except Arequipa, which is on 50 cycles. Plugs are two-pronged, and usually accept both flat prongs (found in North America) and round ones (found in Europe).

## WEIGHTS & MEASURES

Peru uses the metric system, as does this book. For reasons I haven't figured out, gasoline is sold in gallons, but everything else is metric. A conversion table is at the back of the book.

## LAUNDRY

Self-service laundry machines can be found in only a few major cities. This means that you have to find someone to wash your clothes or else wash them yourself. In most towns, there are laundries (*lavanderías*) where you leave your clothes for a full day or overnight. Some lavanderías only do dry-cleaning, so check.

If you wash clothes yourself, ask the hotel staff where to do this. Some of the cheaper hotels will show you a huge cement sink and scrubbing board, which is much easier to use than a bathroom sink. Often there is a well-like section full of clean water next to the scrubbing board. Don't dunk your clothes in this water to soak or rinse them, as it is used as an emergency water supply in case of water failure. Use a bowl or bucket to scoop water out instead, or run water from a tap.

Some towns suffer from water shortages and prohibit clothes-washing in hotel rooms.

## TOILETS

Peruvian plumbing (except in top-end hotels and restaurants) leaves something to be desired. Flushing a toilet can lead to an overflow, so you should avoid putting anything other than human waste into the toilet. Even putting toilet paper into the bowl can clog up the system and so a waste receptacle is routinely provided for the paper. This may not seem particularly sanitary, but is better than clogged bowls and water on the floor. A well-run hotel or restaurant, even a cheap one, will ensure that the receptacle is emptied and the toilet cleaned every day.

Public toilets are rare, outside of transportation terminals and restaurants. Those in transportation terminals are often dirty. It is not unusual to see men urinating against walls on side streets. Both men and women can ask to use the bathroom in a restaurant, even if they are not patrons. Occasionally, permission isn't granted because, you're told, the facility isn't functioning properly, in which case you should simply try a second restaurant. Toilet paper is provided only in the better hotels and restaurants, and travelers should carry a supply of their own.

## HEALTH

Travel health depends on your predeparture preparations, your day-to-day health care while traveling and how you handle any medical problem or emergency that does develop. While the list of potential dangers can seem frightening, with a little luck, some basic precautions and adequate information, few travelers experience more than upset stomachs.

### Travel Health Guides

There are a number of books on travel health, including:

*Staying Healthy in Asia, Africa & Latin America,* Dirk G Schroeder. Probably the best all-round guide to carry, as it's compact but very detailed and well organized.

*Travel with Children,* Maureen Wheeler. Includes basic advice on travel health for younger children.

*Where There is No Doctor,* David Werner. A very detailed guide intended for someone like a Peace Corps worker going to work in an underdeveloped country rather than for the average traveler.

### Predeparture Preparations

**Travel Insurance** A travel insurance policy to cover theft, loss and medical problems is a wise idea. There are a wide variety of policies, and your travel agent will have recommendations. The international student-travel policies handled by STA Travel or other student-travel organizations are usually a good value. Some policies offer lower and higher medical-expense options, but the higher coverage is chiefly for countries like the USA, where medical costs are extremely high. Check the small print on your insurance form:

- Some policies specifically exclude 'dangerous activities,' which can include scuba diving, motorcycling, even trekking. If such activities are on your agenda, you don't want that sort of policy.

- A locally acquired motorcycle license may not be valid under your policy.

- You may prefer a policy that pays doctors or hospitals directly, rather than your having to pay on the spot and make a claim later. If you have to claim later, make sure you keep all documentation. Some policies ask you to call back (reverse charges) to a center in your home country where an immediate assessment of your problem is made.

- Check if the policy covers ambulances or an emergency flight home. If you have to stretch out, you will need two seats, and somebody has to pay for them! Some policies are designed specifically to cover the cost of emergency medical evacuation in the case of serious injury or illness.

**Health Preparations** Make sure you're healthy before you start traveling. If you are embarking on a long trip, make sure your teeth are OK; there are lots of places where a visit to the dentist would be the last thing you'd want.

If you wear glasses, take a spare pair and your prescription. Losing your glasses can be a real problem, although in many places you can get new spectacles made up quickly, cheaply and competently.

If you require a particular medication, take an adequate supply, as it may not be available locally. Take the prescription or, better still, part of the packaging that shows the generic rather than the brand name (which may not be locally available), as it will make getting replacements easier. It's a wise idea to have a legible prescription with you to show that you use the medication legally – it's surprising how often over-the-counter drugs from one place are illegal without a prescription or even banned in another.

**Immunizations** Vaccinations provide protection against diseases you might meet along the way. Although no immunizations are currently necessary to enter Peru, the farther off the beaten track you go, the more sensible it is to take precautions.

It is important to understand the distinction between vaccines recommended for travel in certain areas and those required by law. Essentially, the number of vaccines subject to international health regulations has been dramatically reduced over the last 10 years. Currently, yellow fever is the only vaccine subject to international health regulations. Vaccination as an entry requirement is usually only enforced when coming from an infected area.

On the other hand, a number of vaccines are recommended for travel in certain areas. These may not be required by law, but are recommended for your own personal protection.

All vaccinations should be recorded on an International Health Certificate, which is available from your physician or government health department.

Plan ahead for getting your vaccinations: some of them require an initial shot followed by a booster, while some vaccinations should not be given together. It is recommended you seek medical advice at least six weeks prior to travel. Be prepared for some

---

## Medical Kit Checklist

Consider taking a basic medical kit that includes:

- ❑ **Aspirin** or **paracetamol** (acetaminophen in the USA) – for pain or fever

- ❑ **Antihistamine** (eg, Benadryl) – for colds and allergies, insect bites and stings, and motion-sickness prevention; may cause sedation and may interact adversely with alcohol, so care should be taken when using; take a brand you know and have used before.

- ❑ **Antibiotics** – useful for traveling off the beaten track, but they must be prescribed; carry the prescription with you.

- ❑ **Lomotil** or **Imodium** – for diarrhea; prochlorperazine (eg, Stemetil) or metaclopramide (eg, Maxalon) for nausea and vomiting

- ❑ **Rehydration mixture** – for severe diarrhea; important when traveling with children

- ❑ **Antiseptic** such as povidone-iodine (eg, Betadine) – for cuts and scrapes

- ❑ **Multivitamins** – especially useful for long trips when dietary vitamin intake may be inadequate

- ❑ **Calamine lotion** or **aluminum sulfate spray** (eg, Stingose) – to ease irritation from bites or stings

- ❑ **Bandages** and **Band-Aids**

- ❑ **Scissors, tweezers** and a **thermometer** (note that mercury thermometers are prohibited by airlines)

- ❑ **Cold and flu tablets** and **throat lozenges** – pseudoephedrine hydrochloride (Sudafed) may be useful if flying with a cold, to avoid ear damage.

- ❑ **Insect repellent, sunscreen, lip balm** and **water-purification tablets**

- ❑ **A couple of syringes** – in case you need injections in a country with medical hygiene problems; ask your doctor for a note explaining why they have been prescribed.

soreness and other side effects from immunizations – don't leave them for the day you are packing for the trip. Ask your doctor about your choice of vaccines and their various possible side effects.

Most travelers from developed countries will have been immunized against various diseases during childhood, but your doctor may still recommend booster shots against diphtheria-tetanus, measles or polio. The period of protection offered by vaccinations differs widely, and some are contraindicated if you are pregnant.

In some countries, immunizations are available from airport or government health centers. Travel agents or airline offices will tell you where. Vaccinations include:

**Cholera** This vaccination is not required by law, and the disease is currently not a problem in Peru. Protection is poor and lasts only six months. It is contraindicated in pregnancy.

**Infectious Hepatitis** This is the most common travel-acquired illness that can be prevented by vaccination. Protection can be provided in two ways – either with the antibody gamma globulin or with a new vaccine called Havrix. In the USA, this is called the Hepatitis A vaccine. Havrix is more expensive and must be taken at least three weeks before departure, but is recommended because it provides up to 10 years of immunity. Gamma globulin lasts only six months and may interfere with the development of immunity to other diseases, so careful timing is important with its use.

**Tetanus & Diphtheria** Boosters are necessary every 10 years, and protection is highly recommended.

**Typhoid** This vaccination is available either as an injection or in oral capsules. Protection lasts from one to three years and is useful if you are traveling for a long time in rural, tropical areas.

**Yellow Fever** Travelers to Peru should get this vaccination if planning a trip to the Amazon, but it is not necessary for visits to the coast or Andean highlands. Protection lasts 10 years. You usually have to go to a special yellow-fever vaccination center. Vaccination is contraindicated during pregnancy, but if you must travel to a high-risk area, it is probably advisable.

## Basic Rules

Being careful about what you eat and drink is the most important health rule; stomach upsets are the most likely travel health problem (between 30% and 50% of travelers in a two-week stay experience this), but the majority of these upsets will be relatively minor. Don't become paranoid; after all, trying the local food is part of the experience of travel.

**Water** The number-one rule is *don't drink the water* – and that includes ice. If you don't know for certain that the water is safe, always assume the worst. Commercial bottled water or soft drinks are generally fine. Take care with fruit juice, particularly if water may have been added. Tea or coffee should be safe since the water should have been boiled.

**Water Purification** The simplest way of purifying water is to boil it thoroughly. Vigorously boiling for five minutes should be satisfactory; however, at high altitude, water boils at a lower temperature, so germs are less likely to be killed.

Water filters may or may not remove all dangerous organisms, so read the manufacturer's literature carefully before purchasing one. If you cannot boil water, chemical treatment may be more reliable than a filter. Chlorine tablets (Puritabs, Steritabs or other brands) will kill many but not all pathogens, including giardia and amoebic cysts. Iodine is very effective in purifying water and is available in tablet form (such as Potable Aqua), but follow the directions carefully and remember that too much iodine can be harmful.

If you can't find tablets, tincture of iodine (2%) or iodine crystals can be used. Four drops of tincture of iodine per liter or quart of clear water is the recommended dosage; the treated water should be left to stand for 20 to 30 minutes before drinking.

**Food** Salads and fruit should be washed with purified water or peeled when possible. Ice cream is usually safe if it is a reputable brand name, but beware of street vendors and of ice cream that has melted and been refrozen. Thoroughly cooked food is safest, but not if it has been left to cool or if it has been reheated. Shellfish such as mussels, oysters and clams should be avoided, as should undercooked meat, particularly in the form of minced or ground beef. Steaming does not make bad shellfish safe for eating. Having said that, it is difficult to resist Peruvian seafood dishes like *ceviche*, which is marinated but not cooked. This is rarely a problem, as long as it is served fresh in a reputable restaurant.

If a place looks clean and well run, and if the vendor also looks clean and healthy, then the food is probably safe. In general, places that are packed with travelers or locals will be fine, while empty restaurants are questionable. The food in busy restaurants is cooked and eaten quite quickly with little standing around and is probably not reheated.

**Nutrition** If your food is poor or limited in availability, if you're traveling hard and fast and therefore missing meals, or if you simply lose your appetite, you can soon start to lose weight and place your health at risk.

Make sure your diet is well balanced. Eggs, beans, lentils and nuts are all safe ways to get protein. Fruits you can peel (bananas, oranges or mandarins, for example) are always safe and a good source of vitamins. Try to eat plenty of grains (rice) and bread. Remember that although food is generally safer if it is cooked well, overcooked food loses much of its nutritional value. If your diet isn't well balanced or if your food intake is insufficient, it's a good idea to take vitamins and iron supplements on a long trip.

In hot climates, make sure you drink enough – don't rely on feeling thirsty to indicate when you should drink. Not needing to urinate or very dark yellow urine is a danger sign. Always carry a water bottle with you on long trips. Excessive sweating can lead to loss of salt, which causes muscle cramping. Salt tablets are not a good idea as a preventative, but in places where salt is not already used, adding some to your food can help.

**Everyday Health** Normal body temperature is 37°C (98.6°F); more than 2°C (4°F) higher indicates a 'high' fever. The normal adult pulse rate is 60 to 80 per minute (for children, 80 to 100 beats per minute; for babies, 100 to 140 beats per minute). You should know how to take a temperature and a pulse rate. As a general rule, the pulse increases by about 20 beats per minute for each degree-Celsius rise in fever.

Respiration (breathing) rate is also an indicator of illness. Count the number of breaths per minute: between 12 and 20 is normal for adults and older children (up to 30 for younger children, 40 for babies). People with a high fever or serious respiratory illness (like pneumonia) breathe more quickly than normal. More than 40 shallow breaths a minute usually means pneumonia.

Illnesses ranging from the common cold to cholera have been proven to be easily transmitted through manual contact. Try not to put your hand to your mouth, and wash your hands before meals. Clean your teeth with purified water rather than straight from the tap. Avoid climatic extremes: Keep out of the sun when it's hot, dress warmly when it's cold. Avoid potential diseases by dressing sensibly. You can get worm infections by walking barefoot. You can avoid insect bites by covering bare skin when insects are around, by screening windows or beds and by using insect repellents. Seek local advice: If you're told the water is unsafe due to jellyfish, piranhas or schistosomiasis, don't go in. In situations where there is no information, discretion is good practice.

## Medical Problems & Treatment

Self-diagnosis and treatment can be risky, so wherever possible, seek qualified help. Drug dosages given in this section are for emergency use only.

An embassy or consulate can usually recommend a good place to go for such advice. So can the best hotels, although they often recommend doctors with the highest prices. (This is when that medical insurance really comes in useful!) Generally speaking, though, Peruvian doctors charge less than their counterparts in North America or Europe. In some places, standards of medical attention are so low that for some ailments, the best advice is to get on a plane and go somewhere else. Adequate medical care is available in the major cities, and the best places are mentioned in the city chapters of this book.

Ideally, antibiotics should be administered only under medical supervision and should never be taken indiscriminately. Take only the recommended dose at the prescribed intervals and continue using the antibiotic for the prescribed period, even if the illness seems to be cured earlier. Antibiotics are quite specific to the infections they can treat. Stop immediately if there are any serious reactions, and don't use the antibiotic at all if you are unsure that you have the correct one.

In Peru, if a medicine is available at all, it will generally be available over the counter, and the price will be much cheaper than in North America or Europe. It is possible that drugs that are no longer recommended or are even banned in more industrialized countries are still being dispensed in Peru.

It may be a good idea to leave unwanted medicines and syringes with a local clinic rather than carry them home.

## Climatic & Geographical Considerations

**Sunburn** In the tropics, the desert, or at high altitude, you can get sunburned surprisingly quickly, even through cloud cover. Use sunscreen (SPF 15 minimum), and take extra care to cover areas that don't normally see sun – eg, your feet. A hat provides added protection, and you should also use zinc cream or some other barrier cream for your nose and lips. Calamine lotion is good for mild sunburn.

**Prickly Heat** Prickly heat is an itchy rash caused by excessive perspiration trapped under the skin. It usually strikes people who have just arrived in a hot climate and whose pores have not yet opened sufficiently to cope with greater sweating. Keeping cool but bathing often, using a mild talcum powder or even resorting to air-conditioning may help until you acclimatize.

**Heat Exhaustion** Dehydration or salt deficiency can cause heat exhaustion. Take time to acclimatize to high temperatures, and make sure you get sufficient liquids. Wear loose clothing and a broad-brimmed hat. Do not do anything too physically demanding.

Salt deficiency is characterized by fatigue, lethargy, headaches, giddiness and muscle cramps, and in this case, salt tablets may help. Vomiting or diarrhea can deplete your liquid and salt levels.

**Heat Stroke** This serious – and sometimes fatal – condition can occur if the body's heat-regulating mechanism breaks down and the body temperature rises to dangerous levels. Long, continuous periods of exposure to high temperatures can leave you vulnerable to heat stroke. You should avoid excessive alcohol or strenuous activity when you first arrive in a hot climate.

The symptoms of heat stroke are feeling unwell, not sweating very much or at all, and a high body temperature (over 39°C, or 102°F). Where sweating has ceased, the skin becomes flushed and red. Severe, throbbing headaches and lack of coordination will also occur, and the sufferer may be confused or aggressive. Eventually the victim will become delirious or convulse. Hospitalization is essential, but meanwhile, get the victim out of the sun, remove their clothing, cover them with a wet sheet or towel and then fan continually.

**Fungal Infections** Hot-weather fungal infections are most likely to occur on the scalp, between the toes or fingers (athlete's foot), in the groin (jock itch or crotch rot) and on the body (ringworm). You get ringworm (which is a fungal infection, not a worm) from infected animals or by walking on damp areas, like shower floors.

To prevent fungal infections, wear loose, comfortable clothes, avoid artificial fibers, wash frequently and dry carefully. If you do get an infection, wash the infected area daily with a disinfectant or medicated soap and water, and rinse and dry well. Apply an antifungal powder like the widely available Tinaderm or Tinactin. Try to expose the infected area to air or sunlight as much as possible, and wash all towels and underwear in hot water, in addition to changing them often.

**Cold** Too much cold is just as dangerous as too much heat, as it may cause hypothermia. If you are trekking at high altitudes or simply taking a long bus trip over mountains, particularly at night, be prepared. In the high Andes, you should always be prepared for cold, wet or windy conditions, particularly when walking, backpacking or trekking.

Hypothermia occurs when the body loses heat faster than it can produce it, and the core temperature of the body falls. It is surprisingly easy to progress from very cold to dangerously cold due to a combination of wind, wet clothing, fatigue and hunger, even if the air temperature is above freezing. It is best to dress in layers; silk, wool and some of the new artificial fibers are all good insulating materials. A hat is important, as a lot of heat is lost through the head. A strong, waterproof outer layer is essential, because keeping dry is vital. Carry basic supplies, including food containing simple sugars to generate heat quickly, and lots of fluid to drink. A space blanket – an extremely thin, lightweight emergency blanket made of a reflective material that keeps heat in – is something all travelers in cold environments should carry.

Symptoms of hypothermia are exhaustion, numb skin (particularly toes and fingers), shivering, slurred speech, irrational or violent behavior, lethargy, stumbling, dizzy spells, muscle cramps and violent bursts of energy. Irrationality may take the form of sufferers claiming they are warm and trying to take off their clothes.

To treat mild hypothermia, first get the person out of the wind and/or rain, remove their clothing if it's wet and replace it with dry, warm clothing. Give them hot liquids – no alcohol – and some high-calorie, easily digestible food. Do not rub victims, as rough handling may cause cardiac arrest. This should be enough to treat the early stages of hypothermia. The early recognition and

treatment of mild hypothermia is the only way to prevent severe hypothermia, which is a critical condition.

**Altitude Sickness** Acute mountain sickness, or AMS, occurs at high altitude and can be fatal. The lack of oxygen at high altitudes affects most people to some extent.

A number of measures can be adopted to prevent acute mountain sickness:

- Ascend slowly – have frequent rest days, spending two to three nights at each rise of 1000m. When you first arrive at high altitude, try not to over exert yourself.
- Drink extra fluids. The mountain air is dry and cold, and moisture is lost as you breathe.
- Eat light, high-carbohydrate meals for more energy.
- Avoid alcohol, as it may increase the risk of dehydration.
- Avoid sedatives.
- Drink the coca tea *(mate de coca)* available in most Andean hotels and restaurants.

Even with acclimatization, you may still have trouble adjusting. Breathlessness; a dry, irritative cough (which may progress to the production of pink, frothy sputum); severe headache; loss of appetite; nausea; and sometimes vomiting are all danger signs. Increasing tiredness, confusion and lack of coordination and balance are real danger signs. Any of these symptoms individually, even just a persistent headache, can be a warning. Mild altitude sickness *(soroche)* will generally abate after a day or so but if the symptoms persist, or become worse, the only treatment is to descend – even 500m can help.

There is no hard and fast rule as to how high is too high: AMS has been fatal at altitudes of 3000m, although 3500m to 4500m is the usual range. It is always wise to sleep at a lower altitude than the greatest height reached during the day.

The prescription drug Diamox (acetazolamide) has been shown to help with acclimatization if taken the day before the ascent and during the first few days at high altitude. There are some mild side effects, such as increased urination, tingling sensations in the extremities and making fizzy drinks taste funny. If you are interested in trying Diamox, talk to your doctor.

**Motion Sickness** Eating lightly before and during a trip will reduce the chances of motion sickness. If you are prone to motion sickness, try to find a place that minimizes disturbance – near the wing on aircraft, close to midships on boats and near the center on buses. Fresh air usually helps; reading and cigarette smoke don't. Commercial motion-sickness preparations, which can cause drowsiness, have to be taken before the trip commences; when you're feeling sick it's too late. Ginger is a natural preventative and is available in capsule form.

**Jet Lag** Jet lag is experienced when a person travels by air across more than three time zones. It occurs because many of the functions of the human body are regulated by internal 24-hour cycles called circadian rhythms. When we travel long distances rapidly, our bodies take time to adjust to the 'new time' of our destination, and we may experience fatigue, disorientation, insomnia, anxiety, impaired concentration and loss of appetite.

These symptoms will usually be gone within three days of arrival, but doing the following can help to minimize the severity and duration of jet lag:

- Rest for a couple of days prior to departure; try to avoid late nights and excessive anxiety such as last-minute dashes for traveler's checks, passport, etc.

- Try to select flight schedules that minimize sleep deprivation; arriving late in the day means you can go to sleep soon after you arrive. For very long flights, try to organize a stopover.

- Make yourself comfortable by wearing loose-fitting clothes and perhaps bringing an eye mask and ear plugs to help you sleep.

- Avoid excessive eating and alcohol during the flight. Drink plenty of noncarbonated, nonalcoholic drinks – such as fruit juice or water.

- Avoid smoking – it causes greater fatigue.

## Diseases of Poor Sanitation

**Diarrhea** A change of water, food or climate can all cause the runs; diarrhea caused by contaminated food or water is more serious. Despite all your precautions, you may still have a mild bout of traveler's diarrhea but a few rushed toilet trips with no other symptoms is not indicative of a serious problem. Moderate diarrhea, involving half a dozen loose bowel movements in a day, is more of a nuisance.

Dehydration is the main danger with any diarrhea – children dehydrate particularly quickly. Fluid replacement remains the mainstay of management. Weak black tea with a little sugar, soda water, or soft drinks allowed to go flat and diluted 50% with water are all good. With severe diarrhea, a rehydrating solution is necessary to replace minerals and salts. Commercially available ORS (oral rehydration salts) are very useful; add the contents of one sachet to a liter of boiled or bottled water. In an emergency, you can make up a solution of eight teaspoons of sugar to a liter of boiled water and provide salted cracker biscuits at the same time. You should stick to a bland diet as you recover.

Lomotil or Imodium can be used to bring relief from the symptoms, although they do not actually cure the problem. Only use these drugs if absolutely necessary – that is, if you *must* travel. For children, Imodium is preferable, but under all circumstances, fluid replacement is the most important thing to remember. Do not use these drugs if the person has a high fever or is severely dehydrated.

Antibiotics may be needed for diarrhea that lasts for more than five days, or if it is severe, or for watery diarrhea with fever and lethargy or with blood and mucus (gut-paralyzing drugs like Imodium or Lomotil should be avoided in this situation).

The recommended drugs (adults only) would be either norfloxacin (400mg) or ciprofloxacin (500mg; this drug is expensive and hard to find) twice daily for three days. Bismuth subsalicylate may be useful but is not available in Australia. Two tablets for adults and one for children can be taken every hour up to eight times a day. Recommended drugs for children are co-trimoxazole (Bactrim, Septrin, Resprim); dosage is dependent on weight.

**Giardiasis** The parasite causing this intestinal disorder is present in contaminated water. The symptoms are stomach cramps, nausea, a bloated stomach, watery, foul-smelling diarrhea and frequent gas. Giardiasis can appear several weeks after you have been exposed to the parasite. The symptoms may disappear for a few days and then return; this can go on for several weeks. Tinidazole, known as Fasigyn, or metronidazole (Flagyl) are the recommended drugs for treatment. Either can be used in a single-treatment dose. Antibiotics are of no use.

**Dysentery** This serious illness is caused by contaminated food or water and is characterized by severe diarrhea, often with blood or mucus in the stool. There are two kinds of dysentery. Bacillary dysentery is characterized by a high fever and rapid onset; headache, vomiting and stomach pains are also symptoms. It generally does not last longer than a week, but it is highly contagious.

Amoebic dysentery is often more gradual in the onset of symptoms, with cramping abdominal pain and vomiting being less likely; fever may not be present. It is not a self-limiting disease: It will persist until treated and can recur and cause long-term health problems.

A stool test is necessary to diagnose which kind of dysentery you have, so you should seek medical help urgently. In an emergency, the recommended drugs for bacillary dysentery are norfloxacin (400mg), ciprofloxacin (500mg; expensive and hard to find) or co-trimoxazole (160/800mg; Bactrim, Septrin, Resprim) twice daily for seven days. Co-trimoxazole is also the recommended drug for children.

For amoebic dysentery, the recommended adult dosage of metronidazole (Flagyl) is one 750mg to 800mg capsule three times daily for five days. Children between the ages of 8 and 12 years should take half the adult dose; the dosage for younger children

is one-third the adult dose. An alternative to Flagyl is Fasigyn, taken as a 2g daily dose for three days. Alcohol must be avoided during treatment and for 48 hours afterward.

**Cholera** Cholera vaccination is not very effective. The bacteria responsible for this disease are waterborne, so attention to the rules of eating and drinking should protect the traveler.

Outbreaks of cholera are generally widely reported, so you can avoid such problem areas. The 1991 epidemic in Peru was confined to extremely poor neighborhoods that, for the most part, lacked running water and a proper sewage system. These are not places where the traveler would normally go.

The disease is characterized by a sudden onset of acute diarrhea with 'rice water' stools, vomiting, muscle cramps and extreme weakness. You need medical help – but first begin treatment for dehydration, which can be extreme, and if there is considerable delay in getting to a hospital, then begin taking 250mg of tetracycline four times daily. It is not recommended for children aged eight or under, nor for pregnant women. Sun-sensitivity is a side effect of the drug, so avoid prolonged exposure if you are taking tetracycline. An alternative drug is Ampicillin. Remember that while antibiotics might kill the bacteria, it is the toxin produced by the bacteria that causes the massive fluid loss. Fluid replacement is by far the most important aspect of treatment.

**Viral Gastroenteritis** This is caused not by bacteria but, as the name suggests, by a virus. It is characterized by stomach cramps, diarrhea and sometimes by vomiting or a slight fever. All you can do is rest and drink lots of fluids.

**Hepatitis** Hepatitis A is a very common problem among travelers to areas with poor sanitation. With good water and adequate sewage disposal in most industrialized countries since the 1940s, very few young adults now have any natural immunity, so they must be protected. Protection is through the new vaccine Havrix (hepatitis A vaccine) or the antibody gamma globulin.

The disease is spread by contaminated food or water. The symptoms are fever, chills, headache, fatigue, feelings of weakness and aches and pains. These symptoms may be followed by loss of appetite, nausea, vomiting, abdominal pain, dark urine, light-colored feces, jaundiced skin and/or eyes. In some cases, the infected person may feel tired, have no appetite, or experience aches and pains. You should seek medical advice, but in general, there is not much you can do apart from resting, drinking lots of fluids, eating lightly and avoiding fatty foods. People who have had hepatitis must forego alcohol for six months after the illness to allow the liver to recover from the hepatitis attack.

Hepatitis B, which used to be called serum hepatitis, is spread through contact with infected blood, blood products or bodily fluids – especially through sexual contact, unsterilized needles and blood transfusions. Other risk situations include getting a shave, tattoo or piercing done in a local shop. The symptoms of type B are much the same as type A, except that they are more severe and may lead to irreparable liver damage, or even liver cancer. Although there is no treatment for hepatitis B, an effective vaccine is readily available in most countries. The immunization schedule requires two injections at least a month apart, followed by a third dose five months after the second. Persons who should receive a hepatitis B vaccination include anyone who anticipates contact with blood or other bodily secretions, either as a health-care worker or through sexual contact with the local population, particularly those who intend to stay in the country for a long period of time.

Hepatitis Non-A Non-B is a blanket term formerly used for several different strains of hepatitis that have now been separately identified. Hepatitis C is similar to B but is less common. Hepatitis D (the 'delta particle') is also similar to B and always occurs in concert with it; its occurrence is currently limited to intravenous drug users. Hepatitis E, however, is similar to A and is spread in the same manner – by water or food contamination.

Tests are available for these strains, but they are very expensive. Travelers shouldn't be too paranoid about this apparent proliferation of hepatitis strains; they are fairly rare (so far), and following the same precautions as for A and B should be all that's necessary to avoid them.

**Typhoid** Typhoid fever is another gut infection that travels the fecal-oral route. Contaminated water and food are responsible. Vaccination against typhoid is not totally effective, and it is one of the most dangerous infections, so medical help must be sought.

In its early stages, typhoid resembles many other illnesses: Sufferers may feel as if they have a bad cold or are in the initial stages of a flu, as early symptoms are a headache, a sore throat and a fever, which rises a little each day until it is around 40°C or more. The victim's pulse is often slow relative to the degree of fever present, and gets slower as the fever rises – unlike a normal fever, where the pulse increases. There may also be vomiting, diarrhea or constipation.

In the second week, the high fever and slow pulse continue, and a few pink spots may appear on the body; trembling, delirium, weakness, weight loss and dehydration are other symptoms. If there are no further complications, the fever and other symptoms will slowly diminish during the third week. Still, you must get medical help, since pneumonia (an acute lung infection) or peritonitis (perforated bowel) are common complications, and typhoid is very infectious. The fever should be treated by keeping the victim cool and dehydration should also be watched for.

The drug of choice is ciprofloxacin at a dose of 1g daily for 14 days. It is quite expensive and may not be available. The alternative, chloramphenicol, has been the mainstay of treatment for many years. In many countries, it is still the recommended antibiotic, but there are fewer side effects with Ampicillin. The adult dosage is two 250mg capsules, four times a day. Children between the ages of 8 and 12 years should have half the adult dose; younger children should have one-third the adult dose. People who are allergic to penicillin should not be given Ampicillin.

**Worms** These parasites are most common in rural, tropical areas. They can be present on unwashed vegetables or in undercooked meat, and you can pick them up through your skin by walking in bare feet. Infestations may not show up for some time, and although they are generally not serious, if left untreated, they can cause severe health problems. A stool test is necessary to pinpoint the problem, and medication is often available over the counter.

## Diseases Spread by Animals & People

**Tetanus** This potentially fatal disease is found in undeveloped tropical areas. It is difficult to treat, but it is preventable with immunization. Tetanus occurs when a wound becomes infected by a germ that lives in the feces of animals or people, so clean all cuts, punctures or animal bites. Tetanus is also known as lockjaw, and the first symptom may be discomfort in swallowing, or stiffening of the jaw and neck; this is followed by painful convulsions of the jaw and whole body.

**Rabies** Rabies is caused by a bite or scratch by an infected animal. Dogs are noted carriers, as are monkeys and cats. Any bite, scratch or even lick should be cleaned immediately and thoroughly. Scrub with soap and running water, and then clean with an alcohol solution. If there is any possibility that the animal is infected, medical help should be sought immediately. Rabies takes at least five days and sometimes several weeks to develop, but once it develops, it is always fatal. A vaccination after the bite occurs but before rabies appears generally results in complete recovery. Even if the animal is not rabid, all bites should be treated seriously, as they can become infected or can result in tetanus. A rabies vaccination is now available and should be

considered if you are in a high-risk category – particularly if you intend to explore caves (bat bites can be dangerous) or work with animals.

**Meningococcal Meningitis** This rare (in Peru) but very serious disease attacks the brain and can be fatal. A scattered, blotchy rash, fever, severe headache, sensitivity to light and neck stiffness that prevents bending the head forward are the first symptoms. Death can occur within a few hours, so immediate treatment is important.

Treatment is large doses of penicillin given intravenously, or, if that is not possible, intramuscularly (in the buttocks). Vaccination offers good protection for over a year, but you should also check for reports of current epidemics.

**Tuberculosis (TB)** Although this disease is widespread in many developing countries, it is not a serious risk to travelers. Young children are more susceptible than adults, and vaccination is a sensible precaution for children under 12 traveling in endemic areas. TB is commonly spread by coughing or by unpasteurized dairy products from infected cows.

**Schistosomiasis** Also known as bilharzia, this disease is carried in slow-moving water (especially behind dams) by minute worms. It is quite common in the Brazilian Amazon, less so in Peru.

The worms attach themselves to your intestines or bladder, then produce large numbers of eggs. The worm enters through the skin, and the first symptom may be a tingling and sometimes a light rash around the area where it entered. Weeks later, when the worm is busy producing eggs, a high fever may develop. A general ill feeling may be the first symptom; once the disease is established, abdominal pain and blood in the urine are other signs.

Don't swim in fresh water where bilharzia is present. Even deep water can be infected. If you do get wet, towel off quickly, as the worms supposedly burrow into the skin as the water evaporates. Dry your clothes as well. Seek medical attention if you have been exposed to the disease, and tell the doctor your suspicions, as schistosomiasis in the early stages can be confused with malaria or typhoid. If you cannot get medical help immediately, praziquantel (Biltricide) is the recommended treatment. The recommended dosage is 40 mg/kg in divided doses over one day. Niridazole is an alternative drug.

**Diphtheria** Diphtheria can be a skin infection or a more dangerous throat infection. It is spread by contaminated dust contacting the skin or by the inhalation of infected cough or sneeze vapor. Frequent washing and keeping the skin dry will help prevent skin infection. A vaccination is available to prevent the throat infection.

**Sexually Transmitted Diseases** STDs are spread through sexual contact with an infected partner. Abstinence is the only 100% effective preventative, but monogamous sexual activity is safe as long as both partners are healthy and remain trustworthy. Using condoms is also effective. Gonorrhea and syphilis are common STDs; sores, blisters or rashes around the genitals and discharges or pain when urinating are common symptoms. Symptoms may be less marked or not observed at all in women. Syphilis symptoms eventually disappear completely, but the disease continues and can cause severe problems in later years. The treatment of gonorrhea and syphilis is by antibiotics. There is no cure for herpes (which causes blisters but is not normally very dangerous) or for AIDS.

**HIV/AIDS** HIV, the Human Immunodeficiency Virus, may develop into AIDS, Acquired Immune Deficiency Syndrome (SIDA in Spanish). HIV is a significant problem in neighboring Brazil, and the virus is spreading to the Peruvian population, particularly among prostitutes of both sexes. Any exposure to blood, blood products or bodily fluids may put an individual at risk. Transmission is predominantly through heterosexual sexual activity. This is quite different from industrialized countries, where

transmission is mostly through sexual contact with homosexual or bisexual males, or via contaminated needles shared by intravenous drug users. Apart from abstinence, the most effective preventative is to practice safe sex, using condoms. Condoms *(preservativos)* are available in some Peruvian pharmacies, though they are expensive and of low quality. It is impossible to detect the HIV-positive status of an otherwise healthy-looking person without a blood test.

HIV/AIDS can also be spread through infected blood transfusions; if you need a blood transfusion, go to the best clinic, as they normally will screen blood for transfusions. It can also be spread by dirty needles – vaccinations, acupuncture, tattooing and piercing can potentially be as dangerous as intravenous drug use if the equipment is not clean. If you do need an injection, ask to see the syringe unwrapped in front of you, or better still, take a needle and syringe pack with you – it is a cheap insurance package against infection with HIV.

Fear of HIV infection should never preclude treatment for serious medical conditions. The risk of infection remains very small.

## Insect-Borne Diseases

**Malaria** This serious disease is spread by mosquito bites. If you are traveling in endemic areas, it is extremely important to take malarial prophylactics. Symptoms include headaches, fever, chills and sweating, which may subside and recur. Without treatment, malaria can develop more serious, potentially fatal effects.

Antimalarial drugs do not prevent you from being infected, but kill the parasites during a stage in their development.

There are several types of malaria. The problem in recent years has been the increasing resistance to commonly used antimalarials like chloroquine, maloprim and proguanil. Newer drugs such as mefloquine (Lariam) and doxycycline (Vibramycin, Doryx) are often recommended for chloroquine- and multidrug-resistant areas. In Peru, chloroquine is still considered effective, but it is only a matter of time until chloroquine-resistant strains begin to establish themselves, as they already have in neighboring Ecuador.

Expert advice should be sought, as there are many factors to consider when deciding on the type of antimalarial medication, including the area to be visited, the risk of exposure to malaria-carrying mosquitoes, your current medical condition, and your age and pregnancy status. It is also important to discuss the side-effect profile of the medication, so you can work out some level of risk-versus-benefit ratio. It is also very important to be sure of the correct dosage of the medication prescribed to you. Some people have inadvertently taken weekly medication (chloroquine) on a daily basis, with disastrous effects. It is often advisable to pack the dosages required for treatment, especially if your trip is through a high-risk area that would isolate you from medical care.

Note that, in Peru, malaria occurs only in the Amazon Basin and parts of the far north coast, so you needn't worry about the disease if you aren't spending time in those regions.

The main messages are the following:

- The mosquitoes that transmit malaria bite from dusk to dawn, so during this period, wear light-colored clothing; wear long pants and long-sleeved shirts; use mosquito repellents containing DEET on exposed areas; avoid perfumes or scented aftershave; use a mosquito net – it may be worthwhile carrying your own.

- While no antimalarial is 100% effective, taking the most appropriate drug significantly reduces the risk of contracting the disease.

- No one should ever die from malaria. It can be diagnosed by a simple blood test. Contrary to popular belief, once a traveler contracts malaria, he or she does not have it for life. Malaria is curable, as long as the traveler seeks medical help when symptoms occur.

**Dengue Fever** There is no prophylactic available for this mosquito-spread disease; the main preventative measure is to avoid mosquito bites. A sudden onset of fever, headaches and severe joint and muscle pains are the first signs before a rash starts on the trunk of the body and spreads to the limbs and face. After a few days more, the fever will subside, and recovery will begin. Serious complications are not common, but full recovery can take up to a month or more. Though quite common in neighboring Brazil, it is rare in Peru.

**Yellow Fever** This disease is endemic in the Amazon Basin. It is a viral disease transmitted to humans by mosquitoes; the initial symptoms are fever, headache, abdominal pain and vomiting. There may appear to be a brief recovery before the disease progresses to more severe complications, including liver failure. There is no medical treatment, apart from keeping the fever down and avoiding dehydration, but yellow-fever vaccination gives good protection for 10 years.

**Chagas' Disease** In remote rural areas of Latin America, this parasitic disease is transmitted by a bug that hides in crevices and palm fronds and often takes up residence in the thatched roofs of huts. It comes out to feed at night. A hard, violet-colored swelling appears at the site of the bite in about a week. Usually, the body overcomes the disease unaided, but sometimes it continues and can eventually lead to death years later. Chagas' disease can be treated in its early stages, but it is best to avoid thatched-roof huts, sleep under a mosquito net and use insecticides and insect repellents. Always check bedding for hidden insects.

**Typhus** Typhus is spread by ticks, mites or lice. It begins as a bad cold, followed by a fever, chills, headache, muscle pains and a body rash. There is often a large painful sore at the site of the bite, and nearby lymph nodes are swollen and painful.

Tick typhus is spread by ticks. Seek local advice on areas where ticks pose a danger, and always check your skin carefully for ticks after walking in a high-risk area such as a tropical forest. A strong insect repellent can help, and serious walkers in tick areas should consider having their boots and trousers impregnated with benzyl benzoate and dibutylphthalate. Typhus is present but not very common in Peru.

## Cuts, Bites & Stings

**Cuts & Scratches** Skin punctures can easily become infected in hot climates and may be difficult to heal. Treat any cut with an antiseptic such as Betadine. Where possible, avoid bandages and Band-Aids, which can keep wounds wet.

**Bites & Stings** Bee and wasp stings are usually painful rather than dangerous. Calamine lotion will give relief, and ice packs will reduce the pain and swelling. There are some spiders with dangerous bites, but these are not usually fatal, and antivenins are usually available. Scorpion stings are notoriously painful but are very rarely fatal. Scorpions, spiders, ants and other biting creatures often shelter in shoes or clothing. Develop the habit of shaking out your clothing before putting it on, especially in the lowlands. Check your bedding before going to sleep. Don't walk barefoot, and look where you place your hands when reaching to a shelf or branch.

**Snakes** To minimize your chances of being bitten, always wear boots, socks and long trousers when walking through undergrowth where snakes may be present. Don't put your hands into holes and crevices, and be careful when collecting firewood.

Snake bites do not cause instantaneous death, and antivenins are usually available. If bitten, keep calm and still, wrap the bitten limb tightly, as you would for a sprained ankle, and then attach a splint to immobilize

it. Then seek medical help, if possible with the dead snake for identification. Don't attempt to catch the snake if there is even a remote possibility of being bitten again. Tourniquets and sucking out the poison are now widely discredited as treatment for snake bites.

**Jellyfish** Local advice is the best way of avoiding contact with these sea creatures, which have stinging tentacles. The stings from most jellyfish are rather painful but not lethal. Dousing in vinegar will de-activate any stingers that have not 'fired.' Calamine lotion, antihistamines and analgesics may reduce the reaction and relieve the pain.

**Bedbugs & Lice** Bedbugs live in various places, but particularly in dirty mattresses and bedding. Spots of blood on bedclothes or on the wall around the bed can be read as a suggestion to find another hotel. Bedbugs leave itchy bites in neat rows. Calamine lotion may help.

All lice cause itching and discomfort. They make themselves at home in your hair (head lice), your clothing (body lice) or in your pubic hair (crabs). You catch lice through direct contact with infected people or by sharing combs, clothing and the like. Powder or shampoo treatment will kill the lice, and infected clothing should then be washed in very hot water.

**Other Creatures** Scabies are mites that burrow into your skin and cause it to become red and itchy. To kill scabies, wash yourself with a benzene benzoate solution, and wash your clothes too. Both benzene hexachloride and benzoate are obtainable from pharmacies in Peru.

Ticks (also see Typhus under Insect-Borne Diseases) are best removed by gripping them gently with tweezers and working them back and forth. Don't leave the head stuck in your skin.

Chiggers are tiny mite larvae that burrow under the skin and feed on you for several days. They itch like crazy and are best avoided by not walking through long grass without long trousers and insect repellent.

Botfly eggs are deposited under the skin. When they hatch, the larvae burrow deeper, and you can feel them moving around – disconcerting and uncomfortable but not dangerous. It is hard to remove them, though various suggestions are offered. Try putting Vaseline or nail polish over the hole in the skin, thus suffocating the beasts and causing them to stick their heads out, at which time they can be pulled out with tweezers. Many travelers have concluded, however, that botflies have to be removed surgically.

Sandflies can cause the disfiguring disease leishmaniasis, and are small enough to crawl through mosquito nets. Use insect repellents, particularly when sleeping on the ground in the lowlands.

Your worst nightmare might be the candirú fish (also known as the orifish), a nasty little bugger that can swim up your urethra, supposedly when you are urinating, and then become embedded in the urinary tract. Surgical removal is the best 'cure.' A better option is not to pee in the river and not to swim naked in the Amazon Basin.

## Women's Health

**Gynecological Problems** Poor diet, lowered resistance due to the use of antibiotics for stomach upsets, and even contraceptive pills can lead to vaginal infections when traveling in hot climates. Wearing skirts or loose-fitting trousers and cotton underwear will help to prevent infections.

Yeast infections, characterized by a rash, itch and discharge, can be treated with a vinegar-and-water or lemon-juice-and-water douche, or with yogurt. Nystatin suppositories are the usual medical prescription. Trichomoniasis is a more serious infection; symptoms are a discharge and a burning sensation when urinating. Male sexual partners must also be treated, and if a vinegar-water douche is not effective, medical attention should be sought. Metronidazole (Flagyl) is the prescribed drug.

**Pregnancy** Most miscarriages occur during the first three months of pregnancy, so this is the most risky time to travel as far as your own health is concerned. Miscarriage is not uncommon, and can occasionally lead to severe bleeding. The last three months of pregnancy should also be spent within reasonable distance of good medical care. A baby born as early as 24 weeks stands a chance of survival, but only in a good modern hospital. Pregnant women should avoid all unnecessary medication, but vaccinations and malarial prophylactics should still be taken where possible. Take additional care to prevent illness, and pay particular attention to diet and nutrition. Alcohol and nicotine, for example, should be avoided.

Women travelers often find that their periods become irregular or even cease while they're on the road. Remember that a missed period in these circumstances doesn't necessarily indicate pregnancy. There are health posts or family-planning clinics in many urban centers, where you can seek advice and have a urine test to determine whether or not you are pregnant.

## WOMEN TRAVELERS
### Attitudes Toward Women

Generally, women travelers will find Peru safe and pleasant to visit.

That is not to say, however, that machismo is a thing of the past. On the contrary, it is very much alive and practiced. Peruvian men generally consider *gringas* to be more liberated (and therefore, easier sexual conquests) than their Peruvian counterparts. Local men will often make flirtatious comments, whistles and hisses to single women – both Peruvian and foreign. Women traveling with other women are not exempt from this attention. Peruvian women usually deal with this by looking away and completely ignoring the man – this works reasonably well for gringas too. Women who firmly ignore unwanted verbal advances are normally treated with respect. Wearing a ring on the wedding finger (whether married or not) acts as a good deterrent.

Traveling with another woman may give you some measure of psychological support. Traveling with a man tends to minimize the attention that Peruvian men may direct toward women travelers. Increasing numbers of Peruvian men are becoming sensitive to the issue of machismo – they may practice it with their buddies, but won't hassle every gringa they see.

Occasionally, you hear about a woman traveler being raped. A rape-prevention counselor who worked with women in the US Peace Corps suggests that a lone woman should never wander around poorly lit areas at night or remote places at any time. Other suggestions include carrying a metal whistle (in your hand – not in your backpack). This produces a piercing blast and will startle off most would-be rapists long enough for a woman to get away.

Many women have traveled safely, and alone, throughout Peru. Many have made friends with Peruvian men and found them charming and friendly. However, unless you are attracted to a local man, you should avoid going somewhere with him alone, as that indicates that you are interested in sleeping with him, and you will be pressured to do so. Friendships are best developed in public group settings.

Women should avoid dimly lit or deserted areas at night. If taking a taxi alone after dark, avoid 'pirate' taxis flagged down on the street and stick with a reputable regulated taxi. Regulated taxis can be called by phone; in smaller towns, they should at least have their number clearly painted on the vehicle.

The following books are recommended for women interested in solo travel: *Travelers' Tales: Gutsy Women, Travel Tips, and Wisdom for the Road*, by Marybeth Bond, and *A Journey of One's Own: Uncommon Advice for the Independent Woman Traveler*, by Thalia Zepatos.

### Organizations

There is not much in the way of local resources for women travelers. Movimiento Manuela Ramos is an organization that organizes workshops to teach local women about starting small businesses, family planning, preventing abuse and other useful topics. They can be contacted at their crafts shop (see Shopping in the Lima chapter). The South American Explorers' clubhouses in Lima and Quito are often staffed by women – these friendly and wonderful people can offer straightforward advice.

*Journeywoman* (www.journeywoman.com) is an online magazine with many useful links. Also check out *Maiden Voyages* (www.maiden-voyages.com), which has both text and online versions, as well as links to travel books for and about women.

Women travelers are encouraged to send any practical advice for other women travelers by email to info@lonelyplanet.com or by letter or postcard to the US Lonely Planet office at 150 Linden St, Oakland, CA 94607.

## GAY & LESBIAN TRAVELERS

Gay rights in a political or legal context don't even exist as an issue for most Peruvians. Sexuality is more stereotyped in Peru (and in many Latin countries) than it is in Europe and North America, with the man playing a dominant macho role and the woman tagging along with that. This attitude spills over into homosexuality: 'Straight-acting,' macho men are not considered to be gay, even if they are, while an effeminate man, even if he is straight, will be called a *maricón* – a derogatory term for a homosexual man. Public displays of affection are very rarely seen and may be received with derision, indifference, hostility or laughter. Relatively few gay men in Peru are exclusively homosexual. This means that AIDS is often transmitted heterosexually and is a growing problem in Peru (see HIV/AIDS under Health earlier in this chapter).

Lesbians are an almost ignored segment of the population – most Peruvians realize they exist but don't really think much about it.

### Organizations

Peru's best-known, and possibly only, gay organization is Movimiento Homosexual-Lesbiana (MHOL, ☎ 433-6375, fax 433-5519, Mariscal Miller 828, Jesús María, Lima). Their phone is open 24 hours, and they have English-speaking staff in the evenings.

Various gay-oriented travel guidebooks that are available (you won't find them in Peru) rarely have much information about Peru. From time to time, South American countries are covered in the gay-travel newsletter *Out and About*. The organization's website, www.outandabout.com, has general information on gay travel and allows you to order back issues.

In the USA, Matthew Seats (☎ 757-220-9427, vacations@erols.com) is an IGLTA-certified gay-travel specialist who can arrange tours and travel to Peru (and anywhere else) for all travelers, regardless of sexual orientation. He can advise clients about the ever-changing world of gay-friendly discos and bars in Lima (they are almost unheard of outside the capital).

## DISABLED TRAVELERS

A new chain of 1st-class hotels, the Posadas del Inca (www.posadas.com.pe), all have two or more rooms and bathrooms designed for wheelchair access. Their five hotels are in Lima (2), Cuzco, Yucay and Puno.

Jóse (Pepe) Lopez (☎ in Lima 442-3886, fax 422-5247, pepelopz@hotmail.com, Bellavista 518, Miraflores, Lima, ☎ in Cuzco 24-2030, Garcilaso 265, Cuzco) operates Apumayo Expeditions, an adventure tour company that has begun working with disabled travelers. He has led disabled travelers on tours to Machu Picchu, Cuzco and other historical sites as well as river running. Trips to the Tambopata Reserve in the Amazon rainforest are also being planned.

For more information about traveling through Peru with physical disabilities, see the article 'Peru – A Cross-Disability Adventure' in the magazine *Open World: For Disability and Mature Travel* (Summer 1998). This magazine is published by the Society for the Advancement of Travelers with Handicaps (☎ 212-447-7284, fax 212-725-8253, email sathtravel@aol.com, 347 5th Ave, Suite 610, New York, NY 10016, USA).

Unfortunately, Peru's infrastructure offers few other conveniences for disabled travelers, as is the case in most third-world countries. Wheelchair ramps are few and far between, and pavement is often badly potholed and cracked. Bathrooms and toilets are often barely large enough for an able-bodied person to walk into, so very few

indeed are accessible to wheelchairs. Features such as signs in braille or telephones for the hearing-impaired are virtually nonexistent. Nevertheless, there are disabled Peruvians who get around, mainly through the help of others. It is not particularly unusual to see disabled travelers being carried bodily to a seat on a bus, for example.

## SENIOR TRAVELERS

Discounts for senior travelers are virtually unknown in Peru.

## TRAVEL WITH CHILDREN

Children pay full fare on buses if they occupy a seat, but often ride for free if they sit on a parent's knee. Children under 12 pay half fare on domestic airline flights and get a seat, while infants under two pay 10% of the fare but don't get a seat.

In hotels, the general rule is simply to bargain. Children should never have to pay as much as an adult, but whether they stay for half price or free is open to discussion.

While 'kids' meals' (small portions at small prices) are not normally offered in restaurants, it is perfectly acceptable to order a meal to split between two children or an adult and a child.

Foreigners traveling with children are still a curiosity in Peru and will meet with extra, generally friendly, attention and interest.

For more suggestions, see Lonely Planet's *Travel with Children*.

## USEFUL ORGANIZATIONS

The single most useful organization is the recommended South American Explorers. They have four offices – in the USA, Ecuador, Lima and Cuzco. Full details are given in the Lima chapter.

You can get up-to-date information on safety, political and economic situations, health risks and costs for all the Latin American countries (including Peru) from *The Latin American Travel Advisor* (☎ 888-215-9511 in North America, fax 2-562-566, lata@pi.pro.ec, PO Box 17-17-908, Quito, Ecuador). This is an impartial, 16-page, quarterly newsletter published in Ecuador. Four issues are US$39, the most recent issue is US$15 and back issues are US$7.50.

The government-run consumer-protection and tourist-complaint bureau, INDECOPI (in Lima ☎ 224-7777, fax 224-0348, in the provinces ☎ 0-800-44040, postmaster@indecopi.gov.pe, www.indecopi.gob.pe, Calle de Prosa 138, San Borja, Lima) accepts complaints regarding airlines, customs, restaurants, hotels, travel agencies, etc. They are helpful and, sometimes, quite effective at righting wrongs.

## DANGERS & ANNOYANCES
### Theft

Peru has a reputation for thievery and unfortunately, it is fully warranted. Every year, I receive letters from people who have been ripped off or meet travelers who have been robbed. However, by taking some basic precautions and exercising a reasonable amount of vigilance, you probably won't be robbed. What normally happens is that travelers are so involved in their new surroundings and experiences that they forget to stay alert – and that's when something is stolen. It's good to know that armed theft is not as frequent as sneak theft. Remember that crowded places are usually the haunts of pickpockets – this means badly lit bus and train stations or bustling markets and fiestas.

Thieves look for easy targets. Tourists who carry a wallet or passport in a hip pocket are asking for trouble. Leave your wallet at home; it's an easy mark for a pickpocket. A small roll of bills loosely wadded under a handkerchief in your front pocket is as safe a way as any of carrying your daily spending money. The rest should be hidden. Always use at least a closable inside pocket – or preferably a body pouch, money belt or leg pouch – to protect your money and passport.

You can carry some of your money as traveler's checks. These can be refunded if lost or stolen, often within a few days in Lima. However, exchange rates for traveler's checks are less than US cash by several percent, depending on the exchange

regulations at the time you visit. Some airlines will reissue your ticket if it is lost. You must give details such as where and when you got it, the ticket number and which flight was involved. Usually a reissuing fee (about US$20) is charged, but that's much better than buying a new ticket. Stolen passports can be reissued at your embassy. For this, you need a police report of the theft and positive identification.

Pickpockets are not the only problem. Snatch theft is also common, so don't wear gold necklaces and expensive wristwatches, or you're liable to have them snatched from your body. I've seen it happen to someone walking with me, and by the time I realized that something had been stolen, the thief was 20m away and jumping onto a friend's motorcycle. Snatch theft can also occur if you carry a camera loosely over your shoulder or place a bag on the ground for just a second.

Thieves often work in pairs or groups. While your attention is being distracted by one partner, another is robbing you. The distraction can take the form of a bunch of kids fighting in front of you, an old lady 'accidentally' bumping into you, someone dropping something in your path or spilling something on your clothes – the possibilities go on and on. The only thing you can do is try, as much as possible, to avoid being in very tight crowds and to stay alert, especially when something out of the ordinary occurs.

To worry you further, there are the razor-blade artists who slit open your luggage when you're not looking. A pack on your back or luggage in the rack of a bus or train – or even your trouser pocket – are all vulnerable. Many travelers carry their day packs on their chests to avoid having them slashed during day trips to markets and other crowded public spaces. When walking with my large pack, I move fast and avoid stopping, which makes it difficult for anyone intent on cutting the bag. If I have to stop, at a street crossing for example, I tend to gently swing from side to side so I can feel if anyone is touching my pack and I look around a lot. I never place a bag on the ground unless I have my foot on it. It is always a good idea to walk purposefully wherever you are going, even if you are lost.

One of the best solutions to the rip-off problem is to travel with a friend and to watch one another. An extra pair of eyes makes a big difference. I often see shifty-looking types eyeing luggage at bus stations, but they notice if you are alert and are less likely to bother you. If you see a suspicious-looking character, look them directly in the eye and point them out to your traveling companions. They'd much rather steal something from the tired and unalert traveler who has put their bag on a chair while buying a coffee, and who, 10 seconds later, has their coffee but no bag!

It is a good idea to carry an emergency kit somewhere separate from all your other valuables. This kit could be sewn into a jacket or even carried in your shoe. It should contain a photocopy of the important pages of your passport in case it's lost or stolen. On the back of the photocopy, you should list important numbers, such as all your traveler's-check serial numbers, airline-ticket numbers, credit-card or bank-account numbers, telephone numbers etc. Also keep one high-denomination bill with this emergency stash. You will probably never have to use it, but it's a good idea not to put all your eggs into one basket.

Take out traveler's insurance, but don't get paranoid. Stay alert and you can spend months in Peru without anything being stolen.

## Discrimination

Nonwhite people are sometimes discriminated against, especially in upscale bars, nightclubs and discos in Lima; less so elsewhere. During 1998, several nightclubs were temporarily closed for not allowing nonwhites (including Peruvian highland Indians and black US Embassy personnel) into their establishments, even though they were wearing appropriate dress. This has been going on for years and is illegal, but it wasn't until 1998 that something began to be done about it.

There is also discrimination against Peruvians in some hotels that prefer to cater to foreign travelers.

## Drugs

Definitely avoid any conversation with someone who offers you drugs. In fact, talking to any stranger on the street can hold risks. It has happened that travelers who have talked to strangers have been stopped soon after by plainclothes police officers and accused of talking to a drug dealer. In such a situation, never get into a vehicle with the 'police,' but insist on going to a bona fide police station on foot. Be wary of false or crooked police who prey on tourists. Note that the Policía de Turismo, listed in major cities, is usually helpful with legal problems.

Be aware that there are draconian penalties for the possession of even a small amount of drugs for personal use. There's no chance of a fine and probation – minimum sentences are several years in jail.

## Altitude Sickness

Cuzco and Lake Titicaca are both high on the list of many travelers' destinations, and they are high in the mountains too. Many visitors fly in from Lima, at sea level, and usually experience some mild altitude sickness during the first day or two. Make sure that you allow for a rest day at the beginning of your visit to the highlands to allow you to acclimatize. See Health earlier in this chapter for more details.

## Terrorism

There are two guerrilla groups in Peru, the MRTA and the Sendero Luminoso. As described in the previous chapter, the main leaders of both groups were captured and imprisoned in 1992 and, since then, travel safety has improved dramatically. Occasional attacks by a few remaining Senderistas are still reported, but these are infrequent and not generally aimed at tourists. The MRTA were responsible for taking over the Japanese Embassy in Lima in 1996; likewise, their actions are limited and not aimed at tourists. The chances of a traveler's being subject to terrorist attack in Peru are probably no greater than in most other countries.

## Earthquakes

Peru is in an earthquake zone, and small tremors are frequent. Every few years, a large earthquake results in loss of life and property damage. Should you be caught in an earthquake, the best advice is to take shelter under a solid object, such as a desk or doorframe. Do not stand near windows or heavy objects. Do not run out of the building. If you are outside, attempt to stay clear of falling wires, bricks, telephone poles and other hazards. Avoid crowds in the aftermath.

## Dangerous Travel Areas

Peru is generally safe to travel in, but it is best to avoid the Río Huallaga valley between Tingo María and Juanjui. This is where the majority of Peru's illegal drug-growing takes place, and the area is somewhat dangerous. Some remote areas of Peru have isolated incidents of terrorism, but they don't happen on the well-traveled routes.

It is always safer (and more scenic) to take buses during the day, as night buses are occasionally held up in remote areas of the country. This doesn't happen very often, and in some cases, you have no choice but to travel at night. The situation can change, so you should seek local advice.

## LEGAL MATTERS

Be aware that some police are corrupt (see Drugs under Dangers & Annoyances earlier in this chapter). Also be aware that your own embassy is of limited help if you get into trouble with the law (see Embassies & Consulates earlier in this chapter). Should you be stopped by a plainclothes policeman, don't hand over any documents or money, and insist on going to a police station. Don't go into the policeman's car. I once was stopped by a 'plainclothes policeman' for no reason, and he just didn't seem like a cop to me. I turned around and simply walked quickly the other way, pretending not to understand! (I don't know if this is good advice, unless you are feeling pretty sure of yourself.)

Bribery is illegal. However, you'll often see a Peruvian driver slipping a policeman some money in order to smooth things along. The idea here is not to offer an (illegal) bribe, but simply a 'gift' or 'on-the-spot fine' so that you can get on your way. For most travelers, who won't have to deal with traffic police, the most likely place that you'll be expected to pay officials a little extra is (sometimes) at land borders. This too is illegal, and if you have the time and fortitude to stick to your guns, you'll eventually be allowed in without paying a fee.

Police occasionally do random room checks in a hotel, looking either for passport/visa violations, or for illegal items (drugs and firearms). Firearms are generally illegal, and you can be locked up for carrying one. If your room is being searched, be polite but insistent that you are completely innocent and are horrified at the very idea of drugs. Watch the searchers like a hawk to avoid the slight possibility of having drugs planted or something stolen from your luggage.

If you are driving and are involved in an accident that results in injury, know that drivers are routinely imprisoned for several days or even weeks until innocence has been established. If you are imprisoned for any reason, make sure someone knows about it. Prison food is extremely poor, and Peruvians routinely bring food to family members who are in prison.

## BUSINESS HOURS

Hours are variable and liable to change. Some places may have posted hours and not adhere to them. Many shops and offices close for an extended lunch break. Weekend hours are limited or nonexistent for government offices. Recently, a few 24-hour supermarkets have opened in Lima and some other major cities. Cabdrivers often know where late-night stores are. Be flexible and patient when needing to get things done.

## PUBLIC HOLIDAYS & SPECIAL EVENTS

Many of Peru's main festivals favor the Roman Catholic liturgical calendar. They are often celebrated with great pageantry, especially in highland Indian villages, where the Catholic feast day may well be linked with some traditional agricultural festival (such as spring or harvest) and be the excuse for a traditional Indian fiesta, with much drinking, dancing, rituals and processions. Other holidays are of historical or political interest, such as Fiestas Patrias (National Independence) on July 28 and 29. On major holidays, banks, offices and other services are closed, and transportation tends to be very crowded, so book ahead if possible.

The following list describes the major holidays, which may be celebrated for several days around the actual date. Those marked by an asterisk (*) are official public holidays, when banks and other businesses are closed; others are more local holidays. If an official public holiday falls on a weekend, offices close on the following Monday. If an official holiday falls midweek, it may or may not be moved to the nearest Monday to create a long weekend.

**January**

Año Nuevo* (New Year's Day, January 1) – This holiday is particularly important in Huancayo, where a fiesta continues until January 6.

**February**

La Virgen de la Candelaria (Candlemas) – This is a colorful fiesta in the highlands, particularly in the Puno area (February 2).

Carnaval – Held on the last few days before Lent, this holiday is often celebrated with water fights, so be warned. It's a particularly popular feast in the highlands, with the Carnaval de Cajamarca being one of the biggest.

**March-April**

Semana Santa* (Holy Week) – This takes place the week before Easter. Maundy Thursday afternoon and all of Good Friday are public holidays. Holy Week is celebrated with spectacular religious processions almost daily, with Ayacucho being recognized as having the best in Peru. Cuzco is also good for Easter processions.

**May**

Labor Day* (May 1)

**June**

Corpus Christi – The processions in Cuzco are especially dramatic (the ninth Thursday after Easter).

Inti Raymi* (also St John the Baptist and Peasant's Day) – This is a public half-day holiday. Inti Raymi celebrates the winter solstice and is the greatest of the Inca festivals. It's certainly the spectacle of the year in Cuzco and attracts many thousands of Peruvian and foreign visitors. Despite its commercialization, it's still worth seeing the street dances and parades, as well as the pageant held in Sacsayhuamán. It's also a big holiday in many of the jungle towns (June 24).

San Pedro y San Pablo* – Feast of St Peter & St Paul (June 29)

**July**

La Virgen del Carmen – This holiday is mainly celebrated in the southern sierra, with Paucartambo and Pisac near Cuzco and Pucara near Lake Titicaca being especially important (July 16).

Fiestas Patrias (Peru's Independence) – While celebrated throughout the country, in the southern sierra, festivities can begin three days ahead with the feast of St James on July 25. This is perhaps the biggest national holiday, and the whole nation seems to be on the move. Buses and hotels are booked long in advance. Hotel prices can triple (July 28-29).

**August**

Santa Rosa de Lima* – This involves major processions in Lima to honor the patron saint of Lima and of the Americas (August 30).

**October**

Battle of Angamos (October 8)

El Señor de los Milagros (Lord of the Miracles) – This is celebrated with major religious processions in Lima; people wear purple (October 18).

**November**

Todos Santos* – All Saint's Day (November 1)

Día de los Muertos (All Soul's Day) – This is celebrated with gifts of food, drink and flowers taken to family graves; it is especially colorful in the sierra. Some of the 'gift' food and drink is consumed, and the atmosphere is festive rather than somber (November 2).

Puno Day – Several days of spectacular costumes and street dancing in Puno help celebrate the legendary emergence of the first Inca, Manco Capac, from Lake Titicaca (November 5).

**December**

Fiesta de la Purísima Concepción – the Feast of the Immaculate Conception (December 8)

Navidad* – Christmas Day (December 25)

Local fiestas and festivals are held somewhere in Peru every week. Many are mentioned in the individual town descriptions.

## ACTIVITIES
### Visiting Archaeological Sites

Visiting Peru without seeing the Inca ruins in the Cuzco area (especially Machu Picchu) is a bit like visiting Egypt without seeing the pyramids. If you're interested in more than just the Inca Empire, however, I recommend the following.

Trujillo is an excellent base for seeing Chan Chan (the huge adobe capital of the Chimu), as well as Moche pyramids and good museums. If you have any spare time in Huaraz, the 2500-year-old ruins of the Chavín are worth a day trip. The artifacts of Paracas are best seen in museums, and the Nazca Lines can only be appreciated properly from the air. The newly excavated site of El Señor del Sipán near Chiclayo is interesting if you want to see archaeology in action, but the highlight is the display in the nearby Bruning Museum. The funerary towers at Sillustani, near Lake Titicaca, are worth seeing if you have a spare day in Puno. Kuélap is great if you have the energy to go to such a remote area. Other sites, while worthwhile for someone who is particularly interested in archaeology or has plenty of time in Peru, don't offer as many rewards as those mentioned here.

### Wildlife-Watching

Sea lions, seabirds, vicuñas, condors, scarlet macaws, hummingbirds, sloths, leaf-cutter ants, monkeys, caimans, toucans, iguanas, parrots, freshwater dolphins – the list of Peruvian wildlife seems endless, and there are many opportunities to see these animals. Many people come specifically to spend their days watching wildlife or birds, and many companies arrange guided natural-history tours.

Tours aren't cheap and will be beyond the pocketbooks of many travelers on a budget. Here are some tips for budget travelers who want to view as much wildlife as possible (though travelers on an expensive tour should also follow these suggestions). The national parks and preserves are all good places for observation, but private areas such as jungle lodges can also yield a good number of birds, insects, reptiles, and even monkeys. Always be alert for these possibilities. Early morning and late afternoon are the best times to watch for wildlife activity anywhere; the hot and bright middle of the day is when many animals rest. Carry binoculars. An inexpensive lightweight pair brought from home will improve wildlife observation tremendously; they don't have to be the most expensive.

Have realistic expectations. The desert has limited wildlife – go to the Paracas Peninsula and Islas Ballestas for the best experience. The rugged highlands have Andean wildlife, but much of it has been hunted out, so visit remote trekking areas. The rainforest is a fantastic environment with plenty of wildlife, but animals are hard to see because the vegetation is so thick. You could be 15m from a jaguar and not even know it is there. Don't expect to see jaguars, ocelots, tapirs, and many other mammals, which are shy, well camouflaged, and rare. Concentrate on things that are easier to observe and enjoy them – most of the animals listed at the beginning of this section can be seen fairly easily if you visit different parts of the country. Walk slowly and quietly; listen as well as look.

### Trekking & Backpacking

These activities are very rewarding during the May-September dry season in the Andes. It is certainly possible to hike during the wet season; just be prepared for rain!

The main hiking centers are Cuzco (for the world-famous Inca Trail to Machu Picchu and exploring Ausangate), and Huaraz (for the spectacular Cordillera Blanca and Cordillera Huayhuash). Details are given under those towns.

Both Cuzco and Huaraz have outfitters who will provide everything you might need in the way of rental equipment and guides. Competition is fierce, which results in many cheap operations that cut their profits to the thinnest margins. The downside of this is that local porters and camp crews are woefully underpaid, groups can be large, equipment and food may be mediocre or poor, and environmental responsibility is sadly lacking (see the boxed text 'Inca Trail Tours' in the Cuzco Area chapter for a discussion of this).

## Mountaineering

The Cordillera Blanca, with dozens of peaks exceeding 5000m, is arguably the most inspiring climbing area in South America. It is accessed from the town of Huaraz, where guides, information and climbing equipment can be hired, though it is best to bring your own for more serious ascents.

Mountains range from Ishinca (5530m) to Pisco (5752m) and are considered easy enough for relatively inexperienced climbers. These two mountains are also good warm-up climbs for experienced climbers who are acclimatizing for bigger adventures, such as Huascarán (6768m), the highest in Peru and a fairly challenging climb. In between are many more difficult peaks, including the knife-edged Alpamayo (5947m), considered by many to be the most beautiful mountain in Peru, as well as dozens of possible new routes for the most experienced climbers. South of the Cordillera Blanca, the Cordillera Huayhuash offers many other possibilities, including Yerupajá (6634m), Peru's second-highest peak.

High-altitude climbing is best done during the dry season, with mid-June to mid-July considered the best time of all. Acclimatization is essential, and expeditions need to budget at least a week before attempting the most difficult high peaks. Many climbers arrive in Peru specifically to take a bus to Huaraz and climb for their entire trip, sometimes reaching summits of several 6000m-high peaks.

Outside of the dry season, you can try climbing mountains in the Arequipa area, where conditions are generally drier year round.

## River Running

River running is a popular activity year round. Now that remote areas are again accessible (after the guerrilla years), increasing numbers of travelers are discovering the unspoiled rivers plunging from the Andes into the lush canyons of the upper Amazon. Commercial rafting trips and kayaking are both possible; trips can range from a few hours to over two weeks.

Cuzco is undoubtedly the main town to find the greatest variety of river possibilities, ranging from a few hours of mild rapids on the Urubamba (the most popular river day trip in Peru) to several days on the Apurímac (technically the source of the Amazon and with some world-class whitewater rafting) or Tambopata rivers (a whitewater trip that tumbles down the eastern slopes of the Andes, culminating in a couple of days of floating in unspoiled rainforest). Other areas include Arequipa and Huaraz in the highlands and Cañete – more details are given in those sections.

Rafting has more dangers associated with it than many participants realize. On the more difficult Apurímac and Tambopata rivers, paying customers and guides have died in accidents in recent years. These and other rivers are remote, and rescues can take days. Therefore it is worth investing in a well-run expedition with a reputable company and avoid the cut-price trips.

A good operator will have insurance, provide you with a *Boleta de Venta* (a legal document indicating the operator is registered and paying taxes), have highly experienced guides with certified first-aid training, carry a well-stocked and up-to-date medical kit, serve hygienically prepared food (enduring the runs while running a river is a definite bummer for you and your raft-mates) and provide top-notch equipment: self-bailing rafts, US Coast Guard-approved life jackets, 1st-class helmets, wet bags in good condition (to make sure your sleeping bag and other gear stays dry throughout the trip), rain- and insect-proof tents, wet suits or splash jackets on the colder rivers, and plastic paddles and spares (not homemade wooden ones).

While it's possible to run rivers more cheaply with less-than-state-of-the-art equipment, you have to decide where your priorities lie – saving money or saving your skin if the river turns rough. Many good companies raft rivers accompanied by a kayaker who is experienced in river rescue.

As with the cheaper trekking outfitters, some river runners are not environmentally sensitive, which results in dirty camping beaches. The only way to protect yourself and the river is to ask the tough questions and inspect equipment.

## Mountain Biking

Mountain biking is a fledgling sport in Peru. See the Cuzco, Huaraz and Huancayo chapters for options. Be aware that, with the exception of Huaraz, rental mountain bikes tend to be pretty basic, so if you are planning on some serious biking, it's best to bring your own bike. Domestic flights may cost from US$10 to US$50 extra for a bike, so shop around for the best deal. Even with your own bike, it's worth hiring a guide or getting local information about the best biking routes. Most of them aren't very well known.

For cycling around Peru, see Bicycle in the Getting Around chapter.

## Surfing

Surfing is an activity enjoyed mainly by a few local middle- and upper-class young people and a handful of international surfers. The surfing is considered to be good, uncrowded and with plenty of new places to explore.

The water is cold from April to December (as low as 13°C), when locals wear wet suits to surf. Indeed, surfers wear wet suits year round, even though they could get away with not using them in the January to March period, when the water is a little warmer (around 20°C in the Lima area). The far north coast (north of Talara) stays above 21°C most of the time. The surfing is quite challenging, but available facilities and equipment are limited and expensive – see the Lima chapter for a list of surf shops.

The following are the main surfing areas, listed north to south. They are abridged from an excellent article, *Gimme a Breaker: Surfer's Guide to Peru*, by Christopher James, published in the *South American Explorer*, No 45, Autumn 1996.

**Far Northern Peru** October through March are the best months, with Cabo Blanco one of the most popular areas. There is a fairly technical left here, and it becomes crowded when conditions aren't too intimidating. Farther north, Mancora and Zorritos has good lefts as well. To the south, the slightly cooler area around Bayovar has a good left but can only be reached by 4WD vehicle and there is nowhere to stay unless you camp.

**Chicama Area** Several surfing waves are found near here, with the most famous being at Puerto Malabrigo where rides of over a kilometer in length are possible, on a wave considered the world's longest. Pacasmayo, just to the north, is also good.

**Lima Area** Visitors to the capital can go to the Miraflores and Costa Verde beaches to watch surfers – these are the country's most crowded beaches. Slightly south, Herradura, with an outstanding left, can also get crowded when there is a strong swell. In-the-know surfers prefer the smaller crowds farther south at Punta Hermosa with several good waves. Near here is Punta Rocas, where International and National championships are held annually. Nearby, Pico Alto is surfed very occasionally when the surf is really large – it can provide one of the few rideable waves of over 6m.

**Southern Peru** Still largely unexplored with difficult access, cold water but unlimited possibilities for self-sufficient adventurers with 4WD and all camping gear. Isla San Gallán, an island off the Península de Paracas, is accessible only by boat (ask local fishermen or at the hotels) and provides an excellent right in a land of lefts.

## Swimming

This is locally popular from January to March, when the water is warm, although the beaches are very contaminated near the major coastal cities, and there are many dangerous currents. Only north of Talara is the water warm year round. Most beaches are barren and not very attractive.

## Diving

There is limited scuba diving. The water is generally cold except from December to March, and the water is the cloudiest then because of run-off from mountain rivers. There is a dive shop in Lima. The best diving areas are the warm waters near the Ecuadorian border and the clear waters around the Península de Paracas.

## Gambling

Peru has suffered from a glut of 'casinos' (most are slot-machine parlors) in recent years. Every town of any size has one, and larger towns and cities have many. They don't offer very good odds compared to the slots of Las Vegas. The major cities also offer casinos with gambling, such as roulette and blackjack. These are usually found in the best hotels.

## LANGUAGE COURSES

Peru is less known for Spanish-language courses than some other Latin American countries. However, there are a few schools listed under the Language Courses section in the Lima chapter and the Classes section in the Cuzco chapter.

## WORK

Officially you need a work visa to work in Peru. You can, however, possibly get a job teaching English in language schools without a work visa, usually in Lima. This is, however, illegal and becoming increasingly difficult without a work visa (though travelers do it anyway). Schools occasionally advertise for teachers in the newspapers, but more often, jobs are found by word of mouth. They expect you to be a native English-speaker, and the pay is usually low – US$100 per week is quite good, if you are an unqualified teacher.

If, in addition to speaking English like a native, you actually have a bona fide teaching credential, so much the better and I have heard a few reports of much higher rates for qualified teachers. American and British schools in Lima will sometimes hire teachers of math, biology and other subjects and can often help you get a work visa if you want to stay. They also pay much better than the language schools. Members of the South American Explorers may find that their Lima office has contacts with schools that are looking for teachers.

Some enterprising travelers make money selling jewelry or art in crafts markets. Most other jobs are obtained by word of mouth (eg, bartenders, jungle guides), but the possibilities are limited.

## ACCOMMODATIONS

There is a lot of variety and no shortage of places to stay in Peru. These come under various names, such as *pensión, residencial, hospedaje* and *hostal*, as well as simply hotel. In most cases, a *pensión* or a *hospedaje* offers cheap and basic lodging. A *residencial* is usually cheap but perhaps a little better. *Hostal* and *hotel* are catch-all terms that can be applied to both the cheapest and most expensive hotels in town.

It is rare to arrive in a town and not be able to find someplace to sleep, but during major fiestas or the high tourist season, accommodations can be tight. This is especially true around Christmas and the New Year, and for several days around the Fiestas Patrias (Peru's Independence) on July 28. At these times you may find yourself paying several times more than your normal budget – or instead sleeping on someone's floor in a sleeping bag! Plan ahead for both accommodations and public transport during major fiestas.

Because of the lack of rooms during fiestas, as many hotels as possible are marked on the town maps in this book. The fact that a hotel is marked on a map does not necessarily imply that it is recommended – in some cases they are there only so you can find them if everywhere else is full. Similarly, if a hotel has something more than a roof and a bed to recommend it, it is mentioned and briefly described in the text. If you are going to a town specifically for a market or fiesta, try to arrive a day or so early if possible.

Sometimes it's a little difficult to find single rooms (particularly in cheap hotels), and you may get a room with two or even three beds. In most cases, though, you are charged for one bed and don't have to share, unless the hotel is full. Ensure in advance that you won't be asked to pay for all the beds or share with a stranger if you don't want to. This is no problem 90% of the time. In better hotels, the rates for singles and doubles is often almost the same (as is common in many first-world countries).

Because many Peruvian homes are very crowded, couples may rent a budget hotel room for private lovemaking. This is an accepted behavior; if you happen to stay in a budget hotel that seems to have numerous 'short-stay' couples, don't assume they are prostitutes with their johns. Often, they are just a decent young couple looking for a few hours of privacy.

Most of the following comments apply particularly to budget hotels, though they may often apply to mid-range hotels and even to top-end places.

If you are traveling as a couple or in a group, don't assume that a room with two or three beds will always be cheaper per person than a room with one bed – often it isn't. In this book, if prices are given per person, then a double or triple room will usually cost two or three times a single, though you should always try to bargain in these situations. If more than one price is given, this indicates that doubles and triples are cheaper per person than singles. Travelers on a tight budget should know that rooms with four or more beds are available in many cheap hotels, and these work out cheaper per person if you're traveling in a group. Couples sharing one bed (*cama matrimonial*) are usually, though not always, charged a little less than a double room with people in separate beds.

Remember to look around a hotel if possible. The same prices are often charged for rooms of widely differing quality. If you are on a tight budget and are shown into a horrible airless box with just a bed and a bare lightbulb, you can ask to see a better room without giving offense, simply by asking if they have a room with a window, or explaining that you have to write some letters home and is there a room with a table and chair.

You'll often be amazed at the results. If the bathrooms are shared, ask to see them and make sure that the toilet flushes and the water runs. If they aren't acceptably clean, there's probably a better hotel at the same price a few blocks away.

Cheap hotels don't always have hot water, or it might only work during certain hours. Ask when (not if) hot water is available. Another intriguing device you should know about is the **electric shower**. This consists of a cold-water showerhead hooked up to an electric heating element that is switched on when you want a hot (more likely tepid) shower. Don't touch anything metal while you're in the shower to avoid a possible electric shock. In many years of using these types of showers, I've only had a couple of mild electric jolts from them, and I have never heard of anyone getting a serious injury from one. Some hotels charge extra for hot showers, and a few simply don't have any showers at all.

Most hotels will provide a key to lock your room, and theft is not very frequent. Nevertheless, carrying your own padlock is a good idea if you plan on staying in the cheapest hotels or in remote areas. Once in a while, you'll find that a room doesn't look very secure – perhaps there's a window that doesn't close, or the wall doesn't come to the ceiling and can be climbed over. In such cases, it's worth looking for another room – assuming you're not in some tiny jungle town where there's nothing else.

You should never leave valuables lying around the room – they can be too tempting for a maid who earns just US$4 a day. Money and your passport should be in a secure body pouch, while other valuables can usually be kept in the hotel strongbox. (Some cheaper hotels might not want to take this responsibility.) If you leave valuables in a hotel, place them in a carefully sealed package so that it will be obvious if it has been tampered with. Always get a receipt. If you leave valuables in your room (eg, camera gear), pack them out of sight at the bottom of a locked bag or closed pack. Don't become paranoid though. In 18 years of traveling in Peru, I have rarely had something taken from my hotel room. Usually, it was partly my fault. I left my camera on the bed instead of at the bottom of a closed pack, and it was gone when I got back. I rarely hear of people who have been ripped off from their hotel rooms, particularly if they take basic precautions.

If you're really traveling off the beaten track, you may end up in a village that doesn't even have a basic pensión. You can usually find somewhere to sleep by asking around, but it might be just a roof over your head rather than a bed, so carry a sleeping bag or at least a blanket. The place to ask at first is probably a village store – the store owner usually knows everyone in the village and will know who is in the habit of renting rooms or floor space. If that fails, you may be offered floor space by the mayor (alcalde) or at the policía and allowed to sleep on the floor of the schoolhouse, jail or village community center.

In this book, hotels are usually listed in a roughly ascending order of price. Budget hotels are the cheapest, but not necessarily the worst. Although these are usually quite basic, with just a bed and four walls, they can nevertheless be well looked-after and very clean. They are often good places to meet other travelers, both Peruvian and foreign. Prices in this category start at about US$3 and go to about US$10 per person.

Every town has hotels in the budget price range. Many small towns have one or two hotels in the middle range. Although you'll usually have to use communal bathrooms in the cheapest hotels, rooms with a private bathroom can sometimes be found for under US$6 per person.

Youth hostels as we know them in other parts of the world are not common in Peru, but the cheaper hotels make up for this deficiency. There are almost no campsites in the towns; again, the constant availability of cheap hotels make town campsites unnecessary for travelers on a budget.

Hotels in the middle price range usually cost from about US$20 for a double (more in Lima and Cuzco). They are not always better than the best hotels in the budget group. However, you can find some very

good bargains here. Even if you're traveling on a budget, there are always special occasions (your birthday?) when you can indulge in comparative luxury for a day or two.

If you're not a shoestring traveler, most towns have pricier hotels with clean, private bathrooms.

Taxes of 28% are charged in some mid-range and all top-end hotels, but rarely in budget accommodations.

## FOOD
It is worth remembering that the main meal of the day is usually lunch (almuerzo). Breakfast is often minimal, although desayuno Americano (American breakfast) is always available at better hotels and restaurants. Dinner (cena) is usually served late – don't expect much dinner action before 8 pm.

If you're on a tight budget, food is undoubtedly the most important part of your trip expenses. You can stay in rock-bottom hotels, travel 2nd class and never consider buying a souvenir, but you've got to eat well. This doesn't mean expensively, but it does mean that you want to avoid spending half your trip sitting on the toilet.

The worst culprits for causing illness are salads and unpeeled fruit. Stick to fruit that you can peel, such as bananas, oranges and pineapples. With unpeeled fruit or salads, wash the ingredients yourself in purified water.

As long as you take heed of the salad warning, you'll find plenty of good things to eat at reasonable prices. You certainly don't have to eat at a fancy restaurant (where kitchen facilities may not be as clean as the white tablecloths). If a restaurant is full of locals, it's usually a good sign.

If you're on a tight budget, you can eat from the street and market stalls if the food is hot and freshly cooked, though watch to see if your plate is going to be dunked in a bowl of cold greasy water and wiped with a filthy rag.

Also worth remembering (if you're trying to stretch your money) is that chifas (Chinese restaurants) can offer a good value. The key word here is tallarines, which are noodles. Most chifas will offer a tallarines dish with chopped chicken, beef, pork or shrimp for under US$2. Other dishes are also good but not quite as cheap. Many restaurants offer an inexpensive set meal of the day (especially at lunchtime), which is usually soup and a second course. This is called simply *el menú*. If you want to read a menu, ask for *la carta*. Some menus have English translations, though these are often amusingly garbled. 'Fred Chicken' and 'Gordon Blue' may play starring roles.

If you aren't on a tight budget, you'll find plenty to choose from in the major cities. Most average restaurants will have meals in the US$4 to US$10 range; only the big cities have fancy restaurants charging more. The really luxurious places, with food and ambiance to rival a good restaurant anywhere in the world, may have meals as high as US$50 a person, including wine, taxes and

tip. Errors on bills (usually in the restaurant's favor) are not uncommon. Check the bill carefully. (See Taxes under Money earlier in this chapter.)

Typical Peruvian dishes are tasty, varied and regional. This stands to reason – seafood is best on the coast, while the Inca delicacy, roast guinea pig, can still be sampled in the highlands. A description of some regional dishes is given in the Places to Eat sections of the major cities. Spicy foods are often described by the term *a la criolla*. Here is a brief overview of some of Peru's most typical dishes:

Lomo Saltado – chopped steak, fried with onions, tomatoes and potatoes and served with rice. This is a standard dish served everywhere, especially at long-distance bus meal stops.

Ceviche de Corvina – white sea bass marinated in lemon, chili and onions and served cold with a boiled potato or yam. It's delicious. If any one dish is to be singled out as most typical of Peru, it is this.

Ceviche de Camarones – the same thing made with shrimp. These dishes are large appetizers or small meals.

Ceviche de Mariscos – mixed-seafood ceviche

Sopa a la Criolla – a lightly spiced noodle soup with beef, egg, milk and vegetables. It's hearty and filling.

Palta a la Jardinera – avocado, stuffed with cold vegetable salad

Palta a la Reyna – avocado, stuffed with chicken salad. This is one of my favorite appetizers, and it can make a light meal.

Most foodstuffs available at home are available in one form or another in Peru. A simple food glossary can be found in the Language chapter.

## DRINKS
## Nonalcoholic Drinks

**Tea & Coffee** Tea *(té)* is served black with lemon and sugar. If you ask for tea with milk, British style, you'll get a cup of hot milk with a tea bag to dunk in it. *Maté* or *té de hierbas* are herb teas. *Maté de coca* is a tea made from coca leaves and served in many restaurants in the highlands. It's supposed to help the newly arrived visitor in acclimatization.

Camote (Sweet Potato)

Guanábana (Soursop)

Jícama

Granadilla (Passionfruit)

Guayaba (Guava)

Apilla (Oca)

Chayote

Añú

Some native fruits and vegetables

Coffee is available almost everywhere, but it is often disappointing. Sometimes it is served in cruets as a liquid concentrate that is diluted with milk or water. It looks very much like soy sauce, so always check before pouring it into your milk (or over your rice)! Instant coffee is also served. Espresso and cappuccino are sometimes available but only in the bigger towns. *Café con leche* is milk with coffee, and *café con agua* or *café negro* is black coffee. Hot chocolate is also popular.

**Water** I don't recommend drinking tap water anywhere in Latin America. *Agua potable* means that the water comes from the tap, but it's not necessarily healthy. Even if it comes from a chlorination or filtration plant, the plumbing is often old, cracked and full of crud. (Salads washed in this water aren't clean.) One possibility is to carry a water bottle and purify your own water (see Health earlier in this chapter). If you don't want to go through the hassle of constantly purifying water, bottled mineral water, *agua mineral*, is available in bottles ranging up to two liters in size. *Agua con gas* and *agua sin gas* are carbonated and noncarbonated mineral water, respectively.

**Soft Drinks** Many of the usual soft drinks are available, as are some local ones, with such tongue-twisting names as Socosani or the ubiquitous Inca Cola, which is appropriately gold-colored and tastes like fizzy bubble gum. Soft drinks are collectively known as *gaseosas*, and the local brands are very sweet. You can also buy Coca-Cola, Pepsi Cola, Fanta or Orange Crush (called *croosh*) and Sprite – the latter pronounced 'essprite.' Ask for your drink *helada* if you want it out of the refrigerator, *al clima* if you don't. Remember to say *sin hielo* (without ice) unless you really trust the water supply. Diet soft drinks have recently become available.

**Fruit Juice** Juices *(jugos)* are available everywhere and, to my taste, are usually better than gaseosas, but cost more. Make sure you get *jugo puro* (pure juice) and not *con agua* (with water). The most common kinds are listed in the Food section of the Language chapter.

## Culinary No-Nos

In some areas of Peru – especially in the jungle – meals are prepared from endangered or protected species. Recent Peruvian TV reports have denounced the availability of dolphin (*chancho marino* or *muchame*) in some coastal restaurants. In the jungle, you occasionally may be offered tortoise eggs (*huevos de charapa*), turtle (*motelo*), paca or agouti (*majas*), monkey (*mono*), armadillo and others.

Also, a jungle radio broadcast claimed that poor people are hunting some animals with rat poison, because it is cheaper than shotgun shells, and that the meat can be dangerous for humans. Readers are advised to avoid eating protected wildlife and perhaps to discuss conservation issues with jungle guides or restaurant owners.

## Alcoholic Drinks

Finally we come to those beverages that can loosely be labeled 'libations.' The selection of beers is limited to about a dozen types, but these are quite palatable and inexpensive. Beer comes in various sizes – 355ml, 620ml, 1L and 'litro cien' (1100ml, locally nicknamed a *margarito*). Light lager-type beers *(cerveza)* and sweet dark beers *(malta* or *cerveza negra)* are available. Most have a 5% alcohol content.

The best known coastal beers are Pilsen and Cristal, both good and each with its own devotees. Peru's priciest domestic beer is Bremen.

Two highland towns known for their beer are Cuzco and Arequipa which make Cuzqueña and Arequipeña respectively. Both are available in lager and dark. Cuzqueña is Peru's best beer, according to many drinkers. Arequipeña tastes slightly sweet. In the jungle, there is San Juan, which is brewed in Pucallpa and advertises itself as 'the only beer brewed on the Amazon.' It's not a bad light beer. Imported beers are usually expensive.

Peru has a thriving wine industry and produces acceptable wines, though not as good as Chilean or Argentine varieties. The best wines are from the Tacama and Ocucaje wineries and begin at about US$4 a bottle (more in restaurants). The usual selection of reds, whites and rosés is available – I'm afraid I'm not a connoisseur, so experts will have to experiment for themselves.

Spirits are expensive if imported, and not very good if made locally, though there are some notable exceptions. Rum is cheap and quite good; a white-grape brandy called *pisco* (the national drink) is usually served as a pisco sour – a tasty cocktail made from pisco, egg white, lemon juice, sugar, syrup, crushed ice and bitters. *Guinda* is a sweet cherry brandy, and the local firewater, *aguardiente*, or sugar-cane alcohol, is an acquired taste and very cheap.

## SPECTATOR SPORTS

Soccer (called *fútbol*) and bullfighting are the best attended of spectator sports. Basketball is also quite popular. Although tennis is not especially popular in Peru, the Peruvian tennis player Jaime Yzaga is one of the country's few athletes whose name might be recognized by non-Peruvians.

The soccer season is late March to November. There are many teams, though their abilities on the whole are not exceptional. The best teams are from Lima, and the traditional *clásico* is the match between Alianza Lima and Universitario (La U). These matches are played in the Estadio Nacional in Lima, and entrance fees start at about US$2.50 in the popular section (not recommended, as most of the fan violence happens here), go up to US$7 in the better *oriente* (eastern) section, and reach US$15 to US$30 for the best seats in the *occidente* (western) section. Weekend matches are often doubleheaders (two games, four teams).

The bullfighting season in Lima is from early October through early December and attracts internationally famous matadors. See the Lima chapter for more details. Outside of Lima, bullfights may occur at a variety of fiestas, but they are not of an international level.

## SHOPPING

Souvenirs are good, varied and cheap. Although going to villages and markets is fun, you won't necessarily save a great deal of money – similar items for sale in shops are often not much more expensive. In markets and smaller stores, bargaining is acceptable, indeed expected. In tourist stores in the major cities, prices are sometimes fixed. Some of the best stores are quite expensive, but the quality of their products is often superior.

You can buy everything in Lima, be it a blowpipe from the jungle or a woven poncho from the highlands. Although it is usually a little more expensive to buy handicrafts in Lima, the choice is varied, the quality is high and it's worth looking around some of Lima's gift shops and markets to get an idea of the items you'd like to buy. Then you might go to the areas where the items you're interested in are made – but often, the best pieces are in Lima.

Cuzco also has a great selection of craft shops, but the quality is no higher than in Lima. Old and new weavings, ceramics, paintings, woolen clothing and jewelry are all found here. Cuzco has a good selection of the more traditional weavings.

The Puno-Juliaca area is good for knitted alpaca sweaters and knickknacks made from the totora reed, which grows on Lake Titicaca. The Huancayo area is good for carved gourds, as well as for excellent weavings and clothing in the cooperative market. The Ayacucho area is famous for modern weavings and stylized ceramic churches. San Pedro de Cajas is known for its peculiar weavings, which are made of rolls of yarn stuffed with wool (you'll recognize the style instantly when you see it). The Shipibo pottery sold in Yarinacocha near Pucallpa is among the best of the jungle artifacts available. Superb reproductions of Moche and Mochica pottery are available in Trujillo. Shopping for these is described in more detail under the appropriate towns.

Crafts as souvenirs or gifts are relatively cheap by western standards. A good rule of thumb is if you like something very much, buy it (assuming you can afford it). You may not find exactly the same thing again, and if you do find a better example, you can always give the first one away as a gift.

Souvenirs made from animal products are not normally allowed into most western nations. Objects made from skins, feathers, turtle shells and so forth should not be bought, because their purchase contributes to the degradation of the wildlife in the rainforests.

Shipping goods home is extremely expensive (see Post & Communications earlier in this chapter). It's cheaper to pay excess baggage charges and hire skycaps at the airport.

# Getting There & Away

## AIR

### Airports & Airlines

Jorge Chávez International Airport in Lima is the main hub for flights to the Andean countries from Europe and North America, so it is easy to fly to Peru from those continents. There are also some international flights to Iquitos (in Peru's Amazon region). Cuzco has international flights from Bolivia. Following AeroPerú's shutdown in 1999, Peru has no international airline. Talk of reopening AeroPerú in some form is ongoing.

### Buying Tickets

The high season for air travel to and within Peru is June through early September and December through mid-January. Lower fares may be offered at other times.

Regular round-trip fares are almost always cheaper than two one-way tickets. They are also cheaper than open-jaw tickets, which enable you to fly into one city (eg, Lima) and leave via another (eg, Rio de Janeiro).

**Youth & Student Fares** Students with international student ID cards and anyone under 26 can get discounts with most airlines. Although youth and student fares can be arranged through most travel agents and airlines, it is a good idea to go through agents that specialize in student travel – several are listed in the country sections that follow. Note that student fares are not only cheap, but often include free stopovers, don't require advance purchase, and may be valid for up to a year – a great deal if you are a student.

**Airline Deals** If you can purchase your ticket well in advance and stay a minimum length of time, you can buy a ticket usually about 30% or 40% cheaper than the full economy fare. These are often called APEX, excursion, or promotional fares, depending on the country you are flying from and the rules and fare structures that apply there.

Often the following restrictions apply: You must purchase your ticket at least 21 (sometimes more or fewer) days in advance; you must stay a minimum period (about 14 days on average); and you must return within 180 days (sometimes less – for example, passengers from the USA must return within 30 days to qualify for the lowest APEX fares). Individual airlines have different requirements, and they change from time to time. Most of these tickets do not allow stopovers, and there are extra charges if you change your destinations or dates of travel. These tickets are often sold out well in advance, so try to book early.

**Discounted Tickets** The cheapest way to go is with a ticket sold by companies specializing in air travel ('consolidators' or 'bucket shops') that are legally allowed to sell discounted tickets to help airlines and charter companies fill their flights. These tickets often sell out fast, and you may be limited to only a few available dates and have other restrictions. While APEX, economy and student tickets are available directly from the airlines or from a travel agent, discounted tickets are available only from the discount ticket agencies themselves. Most of them are good, reputable, legalized and bonded companies, but once in a while, a fly-by-night operator comes along and takes your money for a supercheap flight and gives you an invalid or unusable ticket, so check what you are buying carefully before handing over your money.

Discount ticket agencies often advertise in newspapers and magazines; there is much competition, and a variety of fares and schedules are available. Fares to South America have traditionally been relatively expensive, but ticket agencies have recently been able to offer increasingly economical fares to the continent.

See the boxed text 'Useful Web Addresses' in this chapter for consolidator websites.

**Courier Travel** If you are flexible with dates and can manage with only carry-on luggage, you can fly to Peru as a courier. This is most practical between major US gateways and Lima. Couriers are hired by companies that need to have packages delivered to Peru (and other countries). The companies will give the courier exceptionally cheap tickets in return for using his or her baggage allowance. These are legitimate operations – all baggage that you are to deliver is completely legal. And it is amazing how much you can bring in your carry-on luggage. I have heard of couriers boarding an aircraft wearing two pairs of trousers and two shirts under a sweater and rain jacket and stuffing the pockets with travel essentials. Bring a folded plastic shopping bag and, once you have boarded the aircraft, you can remove the extra clothes and place them in the plastic bag. (Try not to have metal objects in inside pockets when you go through the metal detector at the airport! Also bear in mind that most courier companies want their couriers to look reasonably neat, so you can't overdo the 'bag lady' routine.) Remember, you can buy things like T-shirts, towels and soap after you arrive at your destination, so traveling with just carry-on luggage is certainly feasible.

## Travelers with Special Needs

Most airlines can accommodate travelers with special needs, but only if requested some days in advance. On flights with meals, a variety of special cuisine can be ordered in advance at no extra charge. These may include most of the following: vegetarian, low fat, low salt, children's, kosher, Muslim and/or others.

Airlines can easily accommodate travelers requiring physical assistance. Wheelchairs designed to fit in aircraft aisles, plus an employee to push the chair if necessary, are available with advance notice. Passengers can check their own wheelchairs as luggage. Blind passengers can request to have an employee take them through the check-in procedure and all the way to their seats. Again, ask if you have special needs – airlines usually work to oblige.

### Warning

The information in this chapter is particularly vulnerable to change: Prices for international travel are volatile, routes are introduced and canceled, schedules change, special deals come and go, and rules and visa requirements are amended. Airlines and governments seem to take a perverse pleasure in making price structures and regulations as complicated as possible. You should check directly with the airline or a travel agent to make sure you understand how a fare (and ticket you may buy) works. In addition, the travel industry is highly competitive, and there are many lurks and perks.

The upshot of this is that you should get opinions, quotes and advice from as many airlines and travel agents as possible before you part with your hard-earned cash. The details given in this chapter should be regarded as pointers and are not a substitute for your own careful, up-to-date research.

## Departure Tax

Peruvian airport departure tax is US$25 for international flights, payable in either US dollars or nuevos soles. Cash or traveler's checks are accepted; if you only have plastic, use an airport ATM to obtain cash.

## The USA

From the USA, there are direct flights to Lima from Los Angeles, New York, Atlanta, Dallas, Houston and Miami. American Airlines, United, Delta and Continental are the US carriers, and some Latin American carriers stop in Lima en route to somewhere else.

Generally speaking, the USA does not have such a strong discount-ticket tradition as Europe or Asia, so it's harder getting heavily discounted flights from here to South America. In recent years, however, 'consolidators' (as discount ticket agencies in the USA are called) have begun to

## Air Travel Glossary

**APEX** Also known as 'advance purchase excursion,' this is a discounted ticket that must be paid for in advance. There are penalties if you wish to make changes to it.

**Baggage Allowance** This will be written on your ticket and usually includes one 20kg item to go in the hold, plus one item of hand luggage.

**Bucket Shop** These are unbonded travel agencies specializing in discounted airline tickets.

**Bumped** Just because you have a confirmed seat doesn't mean you're going to get on the plane (see Overbooking).

**Cancellation Penalties** If you have to cancel or change a discounted ticket, there are often heavy penalties involved; insurance can sometimes be taken out against these penalties. Some airlines impose penalties on regular tickets as well, particularly for 'no show' passengers.

**Check-In** Airlines ask you to check in a certain time ahead of the flight departure (usually 1½ hours on international flights). If you fail to check in on time and the flight is overbooked, the airline can cancel your booking and give your seat to somebody else.

**Confirmation** Having a ticket written out with the flight and date you want doesn't mean you have a seat until the agent has checked with the airline that your status is 'OK' or confirmed. Meanwhile you could just be 'on request.'

**Courier Fares** Businesses often need to send urgent documents or freight securely and quickly. Courier companies hire people to accompany the package through customs and, in return, offer a discount ticket that is sometimes a phenomenal bargain. In effect, what the companies do is ship their freight as your luggage on regular commercial flights. This is a legitimate operation, but there are two shortcomings – the short turnaround time of the ticket (usually not longer than a month) and the limitation on your luggage allowance. You may have to surrender all your allowance and take only carry-on luggage.

**ITX** An ITX, or 'independent inclusive tour excursion,' is often available on tickets to popular holiday destinations. Officially, it's a package deal combined with hotel accommodations, but many agents will sell you one of these for the flight only and give you phony hotel vouchers in the unlikely event that you're challenged at the airport.

**Lost Tickets** If you lose your airline ticket, an airline will usually treat it like a traveler's check and, after inquiries, issue you another one. Legally, however, an airline is entitled to treat it like cash; and if you lose it, then it's gone forever. Take good care of your tickets.

**MCO** An MCO, or 'miscellaneous charge order,' is a voucher that looks like an airline ticket but carries no destination or date. It can be exchangted through any International Air Transport Association (IATA) airline for a ticket on a specific flight. It's a useful alternative to an

# Air Travel Glossary

onward ticket in those countries that demand one, and it is more flexible than an ordinary onward ticket in those countries that demand one, and it is more flexible than an ordinary ticket if you're unsure of your route.

**No-Shows** No-shows are passengers who fail to show up for their flight. Full-fare passengers who fail to turn up are sometimes entitled to travel on a later flight. The rest are penalized (see Cancellation Penalties).

**On Request** This is an unconfirmed booking for a flight.

**Onward Tickets** An entry requirement for many countries is that you have a ticket out of the country. If you're unsure of your next move, the easiest solution is to buy the cheapest onward ticket to a neighboring country or a ticket from a reliable airline that can later be refunded if you do not use it.

**Open-Jaw Tickets** These are round-trip tickets with which you fly out to one place but return from another. If available, these can save you backtracking to your arrival point.

**Overbooking** Airlines hate to fly with empty seats, and since every flight has some passengers who fail to show up, airlines often book more passengers than they have seats. Usually, excess passengers make up for the no-shows, but occasionally, somebody gets bumped. Guess who it is most likely to be? The passengers who check in late.

**Point-to-Point Tickets** These are discount tickets that can be bought on some routes in return for passengers waiving their rights to a stopover.

**Reconfirmation** At least 72 hours prior to departure time of an onward or return flight, you must contact the airline and 'reconfirm' that you intend to be on the flight. If you don't do this, the airline can delete your name from the passenger list and you could lose your seat.

**Restrictions** Discounted tickets often have various restrictions on them – such as advance payment, minimum and maximum periods you must be away (eg, a minimum of two weeks or a maximum of one year) and penalties for changing the tickets.

**Round-the-World Tickets** RTW tickets give you a limited period (usually a year) in which to circumnavigate the globe. You can go anywhere the carrying airlines go, as long as you don't backtrack. The number of stopovers or total number of separate flights is decided before you set off, and they usually cost a bit more than a basic return flight.

**Stand-By** This is a discounted ticket on which you only fly if there is a seat free at the last moment. Stand-by fares are usually available only on domestic routes.

**Travel Periods** Ticket prices vary with the time of year. There is a low (off-peak) season and a high (peak) season, and often a low-shoulder season and a high-shoulder season as well. Usually the fare depends on your outward flight – if you depart in the high season and return in the low season, you pay the high-season fare.

appear. Sometimes the Sunday travel sections in the major newspapers (the *Los Angeles Times* on the west coast and the *New York Times* on the east coast) advertise cheap fares to South America, although these are sometimes no cheaper than APEX fares. Several useful books about this have been published; a large bookstore with a good travel section (or a travel bookstore) will advise you of recent ones.

A travel agent that can find you the best deal to Peru (and anywhere else in the world) is Council Travel, a subsidiary of the Council on International Educational Exchange (CIEE). You can find their address and telephone numbers in the telephone directories of many North American cities, particularly those with universities. Contact their headquarters at (☎ 212-661-1414, 800-226-8624, fax 212-972-231, 205 E 42nd St, New York, NY 10017). They work with all age groups. Also good for cheap airfares, mainly for students, is STA Travel (☎ 800-777-0112, 800-781-4040), which has offices in many towns; the 800 number automatically connects you to the nearest. Another excellent source for cheap tickets is eXito Latin America Travel Specialists (☎ 800-655-4053, fax 510-655-4566, exito@wonderlink.com, 1212 Broadway, Suite 910, Oakland, CA 94612). They specialize in Latin America and can do both short- and long-term tickets with multiple stopovers if desired.

Typical round-trip APEX fares start at US$500 from Miami, US$600 from New York and US$700 and US$800 from Los Angeles. Low-season discounts can knock the fare down by up to US$100. Fares may be more expensive if you want to stay a few months. People are often surprised that fares from Los Angeles in southern California are so much higher than from northerly New York. A glance at a world map soon shows why. New York, at 74° west, is almost due north of Lima, at 77°. Thus planes can fly a shorter, faster and cheaper north-south route. Los Angeles, on the other hand, is 118° west, and therefore much farther away from Lima than New York.

Courier flights to South America are more common from the USA than Europe. This is a good option for people flying from New York or Miami. For up-to-date information, contact Travel Unlimited (PO Box 1058, Allston, MA 02134), which publishes monthly listings of courier and other cheap flights to Peru and many other countries – this newsletter is recommended for cheap-fare hunters. A year's subscription costs US$25 in the USA, US$35 elsewhere. You can get a single issue for US$5. Also contact the Association of Air Travel Couriers (☎ 561-582-8320).

## Canada

From Canada, American Airlines, United and Delta have connections from Calgary, Montreal, Toronto and Vancouver to US gateways and on to Lima. Canadian Airlines and Air Canada fly to US gateways, connecting with other carriers. APEX fares to Lima are about US$800 to US$1000.

Travel CUTS (☎ 416-614-2887, 800-667-2887, fax 416-614-9670, 200 Ronson Dr, Ste 300, Toronto, ON M9W-5Z9), which has about 60 offices nationwide, is a good choice for student, youth and budget airfares. STA (☎ 416-977-5228, fax 416-977-7112, www.statravel.com, 187 College St, Toronto, ON M5T 1P7) also has travel offices in Montreal, Calgary, Edmonton and Vancouver.

See the USA for eXito Latin American Travel Specialists, which can arrange discounted fares from Canada.

## Australia

The most direct route is with Aerolíneas Argentinas via Auckland, New Zealand, to Buenos Aires with connections to Lima, Peru. Qantas is now sharing this route with Aerolíneas Argentinas. Fares are usually the same from Melbourne, Sydney or Brisbane, but from other Australian cities you may have to add the cost of getting to Sydney. Low-season excursion fares from Sydney or Melbourne are A$1449 for a stay of up to 35 days, A$1640 for up to 45 days.

The other South American route is with Qantas or Air New Zealand connecting with LanChile in Los Angeles or other stopovers. In the past, discount excursion fares from Sydney to various South American cities have been as low as A$1599 for 45 days.

In terms of airfares only, it may be marginally cheaper to go to South America via the USA, but even a day or so in Los Angeles would cost more than the savings in airfares, so it's not a good value unless you want to visit the US anyway. It may be worth it for travel to Colombia or Venezuela, but not for countries farther south.

The best RTW options are probably those with Aerolíneas Argentinas combined with other airlines (including Air New Zealand, British Airways, Iberia, Singapore Airlines, Thai Airways or KLM). The new Qantas version of an RTW ticket is its 'OneWorld Explorer' fare, which allows you to visit up to six continents with three stopovers in each one. Prices start at A$1999 for three continents in the low season, or A$2599 in the peak season. Rules are quite complicated, but a routing via South America will probably need to include Europe.

The following South American airlines have offices in Australia:

Aerolíneas Argentinas
  Level 2, 580 George St, Sydney 2000
  (☎ 02-9283-3660)
  Level 6, Nauru House, 80 Collins St,
  Melbourne 3000 (☎ 03-9650-7111)
LanChile
  64 York St, Sydney 2000 (☎ 02-9244-2333)
  310 King St, Melbourne 3000 (☎ 03-9920-3881)
Varig
  403 George St, Sydney 2000 (☎ 02-9244-2111)
  310 King St, Melbourne 3000 (☎ 03-9920-3856)

A number of agents offer cheap air tickets out of Australia. STA has offices in all capital cities and on many university campuses. Flight Centres International also specializes in cheap airfares and has offices in most capital cities and branches in many suburban areas. Inca Tours (☎ 02-4351-2133, 800-024-955) is staffed by very knowledgeable people who arrange tours to South America in addition to giving advice and selling tickets to independent travelers. Destination Holidays (☎ 03-9725-4655, 800-337-050) also specializes in travel to Latin America. Check the advertisements in Saturday editions of newspapers, such as Melbourne's *Age* or the *Sydney Morning Herald*.

## New Zealand

The two chief options are to fly Aerolíneas Argentinas (☎ 09-379-3675) from Auckland to Buenos Aires (with connections to neighboring countries) or to fly with Air New Zealand (☎ 09-357-3000) from Auckland to Papeete, Tahiti, connecting with a LanChile (☎ 09-309-8673) flight via Easter Island to Santiago. The excursion fare from Auckland to Santiago or Buenos Aires is about the same for both routes – NZ$1899/2099 in low/high season for 10 to 45 days, NZ$2099/2299 for 21 to 90 days and NZ$2986 for up to one year (high season is roughly December through February). You might also be able to get a low-season promotional fare of NZ$1499 for a 10- to 35-day stay.

Onward tickets to Lima are much cheaper if purchased in conjunction with a long-haul flight from the same carrier. A 'Visit South America' fare, good for three months, allows you two stops in South America plus one in the USA, and then takes you back to Auckland. Various open-jaw options are possible, and you can make the trip in either direction. It costs NZ$2986/3293 in low/high season.

For discount fares, try STA (☎ 09-309-0458, 10 High St, Auckland) or Flight Center (☎ 800-354-488, National Bank Tower, 205-225 Queens St, Auckland). Both have offices in other cities.

## The UK & Continental Europe

Discount ticket agencies generally provide the cheapest fares from Europe to South America. Fares from London are often cheaper than from other European cities, even though your flight route may take you from London through a European city. Many European (especially Scandinavian) budget travelers buy from London ticket agencies, as cheap fares are difficult to find in their own countries. Discounted tickets available from these ticket agencies are often several hundred dollars cheaper than official fares and usually carry certain restrictions, but they are valid and legal.

In London, competition is fierce. Discount flights are often advertised in the classifieds of newspapers. Consistently good reports have been received about Journey

Latin America (JLA) (☎ tours 020-8747-8315, flights 020-8747-3108, fax 020-8742-1312, 12 & 13 Heathfield Terrace, Chiswick, London W4 4JE). They specialize in cheap fares to Peru and the entire continent, as well as arranging itineraries for both independent and escorted travel. They will make arrangements for you over the phone or by fax. Ask for their free magazine *The Papagaio*, which has helpful information. Flightbookers (☎ 020-7757-2611, 177 Tottenham Court Rd, London W1P OLX) recently had some of the cheapest flights from the UK.

Council Travel (see USA earlier in this section for more information) has the following offices:

28A Poland Street, (Oxford Circus), London, W1V 3DB, UK (☎ 020-7437-7767)

16, rue de Vaugirard, 75006 Paris, France (☎ 1-44-41-89-89, 0800-148-188, fax 1-40-51-89-12)

12, rue Victor-Leydet, 13100 Aix-en-Provence, France (☎ 4-42-38-58-82, fax 4-42-38-94-00)

35, rue Victor-Hugo, 69002 Lyon, France (☎ 4-78-38-78-38, fax 4-78-38-78-30)

Graf Adolf Strasse 64, 40212 Dusseldorf, Germany (☎ 211-36-30-30, CouncilTravelDusseldorf@ciee.org)

Adalbert Strasse 32, 80799 Munich, Germany (☎ 089-39-50-22, CouncilTravelMunich@ciee.org)

STA Travel (see USA for contact information) has many offices in Germany and Switzerland, as well as an office each in Denmark, Finland and Sweden.

The cheapest fares from London may start at under UK£500, which is an incredible deal considering the distance. Restrictions are usually that the flights may leave only on certain days, the tickets may be valid for only 90 days, and there may be penalties for changing your return date. A UK£10 departure tax is added.

Aeroflot, Iberia, KLM and Lufthansa have direct flights from Europe to Peru (no change of planes is required at the stops).

## Africa

Most travelers will need to make lengthy and expensive connections via Europe. The main exception is South Africa, which has flights to some South American cities (not Lima). STA Travel (see USA for contact information) has offices in Cape Town, Johannesburg and Pretoria.

## Asia

The normal route is to fly from Asia to the US west coast and connect to Lima from there. Council Travel has a Tokyo office (☎ 3-5467-5535, fax 3-5467-7031, Cosmos Aoyama, Gallery Floor, 5-53-67 Jingumae, Shibuya-ku, Tokyo 150, Japan). STA Travel has a head office in Toyko (☎ 81-3-5391-2889, fax 81-3-5391-2923, 7th floor, Nukariya Building 1-16-20 Minami-Ikebukuro Toshima-Ku), as well as three branch offices in Japan; three in Singapore; and one each in Kuala Lumpur, Malaysia, and Bangkok, Thailand.

## Latin America

Flights from Latin American countries are usually subject to high tax, and good deals are not often available.

Many Latin American airlines fly to Lima, including Aerolíneas Argentinas, Aeroméxico, Mexicana, Servivensa (Venezuela), Avianca (Colombia), Copa (Panamá), Grupo Taca (Central America), LanChile, Lloyd Aéreo Boliviano, Ecuatoriana and Saeta (Ecuador) and Varig (Brazil). In addition, several US companies have flights between some Latin American cities and Lima.

## LAND

If you live in the Americas, it is possible to travel overland by bus. However, if you want to start from North or Central America, the Carretera Panamericana stops in Panamá and begins again in Colombia, leaving a 200km roadless section of jungle known as the Darien Gap. This takes about a week to cross on foot and by canoe in the dry season (January to mid-April) but is much heavier going in the wet season. This overland route has become increasingly dangerous because of banditry and drug-related problems, especially on the Colombian side. Most overland travelers fly or take a boat around the Darien Gap.

Once in South America, it is relatively straightforward to travel by public bus from

Frog, Zona Reservada Tambopata-Candamo

KEVIN SCHAFER

Llama at Llulluchupampa, along the Inca Trail

CRAIG LOVELL

quirrel monkey, Amazon rainforest

VICTOR ENGLEBERT

Male cock-of-the-rock at a lek in southeast Peru

KEVIN SCHAFER

KEVIN SCHAFER

Machu Picchu - shrouded in mist and mystery

## Useful Web Addresses

### Airlines with Flights to Peru

| | |
|---|---|
| Aeroflot | www.aeroflot.org |
| Aerolíneas Argentinas | www.aerolineas.com.ar |
| Aeroméxico | www.aeromexico.com |
| American Airlines | www.americanair.com |
| Continental | www.continental.com |
| Copa | www.copaair.com/ |
| Delta | www.deltaairlines.com |
| Iberia | www.iberia.com |
| KLM | www.klmuk.com |
| LanChile | www.lanchile.com |
| Lloyd Aéreo Boliviano | www.labairlines.com |
| Lufthansa | www.lufthansa.com |
| Mexicana | www.mexicana.com.mx |
| Saeta | www.saeta.com.ec/ |
| Servivensa | www.avensa.com.ve/ |
| United | www.ual.com |
| Varig | www.varig.com |

### Adventure Tours

| | |
|---|---|
| Adventure Associates | www.adventureassociates.com |
| Amazonas Explorer | www.amazonas-explorer.com |
| Inca Tours | www.southamerica.com.au (from Australia) |
| Wilderness Travel | www.wildernesstravel.com |

### Online Travel Deals & Booking Agents

| | |
|---|---|
| Airlines of the Web | www.flyaow.com/ |
| Association of Air Travel Couriers | www.courier.org |
| Cheap Tickets | www.cheaptickets.com (from N. America) |
| CNN Interactive's Travel Guide | www.cnn.com/Travel |
| Council Travel | www.counciltravel.com |
| ETN | www.etn.nl (from Europe) |
| Excite Travel by City.Net | www.city.net |
| eXito | www.exitotravel.com |
| Flightbookers | www.flightbookers.net |
| Flight Centres International | www.flightcentre.com.au (from Australia only) |
| Internet Travel Network | www.itn.net |
| Journey Latin America | www.journeylatinamerica.co.uk |
| Preview Travel | www.previewtravel.com |
| STA Travel | www.statravel.com |
| Travel.com | www.travel.com.au |
| Travel CUTS | www.travelcuts.com (from Canada only) |
| Travelocity | www.travelocity.com |

the Andean countries (Colombia, Ecuador, Chile and Bolivia), although this is a fairly slow option. See the Lonely Planet guides to those countries for full details.

Some companies offer international buses to other countries. In Lima, Ormeño Internacional (☎ 472-1710, Javier Prado 1059, Santa Catalina) has buses from and to Quito, Ecuador (1½ days); Bogotá, Colombia (3 days); Caracas, Venezuela (4 days and 4 hours); Santiago, Chile (2 days and 6 hours); and Buenos Aires, Argentina (4 days). Fares are about US$50 per day, and luggage is limited to 20kg. Also in Lima, Caracol (☎ 445-4879, Enrique Palacios 954, Miraflores) has services to most of these countries plus Uruguay and Brazil. El Rápido (☎ 422-9508, Rivera Navarrete 2650, Lince) has buses to Argentina and Uruguay. Cruz del Sur (☎ 424-1005, 427-1311, 423-1570, Quilca 531) has buses to La Paz, Bolivia. Check carefully with the company about what is included, and whether the service is direct or involves a transfer at the border. It is always much cheaper to buy tickets to the border, cross, and the buy onward tickets on the other side.

## SEA
It is possible to arrive in Lima's port of Callao both by expensive ocean liners and cheaper freight vessels. Few people arrive by sea, however, because services are infrequent and are normally more expensive and less convenient than flying.

## RIVER
It is possible to travel by river boat all the way from the mouth of the Amazon (at Belém, Brazil) to Iquitos, Peru. Passengers will need to break up the journey into several stages, because single boats don't do the entire trip.

The easiest way is to take one boat from Belém to Manaus in central Brazil, and then a second boat from Manaus to Benjamin Constant, which is on the Brazilian side of the Peruvian-Brazilian-Colombian border. At this point, you can take local motorboats across the border to the small Colombian port of Leticia, from where you can easily find boats into Peru.

The journey from Belém to Leticia will take about two weeks, depending on the currents and speed of the boat. From Leticia to Iquitos takes another one to three days. The entire trip will cost roughly US$100 or less if traveling on the lower decks.

There's also the option of entering Peru from the Bolivian border via river boat along the Madre de Dios, but finding a boat going in this direction (against the current) is difficult. More information about river travel in Peru is found in the Getting Around and Amazon Basin chapters.

## ORGANIZED TOURS
Many of the travel agencies listed earlier in your departure country can help arrange tours. The following specialize in organized tours.

**From North America** Because of the easy flight connection to Peru, the USA has far more companies offering tours than the rest of the world put together. There must be well over a hundred companies that offer tours to Peru. You can find their addresses in advertisements in outdoor and travel magazines such as *Escape* and *Outside*, as well as more general magazines, such as *Natural History, Audubon* and *Smithsonian*. The following are some of the best and longest-established companies. (Also refer to Organized Tours in Getting Around for Peruvian operators.)

Wilderness Travel (☎ 510-558-2488, 800-368-2794, fax 510-558-2489, 1102 Ninth St, Berkeley, CA 94710) has been sending small groups (4 to 15 participants) to Peru (and many other countries) since the 1970s, and is one of the best in the business. They offer a good variety of treks – ranging from four nights on the Inca Trail to two weeks in the remote Cordillera Huayhuash – combined with hotel portions in the Cuzco-Machu Picchu area. They also offer comfortable hotel-based tours to the most interesting areas of Peru.

International Expeditions (☎ 205-428-1700, 800-633-4734, fax 205-428-1714, amazon@ietravel.com, One Environs Park, Helena, AL 35080) offers the best variety of tours in the

Amazon. Their tours involve visits to both the northern and southern Peruvian rainforests, stays in jungle lodges (including the ACEER, which has a rainforest canopy walkway) and river boat trips that emphasize natural history. More details are given in the Amazon Basin chapter. They can combine Amazon trips with visits to other parts of Peru. Other companies going to the Amazon tend to specialize in one area and are mentioned in the appropriate parts of that chapter.

Wildland Adventures (☎ 206-365-0686, 800-345-4453, fax 206-363-6615, info@ wildland.com, 3546 NE 155th St, Seattle, WA 98155) has a variety of treks, including Inca Trail clean-up campaigns, and general tours with an emphasis on ecology and local culture. They come well recommended. Mountain Travel-Sobek (☎ 510-527-8100, 888-687-6235, fax 510-525-7710, info@ mtsobek.com, 6420 Fairmont Ave, El Cerrito, CA 94530) is good for trekking and river-running tours. Backroads (☎ 510-527-1555, 800-462-2848, fax 510-527-1444, goactive@ backroads.com, 801 Cedar St, Berkeley, CA 94710) has biking tours in the Cuzco area.

In Canada, Adventures Abroad (☎ 604-303-1099, 800-665-3998, fax 604-303-1076, adabroad@infoserve.net, Suite 2148, 20800 Westminster Hwy, Richmond, BC V6V 2W3) has one-week tours of the Cuzco-Lake Titicaca areas.

**From the UK** JLA (see UK & Continental Europe under Air earlier in this chapter) offers group and customized itineraries. There's also Encounter Overland (☎/fax 020-7370-6845, adventure@encounter.co.uk, 267 Old Brompton Rd, London SW5 9JA) and Exodus (☎ 020-8675-5550, fax 020-8673-0779, sales@exodustravel.co.uk, 9 Weir Rd, London SW12 ULT). Both companies have

long-distance expeditions using specially equipped trucks, and the trips often include camping. These trips are popular with young, adventurous budget travelers.

Amazonas Explorer (☎/fax 01437-891743, sales@amazonas-explorer.com, Riverside, Black Tar, Llangwm, Haverfordwest, Pembs, Wales SA62 4JD) specializes in high-adventure multiday rafting trips on several of the most exciting rivers in southern Peru. Rafting trips can be combined with mountain biking, visits to Machu Picchu or the Inca Trail, extreme trekking or customized itineraries. The owners are super-knowledgeable and have an Arequipa office (☎ 54-21-2813, fax 54-22-0147).

For all-inclusive, 21-day mountain-biking adventures, the following have been recommended: Discover Adventure (☎/fax 01722-741123, discover@adventure.u-net .com, 5 Netherhampton Cottages, Netherhampton, Salisbury) and KE Adventure Travel (☎ 017687-73966, fax 017687-74693, keadventure@enterprise.net, 32 Lake Road, Keswick, Cumbria, CA12 5DQ).

**From Australia and New Zealand** For tours to Peru from Australia and New Zealand, contact Adventure Associates (☎ 02-9389-7466, fax 02-9369-1853, 197 Oxford St, Bondi Junction, Sydney, NSW 2022); they handle standard one-week tours plus independent travel arrangements. Another option is Adventure World (☎ 02-9956-7766, 800-221-931, 73 Walker St, Sydney) and (☎ 09-524-5118, fax 09-520-6629, 101 Great South Road, Remuera, Auckland). For a good variety of Latin American tours at mid- to lower-top-end prices, contact Contours (☎ 03-9670-6900, fax 03-9670-7558, contours@compuserve.com, 1/84 William St, Melbourne, VIC 3000).

# Getting Around

Public buses are frequent and reasonably comfortable on the major routes and are the normal form of transport for most Peruvians and budget travelers. Less-traveled routes are served by older and less-comfortable vehicles. There are two railway systems, which can make an interesting change from bus travel. Travelers in a hurry or desiring greater comfort or privacy can hire a car with a driver, which is often not much more expensive than renting a self-drive car. Air services are widespread and particularly recommended for those short on time. In the jungle regions, travel by river boat or by air is normally the only choice.

Whichever form of transport you use, remember to have your passport on your person at all times – not packed away in your luggage or left in the hotel safe. You may need to show your passport to board a plane. Buses may have to go through a transit police check upon entering and leaving major towns; in the past, passports had to be shown, but this rarely occurred on my last trip. Regulations change frequently, so be prepared. If your passport is in order, these procedures are no more than cursory. If you're traveling anywhere near the borders, you can expect more-frequent passport controls.

## AIR
### Domestic Airports
The main airports are shown on the accompanying Internal Air Flights map, but there are many others that are often no more than a grass strip in the jungle. They can be reached on some of the smallest airlines or by chartered light aircraft. Note that the routes shown on this map are subject to frequent change. For example, the short flight from Chiclayo to Trujillo may occasionally be offered if the airline can combine a Chiclayo-Lima flight with a Trujillo-Lima flight. Also note that some routes are not served every day.

### Domestic Airlines
Once you have arrived in Peru, you'll find that the only major carrier, Aero Continente (☎ toll-free in the USA: 877-359-7378, www.aerocontinente.com.pe) serves most domestic routes. Four other major domestic airlines (including international carriers Faucett and AeroPerú) have closed their doors from 1997 to 1999, creating a shortage of domestic flights at this time. Aero Continente is not on the international reservation system, so reservations must be made either in Peru or through a tour operator that works with Peruvian agents. Currently, flights are often full, and getting reservations on short notice can be difficult. In July 1999, LanPeru, jointly owned by LanChile and a Peruvian company, began domestic flights. Check www.traficoperu.com for details of any new airlines that may start up.

TdobleA flies to more remote towns (such as Andahuaylas, Ayacucho, Chachapoyas, Huánuco, Tingo María, Tarapoto). Their destinations change often. TANS, a civilian airline operated by the Peruvian air force, has filled in for the recent demise of Aero-Perú with daily flights from Lima to Cuzco, Arequipa and Iquitos, and several flights a week to Pucallpa, Tarapoto, Yurimaguas and other jungle towns. AeroCóndor has tour flights from Lima to the Nazca Lines (see Nazca in the South Coast chapter) and also flies to Cajamarca.

There are also a handful of small airlines flying to remote destinations in light aircraft; these are detailed in the appropriate parts of the text. Very cheap flights are offered by Grupo 8, the military airline, but these are infrequent and hard to get on because Peruvians have priority.

Fares, schedules and airlines change frequently (!!), so you need to check the latest details. In early 1999, discounted, one-way flights between major cities were US$49; after AeroPerú closed in March 1999, prices rapidly climbed to about US$100. Therefore

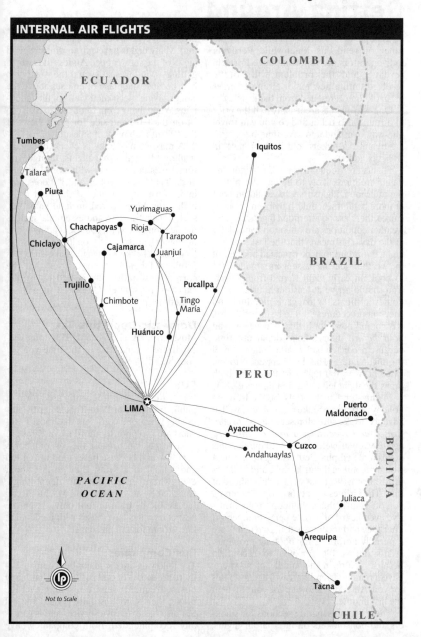

INTERNAL AIR FLIGHTS

COLOMBIA

ECUADOR

Tumbes

Talara

Piura

Iquitos

Yurimaguas

Chachapoyas   Rioja

Chiclayo                    Tarapoto

Cajamarca        Juanjuí

BRAZIL

Trujillo

Chimbote                   Pucallpa

Tingo
María

Huánuco

PERU

LIMA

Puerto
Maldonado

Ayacucho
Cuzco

Andahuaylas

BOLIVIA

PACIFIC
OCEAN

Juliaca

Arequipa

Not to Scale

Tacna

CHILE

I am unable to quote fares. There could well be a couple of new airlines in business by the time you read this. Meanwhile, Peruvian tour operators are reporting huge losses in revenue, and the problem will not be resolved until a new major airline emerges or an old one is rescued from bankruptcy.

One-way tickets are usually half the price of a round-trip ticket and so you can travel one-way overland and save time by returning by air. All tickets sold in Peru have an 18% tax added.

Flights are frequently late. Early morning flights are more likely to be on time, but by the afternoon, flights may have slid an hour or more behind schedule. If flying in or out of Cuzco, there are no afternoon flights, because weather conditions are often too windy later in the day. This means that the last morning flight, if it is late, may be canceled because of the weather -leaving passengers stranded. Try to book an early flight to and from Cuzco. You should arrive at least an hour early for domestic flights, as baggage handling and check-in procedures tend to be chaotic. Also, it is not unknown for flights to leave up to an hour *before* their official departure time because predicted bad weather might cancel the flight later. (This has happened to me twice in over 100 flights in Peru, and both times, the flight left about 15 minutes early.)

Flights tend to be fully booked during holiday periods, so make reservations well in advance. Make sure all reservations are *confirmed and reconfirmed and reconfirmed again*. Many travelers have told me that this needs to be emphasized. As a general rule, I would reconfirm flights both 72 and 24 hours in advance, as well as a week or two ahead of time. The airlines are notorious for bumping you off your flights if you don't reconfirm – I've even heard of people being bumped off after they had reconfirmed. Cuzco flights are especially notorious for booking problems. If it's impossible for you to reconfirm because you're in the middle of nowhere, have a reliable friend or travel agent do this for you. And don't show up for your flight at the last minute.

There are no separate sections for smokers and nonsmokers on internal air flights;

nonsmokers have to suffer (though some flights have now been declared nonsmoking). Many flights have extraordinarily good views of the snowcapped Andes – it is worth getting a window seat even if the weather is bad, because the plane often rises above the clouds, giving spectacular views of the mountains. When flying from Lima to Cuzco, try to sit on the left-hand side for great views of the 6271m-high peak of Salcantay.

A maximum of 20kg of checked luggage is allowed on internal flights, though you sometimes can get away with more. Luggage doesn't get lost very often and, if it does, normally turns up on one of the next day's flights, but be prepared: include valuables, such as camera gear, and essentials, such as medication or a warm coat (if heading to the highlands), in your carry-on luggage. Always lock your checked luggage, make sure it is properly labeled and try to see that the correct destination tag is tied on by the check-in personnel. Unlocked luggage is sometimes pilfered.

## Domestic-Departure Tax

Most airports charge a US$3 domestic-departure tax, payable at the time you get your boarding pass.

## BUS

Buses are the most frequently used form of public transport in Peru. This is hardly surprising when one considers that most Peruvians are too poor to afford a car. Fares are relatively cheap, because the cost of labor is very low, and because buses tend to run full and sell all their seats. They go just about everywhere except for the deep jungle (reached by air or river) and Machu Picchu (accessible by train or foot only). Even the best companies have buses with inadequate knee-room for tall passengers.

### Bus Companies

The following are the major bus companies – there are scores of others. Ormeño has many buses, frequent departures and average prices; their service is quite good. Cruz del Sur also has extensive services and is generally recommended. Both companies have several subsidiary companies that leave from the same terminal as the mother company in the main cities. Other large companies include Expreso Sudamericano, which is one of the cheapest and slowest, with more frequent delays, but they get there. CIVA is usually OK as well. TEPSA has a poor reputation for driving too fast using old buses and is among the most expensive. The bigger companies often have luxury buses (called Imperial or similar), charging 30% to 100% more and providing express service, with toilets, snacks, videos and air-conditioning. Note that the toilets are, as one company announces during their 'in-flight announcements,' for 'urination only.' On trips in excess of eight hours, bathroom stops are made. Smaller companies are detailed in the text.

## General Information

The scores of competing bus companies all have their own offices. In some towns, the different bus companies have their offices in a main bus terminal. In other cities, bus companies are clustered around a few city blocks, while elsewhere, the terminals may be scattered all over town. Slowly, cities are moving toward having one long-distance bus terminal. I have tried to mark as many companies as possible on my city maps, and the accompanying text will tell you which destinations are served by which companies.

I suggest buying your ticket in advance, which enables you to check out the schedules and prices of different companies without being encumbered by your luggage. There is sometimes a separate 'express' ticket window for buying tickets for another day. Schedules and fares change frequently and vary from company to company; therefore, I give only approximations. Exact fares and schedules would be obsolete within weeks. Students with international student cards may be able to get a 10% discount. Travelers on a tight budget should shop around for the best fares. Prices vary substantially, but so does the quality of the buses. At low travel periods, some companies offer discounted bus fares – conversely, fares can double during peak periods or around holidays such as Christmas or Independence Day (July 28), when tickets may be sold out several days ahead of time. Buses can be much delayed during the rainy season, especially in the highlands and jungles. From January to April, journey times can double or even triple because of landslides and bad road conditions.

When buying your ticket, avoid seats at the back of the bus, because the ride is bumpier. On some rough mountain roads, you can literally be thrown out of your seat in the back of the bus. Also try to avoid the seats over the wheel wells, because you'll lose leg space. Always ask where the bus is leaving from, because the ticket office and bus stop are sometimes on different streets.

When waiting in bus terminals, watch your luggage very carefully. Snatch theft is common, and thieves work in pairs – one may distract you while the other grabs your bag. Razor-blade artists abound, too. While you're dozing off, leaning against your pack, somebody may try to slash through the pockets. Keep luggage where you can see it, and stay alert. I hear depressingly frequent stories of theft in bus stations. Thieves are looking for an easy rip-off and won't bother you if you appear to be on top of things. They will bother you, however, if you leave your pack leaning against the wall for 15 seconds when you're buying a bar of chocolate. Turn around with your chocolate and – no pack! See Dangers & Annoyances in the Facts for the Visitor chapter for more information on playing it safe.

During the journey, your luggage will travel in the luggage compartment unless it is small enough to carry on board. This is reasonably safe. You are given a baggage tag in exchange for your bag, which should be securely closed or locked if possible. I like to watch my pack getting loaded onto the bus, and I usually exchange a few friendly words with the loader (who is often the driver's assistant), just to make sure that my bag is properly loaded and going to the right destination. During a long trip, I get off and check my bag at stops and generally maintain a high profile. If you're on a night bus, you'll want to sleep, but I've not had any problem with anyone claiming my luggage in the middle of the night. Your hand luggage is a different matter. If you're asleep with a camera around your neck, you might wake up with a neatly razored strap and no camera at the end of it. Hide valuables! I sleep with my carry-on bag (usually a day pack) strapped on to my person and with my arms around it.

Some travelers prefer to bring their luggage on the bus with them, because there are occasional reports of theft from the luggage compartment. This works if your pack is reasonably sized (luggage racks are either nonexistent or just big enough for a briefcase, so you have to be able to shove it between your legs or on your lap).

Distances are great in Peru, and you'll probably take some trips at night. In some cases, night trips are impossible to avoid, because many buses travel at night. On the whole, day travel is the best, both to be able to see the scenery and because night trips are (rarely) subject to banditry (currently not a problem). It takes roughly 20 to 24 hours to get from either the Ecuadorian or Chilean border to Lima along the (mainly) paved Carretera Panamericana (Pan-American Hwy), which is the best long-distance highway in Peru.

Buses using the Panamericana are reasonably comfortable and have reclining seats. The same kinds of buses may be used on the rougher roads into the mountains, but they are generally less comfortable, because the constant bumping and jarring has often broken the reclining mechanism on some of the seats. How good a seat you get is largely a matter of luck. On the more remote highways, the buses are often of the uncomfortable 'school bus' type. An irritating habit that bus companies have is to shift all the rows of seats forward so that they can get another row or two in the bus. This is fine if you're short or medium-sized, but can be a real pain if you're tall. The heating in buses rarely works, and it can literally get down to freezing inside the bus when traveling in the mountains at night, so bring a blanket, sleeping bag or warm clothes as hand luggage. Conversely, the air-conditioning rarely works, and so it can get very hot and sweaty

on some of the lowland trips, especially if the windows can't be opened.

Long-distance buses stop for three meals a day (unless you travel on one of the luxury buses, which serve snacks and don't stop). The driver will announce how long the stop will be, but it's usually worth asking again unless you're sure you heard right. '*Diez minutos*' and '*treinta minutos*' sound very much alike when the driver mumbles the words while stifling a yawn; it's your responsibility to be on the bus when it leaves. Many companies have their own special rest areas, and they are sometimes in the middle of nowhere, so you don't have any choice but to eat there. The food is generally inexpensive but not particularly appetizing. I generally eat the *lomo saltado* (chopped beef fried with vegetables and served with rice) and find it's one of the standard, more edible dishes. Some travelers prefer to bring their own food.

These rest stops double as lavatory stops. Some of the better long-distance buses do have toilet cubicles aboard, but don't rely on them. Sometimes they don't work and are locked, at other times they are used as an extra luggage compartment and, if they do work, somebody invariably vomits over the whole thing just before you go to use it. Rule number one of travel in Peru is to always carry your own roll of toilet paper, because you will never find any in the toilets. Most rest-stop areas have a place that sells essentials like toilet paper, toothpaste, chocolate and other snacks.

If you're traveling during long holiday weekends or special fiestas, you may find that buses are booked up for several days in advance, so *book as early as you can* for these periods.

Whenever you travel, be prepared for delays, and don't plan on making important connections after a bus journey. Innumerable flat tires, a landslide, or engine trouble can lengthen an 18-hour journey into a three-day odyssey. Such lengthy delays are not very common, but a delay of several hours can be expected quite frequently.

A useful thing to carry on an overnight bus is a flashlight, because the driver nearly always shuts off the interior lights when the bus is under way. Being so close to the equator, it is dark for 12 hours, and a flashlight enables you to read a book for a few hours before going to sleep. And, when you do decide to sleep, ear plugs are a good idea.

## TRUCK

In remote areas, trucks may double as buses. Sometimes they are pickup trucks with rudimentary wooden benches, and at other times, they are ordinary trucks; you just climb in the back, often with the cargo. I once had a ride on top of a truck carrying two bulls – for 12 hours, my feet dangled just centimeters away from a pair of impressively large horns. If the weather is OK, you can get fabulous views as you travel in the refreshing wind (dress warmly). If the weather is bad, you hunker down underneath a dark tarpaulin with the other passengers – unless the cargo happens to be two bulls, in which case you stay on top and get soaked to the bone. It certainly isn't the height of luxury, but it may be the only way of getting to some areas, and if you're open-minded about the minor discomforts, you may find these rides among the most interesting in Peru.

Payment for these rides is determined by the driver and is a standard fare, depending on the distance. Ask other passengers how much they are paying; usually you'll find that because the trucks double as buses, they charge almost as much as buses.

## TRAIN

The Peruvian railroad (INAFER), which is currently government-owned but is facing imminent privatization, goes from the coast to the highlands and was a major communication link between the sierra and the coast before the advent of roads and air travel. Trains are less used today, but they nevertheless still play a part in Peru's transportation system.

The central railroad runs from Lima to the mining town of La Oroya, where it branches north and south. The northbound line goes to Cerro de Pasco, but has been closed to all but freight trains since the early 1980s. The southbound line goes to Huancayo but did not carry passengers through most of the 1990s. In 1998, passenger trains began running from Lima to Huancayo on the last Saturday of every month, returning on the following Monday. In the 1999 dry season, this service was increased to four times a month. Depending on the continued success of this service, schedules may be increased or canceled, and it normally doesn't run during the rainiest months. This journey passes through the station of Galera, which is 4781m above sea level and the highest standard-gauge train station in the world. In Huancayo, you can change train stations and then continue to Huancavelica. The Huancayo-to-Huancavelica section is running daily at this time.

The southern railroad runs from the coast at Mollendo through Arequipa to Lake Titicaca and Cuzco. The Mollendo-Arequipa route is for freight only. The Arequipa-Lake Titicaca-Cuzco section is for passengers as well as freight. Trains from Arequipa to Puno, on the shores of Lake Titicaca, run three nights a week. You can change at Juliaca, about 40km before Puno, for trains to Cuzco. The Arequipa-Juliaca (or Puno) service takes a whole night; the Puno-Cuzco service takes a whole day. This trip is more expensive and takes longer than the bus, so it is for train fans only. In Cuzco, there are two train stations a few kilometers apart; one for the service described above, and the other for services to Machu Picchu. You cannot go directly from Arequipa or Lake Titicaca. There are several trains from Cuzco to Machu Picchu every day.

The last segment of Peru's southern railway is found in the extreme south of the country. It is a border train that runs several times a week between Tacna in Peru and Arica in Chile.

There are several classes. Second class is the cheapest, very crowded, uncomfortable and prone to theft. First class is about 25% more expensive, safer, and much more comfortable. Then there are Pullman cars (also called Tourist or Inca Class), which require a significant surcharge. They are heated and give access to food service.

In addition to the normal train *(tren)*, there is a faster electric train called the *autovagón*. This is smaller and more expensive than the ordinary train and runs on only a few routes.

The main drawback to traveling by train is thievery. The night train from Arequipa to Puno is especially notorious, particularly in the crowded and poorly lit 2nd-class carriages, where a dozing traveler is almost certain to get robbed. Dark train stations are also the haunts of thieves, who often work in pairs or small groups. The answer to the problem is to travel by day and stay alert, to travel with a friend or group, and to travel 1st class. Above all, stay alert. The Pullman classes have a surcharge and are the safest carriages to ride in because only ticket holders are allowed aboard. However, the high surcharge discourages Peruvians, and many travelers prefer to travel 1st class to be with the locals.

For all services, it is advisable to buy tickets in advance – the day before is usually best. This way, you don't have to worry about looking after your luggage while lining up to buy a ticket at a crowded booking-office window. Often, advance tickets are hard to buy at the train stations, because travel agencies buy them up in bulk and sell them at a US$2 or US$3 surcharge – convenient if you can afford it, but very irritating if you are traveling on a budget.

## CAR & MOTORCYCLE
### Car Rental
The major car-rental companies (Budget, Avis, National and Hertz) are found in Lima, and a few are found in the other major cities. In general, car rental is not cheap (averaging US$50 a day for a car). There are plenty of hidden charges for mileage (per kilometer), insurance and so on, so make sure you understand the rental agreement before renting a car. A deposit by credit card is usually required, and renters normally need to be over 25. Your own driver's license should be accepted for driving in Peru.

If you really want to drive, bear in mind that it is a long way from Lima to most major tourist destinations, and it is suggested that you use bus or air to wherever you want to go and rent a car when you get there. Also bear in mind that the condition of the rental vehicles is often not very good, roads are badly potholed (even the paved Panamericana) and drivers are extremely aggressive. Road signs, where they exist, are often small and unclear. Gas stations are few and far between. Vehicles such as 4WD jeeps are very expensive, and many companies are reluctant to rent ordinary cars for anything but short coastal runs. Theft is all too common, so you should not leave your vehicle parked in the street or you'll lose your hubcaps, windshield wipers, or even your wheels. Driving at night is not recommended because of poor road conditions, speeding buses, and slow-moving, ill-lit trucks. When stopping overnight, park the car in a guarded lot (the better hotels have them). Generally, I do not recommend self-drive car rental.

### Buying a Car
I don't recommend trying to buy, drive and then resell a car unless you are planning on a long stay and are prepared to put up with a lot of red tape. Using public transport is generally more efficient, given the negative points outlined earlier.

### Taxis
Renting a taxi for long-distance trips costs little more than renting a car and takes care of many of the problems outlined earlier. Not all taxi drivers will agree to drive long distances, but if one does, you should check the driver's credentials before hiring.

### Motorcycle Rental
Motorcycle rental seems to be an option mainly in jungle towns like Iquitos and Puerto Maldonado, where bikers can go for short runs around town and into the surroundings, but not much farther.

## BICYCLE
Each year, there are a handful of cyclists who attempt to cycle from Alaska to Argentina, or shorter long-distance rides,

and they manage to get through Peru OK. They report that the Panamericana is incredibly long, boring, windy, sandy, miserable, and there is a good chance that you will be knocked off by kamikaze truck and bus drivers who will not stop to see if you're OK. Cycling in the Andes is more fun and visually rewarding, though hard work. Mountain bikes are recommended, road bikes won't stand up to the poor roads.

Renting bikes is only a recent option in Peru and is described under the towns of Huaraz, Huancayo and Cuzco. These are rented to people who want to stay in the general area of those towns, not travel all over the country. The bicycles that are available aren't bad, but if you're a dedicated biker, you're probably better off bringing your own. Most airlines will fly them at no extra cost if you box them. However, boxing the bike gives baggage handlers little clue to the contents, and the box is liable to be roughly handled, possibly damaging the bike. An alternative is wrapping it in heavy-duty plastic – baggage handlers are less likely to drop or throw the bike in this case. Airlines' bicycle-carrying policies do vary a lot, so shop around.

Be wary at Peruvian Customs if agents try to sting you for a '25% of value, fully refundable bond.' It's not clear if this is legal or not, but if you are insistent enough, you may persuade the customs agent that it's your personal baggage, not for resale in the country. If you can't get around the bond, undervalue your bike as much as you dare, because it will be difficult and time-consuming to get your bond back when you leave.

Bicycle shops are few and far between in Peru and used to carry a completely inadequate selection of parts. This has improved recently with the lifting of prohibitive taxes on bike parts.

## HITCHHIKING

Hitching is never entirely safe in any country in the world and is not recommended. Travelers who decide to hitch should understand that they are taking a small but potentially serious risk. People who do choose to hitch will be safer if they travel in pairs and let someone know where they are planning to go.

Hitchhiking is not very practical in Peru for three reasons: There are few private cars, public transport is relatively cheap, and trucks are used as public transport in remote areas, so trying to hitch a free ride on one is the same as trying to hitch a free ride on a bus. Many drivers of *any* vehicle will pick you up, but will also expect payment. If the driver is stopping to drop off and pick up other passengers, ask them what the going rate is. If you are the only passenger, the driver may have picked you up just to talk with a foreigner, and he may wave aside your offer of payment. If you do decide to try hitching, make sure in advance of your ride that you and the driver agree on the subject of payment.

## BOAT

Although Peru has a long coastline, travel along the coast is almost entirely by road or air, and there are no coastal passenger steamer services, although international cruise ships arrive at the port in Callao once in a while.

In the highlands, there are boat services on Lake Titicaca, which, at just over 3800m, is the highest navigable lake in the world. Boats are usually small motorized vessels that take about 20 passengers from Puno to visit the various islands on the lake. There are departures every day, and costs are low. There used to be a couple of larger steamships crossing the lake from Puno to Bolivia, but this service no longer exists, although the *Yavari* (see the boxed text 'The Yavari Project' in the Lake Titicaca chapter) is being restored and will offer tours in the next few years. Meanwhile, an expensive hydrofoil can be booked through travel agents (details are given under Puno in the Lake Titicaca chapter). It is much cheaper to take a bus from Puno to La Paz, Bolivia, which gives you the opportunity to 'cross' Lake Titicaca by a ferry over the narrow Estrecho de Tiquina.

In Peru's eastern lowlands, however, boat travel is of major importance. Boats are mainly of two types – small dugout canoes or larger cargo boats. The dugout canoes are usually powered by an outboard engine and act as a water taxi or bus on some of the smaller rivers. Sometimes they are powered by a strange arrangement that looks like an inboard motorcycle engine attached to a tiny propeller by a 3m-long propeller shaft. Called *peki-pekis*, these canoes are a slow and rather noisy method of transportation, but are OK for short trips; they are especially common on Yarinacocha (a lake near Pucallpa). In some places, modern aluminum launches are found, but dugouts are still more common. As one gets farther inland and the rivers widen, larger cargo boats are normally available.

## Dugout Canoe

Dugout canoes often carry as many as 24 passengers and are the only way to get around many roadless areas. Hiring one yourself is expensive. Taking one with other passengers is much cheaper, but not as cheap as bus travel over a similar distance. This is because an outboard engine uses more fuel per passenger per kilometer than a bus engine, and because a boat travels slower than a bus.

Many of the boats used are literally dugouts, with maybe a splashboard added to the gunwales. They are long in shape, but short on comfort. Seating is normally on hard, low, uncomfortable wooden benches accommodating two people each. Luggage is stashed forward under a tarpaulin, so carry hand baggage containing essentials for the journey.

If it is a long journey, you will be miserable if you don't take the following advice – advice that is worth the cost of this book! *Bring seat padding!* A folded sweater or towel will make a world of difference to your trip. Pelting rain or glaring sun are major hazards, and an umbrella is excellent defense against both. Bring sunblock and wear long sleeves, long pants and a sun hat – I have seen people unable to walk because of second-degree burns on their legs from a six-hour exposure to the tropical sun. As the boat motors along, the breeze tends to keep insects away, and it also tends to cool you

down, so you don't notice the burning effects of the sun. If the sun should disappear or the rain begin, you can get quite chilled, so bring a light jacket. Insect repellent is useful during stops along the river. A water bottle and food will complete your hand luggage. Remember to stash your spare clothes in plastic bags, or they'll get soaked by rain or spray.

A final word about dugout canoes – they feel very unstable! Until you get used to the motion, you might worry about the whole thing just rolling over and tipping everybody into the piranha-, electric eel-, or boa constrictor-infested waters. Clenching the side of the canoe and wondering what madness possessed you to board the flimsy contraption in the first place doesn't seem to help. But dugouts feel much less stable than they really are, so don't worry about a disaster; it almost never happens. I've ridden many dugouts without any problems, even in rapids. Nor have I met anyone who was actually dunked in.

## River Boat

This is the classic way to travel down the Amazon – swinging in your hammock aboard a banana boat piloted by a grizzled old captain who knows the waters better than the back of his hand. You can travel from Pucallpa or Yurimaguas to the mouth of the Amazon this way, although boats don't do the entire trip. Instead, you'll spend a few days getting to Iquitos, where you'll board another, slightly larger boat and continue for two more days to the border with Brazil and Colombia. From there, more boats can be found for the week-long passage to Manaus (Brazil) in the heart of the Amazon Basin.

Although cargo boats ply the Ucayali from Pucallpa to Iquitos, and the Marañon from Yurimaguas to Iquitos, they tend to leave only once or twice a week. The boats are small, but have two decks. The lower deck is normally for cargo, and the upper for passengers and crew. Bring your own hammock. Food is usually provided, but it is basic and not necessarily very hygienic; you may want to bring some of your own. To arrange a passage, ask around at the docks until you hear of a boat going where you want to go, then find out who the captain is. It's usually worth asking around about the approximate cost to avoid being overcharged, though some captains will charge you the same as anybody else. Departure time often depends on a full cargo, and *mañana* may go on for several days if the hold is only half full. Usually, you can sleep on the boat while you are waiting for departure if you want to save on hotel bills. At no time should you leave your luggage unattended.

Boats to Iquitos are relatively infrequent and rather small, slow and uncomfortable. Beyond Iquitos, however, services are more frequent and comfortable. Things are generally more organized too; there are chalkboards at the docks with ship's names, destinations and departure times displayed reasonably clearly and accurately. You can look over a boat for your prospective destination and wait for a better vessel if you don't like what you see. Some boats even have cabins, though these tend to be rather grubby, airless boxes, and you have to supply your own bedding. I prefer to use a hammock. Try to hang it away from the engine room and not directly under a light, as these are often lit far into the evening, precluding sleep and attracting insects. Food is usually included in the price of the passage, and may be marginally better on some of the bigger and better ships. If you like rice and beans – or rice and fish, or rice and tough meat, or rice and fried bananas – you'll be OK. If you don't like rice, you'll have a problem. Bottled soft drinks and beers are usually available and priced very reasonably – ask about this before the boat leaves, because you definitely don't want to drink the water. Sanitary facilities are basic but adequate, and there's usually a pump shower on board.

Boats from Iquitos used to go all the way to the mouth of the Amazon, though this is almost unheard of these days. However, the very fact that oceangoing vessels are capable of reaching Iquitos indicates how vast this river is. Many people have misconceptions about sailing down the Amazon, watching monkeys swinging in the tree tops, snakes gliding among the branches, and parrots and macaws flying across the river in front of you. In reality, most of the banks have been colonized, and there is little wildlife there. Also, the boats often navigate the midstream, and the shoreline is seen only as a rather distant green line. In fact, some people find the monotonous diet and long days of sitting in their hammocks to be boring, and they don't enjoy the trip. For others, it's a great experience – I hope my descriptions help you decide whether this is something you'd like to attempt or want to avoid. See the boxed text 'A Week on the Amazon' for more on Amazon travel. If you'd like to do it in greater comfort, there are much more expensive boats with air-conditioned cabins available, which are for tourists rather than cargo and river passengers. See Cruises under Exploring the Jungle in the Amazon Basin chapter for details.

## LOCAL TRANSPORT

There are no underground or surface trains in any city in Peru. Local transport is therefore limited to bus or taxi.

### Bus

Local buses are usually slow and crowded, but cheap. Local buses often go out to a nearby village, and this is a good way to see an area. Just stay on the bus to the end of the line, pay another fare and head back again, sitting in the best seat on the bus. If you make friends with the driver, you may end up with an entertaining tour as he points out the local sights, in between collecting other passengers' fares.

When you want to get off a local bus, yell *Baja!*, which means 'Down!' (as in 'The passenger is getting down'). Telling the driver to stop will make him think you're trying to be a backseat driver, and you will be ignored. He's only interested if you're getting off, or down from the bus. Another way of getting him to stop is to yell *Esquina!*, which means 'Corner!' He'll stop at the next one. A *por favor* doesn't hurt, and makes everyone think you speak excellent Spanish. If you don't actually speak Spanish and someone tries to converse after your display of linguistic brilliance, a smile and a sage nod should suffice until you get down from the bus.

## Taxi

For short hops around a city, just flag down one of the many taxis that seem to be every-where. They are recognizable by the small red taxi sticker in the windshield. The cars themselves can be of almost any model and color. Regulated taxis called by telephone are available in Lima and some of the other major cities, and are listed in applicable

---

### A Week on the Amazon

Once, I traveled by boat from Iquitos all the way to Manaus and had a great time. I was already aware of the lack of wildlife in this well-traveled and colonized sector, so I brought a couple of very thick books. Yet I found I barely had the time to read them; there was so much to do. The views of the great river stretching all around were often very beautiful, particularly during the misty dawns and the searing sunsets.

Quarters were close on the passenger deck, and my elbows literally touched my neighbor's when I was in my hammock. Friendliness and an easygoing attitude are essential ingredients

for a river trip. Most of the passengers are friendly and fun, and you can have a great time getting to know them.

On the first evening of the seven-day trip from the Peruvian border to Manaus, I was sitting in the bow, enjoying the cooling breeze and watching the sun go down. Soon, a small crowd of Peruvian, Colombian and Brazilian passengers and crew gathered, and a rum bottle and guitar appeared.

Within minutes, we had a first-rate party with singing, dancing, hand clapping and an incredible impromptu orchestra. One of the crew bent a metal rod into a rough triangle that he pounded rhythmically, someone else threw a handful of beans into a can and started shaking, a couple of pieces of polished wood were clapped together to interweave yet another rhythm, a mouth harp was produced, I blew bass notes across the top of my beer bottle and everyone had a great time. A couple of hours of rhythmic music as the sun went down became a standard part of the ship's routine and gave me some of my most unforgettable moments of South American travel.

Once or twice a day, the boat would pull into some tiny Amazon port to load or off-load passengers and cargo. The arrival of a big boat was often the main event of the day in one of these small river villages, and the entire population might come down to the riverbank to swap gossip and watch the goings-on. This, too, added to the interest of the trip.

Don't expect to see much wildlife when traveling on an Amazon passenger/cargo boat, but do expect to interact with the locals and enjoy the views and the river life.

chapters. These are more expensive than taxis flagged down on the street, but are also safer and more reliable. Those flagged down on the street are not regulated, and although I've never had a problem with one, I would avoid taking one of those if carrying a large amount of money or going to the airport with all my luggage. Single women should stick to regulated taxis, especially at night.

The taxis outside the expensive hotels are usually the most convenient, comfortable and reliable, and some of their drivers speak English. They do a brisk trade in taking well-heeled tourists to the airport or local museums. They are also the most expensive and have set rates, which are often two or three times the rate of a taxi flagged down on the street.

Shared taxis, or *colectivos*, do set runs and are especially found in Lima. The driver drives along with one hand out of the window holding up as many fingers as the number of seats available. You can flag them down on any corner and get off wherever you like. There used to be more *comités*, or shared intercity taxis, but these have been displaced by improved bus and plane services. Note that the term colectivo is also used to denote a bus, especially a minibus or van.

Whatever kind of taxi you take, there are two things to remember: Fares are invariably cheaper than in North America or Europe, and you must always ask the fare in advance, because there are no meters. It is quite acceptable to haggle over a taxi fare – drivers often double or triple the standard rate for an unsuspecting foreigner. Try to find out what the going rate is before taking a cab. Recently, S/2 (about US$0.60) was the standard fare for short runs in most cities.

Finally, you can hire a taxi with a driver for several hours, or even days. The cost varies depending on how far you expect to drive in a day and on how luxurious a vehicle you get. If you speak Spanish and make your own arrangements with a driver, you could start around $40 per day if you are driving on better roads and making occasional stops, more if driving a long way or on poor roads. On the other hand, a tourist agency could arrange a comfortable car with an English-speaking driver for about twice as much. Often, your hotel can help arrange a taxi for you. If you hire one for several days, make sure that you discuss eating and sleeping arrangements. Some drivers will charge enough to be able to make their own arrangements, while others will expect you to provide a room and three meals.

Tipping is not the norm, especially for short hops within the city. If you hire a driver for the day and he is particularly helpful or friendly, you may want to tip.

## On Foot

Walking around cities is generally safe, even at night, if you stick to the well-lit areas. Always be on the alert for pickpockets though, and make inquiries before venturing into an area you don't know.

## ORGANIZED TOURS

Most people who take tours in Peru either arrange them in their home countries with a reputable outfitter (some of which are mentioned in the Getting There & Away chapter) or take local tours in Peru. Some travelers come to Lima to buy a tour covering much of Peru, and a few agencies in Lima are set up for this kind of travel. Many agencies will book your flights and hotels and arrange to have you met by a local tour representative in the towns you wish to visit, in effect combining a series of local tours.

The best-known and most-experienced of these agencies in Lima is Lima Tours (☎ 424-7560, 424-6410, 424-5110, fax 330-4488, inbound@limatours.com.pe, Jirón Belén 1040, Lima 1) although they are also among the most expensive. Condor Travel (☎ 442-9026, 442-7503, fax 442-0935, Calle Blondet 249, San Isidro) is also well recommended for top-end touring. Travelers will find it cheaper to make their own travel and hotel arrangements to the towns of their choice, and then take local tours with one of the agencies available in the most popular destinations. The better agencies are listed under the appropriate city. A smaller travel agent with an excellent reputation for helping travelers is Fertur Peru (☎ 427-1958, fax 428-3247, fertur@correo.dnet.com.pe, Jirón Junín

211, Lima 1), owned by Siduith Ferrer Herrera, who speaks English.

An excellent Peruvian company that owns lodges in the Amazon and arranges tours to several other parts of Peru is InkaNatura (☎ 84-243-408, 84-623-666, ☎/fax 84-226-392, inkanatura@chavin.rcp.net.pe, www.inkanatura.com, Avenida Sol 821, 2nd floor, Cuzco). InkaNatura's profits go toward funding two Peruvian conservation organizations. One of the directors is macaw expert Dr Charles Munn (see *National Geographic*, January 1994). They have a US office at (☎ 215-923-3641, fax 215-923-5535, kit@inkanatura.com) 620 Chestnut St, Public Ledger Building, Suite 668, Philadelphia PA 19106-3474.

For expeditions in specially converted 4X4 vehicles, contact Rafael Belmonte at Peru Expeditions Overland (☎ 447-2057, fax 445-9683, peruexpe@amauta.rcp.net.pe, www.peru-expeditions.com, Avenida Arequipa 5241, office 504, Miraflores, Lima 18). Apart from vehicle tours from Lima to many parts of the country, which include camping in remote areas, they also arrange trekking, mountain-biking, rafting and Amazon expeditions. They have English-speaking guides and international passengers. Most tours cost a little over US$100 per day.

Another option, Aventours (☎ 444-9060, fax 444-1067, aventours@correo.dnet.com.pe, www.aventours.com) has fixed, eight-day bus departures throughout the year. Two main trips are offered; one is the traditional southern circuit: Lima-Paracas-Nazca-Colca-Arequipa-Titicaca-Cuzco, and the other is a northern archaeological circuit: Lima-Trujillo-Chiclayo-Chachapoyas-Kuélap-Leymebamba-Celendín-Cajamarca-Lima. Both trips travel by comfortable private bus (return by plane) and use a combination of camping and staying in comfortable hotels. Rates are US$800 per person, including everything with the exception of a couple of dinners in cities.

One of the best established adventure-travel companies, specializing in trekking, is Explorandes (☎ 445-8683, 445-0532, fax 445-4686, Calle San Fernando 320, Miraflores, Lima).

There are hundreds of smaller agencies specializing in their own areas. The best of these are listed in appropriate areas of the book.

# Lima

☎ 01

If, like me, you read the *Paddington Bear* books in your youth, Lima in 'darkest Peru' may conjure up images of an exotic city in the heart of a lush tropical jungle. Unfortunately, this is far from the reality. The city, sprawled untidily on the edge of the coastal desert, is mainly modern and not particularly exotic. Despite its many urban problems, most visitors find Lima an interesting, if nerve-racking, place to visit.

Lima is the capital of Peru. Almost a third of Peru's 24 million inhabitants now live in Lima, making most of the city overcrowded, polluted and noisy. Much of the city's population growth can be attributed to the influx of very poor people from other areas of Peru, especially the highlands. They come searching for a better life with a job and, perhaps, opportunities for their children. Most end up living in the *pueblos jovenes*, or 'young towns.' These shantytowns, which surround the capital, lack electricity, water and adequate sanitation. Jobs are scarce; many work as *ambulantes*, or street vendors, selling anything from chocolates to clothespins and earning barely enough for food. Their chances of improving their lot are very slim.

Lima's location in the center of Peru's desert coastline gives it a climate and environment that can only be described as dismal. From April to December, the coastal fog, known as *garúa*, blots out the sun and blankets the city's buildings in a fine gray mist. Unless repainted annually, the buildings soon take on a ghostly pallor from the incessant mist that coats the rooftops with a thin, concretelike layer of hardened gray sludge. The situation is not much better during the few months of Lima's short summer – although the sun does come out, smog makes walking the city streets a sticky and unpleasant activity.

As the waste products of nearly 8 million Lima residents mostly end up in the Pacific, the beaches are overcrowded cesspools, and the newspapers carry daily health warnings during summer.

Having read this far, you might well be wondering how to avoid Lima. However, if you're planning any kind of extensive traveling in Peru, you will find it virtually impossible to avoid the desert coastline and, in turn, Lima. Despite the city's drawbacks, having no choice is not the only reason to visit Lima. Its people are generally friendly and hospitable, there are superb opportunities for dining, nightlife and other entertainment and, perhaps most important of all, the great selection of museums includes some of the best in Peru. So it's worth trying to ignore the traffic jams and the crowds and getting to know something of the people and the culture of Peru.

## History

Because it was founded by Francisco Pizarro on January 6, 1535, the Catholic feast of Epiphany, or the Day of the Kings, its first name was the City of the Kings. A university opened in 1551, and Lima became the seat of the Spanish Inquisition in 1569. The city grew quickly and was the continent's richest and most important town during early colonial times.

This changed in 1746, when a disastrous earthquake wiped out most of the city, leaving only a few churches and houses standing, some of which can still be visited. Because of Lima's importance, rebuilding was rapid, and most of the old colonial buildings that can still be seen here date from after the earthquake. After the wars of independence from Spain in the 1820s, other cities became increasingly important as capitals of the newly independent states, and Lima's importance as a colonial center vanished.

Unfortunately, much of Lima's original colonial charm has been overwhelmed by a recent population explosion. For almost 400 years, Lima was a relatively small city. Then,

LIMA

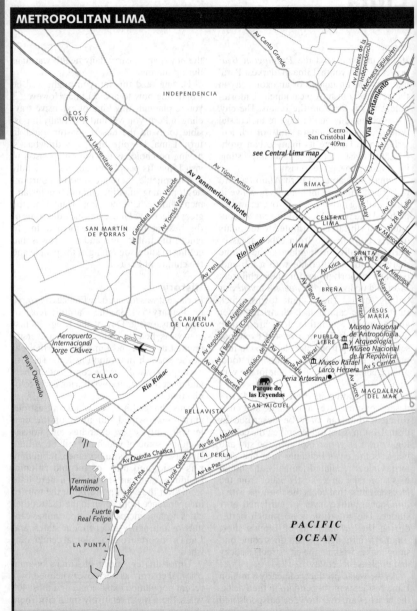

## METROPOLITAN LIMA

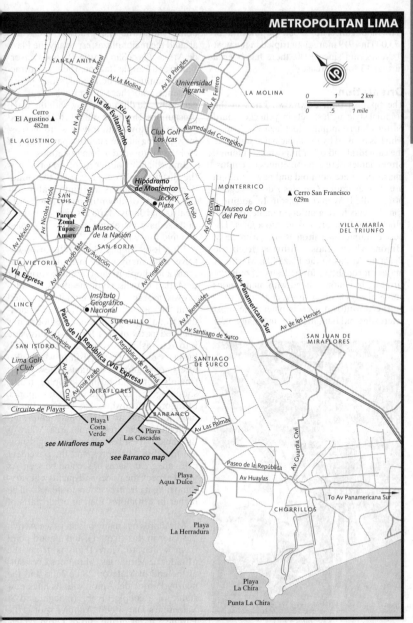

## METROPOLITAN LIMA

SANTA ANITA

Av La Molina

Av J P Pringles

Universidad Agraria

LA MOLINA

Carretera Central

Av N Ayllon

Cerro El Agustino ▲ 482m

Vía de Evitamiento

Río Surco

Av R Ferrero

Alameda del Corregidor

EL AGUSTINO

Club Golf Los Icas

Hipódromo de Monterrico

MONTERRICO

▲ Cerro San Francisco 629m

SAN LUIS

Av Cañada

Jockey Plaza

Av El Polo

🏛 Museo de Oro del Peru

VILLA MARÍA DEL TRIUNFO

Av Nicolas Arriola

Parque Zonal Túpac Amaru

🏛 Museo de la Nación

SAN BORJA

Av de Molina

Av Mexico

Av Javier Prado Este

Av Aviación

LA VICTORIA

Vía Expresa

Av Primavera

Av Panamericana Sur

LINCE

Instituto Geográfico ● Nacional

SURQUILLO

Av A Benavides

Av de los Heroes

Paseo de la República

Av Arequipa

Av República de Panamá

Av Santiago de Surco

SAN JUAN DE MIRAFLORES

SAN ISIDRO

Lima Golf ↑ Club

Paseo de la República (Vía Expresa)

Av Santa Cruz

Av José Pardo

SANTIAGO DE SURCO

MIRAFLORES

Circuito de Playas

Playa Costa Verde

see Miraflores map

BARRANCO

Playa Las Cascadas

Av Las Palmas

see Barranco map

Av Guardia Civil

Paseo de la República

Playa Aqua Dulce

Av Huaylas

To Av Panamericana Sur

CHORRILLOS

Playa La Herradura

Playa La Chira

Punta La Chira

0    1    2 km

0    .5    1 mile

in the 1920s, unprecedented population growth began. The urban population of 173,000 in 1919 more than tripled in the next 20 years, and since 1940, there has been a further 13-fold increase.

## Orientation

The Spanish built downtown Lima in the colonial style, with streets in a checkerboard pattern surrounding the Plaza de Armas, which is flanked by the Palacio de Gobierno, the cathedral and other important buildings. Street names here can sometimes be confusing, as there are both old and new names in use. For example, Garcilaso de la Vega is often called Avenida Wilson. In addition, some streets have a different name for each block, and these are linked into a *jirón*. The best example of a jirón is the Jirón de la Unión, which leads southwest from the Plaza de Armas to the Plaza San Martín. A major thoroughfare for pedestrians only, the Jirón de la Unión is lined with many shops and is always lively with street action.

The downtown area is where the most interesting old buildings are, and many have been recently renovated after decades of being rundown. The prettiest areas are around the major plazas, especially the Plaza de Armas, Plaza San Martín, Parque Universitario and Parque Italiano. There are attractively planted gardens and more police presence, and these downtown areas are generally safe during the day, with the usual precautions. There are still several very good hotels downtown, but travelers are increasingly staying in the suburbs, particularly if looking for top-end accommodations.

Immediately southwest of downtown is the district of Breña, home of the South American Explorers and immigration offices. South of downtown are the Santa Beatriz and Jesús María districts – all three of these have increasing numbers of budget and mid-range hotels.

Miraflores, about 8km south of downtown, with many excellent hotels, restaurants and shops, is the current favorite for upmarket tourists. Until the 1940s, Miraflores was a beachfront community separated from the capital by countryside and haciendas. Lima's recent population boom has changed parts of this former countryside into the fashionably elegant residential/business district of San Isidro, which also offers some good restaurants, a few hotels (mainly aimed at businesspeople), major shopping centers and pleasant parks. Miraflores, meanwhile, has become Lima's most important hotel, shopping, entertainment and upscale residential area. Many of the capital's best restaurants and nightspots are found in Miraflores, and the pavement cafés are great places to see and be seen. As you'd expect, the prices and quality of everything ranging from sweaters to steaks will be higher in Miraflores than in other parts of the city.

Miraflores has many beaches (see Activities later in this chapter), and a good point from which to view them is from the Mirador de Miraflores (Miraflores Lookout) at the end of Malecón 28 de Julio and the nearby Parque del Amor, with its huge new statue of a couple kissing (inaugurated St Valentine's Day, 1993). Another spot is the Parque Salazar at the end of Larco, which,

Say 'queso'!

CRAIG LOVELL

since 1998, also offers American-style restaurants, as well as a modern bowling alley, a good bookstore and a 12-screen movie theater.

The main bus route joining downtown with San Isidro and Miraflores is along Tacna, Garcilaso de la Vega and Arequipa – a congested route. Taxis prefer to take the Vía Expresa, marked on many maps as the Paseo de la República, which is the only freeway with limited entry and exits in the city. Because it is sunken below ground level, it is locally nicknamed *el zanjón* (the ditch). The Vía Expresa continues about 2km beyond Miraflores to the small cliff-top community of Barranco, which is something of an artists' and poets' colony and is currently the liveliest suburb for nightlife. If you are looking for a night out on the town, this is where to go – and not all of it is very expensive. Because the bars and clubs are found all within a few blocks of the main plaza, it is easy to go clubhopping or bar-crawling on foot. Barranco is also known for its attractive 19th- and early 20th-century Peruvian architecture and the romantic El Puente de los Suspiros (the Bridge of Sighs). This is the place for a special date. Unfortunately, there are almost no hotels here.

The international airport is in Callao – about 12km west of downtown or 16km northwest of Miraflores – but there is no expressway connecting the airport with the main parts of the city. Roads joining the airport to the rest of Lima are crowded, and during rush hours, it can take almost an hour for a taxi to reach the airport. Callao also features Lima's shipping port, naval base and an old colonial fort.

Other suburbs of interest to the visitor are Pueblo Libre, San Borja and Monterrico, where some of the best museums are found.

Throughout this chapter, addresses are followed with the suburbs they are found in, except for those addresses found in the center of Lima itself.

**Maps** Lima is so huge that it is impossible, in a book such as this, to do more than map the central city area and major suburbs. You are strongly advised to buy a street map of the city, if you want to spend a few days looking around outside of the main areas. The best is published by Lima 2000 (☎ 440-3486, fax 440-3480, Avenida Arequipa 2625, Lince).

Many maps are sold in bookstores or by street vendors around the Plaza San Martín area. The quality varies widely, and prices tend to be high, so try bargaining. Some supermarkets also sell maps.

The South American Explorers' clubhouse has trail maps of the main hiking areas, road maps of Peru and detailed street and bus maps of Lima. If they don't have the maps you want, they'll know where you can get them.

For topographical maps, go to the Instituto Geográfico Nacional, or IGN (☎ 475-9960, fax 475-3075, Aramburu 1198, Surquillo). It's open from 9 am to 4 pm (limited entry after 3 pm) on weekdays; you need your passport, and you can't wear shorts. In January, they close around lunchtime. Their maps are for sale or for reference on the premises. Their good road map of Peru (1:2,000,000) is US$8, and a four-sheet 1:1,000,000 topographical map of Peru costs US$33. Departmental maps at various scales are US$6.50. High-scale topographic maps for backpacking are available, though some sheets of border areas might be hard to get. Geological and political maps are also sold. The Servicio Aerofotográfico Nacional at Las Palmeras Air Force base in Surco sells aerial photographs from 8 am to 2 pm on weekdays. Some of these aerial photos are also available from the IGN.

## Information
**Tourist Offices** There is no government-run tourist office freely dispensing maps and advice, so you have to rely on private offices that also would like to sell services.

Fertur Peru (☎ 427-1958, fax 428-3247, fertur@correo.dnet.com.pe, Jirón Junín 211) is recommended for countrywide information and good prices on national and international flights, with discounts for international student ID cards and members of the South American Explorers; ask for Siduith Ferrer Herrera. They are open most days from 9 am to 7 pm.

Infotur (☎ 431-0117, Jirón de la Unión 1066 – also known as Jirón Belén) has information about transportation, hotels and sightseeing throughout the more frequently visited parts of Peru. Hours are 9:30 am to 6 pm weekdays and 10 am to 2 pm on Saturday. Fertur Peru also maintains a desk here.

At the airport, there is also a tourist-information office that will find a hotel by phone if necessary, though they discourage budget travelers and work with the pricier taxis. The Hostal España (see Places to Stay – Budget for Lima later in this chapter) has budget-travel information. A useful source of general information is the *Peru Guide*. This free booklet is published monthly by Lima Editora and can be found at some of the better hotels, restaurants and tourist spots in Lima, though their information is not always completely up-to-date.

The Trekking and Backpacking Club (☎ 423-2515, fax 428-0666, tebac@hotmail .com, Huascar 1152, Jesús María, Lima 11) provides information (in Spanish) for independent trekkers and has maps, brochures, equipment rental and guides.

**South American Explorers (SAE)** For many long-term travelers, journalists, academics, scientists and expat residents, this club has become something of a legend. Since it was founded by Don Montague and Linda Rojas in 1977, SAE has been involved in activities ranging from the 1980 cleanup of the Inca Trail to the cleanup of erroneous media reports about discoveries of 'lost' Peruvian cities in 1985, as well as the organization of clothing and medicine drives for local nonprofit organizations. Primarily, however, it functions as an information center for travelers (like you!), adventurers and scientific expeditions, and the Lima clubhouse can provide excellent advice about Latin American travel, with an emphasis on Peru, Ecuador and Bolivia. A Cuzco clubhouse opened in 1999 (see the Information section of the Cuzco Area chapter).

The club has an extensive library of books, maps and trip reports of other travelers, indexed by region and date. Various useful books and maps are sold, and there are trail maps for the Inca Trail, Mt Ausangate area, Cordillera Blanca and Cordillera Huayhuash, as well as general maps of South America. You can also get useful current information on travel conditions, currency regulations, weather and so on.

The club is a member-supported, nonprofit educational organization. Annual membership costs US$40 per person (US$70 for a couple), which covers four issues of their excellent and informative quarterly *South American Explorer* magazine. (Membership dues and donations to the club are US tax-deductible. Members outside the USA have to add US$10 for postage.) Members receive full use of the clubhouse and its facilities. These include an information service and library; introductions to other travelers and notification of expedition opportunities; luggage storage (anything from small valuables to a kayak); storage or forwarding of mail addressed to you at the club; a relaxing place to read, do research or just have a cup of tea and a chat with the friendly staff; a book exchange; buying and selling of used equipment; and discounts on the books, maps and gear sold at the club and other services. (Note: all imported merchandise sold at the Peru SAEs is reserved for members only.) The storage facilities are particularly useful if you plan on returning to Peru; I leave climbing gear and other heavy stuff here from year to year. Services for nonmembers are limited: the staff is happy to answer a few quick questions about travel in South America and show you around the club. But staff are volunteers, and members' needs come first. Much of the club is designated for 'Members Only.' Paid-up members can stay all day – a welcome relief from the maddening bustle of Lima. The club is highly recommended.

If you're in Lima, simply go to the clubhouse (☎/fax 425-0142, montague@amauta .rcp.net.pe, República de Portugal 146) and sign up. Otherwise, mail your US$40 (and any questions you have) direct to the club at Casilla 3714, Lima 100. The club is about a 15-minute walk from the Plaza San Martín. Hours are 9:30 am to 5 pm weekdays (extended to 8 pm on Wednesday); it is closed weekends.

The club's US office (☎ 607-277-0488, fax 277-6122, explorer@sameplo.org, 126 Indian Creek Rd, Ithaca, NY 14850) publishes the magazine; send them US$6 for a sample copy of the *South American Explorer* and further information. Nonmember subscriptions are US$22 for four issues and US$35 for eight issues.

The Ecuador clubhouse (☎/fax 593-2-225-228, explorer@saec.org.ec, Jorge Washington 311, Quito) was founded in 1989 and has facilities similar to Lima's. Watch for a Cuzco clubhouse in 1999, and possibly La Paz and other branches in the next millennium.

**Foreign Consulates** See the Embassies & Consulates in Peru section in Facts for the Visitor chapter for a list of embassies in Lima.

**Visas** Lima is one of the easiest places in Peru to have your tourist permit extended. Most foreign visitors receive a 90-day permit on arrival that can be extended for a further 90 days at a cost of about US$30 per 30 days; you must return for each 30-day extension. Foreigners requiring tourist visas can also renew. Once your maximum of 180 days is up, you must leave the country. However, there is no law against crossing the border to a neighboring country and returning the next day to start the process over again.

The Lima immigration *(migraciones)* office (☎ 330-4144, 330-4030, Avenida España 700, Breña) is open 9 am to 2 pm weekdays, and it's best to go first thing in the morning if you want to get your extension the same day. Specially stamped paperwork is required and can be bought at the Banco de la Nación (it costs almost US$7). This bank is in the immigration office. You will need your passport and the white or blue immigration slip you received upon entry (it's not a disaster if you lose it, but the process becomes more time-consuming and expensive). These documents are presented with a fee of US$20 (payable in US cash or nuevos soles). Sometimes (especially on your last 30-day extension), you may be asked for a ticket out of the country, though you can get around this by showing enough money.

The more affluent you look, the less hassle you'll have. Remember that regulations change frequently in Latin America, and Lima is no exception! (The new office is three blocks from the South American Explorers' clubhouse, and members should stop by to ask about the latest regulations.)

A bus ticket from Lima to the Ecuadorian, Bolivian or Chilean border will cost less than renewing your visa, so if you're on a tight budget, you might want to spend your money traveling to a convenient border and reentering the country instead.

As for student visas, you can get one if you're studying in Peru, but as they're usually more hassle than they're worth, many foreign students prefer to use tourist permits if they are taking a Spanish course.

**Money** Most Lima bank hours are 9 am to 6 pm weekdays, and they are often open Saturday morning. Many banks have 24-hour ATMs; see the Facts for the Visitor chapter for general ATM information. Visitors will find many bank branches in central Lima and near the Parque Kennedy in Miraflores, as well as all over the city. Expect long lines in banks, especially on Monday mornings (although some banks have express windows for foreign-currency transactions). The following lists some of the most useful banks and branches – there are dozens more. Use caution when making withdrawals from ATMs, especially at night.

Banco Continental
  Larco at Benavides, Miraflores
  Jirón Cusco 286, Lima (Visa representatives)
  Hours: 9 am to 6 pm weekdays, 9:30 am to 12:30 pm on Saturday
Banco de Crédito
  Pardo 491, Miraflores; Larco at José Gonzales, Miraflores (both with 24-hour ATMs)
  Jirón Lampa 499, Lima (main branch)
  Hours: 9 am to 6 pm weekdays, 9:30 am to 12:30 pm on Saturday
Banco Latino
  Larco 337, Miraflores (24-hr ATM)
  Paseo de la República 3505, San Isidro (main branch)
  Hours: 8:30 am to 8 pm weekdays, 9 am to 1 pm on Saturday

Banco Wiese
 Larco 1123, Miraflores
 Jirón Cusco 245, Lima (MasterCard
 representatives)
 Hours: 9:15 am to 6 pm weekdays, 9:30 am to
 12:30 pm on Saturday
Interbanc
 Pardo 413, Miraflores; Larco 690, Miraflores
 (both with 24-hr ATM)
 Jirón de la Unión 600, Lima (main branch)
 Hours: 9 am to 6 pm weekdays

The American Express office (☎ 330-4481, 330-4482, 330-4484, 330-4485, Jirón Belén 1040; in Lima Tours office) will replace stolen or lost AmEx checks, but will not cash their own checks. Hours are 9 am to 5 pm weekdays and 9 am to 1 pm on Saturday. Someone is usually there after hours to take telephone reports of lost checks. Most banks will cash AmEx checks; the best rates are if you cash them in for nuevos soles. Other traveler's checks are difficult to replace in Peru.

 *Casas de cambio*, or exchange houses, usually give the same (or slightly better) rate as banks for cash; they also tend to be quicker and are open longer. Traveler's checks are either not cashed or are exchanged at a higher commission than banks. There are several casas de cambio downtown on Ocoña (behind the Gran Hotel Bolívar) and on Camaná between Nicolás de Piérola (also called Colmena) and Ocoña. They are also found along Larco in Miraflores. One casa de cambio, P&P, exchanges traveler's checks at either of their two locations: Nicolás de Piérola 805 at Camaná (☎ 428-8653) and Benavides 735, Miraflores (☎ 444-2404). LAC Dólar in central Lima (☎ 428-8127, fax 427-3906, Camaná 779, office 201) and in Miraflores (☎ 242-4069, La Paz 211) is safe, reliable, and changes cash and traveler's checks at reasonable rates. Hours are 8:30 am to 7:30 pm Monday to Saturday, and 9 am to 2 pm on Sunday and some holidays.

 Street moneychangers often hang around the casas de cambio. The corner of Plaza San Martín and Ocoña is a favorite spot – on some days, every person on the block seems to be buying or selling dollars. However, this isn't the safest place to change large sums of money. The changers in the Parque Kennedy area in Miraflores have uniforms and badges and are generally the safest. They are the best option outside of business hours.

**Post**  The main post office (☎ 427-5592, Camaná 195) is inside the city block on the northwest corner of the Plaza de Armas. Mail sent to you at Lista de Correo, Correos Central, Lima, should be collected here (though I have heard reports of loss). The main office is open from 8:15 am to 8:15 pm weekdays and from 9 am to 1:30 pm on Saturday. The Miraflores-branch post office (☎ 445-0697, Petit Thouars 5201) is open the same hours. There are also branch post offices in various districts of Lima, but these are less reliable.

 American Express clients can have mail held for them at AmEx, c/o Lima Tours, Jirón Belén 1040, Lima. You can pick up mail between 9 am and noon and from 3 to 5 pm on weekdays.

 Bring identification when collecting mail from either AmEx or a post office.

 Members of the South American Explorers can have mail held for them at Casilla 3714, Lima 100, Peru.

 Private companies such as DHL, UPS and Federal Express have offices in Lima, but their services are very expensive by US standards and are not worth using in most circumstances. They change addresses often; check the telephone directory or ask locally.

**Telephone & Fax**  Telefónica del Peru has pay phones all over Lima (coins, telephone cards or sometimes both are accepted), though competitor companies are expected to appear in 1999. If you prefer to call from a telephone office, the following are a few of the main ones: Carabaya 937, Lima; Bolivia 347, Lima; Porta 139, Miraflores; Pasaje Tarata 280, Miraflores.

 Call ☎ 103 (no charge) for directory inquiries within Lima and ☎ 109 for assistance with provincial numbers.

 The area code for Lima is 01 when calling from outside Lima but within Peru. From outside Peru, drop the 0.

 Fax services are available at Telefónica del Peru offices.

**Email & Internet Access** Increasing numbers of hotels have Internet access available to guests. Meanwhile, public Internet access for about US$2 an hour or less is available from several agencies at Garcilaso de la Vega (also known as Avenida Wilson) 1132, from 9 am to 9 pm weekdays, or 9 am to 6 pm on Saturday. Dragon Fans Internet (☎ 444-9325, Pasaje Tarata 230, Miraflores) is open 24 hours. There are other public Internet places opening.

**Travel Agencies & Tour Guides** Many travel agencies in Lima can sell airline tickets, make hotel reservations and provide tour services. Tours bought in Lima that visit other parts of Peru will normally be cheaper than tours bought in your home country, but more expensive than tours bought in the nearest major town to the area you wish to visit.

For guided tours of Lima (the city, churches, museums, Lima by night, nearby archaeological sites – such as Pachacamac, and so on), see the agencies listed under Organized Tours in the Getting Around chapter.

For specialized tours for individuals or small groups, you can hire a good Spanish-speaking guide for about US$25 a day plus expenses, although guided tours in English (or other languages) are considerably more expensive. Some guides are cheaper, but they are often students or unregistered guides, and the usual caveat emptor applies – some are good, some aren't. The following are officially registered with AGOTUR (the local guide organization). The telephone numbers are for daytime use only (Peruvian time) – these are private numbers that can't handle middle-of-the-night calls.

Victor Aranda
  ☎ 474-9814; English, French, German, Italian
Gladis Araujo
  ☎ 463-3642, cell 966-4780, fax 448-4080; English
Lucy Guerra
  ☎ 444-0516, cell 966-4820; English
Tino Guzman
  ☎/fax 429-5779, cell 968-3776, tino@amauta.rcp.net.pe; member of South American Explorers; English

Maria Kralewska de Canchaya
  ☎ 470-9888, 265-2134, mariakralewska@lanet.com.pe; Polish
Toshie Matsumura De Irikura
  ☎ 476-5101; Japanese
Hugo Ochoa
  ☎ 449-9499 x5095, cell 972-6117; English, French, German
Angel Rios
  ☎ 438-1060, 442-2040; Hebrew
Silvia Rodrich
  ☎ 446-0391, 446-8185; English
Nila Soto
  ☎ 452-5483, cell 972-8880; English, Italian
Jennie Tang
  ☎ 275-2676, 449-3376, cell 940-0808; Chinese (Mandarin & Cantonese)
Jaime Torres
  ☎ 337-6953; English
Tessy Torres
  ☎ 241-1704, 438-8066, cell 997-1307, fax 242-4688, perubra@mail.cosapidata.com.pe; English, French, Italian, Portuguese
Monica Velásquez
  ☎ 425-5087, cell 991-2160, vcmonica@blockbuster.com.pe; some English, airport pick-ups offered

**Bookstores** The best selection of English-language guidebooks can be found at the South American Explorers' clubhouse, but are sold to members only. The club also has a paperback book exchange for members only. The ABC bookstore (☎ 444-4099, Benavides 455, Miraflores) has a good but expensive selection of English, German and French newspapers; magazines; coffee-table books and guidebooks. For books in Spanish (and a limited number of English books), Epoca Books (☎ 447-8907, Pardo 399, Miraflores, and ☎ 242-2296, Espinar 864, Miraflores) is recommended. Bear in mind that most English-language books about Peru are much cheaper in Britain or the USA than in Peru.

**Libraries** The Biblioteca Nacional (☎ 428-7690), at Abancay and Miró Quesada, has books in Spanish. Hours are 8 am to 7 pm Monday to Saturday. For books in English, German and French, contact one of the following cultural centers.

**Cultural Centers** The Instituto Cultural Peruano-Norteamericano (☎ 241-1940, Arequipa 4798, Miraflores, and ☎ 428-3530, Cusco 446, Lima) offers US newspapers, a library and Spanish courses. You can read British newspapers at the Peruvian-British Cultural Association (☎ 221-7550, Arequipa 3495, San Isidro) or at the British Council (☎ 221-7552, Alberto Lynch 110, San Isidro). These also have English book libraries. German-speakers can head over to the Goethe Institut (☎ 433-3180, Jirón Nazca 722, Jesús María), and French-speakers have the Alianza Francesa (☎ 241-7014, Arequipa 4598, Miraflores, and ☎ 432-3842, Garcilaso de la Vega 1550, Lima). All of these present a variety of cultural programs (plays, film screenings, art shows, or lectures) at irregular intervals.

**Laundry** Many hotels can have your laundry done for you – the more expensive the hotel, the more expensive the laundry. Increasing numbers of lavanderías have opened, especially in Miraflores and San Isidro. Many lavanderías only do dry cleaning, and those that do wash and dry may charge by the item (expensive) rather than by weight (cheaper). Most have overnight laundry; some will have it ready the same day if left first thing in the morning, and a few have self-service.

Burbujitas
  ☎ 241-3592, Porta 293, Miraflores; wash and dry, US$4.50 for 4kg; hours are 9 am to 7 pm Monday to Saturday

Lava Express
  ☎ 263-0845, Alcanfores 964, Miraflores

Lava Philip
  Arica 448, Breña; wash and dry, US$4 per basket

Lavandería 40 Minutos
  ☎ 428-4472, Jirón Lampa 1180, Lima
  ☎ 446-5928, Espinar 154, Miraflores

Lavanderías de Autoservicio
  ☎ 241-5171, Berlin 336, Miraflores; wash and dry, US$4 per load; hours are 8 am to 9 pm Monday to Saturday and 9 am to 6 pm Sunday

Lavarap
  ☎ 241-0759, Schell 601, Miraflores; self-service

**Toilets** In common with other Peruvian cities, public toilets are limited to transport terminals, restaurants and public sites such as museums.

**Left Luggage** Apart from your hotel, you can safely store bags at the airport for US$3 a day.

**Medical Services** The Clínica Anglo-American (☎ 221-3656), on the 3rd block of Salazar in San Isidro, charges up to US$60 for a consultation and stocks yellow-fever (US$17) and tetanus (US$1.50) vaccines. Dr Luis Manuel Valdez (internal medicine) practices here and is recommended. The Clínica Internacional (☎ 433-4306), located at Washington 1471 and 9 de Diciembre in central Lima, is good and charges up to US$35 for consultations. The Clínica San Borja (☎ 475-4000, 475-3141, Avenida Guardia Civil 337, San Borja) is also OK. All of these clinics have 24-hour service and some English-speaking staff.

Hospital del Niño (☎ 330-0022, 330-0033, Brasil 600, Breña) gives free tetanus shots and charges US$17 for yellow-fever jabs. For tropical diseases, try Instituto de Medicina Tropical (☎ 482-3903, 482-3910), in the Cayetano Heredia Hospital, on Avenida Honorio Delgado near the Panamericana in San Martín de Porres. It is also one of the cheapest and is good. Instituto de Ginecología y Reproducción (☎ 434-2130, 434-2426, Monterrico 1045, Monterrico) deals with gynecology. There are many other hospitals and clinics.

The Centro Anti-Rabia de Lima (☎ 425-6313, Austria 1300, Breña) is inexpensive, open from 8 am to 6:30 pm Monday to Saturday, and is the place to go if you are bitten by a dog or other animal and need a rabies shot. For dermatological problems, the best doctors are the English-speaking Dr Francisco Bravo and Dr Alejandro Morales (☎ 446-6250, 241-6121, 446-0484, Angamos Oeste 896, Miraflores).

Dr Victor Aste (☎/fax 421-9169, Antero Aspillaga 415, office 101, San Isidro) is a well-recommended, English-speaking dentist. Dr Carlos Abugattas (☎ 445-7305, Benavides

261, office 301, Miraflores) is a recommended oral surgeon. Dr Juvenal Gonzalez (☎ 421-7011, 421-0867, 421-8936, VV Maúrtua 131, office 204, San Isidro) is recommended for root canals.

If you have a spectacle prescription with you, you can have a spare pair of glasses made cheaply by one of Lima's numerous opticians. There are several along Cailloma in the city center and around Schell and Larco in Miraflores. Having your eyes examined for a new prescription is also cheap, but some ophthalmologists practicing in Peru have archaic equipment and don't do a very good job. If you need a new prescription, ask at your embassy for a recommended ophthalmologist.

There are hundreds of pharmacies (see Lima yellow pages under 'Boticas y Farmacias'). The following, all in Miraflores, are modern, well-stocked and open 24 hours. Superfarma (☎ 222-1575, 222-1577, Benavides 2849 and Armendariz 215) and Botica Fasa (☎ 242-1378, Pardo 715).

**Emergency**  For emergencies ranging from robbery to rabies, you can contact the Policía de Turismo (☎ 225-8699, 225-8698, Museo de la Nación, 5th floor, Javier Prado Este 2465, San Borja) for advice and assistance. They have been recommended to me by several people for their courtesy and helpfulness. English-speaking police are usually available, and they can cut down on a lot of red tape if you need a police report to make an insurance claim or get a traveler's-check refund. They are open 24 hours.

Other emergency telephone numbers are for the police (☎ 105) and fire (☎ 116).

Also see INDECOPI under Useful Organizations in the Facts for the Visitor chapter.

**Visiting Prisoners**  People wishing to visit foreign (English-speaking) prisoners (mainly in jail on drug charges) can ask the SAE for a list of prisoners, prison addresses, and visiting hours.

**Dangers & Annoyances**  With literally millions of very poor and unemployed people, it is hardly surprising that Lima has a crime problem. Don't be overly worried – you are unlikely to be mugged or otherwise physically hurt, but travelers do have their belongings stolen. Please reread the Dangers & Annoyances section of the Facts for the Visitor chapter before arriving in Lima.

I've traveled in Peru almost every year since 1981 (I missed 1988) and have come to the conclusion that Lima is as safe as any other major city, if you take the necessary precautions outlined in the Facts for the Visitor chapter. If you don't take those precautions, you can expect to have that Rolex ripped off your wrist.

Downtown Lima has many pickpockets. Be especially careful here. But don't assume that ritzy Miraflores is free of thieves. Take proper precautions throughout Lima and Peru.

## Things to See
The numerous museums, churches and colonial houses in Lima are enough to keep the sightseer occupied for several days. Most are described below. Unfortunately, opening hours are subject to frequent change; call the museum or check with a tourist office or at the SAE for up-to-date times. Entrance fees may also vary noticeably from those given here; if you are on a tight budget, you should check before you go.

Lima's museums are described first, followed by religious buildings and other sights. Lima's many colonial churches, monasteries and convents are a very welcome break from the city's noisy traffic and incessant crowds. Opening hours tend to be even more erratic than those of the museums – churches are often closed for restoration, religious services or because the caretaker is having an extended lunch – so you have to take your chances. While the museums and religious buildings will undoubtedly take up most of the visitor's sightseeing time, Lima also has many plazas, buildings and other sites of interest.

**Museo de la Nación**  This museum (☎ 476-9875, Javier Prado Oeste 2466, San Borja) has excellent models of Peru's major ruins, as well as exhibits about Peruvian archaeology.

## CENTRAL LIMA

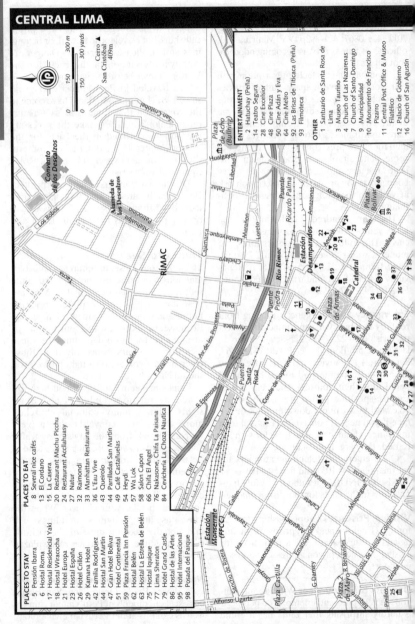

**PLACES TO STAY**
5   Pensión Ibarra
6   Hostal Roma
17  Hostal Residencial Yaki
18  Hostal Wiracocha
21  Hotel Europa
23  Hostal España
26  Hotel Crillón
29  Kamana Hotel
42  Familia Rodriguez
44  Hostal San Martin
47  Gran Hotel Bolivar
51  Hotel Continental
59  Plaza Francia Inn Pensión
62  Hostal Belén
63  Hostal La Estrella de Belén
75  Hostal Iquique
79  Hotel Grand Castle
86  Lima Sheraton
95  Hostal de las Artes
95  Hotel Internacional
98  Posada del Parque

**PLACES TO EAT**
8   Several nice cafés
13  El Cordano
15  La Casera
20  Restaurant Machu Picchu
24  Restaurant Accllahuasy
27  Natur
32  Raimondi
33  Manhattan Restaurant
36  L'Eau Vive
43  Queirolo
44  Parrilladas San Martin
49  Café Castañuelas
54  Heydi
57  Wa Lok
58  Salon Capon
66  Chifa El Angel
76  Nakasone, Chifa La Paisana
84  Cevichería La Choza Nautica

**ENTERTAINMENT**
2   Hatuchay (Peña)
14  Teatro Segura
28  Cine Excelsior
48  Cine Plaza
50  Cine Adán y Eva
77  Cine Metro
92  Las Brisas de Titicaca (Peña)
93  Filmoteca

**OTHER**
1   Santuario de Santa Rosa de Lima
3   Museo Taurino
7   Church of Las Nazarenas
7   Church of Santo Domingo
9   Municipalidad
10  Monumento de Francisco Pizarro
11  Central Post Office & Museo Filatélico
12  Palacio de Gobierno
16  Church of San Agustín

## CENTRAL LIMA

19 Fertur Peru
22 Church of San Francisco & Catacombs
25 Museo de la Cultura Peruana
30 Interbanc
31 Church of La Merced
34 Museo del Banco Central de Reserva
35 Banco de Crédito
37 Palacio Torre Tagle
38 Church of San Pedro
39 Museo de la Inquisición
40 Congreso
41 Cruz del Sur
45 P&P Casa de Cambio
46 LAC Dólar & other casas de cambio
52 Banco Continental
53 Banco Wiese
55 Instituto Cultural Peruano-Norteamericano
56 Biblioteca Nacional
60 Infotur
61 Lima Tours & American Express
64 Telefónica del Peru
65 South American Explorers
67 Telefónica del Peru
68 Internet services
69 Museo de Arte Italiano
70 TEPSA
71 Transportes Rodríguez
72 Transportes Atahualpa
73 Móvil Tours
74 Santa Catalina Convent & Plaza
78 Palacio de Justicia
80 Ormeño & subsidiaries
81 TUBSA
82 Buses to Pachacamac
83 Buses to Pucusana
85 Minibuses to Chosica
87 Clínica Internacional
88 CIVA, Mariscal Cáceres
89 Expreso Sudamericano
90 Expreso Molina
91 Olano
93 Museo de Arte
94 Polvos Azules Market
96 Royal Tours
97 Transportes León de Huánuco
99 Cruz del Sur (Ideal & Imperial Service)

This museum now offers the nation's best overview of its archaeological heritage at a much more affordable price than some of the private collections. Chavín stone carvings, Nazca ceramics and Paracas weavings are all displayed here, along with collections of the best artifacts from all major Peruvian cultures. There are also exhibits from the now defunct Museo de Ciencias de la Salud that describe medical practices in pre-Columbian times, as well as 18th- and 19th-century medical instruments. Besides the permanent collections, there are often special shows on the ground floor, as well as lectures and other events. The most recent special show was 'The Lord of Sipán' (see the North Coast chapter), which was by far the most sophisticated and well-presented museum event in Peru. After three years at this museum, the show is slated to move to Lambayeque in 1999.

Hours are 9 am to 9 pm Tuesday to Friday, and 10 am to 7 pm Saturday and Sunday. Admission is US$1, or US$3.30 for special shows.

**Museo de Oro del Peru** This museum (☎ 345-1271, Alonso de Molina 1100, Monterrico) has two separate collections in the same private building, owned by the Mujica Gallo family. The incredibly rich Gold Museum is in a huge basement vault. The thousands of gold pieces range from ear plugs to ponchos embroidered with hundreds of solid-gold plates. In addition, there are numerous other artifacts made of silver and precious stones and gems such as lapis lazuli, emeralds and pearls. Unfortunately, this superb collection is not very well labeled, but it is still worth seeing.

The Arms Museum, housed in the top half of the building, is reputed to be one of the world's best. Even if, like me, you have no interest in guns, you'll probably be fascinated by the thousands of ancient and bizarre firearms from all over the world that are displayed here. One of my favorite exhibits is a huge, ornately decorated blunderbuss. It's about 2m long, with a 5cm bore and a flaring, trumpetlike muzzle, and dates from the 19th century. Although it looks more suitable for hunting elephants, it's labeled as a duck-hunting rifle!

The Gold Museum's private collection is high on the 'must see' list for many tourists. Admission is US$6 per person, which includes both the Gold and Arms museums; separate tickets are not sold. Photography is prohibited, but postcards and color slides are for sale. Hours are 11:30 am to 7 pm daily. There are high-quality (but expensive) gift shops on the grounds.

**Museo Rafael Larco Herrera** This private museum (☎ 461-1312, 261-3397, Bolívar 1515, Pueblo Libre) has one of the most incredible ceramics collections to be found anywhere. It is said to include about 55,000 pots. Many of the items were collected in the 1920s by a former vice president of Peru. Entering the first rooms is like walking into a museum store – one is overwhelmed by shelf after shelf stacked to the high ceilings with thousands of ceramics grouped roughly into categories such as animals, people and medical practices.

Further into the museum, the best pieces are displayed in the uncluttered manner they deserve. The museum also has mummies, a gold room, a small cactus garden, textiles made from feathers and a Paracas weaving that contains 398 threads to the linear inch – a world record. In a separate building is the famous collection of pre-Columbian erotic pots that illustrate, with remarkable explicitness, the sexual practices of several Peruvian cultures. All in all, this museum is highly recommended to everyone and certainly should not be missed by the ceramist.

Hours are 9 am to 6 pm daily except Sunday, when it closes at 1 pm. Admission is US$3. Photography is not allowed.

**Museo de Arte** Lima's Art Museum (☎ 423-4732) is housed in a very handsome building at Paseo de Colón 125 (the popular name for 9 de Diciembre) in Parque de la Exposición. It exhibits far more than art, and its collection ranges from colonial furniture to pre-Columbian artifacts, as well as canvases spanning 400 years of Peruvian art. It's well worth a visit.

Hours are 10 am to 5 pm Tuesday to Sunday. Admission is US$1.50, and photography is not allowed. Occasional temporary shows may cost extra. There is a café. On many evenings, the museum's Filmoteca shows a diverse range of films (see Entertainment later in this chapter).

**Museo de Arte Italiano** Housed in a fairy-tale neoclassical building in a park on the 2nd block of Paseo de la República in central Lima, the Museum of Italian Art (☎ 423-9932) exhibits paintings, sculptures and prints mainly from the early 20th century. Italian and other European art is represented. The detailed mosaic murals on the outside walls should be looked out for. Hours are 9 am to 4:30 pm weekdays. Admission is about US$1.

**Museo Amano** Those interested in Peruvian archaeology will want to visit this museum (☎ 441-2909, Retiro 160, Miraflores). Its fine private ceramics collection is arranged chronologically to show the development of pottery through Peru's various pre-Columbian cultures. The museum specializes in the little-known Chancay culture, of which it has a remarkable collection of textiles.

Tours are free and are available for small groups only (no individuals or large groups) on weekdays at 2, 3, 4 and 5 pm; you must make an appointment in advance. All groups are met punctually at the door by a guide who will show you around for exactly one hour – it's best if you understand Spanish or have someone along to translate. You cannot wander the museum's halls at will, but by listening to the guide, you'll learn a good deal about the development of pottery in Peru and about the Chancay culture. Donations are appreciated.

**Museo Pedro de Osma** This private museum (☎ 467-0915, 467-0019, Pedro de Osma 421, Barranco) has a fine collection of colonial art, furniture, sculpture, metalwork and much more from all over Peru. They also have changing art shows. The museum is in one of Barranco's older mansions and is open from 10 am to 6 pm Tuesday to Sunday. Admission is US$3 and includes a one-hour guided tour.

**Museo de la Electricidad** The Electricity Museum (☎ 477-6577, Pedro de Osma 105, Barranco) has a small exhibit about the historical development of electricity in Lima, including the electric tramway system that used to link Barranco with Miraflores and Lima. Outside, a restored electric tram runs along rails on a few blocks of Pedro de Osma on request. Hours are 9 am to 1 pm and 2 to 5 pm Tuesday to Sunday. A tram ride costs US$0.75.

**Museo Nacional de Antropología y Arqueología** This used to be the best collection tracing the prehistory of Peru chronologically from the earliest archaeological sites to the arrival of the Spaniards. Some of the pieces formerly exhibited here have been moved to the new Museo de la Nación, but a worthwhile collection remains. Look for enlightening scale models of Machu Picchu and other sites, as well as some of the original stelae and obelisks from Chavín. The museum building and grounds are attractive and quiet and there is a simple café.

The museum (☎ 463-5070) is at Plaza Bolívar, at the intersection of San Martín and Vivanco in Pueblo Libre. Hours are 9 am to 6 pm Tuesday to Sunday. Admission is US$2.

**Museo Nacional de la República** Also known as the Museo Nacional de Historia (☎ 463-2009), this building once was the home of the revolutionary heroes San Martín (from 1821 to 1822) and Bolívar (from 1823 to 1826). The museum contains late colonial and early republican paintings, furnishings and independence artifacts, and is mainly of interest to students of the Peruvian revolution. The building is next to the Museo Nacional de Antropología y Arqueología, and entrance details are the same.

**Museo del Banco Central de Reserva** This archaeological museum (☎ 427-6250), in the Banco Central de Reserva at the corner of Ucayali and Lampa, specializes in ceramics from the

Vicus culture, in addition to housing a small collection of other pre-Columbian artifacts and 19th- and 20th-century Peruvian art. In the heart of the city center, it represents a welcome haven from the hustle and bustle of changing money or reconfirming airline tickets, but it is also worth visiting in its own right.

Hours are 10 am to 4 pm Tuesday to Friday and 10 am to 1 pm on weekends. Admission is free, but you need to show a passport or national ID card to get in.

**Museo de la Inquisición** The building housing this museum (☎ 428-7980, 427-0365, Jirón Junín 548) was used by the Spanish Inquisition from 1570 to 1820 and subsequently became the senate building. It is now a university library. Visitors can walk around the basement where prisoners were tortured, and there's a ghoulish waxwork exhibit of lifesize unfortunates on the rack or having their feet roasted. In the library upstairs is a remarkable wood ceiling.

Hours are 9 am to 1 pm and 2:30 to 5 pm weekdays. Admission is free, and guided tours in Spanish are offered about every half hour.

**Museo de la Cultura Peruana** This small museum (☎ 423-5892, Alfonso Ugarte 630) specializes in items more closely allied to popular art and handicrafts than to archaeology and history. Exhibits include ceramics, carved gourds, recent art, traditional folk art and costumes from various periods and places.

Hours are 10 am to 4:30 pm Tuesday to Friday and 10 am to 2 pm on Saturday. Adults/students pay US$0.50/0.25, and there is a US$2.50 fee for photography.

**Museo de Historia Natural** The Natural History Museum (☎ 471-0117, Arenales 1256), one block west of the 12th block of Arequipa, has only a modest taxidermy collection, but if you want to familiarize yourself with the fauna of Peru, it warrants a visit. Mammals, birds, reptiles, fish and insects are all represented.

Hours are 9 am to 3 pm weekdays, 9 am to 5 pm on Saturday and 9 am to 1 pm on Sunday. Adults pay US$1; students pay US$0.50.

**Museo Filatélico** Appropriately housed in the main post office in Lima, the Philatelic Museum (☎ 428-7931, 428-0400) allows you to examine, buy and trade Peruvian stamps. (The collection of Peruvian stamps is incomplete.) Hours are 8:30 am to 1 pm and 2 to 6:30 pm weekdays. Entry is free.

If you want to buy stamps for your collection, you'll find the museum shop open from 8 am to noon and 2 to 3 pm weekdays. Ask at the museum when collectors and dealers meet to buy, sell and trade stamps.

**Museo Taurino** The Bullfight Museum (☎ 482-3360) is at the Plaza de Acho, Lima's bullring, at Hualgayoc 332, Rímac. Even if you oppose bullfighting, you might want to visit the museum just to see the matadors' relics. These include a holed and blood-stained costume worn by a famous matador who was gored and killed in the Lima bullring some years ago. Score one for the bulls! (A recent report claims that this item is not currently exhibited.) Also worth seeing are some very good paintings and drawings of bullfighting scenes by various artists, notably Picasso. Hours are 9 am to 3 pm weekdays and 10 am to 2 pm on Saturday. Admission is US$0.75.

**Fuerte Real Felipe** This historic fort (☎ 429-0532, Plaza Independencia, Callao) is where the Spanish royalists made their last stand during the battles of independence in the 1820s. There's an on-site military museum, and Spanish-speaking guides are available. Hours are 9:30 am to 2 pm Tuesday to Sunday, and admission is US$1.25. Note that the nearby dock area is a rough neighborhood.

**La Catedral** Completed in 1555, the original cathedral, on the southeast side of the Plaza de Armas, was soon deemed too small, and another planned in its place. Work on the new cathedral began in 1564, and the building was still unfinished when it was consecrated in 1625. It was more or less complete by 1649,

Cathedral at dusk on the Plaza de Armas, Lima

Book browsing on Paseo de la República, Lima

Lima's daily grind

Oasis at Huacachina, near Ica

Sea lions, Islas Ballestas

but it was badly damaged in the 1687 earthquake and almost totally destroyed by another earthquake in 1746. The present reconstruction is based on the early plans.

The interior is stark compared to many Latin American churches. Of particular interest are the coffin and remains of Francisco Pizarro in the mosaic-covered chapel just to the right of the main door. For many years, there was debate over whether the remains were actually those of Pizarro. Recent investigations revealed that the remains previously on display were, in fact, those of an unknown conquistador. Now that Pizarro's real remains (discovered in the crypt in the early 1980s) have been transferred to the chapel, most authorities agree that the exhibit is now authentic. Also of interest is the well-carved choir and the small religious museum in the rear of the cathedral.

The cathedral's opening hours have changed regularly over the years. At last check, they were 10 am to 1 pm and 3 to 5 pm Monday to Saturday. Adults/students pay US$2/1 including entry to the religious museum (☎ 427-9647). Tours in English are available. Some photography is allowed, and color slides and postcards are on sale.

**San Francisco** This Franciscan church and monastery is famous for its catacombs. It is less well known for its remarkable library, where you can see thousands of antique texts – some dating back to the time of the conquistadors.

The church is one of the best preserved of Lima's early colonial churches. Finished before the earthquake of 1687, which badly damaged most of Lima's churches, San Francisco withstood both this and the earthquake of 1746 better than the others. However, the 1970 earthquake caused considerable damage. Much of the church has been well restored in its original baroque style with Moorish influence.

The monastery is at the corner of Lampa and Ancash, and hours are 7 am to 5:30 pm. The US$2 admission includes a 45-minute guided tour. Spanish-speaking tours leave several times an hour, and there are also tours led by English-speaking guides at least

once an hour. These tours visit the catacombs, library, cloister and a very fine museum of religious art. The underground catacombs are the site of an estimated 70,000 burials and the faint-hearted may find the bone-filled crypts slightly unnerving.

**Convento de los Descalzos** This infrequently visited convent and museum (☎ 481-0441) lies at the end of the Alameda de los Descalzos, an attractive if somewhat forgotten avenue in the Rímac district, north of central Lima across the Río Rímac. (Though one of the poorer areas of Lima, Rímac is safe to visit during the day.) Visitors can see old wine-making equipment in the 17th-century kitchen, refectory, infirmary, typical cells of the Descalzos (or 'the Barefooted,' a reference to the Franciscan friars) and some 300 colonial paintings of the Quito and Cuzco schools. It's a great place to get away from the tourist crowds.

Hours are 10 am to 1 pm and 3 to 6 pm daily except Tuesday. Admission is US$1.50, and Spanish-speaking guides will show you around. A tour lasts about 45 minutes, and a small tip is appreciated.

**Santuario de Santa Rosa de Lima** Saint Rose, the first saint of the western hemisphere, is particularly venerated in Lima, where she lived, and a garden and small church have been built on the 1st block of Tacna, roughly at the site of her birth. The sanctuary itself is a small adobe hut, built by Saint Rose in the early 17th century as a private room for prayer and meditation.

Hours (☎ 425-1279) are 9 am to 12:30 pm daily, and 4:30 to 6:30 pm Monday to Saturday. Admission is free.

**Santo Domingo** This church (☎ 425-1279) is on the 1st block of Camaná, across from the post office. It is one of Lima's most historic churches because it was built on the land granted by Francisco Pizarro to the Dominican Friar Vicente Valverde in 1535. The friar accompanied Pizarro throughout the conquest and was instrumental in persuading him to execute Atahualpa after the Inca had been captured and ransomed in Cajamarca.

Construction of the church of Santo Domingo began in 1540 and was finished in 1599. Although the structure survived the earthquakes reasonably well, much of the interior was modernized late in the 18th century. The church contains the tombs of Saint Rose and Saint Martín de Porres (also of Lima and one of the few black saints), as well as an alabaster statue of Saint Rose that was presented to the church by Pope Clement in 1669. There is also fine tile work showing the life of Saint Dominic and pleasantly quiet cloisters in which you can walk and relax.

The monastery and tombs are open 9 am to 12:30 pm and 3 to 6 pm Monday to Saturday, and 9 am to 1 pm on Sunday. Admission is US$1.

**La Merced** On the busy pedestrian street of Jirón de la Unión at Miró Quesada, La Merced (☎ 427-8199) is another historic church with a long and colorful history. The church was built on the site of the first mass celebrated in Lima in 1534, before Pizarro's official founding of the city in 1535. The original building, a temporary affair, was soon replaced by a larger church. This, in turn, was torn down, and construction of a third building began in 1628. The structure was seriously damaged by the 1687 earthquake, but once again, rebuilding was soon under way. Work started on a new facade after damage in the 1746 earthquake, and in 1773, the church suffered further damage when a fire destroyed all the paintings and vestments in the sacristy. Thus, most of today's church dates to the 18th century. An attempt was made to modernize the facade early this century, but in 1936, it was restored to its original appearance. Inside the church is an ornately carved chancel and an attractively decorated cloister.

Further renovation is currently under way, but the church can still be visited 8 am to noon and 4 to 8 pm daily.

**San Pedro** Many experts consider this small baroque church (☎ 428-3017) to be one of the finest examples of early colonial architecture in Lima. It's on the corner of Azangaro and Ucayali in the old center. It was consecrated by the Jesuits in 1638 and has changed little since. The interior, sumptuously decorated with gilded altars, Moorish-influenced carvings and an abundance of beautiful glazed tile work, is well worth seeing. Hours are noon to 5 pm Monday to Saturday. Admission is free.

**San Agustín** This church (☎ 427-7548) is on the corner of Ica and Camaná. In contrast to San Pedro, the church of San Agustín has been altered much more than Lima's other early churches. The churrigueresque (an elaborate and intricately decorated Spanish style, named for the architect José Churriguera and common in colonial Latin America) facade dates from the early 1700s and is the oldest part of the church to have remained intact. Much of the church was reconstructed at the end of the 19th century, and again after the extensive damage of the 1970 earthquake.

The hours that this church is open to the public are very limited and change very frequently.

**Las Nazarenas** This church (☎ 423-5718), on the corner of Huancavelica and Tacna, was built in the 18th century and is not, in itself, of great interest. The site on which it is built, however, plays a part in one of the most passionate of Lima's traditional religious feasts.

The site used to be a shantytown inhabited mainly by liberated black slaves. Early in the 17th century, an ex-slave painted one of the walls of the shantytown with an image of the crucifixion of Christ. Although the area was destroyed by an earthquake in 1655, the wall with the mural survived. This was considered a miracle, and the church of the Nazarene was later built around the wall. On October 18 of each year, a copy of the mural, known as the Lord of the Miracles, is carried around in a huge procession of many thousands of the faithful. The procession continues for two or three days, with the holy image being taken from church to church before being returned to Las Nazarenas.

Hours are 7 am to noon and 5 to 8:30 pm Monday to Saturday; 6:30 am to 1 pm and 4 to 8:30 pm on Sunday. Admission is free.

**Plaza de Armas** The central and most important plaza in any Peruvian town is called the Plaza de Armas, and Lima is no exception (though it is also called the Plaza Mayor). This large plaza (140 sq meters) was once the heart of Lima, but not one original building remains. The oldest surviving part – the impressive bronze fountain in the center – was erected in 1650, and the oldest building on the plaza – the cathedral – was reconstructed after the 1746 earthquake.

The exquisitely balconied Archbishop's palace to the left of the cathedral is a relatively modern building, dating to 1924. The Palacio de Gobierno on the northeast side of the plaza was built in the same period. Here, a handsomely uniformed presidential guard is on duty all day, and the daily ceremonial changing of the guard takes place at noon (get there by 11:45 am). The other buildings around the plaza are also modern: the municipalidad (town hall) built in 1945, the Unión Club and various stores and cafés. The plaza was completely renovated in 1997.

On the corner of the plaza, opposite the cathedral, there is an impressive statue of Francisco Pizarro on horseback (actually, he was a mediocre horseman). Apparently, the equestrian statue was once in the center of the plaza, but as the clergy took a dim view of the fact that the horse's rear end faced the cathedral, the statue was moved to its present position. I'm told that there is an identical statue in Pizarro's hometown of Trujillo, Spain.

**Plaza San Martín** Dating from the early 20th century and renovated in 1997, the Plaza San Martín is one of the major plazas in central Lima. The bronze equestrian statue of the liberator General San Martín was erected in 1921.

**Jirón de la Unión** Five blocks of this street join the Plaza de Armas and the Plaza San Martín. These five blocks are a pedestrian precinct and contain stores and movie theaters, as well as the church of La Merced. It is always very crowded with shoppers, sightseers, street performers, ambulantes and, inevitably, pickpockets. Few visitors to Lima miss this street, but it is essential to keep your valuables in an inside pocket or money belt.

**Palacio Torre Tagle** Built in 1735, this mansion (☎ 427-6064, 427-3860, Ucayali 363) is considered to be the best surviving colonial house in Lima. It now contains the offices of the Foreign Ministry, so entry on weekdays is either prohibited, restricted to the patio or allowed by special appointment. On some Saturdays, you can enter the building; a tip to the caretaker may allow you access to the fine rooms and balconies upstairs.

**Casa Aliaga** The Aliaga house (☎ 427-6624) is at Jirón de la Unión 224. This is one of Lima's most historic houses and is furnished completely in the colonial style. It stands on land given to Jerónimo de Aliaga by Pizarro in 1535 and has been occupied by the Aliaga family ever since. The house can be visited only by appointment or through local tour agencies.

Statue of Francisco Pizarro in the Plaza de Armas

VICTOR ENGLEBERT

**Other Colonial Houses** Other colonial houses are easier to visit, though they are not as important as those already mentioned. The Casa Pilatos (☎ 427-7212, Camaná 390) now houses the National Culture Institute and is easiest to visit outside of office hours, especially from 2 to 6 pm weekdays or 9 am to 5 pm weekends. If you knock on the closed door, a guard will usually let you in for a look around. The Casa de la Riva (Ica 426) is run by the Entre Nous Society and is open from 10 am to 1 pm and 2 to 4 pm. Admission is US$1. The Casa de Riva-Aguero (☎ 427-9275, Camaná 459) houses a small folk-art collection. Hours for the collection are 1 to 8 pm weekdays and 9 am to 1 pm weekends. The rest of the house is shown only by appointment. The Casa de Ricardo Palma (☎ 445-5836, Gral Suarez 189, Miraflores) was the home of the Peruvian author of that name from 1913 until his death in 1919. Hours are 9:15 am to 12:45 pm and 2:30 to 5 pm weekdays. Adults/students pay US$1/0.25. The Casa de Oquendo (☎ 428-7919, Conde de Superunda 298) is a 19th-century house with an art gallery; call to obtain visiting hours.

**Zoo** The zoo (☎ 452-6913), in the Parque de las Leyendas between Lima and Callao, is divided into three areas representing the three major geographical divisions of Peru: the coast, the sierra (or Andes) and the Amazon Basin. Peruvian animals make up most of the exhibits, though there are a few more typical zoo animals, such as elephants. The zoo has recently been modernized, and hours are 9 am to 5:30 pm daily. Admission is US$2.

**Cerro San Cristóbal** This 409m-high hill overlooking central Lima from the northeast can be visited. At the top is a *mirador* (lookout) with views of the bullring, the Río Rímac, the Plaza de Armas and the rest of Lima and its suburbs fading off into the garúa. A huge cross, built in 1928 and illuminated at night, is a Lima landmark and is the object of a pilgrimage every May 1. There is also a small museum, open 10 am to 5 pm Tuesday to Sunday, with a US$0.35 fee.

The streets leading up to the mirador go through a poor part of Lima, and it's probably safest to take a taxi and have it wait for you, though I'm told that increased police presence on the streets has made it reasonably safe to climb during the day, if you don't stray off the main streets (those that have signs and are paved) and if you don't flash your camera around.

**Archaeological Sites** There are a few minor pre-Inca ruins in the Lima metro area. Also known as Pan de Azúcar, the Huaca Huallamarca (☎ 222-4124), on the corner of avenidas El Rosario and Nicolás de Riviera in San Isidro, is a restored Maranga adobe pyramid dating from about 200 AD to 500 AD. Hours are 9 am to 5 pm daily except Monday, and there is a small on-site museum. Admission is US$1.

The Huaca Juliana, near the intersection of Pezet and Belén in San Isidro, is a good example of the Lima culture; it dates to about 400 AD. The on-site museum is open 9 am to 5 pm daily except Tuesday; admission is US$0.50. The Huaca Pucllana, at the intersection of Borgona and Tarapaca in Miraflores, is also of the Lima culture but is open only to guided tours.

**Street Markets** There are several street markets ranging from the busy general market in central Lima to the leisurely and relaxed artists' market in Miraflores.

Lima's Mercado Central (main market) is at Ayacucho and Ucayali to the southeast of Abancay. You can buy almost anything here, but it can be crowded. East of the Mercado Central is Lima's Barrio Chino (Chinatown).

South of the Plaza Grau is a black-market area known as Polvos Azules, or 'blue powders.' This is the place to find smuggled (or stolen) luxuries such as ghetto blasters and perfume, as well as a remarkable variety of other consumer goods and a few handicrafts. The government turns a blind eye to these activities, and people from all social strata wander around, though you should watch your pockets and belongings carefully.

At Puente Santa Rosa (Santa Rosa bridge), where Tacna crosses the Río Rímac,

Lima's main flower market is a kaleidoscopic scene of beautiful flowers at bargain prices. The selection is best in the morning, though it's open until dusk every day.

The Feria Artesanal (Artisans' Market) is along the north side of Avenida de la Marina from the 6th to 10th blocks in Pueblo Libre. The selection of handicrafts here is extremely varied, as are prices, so shop carefully. Better quality at much higher prices can be found at various handicraft stores in Miraflores (see Shopping later in this chapter).

An artists' and artisans' market functions on Parque Kennedy, in the heart of Miraflores, from 5 to 11 pm daily (weekend hours start earlier). It is a good place to see local artists' work, which ranges from garish 'painting by number' monstrosities in oil to some good watercolors.

## Activities

Swimming and surfing are popular with Limeños during the summer months of January, February and March. Playa Costa Verde in Miraflores (also called Waikiki) is a favorite of local surfers, and they can be seen here year round, wearing wet suits. The following stores in Miraflores sell surfing equipment and provide information: Klimax (☎ 447-1685, José Gonzales 488), O'Neills (☎ 445-0406, Santa Cruz 851), Gordo Barreda (☎ 445-9621, Atahualpa 287) and Billa Bong (☎ 421-8217, Ignacio Merino 711).

There are seven other beaches in Miraflores and four more in Barranco. However, the water is heavily polluted at all of Lima's beaches, and newspapers warn of the serious health hazard posed by swimming and surfing. In addition, there are plenty of thieves, so you can't leave anything unattended for a second. Despite the health warnings, Limeños visit the beaches in large numbers in summer, and it's very crowded on weekends. It's best to go in a sizable group – if you want to go at all. Cleaner beaches are found south of Lima (see Around Lima at the end of this chapter).

Peru Divers (☎ 441-3282, fax 421-7814, perudivers@bellnet.com.pe, Conquistadores 946, San Isidro) is an excellent dive shop that is owned by Luis Rodríguez, a PADI-certified instructor who has information, arranges certification and diving trips and sells gear.

Lima has several tennis and golf clubs, and the 1st-class hotels and tour agencies can help organize a game for you. Sudex Agency (☎ 442-2737, 442-3684) may be able to help with tennis and golf in Lima. You can go tenpin bowling (US$3) and play pool at the Brunswick Bowl (☎ 445-5683, Malecón Balta 135, Miraflores); hours are 9 am to 3 am. Several other pool halls have appeared in Miraflores; a good one is Strokers (Benavides at Colón). Lima Cricket and Football Club (☎ 264-0027, Justo Amadeo Vigil 200, Magdalena) may allow (at their discretion) English-speaking visitors with passports to obtain temporary membership for a small fee. This club is popular with expats and offers many other sports activities beyond the obligatory cricket and football; it also has a reasonably priced bar and restaurant.

Several hotels (see Places to Stay later in this chapter) have casinos. There are also many slot-machine entertainment places scattered around Lima, especially in Miraflores. Betting is in US cash, and rules are similar to Nevada rules, with minor differences. One difference is that Blackjack (21) players must bet in exact multiples of the table minimum, so that on a US$2-minimum table, you can bet US$4 or US$6, but not US$5. Slot machines at these casinos have a reputation for being very tight.

Expediciones Viento Sur (☎ 949-4967, 922-3076, fax 429-1414, Grau 855, La Punta, Callao) offers sailboat rides to islands near the Lima coast. Sea lions and seabirds can be observed. Four-hour cruises leave La Punta at 9:30 am and 2 pm and cost US$30, or US$20 for children under 13.

## Language Courses

Asociación Cultural Peruano-Britanico
  ☎ 221-7550, Arequipa 3495, San Isidro
  US$33 per month for three 90-minute group classes per week

Instituto Cultural Peruano-Norteamericano
  ☎ 241-1940, 428-3530, Arequipa 4798, Miraflores
  US$95 per month for five two-hour group classes per week

# MIRAFLORES

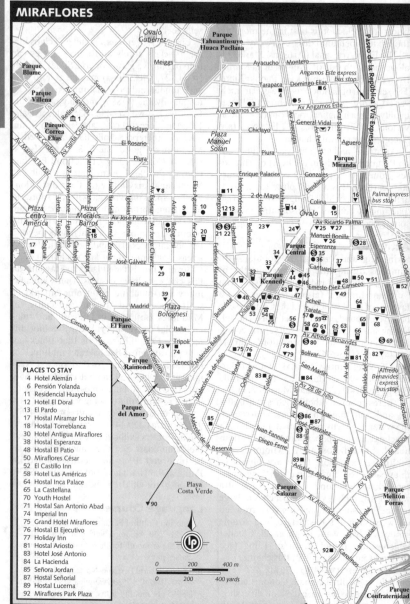

**PLACES TO STAY**
4 Hotel Alemán
6 Pensión Yolanda
11 Residencial Huaychulo
12 Hotel El Doral
13 El Pardo
17 Hostal Miramar Ischia
18 Hostal Torreblanca
30 Hotel Antigua Miraflores
38 Hostal Esperanza
48 Hostal El Patio
50 Miraflores César
52 El Castillo Inn
58 Hotel Las Américas
64 Hostal Inca Palace
65 La Castellana
70 Youth Hostel
71 Hostal San Antonio Abad
74 Imperial Inn
75 Grand Hotel Miraflores
76 Hostal El Ejecutivo
77 Holiday Inn
81 Hostal Ariosto
83 Hotel José Antonio
84 La Hacienda
85 Señora Jordan
87 Hostal Señorial
89 Hostal Lucerna
92 Miraflores Park Plaza

## MIRAFLORES

**PLACES TO EAT**
2   Quattro D
4   Hotel Alemán
8   Pizza Hut
16  Il Postino
23  La Tranquera
24  Haiti
25  La Tiendecita Blanca
26  La Trattoria
27  Vivaldi
29  Cebichería Don Beta
33  La Pizzería & other Italian
    restaurants ('Pizza Street')
34  Café Café
37  Astrid y Gaston
39  Las Brujas de Cachiche
47  El Parquecito, Café Paris
49  Las Tejas
51  Bircher Benner
63  Carlin, El Suche
68  Govinda
73  Sí Señor
79  Chifa Kun Fa
82  Pardo's Chicken
90  La Rosa Nautica
91  El Rincón Gaucho
92  Ambrosia

**ENTERTAINMENT**
14  The Brenchley Arms (Bar)
20  Mamut (Disco)
24  Cine Pacifico
31  Gitanos (Disco)
32  The Old Pub
40  Teatro Britanico
41  Media Naranja (Bar)
42  Cine Romeo, Cine Julieta
43  Tequila Rocks (Disco)
53  Brunswick Bowl
55  Downtown (Bar)
62  Treff's (Bar)
66  Mitos (Disco)
67  O'Murphy's Irish Pub
78  Cine Club Miraflores

**OTHER**
1   Museo Amano
3   Todo Camping
5   Instituto Cultural Peruano-
    Norteamericano
7   Post Office
9   TdobleA
10  Aero Continente
15  Casa de Ricardo Palma
19  Santa Isabel Supermarket
21  Banco de Crédito
22  Banco Latino
28  LAC Dólar Casa de Cambio
35  Banco Latino
36  Alpamayo Camping Store
44  Church of  La Virgen
    Milagrosa
45  Municipalidad
46  Centro Cultural de Miraflores
54  Telefónica del Peru
56  Interbanc
57  Dragon Fans Internet
59  Telefónica del Peru
60  ABC Bookstore
61  Santa Isabel Supermarket
    (24 hours)
63  Centro Comercial El Suche
    Shopping Arcade
69  P&P Casa de Cambio
72  Taller de Fotografía
    Profesional
78  Centro Cultural Ricardo
    Palma
80  Banco Continental
86  Banco de Crédito
88  Banco Wiese

Instituto de Idiomas (Universidad Católica)
☎ 442-8761, 442-6419, Camino Real 1037,
San Isidro
US$120 per month for five two-hour group
classes per week

Instituto de Idiomas (Universidad del Pacífico)
☎ 421-2969, Prescott 333, San Isidro
US$290 for three months with three 90-minute
group classes per week

Private Teachers (US$5 per hour)
Susy Arteaga, ☎ 534-0208, beginners only
Patty Felix, ☎ 533-3713, beginners only
Lourdes Galvaz, ☎ 435-3910, Spanish and
Quechua
Llorgelina Savastiazagal, ☎ 438-2676

## Special Events

There are major processions in Lima on
August 30 in honor of Saint Rose, the patron
saint of Lima and the Americas. October 18
sees huge religious processions in the capital
in honor of the Lord of the Miracles (smaller
processions occur on most Sundays in
October). See Public Holidays & Special
Events in the Facts for the Visitor chapter
for details on national holidays.

## Places to Stay

Lima offers literally scores of hotels,
ranging from US$3-per-night cheapies to
luxury hotels charging over US$200. It is
impossible and unnecessary to list them all,
but this selection should include something
that suits you.

Generally speaking, hotels are more
expensive in Lima than in other Peruvian
cities (except the tourist mecca of Cuzco).
Most of the cheapest are in central Lima,
with some well-known budget hotels to be
found within a few blocks of the Plaza de
Armas. At night, the city center is not as safe
as some of the more upmarket neighborhoods (such as Miraflores) and is also dirtier
and noisier. However, there's no real
problem, as long as you don't parade around
with a gold chain on your neck and a wallet
peeking out of your hip pocket.

Mid-range and expensive hotels are all
over Lima; there are some excellent luxury
hotels both in the heart of the city and in
Miraflores. San Isidro also has good hotels,
often aimed at businesspeople.

Whether you are staying in cheap or expensive accommodations, always ask about discounts if you plan to spend some time in Lima. Most places will offer cheaper weekly rates and may give you a discount for a stay of just a few days.

## Places to Stay – Budget

**Lima** *Hostal España* (☎ 428-5546, *Azangaro 105*) is a rambling old mansion full of plants, birds and paintings and a favorite place for gringo shoestring travelers, although the management won't allow Peruvians to stay here. Accommodations are basic, but clean and safe, and cost about US$3 per person in shared rooms and US$6/9 for singles/doubles. There are hot showers early in the morning or late in the evening, laundry facilities, and a small café. Nearby is the equally cheap *Hotel Europa* (☎ 427-3351, *Ancash 376*), which is also popular with backpackers. Their communal showers sometimes have hot water.

The reasonably clean *Hostal Belén* (☎ 427-8995, *Jirón Belén 1049*) is in a large old building, has very hot water, is popular with young Europeans and has received recommendations. Rooms cost US$7/10. The friendly *Familia Rodríguez* (☎ 423-6465, fax 424-1606, jjr-art@mail.cosapidata.com.pe, *Nicolás de Piérola 730, 2nd floor, No 3*) is very popular and recommended. Dormitory-style rooms are US$6 per person including breakfast. They are helpful to their visitors. *Hostal Residencial Yaki* (☎ 427-9506, *Jirón de la Unión 411*) has clean rooms with shared showers for US$5/7/10 for one/two/three people and doubles with bath for US$10. *Casa Hospedaje Machu Picchu* (☎ 424-3479, fax 447-9247, *Juan Pablo Ferandini 1015, Breña*), a block off the 10th block of Brasil, is friendly, secure, has kitchen privileges and charges just US$4 per person. Susy Arteaga (see Language Courses earlier in this chapter) also has a few budget rooms, especially useful if you are taking Spanish lessons from her.

The new *Plaza Francia Inn Pensión* (☎ 330-6080, franciasquareinn@yahoo.com, *Rufino Torrico 1117*) has very clean dorm rooms with shared hot showers at US$7 per person. SAE and Youth Hostel members get 10% off. (The owners also run the excellent mid-range Posada del Parque.) The well-recommended *Pensión Ibarra* (☎/fax 427-8603, *Tacna 359, 14th and 15th floors*) is run by the helpful Señora Ibarra, who makes a real effort to keep this place safe, comfortable and clean. Kitchen facilities are available. Rates are $10 per person including breakfast. The friendly *Hostal Wiracocha* (☎ 427-1178, *Jirón Junín 284*) has rooms with private hot showers for US$10/12. Rooms without bath are cheaper, but the communal showers lack hot water.

The highly recommended *Hostal Iquique* (☎ 433-4724, *Iquique 758*) is very clean, safe, near the SAE and has warm showers at any time. Kitchen facilities are available – the amiable owner, Fernando, is an excellent cook, and if you're lucky, he might help you with a good meal. Rooms with shared bath are US$7.50/11 for one/two beds and US$11/13 with private bath. TVs are available on request. The friendly *Hostal Roma* (☎ 427-7576, fax 427-7572, resroma@peru.itete.com.pe, *Ica 326*) is clean, central and attractive and has rooms with bath and hot water for US$15/20 and rooms with shared bath for US$10/15. There is a restaurant at the hotel. The Dutch/Peruvian-owned *Hostal de las Artes* (☎ 433-0031, artes@telematic.com.pe, *Chota 1469*) has rooms with private bath and hot water for US$9/11. The hostel is in an atmospheric older house, serves soft drinks at any time, is gay-friendly and is on a quiet street. The owners also own a cheaper, more basic hostel around the corner if this one is full. Another good choice is *Hostal La Estrella de Belén* (☎ 428-6462, *Jirón Belén 1051*), which is clean and safe and charges US$12/14.

**Miraflores** The *Youth Hostel* (☎ 444-8187, *Casimiro Ulloa 328*) charges US$11 per person in shared rooms or US$36 for a private double with bath. The hostel offers laundry facilities, travel information and minimal kitchen facilities. The clean *Pensión José Luis* (☎ 444-1015, hsjluis@telematic .edu.pe, *Paula de Ugarriza 727; no sign*) is on

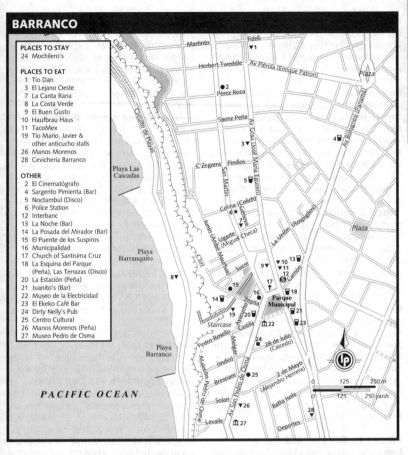

**BARRANCO**

**PLACES TO STAY**
24  Mochilero's

**PLACES TO EAT**
1   Tío Dan
3   El Lejano Oeste
7   La Canta Rana
8   La Costa Verde
9   El Buen Gusto
10  Haufbrau Haus
11  TacoMex
19  Tío Mario, Javier &
    other anticucho stalls
26  Manos Morenos
28  Cevichería Barranco

**OTHER**
2   El Cinematógrafo
4   Sargento Pimienta (Bar)
5   Noctambul (Disco)
6   Police Station
12  Interbanc
13  La Noche (Bar)
14  La Posada del Mirador (Bar)
15  El Puente de los Suspiros
16  Municipalidad
17  Church of Santisima Cruz
18  La Esquina del Parque
    (Peña), Las Terrazas (Disco)
20  La Estación (Peña)
21  Juanito's (Bar)
22  Museo de la Electricidad
23  El Ekeko Café Bar
24  Dirty Nelly's Pub
25  Centro Cultural
26  Manos Morenos (Peña)
27  Museo Pedro de Osma

*PACIFIC OCEAN*

a quiet residential street off 28 de Julio, four
blocks east of the Vía Expresa. You must
make a reservation at this popular pensión,
which has rooms of various sizes, some with
kitchenettes. All but three of the rooms have
private baths, and there is 24-hour hot water.
Rates are US$12 per person.

If you want to stay with a family, try
calling the following to see if space is available. *M Luisa Chávez* (☎ 447-3996, *Genaro
Castro Iglesias 273*) charges US$10 per
person with breakfast. Baths are shared.
*Señora Jordan* (☎ 445-9840, *Porta 724*) is
friendly and charges US$15 per person

including breakfast. The house is quiet.
*Pensión Yolanda*, run by the friendly,
English-speaking Yolanda Escobar (☎ 445-
7565, *Domingo Elías 230*) charges US$12/20
for singles/doubles. *El Castillo Inn* (☎ 446-
9501, *Diez Canseco 580; no sign*) is quiet and
has spacious rooms with private bath for
US$10 per person. *Imperial Inn* (☎ 445-
2504, *Bolognesi 641*) is in a residential neighborhood and charges just US$12 per room.

**San Isidro** *Malka Youth Hostel* (☎ 442-0162,
*fax 222-5589, cell 936-4451, alberguemalka@
hotmail.com, Los Lirios 165; no sign*) has

large clean rooms sleeping four to eight people at US$6 per person. There are kitchen and laundry facilities, a TV room and a games room, luggage storage and 24-hour hot water.

**Barranco** The friendly *Mochilero's* (☎ 477-4506, cell 903-6702, backpacker@amauta .rcp.net.pe, Pedro de Osma 135) is in a beautiful 100-year-old house just a couple of blocks from Barranco's nightlife. There is an Irish pub on the premises. Dorm rooms with shared baths and 24-hour hot showers are US$8 per person, and private rooms are planned. The young owners speak English.

**Other Suburbs** I have received recommendations about the following budget accommodations. *Gustavo Ruiz* (☎ 424-6581, cell 949-7054, preciso@computextos .com.pe, Mello Franco 170, Jesús María) rents rooms in his house starting at US$3 per person and suggests you contact him in advance. *La Casa Nahum* (☎ 462-6225, Pershing 550 G, Magdalena del Mar) rents rooms at US$5 per person and is popular with Israeli backpackers (Hebrew is spoken here). There are kitchen and laundry facilities, as well as tourist information. *Paseo Las Palomas* ( 463-3161, ☎/fax 261-1206, cosy-coyllor@yahoo.com, Parque Ayacucho 126, Pueblo Libre) is clean and friendly; English is spoken. Rates are US$5/6 per person without/with breakfast.

## Places to Stay – Mid-Range
**Lima** The well-recommended *Posada del Parque* (☎ 433-2412, cell 945-4260, fax 332-6927, monden@telematic.com.pe, Parque Hernán Velarde 60) is a lovely house on a quiet cul-de-sac in the residential Santa Beatriz neighborhood. The hostel – run by a friendly and helpful young couple, Monica and Leo (who speaks English) – features spotless rooms with excellent beds and attractive furniture and artwork. All rooms have private baths and cable TV. Rates are US$25/30/40/48 for one to four people, and continental breakfast (which can be taken indoors or on a patio) is US$3. Airport pick-up can be arranged at any time.

*Hostal San Martín* (☎ 428-5337, fax 423-5744, Nicolás de Piérola 882), on Plaza San Martín, has a decent restaurant, is quite helpful and boasts air-conditioned rooms with private baths, hot water, TV, minibars, telephones. Rooms are US$30/42 for singles/doubles including breakfast, and it's a decent value.

*Hotel Grand Castle* (☎ 428-3181, 428-3185, fax 428-6241, Carlos Zavala Loayza 218) is opposite the Ormeño bus terminal. This is not a very good area, but it is convenient for the bus. Rooms all have private bath, hot water and phone; there is a decent restaurant, and a small breakfast is included. Rates are US$20/30. *Hotel Internacional* (☎ 433-5517, fax 330-4754, 28 de Julio 763) is OK at US$21/30.

The newly renovated *Kamana Hotel* (☎ 426-7204, fax 426-0790, Camaná 547) is clean and good. Rates are US$37/46. The *Hotel Continental* (☎ 427-5890, fax 426-1633, Puno 196) has 90 rooms on 11 floors and charges US$36/45 including breakfast. The 7th floor and up have newer rooms with cable TV.

**Miraflores** There are plenty of good, small, mid-range hotels in Miraflores. All of the following have private baths and hot water. *Hostal El Patio* (☎ 444-2107, 444-4884, fax 444-1663, ossa@mail.cosapidata.com.pe, Diez Canseco 341a) is friendly, a good value and recommended. Rooms are US$38/48 with breakfast; for a few dollars more, you can have a kitchenette. *Hostal San Antonio Abad* (☎ 447-6766, 444-5475, fax 446-4208, gfer@amauta.rcp.net.pe, Ramón Ribeyro 301) is popular and pleasant. Rooms with TV and telephone are US$50/60 including breakfast and airport pick-up with advance notice. The friendly *La Castellana* (☎ 444-3530, fax 446-8030, Grimaldo del Solar 222) is in an attractive colonial-style house with pleasant rooms and cable TV for US$55/70 including continental breakfast. Rooms have added features, such as hairdryers and shaving outlets. Outside is a grassy garden. Also good is *Hostal Señorial* (☎ 445-9724, fax 444-5755, José Gonzalez 567), which has a nice garden with an outdoor eating area.

Good-sized rooms with TV are US$43/60 including breakfast.

The comfortable *Hostal Lucerna* (☎ 445-7321, *Las Dalias 276*) has rooms with TV for US$45/53. The clean *Hostal Inca Palace* (☎ 444-3714, *Shell 547*) is US$52/64 including continental breakfast. *Residencial Huaychulo* (☎ 241-3136, ☎/fax 231-3130, *2 de Mayo 494*) is safe and friendly. Rooms are US$40/45. *Hostal Esperanza* (☎ 444-2411, fax 444-0834, *Esperanza 350*) is safe and spotless. Rooms with TV and phone are US$45/60. The friendly *Hostal El Ejecutivo* (☎ /fax 241-3575, *28 de Julio 245*) offers good clean rooms with phone and TV for US$50/60 including breakfast.

The very clean, quiet and secure *Hotel Alemán* (☎ 445-6999, 241-1500, fax 447-3950, *haleman@correo.dnet.com.pe, Arequipa 4704*) charges US$60/65 including an excellent buffet breakfast for spacious rooms with cable TV. Light snacks are available during the day. They give discounts for long stays or businesses. *Hostal Torreblanca* (☎ 447-9998, ☎/fax 447-3363, *torreblc@peru.itete.com.pe, Pardo 1453*) offers singles/doubles for US$40/50 including continental breakfast and free airport pick-up.

Also recommended is the comfortable and friendly *Hostal Miramar Ischia* (☎ 446-6969, 446-8174, fax 445-0851, *ischia@bellnet.com.pe, Malecón Cisneros 1244*), near Plaza Centro America. Some of the rooms have an ocean view, and rates are US$64/83 including breakfast. *Hotel El Doral* (☎ 447-6305, fax 446-8344, *Pardo 486*) has a swimming pool and rooms with TV, minibars and small sitting rooms. Rates are US$75/81. Also good is the *Grand Hotel Miraflores* (☎ 241-4647, fax 446-5518, *postmast@ghotelm.com.pe, 28 de Julio 151*) with rooms for US$70/86. They have a casino.

## Places to Stay – Top End

**Lima** The venerable *Gran Hotel Bolívar* (☎ 428-7671, 428-7672, fax 428-7674, *bolivar@chavin.rcp.net.pe, Jirón de la Unión 958*), near Plaza San Martín, is the oldest top-class hotel in town and a delightful place in which to wander. The hotel reputedly serves one of the better pisco sours in town,

and if you can't afford a room, you can still luxuriate with an (expensive) drink in the bar. A string quartet plays light classical pieces in the beautiful, domed, stained-glass rotunda during afternoon tea (pricey but charming). If you stay here, try to get rooms on the 2nd or 3rd floors – the upper floors seem less used and slightly musty. Rooms are spacious and comfortable and have luxurious bathrooms. They go for US$102/115, and some suites are US$134/198.

A few blocks away, the modern and excellent *Hotel Crillón* (☎ 428-3290/1/2/3, fax 426-5920, *Nicolás de Piérola 589*) has a Sky Room restaurant and bar on the top floor with occasional live music and stupendous views of Lima. There is also another restaurant and casino. Large comfortable rooms are well appointed, with writing desks, plenty of storage space and big bathrooms. Rates are US$154/172, and suites are US$212/285. *Lima Sheraton* (☎ 433-3320, fax 433-5844, *sheraton@correo.dnet.com.pe, Paseo de la República 170*) charges US$184/202 for a typical Sheraton room – clean, modern, comfortable and spacious. With over 400 rooms, this hotel is one of the biggest and has a casino.

**Miraflores** My favorite in this category is *Hotel Antigua Miraflores* (☎ 241-6116, fax 241-6115, *hantigua@amauta.rcp.net.pe, Grau 350*). Unlike most of the other top-end hotels housed in modern buildings, the Hotel Antigua, as its name suggests, is in an older mansion that has been converted into a hotel in a quiet neighborhood that is only a few blocks from central Miraflores. The public spaces are elegant and decorated with Peruvian art (both colonial and modern), and the rooms, while comfortable and with all modern facilities (including bathtubs), have interesting antique flourishes. The staff is handpicked, friendly and helpful. Rooms vary in size and range from US$70 to US$100 for a single and US$85 to US$115 for a double including continental breakfast. The small restaurant also serves snacks, lunches and dinners.

*Posada del Inca* (☎ 241-7688, 444-3975, fax 447-8199, *posada_ventas@el-olivar.com.pe,*

*Alcanfores 329)* is one of a small chain of 1st-class hotels (others are in San Isidro, Cuzco, the Sacred Valley and one is being built in Puno). Each features some rooms with wheelchair access. The 28 rooms have Jacuzzi tubs, air-conditioning, minirefrigerators, cable TV and telephones renting for US$90/105 single/double including breakfast.

The helpful *Hostal Ariosto (☎ 444-1414, 444-1416, fax 444-3955, La Paz 769)* seems to attract famous people such as jazz musicians and writers, as well as a fair sprinkling of international businesspeople and tourists. There is 24-hour restaurant service and a small but attractive plant-filled courtyard. Rooms cost US$100/120 including continental breakfast and airport pick-up, but discounted rates can be arranged for large groups and long stays. Also recommended in this price range are *Hotel José Antonio (☎ 445-0428, 445-1366, fax 446-8295, 28 de Julio 398)* and *La Hacienda (☎ 444-4346, 242-0109, fax 444-1942, lahacien@amauta .rcp.net.pe, 28 de Julio 511)*. Both have decent restaurants, and the Hacienda has a

casino. *Holiday Inn (☎ 242-3200, fax 242-3193, donquijote@llulitec.com.pe, Benavides 300)* is a good hotel for businesspeople and has a business center. The 68 executive suites feature kitchenettes, soundproof walls and two telephone lines. Rates are US$140 for a single or double.

*Miraflores César (☎ 444-1212, fax 444-4440, La Paz 463)* charges US$250/270 for some of the most luxurious rooms in town (though discounts can be arranged). There's a great view-bar on the 18th floor, swimming pool, sauna, exercise room, three restaurants (one is open 24 hours) and plenty of antiques to set off the essentially modern quality of the place. Service is excellent. *Miraflores Park Plaza (☎ 242-3000, fax 242-3393, mirapph@ibm.net, Malecón de la Reserva 1035)* is one of the newest and best of Lima's luxury hotels, with 81 suites, ocean views and all the amenities expected of a five-star hotel – including an international gourmet restaurant. Rates are US$270 for a single or double.

Other luxury hotels include *El Pardo (☎ 444-2238, 444-2236, ☎/fax 447-8105,*

Churro vendor

*pardohot@si.com.pe, Pardo 420)*, which charges US$211 for rooms, all of which have two beds. They have a gym (one of Lima's most well-equipped) with a pool and sauna and 24-hour room service. *Hotel Las Américas (☎ 241-2820, 444-7272, fax 444-1137, Benavides 415)* has rooms for US$250 and has full five-star services. Travel agents can guide you to several other hotels in Miraflores in this price range. Businesspeople can often get corporate discounts at these top-end places.

**San Isidro** The *Posada del Inca (☎ 222-4373, fax 222-4370, posada_ventas@el-olivar.com.pe, Libertadores 490)* has 45 modern air-conditioned rooms and five minisuites with kitchenettes at US$90/105 for singles/doubles including breakfast; you'll pay US$150 for a suite. A restaurant and bar are on the premises. *Hotel Oro Verde (☎ 421-4400, fax 421-4422, peovl@ibm.net, Vía Central 150)* is a well-run, full-service business hotel with 244 rooms at US$250/282. *Los Delfines Hotel (☎ 215-7000, fax 215-7070, Los Eucaliptos 555)* is known for its restaurant and lobby bar, which have views of live dolphins (although the hotel has been criticized for providing an inadequate environment for them). The more than 200 rooms cost US$282.

## Places to Eat

As with hotels, Lima has a vast selection of restaurants of every price range and quality. Note that taxes and service charges on meals can be exorbitant. Cheap restaurants rarely charge extra, but check first if you're on a tight budget. The fancier restaurants may add up to 28% to your bill in combined taxes and service charges. You can add up to 5% of the pretax bill if the service really is excellent. Check the menu to see if taxes *(impuestos or IGV)* are included *(incluido)*.

## Places to Eat – Budget

**Lima** Set-lunch menus that cost under US$2 can be found in the cheaper restaurants. *Restaurant Machu Picchu (Ancash 312)*, near the backpackers' hotels, is popular with gringos and is good and cheap. Nearby, *Restaurant Acllahuasy (Ancash 400)* is

another good choice. The friendly, family-run *Natur (Moquegua 132)* is inexpensive and recommended for vegetarian meals. *Heydi (Puno 367)* is a very popular cevichería open only for lunch. Near the Plaza San Martín, *Café Castañuelas (☎ 426-6453, Jirón de la Unión 873)* is good for a light meal.

For cheap, large portions of good food, try *Nakasone*, near the SAE, for fried chicken; *Chifa La Paisana*, *Chifa El Angel* and others on the 13th block of Alfonso Ugarte; and *Razato (☎ 423-4369, Arica 298)*.

*El Cordano (Ancash 202)* is somewhat pricier but is a long-standing downtown restaurant with an interesting 1920s decor; a varied menu of typical Peruvian snacks and meals; and a great selection of Peruvian beers, wines and piscos. Hours are 9:30 am to 9 pm, but it's often dead at night. Another atmospheric old restaurant – *Queirolo* – is very popular for set lunches and as a drinking-and-gathering spot for Limeños; it is located on the corner of Camaná and Quilca. *La Casera (Huancavelica 244)* also has a good range of typical Peruvian food at reasonable prices.

**Miraflores** Here, restaurants are more expensive. The vegetarian places are among the cheapest. These include *Govinda (Schell 634)*, run by the Hare Krishnas, and *Bircher Benner (Diez Canseco 487)*, which has good food but slow service. The lunch menu here is US$3.

Also fairly cheap are the US-style fast-food joints found around the Parque Kennedy area and at the Óvalo Gutiérrez, at the intersection of Santa Cruz and Espinar, just north of the map of Miraflores. Cheap set lunches are served in several restaurants on Berlin between Grau and Diagonal, as well as at *El Parquecito (Diez Canseco 150)* and *Café Paris (☎ 242-2469, Diez Canseco 180)*.

**Barranco** The passageway under El Puente de los Suspiros leads to several *anticucho* stalls and restaurants. Although food sold on the street is generally suspect, the delicious beef-heart shish kebabs served up here come right off the grill and so won't make you sick. Both *Tío Mario* and *Javier* are recommended; a *porción* of four small sticks is US$2.50. Reasonably priced pizza and Italian food is served at *Tío Dan*, on Grau at Piérola. Nearby is a stand that sells big cheap sandwiches. *TacoMex (Grau 302)* has cheap, fast Mexican food.

## Places to Eat – Mid-Range

**Lima** Half a block from the Plaza de Armas, the tiny Pasaje Viejo has pleasant benches to relax on and several upscale cafés (including branches of those in Miraflores), ice-cream shops and art galleries.

*Raimondi* (☎ 427-7933, *Miró Quesada 158*) is a good lunchtime restaurant that is popular with Lima's businesspeople. There's no sign, and the exterior gives no indication of the spacious comfort and lovely ceiling within. A set lunch is US$5, and there is a wide variety of other, more expensive, options. *Manhattan Restaurant (Miró Quesada 253)* also caters to businesspeople and has good lunches in the US$5 to US$10 range, as well as a happy hour from 5 to closing time at 7 pm. *Parrilladas San Martín*, on the plaza of the same name, is a decent place for a meaty meal; grills are the speciality. Prices are upper mid-end.

There are authentic Chinese restaurants in the small but lively Barrio Chino, or Chinatown, in Lima. One of the best is *Wa Lok* (☎ 427-2656, *Paruro 864*), whose friendly owner, Liliana Com, speaks English. Meals here are about US$7 to US$10. Across the street, *Salon Capon (Paruro 819)* has great dim sum. There are several others within one or two blocks.

I enjoy eating the good seafood at *Cevichería La Choza Nautica* (☎ 424-1766, *Breña 204*), at Pasaje Río Bravo. Most plates are US$7 to US$10. ('La choza' means 'the shack,' and I like the play on words; think of the upscale La Rosa Nautica; see Places to Eat – Top-End for Miraflores later in this chapter.) They are closed Sunday and Monday evenings, though there are a couple of other nearby seafood restaurants.

**Miraflores** The trendiest spot in Miraflores is *Café Café* (☎ 445-1165, *Martír Olaya 250*), which advertises 120 different drinks,

coffees, sandwiches and desserts. Various gourmet coffees are US$1 and up, and sandwiches are about US$5. This is the place to see and be seen. Miraflores also has many pavement cafés that are great for people-watching. *Haiti* (☎ 445-0539), on the óvalo next to El Pacífico cinema, is an excellent place to watch the world go by while you have a coffee. I'm told that this is a gay-friendly place, though it's equally popular with families, straights, little old ladies ... the waiters are very suave with their black bow ties, but the food receives mixed reviews, ranging from mediocre to very good. *La Tiendecita Blanca* (☎ 445-9797, *Larco 111*), on the other side of the óvalo, has been a Miraflores landmark for over half a century and has a superb, if pricey, pastry selection. Nearby, *Vivaldi* (☎ 447-1636, *Ricardo Palma 258*) is also pricey, but has good coffees. There are several others in the area.

*Sí Señor* (☎ 445-3789, *Bolognesi 706*) has a lively atmosphere and serves Tex-Mex food in the US$6 to US$8 range. Mexican beer and tequila are featured. A good seafood restaurant is *Cebichería Don Beta* (☎ 446-9465, *José Gálvez 667*). Don't be put off by the tiny exterior – it opens up inside. This place is very popular among Peruvians for lunch but is quiet in the evenings. Ceviches start around US$8. There are several other seafood restaurants on this street. Several US-style restaurants (*TGIF, Outback Steakhouse*) are found at Óvalo Gutiérrez.

For a good variety of standard Peruvian fare, try *Las Tejas* (☎ 444-4360, *Diez Canseco 340*). Most meals here are US$10 to US$15, and they have live *criolla* music starting at 8 pm Thursday to Saturday. *Chifa Kun Fa* (☎ 447-8634, *San Martín 459*) has good Chinese food – Peruvian style, of course! *Pardo's Chicken* (☎ 446-4790, *Benavides 730*) is a very popular chicken-and-fries restaurant – they do ribs and anticuchos also. *El Suche* (☎ 242-7090, *La Paz 646*), in the Centro Comercial El Suche, has a pleasant ambiance and upscale international food at reasonable prices.

Lovers of Italian food will find several pizzerias by Parque Kennedy in Miraflores. On Diagonal, nicknamed 'Pizza Street,' is the pricey *La Pizzería* (☎ 446-7793, *Diagonal 322)* and other places that are cheaper but none are outstanding. Some people say that the *Pizza Hut* (☎ 446-4785, *Espinar 202)* has the best pizza. *La Trattoria* (☎ 446-7002, *Manuel Bonilla 106)* is recommended for tasty, homemade pasta (that you can watch them make). Meals here are about US$8 to US$15. Perhaps the best Italian ice cream, as well as delicious cakes and good coffee, is found at *Quattro D* (☎ 447-1523, *Angamos Oeste 408).*

Several British-style pubs in Miraflores offer meals and drinks. See Entertainment later in this chapter for details.

**Barranco** *La Canta Rana*, or 'the Singing Frog' (☎ 445-0498, *Génova 101)*, is a great cevichería, with ceviches starting around US$8. All kinds of other seafood are also available, though portions tend to be small. It's open for lunch only and has a great weekend ambiance. *Cevichería Barranco* (☎ 467-4560, *Panamá Sur 270)* is cheaper and also very good.

The elegant *El Buen Gusto* (☎ 477-4199, *Grau 323)* has good service, tasty sandwiches and light meals. Nearby, *Haufbrau Haus (Grau 340)* has been recommended; I guess they do German-influenced food. Carnivores can chow down at *El Lejano Oeste*, on Grau near Peña, where a meal is about US$10.

**San Isidro** *Segundo Muelle* (☎ 264-3323, *Pezet 1455)*, two blocks southwest of Lima Golf Club, serves excellent ceviche and is popular with young adults. The more expensive *Punta Sal* (☎ 441-7431, *Conquistadores 958)* also has good seafood. *Al Dente* (☎ 441-9877, *2 de Mayo 759)* does good Italian fare. *Aromas Peruanos* (☎ 224-1482, *Guardia Civil 856)* is recommended for Peruvian food. *La Reserve de Jean Patrick* (☎ 440-0952, *Las Flores 326)* has great French, Italian and Peruvian cuisine, though it is close to top end in price.

## Places to Eat – Top End

**Lima** *L'Eau Vive* (☎ 427-5612, *Ucayali 370)* has food prepared and served by a French order of nuns; it features dishes from all over the world, as well as some exotic cocktails. It's in an extremely quiet colonial-style house and is a welcome relief from the Lima madhouse. Lunches are about US$10, and evening dinners run around US$25, but profits go to charity. Hours are 12:30 to 2:45 pm and 8:30 to 10:30 pm daily except Sunday. The nuns sing an 'Ave María' at the end of dinner.

Otherwise, the best restaurants downtown are in the top-end hotels.

**Miraflores** *El Señorio de Sulco* (☎ 441-0389, *Malecón Cisneros 1470)*, at the end of Pardo and overlooking the sea, is known for its excellent *criollo* (coastal Peruvian) seafood and meats. Meals here run around US$25. The cozy, elegant and delightful *Carlin* (☎ 444-4134, *La Paz 646)* is one of the capital's best international restaurants and specializes in French cuisine. They are closed on Sunday.

*El Rincón Gaucho* (☎ 447-4778, *Armendariz 289)*, at Parque Salazar, is the best place for Argentine steaks for around US$20. They were closed in 1998/99 for complete remodeling. Another recommendation for meateaters is *La Tranquera* (☎ 447-5111, *Pardo 285)*. They serve a US$80 *parrillada* (mixed grill) that supposedly serves five, though the waiter claims it will serve 10 people. They also have a special selection of meats, such as *cuy* (guinea pig), rabbit and game.

*Las Brujas de Cachiche* (☎ 444-5310, *Bolognesi 460)* is one of the best places for Peruvian food. Meals are around US$30. *Il Postino* (☎ 446-8381, *Colina 401)* is one of Miraflores' very best Italian restaurants. The international (French cuisine a speciality) gourmet meals served at *Ambrosia* (☎ 242-3000, *Malecón de la Reserva 1035)*, in the Miraflores Park Plaza hotel, have received wide acclaim locally. It's expensive. Also locally popular among upper-class Limeños is *Astrid y Gaston* (☎ 444-1496, *Cantuarias 175)*, which has excellent local and international cuisine.

*La Rosa Nautica* (☎ 447-0057) is in a fabulous building at the end of a pier at Playa Costa Verde in Miraflores. The ocean is floodlit, and surfers sometimes skim through the piling. To get there, take a taxi to the pier and then a bicycle rickshaw the last 100m along the boardwalk to the restaurant door. A meal for two à la carte will easily go over US$100 here, but they have good set menus for around US$25 to US$35 (including wine and perhaps a pisco sour) that are a better value.

**Barranco** *La Costa Verde* (☎ 477-2424), at Playa Barranquito, is recommended for its excellent seafood. They have a Sunday buffet for about US$55 per person including wine. *Manos Morenas* (☎ 467-0421, Pedro de Osma 409) has top-notch criollo food with live music (after 10 pm) from Thursday to Saturday.

## Entertainment

Cinemas, theaters, art galleries and music shows are listed in *El Comercio* daily newspaper, with the most detailed listings on Friday. If your Spanish is not up to this, the English-language *Lima Times* and *Lima Herald* have general guides to forthcoming events.

Generally speaking, nightlife starts late and continues until 3 or 4 am, so it tends to be more popular on weekends. Cultural events, such as the theater and the symphony, start earlier; films run from early afternoon.

**Cinemas** Non-Peruvian films are usually screened with their original sound track and Spanish subtitles. Admission varies from US$2 in the center of Lima to about US$5 in the better suburbs, where the better cinemas are. Some may offer a half-price night midweek. You can often see the latest Oscar nominees or Cannes winners, along with current Hollywood movies. Cinema clubs show more esoteric films – these are listed in the newspapers' cultural-events section, separately from the cinema listings. *Filmoteca* (☎ 423-4732), at Lima's Museo de Arte, shows a wide range of films, often with particular themes for a week. Admission is US$2 to US$3. *El Cinematógrafo* (☎ 477-1961, Pérez Roca 196, Barranco) screens excellent films with good sound quality for US$3.50; less midweek. *Cine Club Miraflores* (☎ 446-2649, Larco 770, Miraflores),

in the Centro Cultural Ricardo Palma, is another choice.

**Theater & Music** Unfortunately, the beautiful *Teatro Municipal* (Ica 300) burnt down in 1998, but there is talk of rebuilding. It was the premier venue for symphony, opera, plays and ballet. Another good venue is the *Teatro Segura* (☎ 427-7437, Huancavelica 265), which is picking up some of the losses. Others include *Teatro Canut* (☎ 422-5373, Petit Thouars 4550, Miraflores) and *Teatro Britanico* (☎ 447-9760, Bellavista 527, Miraflores), which sometimes has plays in English.

**Peruvian Music** Live Peruvian music is performed at *peñas*, where you can often sing along and dance. Drinks and (sometimes) food are served. They are generally open from Thursday to Saturday. There are two main types of Peruvian music – *folklórico* and *criolla*. The first is more typical of the Andean highlands – and therefore less popular in Lima – while the second is more coastal. The *Hatuchay* (☎ 427-2827, 433-0455, Trujillo 228, Rímac) is in a huge barn of a place just across the bridge behind the presidential palace. The music is mainly folklórico, and there is plenty of audience participation and dancing during the second half. Typical Peruvian snacks are served, as well as drinks. Call for entrance prices, which are usually not very expensive. Doors open at about 9 pm, and music starts around 10 pm. Get there early or make advance reservations to ensure a good seat. A taxi to get there isn't a bad idea.

A well-recommended folklórico peña that is very popular with Limeños is *Las Brisas de Titicaca* (☎ 423-7405, Wakuski 168), near Plaza Bolognesi. The cover charge is about US$7, and they open about 9:30 pm.

For criolla music, there are good places in Barranco. *La Estación* (☎ 477-5030, Pedro de Osma 112) is one of the best known, and covers vary from US$7 to US$15. Readers recommend *La Esquina del Parque* (☎ 477-2072, Sanchez Carrión at Grau). Also see *Manos Morenas* in Places to Eat – Top-End for Barranco earlier in this chapter. There are several others nearby. In Miraflores,

**LIMA**

*Sachun Peña (☎ 441-0123, 441-4465, Avenida del Ejército 657)*, away from the center, has been recommended for a variety of acts that get under way around midnight. The cover is about US$10.

**Bars** Unfortunately, several bars and nightclubs discriminate against nonwhites (see Discrimination in the Facts for the Visitor chapter). Readers who encounter this are encouraged to contact me so that I can remove flagrant offenders from the next edition.

There has been a proliferation of British-style pubs in Miraflores and Barranco in recent years. These are the haunts of upper-class Limeños, British and American expatriates who work for oil companies, schools or embassies and foreign visitors. British beer is not imported into Peru, but the local Pilsen and Cristal seem to do the trick; note that prices are high compared to grabbing a beer in a budget restaurant.

One of the oldest is the Peruvian-managed *The Brenchley Arms (☎ 445-9680, Atahualpa 176, Miraflores)* with a small dinner menu offering good English pub food. Prices are in the US$6 to US$14 range. There is a dart board, and you can read British newspapers. Meals are served until 10 pm. They are closed on Sunday. *The Old Pub (☎ 242-8155, San Ramón 295, Miraflores)* is an attractive bar owned by four expats from England, Scotland, Australia and the USA. They have two dart boards (Tuesday is darts night), a TV tuned in to sports coverage and an international dinner menu specializing in beef. The pub opens at 6 pm daily, or at 4 pm on weekends. *O'Murphys (Schell 627, Miraflores)* is a newer and busy Irish pub that has recently been very popular with younger patrons.

*Media Naranja (Schell 130, Miraflores)* is an open-air Brazilian bar with typical drinks from that country. They also have expensive food. *Treff's (☎ 440-0148, Benavides 571, Miraflores)* is a German tavern. *The Jazz Zone Pub (☎ 242-7090, La Paz 656, Miraflores)*, in Pasaje El Suche, has live music sometimes.

At night, Barranco is the most happening place. Friday and Saturday nights are like big, crowded parties. It's quieter midweek. The following are all in Barranco. *Dirty Nelly's Pub (Pedro de Osma 135)*, in the Mochilero's hostel, is a cozy and attractive Irish pub. The popular hangout *Juanito's (Grau 274)*, one of the oldest haunts, is a leftist peña of the 1960s that retains its early simple decor. The party crowd is often to be found in *La Noche (☎ 477-4154, Bolognesi 317)*, which nestles snugly at the end of a street crammed with trendy bars. A lot of these have happy hours during the week, but not during the crowded weekends. *El Ekeko Café Bar (☎ 477-5823, Grau 2660)* is another popular choice and has free poetry readings on Monday and live music (US$7 cover) on weekends. *Sargento Pimienta (☎ 477-0308, Bolognesi 755)* has live rock bands and is very popular. *La Posada del Mirador*, near El Puente de los Suspiros, has ocean views. There are many more around Barranco's Parque Municipal.

**Nightclubs** There are numerous discos that tend to be dead until about 11 pm or midnight. Many are expensive, with a approximately US$10 cover charge, which may include the first drink. Most have recorded music and are aimed at patrons who want to do a lot of dancing and are not planning on doing much the next day! The biggest is the very popular, appropriately named *Mamut (☎ 241-0460, 241-0470, Berlin 438, Miraflores)*, with three dance floors, each with different music. Other popular spots for dancing in Miraflores include *Tequila Rocks (Diez Canseco 146)*, the architecturally interesting *Mitos (Benavides 621)* and *Downtown (Los Pinos 162)*. *Gitanos (☎ 446-3435, Berlin 231)* is one of several gay-friendly places.

In Barranco, the large and modern *Noctambul (☎ 247-0044, Grau 627)* was once Lima's favorite, though Mamut has eclipsed it. No doubt this will change again by the time you read this book – nightlife has a way of doing that! Noctambul has a US$15 cover (half price for women), which reportedly includes as many drinks as you want. Also try *Las Terrazas (Grau 290)* and several others nearby.

## Spectator Sports

Soccer, called *fútbol*, is the national sport, but is closely rivaled by volleyball, which is of a high standard. Peru's Estadio Nacional, off the 7th, 8th and 9th blocks of the Paseo de la República, is the venue for the most important soccer matches and other events.

Horse racing is also popular. *The Jockey Club Of Peru* (Hipódromo de Monterrico), at the junction between the Panamericana Sur and Javier Prado, has horse races every Tuesday and Thursday at 6 pm and weekends at 2 pm. Betting starts at US$0.70. The members' stand (which has a decent restaurant) is open to nonmembers for US$3. For information about *caballos de paso*, or pacing horses (see Trujillo in the North Coast chapter), contact the *Asociación Nacional de Caballos de Paso* (☎ 447-6331).

Bullfighting has a good following in Lima. The bullfighting season is late October to late November (Sunday at 3 pm), and there is also a short season in March. Matadors, most of whom are Spanish, fight in the *Plaza de Acho* bullring (☎ 481-1467, Hualgayoc 332, Rímac), and in 1993, Spanish matador Cristina Sanchez was the first woman to fight in Lima. Rafael Castañeta is the best-known Peruvian matador. Bullfights are widely advertised in the major newspapers, and tickets are sold well in advance. Prices are expensive, ranging from US$20 to US$100 for one event and up to US$600 for season tickets. Tickets are sold at *Farmacia Deza* (☎ 440-8911, Conquistadores 1140, San Isidro). Cockfighting is also popular, and events are advertised locally.

## Shopping

A wide variety of handicrafts from all over Peru is available in Lima. Jewelry – including gold, silver and turquoise – is also popular and reasonably priced. The best selections of top-quality arts and crafts are found in shops and shopping arcades. Shopping hours are generally 10 am to 8 pm Monday to Saturday, with variable lunchtime closing hours. Shop prices tend to be high, but they vary, so it pays to shop around. Cheaper crafts are found in the markets (see Street Markets earlier in this chapter). Prices are fixed in some stores, but you can bargain in others. If you're buying several items in one place, it's always worth asking for a discount. Remember: carry cash in a safe, inside pocket or money belt when shopping. US cash can be used in some of the better stores, and exchange rates are often within 1% of the best rates in town. Traveler's checks and credit cards can also be used, but often receive less favorable rates.

Miraflores has some very nice shops, and although they tend to be expensive, the quality and shopping atmosphere are as good as or better than you'll find anywhere. Highly exclusive jewelry and handicrafts stores are to be found in the very attractive Centro Comercial El Suche arcade, off the 6th block of La Paz in Miraflores. The 5th block of La Paz is also good – the El Alamo shopping arcade is recommended. Alpaca 859 (☎ 447-7163, Larco 859) has high-quality alpaca products. Also good is La Casa de la Alpaca (☎ 447-6271, La Paz 665). There are many other stores in this area. For high-quality antiques, Porta 735 (☎ 447-6158, Porta 735, Miraflores) and Borkas (☎ 441-8306, Las Flores 249, San Isidro) are both open weekdays only. The several stores in the gardens of the Museo de Oro have high-quality crafts and jewelry.

La Casa de la Mujer Artesana Manuela Ramos (☎ 423-8840, Juan Pablo Fernandini, formerly Avenida Perú, 1550, Pueblo Libre), at the 15th block of Brasil, is a crafts cooperative with good-quality work from all over Peru. Hours are noon to 8 pm weekdays, and proceeds support women's programs that are funded by the Movimiento Manuela Ramos.

For camping gear, try the expensive Alpamayo (☎ 445-1671, Larco 345, Miraflores). Todo Camping (☎ 447-6279, Angamos Oeste 350) sells camping gas cartridges and imported insect repellent.

Slide- and print-film developing tends to be mediocre. Taller de Fotografía Profesional (☎ 241-1015, 242-7575, 446-7621, Benavides 1171, Miraflores) is the best photo shop in Lima, with top-quality processing, camera repairs and sales.

There are many supermarkets loaded with both local and imported food, drink, toiletries, and medicines. One of the best is the 24-hour Santa Isabel on Benavides at Alcanfores in Miraflores. On a Saturday night, this place is packed with young Mirafloreños buying six-packs of beer or grabbing a sandwich while they hang out with their friends. It's quite a scene and easily rivals any North American mall hangout. There are several other Santa Isable supermarkets as well.

The huge Jockey Plaza is a US-style mall that opened in 1997. Department stores, a movie theater, food court and speciality stores will make you forget you are in Peru. It's next to The Jockey Club Of Peru (see Spectator Sports earlier in this chapter). The smaller Centro Comercial Larco Mar, at the Parque Salazar in Miraflores, is another US-style mall.

## Getting There & Away

**Air** Lima's Aeropuerto Internacional Jorge Chávez is divided into two sections. As you look at the building from the parking area, the national arrivals and departures section is to your right. To the left is the international section. If arriving by air, reread Visas & Documents and Customs sections in the Facts for the Visitor chapter. Immigration procedures are usually straightforward, though occasionally officials routinely stamp 30 days into your passport; be sure to ask for more than 30 days if you are planning on a lengthy stay. In the baggage claim area, you'll find a bank where you can change money (see Money under Information earlier in this chapter for general information on changing money). After passing through customs, it's only a few meters to taxis and other transportation, so avoid porters in the baggage claim area, unless you want to have your luggage trundled 20m outside the door and dumped into the most expensive taxi available. When several flights arrive at once, it can be a real zoo, so keep your wits and your luggage about you!

The usual airport facilities are available in the terminal. Local, long-distance, and international phone offices; public phones; banks; snack bars; sundry stores and a post office are on the ground floor. Another post office

(supposedly open 24 hours) and restaurants are upstairs. A 24-hour, left-luggage room charges about US$2.50 per piece per day.

Well over 30 international airlines have offices in Lima. Check the yellow pages under 'Lineas Aereas' for telephone numbers, and call before you go, as offices change addresses frequently.

If departing internationally, check in at least two hours early (local agents suggest three hours), as many flights are over-booked. There is a US$25 international-departure tax, payable in US cash or nuevos soles. For domestic flights, it is best to check in about 90 minutes early to avoid possible hassles. There is a domestic-departure tax of about US$3.50 (payable in nuevos soles) at the Lima airport.

Airlines offering domestic flights include:

Aero Continente
    Aguirre 110, Miraflores (☎ 241-4818, 242-8808, 242-4260, reservations 242-4242)
AeroCóndor
    Juan de Arona 781, San Isidro (☎ 442-5215, 442-5663, 941-8675)
TANS
    Arequipa 5200, Miraflores (☎ 445-7327, fax 445-7107)
TdobleA
    Pardo 640, Office T-2, Miraflores (☎ 242-1980, 445-4342)

Domestic-flight schedules and ticket prices change frequently. Recent one-way fares from Lima were US$50 to US$100, depending on distance. The lower fares are often 'special offers' that you may need to ask about. For destinations reached from Lima, see the Internal Air Flights map in Getting Around. AeroCóndor has flights over the Nazca Lines in light aircraft on a daily basis and has a few intercity flights. A day tour over the Nazca Lines from Lima, including lunch, is well over US$300. (It's much cheaper to take a bus to Ica or Nazca and fly from there.)

More remote towns require connecting flights, and smaller towns are not served every day. Getting flight information, buying tickets and reconfirming flights are best done at the airline offices (or a reputable travel agent) rather than at the airport counters, where things can be chaotic. You can buy tickets at the airport on a space-available basis. Note that it is almost impossible to buy tickets just before the major holidays of Semana Santa (the week before Easter) and Fiestas Patrias (last week in July). Book ahead for those times.

Grupo 8 (the military airline) has flights to Cuzco, Puerto Maldonado, Pucallpa and some small jungle towns. These used to be weekly, but schedules are very erratic and subject to overbooking and cancellation, so I wouldn't rely on them.

Overbooking is the norm on domestic flights, so be there 90 minutes early. Officially, you should reconfirm 24 to 72 hours in advance, but it's best to reconfirm upon arrival, then both 72 and 24 hours in advance – and perhaps a couple of other times as well. Flights are changed or canceled with depressing frequency, so it's worth calling the airport or airline just before leaving for the airport.

If you're going to be traveling in a remote part of Peru, try to find a responsible travel agent or other person to reconfirm for you 72 hours before your flight. (Members of the South American Explorers' clubhouse can have the club reconfirm for them.) Passengers may be stranded for days because, having failed to reconfirm, they were bumped off their flight and found that all flights for several days were full. This is especially true during the busy months of July and August, when tourists trying to get on flights, particularly to and from Cuzco, are literally driven to tears. *Reconfirm!* – then reconfirm again. Several readers have echoed this comment. Get to the airport early and, obnoxious as this may sound, push if you have to – it can get very crowded.

**Bus** Both national and foreign destinations are served from Lima. For foreign destinations, see the Getting There & Away chapter.

The most important road out of Lima is the Carretera Panamericana (Pan-American Highway), which runs northwest and southeast roughly parallel to the coast.

Long-distance north and southbound buses leave Lima every few minutes; it takes about 24 hours to drive to either the Ecuadorian or the Chilean border. Other buses ply the much rougher roads inland into the Andes and across into the eastern jungles.

There is no central bus terminal; each bus company runs its own offices and terminals. Lima's bus stations are notorious for theft, so it makes sense to find the station and buy your tickets in advance, unencumbered by luggage. Note that La Victoria and the area around Avenida Carlos Zavala are both poor neighborhoods – use a taxi to get there if you are laden with luggage or traveling at night. It's OK to walk there in the daytime with no valuables to get a ticket. Some major companies have two terminals or are opening new terminals; clarify where the bus leaves from when buying tickets. For a description of the major bus companies and general bus information, see Bus in the Getting Around chapter. Note that there are scores of long-distance bus companies operating from Lima – I give only the best known or most useful here.

The busiest times of year are Semana Santa (the week before Easter) and the week before and after Fiestas Patrias (July 28-29). At these times, thousands of Limeños want to get out of town, bus fares may double or more, and buses often are booked up a week or more in advance. Plan ahead!

The biggest bus company in Lima (supposedly the biggest privately owned bus company on the continent) is Ormeño (☎ 427-5679, 428-8453, Carlos Zavala 177). There are various subsidiaries at the same address, such as Expreso Ancash (to the Huaraz area), Expreso Continental (to North Coast cities), Expreso Chinchano (to Cañete and Chincha), Expreso Ormeño (to South Coast cities, Arequipa, and connections to Cuzco), San Cristóbal (to Juliaca and Puno), and Costa Sierra (to Huancayo). Fast, more comfortable, more expensive long-distance services are offered to Trujillo, Tumbes, Chicalyo, Ica, Arequipa and Tacna. There is talk of closing the Carlos Zavala terminal and moving it to the international terminal (☎ 472-1710, Javier Prado Este 1059, La Victoria).

Cruz del Sur (☎ 424-1005, 427-1311, 423-1570, Quilca 531) serves the entire coast plus Huaraz, Huancayo, Arequipa, Puno and Cuzco. This terminal may become a 'tickets and information only' office in 1999 or 2000. Cruz del Sur has two new terminals that currently deal with only *Ideal* service (a slightly better bus, with video and fewer stops) and *Imperial* service (includes food and videos and rarely stops; about twice the cost of *Normal* service). You can reach the new terminals at ☎ 332-3210, 332-4000, 332-3209; Paseo de la República 801 and ☎ 225-6163, 225-6200, 225-6027, 225-6028, 225-6068, Javier Prado Este 1109.

Most of the coastal destinations and many inland places are also served by Expreso Sudamericano (☎ 427-6548, Montevideo 618), TEPSA (☎ 427-5642/3, Lampa 1237), Olano (☎ 431-2395, 428-2370, 427-3519, Grau 617) and others. Fares with these companies may be a little cheaper, but their buses are often older, slower and more crowded and the service is often less reliable. Avoid them if possible.

For the Huaraz area, several newer companies are competing with the traditional companies by offering new buses and reasonable prices. These include Transportes Rodríguez (☎ 428-0506, Roosevelt 354) and Móvil Tours (☎ 427-5309, 428-0740, Abancay 947). If going to Chiquian, try Turismo Cavassa (☎ 427-7673, Ayacucho 942).

For the Cajamarca, Celendín and Chachapoyas areas, there's CIVA (☎ 428-5649, 426-4926, Carlos Zavala 211) or Transportes Atahualpa (☎ 427-5838, Jirón Sandía 266).

For the Huancayo area, apart from Cruz del Sur there's the recommended Mariscal Cáceres (☎ 427-2844, Carlos Zavala 211).

For Pucallpa (via Huánuco and Tingo María), there are Transportes León de Huánuco (☎ 432-9088, 28 de Julio 1520, La Victoria) and Royal Tours (☎ 330-5346, Paseo de la República 565).

For Tarma and La Merced, use Transportes Chanchamayo (☎ 265-1052, 470-1189, 265-6850, Manco Cápac 1052, La Victoria).

Transportes Molina (☎ 428-0617, Ayacucho 1141) has fast services to Ayacucho via the newly paved road from Pisco.

For approximate fares and journey times, see the respective cities.

**Train** The train from Lima goes inland to Huancayo, climbing from sea level to 4781m – the highest point for passenger trains in the world – before descending to Huancayo at 3260m. It's an exciting trip, with dozens of tunnels and bridges and interesting views. From 1991 to 1998, the line was for freight only, but in 1998, limited passenger service was reinstated. Trains leave Lima at 7:40 am on the last Saturday of each month, arriving in Huancayo about 6 pm. The return trip is on Monday at 7 am (to allow passengers to visit Huancayo on its Sunday market day). In the 1999 dry season, service was increased to about once a week, but travelers should check locally for curent schedules. Round-trip fare is US$20 (one class only) and ticket-holders are guaranteed a seat. The train carries oxygen and has food service and bathrooms.

Another train excursion is every Sunday at 8:30 am with service to San Bartolomé, 1600m above sea level and about 70km inland. The train arrives at 10:45 am, and the return starts at 4 pm. The fare is US$4. Food service is available on board.

Lima's train station, Desamparados (☎ 428-9440, 427-6620, 427-4387, Ancash 201), is open from 8 am to 4 pm weekdays for ticket sales.

**Car Rental** Renting a car in Lima is not convenient – Lima is very congested and parking is difficult, so you are better off taking a taxi. See Car Rental under Car & Motorcycle in the Getting Around chapter. Avis (☎ 575-1637), Budget (☎ 575-1674), Dollar (☎ 575-1710), Hertz (☎ 575-1590) and National (☎ 575-1111) all have 24-hour desks at the airport. Call them for other locations.

**Boat** Lima's port is in Callao, only 15km from the city center. Very few travelers arrive in Peru by ship, and most of the vessels docking at Callao carry freight rather than passengers. The docks area is not particularly attractive and has a reputation for being somewhat dangerous for the unwary.

## Getting Around

**To/From the Airport** Taxis directly outside the airport-terminal exit charge about US$15 to US$20 for trips to Lima and Miraflores. Walking past these into the parking lot will yield taxis for about US$10. If you speak Spanish, are used to travel in Latin America, and don't have a lot of luggage, turn left outside the terminal and walk about 100m to the pedestrian gate, turn right and walk another 100m to the road outside the airport. Here, you can get a cab for US$3.50 to US$7 to Lima or a bit more to Miraflores, depending on how well you bargain and what time of day (or night) it is.

There are colectivo taxis and hotel buses available that charge about US$5 per person and drop you off at your chosen hotel. A travel desk at the airport can arrange taxis and make hotel reservations, but these tend to be expensive.

The cheapest way to get to or from the airport is by the city buses (signed 'Faucett' or 'Aeropuerto') that run south along Alfonso Ugarte and cost US$0.30. If you have a pile of luggage, this isn't recommended.

Getting to the airport by taxi is cheapest if you just flag one down and bargain. If you want to pay the full US$15 from Miraflores, you can call a taxi in advance (see the list under Taxi later in this chapter).

Some hotels will provide airport pick-up if you have a reservation – fees vary. A few of the tour guides recommended in Travel Agencies & Tour Guides (see earlier in this chapter) also provide airport pick-ups.

Recent road construction around the airport has led to lengthy delays. Allow at least an hour to the airport if you are traveling during the week, more during rush hours – the exception is before 6:30 am, when traffic is light.

**Bus** Taking the local buses around Lima is something of a challenge. They're often slow and crowded, but they will get you to your destination very cheaply (fares are generally about US$0.30), along with the millions of Lima commuters who rely on the capital's bus service every day. Bus lines are identifiable by the destination cards placed in the windshield; ignore signs on the side of the bus.

The most useful routes link Lima with Miraflores along Avenida Arequipa or the Vía Expresa. Buses going Garcilaso de la Vega (also called Wilson) and Arequipa are labeled 'Larco/Schell/Miraflores' when heading to Miraflores and 'Wilson/Tacna' when leaving Miraflores for Lima. Catch these along Larco in Miraflores.

From Plaza Grau (with a stop in front of the Museo de Arte Italiano), buses travel along the Vía Expresa, stopping at avenidas Mexico, Canada, Javier Prado, Corpac, Aramburu, Angamos, Ricardo Palma (for central Miraflores) and Benavides.

For Barranco, catch a Lima 2000 bus from in front of the Museo de Arte or along Alfonso Ugarte by España. From Miraflores, take a bus with the sign 'Chorillos/Huaylas/Metro' (or at least one of those) from Diagonal in front of the pizza restaurants. Don't take a bus marked 'Barranco,' as it doesn't go into central Barranco.

It takes a certain sense of adventure to use Lima's bus system, but if you can put up with the crush and bustle, it's a lot of fun. Several readers have written that they enjoyed the cheap and often interesting rides. Don't forget to keep your money in a safe place – pickpockets haunt the crowded buses.

**Taxi Colectivo** There are taxis that drive up and down the same streets all day long. The most useful goes from Lima to Miraflores along avenidas Tacna, Garcilaso de la Vega and Arequipa. Another goes from Plaza San Martín to Callao (passing the airport). A third goes along Paseo de la República onto the Vía Expresa down to Barranco and Chorillos. These taxis are identified by red window stickers, and when seats are available, the driver often holds his hand out of the window indicating how many seats are left. You can flag them down and get off anywhere on the route. The fare is about US$0.50.

LIMA

**Taxi** If you can't face the crowded buses, you'll find that taxis are generally reasonably priced and efficient. If there are three or four of you, they can be quite cheap. You'll pay less if you speak some Spanish and are prepared to bargain – taxis don't have meters, so you have to agree on a price with the driver before you get in. As a rough guide, a trip from the city center to Miraflores will be about US$2 to US$3, and to the Gold Museum or airport about US$3 to US$4. The trip from Miraflores to the airport is about US$5 to US$6. Gringos are often, though not always, charged more. These fares can be negotiated only with taxis flagged down on the streets.

Street taxis can be identified by the (usually) red-and-white taxi sticker on the windshield. Taxis can be any make or color, with dilapidated Volkswagen Beetles and newer Daewoo Ticos (from Korea) being the most common. Many of the older taxis lack seat belts. These taxis are usually private cars creating a source of income (or an extra job) for their owners. A recent survey indicates that one vehicle in seven is a taxi in Lima.

I haven't heard many stories of these taxis ripping off or harassing customers (apart from trying to charge a high rate) but if you are traveling with valuables or as a single woman after dark, you are safest with one of the officially registered taxi companies, which can be called by phone or from a taxi stand. Their vehicles have a licensed number painted on the sides and cost two or three times more than regular street taxis and can be hired by the hour (about US$10 and up). Those few that are actually licensed usually have a yellow paint job. The following all work 24 hours and accept advance reservations.

| company | telephone |
| --- | --- |
| Lima Driver | ☎ 476-2121 |
| Moli Taxi | ☎ 479-0030 |
| Taxi Miraflores | ☎ 446-3953 |
| Taxi Móvil | ☎ 422-6890 |
| Taxi Phono | ☎ 422-6565 |
| Taxi Real | ☎ 470-6263 |
| Taxi Seguro | ☎ 438-7210 |

Willy García (☎ 452-7456, cell 975-5871) speaks English and has been recommended. He charges about US$10 an hour.

**Bicycle** Dozens of bicycle shops are listed in Lima's yellow pages under 'Bicicletas.' Some sell high-quality mountain bikes and parts, have information and do repairs. I couldn't find a rental company. The following have been locally recommended: Cicloroni (☎ 221-7643, 222-6358, Las Casas 019, San Isidro), at the 32nd block of Petit Thouars; Peru Bike (☎ 467-0757, Pedro de Osma 560, Barranco); and Willy Pro (☎ 222-0289, 2 de Mayo 430, San Isidro).

# Around Lima

The following day or weekend trips can all be done using public transport.

## PACHACAMAC

The Pachacamac ruins are the closest major archaeological site to Lima and the most frequently visited. They are about 31km south of the capital and are easily accessible by public transport.

Although Pachacamac was an important Inca site and a major city when the Spanish arrived, it had been a major ceremonial center on the central coast 1000 years before the expansion of the Inca Empire. Most of the buildings are now little more than walls of piled rubble, except for the main temples that are huge pyramids. These have been excavated, but to the untrained eye, they look like huge mounds with rough steps cut into them. One of the most recent of the complexes, the Mamacuña, or 'House of the Chosen Women,' was built by the Incas. It has been excavated and rebuilt, giving some idea of Inca construction. The complex is surrounded by a garden and, as the roof beams are home to innumerable swallows, it is of interest to ornithologists as well as archaeologists.

The site is extensive, and a thorough visit takes some hours. Near the entrance is a visitor's center with a small museum and a cafeteria. From there, a dirt road leads around the site. Those with a vehicle can drive from complex to complex, leaving their car in various parking spots to visit each section. Those on foot can walk around the site. This takes about an hour at a leisurely pace if you don't stop for long at any of the sections. Although the pyramids are badly preserved, their size is impressive. You can climb the stairs to the top of some of them – on a clear day, they offer excellent views of the coast.

Various tour agencies such as Lima Tours offer guided tours to Pachacamac including round-trip transport and a guide. Costs depend on the size of the group, the quality of the guide and the length of the tour, but start at US$20 per person.

Those wishing to visit Pachacamac without a guided tour can do so by catching a minibus from the corner of Montevideo and Ayacucho in Lima. The bus is signed 'Pachacamac' and leaves every 15 minutes. The fare is about US$0.50. The journey takes 45 minutes – tell the driver to let you off near the *ruinas* or you'll end up at Pacha-camac village, about 1km beyond the entrance. This is a poor area, so hide cameras and other valuables carefully. You can also catch a bus signed 'Pachacamac/ Lurin' at Angamos, where it crosses the Panamericana (climb up the stairs), for the same cost.

The ruins are open daily except Monday from 9 am to 5 pm. Entry costs US$1.50, and a bilingual booklet describing the ruins is available for US$1. When you're ready to leave, flag down any bus outside the gate. Some of the passing buses are full, but you can usually get onto one within 30 minutes or so. It's advisable not to wait until late in the afternoon, as buses are likely to be full and you don't want to be stuck in the dark trying to get on a bus.

You can hire a taxi from Lima that will wait for you at the ruins for two or three hours. Expect to pay about US$40 to US$50.

## BEACHES

There are several beaches south of Lima. These include El Silencio, Señoritas, Caballeros, Punta Hermosa, Punta Negra,

San Bartolo, Santa María, Naplo and Pucu-sana. They are crowded with Limeños during the January-to-March summer. Many beaches have a strong current, and there are drownings every year, so inquire locally before swimming. Some beaches have private clubs used by Limeños, and camping is possible on most beaches outside of the Lima metro area, although facilities are minimal or nonexistent. Theft is a real problem, so you should go with a large group and watch your belongings. A few beaches, including El Silencio, Punta Hermosa and San Bartolo, have hostels near the beach at budget to mid-range rates during the busy summer. Pucusana (68km from Lima) has several cheap hotels (see the South Coast chapter).

To get to the beaches, take a bus signed 'San Bartolo' from the Panamericana Sur at the intersection with Angamos. You can get off where you want and hike down to the beach, which is often 1km or 2km away from the highway.

Although the beaches are popular with Limeños, the strong currents, thieves, poor access, lack of facilities and shadeless desert landscape make them unattractive to me. If you have friends in Lima with a car, you may enjoy the beaches more, but travelers on their own should realize that these are not beautiful, tropical beach resorts.

## THE CENTRAL HIGHWAY

The Carretera Central heads directly east from Lima, following the Rímac valley into the foothills of the Andes. You'll find several places of interest along the first 80km of the road east of Lima. Various confusing systems of highway markers and distances are used in different guidebooks, but bus drivers usually know where you need to get off. The road continues to La Oroya (see the Central Highlands chapter).

### Puruchuco

Puruchuco consists of a reconstructed Inca chief's house with one room identified as a guinea pig ranch. Although this is only a minor site, the small museum here is quite good and the drive out gives you a look at some of Lima's surroundings. Puruchuco is about 5km from Lima along the Central Highway (using the highway distance markers) and 13km from central Lima. It is in the suburb of Ate, just before the village of Vitarte, and is marked by a clear signpost on the highway. The site, several hundred meters along a road to the right, is open from 8:30 am to 6 pm daily. Admission is US$1. Information on how to get there is given later in this chapter in Getting There & Away.

## Cajamarquilla

This large site dates to the Wari culture of 700 to 1100 AD and consists mainly of adobe mud walls, some sections of which have been restored. Admission is from 9 am to 5 pm daily and costs US$0.50. A road to the left at about Km 10 (18km from central Lima) goes to the Cajamarquilla zinc refinery, almost 5km from the highway. The ruins are located about halfway along the refinery road and then to the right along a short, rough road. They aren't very clearly marked, though there are some signs, so ask if you have trouble finding them.

## Santa Clara

This village, at about Km 12 (20km from central Lima), is the site of the **Resort & Centro de Convenciones El Pueblo** (☎ 444-1599, 356-0042, 356-0020, fax 356-0024, ameripue@chavin.rcp.net.pe). It resembles a country club and features a swimming pool, golf course, tennis courts and so on. El Pueblo is also used for conventions, and rooms are US$80/95.

## Chaclacayo

The village of Chaclacayo is at Km 27, about 660m above sea level – just high enough to rise above Lima's coastal garúa. Normally, you can bask in sunshine here while about 7 million people in the capital below languish in the gray fog. A double cabin at one of the 'vacation hotels,' such as **Centro Vacacional Huampani** (☎ 497-1188) and **Centro Vacacional Los Cóndores** (☎ 497-1783, 461-6958, Garcilaso de la Vega 900), are mostly mid-range in price. There are pleasant dining, swimming and horse-riding facilities, though the rooms are pretty simple. Peruvians often come here for a day trip.

## Chosica

The resort town of Chosica, 860m above sea level and almost 40km along the Central Highway, was very popular with Limeños early in the 20th century. Today, its popularity has declined, though escapees from Lima's garúa will still find it the most convenient place to take advantage of several variously priced hotels in the sun.

From Chosica, a minor road leads to the ruins of Marcahuasi, described in the Central Highlands chapter.

## Getting There & Away

Buses to Chosica leave frequently from Lima and can be used to get to the intermediate places mentioned in this section. Many are minibuses signed 'Chosica,' and they can be picked up at Arica at the Plaza Bolognesi, or along 9 de Diciembre or Grau (though Grau gets into the dodgy bus-terminal area). Fares are about US$0.75 to Chosica.

# The South Coast

The entire coastal lowlands of Peru are desert interspersed with oases clustered around the rivers that flow down the western slopes of the Andes to the ocean. Running through these desert lowlands is the Carretera Panamericana, which joins the Ecuadorian border in the north with the Chilean border in the south – a driving distance of about 2675km. Most of this is paved, and it is the best highway in the country. Lima lies roughly in the middle of the Peruvian coastline.

The south coast generally has more travelers than the north. This is because the Panamericana south of Lima goes through several interesting places and is the overland route (through Arequipa) to those hugely popular destinations for the traveler in South America – Lake Titicaca and Cuzco.

The main towns of interest for travelers along the south coast are Pisco for the nearby wildlife, Ica for its museum and wine industry, Nazca for the famous Nazca Lines, Arequipa (see the Arequipa chapter) for its beautiful colonial buildings nestled under a perfect cone-shaped volcano, and Tacna for travelers heading to Chile. There are many other places worth visiting if you have the time.

## PUCUSANA
This small fishing village, 68km south of Lima, is a popular beach resort. From January to April, it can get very crowded, especially during weekends, but for the rest of the year, you can often have the place to yourself.

A few kilometers south of the Pucusana turnoff from the Panamericana is the village of Chilca and a mineral-rich mud lagoon called La Milagrosa that supposedly has healing properties. It's popular with Limeños, who come to wash their ills away. There are some places to eat and some cheap hotels.

## Beaches
There are four beaches in this area. The Pucusana and Las Ninfas beaches are small and on the town's seafront, so they tend to be the most crowded. La Isla, a beach on an island in front of the town, can be waded out to at very low tide. Boats frequently go there from the small harbor. The most isolated beach is Naplo, which lies almost 1km away and is reached by walking through a tunnel. There are good views from the cliffs around the town.

## Places to Stay & Eat
There are four hotels, none of which are very fancy. The best is the new **Salón Blanco** (☎ 430-9007, 430-9542). There is also an old Salón Blanco, which is not so good. The **Hotel Bahía** is quite good, and its restaurant is recommended. The cheapest place to stay is the **Hotel Delicias**. All of these can be found on or within a block of the seafront, as can several seafood restaurants. Hotel prices are around US$10 for a double (US$20 in the Salón Blanco), but are usually higher during the busy summer weekends, which are best avoided.

## Getting There & Away
Because Pucusana is about 8km off the Carretera Panamericana, the main bus companies running along the coast don't normally stop there. From Lima, you must take the Pucusana colectivo 97 (US$1, 2 hours), which frequently departs from the corner of Nicolás de Piérola (Colmena) and Andahuaylas, near the Plaza Santa Catalina (the forecourt area in front of the Santa Catalina Convent).

## CAÑETE
☎ 034
The full name of the small town of Cañete, about 144km south of Lima, is San Vicente de Cañete. About 15km north of town along the Panamericana is Cerro Azul, where

there is a locally popular beach with surfing from March to November (bring everything you need) and a small Inca ruin. The road to Lunahuana (see the Lunahuana section later in this chapter) is accessible from Cañete.

## Places to Stay & Eat
There are a couple fairly basic, but clean and adequate, hotels on the Plaza de Armas charging about US$8 to US$12 for a double with bath and cold water. Better hotels include *Hostal Costa Azul* and *Hostal Las Palmeras* (☎ 84-6005). There are several inexpensive restaurants on or close to the plaza. The best restaurant is *El Piloto* on the Panamericana. There are reportedly a couple of very basic cheap hotels near Cerro Azul where surfers can crash.

## Getting There & Away
Buses for Pisco or Ica can drop you here. It's hard to get back to Lima on Sunday afternoons from January to April, when buses are full.

## LUNAHUANA
From Cañete, a road goes inland up the Río Cañete valley to the pleasant village of Lunahuana, about 40km away. From here, river runners sometimes take inflatable rafts or kayaks back down the Río Cañete. Near Lunahuana are three wineries that can be visited. The best time to go for wine is in March, when there is the Fiesta de la Vendimia (harvest festival), though wine-tasting is offered year round. One winery that also produces pisco and welcomes visitors is *Bodega La Reyna de Lunahuana* (☎ 449-6433, 448-3706) in the village of Catapalla, about 7km from Lunahuana.

The local *níspero* tree is a member of the rose family and produces a small yellow fruit used in making preserves. Fiesta del Níspero is held in late September. The Cañete valley also has several ruins that are under archaeological investigation. Near Lunahuana is the **Ruina Incawasi**, and near Imperial, a village about 8km east of Cañete, is the **Ruina Ungara**. There are others ruins as well.

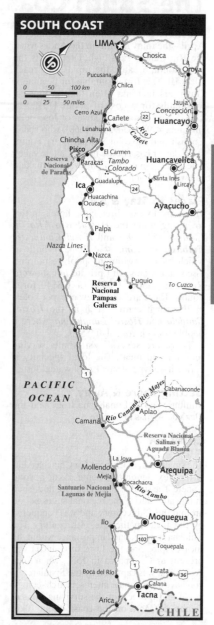

SOUTH COAST

## River Running

The season for river running is December to April – the rainy months in the Andes when the Río Cañete runs high. February is the best month, because the rapids may reach Class III. This trip is suitable for beginners. Outfitters in Lima often take groups on weekends for a cost of about US$20 to US$25 per person. Call Javier or José Bello (in Lima ☎ 946-8309, 438-1060), who speak English and have all the necessary equipment. Javier has a house in the Cañete valley where you can camp if you want to make a full weekend of it.

## Places to Stay & Eat

There are two or three good hotels in this town, including the *Hostal Río Alto (in Lima ☎ 463-5490)* and *Hotel Campestre Embassy (in Lima ☎ 472-3525)*, both of which have a swimming pool, restaurant, disco and rooms with private hot showers. Rates are about US$30 or US$40 for a double. There are also a few cheaper hotels in the town center, such as the *Hostal Candela* and *Hostal Lunahuana*, where a double room is roughly US$10.

There are several restaurants serving seafood and meat. The local specialty is crawfish – a type of small, freshwater lobster.

## Getting There & Away

Minibuses go to Lunahuana from near the Plaza de Armas in Cañete.

## CHINCHA

☎ 034

The small town of Chincha (or Chincha Alta) is the next landmark, some 55km beyond Cañete. The small Chincha Empire flourished in this area during the regional-states period around the 13th century and was conquered by the Incas in the late 14th century. The Chincha state retained importance within the Inca Empire, and the Lord of Chincha was present at Cajamarca in 1532, when Inca Atahualpa was captured by the Spaniards. If you have a passionate interest in archaeology, you'll find the best of the surviving ruins at Tambo de Mora on the coast, about 10km

from Chincha, and at the nearby temple of La Centinela. Both can be visited by taxi.

The Chincha area has a large black population and is known for its Afro-Peruvian music. The best place to hear and dance to this is at the peña (a bar with live traditional music) in the district of El Carmen, which is a 30-minute minibus ride from the Plaza de Armas in Chincha. The best times to go are during Verano Negro at the end of February, Fiestas Patrias in late July, a local fiesta in late October, and Christmas. During these times, minibuses run from Chincha to El Carmen all night long, and the peña is full of Limeños and local blacks dancing – it's quite a scene. There's a cover charge of about US$5.

There is a Banco de Crédito and some other banks.

## Places to Stay & Eat

Most hotels are used by businesspeople rather than tourists. During the festivals mentioned above, the hotels often double or triple their prices and are completely full. Some people avoid this problem by dancing all night and then taking an early morning bus back to Lima.

A few simple hotels in town include the basic *Hostal Residencial San Francisco (Callao 154)* and the *Hotel Sotelo (Benavides 260)*. Each charge about US$7 for a double. The *Hostal Residencial Majestic (Diego del Almagro 114)* is better and charges US$5/8 for single/double rooms or US$7/10 with bath and cold shower. There are a few other places with rooms in this price range. In the town center is the *Hotel Seville (☎ 26-1106, Callao 155)*, which charges US$15/20 for singles/ doubles with private hot shower. Better still is *Hostal El Condado (☎ 26-1216, fax 26-4878, Santo Domingo 188)*, with private baths and cable TV.

On the Panamericana, two acceptable hotels with rates starting at US$20, small pools and rooms with TV and telephone are the *Hostal Sausal (☎ 26-2451, fax 27-1262)* and *Hostal El Valle (☎ 26-4063, ☎/fax 26-2556)*. The latter has the *Restaurant Palacio de los Mariscos*, which is Chincha's best seafood restaurant.

The 200-year-old **Hacienda San José** (☎ 22-1458, in Lima 444-5524) is 5km south on the Panamericana, then 9km inland – take a taxi. It has great buffet lunches, a pool, a pleasant garden and a private chapel with catacombs. Rooms with full board are about US$60 for a double.

## PISCO-PARACAS AREA
☎ 034

Pisco shares its name with the white-grape brandy produced in this region and is the first town south of Lima normally visited by travelers. This fairly important port of about 90,000 people lies 235km south of the capital. Most visitors use Pisco as a base to see the wildlife of the nearby Islas Ballestas and Península de Paracas, but the area is also of historical and archaeological interest.

The resort village of Paracas is about 15km south of Pisco and has many private seaside villas that are empty for most of the year. Because accommodations are pricey and limited, many travelers stay in Pisco and take day trips from there to the Península de Paracas and Islas Ballestas.

### Information
Many of the hotels and travel services provide information.

You can pay for tours with US cash. The Banco de Crédito, on the Plaza de Armas, has a Visa ATM and changes cash and US-dollars traveler's checks. There are other banks and moneychangers nearby.

The post office is at Bolognesi 173. Internet Bill Gates, on the Plaza Bolognesi, provides email service from 7 am to 11 pm daily.

The pedestrian blocks of Comercio, south of the Plaza de Armas, are locally called El Bulevar.

### Tour Agencies
Of the several companies in Pisco, two have been recommended. The newest is Zarcillo Connections (☎/fax 53-6543, cell 66-3072, zarcillo@post.cosapidata.com.pe, San Francisco 111), on the Plaza de Armas at the Hostal Pisco (though unaffiliated), which does daily tours to the Islas Ballestas (US$10) and Reserva Nacional de Paracas (US$8 including entrance fees). English-speaking guides are available. They also do tours to Tambo Colorado (US$15 per person, two-person

**PISCO-PARACAS AREA**

Islas Ballestas
Islas Farallones
Isla Blanca
Isla San Gallan
Pisco
San Clemente
San Andrés
Puerto San Martín
Península de Paracas
Bahía de Paracas
Reserva Nacional de Paracas
Lagunillas
Paracas
PACIFIC OCEAN
To Lima
To Tambo Colorado, Ayacucho
Carretera Panamericana
To Ica

1  Fish-meal factories
2  Playa El Chaco
3  Hotel Paracas & boats to Islas Ballestas
4  Hotel El Mirador
5  Obelisk
6  Museo JC Tello & Information Center
7  Paracas Necropolis
8  Flamingos often seen here
9  'Graveyard' of fishing boats
10 Candelabra
11 Parking, cliff-top trail, sea lions & seabirds

0    5    10 km
0    3    6 miles

## Archaeology in the Paracas Area

Pisco is an oasis watered by the river of the same name, but the surrounding countryside is barren and sandy desert, typical of Peru's coast. Early in the 20th century, no one suspected that the drifting dunes of this arid area had covered the site of a well-developed culture that predated the Incas by more than a thousand years. It was not until 1925 that the Peruvian archaeologist JC Tello discovered burial sites of the Paracas culture, which existed in the area from about 1300 BC until 200 AD. These people are considered to have produced the finest textiles known in the pre-Columbian period.

Little is known about the early Paracas culture, Paracas Antiguo, except that it was influenced by the Chavín Horizon, an early artistic and religious historical period. Most of our knowledge is about the middle and later Paracas cultures, which existed from about 500 BC to 200 AD. This is divided into two periods known as Paracas Cavernas and Paracas Necropolis, named after the main burial sites discovered.

Paracas Cavernas is the middle period (500 BC to 300 BC) and is characterized by communal bottle-shaped tombs dug into the ground at the bottom of a vertical shaft, often to a depth of 6m or more. Several dozen bodies of varying ages and both sexes – possibly family groups – were buried in some of these tombs. They were wrapped in relatively coarse cloth and accompanied by funereal offerings of bone and clay musical instruments, decorated gourds and well-made ceramics.

Paracas Necropolis (300 BC to 200 AD) is the site that yielded the treasure of exquisite textiles for which the Paracas culture is now known. This burial site is about 20km south of Pisco and can still be seen, despite the coverage of drifting sands. It is near the Museo JC Tello on the north side of Cerro Colorado, on the isthmus joining the Península de Paracas with the mainland.

The Necropolis consisted of a roughly rectangular walled enclosure in which more than 400 funerary bundles were found. Each contained an older mummified man (who was probably a nobleman or priest) wrapped in many layers of weavings. It is these textiles that are marveled at

minimum) and will arrange a two-day/one-night trip to Ica/Nazca including transfers and bus tickets, a mid-range hotel and city tour in Ica, a Nazca Lines overflight and a Chauchilla cemetery tour. You get left at a Nazca bus station to continue to Arequipa or

wherever 'your destiny' is. Entry fees and airport tax aren't included. This costs US$80 – you could do it yourself for a few dollars less, but it saves the hassle of arranging it.

One of the oldest companies is Ballestas Travel Service (☎ 53-3095, San Francisco

## Archaeology in the Paracas Area

by visitors now. They average about 1m x 2.5m in size, although one measuring 4m x 26m has been found. This size is in itself remarkable, because weavings wider than the span of the weaver's arms (a bit over a meter) are rarely found in Peru. The textiles consist of a wool or cotton background embroidered with multicolored and exceptionally detailed small figures. These are repeated again and again, until often the entire weaving is covered by a pattern of embroidered designs. Motifs such as fish and seabirds, reflecting the proximity to the ocean, are popular, as are other zoomorphic and geometric designs.

It is best to visit the Lima museums to view the Paracas mummies, textiles and other artifacts. The Museo de la Nación and the Museo Rafael Larco Herrera are particularly recommended. In the Pisco-Paracas region, visit the Museo JC Tello in the Península de Paracas and the excellent Museo Regional in the departmental capital of Ica.

Our knowledge is vague about what happened in the area during the thousand years after the Paracas culture disintegrated. A short distance to the southeast, the Nazca culture became important for several centuries after the disappearance of the Paracas culture. This in turn gave way to Wari influence from the mountains. After the sudden disappearance of the Wari Empire, the area became dominated by the Ica culture, which was similar to and perhaps part of the Chincha Empire. They in turn were conquered by the Incas.

About this time, a remarkable settlement was built by the expanding Incas, one that is perhaps the best-preserved early Inca site to be found in the desert lowlands today. This is Tambo Colorado, so called for the red-painted walls of some of the buildings. Hallmarks of Inca architecture – such as trapezoid-shaped niches, windows and doorways – are evident, although the buildings were made not from rock, but from adobe bricks. It is about 50km inland from Pisco. While not as spectacular as the Inca ruins in the Cuzco area, archaeology enthusiasts or travelers who have time will find it worth a visit.

249). They reliably do tours to the Islas Ballestas and Reserva Nacional de Paracas, but don't offer onward services to Ica/ Nazca. Guests at the Hotel Paracas can arrange reliable tours directly from the hotel, but they are more expensive. Other companies on or near the Plaza de Armas may do slightly cheaper tours, but I have not received recommendations about them.

Alas Peruanas is affiliated with Alegría Tours (see Nazca later in this chapter) and does overflights from the Pisco area to the

Nazca Lines and back for US$130 (three-passenger minimum). Zarcillo Connections also works with Alegría Tours.

## Dangers & Annoyances

In Pisco, the downtown area is safe at any time of the day, but the market and outlying areas should be avoided at night. The beaches (2km west of town) aren't very good and should definitely be avoided at night. Numerous hotel and tour touts meet certain incoming buses (especially at the Ormeño terminal) and aren't all to be trusted. In the confusion, passengers' luggage occasionally disappears, so watch your bags carefully.

## Flora & Fauna

The Península de Paracas (Reserva Nacional de Paracas) and the nearby Islas Ballestas are the most important wildlife sanctuaries on the Peruvian coast. The area is particularly known for its bird and marine life. The birds nest on the offshore islands in such numbers that their nitrogen-rich droppings (guano) collect in quantities large enough to be commercially exploited for fertilizer. This practice dates from at least Inca times. Large sea-lion colonies are also found on the islands.

The most common guano-producing birds are the guanay cormorant, the Peruvian booby and the Peruvian pelican. These are seen in colonies of several thousand birds. Less common, but of particular interest, are the Humboldt penguins on the Islas Ballestas and the Chilean flamingos in the Bahía de Paracas. The Andean condor occasionally descends to the coast and has been seen gliding majestically on the cliff thermals of the peninsula.

Apart from the birds and sea lions, other seashore life is evident. This includes jellyfish, some reaching about 70cm in diameter and trailing stinging tentacles of 1m or more behind them. One calm day, when the sea was glassy smooth, I was crossing the Bahía de Paracas and saw a huge flotilla of jellyfish gently floating in the upper layers of the ocean. There must have been hundreds of them. Often, they are washed up on the shore, where they will quickly dry out in the hot sun and form beautiful mandalic patterns on the sand. Sea hares, ghost crabs and seashells are also found by beachcombers. Swimmers should be wary of jellyfish.

## Islas Ballestas

The only way to see the bird and sea-lion colonies is with a boat tour (landing is prohibited). These trips are inexpensive and worthwhile.

Various places in Pisco offer tours, but basically, they are all similar. The tours leave daily at 7 am and cost US$7 to US$10 per person in Pisco, more in Paracas. Usually, they leave from the plaza or will pick you up from your hotel in a minibus. When everyone has been collected, you will be driven to Paracas to board the boats for the excursion. The cheapest tours are usually pooled into one boat, which may lack life jackets. None of the boats have a cabin, so dress appropriately to protect against the wind, spray, and sun. People who suffer from motion sickness should take medication about an hour

### Of Flags & Flamingos

Local guides tell a perhaps apocryphal story of how the liberator General José de San Martín landed on the beaches of Paracas on September 8, 1820. Tired after a long journey, the general dozed off on the beach. When he awoke, he was dazzled by the view of a flamboyance of flamingos flying by. Their outstretched wings in the setting sun gave San Martín the inspiration for the red outer panels of what is now the Peruvian flag.

before they board the boat. Taking the stuff after you become nauseated doesn't help.

On the outward boat journey, you'll see the so-called Candelabra, which is a giant figure etched into the coastal hills – rather like the figures of the Nazca Lines. No one knows who made the hill drawing or what it signifies, although you'll hear plenty of theories.

About an hour is spent cruising around the islands. You'll see sea lions on the rocks and swimming around your boat, so bring a camera and binoculars. Although you can get close enough to the wildlife for a good look, some species, especially the penguins, are a little less visible. If you show some interest, the boat operator will usually try to point out and name some of the species. Wear a hat, as there are lots of birds in the air, and it's not unusual for someone to receive a direct hit! Some boat drivers reportedly bring their boats in too close and harass the wildlife; don't let your driver do this.

On your return trip, ask to see the flamingos. These are usually found in the southern part of the bay and not on the direct boat route. Sometimes the boat operator will ask for a small tip to pay for the extra fuel and time. The flamingos aren't always there. The best time is supposedly June to August, but I've seen them in October and January too.

On your return to the mainland, a minibus will take you back to Pisco in time for lunch, or you can stay in the port (El Chaco), where there are several seafood restaurants. You can continue on a tour of the Península de Paracas if you wish, or take a minibus back to Pisco later.

## Península de Paracas

Tours to the Península de Paracas from Pisco can be combined with an Islas Ballestas tour to make a full-day excursion. Costs of this tour are a little cheaper than the Islas Ballestas tour, and a discount for combining them can sometimes be arranged. A tour to the peninsula will often include a chance to view a flamingo colony from land. Apart from a tour, you can hire a taxi in Pisco for about US$25 for half a day, or take the colectivo into the village of

Paracas and walk, but allow yourself plenty of time. Bring food and, more importantly, plenty of drinking water.

Near the entrance to the village of Paracas is an **obelisk** commemorating the landing of the liberator General Jose de San Martín. The bus continues further in and will drop you in front of the Hotel Paracas if you ask the driver. Continue on foot either along the tarmac road south of Paracas, or walk along the beach from the hotel and look for seashore life.

About 3km south of the hotel on the road is a park entry point, where a US$2 fee is charged (if on a tour, ask if this is included). About 2km beyond the entrance is an information center and the **Museo JC Tello**. The information center is free, and the museum charges about US$1 for entry. Unfortunately, the museum's best pieces were stolen a few years ago, but a small collection of weavings and other artifacts remains. A few hundred meters behind this complex is the **Paracas Necropolis**, though there's not much to see. Flamingos are often seen in the bay in front of the complex.

Beyond the park complex, the tarmac road continues around the peninsula, past a graveyard of old fishing boats to Puerto San Martín, which has a smelly and uninteresting fish-meal plant and port on the northern tip of the peninsula. It's best to forget the tarmac road and head out on one of the dirt roads crossing the peninsula.

The first dirt road branches left from the tarmac, a few hundred meters beyond the museum. After 6km, it reaches the tiny fishing village of **Lagunillas**, where you'll probably find someone to cook fresh fish for you. The road continues about 5km more, roughly keeping parallel to the coast, then comes to a parking lot from where a footpath leads to a **cliff-top lookout**. Here there are grand views of the ocean, with a sea-lion colony on the rocks below and plenty of seabirds gliding by. Continue further if you're adventurous and carrying enough water. Few people camp, but it is possible – ask at the visitor center for information. The area is covered by topographic map 28-K from the Instituto Geográfico Nacional in Lima.

## Tambo Colorado

This interesting early Inca lowland site is one of the best on the south coast (though it doesn't compare with the Cuzco-area sites). It is about 40km from Pisco. Hire a taxi in Pisco for half a day (about US$25 if you bargain) or take a tour. A bus to the village of Humay, just outside Tambo Colorado, leaves from the Pisco market at about 7 am. Once there, ask the locals about when to expect a return bus, which are infrequent. But if you leave in the morning, you can probably return in the afternoon. An on-site caretaker will answer your questions and collect a fee of about US$1.

## Places to Stay

Pisco is a popular destination during national holidays, especially the Fiestas Patrias (July 28), when every hotel is full and prices reportedly triple for beds and tours.

**Budget** Many hotels are noisy at night with street commotion, and in the morning with tour departees. There is no cable TV in Pisco, so hotels with TVs are limited to a few uninspiring local channels.

The *Hostal Pisco* (☎ 53-2018), on the plaza, charges about US$3.50 per person in rooms with shared and not very clean baths. They have hot water. Rooms with private bath are about US$7/12 for singles/doubles.

Their prices tend to fluctuate. This place is popular with budget travelers, but I've received mixed reports. Readers have described it as friendly, dirty, helpful, a hassle for single women, good, rundown, clean, short on single rooms, having plenty of hot water, overpriced, the cheapest…take your pick. They have business cards that (illegally) reproduce my Pisco map on the back. My lawyer advises me to wait until the Hotel Pisco gets bought by the Hilton chain, then I can sue and retire.

The *Hostal Peru* and *Hostal Callao* charge about US$3 per person, have cold showers and aren't very good. Other hotels near the market, which can be dangerous at night, charge the same. The *Hotel Colonial* and *Hotel Comercio*, on Comercio near the Plaza de Armas, are cheap, basic and have warm showers. The *Hotel Embassy* (☎ 53-2809), on the same block, is a little pricier but not much better, though it does have private showers. Other just-acceptable budget places include *Hostal El César* (☎ 53-2512, 2 de Mayo) and *Hostal Josesito Moreno*, by the Ormeño bus station.

The *Hostal Belén* (☎ 53-3046, fax 53-2948, Arequipa 128) is a decent, clean hotel with warm electric showers. Rates are US$7 for a single (shared shower) and US$12 for a double (private shower).

**Mid-Range** The friendly, popular and recommended *Posada Hispana* (☎/fax 53-6363, andesad@ciber.com.pe, Bolognesi 236) has nine clean rooms (more are planned), most with four beds and all with spotless private bath and hot water. There is a café. Rates are US$8 per person or US$10 single. English, French and Italian are spoken.

The clean *Hostal Residencial San Jorge* (☎/fax 53-2885, Juan Osores 267) has a café and charges US$11/18 for singles/doubles with private hot shower. Under the same ownership, the central *San Jorge Suite Hostal* (☎/fax 53-4200, Comercio 187) has clean rooms (not suites) with TV and private hot showers for US$14/20.

On the Plaza de Armas, the *Regency Plaza Hotel* (☎ 53-5919, fax 53-5920, in Lima 225-1805, Progreso 123) has decent

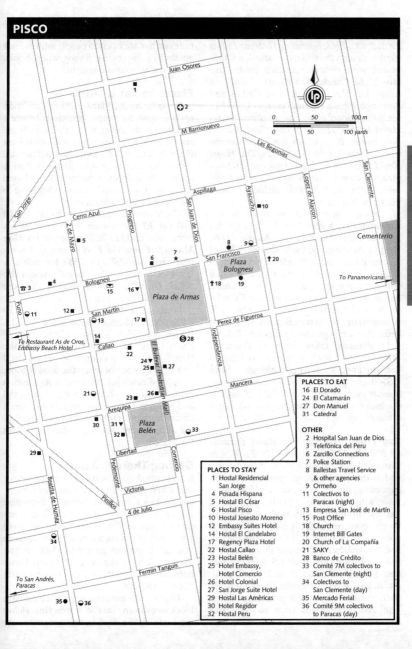

# PISCO

SOUTH COAST

**PLACES TO EAT**
16 El Dorado
24 El Catamarán
27 Don Manuel
31 Catedral

**OTHER**
2 Hospital San Juan de Dios
3 Telefónica del Peru
6 Zarcillo Connections
7 Police Station
8 Ballestas Travel Service
 & other agencies
9 Ormeño
11 Colectivos to
 Paracas (night)
13 Empresa San José de Martín
15 Post Office
18 Church
19 Internet Bill Gates
20 Church of La Compañía
21 SAKY
28 Banco de Crédito
33 Comité 7M colectivos to
 San Clemente (night)
34 Colectivos to
 San Clemente (day)
35 Mercado Ferial
36 Comité 9M colectivos
 to Paracas (day)

**PLACES TO STAY**
1 Hostal Residencial
 San Jorge
4 Posada Hispana
5 Hostal El César
6 Hostal Pisco
10 Hostal Josesito Moreno
12 Embassy Suites Hotel
14 Hostal El Candelabro
17 Regency Plaza Hotel
22 Hostal Callao
23 Hostal Belén
25 Hotel Embassy,
 Hotel Comercio
26 Hotel Colonial
27 San Jorge Suite Hotel
29 Hostal Las Américas
30 Hotel Regidor
32 Hostal Peru

To Restaurant As de Oros,
Embassy Beach Hotel

To Panamericana

Cementerio

To San Andrés,
Paracas

rooms with TV and private hot shower for US$15/24. The *Hostal Las Américas* (☎ 53-3905, fax 53-2948, Beatita de Huamay 150) is similar, though the rooms are smaller. Other places with decent standard rooms are *Hostal El Candelabro* (☎/fax 53-2620, in Lima 435-2156), which is at Callao and Pedemonte, has a café and charges US$17/25 for singles/doubles, and the *Embassy Suites Hotel* (☎ 53-5215, 53-5216, ☎/fax 53-2040, San Martín 202), which has larger rooms with telephones for US$18/29. The *Hotel Regidor* (☎/fax 53-5219, Arequipa 201) has pleasant rooms and bathrooms with bathtubs. Rates are US$20/30 including continental breakfast.

About 1.5km west of town is the *Embassy Beach Hotel* (☎ 53-2568, fax 53-2256, in Lima 435-1951, San Martín 1119). Despite its name, the Embassy Beach Hotel is several hundred meters from the beach. It offers a pleasant swimming pool, a small children's playground, a restaurant and a bar; as well as modern rooms with TV, telephone and minirefrigerator for US$40/50 (one bed) or $60 (two beds or one king-sized bed). They arrange island tours for US$10.

In Paracas, 15km south of Pisco, *El Mirador* (☎ 66-5842) is in the sand dunes at the entrance to town. It charges about US$40 (per person including meals) during holiday periods, and only US$18/25 singles/doubles at other times of the year, when it is often empty.

**Top End** In Paracas, the *Hotel Paracas* (☎ 22-1736, 22-7022, fax 22-5379, 22-7023, in Lima 447-0781, fax 447-6548) is on the bay and is the best, with an excellent (though expensive) dining room, and a garden complete with a swimming pool, a kid's pool, swings, miniature golf, table tennis, and paddle-boat rental. Kids like it. It's also a good spot to see the amazilia hummingbird, and birdwatchers often use this hotel as a base for birding in the area. Singles/doubles cost about US$65/85 from December to April, less in other months. The rooms are fairly standard, but boast pleasant porches. The hotel organizes trips to the Islas Ballestas that cost twice as much as the trips

from Pisco, but it offers English-speaking guides and better, faster boats. The restaurant and bar are open to people who are not guests, as is the small gift shop, where books about the area can be bought.

## Places to Eat & Drink

A few cafés on the Plaza de Armas are open early enough for simple breakfasts before a Ballestas tour and stay open all day. None are especially noteworthy. *La Catedral*, on Plaza Belén, and *El Dorado*, on Plaza de Armas, are both quite good for meals during the day. Shoestring travelers will find basic, cheap meals in several places on Mancera in the block east of Comercio.

There are several places to try on El Bulevar. *El Catamarán* (Comercio 166) is quite good and has Italian specialities. *Don Manuel* (Comercio 179) is one of Pisco's best, charging US$3 to US$8 for meals. A few blocks west of the Plaza de Armas, the *As de Oros* (San Martín 472) is also very good and similarly priced.

Fresh seafood is served in the port of El Chaco (the embarkation point for the Islas Ballestas), which is about 13km south of Pisco. There are several restaurants on the shore that are moderately priced, and although they're not fancy, the food is good.

A local catch sold in some restaurants is turtle – this is reportedly both endangered and protected, but unfortunately still winds up on the menu. Don't encourage the catching of turtles by ordering dishes made with turtle meat.

## Getting There & Away

Bear in mind that Pisco is about 5km west of the Carretera Panamericana, and many coastal buses traveling between Lima and Ica or Nazca don't stop there. There are direct buses to Pisco from both Lima and Ica. If you're not on a direct bus, make sure you ask if the bus goes into Pisco, or you may be left at the turnoff. Local buses between the turnoff and Pisco stop by frequently and charge US$0.30.

The Ormeño bus company has a terminal a block away from Plaza de Armas. Buses leave for Lima (US$3.50, 4 hours) roughly every hour. Ormeño also has several buses a day to Ica (1½ hours) and Nazca (US$3.50, 4 hours), and three buses a day to Arequipa (US$11, 12 to 15 hours). None of these buses goes directly; for example, Ormeño puts you on one of their Lima buses to the Panamericana and has you wait at their 'terminal' (a shack) to connect with southbound buses. They guarantee a seat, and the system works. Note that Arequipa buses leave in the afternoon and travel overnight. Buses go up to Ayacucho (US$5, 7 hours) at 10 am, 6 pm, and 10 pm. The road is now paved to Ayacucho, and more-frequent service may be available.

Other long-distance bus companies include Empresa José de San Martín, with 10 daily buses to Lima and eight direct buses to Ica (US$0.70). SAKY also has frequent service to Ica. These latter companies are easier to use than Ormeño.

## Getting Around

Comité 9M colectivos to Paracas leave from near the market about every half hour and charge US$0.50. At dusk, buses leave from closer to the town center. Buses for San Clemente (where you catch long-distance northbound and southbound buses on the Panamericana) leave frequently from near the market. At night, these buses (Comité 7M colectivos) leave from another location closer to the center of town (see map) to avoid the dangerous market area.

A taxi around town charges about US$0.50, to San Clemente about US$1.60 and to Paracas about US$3.

There is also a small private **zoo** almost a kilometer from the Panamericana at marker Km 235. Cabdrivers know it and can take you there.

## ICA
☎ 034

Ica is a pleasant colonial town of about 150,000 people. Founded by Jerónimo Luis de Cabrera in 1563, it is the capital of the Department of Ica and is about 305km south of Lima and 80km from Pisco. The Carretera Panamericana heads inland from Pisco, rising gently to 420m above sea level at Ica. Because of this, the town sits above

the coastal *garúa* (sea mist), and the climate is dry and sunny. The desert surrounding Ica is noted for its huge sand dunes.

Ica is irrigated by the river of the same name, and the oasis is famous for its grapes. There is a thriving wine and pisco industry, and some distilleries and wineries can be visited. There are attractive colonial churches, an excellent museum and several annual fiestas.

The 1998 El Niño was disastrous in Ica. The Plaza de Armas was flooded a meter deep. The plaza was rebuilt within a few months, but many streets away from the center are still being repaired. Local transport has been disrupted; ask where local buses leave from.

## Information

**Tourist Office** This is at Grau 150. Hours are 8 am to 2:30 pm weekdays. Report losses and problems to the Tourism Police (☎ 22-4553), on Prolongación Arenales, at the Policia Nacional at the southwest end of town.

**Money** The Banco de Crédito on the Plaza de Armas changes traveler's checks and cash and has a Visa ATM. Banco Latino, at Cajamarca 170, has a MasterCard ATM. Moneychangers on the plaza will also change cash.

**Post & Communications** There are several post office branches; one is on Municipalidad just off the plaza. The telephone office on the plaza is open from 7 am to 11 pm. Several places advertise Internet access, but none of them are for the public. This will probably soon change.

**Dangers & Annoyances** I have received reports (as recently as late 1998) of theft in Ica. Stay alert, particularly in the bus terminal and market areas.

## Wineries

Wineries and distilleries (called *bodegas*) can be visited year round, but the best time is during the grape harvest, from late February until early April. At other times, there's not much to see.

# ICA

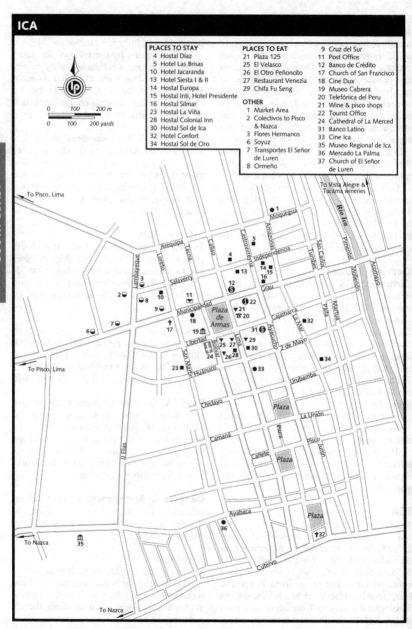

**PLACES TO STAY**
4  Hostal Díaz
5  Hotel Las Brisas
10 Hotel Jacaranda
13 Hotel Siesta I & II
14 Hostal Europa
15 Hostal Inti, Hotel Presidente
16 Hostal Silmar
23 Hostal La Viña
28 Hostal Colonial Inn
30 Hostal Sol de Ica
32 Hotel Confort
34 Hostal Sol de Oro

**PLACES TO EAT**
21 Plaza 125
25 El Velasco
26 El Otro Peñoncito
27 Restaurant Venezia
29 Chifa Fu Seng

**OTHER**
1  Market Area
2  Colectivos to Pisco & Nazca
3  Flores Hermanos
6  Soyuz
7  Transportes El Señor de Luren
8  Ormeño
9  Cruz del Sur
11 Post Office
12 Banco de Crédito
17 Church of San Francisco
18 Cine Dux
19 Museo Cabrera
20 Telefónica del Peru
21 Wine & pisco shops
22 Tourist Office
24 Cathedral of La Merced
31 Banco Latino
33 Cine Ica
35 Museo Regional de Ica
36 Mercado La Palma
37 Church of El Señor de Luren

The best of Peru's wine comes from the **Tacama and Ocucaje wineries**. Unfortunately, they are fairly isolated. The **Vista Alegre winery** makes reasonable wine and is the easiest of the large commercial wineries to visit. In addition to wine, they are a large producer of pisco. Some smaller, family-run wineries can also be visited.

To get to the Vista Alegre winery, walk across the Grau bridge and take the second left turnoff. It's about a 3km walk, and all the locals know it. However, this walk goes through a rough neighborhood, so you may want to take a taxi or bus. It's best to go in the morning, as the winery often closes in the afternoon, despite a sign to the contrary. Reportedly, it closes completely in November. About 8km farther is the Tacama winery, but no buses go there, so hire a taxi. The Ocucaje winery is about 36km south of Ica and a short distance off the Carretera Panamericana. Again, hire a taxi to get there.

The easiest of the small local bodegas to visit are in the suburbs of **Guadalupe**, about 3km from Ica on the road to Lima. There are local buses. In Guadalupe, you'll find the **Bodegas Peña**, **Lovera** and **El Carmel** within a block or two of the plaza. These are very small operations compared to the larger wineries. There are many stalls selling huge bottles of various kinds of piscos and wines.

The tourist office recommends the **Bodega Catador**, which is 7km or 8km south of Ica and can be reached by local bus or taxi. Apart from wine and pisco, they have a gift shop and a restaurant with dancing in the evenings during the harvest. They give tours and explain the wine- and pisco-making process.

Local wines and piscos are sold on Ica's Plaza de Armas.

## Museo Regional de Ica

Don't miss this museum in the southwestern suburbs; it's about 1.5km from the city center and can be reached by taking bus No 17 from the Plaza de Armas. It's also a pleasant walk. The museum is open 8 am to 6 pm weekdays, 9 am to 6 pm on Saturday and 9 am to 1 pm on Sunday. Admission is US\$2.50, or US\$1 for students with ID. There is an extra fee for cameras or video

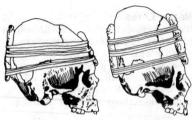

**Pre-Inca method of beautifying skulls**

recorders. This is one of the best small regional museums in Peru. It is very informative and well laid out, and because it's fairly small, you don't feel overwhelmed and can learn a great deal. Interesting maps and paintings can be bought as souvenirs.

There are excellent collections of artifacts from the Paracas, Nazca and Inca cultures and some superb examples of Paracas weavings, as well as textiles made from feathers. There are beautiful Nazca ceramics, well-preserved mummies, trepanned skulls and trophy heads, *quipus* (the knotted strings used by the Incas as mnemonic devices) and many other objects.

## Museo Cabrera

The Cabrera stone museum is on the Plaza de Armas. There's no sign, but you'll find it at Bolívar 170. It's a quirky museum, consisting of a collection of thousands of carved stones and boulders that depict pre-Columbian surgical techniques and day-to-day living. The owner, Dr Javier Cabrera (who is a descendant of the city's founder) claims that these stones are hundreds of years old, but most authorities don't believe him. You can see some of the stones in the museum entrance, but a proper look at them and a guided tour costs US\$5. The museum opens at 9 am, but closing hours vary, and it is usually closed on Sunday.

## Churches

The rather bare **Church of San Francisco** has some fine stained-glass windows. **La Merced**, the cathedral, was rebuilt in 1874 and contains finely carved wooden altars. The **Church of El Señor de Luren** boasts an image of the Lord that is venerated by pilgrims biannually.

## Nazca Lines

It's much cheaper to fly over the Lines from Nazca (see Nazca later in this chapter) but if you're in a hurry, you can do it from Ica for about US$105 per person. A minimum of three people is required. Ask at the Hotel Las Dunas Sun Resort (see Places to Stay later in this section), which has an airstrip.

## Special Events

Ica has more than its share of fiestas. The most famous is the wine-harvest festival held during the first half of March. It's called the Fiesta de la Vendimia. There are processions and beauty contests, cockfights and horse shows, arts and crafts, music and dancing, and of course, free-flowing pisco and wine drinking. The festival site is the Campo Feriado, on the outskirts, and there is a small entry fee. During the week, tasting and buying wine, honey and other food seems to be the thing to do. Most of the other events are held in the evenings or weekends.

In October, the religious pilgrimage of El Señor de Luren culminates in a traditional all-night procession; dates vary. Holy Week celebrations are also quite fervent.

The Carnaval de Yunza takes place in February. Participants dress in beautiful costumes, and there is public dancing. One dance involves circling a tree until it is pulled down. There is also the water-throwing typical of any Latin American carnaval.

The founding of the city on June 17, 1563, is celebrated every June during Ica Week. The more important Ica Tourist Festival is held in the latter half of September.

## Places to Stay

Following the 1998 floods and subsequent street reconstruction, hotels may have water problems. All hotels raise their prices substantially during the festivals, especially during the Fiesta de la Vendimia, when hotels are often fully booked and rates double or even triple in the cheapest hotels. The prices below are average nonfestival rates. The lowest rates are usually during April, May, June, September, November and December. Other months coincide with the Peruvian coastal summer or northern-hemisphere vacation periods.

**Budget** The *Hotel Confort* (☎ 23-3072, La Mar 257) is clean and adequate, and charges US$4 per person for a room with private bath and tepid electric showers. The *Hostal Sol de Oro* (☎ 23-3735, La Mar 371) is clean and friendly and charges US$7/9 singles/doubles with private bath and hot water on request, or US$5/7 with communal showers. The *Hotel Presidente* (☎ 22-5977, Amazonas 223) is good and clean at US$6/9 with bath and hot water. The *Hostal Europa* (Independencia 258) is about US$4/6 for singles/doubles. The rooms are basic, but the beds are clean, and there's a washbasin in each room. The similarly priced *Hostal Díaz* (Independencia 167) is clean and has some rooms with private, cold-water bath for an extra couple of dollars. The *Hostal Colonial Inn* (☎ 21-5582, Lima 262) has basic, clean rooms with communal tepid showers for US$5/8; they claim to be part of the Hostelling International chain. The *Hotel Jacaranda* (☎ 23-2582, Salaverry 355) is a decent basic hotel that charges US$8 for a double with private electric shower. The *Hostal Inti* (☎ 23-3141, Amazonas 235) charges US$5/9 for basic rooms with private cold showers. The *Hostal La Viña* (☎ 22-1043), at San Martín and Huánuco, charges about US$6/8, or US$8/10 for rooms with private bath and hot water.

**Mid-Range** The clean *Hotel Las Brisas* (☎ 23-2737, Castrovirreyna 246) is secure and has rooms with good beds and hot showers for US$11/15. You may need to ask at the desk to have the hot water turned on. The *Hotel Siesta I* (☎ 23-3249, Independencia 194) and the *Hotel Siesta II* (☎ 23-1045, Independencia 160) both have adequate rooms with hot showers and TV for US$17/20. The *Hostal Silmar* (☎ 23-5089, Castrovirreyna 110) has clean carpeted rooms with private bath, TV and telephone for US$17/20. The clean *Hostal Sol de Ica* (☎ 23-6165, fax 23-6168, Lima 265) has small rooms with private bath, TV and telephone at US$20/25. They've had problems with no hot water in the showers. There is also a swimming pool.

A couple of kilometers out of town, **Hostal Los Medanos** (☎ 25-6666), at the 300km marker on the Carretera Panamericana, is pleasant and charges US$20 per double.

**Top End** Out on the Panamericana are more good hotels. The pleasant, colonial-style **Hostal El Carmelo** (☎ 23-2191, in Lima 444-9500), at the 301km marker, has a swimming pool, restaurant and a small winery on the premises. Nice rooms are about US$33/40. The fairly luxurious **Hotel Las Dunas Sun Resort** (☎ 25-6226, in Lima 221-7020, 442-1470, fax 442-4180), at the 300km marker, has comfortable rooms with TV at US$70/85 weekdays and US$90/100 on weekends and holidays. More expensive are suites with a whirlpool bath. The resort offers a swimming pool with water slide, two tennis courts, a small golf course, a children's playground, sandboard rental, a sauna, horseback riding and Nazca Lines overflights and other excursions.

## Places to Eat
There are many cheap restaurants on the streets leading off the Plaza de Armas. Both streets Lima and Municipalidad have several.

The **Restaurant Venezia**, on Lima just off the Plaza de Armas, serves good pizza, as well as more expensive meat and fish dishes, in the $6 to $9 range. Opposite, the **Chifa Fu Seng** has various set meals for US$2. **Plaza 125**, on the plaza, serves hamburgers and chicken. Also on the plaza is **El Velasco**, which serves good cakes, desserts and coffee.

**El Otro Peñoncito** (Bolívar 255) is very clean and serves good meals of all kinds in the US$5 to US$10 range – it's the most upscale restaurant in the town center.

## Entertainment
There's not much happening in Ica outside of fiesta times. Of the two cinemas shown on the map, the **Cine Dux** has the better of a poor movie selection.

## Getting There & Away
**Air** A small local airport used to have scheduled flights from Lima, but doesn't at this time. AeroCóndor has tourist trips over the Nazca Lines.

**Bus** Ica is a main bus destination on the Carretera Panamericana and is easy to get to from Lima, Nazca and Arequipa.

Most of the bus companies are clustered around the west end of Salaverry, so it's easy to wander around comparing prices and schedules. For Lima (4 to 5 hours), Soyuz (☎ 23-3312) has departures every 20 minutes for US$4.50. Cheaper but less frequent service to Lima is available with Cruz del Sur (☎ 22-3333), Ormeño (☎ 21-5600), Transportes El Señor de Luren (☎ 22-3658), Flores Hermanos and others. If going to Pisco, make sure your bus is entering town and not dropping you on the Panamericana 5km from Pisco (though you can easily get a local bus from the junction into Pisco during the day). The easiest way to reach Pisco is to listen for conductors yelling 'Pisco' at the end of Salaverry. Most of the above companies have buses to Nazca during the day, but services to Arequipa (US$10) all seem to be at night. Colectivos and minibuses for Pisco and Nazca leave from Lambayeque at Salaverry when they are full and charge a bit more than buses.

Transportes Oropesa (inside the Flores Hermanos terminal) has overnight buses to Huancavelica leaving at 5:30 pm.

## Getting Around
Ask where buses for Huacachina and Guadalupe leave. They have changed stops since the 1998 flood.

## HUACACHINA
About 5km west of Ica, this tiny resort village nestles next to a small **lagoon** (featured on the back of the S/50 note) surrounded by huge sand dunes. Peruvians swim here because the water is supposed to have curative properties, though it looks murky and uninviting. The surroundings

are pretty – graceful palm trees, colorful flowers, attractive buildings in pastel shades and a backdrop of giant dunes. It's a pleasant side trip from Ica and a very quiet place to rest.

The sand dunes invite hiking and playing. It is possible to rent sandboards for US$1.50 an hour if you want to slide, surf, ski or whatever down the dunes and get sand into all kinds of body nooks and crannies that you probably didn't even want to know. But be careful, for several people have injured themselves (and at least one was killed) when their sandboards went out of control.

### Places to Stay & Eat

There are two hotels, and both are around the lagoon. To the right of the bus stop is the attractive pink *Hotel Mossone* (☎ *21-3630, fax 23-6137, in Lima 221-7020, 442-1470, fax 442-4180*), which has been recently renovated and has simple but stylish rooms around a pleasant courtyard. There is a nice restaurant and an elegant bar, both overlooking the lagoon and a swimming pool. Bicycles and sandboards can be rented. The rooms all have private hot shower and a TV (two channels), and rates are US$50/60 in air-conditioned rooms. Walk-in travelers can get a double without air-conditioning for US$30. One reader reports that the hotel was built in the 1940s by Nazis who escaped from Europe – I don't know if that's true or not.

A little further around the lagoon is the blue *Gran Hotel Salvatierra*, which has doubles for US$8. Ask around for cheap *family hostels* at US$4 per person.

Some people have not been able to resist sleeping in the sand dunes. Beware of thieves.

The Hotel Mossone is the best place to eat. There are several inexpensive restaurants and food vendors by the lagoon, or you could bring a picnic lunch.

### Getting There & Away

Buses leave two or three times an hour from Ica, take 20 minutes and charge US$0.30. A taxi charges about US$1.

## NAZCA
☎ 034

From Ica, the Panamericana heads roughly southeast, passing through the small oasis of Palpa (which is famous for its orange groves), then rises slowly through arid coastal mountains to Nazca, which is 598m above sea level and around 450km south of Lima. Although only a small town of about 30,000 people, Nazca is frequently visited by travelers interested in the Nazca culture and the world-famous Nazca Lines.

A disastrous earthquake in 1996 destroyed about 70% of the town, killing several people and injuring 500. The town's small museum (on the Plaza de Armas) was completely destroyed and has not yet been rebuilt. The government provided loans for rebuilding, and the tourism industry continues unabated. In 1998, Maria Reiche, the famed German mathematician, longtime resident of Nazca and researcher of the Nazca Lines, died at the age of 95. Her house, near the Nazca Lines, is reportedly being turned into a museum.

### History

Like the Paracas culture to the north, the ancient Nazca culture was lost in the drifting desert sands and forgotten until this century. In 1901, the Peruvian archaeologist Max Uhle was the first to excavate the Nazca sites and to realize that he was dealing with a culture distinct from other coastal peoples. Before his discovery, only five Nazca ceramics were known in museums, and no one knew how to classify them. After 1901, thousands of ceramics were found. Most were discovered by *huaqueros* (grave robbers), who plundered burial sites and sold their finds to interested individuals or museums. Despite the amateurish and destructive excavations of the huaqueros, archaeologists have been able to construct a fairly accurate picture of the Nazca culture.

The Nazca culture developed as a result of the disintegration of the Paracas culture around 200 AD. It is divided into three periods: early (200 AD to 500 AD), late (500 AD to 700 AD) and terminal (700 AD to

800 AD). These periods coincide with the types of ceramics studied by archaeologists. Because ceramics are typically better preserved than items made of cloth or wood and are often decorated with representations of everyday life, they are the most important tools for unraveling Peru's ancient past. The designs on the Nazca ceramics depict their plants and animals, fetishes and divinities, musical instruments and household items, as well as the people themselves.

The early Nazca ceramics were very colorful and showed a greater variety of naturalistic designs than later periods. Pots with double necks joined by a stirrup handle have often been found, as well as shallow cups and plates. In the late period, the decoration was more stylized. (The decorations were, in all cases, much more stylized than the rigorously natural styles of the contemporary Moche culture of the northern coast.) The designs painted on the ceramics of the terminal period are poorer and influenced by the Wari culture from the highlands.

Even the most casual observer will soon learn to recognize the distinctive Nazca style. The colors are vivid, and the stylized designs are painted directly onto the ceramic rather than being molded. The effect is strong and attractive. Nazca ceramics can be seen in the museums of Lima and Ica.

## Information

**Money** The Banco de Crédito changes traveler's checks, as do some of the hotels geared toward international tourists.

**Post & Communications** These offices are marked on the map. The Hotel Alegría has public Internet access for US$2 per hour. Nazca Trails Tour Agency also provides email access to travelers.

**Dangers & Annoyances** Robberies on the local land tours have been reported, but they now rarely happen. It's best to go with a reliable agency.

The greatest annoyance for foreign travelers is arriving by bus and being met by touts

trying to sell air and land tours or bring travelers to certain hotels. This happens all over Peru in tourist areas, but Nazca is one of the most annoying. Most of these touts will use the names of places listed below, but aren't to be trusted. They'll tell you anything you want to hear to get you to follow them so they can get a commission. If you do go with a street tout, don't hand over any money until you can talk to the hotel or tour company owner and get a confirmed itinerary in writing.

**Tour Agencies** The biggest tour agency is Alegría Tours, at the Hotel Alegría (☎/fax 52-2444, 52-2702; see Places to Stay later in this section). They offer all the tours described below, plus some off-the-beaten-track options. Their tours are expensive for one or two people, so ask to join up with other travelers to get a group discount if necessary. This is usually easy to arrange. They are reliable, and I have received mostly favorable reports about Alegría's services. They provide guides in English and French, and German in some cases. They also represent Alas Peruanas, which does overflights of the Nazca Lines from both Nazca and Pisco.

Nasca Trails (☎ 52-3710, ☎/fax 52-2858, fax 52-1290, nasca@correo.dnet.com.pe, Bolognesi 550), a smaller agency recommended by several readers, is run by the friendly and multilingual Juan Tohalino Vera. He is an experienced official guide who now manages the agency (and occasionally gives tours) and who speaks excellent English, as well as German, French and Italian. He can arrange tours in those languages. Juan is planning on building his own hotel and giving other agencies a run for their money. I enjoyed the tour he arranged for me with Orlando (Bito) J Flores E (☎ 52-1040), who speaks English.

One of the oldest agencies is at the Hotel Nazca (see Places to Stay later in this section), which provides some of the cheapest but less reliable accommodations, overflights and tours in Nazca. Shoestring travelers wanting to save a few dollars may find this their cheapest option, but be careful. I have

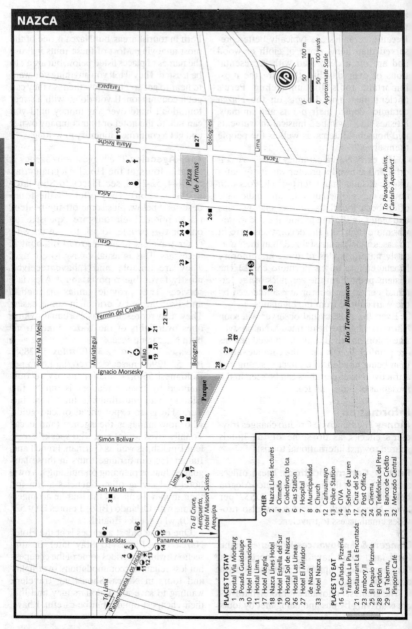

**NAZCA**

To Paradones Ruins,
Cantallo Aqueduct →

*Rio Tierras Blancas*

**PLACES TO STAY**
1   Hostal Vía Morburg
3   Posada Guadalupe
10  Hotel Internacional
11  Hostal Lima
17  Hotel Alegría
18  Nazca Lines Hotel
19  Hostal Estrella del Sur
20  Hostal Sol de Nasca
26  Hostal Las Lineas
27  Hotel El Mirador
    de Nasca
33  Hotel Nasca

**PLACES TO EAT**
16  La Cañada, Pizzeria
    Tratoria La Pua
21  Restaurant La Encantada
23  Jambory II
25  El Puquio Pizzeria
28  El Portón
29  La Taberna,
    Pinpoint Café

**OTHER**
2   Nazca Lines lectures
4   Ormeño
5   Colectivos to Ica
6   Gas Station
7   Hospital
8   Municipalidad
9   Church
12  Carhuamayo
13  Police Station
14  CIVA
15  Señor de Luren
17  Cruz del Sur
22  Post Office
24  Cinema
30  Telefónica del Peru
31  Banco de Crédito
32  Mercado Central

To El Cruce,
Aeropuerto,
Hotel Maison Suisse,
Arequipa

To Lima

Panamericana (Los Incas)

0      50      100 m
0      50      100 yards
Approximate Scale

received mixed reports, including letters from travelers who have been ripped off by touts at the bus stop using the Hotel Nazca name.

The five or so companies that fly over the Lines have offices in the Nazca airport but not in the town. The best, biggest and most expensive company is AeroCóndor (☎ 52-2424), which also has offices in Lima and Ica. The second biggest is AeroIca, which has offices in the Hostal Maison Suisse (opposite the Nazca airport) and in Lima. These and others work primarily with agencies in town. Going to the airport to arrange a flight is not reliable, but you could save a few dollars if you get lucky.

## The Nazca Lines

Once, while traveling on a bus to Nazca, I was amazed to find that one of my (gringo) traveling companions hadn't heard of the Nazca Lines. I naively thought that anyone going to Nazca would have heard all about them. So, what are the Nazca Lines?

Actually, no one completely knows. They are huge geometric designs drawn in the desert and visible only from the air. They were made by the simple expedient of removing the darker sun-baked stones from the surface of the desert and piling them up on either side of the Lines, thus exposing the lighter-colored soil (heavily laden with gypsum) below. Some designs represent a variety of giant animals – such as a 180m-long lizard, a 90m-long monkey with an extravagantly curled tail or a condor with a 130m wingspan. Others are simple but perfect triangles, rectangles or straight lines running for several kilometers across the desert. There are several dozen different figures. The best-known Lines are found in the desert about 20km north of Nazca.

The questions remain: Who constructed the Lines and why? And how did they know what they were doing when the Lines can only be properly appreciated from the air? Maria Reiche, who made the most thorough studies of the Lines, considered that they were made by the Paracas and Nazca cultures during the period from 900 BC to 600 AD, with some additions by the Wari settlers from the highlands in the 7th century. She theorized that the Lines were an astronomical calendar for agricultural purposes.

This explanation is by no means widely accepted by others. Tony Morrison considers the Lines to be ritual walkways linking *huacas* or sites of ceremonial significance. Jim Woodman thinks the Nazca people knew how to construct hot-air balloons and that they did, in fact, observe the Lines from the air. Johann Reinhard has a theory that involves mountain worship. Erich von

KEVIN SCHAFER

**One of the many mysterious Nazca Lines**

Daniken thinks that the Lines are extraterrestrial landing sites. There are other theories.

**Seeing the Nazca Lines** The best way to fully appreciate this enormous archaeological mystery is to take a flight over the Lines. Most people fly from Nazca because flying from Lima or Ica is much more expensive. Although you can make reservations in Lima, it's cheaper to make arrangements when you arrive in Nazca. You can almost always fly on the day you want. Flights can be booked at any of the popular tourist hotels, which will provide transport to the airport, about 3km south of town.

Flights are taken in light aircraft (three to nine seats) in the mornings and early afternoons. There's no point expecting punctuality, because flights depend on the weather. Planes won't take off until there is reasonable visibility, and there's often a low mist over the desert until it warms up at about 9 or 10 am. Strong winds in the late afternoon make flying impractical then. Passengers are usually taken on a first-come, first-served basis, with priority given to those who have made reservations in Lima. Don't worry: 9 times out of 10 there's room for everyone. The flight usually lasts 30 to 45 minutes.

Flight costs have varied considerably in the past. Most recently, they ranged from US$30 to US$40, depending on the company and season (June to August are the busiest months), though occasionally they drop below US$30 or climb above US$50. In addition, there is an airport tax of US$2.

The small aircraft bank left and right so that passengers on both sides can see the Lines. I suggest that you don't eat breakfast before the overflight, and take medication if you are prone to motion sickness. If you feel ill during the flight, looking at the horizon helps.

If you can't or don't want to fly, you can get an idea of what the Lines look like from the *mirador* (observation tower), built on the side of the Carretera Panamericana about 20km north of Nazca. From the top of the mirador, you get an oblique view of three of the figures (lizard, tree and hands), but it's not very good. Don't walk on the Lines, because it's illegal, it damages them and you can't see anything from the ground anyway. To get to the mirador, either take a taxi or catch a northbound bus in the morning and hitchhike back. Don't leave too late, as there's little traffic. You can also take a Nazca Lines mirador tour.

**Nazca Lines Lectures** Lectures about the Nazca Lines, with insights into Maria Reiche's work, are held most evenings at M Bastidas 218. They are free, but US$2 donations are suggested. Signs outside give lecture times. The lectures are given by Viktoria Nikitzki, an English-speaking Austrian who lives in Nazca and was friends with Maria Reiche for the last 10 years of Reiche's life. Nikitzki is also very knowledgeable about the area and is involved in work to reopen a local museum.

### Other Excursions

Many people come to Nazca, take an overflight and go on, but there's a lot more to see. The tour agencies mentioned earlier in this section organize inexpensive and reliable guided tours. Cabdrivers and guides on the street don't know much. Most tours will also include a stop at a potter's and/or goldminer's workshop for a demonstration of the pot-making or gold-mining process. Both demonstrations are worth seeing and include watching the potter form a lump of clay into a perfect hollow sphere in minutes. You should leave a tip or buy a souvenir.

**Cemetery of Chauchilla** One of the most popular tours is to this cemetery, 30km away. Here you'll see bones, skulls, mummies, pottery shards and fragments of cloth dating back to between 1000 and 1300 AD. A few years ago, mummies were visibly sitting on the surface; now they are seen inside 12 tombs below the ground. The extensive cemetery still has bone and cloth fragments littering the ground, though you must now walk a demarcated trail. The tour takes about three hours and costs US$5 to US$12 per person two-person minimum). Entrance is about US$1 (ask if it is included in the tour fee).

**Paredones Ruins & Cantallo Aqueducts** The Paradones ruins (2km southeast of town via Arica over the river) are not very well preserved, but the underground aqueducts (5km farther), built by the Nazcas, are still in working order and provide irrigation to the nearby fields. The stonework is quite fine, and it is possible to enter the aqueducts through the *ventanas* (windows), which the local people use when they clean the aqueducts annually (a wet and claustrophobic experience). Admission is US$1 to the aqueducts. Tours are available for about US$5 per person (four-passenger minimum). You can walk there; don't carry valuables.

**Other Sites** West of the Lines is Cahuachi, the most important known Nazca center. But it is poorly preserved, less visited and harder to get to (25km of dirt road) than the sites mentioned earlier. Tours (3½ hours) include a couple of other minor sites.

Reserva Nacional Pampas Galeras is a vicuña sanctuary high in the mountains 90km east of Nazca and is the best place to see these animals in Peru, though tourist services are virtually nonexistent. In late May or early June is the annual *chaccu*, when local inhabitants round up the vicuñas for shearing and ceremonies.

## Places to Stay
**Budget** The *Hotel Nazca* (☎ 52-2085, *Lima 438*) has basic rooms with communal tepid showers for US$4/7 singles/doubles. Ticket touts hang around offering cheap tours – don't pay for anything until you have it in writing. The *Hotel Alegría* is a mid-range hotel (see Places to Stay – Mid-Range) that keeps its original 13 basic but clean rooms for budget travelers at US$4 per person. These rooms share two bathrooms with hot showers.

The new *Hotel Estrella del Sur* (☎ 52-2764, *Callao 568*) has small but clean rooms with private electric shower and TV. They are a good value at US$7/12 including continental breakfast. The small, family-run *Posada Guadalupe* (☎ 52-2249, *San Martín 225*) is clean, quiet and friendly, with a little garden. Rooms are US$7/12 with private bath and

electric hot showers. There are some cheaper rooms with shared showers. The *Hostal Lima* (☎ 55-22497, *Los Incas 117*), opposite the Ormeño bus terminal, is quite nice and has hot water. Rooms with shared bath are US$7/12, and rooms with private bath are US$8/15, but discounts are often given, especially if you arrange a tour with them.

The clean and secure *Hostal Vía Morburg* (☎ 52-2566, ☎/fax 52-3710, *José María Mejía at Maria Reiche*) has small rooms with cramped showers but lots of hot water for US$8/12. You can get a discount if you take a tour with Nazca Trails. They have a decent and reasonably priced restaurant on the top floor. The *Hotel Internacional* (☎ 55-2166, 52-2744, *Maria Reiche 112*) has basic but larger rooms with private hot showers for US$9/11; bigger bungalows with patios cost US$14 for a double. There's a secure parking lot.

**Mid-Range** The new *Hostal Sol de Nasca* (☎ 52-2730, *Callao 586*) has rooms with TV, telephone and private hot showers for US$11/15 including continental breakfast – a good deal. The *Hotel El Mirador de Nasca* (☎ 52-3121, *Tacna 436*), on the Plaza de Armas, has comfortable rooms with TV, telephone and private hot showers for US$14/21 including continental breakfast. Also on the plaza is the *Hostal Las Lineas* (☎ 52-2488, *Arica 299*), where carpeted rooms with TV and private hot showers cost US$15/22. There is a decent-looking restaurant.

Nazca's most overwhelming success story is Ephraim's *Hotel Alegría* (☎ /fax 52-2444, 52-2702, alegriatours@hotmail.com, *Lima 168*). Once a basic budget hotel, it has now expanded into the town's most popular (among tourists) mid-range hotel. It has a restaurant, bar, small garden, Internet service and a busy travel agency. Comfortable, carpeted rooms with private bath, TV and fan (some boast air-conditioning) are US$14/20; a few slightly older rooms are $15 for a double; basic budget rooms are available (see Places to Stay earlier in this section).

**Top End** The best in town is the *Nazca Lines Hotel* (☎ 52-2293, fax 52-2112, *in Lima* ☎ 221-7020, 442-1470, fax 442-4180), on

SOUTH COAST

Bolognesi, which charges US$60/78. There is a large clean swimming pool, a tennis court, a good restaurant and a quiet lounge. They have 30 rooms and a few more expensive suites. All local tours are quickly arranged. Despite a sign saying that the pool is for guests only, travelers can use the pool if they eat at the hotel restaurant or pay a small fee.

The lovely converted hacienda *Hotel de la Borda* (☎ 52-2576, in Lima 442-6391, fax 440-8430) has pretty gardens and a nice pool, restaurant and bar. It's a few kilometers out of town beyond the airport, so take a taxi. The 39 rooms are large but simple (no TVs) and cost US$55/60, though large discounts are offered on a walk-in basis.

Opposite the airport is the *Hostal Maison Suisse* (☎ 52-2831, ☎/fax 52-2434, in Lima ☎/fax 444-2140). The hotel is comfortable and has a restaurant, bar and small swimming pool. There are 40 rooms with TV and telephone for US$47/58 each, or there are six air-conditioned suites with a Jacuzzi and minirefrigerator for US$104 each. This hotel is also the AeroIca office, and you get a discount if you fly over the Lines with them. The hotel has a large grassy area with hammocks where you can camp at no charge if you are flying with AeroIca.

## Places to Eat

Cheap meals can be found in the center in restaurants (none are noteworthy) near the Plaza de Armas and the market area. Most of the restaurants below cater to tourists and charge US$3 to US$10 for meals, though they'll usually do a set menu for US$2 to US$3.

*El Puquio Pizzería*, on Bolognesi just off the plaza, is a small friendly pizza place run by a charming older couple. *Jambory II* (*Bolognesi 226*) is a small clean place with pizzas, ice cream and Peruvian food. *Restaurant La Encantada*, on Callao at Fermin del Castillo, is also clean if characterless, but has good, reasonably priced food.

On Lima, near the Hotel Alegría, are two restaurants with nice atmosphere. *La Cañada* has good Peruvian food, and the *Pizzería Tratoria La Pua* has a limited and rather pricey Italian menu, but is quite good.

*La Taberna* (*Lima 321*) sometimes has live music on Saturday night and is popular with travelers. Next door, the *Pinpoint Café* offers espresso. *El Portón*, on Lima at Ignacio Morsesky, is one of the most upscale places, with a small patio and Italian and international food.

## Getting There & Away

**Air** You can fly to Nazca from Lima or Ica with AeroCóndor (sometimes with AeroIca). People who fly into Nazca normally fly over the Nazca Lines and return the same day.

**Bus** Nazca is a major destination for buses on the Carretera Panamericana and is easy to get to from Lima, Ica or Arequipa. Unfortunately, buses to Arequipa originate in Lima, and to buy a ticket with a seat, you have to pay the fare from Lima. Ormeño has several buses a day to Lima (US$6, 8 hours), as well as to intermediate points (Ica or Pisco). Señor de Luren (☎ 52-2337) also has several buses a day to Lima and Ica (US$1.75, 3½ hours). CIVA has an overnight bus to Lima.

For Arequipa (US$13.50, 8 to 11 hours), I couldn't find any day buses. Several Ormeño buses leave between 3:30 pm and 3 am. Opposite Ormeño, Carhuamayo has fairly comfortable buses to Arequipa. CIVA and Cruz del Sur (the office is at the Hotel Alegría) also have a late-night bus.

For Cuzco, most travelers go via Arequipa. However, you can go via Puquio and Abancay direct to Cuzco (US$18, 22 hours) at 5 and 10 pm with Empresa Wari, which is at El Cruce – the turnoff for the Puquio road about 2km south of town. There are other companies located along the inland portion of this route – over half of which has now been paved. The journey will be faster in the future, when paving has been completed. The route covers 4300m, and it can become very cold; carry warm clothes onto the bus.

**Colectivo** Fast colectivo taxis and slower minibuses to Ica (US$3, 2½ hours) leave when they are full (usually hourly during the day) from the Panamericana at Lima.

## CHALA
☎ 054

The first town of any importance on the Panamericana southeast of Nazca is the fishing village of Chala, about 170km away. In Inca times, fresh fish was sent by runners from here to Cuzco – an amazing effort. Chala's main attractions are fresh seafood and the opportunity to break the long journey to Arequipa, but most travelers just tough it out and keep going. Maybe that's a good reason to stop, as you won't see too many tourists.

The **Inca ruins** at Puerto Inca, 10km north of town, can be visited. Get there by heading north for 6km on the Panamericana, then turning left near Km 603 and following a dirt road for 4km to the coastal ruins. Also north of town in the desert is **Sacaco**, where the sand is made of crushed fossilized shells, and you might find fossilized crocodile teeth. There is a small site museum (US$2) in the middle of nowhere. You can take a taxi from Nazca to Chala with a stop at Sacaco, or take a taxi from Chala.

## Places to Stay & Eat

The best place is the *Hotel de Turistas* (☎ 50-1111, 50-1114, Comercio 601), at the south end of the beach. The veranda faces the ocean, but the bedrooms don't. It's a nice place for a coffee stop. The restaurant serves breakfast, lunch and dinner. Rooms are about US$26/33 for singles/doubles and have a TV, telephone and private hot shower. Opposite is *Hostal Otero* (☎ 50-1015, Comercio 600), with basic rooms and shared cold showers at US$5 a double. Farther along the beach is the basic *Hostal Grau* (☎ 50-1009, Comercio 701), which is clean and friendly with shared cold showers. Rates are US$4 for a double – ask for a room in the back with ocean views.

## CAMANÁ
☎ 054

From Chala, the Panamericana runs close to the coast until it reaches Camaná, about 220km away. The views of the ocean are often very good, as the highway tortuously clings to sand dunes dropping down to the sea.

Camaná is 175km from Arequipa, and the road is paved, so it's a popular summer beach resort with Arequipeños. The beaches are good, but are 5km from the center, so you must take the local bus to La Punta to visit them. At La Punta, there are private holiday bungalows, but no tourist facilities. Camaná is a convenient place to break the long journey to/from Arequipa.

The Banco de Crédito (9 de Noviembre 139) and Interbanc (28 de Julio 337) change money.

## Places to Stay

Hotels tend to be full during summer weekends (January to March). The basic *Hostal Lima* (☎ 57-2901, Lima 306) is clean and charges US$4 per person for rooms with communal baths and hot water, or US$8 for a double with private cold-water shower. The *Hostal Lider* (☎ 57-1474, Lima 268), next to the bus station, charges US$7/10 for singles/doubles in rooms with private hot showers.

The *Hostal Premier* (☎ 57-1008, García Carbajal 117) charges US$15 for a double with private bath, hot water and TV. Rooms with TV and telephone are US$18/25 including continental breakfast at *Hotel San Diego* (☎/fax 57-2854), on the corner of Ugarte and 28 de Julio, *Hostal Plaza* (☎ 57-1051, fax 57-1756), on the Plaza de Armas, and *Hotel de Turistas* (☎ /fax 57-1113, Lima 138), which has a garden.

## Getting There & Away

Cruz del Sur (☎ 57-1491, Lima 474), Flores Hermanos (☎ 57-1013, Lima 200) and Transportes Zeballos (☎ 57-1572, Lima 268) have the most frequent service.

## MOLLENDO
☎ 054

The Carretera Panamericana leaves the coast at Camaná and heads inland for 135km to the junction of Repartición. Here, a major branch road heads east into the Andes for 42km to Arequipa. The Panamericana turns south toward the coast, and after an additional 15km, it divides again. The southeastern branch goes on toward the Chilean border, while the southwestern branch goes to Mollendo.

This small port of 15,000 people is about 110km southwest of Arequipa and is a popular beach resort for Arequipeños during the January-to-March summer season, but is very quiet for the rest of the year, when the beaches

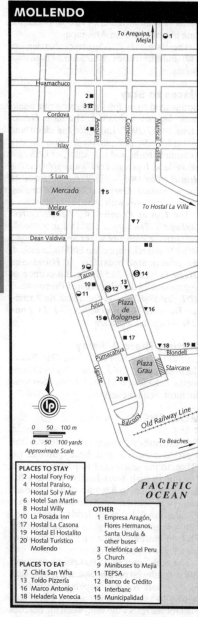

**MOLLENDO**

To Arequipa, Mejía

Huamachuco

Cordova

Islay

S Luna

Mercado

To Hostal La Villa

Melgar

Dean Valdivia

Tacna

Arica

Plaza de Bolognesi

Blondell

Pumacahua

Ugarte

Plaza Grau

Staircase

Balcón

Old Railway Line

To Beaches

0    50    100 m

0    50    100 yards

Approximate Scale

PACIFIC OCEAN

**PLACES TO STAY**
2  Hostal Fory Foy
4  Hostal Paraíso,
   Hostal Sol y Mar
6  Hotel San Martín
8  Hostal Willy
10 La Posada Inn
17 Hostal La Casona
19 Hostal El Hostalito
20 Hostal Turístico
   Mollendo

**PLACES TO EAT**
7  Chifa San Wha
13 Toldo Pizzería
16 Marco Antonio
18 Heladería Venecia

**OTHER**
1  Empresa Aragón,
   Flores Hermanos,
   Santa Ursula &
   other buses
3  Telefónica del Peru
5  Church
9  Minibuses to Mejía
11 TEPSA
12 Banco de Crédito
14 Interbanc
15 Municipalidad

are littered with dead animals. Mollendo is normally reached by road from Arequipa after traveling through desert with delicate brown, pink and gray colors, particularly attractive in the oblique light of early morning. Near La Joya are crescent-shaped gray sand dunes that look as if they have been deliberately poured in unlikely positions on the pinkish rock. Beyond the dunes, the desert becomes very rocky, with tortured-looking cacti eking out an existence in the salt-laden soil.

Mollendo is a pleasant town, with several plazas, attractive hilly streets and a beach. There are customs agencies and shipping offices, but most ships now dock in Matarani 15km to the northwest. One of the best reasons to visit Mollendo is to go to the nearby nature sanctuary at Mejía (see Mejía and the Río Tambo valley later in this chapter).

There is a Banco de Crédito and Interbanc; their locations are shown on the map.

## Places to Stay

Single rooms are difficult to obtain during weekends in the high season, when prices go up. Bargain in the low season. There are several cheap and basic hotels with cold-water showers that charge about US$4 per person. These include **Hostal Fory Foy** (*Arequipa 681*), which is clean and has some rooms with a private bath for a couple of dollars more. (The hostel was formerly named Hostal 45, which Peruvians pronounce as 'fory foy' – hence the odd name.) Others in this price range include the clean and friendly **Hotel San Martín** (with ocean views from the top floor), **La Posada Inn** and **Hostal Willy**.

The **Hostal Sol y Mar** (☎ 53-2265, *Arequipa 569*) has decent rooms for US$10/1. for singles/doubles with private bath and TV, or US$5 per person with communal showers. There is hot water. Next door is the similarly priced **Hostal Paraíso** (☎ 53-2126). **Hostal Turístico Mollendo** (☎ 53-3303 *Arequipa 101*) charges US$10/15 for decen rooms with private bath.

The **Hostal La Casona** (☎/fax 53-2453 *Arequipa 192*) has rooms with cable TV and hot water for US$17/22. **Hostal El Hostalit** (☎ 53-3674, *Blondell 169*) has similar ameni ties plus room telephones for US$19/26. The best is **Hostal La Villa** (☎ 53-5051, 53-4999, Mariscal Castilla 366), with a pool, pleasant garden, parking and restaurant. Clean, carpeted rooms with cable TV and telephone are about US$28/38.

### Places to Eat

The **Marco Antonio** (Comercio 254) is good for coffee and is reasonably priced. It is considered the best restaurant. Nearby, **Toldo Pizzería** serves Italian and other food.

Cheap restaurants are found along Calle Arequipa near the market. The **Chifa San Wha** (Comercio 412) is owned by the mayor of Mollendo and is a reasonable value for Chinese food. For ice cream and snacks, try the **Heladería Venecia**.

### Getting There & Away

The Mollendo-Arequipa train is for freight only.

Most bus terminals are on the 8th block of Mariscal Castilla, including Empresa Aragón (☎ 53-2506), Flores Hermanos (☎ 53-2977) and Santa Ursula (☎ 53-2173). These companies all have numerous departures to Arequipa (US$2, 2¾ hours). TEPSA (☎ 53-2872, Ugarte 320) runs four buses a week direct to Lima.

Minibuses (US$0.30) to the beach resort of Mejía leave from the corner of Tacna and Arequipa. Some continue through Mejía to the Río Tambo valley, La Curva, and Cocachacra to El Fiscal (US$1.50, 2 hours). Empresa Aragón also has buses to Mejía.

### MEJÍA & THE RÍO TAMBO VALLEY

This is an interesting area and is easily visited from Mollendo. Mejía is a summer beach resort for Arequipeños, and is a ghost town from April to December. There are plenty of private homes, a couple of snack bars and an excellent beach, but no hotels.

About 6km southeast of Mejía along the coastal road is the little-known **Santuario Nacional Lagunas de Mejía**. This 690-hectare sanctuary protects coastal lagoons that cover more than 100 hectares. They are the largest permanent lakes in 1500km of desert coastline, hence they attract great numbers of coastal and migratory bird species. Birdwatchers can take one of the morning buses from Mollendo to the Tambo valley or El Fiscal and get off at the reserve. There's a sign, and you can see the lagoons from the road. Buses pass about once an hour during the day.

The road continues along the Río Tambo valley, which has been transformed by an important irrigation project into rice paddies, sugarcane plantations and fields of potatoes and corn. The rice paddies are surrounded by walls of mud. It is interesting to see these huge agricultural areas with a sand-dune and desert backdrop. The road joins the Carretera Panamericana at El Fiscal, which has a gas station and an overpriced fly-blown restaurant. It's the only place in about 100km of desert road. You can wait here to flag down buses to Arequipa or Moquegua.

### MOQUEGUA

Moquegua is a dry and dusty town with some interesting buildings. Many of them, even the cathedral, are roofed with sugarcane stalks covered with dried mud – a type of wattle-and-daub construction. Although the town is built on the Río Moquegua, it is one of the driest towns in Peru and is where the Peruvian coastal desert reaches its driest point. It is here that the desert merges into the Atacama Desert of northern Chile – the driest in the world. The river manages to provide enough moisture for some agriculture (mainly grapes and avocados), but a couple of kilometers from the river, you would never believe that agriculture is possible anywhere nearby. Moquegua's grapes are the basis of Pisco Biondi – one of Peru's best piscos.

Moquegua has a population of about 10,000 and is the capital of the small department of the same name. It is 1412m above sea level and 220km southeast of Arequipa. The small and shady Plaza de Armas – with a wrought-iron fountain, flower gardens and some colonial architecture – is a welcome relief from the desert. It's a nice place to just sit and relax. Some readers told me that they enjoyed watching the old maintenance man on the Plaza de Armas, whose sole duty appears to be chasing the pigeons away from the fountains. Meanwhile, several vendors

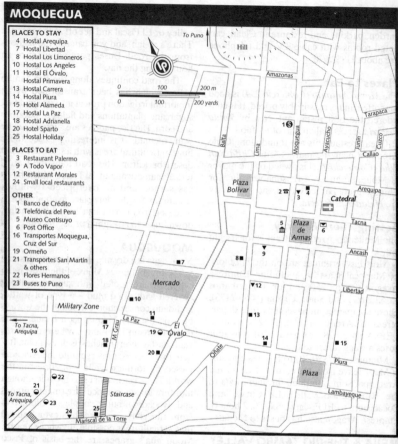

**MOQUEGUA**

PLACES TO STAY
4  Hostal Arequipa
7  Hostal Libertad
8  Hostal Los Limoneros
10  Hostal Los Angeles
11  Hostal El Óvalo,
     Hostal Primavera
13  Hostal Carrera
14  Hostal Piura
15  Hotel Alameda
17  Hostal La Paz
18  Hostal Adrianella
20  Hotel Sparto
25  Hostal Holiday

PLACES TO EAT
3  Restaurant Palermo
9  A Todo Vapor
12  Restaurant Morales
24  Small local restaurants

OTHER
1  Banco de Crédito
2  Telefónica del Peru
5  Museo Contisuyo
6  Post Office
16  Transportes Moquegua,
     Cruz del Sur
19  Ormeño
21  Transportes San Martín
     & others
22  Flores Hermanos
23  Buses to Puno

sell birdseed on the same plaza, resulting in a tragicomical scene that has been happening for years.

The Museo Contisuyo, on the Plaza de Armas, is an excellent new museum of local archaeology. Its exhibits are labeled in English and Spanish. Hours are 10 am to 12:30 pm and 3 to 5:30 pm Wednesday to Monday; 10 am to 1 pm and 4 to 8 pm on Tuesday.

Several other plazas offer pleasant and flowery places to sit. Walk around to see some of the typical local roofs – northeast of the plaza along Moquegua is one of many options.

People are friendly, and the rare foreign visitor doesn't get hassled. There really isn' much to do in Moquegua, but I found it…different. It's worth a stop if you aren't in a hurry

## Places to Stay

**Budget** Single rooms are few, and some hotels insist that single travelers pay the double-room rate if singles are full. As usual the cheapest and most basic are around the market, which seems safer than the marke areas in many Peruvian towns. Some hotel may be used for short stays but aren't sleazy Double rooms, some with bath but few with hot water, cost about US$5 to US$8 at the *Hostals El Óvalo, La Paz, Libertad, Los Angeles* and *Primavera*. Away from the market is the clean, quiet and secure *Hostal Carrera* (☎ 76-2113, *Lima 320)*, where singles with shared bath are US$3.50 and doubles with private cold bath are US$8.50. The decent *Hotel Sparto* (☎ 76-2360, *Balta 165)* has hot water in the mornings and charges US$6/9 for rooms with shared showers and US$7.50/12 with private bath. The *Hostal Holiday* (☎ 76-3163) charges US$5/9 for clean singles/doubles with shared hot showers.

The friendly *Hostal Arequipa* (☎ 76-1338, *Arequipa 360)* charges US$7/11 for clean and pleasant singles/doubles with private bath and hot water (sometimes); a few cheaper rooms have shared baths. The owners also run the similar *Hostal Piura* (☎ 76-3974, *Piura 255)*. *Hostal Adrianella* (☎ 76-3469, *M Grau 239)* is also clean and has rooms with private hot showers and TV (four channels) for US$12/16.

The *Hostal Los Limoneros* (☎ 76-1649, *Lima 441)* has a pleasant garden and clean singles/doubles with a washbasin in the room, but communal toilets and hot showers, for US$7/12. Rooms with private bath, hot water and cable TV are US$15/18.

**Mid-Range** The new *Hotel Alameda* (☎ 76-3971, *Junín 322)* has rooms with hot showers and cable TV for US$21/28. The *Hotel El Mirador de Moquegua* (☎ 76-1765, *fax 786-1895)* is about 3km from the town center. There is a swimming pool, children's playground, and restaurant/bar. Rooms are US$48 for a double, and larger bungalows are US$67.

## Places to Eat

The cheapest places are near the market. The small and clean *Restaurant Morales*, at Lima and Libertad, is one of numerous choices. At the southwest end of town, along Mariscal de la Torre, are several hole-in-the-wall restaurants with views of the city and a limited menu of local dishes, such as *cuy* (roast guinea pig) and *chicharrones* (deep-fried pork skins), at fair prices. Of

several simple restaurants near the Plaza de Armas, the *Restaurant Palermo* is one of the best in town, with a varied menu. Also near the plaza, *A Todo Vapor*, which means 'full steam ahead,' specializes in seafood and is in an older building with character.

## Getting There & Away

The easiest way to get to Moquegua is by bus from either Arequipa or Tacna. Buses leave from small terminals down a hill west of the center. Buses to Lima (US$9 to US$20, 16 to 20 hours) leave several times daily with Ormeño, Cruz del Sur and Angelitos Negros. These buses may make intermediate stops at Camaná, Chala, Nazca and Ica.

Buses to Arequipa (US$3, up to 4 hours) leave with either Cruz del Sur, Ormeño, Transportes Moquegua, Flores Hermanos or Angelitos Negros about every hour. Buses to Tacna (US$2, 2½ hours) depart frequently with the same companies. Cruz del Sur, Flores Hermanos and Transportes Moquegua also have buses to Ilo (US$1.50, 2 hours) several times a day.

Several companies have service on the rough road to Puno (US$5, 9 to 11 hours) but they all leave in the evening.

## ILO
☎ 054

This is the departmental port, about 95km south of Moquegua. It's mainly used to ship out copper from the mine at Toquepala in the Department of Tacna farther south, but some wine and avocados are exported from Moquegua too. In 1992, Bolivia was granted the right to use the port for importing and exporting goods without paying duty, and the importance of Ilo has grown since then.

About 15km inland from Ilo is the modern **Museo El Algarrobal**, which opened in 1994 and has good exhibits pertaining to the area's archaeology and agriculture. The museum has labels in English and is a surprisingly good find in the middle of nowhere. A cab will cost about US$4. Hours are 9 am to 2 pm Tuesday to Friday. More information is available from the Casa de Cultura (☎ 78-1989) in central Ilo.

## Places to Stay & Eat

Hotels are often full with mining engineers and Bolivian businesspeople. The best in the center is the *Hotel Karina* (☎ 78-1397, *Abtao 780*). Good hotels a short distance from the center include the *Gran Hotel Ilo* (☎ 78-2411, fax 78-2421, Cáceres 3007) and *Hotel Chiribaya* (☎ 78-2268, fax 78-3040, Villa del Mar L-10). All of these have a restaurant, bar and comfortable rooms with cable TV, telephone and private bath for about US$30/40.

There are several cheaper hotels, including the *Hotel Paraíso* (☎ 78-1432, Zepita 749), *Hotel San Martín* (☎ 78-1082, Matará 325), *Hotel El Eden* (☎ 78-1950, Moquegua 846) or *Hotel Romicor* (☎ 78-1195, Ayacucho 408) – all of which have fair rooms with private bath and hot water. Also try the cheaper *Hostal Arequipa* (☎ 78-2911, Cuzco 473) or *Hostal Porteño* (☎ 78-2971, Zepita 705).

## Getting There & Away

There used to be flights from Lima, but they were recently suspended. Most people arrive by bus from Arequipa, Moquegua or Tacna. The bus station is north of town; take a cab for under US$1.

## TACNA
☎ 054

At 18° south of the equator and 1293km (by road) southeast of Lima, Tacna is Peru's southernmost city. It is the capital of its department, has a population of approximately 150,000 and lies 560m above sea level. Tacna is situated only 36km from the Chilean border and has strong historical ties with that country. It became part of Chile in 1880 during the War of the Pacific and remained in Chilean hands until 1929, when its people voted to return to Peru. Tacna has some of the best schools and hospitals in Peru; whether this is because of the Chilean influence is a matter of opinion.

Tacna is a clean and pleasant city with an attractive Plaza de Armas, but the main reason to go there is to cross the land border, which is well served by road and rail. (Remember that international-tourist traffic attracts thieves, so be careful.) There are some good rural restaurants where the locals go, which is fun if you like to eat tasty Peruvian food. Most people find that a day is more than enough to stay in Tacna.

## Information

**Consulates** The Chilean Consulate (☎ 72-4391, 72-1846) is near the train station and is open weekdays from 8 am to 12:30 pm. Most travelers just need a tourist card, which is freely available at the border.

The Bolivian Consulate is at the southeast end of town, on Avenida Piura. A taxi costs about US$1. Hours are weekdays from 9 to 11 am.

**Money** Several banks and street money-changers are found at the southeast end of the Plaza de Armas. Peruvian nuevos soles, Chilean pesos and US dollars can all be easily exchanged.

**Post & Communications** The post office is shown on the map. There are several telephone offices around the Plaza de Armas. Internet service is available at San Martín 611 from 9 am to 9 pm Monday to Saturday.

## Plaza de Armas

The plaza, pictured on the front of the S/100 note, features a huge arch – a monument to the heroes of the War of the Pacific. It is flanked by larger-than-life bronze statues of Admiral Grau and Colonel Bolognesi. Nearby, the 6m-high bronze fountain was designed by the French engineer Alexandre Gustave Eiffel (of Eiffel Tower fame) and supposedly represents the four seasons. Eiffel also designed the cathedral, which is noted for its clean lines, fine stained-glass windows and onyx high altar. The plaza is a popular meeting place for *Tacneños* in the evenings and has a patriotic flag-raising ceremony every Sunday at 10 am.

## Parque de la Locomotora

A British locomotive built in 1859 and used as a troop train in the War of the Pacific is the centerpiece of this pleasant downtown park.

## Museo Ferroviario

This is at the train station and is open week-days from about 9 am to 3 pm; go to the front gate and ask the guard to let you in. Admission is US$0.30. There are several early 20th-century engines and other rolling stock, but they are in poor condition. It also has a philatelic section displaying stamps with railway themes from all over the world.

## Museo de Instituto Nacional de Cultura

This small museum is in the Casa de Cultura and is officially open weekdays from 8 am to noon. If it's closed, you can often find someone to open it if you ask in the library below. The main exhibit deals with the War of the Pacific, which is explained by paintings and maps. There is also a small collection of archaeological pieces and local art. Admission is free.

## Museo de Zela

This small museum is housed in a colonial house at Zela 542 and gives a look at the interior of one of Tacna's oldest buildings. Hours are 8:30 am to 1 pm and 3:30 to 7 pm Monday to Saturday; it's free.

## Places to Stay

**Budget** The *Hostal Alameda* (☎ 72-3071, *Bolognesi 780*) is clean and charges US$5/7 for singles/doubles with cold showers. The *Hostal Pacífico* (☎ 71-3961, *Deustua 472*) is reasonably clean, has cold-water showers and charges US$4 per person. The similarly priced *Hostal Bon Ami* (☎ 71-1873, *2 de Mayo 445*) is basic but secure, has occasional hot water and is clean. The basic *Alojamiento Betito* is on the same block and is also secure. There are other basic, cheap places in this area and close to the market.

The *Hostal HC* (☎ 74-2042, *Zela 734*) is clean and quite good at US$8.50/12 with private hot showers. Next door, the *Hostal Lider* (☎ 71-5441, *Zela 724*) has double rooms with hot shower, TV and telephone for· US$10. *Hostal Lido* (☎ 72-1184, *San Martín 876A*) is another decent option at US$6/9.50 with bath and hot water. *Hostal Inclan* (☎ 72-3701, *Inclan 171*) is decent at

US$6/10 with hot shower. *Hostal Virrey* (☎ 72-3061, *Ayacucho 88*) is a similar option.

The small *Hostal Alcazar* (☎ 72-4991, *Simón Bolívar 295*) has clean rooms with bath for US$9.50/13, and you can get hot water if you give an hour's notice. The similarly priced *Hotel Lima* (☎ 71-1912, *San Martín 442*) has a decent restaurant and bar, though the rooms are worn and vary in quality. There is hot water for a couple of hours every morning and evening.

The *Hostal Avenida* (☎ 72-4582, 72-4531, *Bolognesi 699*) has adequate rooms for US$10/13.50 with bath and hot water if you request it in advance. A good choice is the friendly *Hostal Hogar* (☎ 71-1352, 72-6811, *28 de Julio 146*), which charges US$10/15 for clean rooms with TV and hot showers. The *Hostal Copacabana* (☎ /fax 72-1721, *Arias Araguez 370*) has clean rooms with private hot showers for US$13/15, but may be noisy on weekends because of their disco.

**Mid-Range** All the rooms in this section have private bath and hot water. Many raise their rates before Christmas and on weekends, when shoppers from Chile come to town. Prices may drop when hotels are not busy. Most hotels, however, quote rather lower rates than in the last edition of this book.

*Hostal Zapata* (☎ 72-1921, fax 72-4101, *Bolognesi 701*) charges US$12/16 for adequate rooms with a telephone and TV on request. The back rooms are very quiet. The *Hostal Premier* (☎ 71-5943, fax 71-5110, *Bolognesi 804*) has rather small, simple and clean rooms with TVs and telephones. It also has a snack bar. Rates are about US$13/17. The centrally located *Hotel Emperador* (☎ 71-4291, fax 72-2752, *San Martín 558*) has clean rooms with telephone for US$15/20. Opposite, the *Gran Hotel Central* (☎ 71-2281, 71-4841, fax 72-6031, *San Martín 561*) has nicer rooms for US$23/32.

The new *Maximo's Hostal* (☎ 74-2604, fax 74-2605, *Arias Araguez 281*) has a snack bar and clean rooms with phone and cable TV for US$18/23 including continental breakfast. The clean, modern and friendly *Hostal El Mesón* (☎ 72-5841, fax 72-1832,

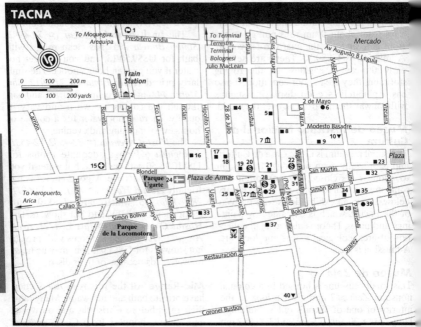

**TACNA**

*Hipolito Unanue 175)* is close to the plaza and has a cafeteria; rooms cost US$23/30. Also in this price range but away from the center is the **Holiday Suites Hotel** (☎ 71-5371, 72-2662, fax 71-1764, Alto de Lima 1476) offers modern and large, but rather bare, rooms with a sitting area. There is a pool, video-pub nightclub and 24-hour cafeteria service. These last four hotels have guarded parking areas.

The **Plaza Hotel** (☎ 72-2101, fax 72-6952, San Martín 421) is on the plaza and offers slightly worn carpeted rooms with TV and phone, some with a minibar, for US$25/30 including breakfast. Rooms vary in attractiveness, so look around. They have a cafeteria.

**Top End** The **Hotel Camino Real** (☎ 72-1952, 72-1891, fax 71-1588, San Martín 855) has nice rooms with minibar, cable TV and phone for US$35/45, as well as minisuites for US$51. They have a good restaurant, bar with dancing, and cafeteria.

The best in town is the **Gran Hotel Tacna** (☎ 72-4193, fax 72-2015, in Lima 442-3090, fax 442-4180, Bolognesi 300). Rooms are about US$58/77 and may include breakfast; bungalows and suites are US$115 a double. Many rooms have balconies. There is a pool, tennis court, pleasant grounds, a restaurant with 24-hour room service and a bar with dancing.

### Places to Eat

One of the best and most popular restaurants in town is the Italian-style **El Viejo Almacén** (☎ 71-4471, San Martín 577). It charges between US$3 and US$8 for a meal and has good steaks, pasta, ice cream, espresso, cheap local wine and desserts. Nearby is the pleasant **Café Genova**, with outdoor tables, espresso, and a variety of snacks, sandwiches, desserts and light meals for US$4 to US$10.

There are plenty of inexpensive, locally popular restaurants serving Peruvian meals, grilled chicken or Chinese food along

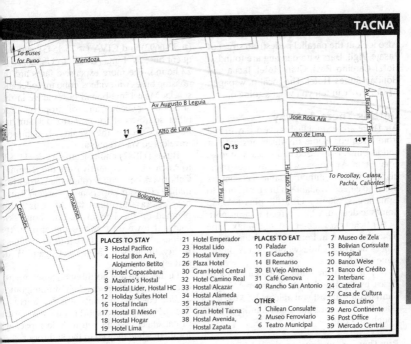

**TACNA**

Ayacucho, south of the Plaza de Armas, and at the intersection of Bolognesi with Ayacucho. Another local favorite is the very clean *Paladar (Meléndez 228)*, where a set-lunch menu is under US$2 and the food is good.

*El Gaucho* (☎ 74-1624, Alto de Lima 436) specializes in Argentine-style *parrilladas* (mixed grills) that cost about US$15 but are very good. They also serve other international foods. The lively *Cevichería El Corsario* (☎ 72-4506, San José 190) is in the southwest corner of town along an unpaved road near the Ciudad Universitaria. Take a taxi to find it. They open at 6 am and serve some of the best *ceviches* and seafood in town. Ceviches start around US$6.

The recommended *Rancho San Antonio* (☎ 72-4392, Coronel Bustíos 298) serves good Peruvian and international food in a garden setting. *El Remanso* (☎ 71-2034, 72-1722, Alto de Lima 2069) also has international food and weekend entertainment. The restaurant at the *Hotel Lima* is quite good

and not expensive, while the one at the *Hotel Camino Real* is good but pricey.

In the campiña, several rustic restaurants really come alive for weekend lunches, offering good food and live music. In Pocollay, 5km northeast of Tacna, there's *Restaurant Don Manuel*, on the Plaza de Armas, with reasonably priced, good local food and a loud but fun band. A few blocks beyond the plaza, *La Huerta* is a nice, quiet, outdoor place with no music. *Restaurant Campestre El Hueco*, on the outskirts of Pocollay on the way to Pachía, has good meals (including cuy) in the range of US$8 to US$15. It has a variety of live music for weekend lunches. Calana, midway between Pocollay and Pachía, has several other rural restaurants.

### Entertainment
The small pedestrian street of *Pasaje Libertad* is the center of Tacna's limited nightlife. Here you'll find three or four pubs and

clubs, some with live music and dancing on weekends, when a cover may be charged. Also look at the parallel pedestrian street of **Pasaje Vigil**. Bars with dancing are found at **Hotel Camino Real, Gran Hotel Tacna** and **Holiday Suites Hotel**. The local newspaper, *El Correos*, can tell you what's going on.

## Getting There & Away

**Air** There are several flights every day to and from Arequipa, some of which originate or end in Lima. For Cuzco or Juliaca, you must connect in Arequipa, which involves overnighting in there, although same-day connections have been available in the past. Fares to Lima are US$60 to US$100, plus a US$3 domestic-departure tax charged at the airport.

Air tickets are subject to a 18% tax if the ticket is bought in Peru. Some airlines have offices in Arica, Chile, where the tax on the same ticket is 2%.

If you fly from Lima to Tacna, cross to Arica by land and then fly from Arica to Santiago, it will cost you at least US$100 less than the international Lima-Santiago fare bought in Peru.

**Bus** There are two bus terminals. Most long-distance departures (except for the Lake Titicaca area) and buses/taxis for Arica leave from the Terminal Terrestre on Hipolito Unanue, at the northeast end of town. A US$0.30 terminal-use tax is levied from all passengers. Terminal Bolognesi, about a kilometer away, is the local terminal for buses to the beach at Boca del Río and other villages outside of the city but within the Department of Tacna. Bus companies to Puno (US$5 to US$8, 12 hours), as well as to the Bolivian border, all leave from Avenida Circumvalación, north of the city and east of the main terminal. There are about a dozen companies with offices lined up next to one another; unfortunately, they all leave in the late afternoon or evening; none during the day.

At the Terminal Terrestre, Flores Hermanos (☎ 72-6691) is the biggest local company, with about 20 buses a day to Moquegua and Arequipa (US$5, 7 hours), 10 buses to Ilo, and a daily 3:45 pm bus (additional departures on weekends) to Toquepala.

Several companies, including Flores Hermanos, Ormeño (☎ 72-4401), Cruz del Sur (☎ 72-6692) and CIVA (☎ 74-1543), run frequent buses to Lima (US$10 to US$20, 18 to 22 hours). The more expensive fares are on nonstop buses with videos, onboard toilet and snacks. Most Lima-bound buses leave in the afternoon or evening and will drop you off at other south-coast towns. Cruz del Sur has buses to Cuzco in the evening, though most travelers go via Arequipa.

Buses (US$2) and colectivo taxis (US$3) to Arica leave frequently from the terminal. Cabdrivers help you through the border formalities (if your papers are in order). But a new bus/taxi terminal for Arica is being planned on the Panamericana, about 2km south of town en route to the airport. It's supposed to open by 2000. If this becomes a reality, things will change yet again. Write and let me know.

Finally, note that northbound buses are frequently stopped and searched by immigration and/or customs officials not far north of Tacna. Have your passport handy, and beware of passengers asking you to hold a package for them while they go to the bathroom.

**Train** Trains between Tacna (☎ 72-4981) and Arica are the cheapest but slowest way to cross the border. Supposedly, there are trains from Tacna at 6 am and 7 am on Monday, Wednesday and Friday, but schedules change often. The 6 am train takes 2½ hours and the faster electric train at 7 am takes 1½ hours. The fare is about US$1. Your passport is stamped at the train station, there is no stop at the actual border and you receive your entry stamp when you arrive near Arica's Plaza de Armas.

## Getting Around

The airport is 5km south of town. A taxi charges about US$4 to Tacna, or you can go direct from the airport to Arica, with the appropriate stop at the border, for US$40. Alternatively, walk out of the airport parking area and get the same services for under half this price.

A taxi from downtown to the bus terminal is about US$0.75.

## Around Tacna

The land around the city is popularly called *la campiña,* or 'the countryside.' The area is known for vineyards, olive groves and orchards set in the desert and irrigated by the Río Caplina, which runs under Bolognesi in Tacna and provides water for the city. Wine is locally made in small bodegas that typically produce a few thousand liters of *vino de chacra* – a rough but pleasing table wine with a high alcohol content, sometimes reaching 18%. March and April are the main production times. Local bodegas can be visited, but none are specifically tourist attractions. Ask a cabdriver if he knows of one. Several suburbs and small villages have good rural restaurants that attract locals and tourists. They often have live bands on weekends, particularly for lunch.

**Pocollay** is a suburb about 5km from Tacna and can be reached by walking east on Bolognesi or by taking a bus along that street. It is popular with Tacneños for its rural restaurants, which are especially busy on Sundays. Popular dishes include *patasca a la tacneña,* a thick, spicy vegetable-and-meat soup; *picante de guatita,* hot peppered tripe (it's better than it sounds); *cazuela de ave,* a thick chicken-and-vegetable soup; *choclo con queso,* hot corn on the cob with cheese; *chicharrones de chancho* deep-fried chunks of pork, usually served with popcorn; *asado de chancho,* roast pork; *cordero a la parrilla,* barbecued lamb; and the typical Peruvian highland dish, *cuy chactado,* roasted guinea pig, which is usually served spicier here than in the mountains.

Continuing northeast of Tacna are the villages of **Calana, Pachía** and **Calientes,** which are 15km, 17km and 24km from Tacna, respectively. The area is known for its pleasant climate and countryside (by desert standards). Both Calana and Pachía have many rural restaurants, and Calientes has hot springs.

Tacna's main seaside resort is **Boca del Río,** about 55km southwest of the city. Buses go from Tacna along a good road. Tacneños have built summer homes there, but there are no hotels. There are several restaurants, and the beach is reportedly good.

The modern copper-mining center of **Toquepala** is near a cave in which rock paintings dating to 8000 BC have been found. They clearly illustrate a guanaco hunt among other things. It's not easy to get there, and there's no hotel, although the people at the mine may be able to help with providing floor space.

## GOING TO CHILE

Border-crossing formalities are relatively straightforward in both directions. Taxis are the quickest way of crossing, while trains are the cheapest. The border closes at 10 pm. Chile is an hour (two hours during daylight-saving time) ahead of Peru.

From Arica, you can continue south into Chile by air or bus, or northeast into Bolivia by air; the train that used to run from Arica has reportedly been canceled. There are plenty of hotels and restaurants; Arica is quite a lively place. For information about travel in Chile, consult Lonely Planet's *Chile & Easter Island.*

# The Arequipa Area

The major city of Arequipa is surrounded by some of the wildest terrain in Peru. This is a land of active volcanoes, thermal springs, high-altitude deserts and some of the world's deepest canyons. The most often visited is the famous Cañón del Colca, but there are many other areas for adventurous travelers to explore.

## Arequipa

☎ 054

At 2325m above sea level in the mountainous desert of the western Andes, Arequipa is a city of the highlands rather than one of the coastal lowlands. It is, however, better connected with the coastal transportation network than it is with the highlands, and is therefore often included in the south-coast sections of many guidebooks.

The Panamericana leaves the coast at Camaná and heads east into the Andes. At Repartición, 135km beyond Camaná, the Panamericana swings south, but a major highway continues climbing eastward for a another 40km to Arequipa, the capital of its department and the main city of southern Peru. *Arequipeños* claim that, with a population of almost 700,000, the city is Peru's second largest, but Trujillo vies for this honor.

It certainly is a beautiful city, surrounded by spectacular mountains. The most famous is the volcano El Misti (5822m), which has a beautiful conical peak topped by snow. It rises majestically behind Arequipa's cathedral and is clearly visible from the Plaza de Armas. If standing in the plaza, to the left of El Misti is the higher and more ragged Chachani (6075m), and to the right is the lower peak of Pichu Pichu (5571m).

Many of the city's buildings date to colonial times, and many are built from a very light-colored volcanic rock called *sillar*. The buildings dazzle in the sun, earning Arequipa

the nickname 'the white city.' Locals, however, sometimes say 'When the moon separated from the earth, it forgot to take Arequipa.'

### History

There is archaeological evidence here of pre-Inca settlement by Aymara Indians from the Lake Titicaca area. Some scholars think the Aymaras named the city (*ari* means 'peak' and *quipa* means 'lying behind' in Aymara); hence, Arequipa is 'the place lying behind the peak' (probably referring to the conical peak of El Misti). Other people claim that it is a Quechua name. An oft-heard legend says that the fourth Inca, Mayta Capac, was traveling through the valley and became enchanted by it. He ordered his retinue to stop, saying, '*Ari quipay,*' which translates as 'Yes, stay.'

The Spaniards refounded the city on August 15, 1540, and the date is remembered with a weeklong fair in Arequipa. The fireworks show in the Plaza de Armas on August 14 is noteworthy.

Unfortunately, the city is built in an area highly prone to earthquakes, and none of the original buildings remain. Arequipa was totally destroyed by earthquakes and volcanic eruptions in 1600. More major earthquakes occurred in 1687, 1868, 1958 and 1960. For this reason, many of the city's buildings are built low for stability. Despite these disasters, several 17th- and 18th-century buildings survived and are frequently visited. Without doubt, the most interesting of these is the Monasterio de Santa Catalina (see the boxed text 'Monasterio Misterioso' and Monasterio de Santa Catalina later in this section).

### Orientation

The city center, with its many hotels and interesting sights, is based on a colonial checkerboard pattern around the Plaza de Armas. Addresses can be confusing, because street

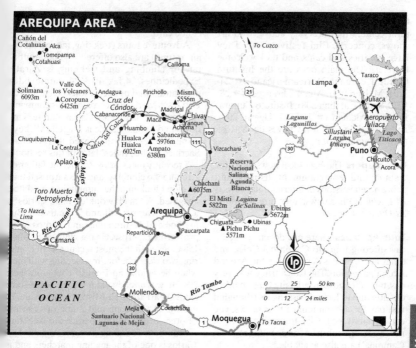

AREQUIPA AREA

change names every few blocks. Generally, streets have different names north, south, east, and west of the plaza. In addition, they change names again farther from the center.

## Information

**Tourist Office** The tourist office (☎ 21-2021) is on the Plaza de Armas at Portal Municipal 112 and is open weekdays from 8 am to 4 pm (sometimes later in the busy month of August, sometimes earlier when things are quiet). The Policía de Turismo (see Emergency later in this section) also provides information.

Visiting hours for churches in Arequipa are erratic. They vary every time I visit the city. The tourist office usually knows when specific churches are open to visitors, but even they can't keep up with the changes. Most churches are normally open from 7 to 9 am and from 6 to 8 pm for worship, and extended hours for tourism.

**Visa Extensions** Migraciónes (☎ 42-1759), at JL Bustamente at Rivero in Urb Quinta Tristán (take a taxi), does tourist-card extensions from 8 am to 1 pm weekdays.

**Money** The Banco de Crédito and Banco Latino are on the 1st block of Jerusalén. Moneychangers are found on nearby streets.

**Post & Communications** The main post office, at Moral 118, is open Monday to Saturday from 8:45 am to 6:45 pm. There are dozens of telephone offices that provide local and international telephone and fax service. The main one is at Alvarez Thomas 201.

There are several places to use the Internet. Cyber Café (Alvarez Thomas 219) is open from 9 am to 10 pm Monday to Saturday and charges US$1.30 an hour. They serve soft drinks and coffee. Readers suggest Don Quixote, on the 2nd block of Moral, where there is also a pub and billiards.

**Cultural Centers** There are several cultural centers that are very active, with art shows, concerts, film festivals, etc. They have libraries and cafés, and they welcome travelers. The main ones are the Instituto Cultural Peruano-Norteamericano (☎ 24-3201, Melgar 109), Alianza Francesa (☎ 28-1770, Santa Catalina 208), Instituto Cultural Peruano-Alemán (☎ 21-8567, Ugarte 207), and Complejo Cultural Cháves de la Rosa (Santa Catalina 101).

**Newspapers** The best local newspaper for cinema and entertainment listings and abbreviated versions of international news is *El Pueblo*. Other newspapers are *Arequipa Al Día* and *Correos*.

**Tour Agencies** There are dozens of agencies offering tours to Cañón del Colca and other nearby areas described in the Around Arequipa section. The Colca trip goes every day, but other advertised daily trips go infrequently due to lack of passengers (though if you pay for a minimum of four places, you can certainly go). City tours and tours of neighboring suburbs and villages ('La Campiña') are also available.

Many travel agencies are found along Santa Catalina or Jerusalén, and I have received mixed or negative reports about some of them, so shop carefully. Most will pool their clients into one bus, even though they may charge different rates. Although large buses are often offered, minibuses are usually provided unless there are plenty of travelers. Unfortunately, the minibuses get overcrowded and don't have adequate legroom for tall people. It may be better to go in a smaller group with a car. Agencies that have been generally well recommended by readers and have a good reputation include Colonial Tours (☎ 28-5980, fax 28-6868, Santa Catalina 106) and Illary Tours (☎ 22-0844, Santa Catalina 205). Expensive private tours can be arranged with Lima Tours (☎ 24-2293, fax 24-1654, Santa Catalina 120).

Guides often speak English and/or other languages, but not all of them do. Some can spout a garbled explanation in poor English, but don't really speak the language fluently.

Guides should be able to produce a Tourist Guide card.

Adventure tours (trekking, mountaineering, rafting) are also offered. The best outfitter for climbing and trekking is Zárate Expediciones (☎/fax 46-3624, zaratexpd@ netcentral.lared.net.pe, Alfonso Ugarte 305, Urb Jesús María, Paucarpata). This company was founded in 1954 by Carlos Zárate Sandoval and its chief guide is Miguel (Mickey) Zárate Flores (see the boxed text 'Human Sacrifice in the Andes' later in this section).

I recently met Carlos Zárate, the father of Arequipeño climbing, and was surprised that he didn't look like the 'mountain man' I had imagined. A small, wrinkled man, Carlos is less than five feet tall and 76 years old. But his book of testimonials and photos soon proved his expertise. He has climbed El Misti 158 times, with the most recent ascent occurring two weeks before my meeting with him when he guided an English couple in their 20s. He was already planning his next excursion! Apart from El Misti, he has made 78 ascents of Chachani and numerous ascents of other peaks. During parades to celebrate Arequipa's founding (every August 15) Carlos is one of the leading marchers and is considered a local gentleman and hero. He is, perhaps, the oldest active mountaineering guide in South America, if not the world.

Zárate Expediciones arranges a variety of overnight expeditions, rents equipment to clients and has a 24-hour information and mountain rescue service. Miguel speaks a few words of English, but Spanish is preferred. They do treks to the local canyons, Valle de los Volcanes, and elsewhere. Trekking rates are about US$30 plus expenses per day for the guide, US$7 per day for a mule and US$7 per day for muleteers. You can trek year round, but January to March is the wettest and least-recommended period. The company arranges climbs of all the local peaks and charges US$50 plus expenses per day for the guide, plus the cost of vehicle rental to get to base camp (US$50 to US$150, depending on the mountain). Another son, Carlos Zárate Flores (☎ 26-3107) is also an experienced guide. If these folks aren't available, they can put you in touch with reliable guides.

Anthony Holley (☎/fax 25-8459, angoho@ lared.net.pe) is an Englishman who has lived in Arequipa since 1938. He offers Land Rover tours anywhere around Arequipa (except Cañón del Colca) and to the beaches and bird sanctuaries of the coast. He can customize a tour for you. He charges about US$150 a day for six people (though his Land Rover can take up to 11). The cost rises proportionately for fewer than six passengers. It's best to call him on weekends or after 5 pm weekdays.

There are other mountain outfitters, though I haven't had any recommended to me. If you go with someone else, let me know how they are. Make sure that the guide you hire has both a guiding card and a booklet listing all the places he or she has guided. For more information on mountain outfitters and excursions or river running, see Around Arequipa later in this chapter.

**Laundry** Clothes can be washed, dried and folded in three hours at Jerusalén 404. They charge by weight, not per item.

**Medical Services** Clínica Arequipa (☎ 25-3424, 25-3416), on Bolognesi at Avenida Puente Grau, is considered the best and most expensive. Clínica San Juan de Dios (☎ 25-2256, Avenida Ejército 1020, Cayma) is also recommended. Slightly cheaper services are available at the Hospital Nacional del Sur (☎ 21-4110, 21-4050), on Peral at Ayacucho.

**Emergency** The Policía de Turismo (☎ 23-9888, Jerusalén 317) provides basic tourist information and helps in the event of emergencies. They are friendly and are open 24 hours a day.

**Dangers & Annoyances** Pickpockets, muggers and other thieves continue to be reported, and travelers are urged to hide their valuables. Areas that have had several robberies reported include San Juan de Dios on the crowded blocks south of Alto de la Luna and Santa Catalina, where there are many tourist services. In both cases, I have walked these streets both day and night with

no problems, but I wasn't carrying a camera or pack. There have been several reports of belongings being stolen from restaurants, so keep your stuff in sight. Thieves work in groups, some distracting you while another snatches your bag. For more information, see the Dangers & Annoyances section in the Facts for the Visitor chapter.

## Monasterio de Santa Catalina

The Monasterio de Santa Catalina, at Santa Catalina 300, wins my 'most fascinating colonial religious building in Peru' award, so even if you've overdosed on churches, you should try to see it. Actually, it's not a monastery, as the name suggests; it's a convent. Nor is it *just* a religious building; it's a good-sized complex of about 20,000 sq meters and covers an entire city block – almost a city within a city. For more description, see the boxed text 'Monasterio Misterioso.'

There are two ways of visiting Santa Catalina. One is to wander around slowly, discovering the intricate architecture of the complex, getting slightly lost and then finding your way again, revisiting the areas you enjoyed the best. This is fun, but if you want to learn a lot about Santa Catalina, it's well worth hiring a guide. Ask when you enter, and you'll be given the next available one. Among them, they speak English, French, German and Italian, and there are plans to add a Japanese-speaking guide. The tours last about 90 minutes, and there is no set cost. A tip is appreciated and well deserved. You are welcome to wander around yourself afterward.

Entrance costs US$4, and hours are 9 am to 5 pm (last tickets are sold at 4 pm) daily. There is a small cafetería that sells delicious homemade snacks cooked by the nuns.

## Museo Santuarios Andinos

In September 1998, the Museo Santuarios Andinos opened at Santa Catalina 210 to exhibit 'Juanita, the ice princess' – the frozen body of an Inca maiden sacrificed on the summit of Ampato (6380m) over 500 years ago (see the boxed text 'Human Sacrifice in the Andes'). A visit consists of an orientation video in Spanish or English, followed by a guided tour (in Spanish or English) of some

## Monasterio Misterioso

The Monasterio de Santa Catalina was built in 1580 and was enlarged in the 17th century. The founder was a rich widow, María de Guzmán, who only accepted nuns from the best Spanish families. All the nuns had to pay a dowry. Traditionally, the second daughter of upper-class families entered a nunnery, supposedly to live in poverty and renounce the material world. In fact, each nun at Santa Catalina had between one and four servants or slaves (usually black), and the nuns were able to invite musicians to perform in the convent, have parties and generally live in the style to which they had become accustomed while growing up.

After about three centuries of these goings-on, the pope complained that Santa Catalina was more like an exclusive club than a convent, and he sent Sister Josefa Cadena, a strict Dominican nun, to straighten things out. She arrived in 1871, sent all the rich dowries back to Europe, and freed all the servants and slaves, giving them the choice of staying on as nuns or leaving.

The convent has always been surrounded by imposing high walls, and the approximately 450 people (about a third of them nuns and the rest servants) who once lived here never ventured outside the convent. Accordingly, the place was shrouded in mystery for almost 400 years. It finally opened to the public in 1970, when the mayor of Arequipa forced the convent to comply with laws, requiring it to install electricity and running water. The nuns, now too poor to do this, opened their doors to tourism to pay for the modernization.

Today, the approximately 20 remaining nuns continue to live a cloistered life, but only in the northern corner of the complex. The rest is open to the public, who are free to wander around. It's like stepping back in time to a forgotten world of narrow twisting streets and tiny plazas, beautiful courtyards and simple living quarters.

Much of Santa Catalina has been excellently restored, and the delicate pastel colors of the buildings are attractively contrasted with bright flowers, period furnishings and religious art. It is a paradise for photographers, who often spend all day capturing the subtle changes in light as the sun moves across the sky. It's a wonderful place to just relax and wind down, write in your journal and perhaps reflect upon your trip.

of the artifacts found at the burial site, and culminates with viewing Juanita and another frozen mummy preserved in glass-walled freezers under carefully monitored conditions. Unguided visits are not permitted, and the whole spectacle is done in a respectful way. Hours are 9 am to 6 pm Monday to Saturday, and a visit costs US$1.75. Allow about an hour. For many travelers, this museum is a highlight of their Arequipa visit.

### La Catedral

The imposing cathedral stands on the Plaza de Armas. The original structure, dating from 1656, was destroyed by fire in 1844. It was rebuilt over the next few years, but was badly damaged by the earthquake of 1868,

and so most of what you see has been rebuilt since then. The outside is impressive, but the inside is surprisingly bare. As with many of Arequipa's churches, the interior emphasizes an airy spaciousness and luminosity, and the high vaults are much less cluttered than churches in other parts of Peru.

The cathedral is the only one in Peru that stretches the entire length of one side of the plaza. The interior has a distinctly international flair. This cathedral is one of less than 100 basilicas in the world that are entitled to display the Vatican flag, which you will see on the right side of the altar. Both the altar and the 12 columns (depicting the 12 apostles) are made of Italian marble. The huge Byzantine-style brass lamp hanging in front of the altar i from Seville, Spain. The pulpit was carved in France from European cedar. In 1870, Belgium provided the very impressive organ, which is reputedly the largest in South America, though it played very poorly for over a century because of damage during shipping. The Belgian authorities sent a specialist over to restore it in the 1980s, and now, concerts are given two or three times a month.

The cathedral is supposedly open from 7 to 10 am and 5 to 7 pm, but this changes frequently (as is the case with all the churches). Entrance is free.

## La Compañía

Just off the southeastern corner of the Plaza de Armas, this church is one of the oldest in Arequipa and is noted for its ornate main facade, which bears the inscription 'Año 1698' (the date of completion after over a century of construction). This Jesuit church was so solidly built that it withstood the earthquakes that toppled the cathedral and other buildings.

The main altar is made of Central American cedar carved in churrigueresque style (a Latin American adaptation of Spanish baroque architecture) and completely covered in 18-karat gold leaf. To the left of the main altar is the San Ignacio chapel, with a wonderful polychrome cupola. Unfortunately, many of the other original murals were covered with plaster and white paint by 19th-century restorers.

Attached to the church are two attractive cloisters, which are now used commercially. There are several stores selling high-quality alpaca goods, locally produced liquors, antiques and other products.

Opening times vary from year to year. Recently, the church was open from 10 am to noon and 5 to 7 pm daily, with free admission. The San Ignacio chapel is open from 9 am to noon and 3 to 6 pm weekdays and costs US$0.30 to visit. The cloisters function from 8 am to 8 pm Monday to Saturday.

## Church of San Francisco

This church was originally built in the 16th century and has been damaged by earthquakes. It still stands, and visitors can see a large crack in the cupola – testimony to the power of the quakes. There is an impressive silver altar, but, by Peruvian standards, the rest of the church has a relatively simple interior.

Hours are 7 to 10 am and 5 to 7 pm, and admission is free to some sections of the church, although an admission of US$1.25 is charged to see the whole complex.

## Monasterio de la Recoleta

A short walk from the city center is the monastery of La Recoleta, originally built on the west side of the Río Chili in 1648 by Franciscan friars. It is now completely rebuilt. This is the most interesting church to visit in Arequipa after Santa Catalina. The Franciscans were among the most active of the Catholic missionaries, and scholarship played a large part in their activities.

Their huge library contains more than 20,000 books, many of which are centuries old. They have several *incunables* (books printed before 1501), and their oldest volume dates from 1494. The library also has several 19th-century Peruvian maps that were printed in Lima that show Iquitos and the territory north of the Río Marañón as part of Ecuador. These territories were part of Ecuador until the Ecuadorian-Peruvian war of 1941.

There is also a museum of Amazonian exhibits collected by the missionaries. These include a large collection of stuffed birds and animals, as well as objects made by the Indians. They have an extensive collection of preconquest artifacts and religious art of the Cuzqueño school. You can also visit the cloisters and monks' cells.

The monastery, at La Recoleta 100, is open from 9 am to 1 pm and from 3 to 5 pm Monday to Saturday. Admission is US$1.75. A Spanish-speaking guide is available (tip expected). Make sure that you don't miss the library, especially if you're a bibliophile.

## Other Churches

If you're particularly interested in churches from the colonial era, then you might also want to visit the churches of San Agustín, Santo Domingo, Santa Teresa and La Merced.

**AREQUIPA AREA**

## Human Sacrifice in the Andes

In 1992, local climber Miguel Zárate was guiding a small French expedition on Ampato (6380m) when he found wooden remnants near the summit. He had worked previously with American mountaineer/archaeologist Johan Reinhard, and so he realized the remnants were indicative of a burial site. Later, he had recurring dreams of a girl who had been left on the mountain. In September 1995, Zárate convinced Reinhard that there was a burial on Ampato, and the two men, accompanied by muleteer Henry Huamani, climbed the peak. They found that recent eruptions of nearby Sabancaya had deposited ash on Ampato. The ash had absorbed solar energy and melted the snow below, thus exposing the burial site.

A statue and other offerings were found, but the stonework of the burial site had collapsed, and there was no sign of a body. The team rolled rocks down the mountain, and by following their path, Zárate found the complete mummy of an Inca girl who had been sacrificed at the summit. Bundled in finely woven blankets, the mummy had rolled down the mountain when the snow had melted. She had been almost perfectly preserved by the icy temperatures for about 500 years. Over 20 similar Inca sacrifices have been discovered atop various Andean mountains since 1954, but this was the first female and one of the best preserved.

It took the men two full days to carry the frozen mummy bundle (it weighed about 36kg) down to the village of Cabanaconde, from where Zárate transported it to Arequipa by road. After arriving in Arequipa, he put the mummy in a large freezer in his house, where it stayed for three days. Then the still-frozen mummy was taken to the Universidad Católica in Arequipa, where it underwent a battery of scientific examinations. Dubbed 'Juanita, the ice princess,' the mummy was temporarily exhibited to the public at the university. In late 1998, she was moved to the Museo Santuarios Andinos. (See Museo Santuarios Andinos earlier in this chapter.)

A month after the discovery of Juanita, Reinhard returned with more climbers and discovered the remains of two more human sacrifices, one well preserved. Reinhard is no stranger to climbing the Andes in search of archaeological remains. A few years earlier, he had been part of a team that discovered the remains of a human sacrifice near the summit of Pichu Pichu (5571m), a few kilometers east of Arequipa. Since these discoveries, he has returned to the area frequently, discovering more mummies on Ampato and Pichu Pichu. Most recently, in September 1998, Reinhard was in a team of archaeologists who discovered six frozen mummies on El Misti. There have been many articles written about these and other discoveries. For further reading, see *Newsweek*, November 6, 1995, and *National Geographic*, March 1992, June 1996 and June 1998.

The Incas considered the mountains to be gods who could kill by volcanic eruption, avalanche or climatic catastrophes. They therefore made human sacrifices to appease the gods. What is most amazing is the ability of the Incas to climb to well over 6000m above sea level – sometimes to construct ritual altars and temples at these elevations – without modern climbing equipment.

## Museo Histórico Municipal

This small local museum, at San Francisco 407, is housed in a colonial building that was one of the first schools in the city and also functioned as an early prison. There are a few paintings, historical documents, photographs, maps and other objects pertaining to the city's history. Most interesting are the photographs of the effects of the 1868 earthquake, photos of the Valle de los Volcanes and a small naval exhibit. It is open from 8 am to 5 pm on weekdays. Admission is US$0.70.

## Colonial Houses

A few beautiful colonial houses – now being used as art galleries, banks or offices – can be visited. One of the best is **Casa Ricketts** (also called Casa Tristán del Pozo), built in 1738. It was first a seminary, then the archbishop's palace, and then a school before passing into the hands of one of Arequipa's upper-crust families, which finally sold it to Banco Central, which in turn sold it to Banco Continental. It now houses a small art gallery and museum, as well as bank offices. It's open 8 am to noon and 3 to 6 pm weekdays; entry is free.

The **Casona Iriberry**, housing the Complejo Cultural Cháves de la Rosa, is a pleasant colonial house with several patios. It dates from the late 18th century. Also worth seeing is the 18th-century **Casa de Moral**, now owned by Bancosur and open during bank hours.

## Yanahuara

The suburb of Yanahuara is within walking distance of the town center and makes a good excursion. Go west on Avenida Puente Grau over the bridge, and continue on Avenida Ejército for about six or seven blocks. Turn right on Avenida Lima, and walk five blocks to a small plaza, where you'll find the church of Yanahuara, which dates from 1750. There's a **mirador** (viewing platform) at the end of the plaza, from where there are excellent views of Arequipa and El Misti.

Head back along Avenida Jerusalén (in Yanahuara), which is the next street parallel to Avenida Lima, and just before reaching Avenida Ejército, you'll see the well-known **Picantería Sol de Mayo**, where you can stop for a good lunch of typical Arequipeño food. The round trip should take under two hours, starting from the town center, but if you get tired, there's a city bus to Yanahuara that leaves Arequipa along Avenida Puente Grau and returns from Yanahuara Plaza to the city every few minutes.

## Cayma

Beyond Yanahuara is Cayma, another suburb with a frequently visited church. The Church of San Miguel Arcángel is open from 9 am to 4 pm, and for a tip, the church warden will take you up the small tower, where you'll have excellent views, particularly in the afternoon. To get there, continue along Avenida Ejército about three blocks beyond Avenida Jerusalén and then turn right on Avenida Cayma and climb up this road for about a kilometer. Alternately, from Yanahuara, take Calle San Vicente and then Avenida Leon Velarde to Cayma. Buses marked Cayma go there from Arequipa along Avenida Puente Grau.

## Paucarpata

This suburb is about 7km southeast of town and features an attractive colonial church on the main plaza, as well as a great local restaurant (see Places to Eat later in this section). Gray buses along Socabaya in Arequipa go there, or take a cab. From Paucarpata, **El Molino de Sabandía** is about a 2km walk away; this mill was built in 1621, fell into disrepair and was restored in 1973. As you walk there, note the Inca terracing en route, particularly around the village of Yumina. You can visit the mill for US$1, and they'll make it work for you. The pleasant surrounding gardens with grazing llamas are a nice place for a picnic in the country with great views of El Misti.

## La Mansión del Fundador

This colonial mansion, complete with its own chapel, has been restored and can be visited 9 am to 5 pm daily for US$1.75. The mansion is in the village of Huasacache, 9km from Arequipa, and is often included in local tours or can be reached by taxi.

## Language Courses

The recommended Centro de Intercambio Cultural is run by Señora Carmen (☎ 23-1759), who charges US$90 for 20 hours of private or semiprivate lessons per week and can arrange family homestays for US$60 a week including meals. Call the Centro, and they'll pick you up in Arequipa. The Instituto

Cultural Peruano-Norteamericano (☎ 24-3201, 24-3841, Melgar 109) offers private Spanish lessons for US$10 per hour and sometimes has group classes. Also ask at the tourist office.

## Special Events

Arequipeños claim that their Holy Week (before Easter) celebrations are similar to the solemn and traditional Spanish observances from Seville. Maundy Thursday, Good Friday and Holy Saturday processions are particularly colorful and, in some districts, end with the burning of an effigy of Judas. Arequipa fills up for the Fiesta de la Virgen de Chapi on May 1, which, if it coincides with Easter, makes hotel rooms very difficult to find. The fiesta itself takes place at the Santuario de la Virgen de Chapi, 45km from Arequipa. Pilgrims walk there, camping en route.

The founding of the city, August 15, is celebrated with parades, fireworks, dancing, beauty pageants and other events over the course of several days. There are several other minor fiestas throughout the year.

## Places to Stay

Arequipa has been experiencing a hotel boom, especially among small mid-range hotels. There are now over 300 lodging establishments in town, and competition is stiff. It's always worth asking for discounts. July and especially August are the high season when prices rise. By September, rates can drop 20% or more.

## Places to Stay – Budget

Several cheap hotels are very popular and are often filled with international budget travelers. Rooms are basic but clean, showers are usually shared and the staff is friendly. Single travelers can often share a room with others to avoid paying the higher single rate. The following places are currently well recommended.

*Casa La Reyna* (☎ 28-6578, *Zela 209*) – look for the 'Rooms For Tourists' sign – has a great rooftop terrace with mountain and monastery views, big laundry sinks and kitchen privileges on request; English is

spoken by the friendly owners. Beds are US$5 single or US$4 per person, and breakfast and pizzas are available. They have about 16 rooms and six bathrooms. The repeatedly recommended *Tambo Viejo* (☎ 28-8195, fax 28-4747, *tamboviejo@yahoo .com, Socabaya 107*) has rooms with shared baths and hot water for US$6 per person, and rooms with private bath at US$10/16/23 singles/doubles/triples. There is a cable TV room, garden, coffee shop, laundry service, book exchange, tourist information and an English-speaking staff. Some rooms have a garden view, and the hotel's terrace has volcano views. The *Colonial House Inn* (☎/fax 22-3533, *colonialhouse@lared.net.pe, Avenida Puente Grau 114*) has five spacious rooms in a colonial house. All the rooms have private bath and hot water, and there is a total of 17 beds. The friendly owners speak English and can provide excellent breakfasts for an extra charge. The inn has good city views from the rooftop and a TV room. Rates are US$5 per person. The *Hotel Regis* (☎ 22-6111, *Ugarte 202*) is clean, safe and friendly; it has 24-hour hot water, a rooftop terrace and rooms with shared baths for US$5 per person.

Some less popular but acceptable shoestring hotels include the following. The really cheap and basic *Hotel Crillon Serrano* (☎ 21-2392, *Peru 109*) is friendly and reasonably clean, but has only cold water. They charge under US$3 per person with communal bath or US$7 for a double with private bath. One reader wrote that the elderly owner offers his guests a shot of pisco in the evening to make up for the lack of hot water. The *Hostal Lider Inn* (☎ 23-8210, *Consuelo 429*) charges US$5 to US$6 for reasonably clean double rooms with private bath and cold water; communal showers are hot. It's popular with young Arequipeño couples, but not particularly sleazy. The reasonably clean *Hostal Royal* (☎ 21-2071, *San Juan de Dios 300A*) has hot water and basic rooms for US$4.25 a person, or US$11 for a double with private bath. The nice *Hostal Wilson* (☎ 23-8781, *Avenida Puente Grau 306*) charges US$4 per person or US$6 per person with private bath. The *Hostal Santa Catalina*

*(☎ 22-1766, 24-3705, Santa Catalina 500)* is basic, fairly clean, and has hot water during the day; it charges US$4/7, or US$8.50/14 for singles/doubles with private bath and hot water. The rooms on the ground floor are noisier than the ones upstairs. There is an adjoining restaurant and a rooftop terrace with good views. Travelers on a budget will find other hotels at about these prices, but many are of poorer quality.

The *Hostal Residencial Núñez* *(☎ 21-8648, Jerusalén 528)* is good, secure, friendly and popular with gringos. There is hot water and a terrace, and breakfast is available. Rooms are US$7/12 singles/doubles with communal baths and US$12/20 in rooms with private bath and TV. The *Hostal Tumi de Oro (San Agustín 311A)* is clean and friendly and has hot water. They charge US$7/10 with shared baths or US$10/14 with private bath and provide kitchen and laundry facilities. The *Hostal Ambassador* *(☎ 28-1048, Jerusalén 619)* has a breakfast cafeteria and good, clean rooms with electric showers for US$8/12 (one bed) or US$15 (two beds). Check the bathroom before paying; some of the showers are very cramped. The safe and popular *Hostal Posada de Sancho* *(☎ 28-7797, 21-8440, fax 28-7797, Santa Catalina 213)* has 24-hour hot water, friendly English- and German-speaking owners and fine views from the rooftop terrace. Breakfast and tour arrangements are available. Most rooms have private bath and cost US$8/18.

Readers highly recommend the new *Los Balcones de Santa Catalina (Moral 226)*, where a triple room with private hot shower costs US$10 per person including continental breakfast.

## Places to Stay – Mid-Range

The *Hotel Señorial* *(☎/fax 28-8061, Carlos Llosa 106)* has average rooms with telephone and cable TV for US$15/23 including continental breakfast. The *Hostal Latino* *(☎/fax 24-4770, Carlos Llosa 135)* has decent rooms with private hot baths, TV and telephone for US$15/22 (US$2 extra for cable TV), as well as a café. They give discounts if you stay a few days. The friendly and clean *La Casa de Melgar* *(☎/fax 22-2459, Melgar*

*108A)* is in an interesting 18th-century building made of sillar blocks. The ground-floor rooms have mysteriously high domed ceilings, and the whole place has a gothic air. Rooms have good beds and private baths, but lack TVs, which is probably just as well. They have a good café. High-season rates are US$17/26, but drop substantially in other months.

Perhaps the best value in its price range is the super-clean, friendly and recommended *Hotel Miamaka* *(☎ 28-8558, fax 22-7906, Hotel_Miamaka@mail.interplace.com.pe, San Juan de Dios 402)*. The 20 variously sized rooms are bright and comfortable, with telephone, cable TV, spotless showers and, in some, a minirefrigerator. There's a small patio (but no hammocks). Rates are US$24/28 for singles/doubles, and up to US$45 for a family room, including continental breakfast. Snack service is available in the cafeteria.

*La Casa de Mi Abuela* *(☎ 24-1206, fax 24-2761, lperezwi@ucsm.edu.pe, Jerusalén 606)* has long been a popular choice. The *abuela* (grandmother) after whom the place is named died in 1994 at the age of 100. Singles/doubles with a private shower and hot water cost US$26/34, or half this price with shared bathrooms. There's an attractive garden full of singing birds, with tables and chairs provided for breakfast. A new section at the back includes a swimming pool, games area, library and restaurant. The rooms are a hodgepodge of differently aged and styled furniture, but each has a stock of beer and soft drinks, which you pay for when you leave. Some rooms have cable TV, telephone or radios. It's well run and secure – you must ring a bell to get in. Avoid the room next to the reception room, as the bell will disturb you.

*Posada de San Juan* *(☎ 24-7209, fax 21-3613, psanjuan@mail.interplace.com.pe, San Juan de Dios 210)* is in an attractive older house that has been completely renovated. There are 18 rooms with private bath and local TV. High-season rates are US$32 to US$40 for one to three people, with discounts in mid or low season. Rates include continental breakfast. The recommended *Tierra Sur Hostal* *(☎ 28-6564, ☎/fax 22-7132,*

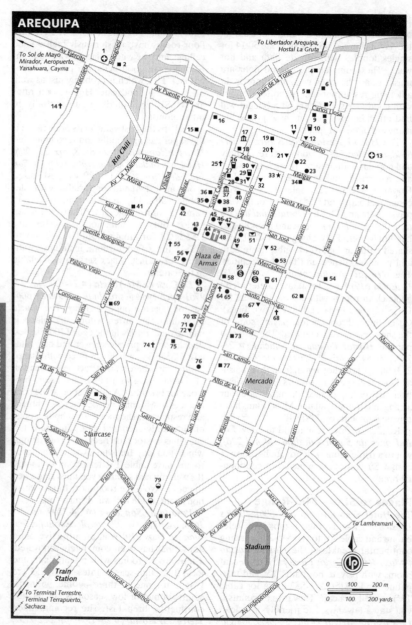

# AREQUIPA

To Libertador Arequipa,
Hostal La Gruta

To Sol de Mayo
Mirador, Aeropuerto,
Yanahuara, Cayma

Río Chili

Av Ejército

Bolognesi

La Recoleta

Av Puente Grau

Juan de la Torre

Carlos Llosa

Ayacucho

Zela

Av La Marina

Ugarte

Av La Moral

Villalba

Bolívar

Santa Catalina

San Francisco

Santa María

Jerusalén

Melgar

Rivero

Pierola

Colón

San José

San Agustín

Puente Bolognesi

Palacio Viejo

Consuelo

Av Lima

Sucre

Cruz Verde

La Merced

Álvarez Thomas

Mercaderes

Plaza de
Armas

Santo Domingo

Valdivia

San Camilo

Mercado

Alto de la Luna

Muñoz

Nuevo Corbacho

Via Circunvalación

28 de Julio

San Martín

Sucre

Pizarro

Garci Carbajal

San Juan de Dios

N de Piérola

Perú

Pizarro

Victor Lira

Garci Carbajal

Salaverry

Staircase

Martínez

Parra

Socabaya

Tacna y Arica

Quiroz

Leticia

Olímpica

Av Jorge Chávez

Romana

To Lambramani

Stadium

Train
Station

To Terminal Terrestre,
Terminal Terrapuerto,
Sachaca

Huascar y Angamos

Av Independencia

| 0 | 100 | 200 m |
| 0 | 100 | 200 yards |

AREQUIPA AREA

## AREQUIPA

**PLACES TO STAY**
2  La Posada del Puente
3  Hostal Santa Catalina
4  Hostal Ambassador
5  Hotel Jerusalén
6  La Casa de Mi Abuela
7  Hostal Latino
8  Hostal Señorial
9  Hostal Residencial Núñez
15  La Hostería
16  Hostal Wilson
18  Casa La Reyna
19  Colonial House Inn
27  La Posada del Monasterio
34  La Casa de Melgar
36  Hostal Posada de Sancho
39  Los Balcones de Santa Catalina
40  Hotel Regis
41  Hostal Tumi de Oro
54  Hotel Conquistador
58  Hotel El Portal
62  Hotel Crillon Serrano
66  Posada de San Juan
69  Hostal Lider Inn
73  Hostal Royal
75  Tierra Sur Hostal
77  Hotel Miamaka
78  Hostal Mansión Dorada
81  Tambo Viejo

**PLACES TO EAT**
11  Govinda

12  Ary Quepay
21  Pizzería Los Leños
30  Casa Mayor
31  La Brochetta
32  Trattoria Gianni
46  Mixtos, La Truffa & others
47  Forum Café
49  Manolo's
52  Bonanza
56  Restaurant Cuzco, El Balcón & others
67  Monzas
72  Cevichería 45

**ENTERTAINMENT**
10  La Quinta, La Troica
18  Kibosch
26  Las Quenas
29  Blues Bar
53  Cine Municipal
61  Champs
65  Cine Fenix
76  Cine Ateneo

**OTHER**
1  Clínica Arequipa
13  Hospital Nacional del Sur
14  Monasterio de la Recoleta
17  Museo Histórico Municipal, Crafts shops
20  Church of San Francisco
22  Laundry

23  Instituto Cultural Peruano-Norteamericano
24  Church of Santa Teresa
25  Monasterio de Santa Catalina
28  Instituto Cultural Peruano-Alemán
33  Tourism Police
35  Illary Tours
37  Museo Santuarios Andinos
38  Alianza Francesa
42  Casa de Moral
43  Complejo Cultural Cháves de la Rosa, Casona Iriberry
44  Colonial Tours
45  Lima Tours
48  Catedral
50  Casa Ricketts (Casa Tristán del Pozo)
51  Central Post Office
55  Church of San Agustín
57  Aero Continente
59  Banco de Crédito
60  Banco Latino
63  Tourist Office
64  Church of La Compañía
68  Church of Santo Domingo
70  Telefónica del Peru
71  Cyber Café
74  Church of La Merced
79  Ormeño (tickets)
80  Cruz del Sur (tickets)

*tierrasur@lared.net.pe, Consuelo 210*) is clean, quiet, modern and reminiscent of a good American motel. There is a restaurant and bar. Rooms with telephone and cable TV are US$28/38 with continental breakfast. In the suburb of Yanahuara, ***Hotel Yanahuara*** (☎ 27-1515, fax 25-3156, *Jerusalén 500*) has similarly priced modern rooms.

***Hotel Conquistador*** (☎ 21-2916, fax 21-8987, *Mercaderes 409*) is friendly, and the manager speaks English. The lobby of the attractive colonial house is elegant, and the rooms, though fairly plain, have telephones and TVs. There is a restaurant. Rates are US$30/39. ***Hotel Jerusalén*** (☎ 24-4481, 24-4441, fax 24-3472, *Jerusalén 601*) has a restaurant, room telephones, and the luxury of a bathtub in some rooms – good if you're fed up with showers. Rates are US$25 in their standard rooms, which are shabby, or

US$35/45 in their deluxe rooms (on the 3rd and 4th floors), which are much nicer, more spacious and have cable TV. The 11-room ***Hostal Mansión Dorada*** (☎ 22-2336, fax 28-3307, *mansiondorada@yahoo.com, 28 de Julio 505*) has cable TV and telephones in the rooms, helpful staff and a nice patio. Rates are US$25/40 including continental breakfast, but the front rooms suffer somewhat from street noise.

## Places to Stay – Top End

The recommended ***Hostal La Gruta*** (☎ 22-4631, fax 28-9899, *hostal_lagruta@LaRed .com.pe, La Gruta 304, Selva Alegre*), less than 2km north of the Plaza de Armas, is a beautiful small hotel on a quiet street. All 13 rooms are differently but comfortably and tastefully furnished, and all have large windows with views of the attractive garden, cable TV, telephone, refrigerator and bar. Minisuites have a fireplace and private garden access. Rates are an exceptional value at US$45/55 or US$65 for the minisuites, and include continental breakfast and airport pick-up on request. The helpful owner speaks perfect English.

The similarly priced and recommended *La Hostería* (☎ 28-9269, fax 28-1779, Bolívar 405) is a charming 11-room hotel close to the center of town. The rooms are very pleasant, but some suffer from street noise; stay in the back. *La Posada del Monasterio* (☎ 28-3076, fax 24-7353, Santa Catalina 300) is in an architecturally delightful colonial building; from the rooftop terrace, there are fine views of the Santa Catalina convent. The comfortable and modern rooms have all the expected facilities, and rates are US$46/60 including breakfast. This hotel is very popular with Europeans.

*La Posada del Puente* (☎ 25-3132, fax 25-3576, hotel@posadadelpuente.com, Avenida Bolognesi 101) is a small hotel with attractive rooms and a good restaurant and bar. Their garden and river views make for a tranquil setting. Rates are US$60/70 or US$105 for minisuites. On the plaza is the very modern *Hotel El Portal* (☎ 21-5530, fax 23-4374, Portal de Flores 116). Good rooms are about US$65/80, plus a 50% surcharge if you have a plaza view. This is one of the best run and most comfortable hotels in town; it even boasts a rooftop swimming pool, as well as a couple of restaurants, a bar and a disco.

*Libertador Arequipa* (☎ 21-5110, fax 24-1933, arequipa@libertador.com.pe, Plaza Bolívar, Selva Alegre), 1.5km north of the Plaza de Armas, charges US$104 for single/double rooms and US$175 for suites. This is the grande dame of Arequipa's hotels, and the recently renovated, spacious rooms and public areas have a charmingly old-fashioned air. The stylish pink building is nicely set in sizable gardens with an unheated swimming pool and playground. Their spa has a sauna, Jacuzzi and gym. There is a sedate restaurant and a fine Sunday brunch.

For business travelers, the *Holiday Inn* (☎ 44-8383, fax 44-8344, holiaqp@lared.net.pe), on the outskirts of the city on the road to

Sabandía, provides the expected services and airport pick-up. Rooms are US$97.

## Places to Eat

In Arequipa, there are several reasonably priced restaurants around the Plaza de Armas, particularly on the Santa Catalina side. The 2nd floors of *El Balcón* (☎ 23-9777), *Restaurant Cuzco* and others on the northwest side of the plaza have views overlooking the plaza, the cathedral and El Misti. The food is OK, and the service tends to be slow, but find your way up there (through a door to the right of the airline offices) to enjoy the views. Below the balcony are a few more cheap to mid-range restaurants.

There are several budget restaurants on the 300, 400 and 500 blocks of Jerusalén. *Govinda* (Jerusalén 505) is a vegetarian place run by the Hare Krishnas, and it's very cheap. *Ary Quepay* (Jerusalén 502) offers traditional plates (including *cuy*, or guinea pig) in a colonial-style building, with live *música folklórica* in the evenings. Good Italian food is available at *Pizzería Los Leños* (☎ 28-9179, Jerusalén 407), where they bake the pizza in a wood-burning oven. Recorded rock music is interspersed with live performances by Peruvian folklórica musicians who wander in during the evening, creating a friendly atmosphere. It's open from 5 pm until late at night Monday to Saturday. There are several other pizzerias.

For coffee drinkers, cafés serving espresso and cappuccino include *Monzas* (☎ 21-2169, Santo Domingo 102), which is one of the oldest. It also serves meals and has a full bar. The popular *Forum Café*, on San Francisco, half a block north of the plaza, and *Bistrot* in the Alianza Francesa (Santa Catalina 208) are both recommended.

*Bonanza* (☎ 21-5371, Jerusalén 114) serves a variety of reasonably priced dishes and is also popular with Arequipeños. Meals are in the US$3 to US$6 range. Good ceviche (and nothing else) is served in the little *Cevichería 45* (☎ 24-2400, Alvarez Thomas 221) from 9 am to 3 pm. *Manolo's* (☎ 21-9009, Mercaderes 113) is a good general restaurant with coffees, ice creams, desserts, sandwiches and other meals.

The alley behind the cathedral on the Plaza de Armas has several small, popular, quaint restaurants. The names and owners of these places change often, but current popular choices are *La Truffa* (☎ 24-2010, *Pasaje Catedral 111*), which serves good Italian food from 11 am to 11 pm Monday to Saturday, and *Mixtos* (☎ 24-7624, *Pasaje Catedral 115*), which does mainly seafood but might not be open in the evening. Main courses in both run about US$4 to US$8.

The 300 block of San Francisco has several good choices. *Trattoria Gianni* (☎ 28-7138, *San Francisco 304*) has pizzas and pastas from 7 pm to midnight Monday to Saturday. Opposite, the newer *La Brochetta* is locally recommended for Italian food, and *Casa Mayor* is a new, reasonably priced steakhouse with a colonial ambiance.

The best places for traditional Arequipeño food are mostly outside the central area. Try *Sol de Mayo* (☎ 25-4148, 27-0391, *Jerusalén 207*), in the Yanahuara district. It is open from 11 am to 7 pm daily and serves good and moderately priced Peruvian food, as well as a set US$3 lunch menu on weekdays. They have live música folklórica from 1 to 2 pm. (A luncheon visit to Sol de Mayo can be combined with a visit to the mirador in Yanahuara.) Slightly farther afield is the locally popular *Tradición Arequipeña* (☎ 42-6467, *Avenida Dolores 111*), near the southeastern suburb of Paucarpata. Most cabdrivers know it, and a trip should cost less than US$2 from the city center. Meals here are in the US$4 to US$10 range, and hours are noon to 7 pm Sunday to Thursday and noon to 10 pm Friday and Saturday. Also try *La Cantarilla* (☎ 25-1515, *Tahuaycani 106*), in the southwestern suburb of Sachaca, with some international fare as well as good Arequipeño food, including local freshwater shrimp. It is open for lunch daily and has a children's playground. Again, take a cab. A recent recommendation is *Picantería Los Guisos Arequipeños* (☎ 46-5151, *Pizarro 111*), in the suburb of Lambramani, about 2km south.

Try *rocoto relleno* (hot peppers stuffed with meat, rice and vegetables), *cuy chactado* (roasted guinea pig), *ocopa* (potatoes with a spicy sauce and fried cheese), *chupe* de camarónes (shrimp soup), *chancho al horno* (suckling pig), *anticucho* (shish kebab of beef or beef hearts) and *ceviche* (marinated seafood); and wash it down with *chicha* (fermented maize beer).

Also see Entertainment for dinner shows.

## Entertainment

Things are generally pretty quiet midweek. An irritating habit of some places is to advertise a nightly peña, when in fact there's rarely anything going on except from Thursday to Saturday nights. An exception is *Las Quenas* (☎ 21-5468, 28-1115, *Santa Catalina 302*), open Monday to Saturday with live music nightly at 9 pm. Music varies, though música folklórica predominates. There is a US$1.75 cover charge, and they serve decent Arequipeño food starting at 8 pm.

Also good for local food and music is *La Quinta* (☎ 23-7149, *Jerusalén 522*), with a US$1.75 cover on Saturday nights, but there might not be a cover charge on other nights when they have music. Next door is *La Troica* (☎ 22-5690, *Jerusalén 522-A*), which also has food and music, including Afro-Peruvian and Latin, as well as folklórica.

The most happening bar is the *Blues Bar* (☎ 28-3387, *San Francisco 319*), with good drinks, pool tables, live Latin American rock music and dancing. It's popular with young Arequipeños, but doesn't get under way until about 11 pm or later. Cover charges vary and can go up to US$6 on Saturday night. Food is served, but it's mediocre – you're here for bands and booze, and the burgers are an afterthought. Their pizzas are better if you get the munchies. Another late-night dance spot with occasional music is *Kibosch* (*Zela 205*).

For a beer, a chat and a game of darts, head over to *Champs* (☎ 21-5054, *Galerías Gamesa 14*), a shopping center off Santo Domingo. Run by a Brit who has lived in Peru for many decades, Champs is the closest you'll get to a British pub.

There's also the usual selection of cinemas, some of which show English-language movies with Spanish subtitles. Also check the various cultural centers for films and other events.

AREQUIPA AREA

## Shopping

Good souvenir shopping is to be had in the stores next to the Museo Histórico Municipal. Lanificio del Perú (☎ 42-9934, 42-4946), on Argentina in the Paucarpata suburb, is a factory outlet selling high-quality alpaca cloth at good prices. High-quality (but not cheap) alpaca, vicuña, leather and natural cotton goods are sold by the Grupo Inca Factory Outlet (Zela 212). El Zaguán (La Merced 125, Room 116) sells alpaca clothing and handicrafts.

## Getting There & Away

**Air** The airport is 9km northwest of the center of town. There are several direct flights to/from Lima, and about two each to Tacna, Cuzco, and Juliaca every day. The Aero Continente office (☎ 28-1815, 21-2989, 21-9788) is on the Plaza de Armas. TANS has recently begun operating daily flights to Lima.

Servicios Aereos AQP (☎ 28-1800, 23-2501, fax 20-1184, San Francisco 106) flies nine-passenger, twin-engined Piper Comanches anywhere you want to go, including local sightseeing spots.

The usual US$3.50 airport departure tax applies.

**Bus** The Terminal Terrestre opened in 1993 on Avenida A Avelino Cáceres, about 3km south of the center of town. Since then, another bus station, called the Terrapuerto, has opened near the Terminal Terrestre. At this time, most buses leaving from the Terminal Terrestre and the Terrapuerto are local buses. The terminal is modern and well organized, with shops, restaurants and a traveler's information office (☎ 24-1735). As always, keep a close watch on your belongings at the terminal. There is a US$0.50 departure tax.

There are many companies at the terminal, and I give some of the biggest or most important below. Your best bet is to go to the station a day ahead to buy a ticket for the best departure for your needs. Roads into the highlands are unpaved and are being improved, but travel times and costs can vary depending on road conditions.

Lima is between 16 and 20 hours away. Ormeño (☎ 42-4187, 42-3546), Cruz del Sur (☎ 23-2014, 21-6625), Flores Hermanos (☎ 23-8741), CIVA and others have several buses a day to Lima, most leaving in the afternoon. Fares range from a standard US$10 to US$20 for nonstop service with food. Ormeño and Cruz del Sur still maintain ticket offices at San Juan de Dios and Socabaya (see map), but buses leave from the terminal.

For intermediate south-coast points, most buses stop in Nazca (starting at US$6, about 9 to 12 hours), as well as Camaná, Chala and Ica, but remember that Pisco is about 5km off the Panamericana, and not all buses go there. Change in Ica if necessary. For north of Lima, change in Lima. There are also many buses a day via Moquegua to Tacna (US$4 to US$6, 6 to 7 hours).

If you're going inland to Lake Titicaca, the bus lines Ormeño, Cruz del Sur and Transportes Jacantay (☎ 23-2061) have one or two buses a day to Juliaca and Puno (US$7 to US$12, about 11 hours), with both daytime and overnight options. Julsa Angeles (☎ 43-0843) and others have buses through Puno all the way to Desagauadero (about 14 hours) on the Bolivian border. Sometimes, services all the way to La Paz, Bolivia, are offered, but these may involve a bus change at the border. The road is in poor shape, it's a bumpy ride and delays are common. These and other companies also have buses to Cuzco (US$12 to US$15, 12 to 18 hours) on a poor road. The journey to Juliaca and Cuzco take longer in wet weather.

Transportes Santa Ursula (☎ 28-5378) has almost hourly departures during the day for the coast at Mollendo. Many of its buses go on to Mejía. For Ilo, Flores Hermanos has several departures a day. Other companies serve all of these routes with less frequency.

Ormeño has international buses about every two days to Santiago, Chile and Buenos Aires, Argentina.

For sightseeing in the Department of Arequipa, try Transportes Andalucía, Transportes Colca, Transportes El Chasqui (☎ 27-1129), Turismo Pluma (☎ 28-4721), Transportes Cristo Rey and other small companies at the Terminal Terrestre for Chivay (US$2.50, 3 hours), continuing through Yanque, Achoma and Maca to Cabanaconde (US$4, 7 hours) on the upper Cañón del Colca. Several buses leave around noon, a few leave at dawn or earlier. It's best to buy a ticket the day before.

For buses to Corire (US$2.50, 3 hours) to visit Toro Muerto petroglyphs, go with Flores Hermanos, Transportes El Chasqui, Transportes Trebol or Transportes del Carpio (☎ 42-7049). Between them, they have departures almost every hour starting at about 5:30 am. El Chasqui also goes to Valle de Majes (US$2) for river running, as do other companies. Transportes Trebol continues through Corire to Andagua (US$7, 10 hours) to visit the Valle de los Volcanes. Andagua can also be reached with Transportes Alianza, which takes a longer route (US$8, 12 hours) via Cailloma.

For Cotahuasi (12 hours), Transportes Reyna (☎ 42-6549, 43-0612) has a 5 pm departure, and Transportes Panorama (☎ 24-3036) has a 3 pm departure, both from the Terminal Terrestre. I don't know of any day buses, but ask around.

Local services change frequently.

**Train** The Arequipa-Juliaca route is bleak, but the views of the altiplano are interesting, and you may see flamingos, vicuñas, alpacas and llamas. Unfortunately, daylight trains do not run, so you can't see much. The journey to Juliaca (and Puno) is less convenient and not much more comfortable by train than by bus.

The night train leaves Arequipa at 8 pm on Wednesday and Sunday and arrives at Juliaca at 6 am the following day. There have been more frequent trains in the past, and this may resume. This train continues to Puno, an hour away, or you can connect with the day train to Cuzco, which leaves Juliaca at 9 am. Thus it is possible to buy a through ticket to Cuzco from Arequipa, arriving at 6 pm. If going to Puno, it is cheaper and quicker to buy a ticket to Juliaca and then catch one of the many minibuses to Puno waiting for the train.

A significant number of people have their bags slashed or stolen or their pockets picked on the night train, particularly in the overcrowded and badly lit 2nd class, and to a lesser extent in 1st class. There are also a large number of thieves at the bustling Arequipa train station waiting for the night train or looking for tired passengers disembarking in Juliaca. Watch your baggage carefully and constantly. You are safest buying the Pullman-class tickets in addition to your 1st-class ticket. The railway company keeps changing the name of Pullman class – it may be called 'Buffet,' 'Turismo,' 'Ejecutivo' or 'Inca' class. First class may be called 'Económico.'

The Pullman car has reclining seats and heated carriages (it gets very cold on the altiplano at night, and most of the journey is at altitudes of more than 4000m). Attendants keep the doors locked and allow only ticket holders into the carriages, and also keep an eye on luggage. Oxygen is available if you begin to suffer from altitude sickness.

Fares from Arequipa change frequently. Since the 1st edition of this book, you could pay anywhere between US$2 and US$13 for a 1st-class ticket to Juliaca, with fares in 2nd class at about 25% lower. There is a surcharge for Pullman class (on top of the 1st-class fare). At this time, fares to Puno are US$13 for Pullman and US$7.50 in 1st (Económico), and more than twice as much to Cuzco. The price of a ticket depends on fluctuating exchange rates and various regulations, so see for yourself what the going rate is when you get there.

It's best to buy tickets in advance rather than trying to do so while guarding your luggage in the predeparture crowds. Ticket-office (☎ 23-3928, 21-5350) opening hours change constantly, and there are usually very long lines, which can mean you'll be waiting for several hours. You can buy tickets from various travel agencies in town. Each charge about a 25% commission but provide a transfer from your hotel to the station. Shop around for the best deal. If the Pullman surcharge to Cuzco is too expensive, consider taking 1st class for the Juliaca-Cuzco section, which occurs in daylight when it is easier to guard your luggage.

**AREQUIPA AREA**

## Getting Around
**To/From the Airport** There are no airport buses, although buses and minibuses marked Río Seco, Cono-Norte or Zamacola go along Avenida Puente Grau and Ejército and pass within a kilometer of the airport – ask the driver where to get off. A taxi from downtown costs about US$3.50. From the airport, shared colectivo taxis charge US$2 per person and take you to your hotel.

**To/From the Bus Terminal** Buses and minibuses go southbound along Bolívar and Sucre to the Terminal Terrestre. A taxi ride will cost about US$1.

**Car & Taxi** Avis (☎ 44-3576), Localiza (☎ 44-4222) and RentAndina (☎ 25-7775, 60-1882) are at the airport. You need to be at least 25 years old and have a major credit card and driver's license. Rentals are pricey, and you can hire a taxi with a driver for less.

**Bicycle** Hoz Bicicletas (☎ 28-8343, 22-3221, Villalba 428) sells spare parts and Trek and Klein bikes. The owner, Mario Ortiz de Zavallos, speaks some English.

# Around Arequipa

☎ 054

Several long-distance excursions can be made from Arequipa. The most popular is the tour of the Cañón del Colca. Others include climbing the volcano El Misti and other mountains, visiting the Majes Canyon and the petroglyphs at Toro Muerto, hiking in the Valle de los Volcanes and exploring the Cañón del Cotahuasi, said to be the world's deepest canyon.

Although many of these places can be visited by public transport, this takes longer than going on a tour. So, taking a tour is sometimes worth the extra money, unless, of course, you have the time and prefer the adventure of taking infrequent ramshackle buses to remote areas. The main advantage of taking a tour is that you can stop at the most interesting points for sightseeing or picture taking; however, on public transport, the bus just keeps going. Nevertheless, many travelers have written to say that they had a great time visiting these areas using a combination of buses and hiking.

If you decide to go on a guided tour, you'll have many options, as there are about a dozen tour companies operating out of Arequipa. Some of them aren't very good, so make sure you discuss exactly what to expect before parting with your money. (See Travel Agencies earlier in this chapter for a few recommendations.) Don't take a trip offered by a street tout. They will simply take you to a travel agency and rake in a commission without providing any extra services. Never pay for a tour except in a tour office, or you might never see the money, or the person you paid, again.

Alternatively, if there is a group of you to split the cost, you could rent a car or hire a taxi and driver. I was quoted US$110 for a taxi and driver for two days, but you could easily bargain this down.

## CAÑÓN DEL COLCA
There has been raging controversy over whether or not this is the world's deepest canyon – current opinion is that the nearby Cañón del Cotahuasi is deeper. The sections that you can see from the road on a standard guided tour are certainly very impressive but are not the deepest parts of the canyon. To see the deepest sections, you have to make an overnight trip and hike. It certainly warrants a visit if you have the time. The deepest sections are reportedly 3400m deep.

The people living in the Cañón del Colca region are known for their traditional clothing, especially the women's clothes. (The women don't particularly enjoy being photographed; ask permission.) Their dresses and jackets are beautifully embroidered, and their hats are distinctive. In the Chivay area at the east end of the canyon, the white hats are usually woven from straw and are embellished with lace, sequins and badges. At the west end of the canyon, the hats are of cotton and are colorfully embroidered.

## Guided Tours

Guided tours are about US$20 for a day trip, which lasts about 12 hours and is rushed, tiring and not recommended. I would take a two-day trip, which cost US$25 to US$50 per person with the cheaper agencies. Costs depend on the size of the group and the comfort of the overnight accommodations. Most tours are US$25 to US$35. The extra cost includes lodging with breakfast in Chivay, but other meals are usually at your own expense.

**One-Day Tour** Most one-day guided tours leave Arequipa (2325m) well before dawn and climb northwest past **Chachani** volcano, following the route of the railway. The old route used to go over a pass between Chachani and El Misti. This road, although shorter, is in very bad condition and not used by tour buses anymore. The road continues through the **Reserva Nacional Salinas y Aguada Blanca**, which covers 367,000 hectares at an average elevation of 3850m. Here, vicuñas are often sighted. Later in the trip, domesticated alpacas and llamas are frequently seen, so it is possible to see three of the four members of the South American Camelid family in one day. Seeing the fourth member, the guanaco, is very hard, as they have almost disappeared from this area.

After two to three hours, a breakfast stop is made at **Vizcachani** (4150m). The road continues through bleak altiplano over the high point of about 4800m, from where the snowcaps of **Ampato** (6380m) are seen. Flamingoes might be seen in this area as well. Then the road drops spectacularly to **Chivay**, which is about 160km from Arequipa.

The thermal **hot springs** of Chivay are sometimes visited (US$1.25; bring swimsuits and towels), and then the tour bus continues west, following the south bank of the upper **Cañón del Colca**. The landscape is remarkable for its Inca and pre-Inca terracing, which goes on for many kilometers and is the most extensive I've seen in Peru. The journey is worthwhile to see the terracing alone. Along the route, there are several villages whose inhabitants are involved in agriculture and continue using the terraces today. At **Yanque**, an attractive church that dates from the early 18th century is sometimes visited.

About 20km beyond Chivay, the bus often stops for the driver to point out a small **carved boulder** that is supposed to represent a pre-Columbian map of the terracing. The end point of the tour is at the lookout known as **Cruz del Cóndor**, about 60km beyond Chivay and an hour's drive before you get to the village of Cabanaconde. As the name suggests, Andean condors are sometimes seen here; early morning or late afternoon are the best times for this, although they have been reported at various hours during the day. From the lookout, the view is impressive, with the river flowing 1200m below. Mismi, on the other side of the canyon, is about 3200m above the canyon, and some guides will tell you that the depth measurement should be taken from Mismi's summit. In fact, deeper sections can be seen if you go farther, but this requires legwork from **Cabanaconde** (3290m). Most tours don't go as far as Cabanaconde, but you can visit it by public transport (see Getting There & Away later in this section).

**Two-Day Tour** The two-day tour essentially follows the same route, but leaves Arequipa at 8 am instead of before dawn and overnights in Chivay, where a peña is often held in the evening. Cruz del Cóndor is visited the following morning instead of the afternoon. Condors have reportedly been spotted at all times, though the morning is supposedly the best. Trekking tours can also be arranged to spend time in the canyon.

## Beyond the Guided Tours

Many travelers avoid taking a tour and use public transport to Chivay or Cabanaconde and make their own hotel arrangements. Travelers doing it alone should read the Guided Tours description for background.

**Pinchollo** is a small village a few kilometers before Cruz del Cóndor. From here, a trail climbs south toward **Nevado Hualca Hualca** (a snowcapped volcano of 6025m) to an active geothermal area, where there is a **geyser** that is continuously erupting. The jet of steam shoots between 15m and 30m into the air, and Arequipeños say it is the only geyser in the world that is continuously active. One reader reports that the geyser stopped erupting after a recent earthquake, but others say that it is still going. At any rate, the scenery is wild and interesting. It takes about four hours to walk to the geyser, but you must be acclimatized to high altitudes, as much of the trail is well over 4000m above sea level. The trail is fairly easy to follow, or you can hire a local guide in Pinchollo. The downhill return will take less than two hours, and the views of the snowcapped mountains are good. You can stay in Pinchollo and continue on to Cruz del Cóndor on foot – about two hours.

Cabanaconde is a good base for continuing on into the deepest parts of Cañón del Colca on foot. Ask for directions, or better, hire a local guide, since there are several trails and it can be confusing. Torrential rain and an earthquake during the 1998 El Niño damaged or closed some of the trails. There are a couple of different long-distance walks outlined in *Peru and Bolivia: Backpacking and Trekking* by Hilary Bradt, Jane Letham and John Pilkington. One goes from Cabanaconde down to the canyon bottom, then up the other side over a 5000m pass to Andagua in the Valle de los Volcanes. This adventure takes about five to seven days.

This area is fairly popular with Peruvian tourists but is still pretty much off the beaten track for international tourism. Travelers should expect basic accommodations.

## Places to Stay & Eat

Chivay, at an altitude of about 3700m, is the capital of the province of Cailloma and has several hotels. On or near the main plaza you'll find *Pensión Tierra del Fuego, Hostal Plaza* and *Hostal Municipal*. These are basic, cold-water hotels charging about US$2 a person, and there are others like this. Better hotels, with hot water and private showers and charging about US$7 for a double, include *Hostal La Casa de Lucila* (☎ 52-1109, in Arequipa 21-6206, Grau 131) and *Hotel Los Leños*, on Bolognesi. The

latter is owned by the same folks that have the Pizzería Los Leños in Arequipa. Both have cafés. *Hostal Anita* (☎ 52-1114, in Arequipa 21-3114, Plaza de Armas 607) is about US$8 for a double with bath and hot water.

Two or three blocks west of the plaza is *Hostal Posada del Inca* (☎ 52-1032, fax 52-1108, Salaverry 325), which has a restaurant. It's about US$7 per person with private bath and hot water. This place is favored by tour groups, but readers have complained about a lack of hot water and an overpriced restaurant that serves food similar to what is available at half the price in little restaurants and *comedores* around the plaza and market. Also in this price range is the seven-room *Hostal Kolping* (☎ 52-1076, fax 25-3744), on the outskirts. The best in town at this time is the *Rumi Llaqti Hotel* (☎/fax 52-1098), also away from the center, with rooms at US$23/32/45 for one/two/three people. They have a good restaurant with live music in the evening. New hotels open every year, as Chivay is becoming more frequently visited.

About 8km from Chivay and across the river is the *Colca Lodge*, an attractive stone and thatch building with modern solar-powered facilities and a nearby hot spring. Rooms start at US$40 for a double including breakfast; other meals are US$6. This hotel can be booked in Arequipa (☎/fax 21-2813, colcalodge@grupoinca.com, Zela 212) or with a tour operator in Arequipa.

If staying in Chivay, visit the hot springs that are 4km to the northeast of the village by road. There are minibuses or you can walk. There is a clean swimming pool, changing rooms, a basic cafeteria and an admission fee of US$1.25. The mineral-laden water is said to have curative properties; one traveler writes that it does a good job of boiling eggs for a picnic lunch. They close at dusk.

In Pinchollo, there is the very basic *El Refugio*, near the main plaza, with a couple of rooms at US$1.50 per person. A sleeping bag and flashlight are recommended, because it is very cold and the village lacks electricity.

Cabanaconde has a few basic family-run pensiones that charge about US$2.50 per person. These include *Hotel Cruz del*

*Cóndor, Hostal San Pedro* and *Hostal Solarex*. Bathroom facilities are poor. There is electricity for a couple of hours each evening. The better *Hostal Valle del Fuego* (☎ 28-0367) has a solar-powered shower and about 10 beds at US$3 per person. The owner, Paolino Hunco, knows a lot about the area and can give directions and arrange mule trips. However, several readers have criticized him for keeping a condor tied up in the yard. Also try the *Hostal Virgen de la Candelaria*.

## Getting There & Away
If you don't want a guided tour, see the Arequipa section for details on bus companies that have daily departures to Chivay. Some continue from Chivay past Achoma and Pinchillo (where you can get off) and on to Cabanaconde. In Chivay, there are bus offices along Calle Zarumilla (one block north and west of the plaza). Buses for Arequipa leave several times a day. Buses also leave Chivay at 6:30 am for Cabanaconde. The section of road beyond Cabanaconde to Huambo veers away from the canyon. It is also the roughest part of the road, and there is little transport.

Buses leave Cabanaconde at 7 am, 9:30 am and noon from the main square for the return to Arequipa via Chivay. There are also predawn buses for Cruz del Cóndor. These times change often, and buses don't always stick to them, so make a careful local inquiry.

## CAÑÓN DEL COTAHUASI
This remote canyon is almost 400km by road (200km as the condor flies) northwest of Arequipa. Parts of it are said to exceed 3500m or 4000m in depth (depending on the reference source), and locals claim that it is the deepest canyon in the world. It has only recently begun to be visited by a handful of adventurous travelers. This is a very rural and traditional area.

The main-access town is appropriately named **Cotahuasi** and is at 2680m above sea level on the southeast side of the canyon. It is the capital of the province of La Unión and has about 3200 inhabitants. There is a hospital and several simple places to stay.

Northeast of Cotahuasi and farther up the canyon are the villages of **Tomepampa** (10km away, 2700m), **Lucha** (17.5km away) and **Alca** (20km, 2750m), which also have accommodations. Alca, with 2500 inhabitants, is the end of the road.

Trails lead into the canyon, and **waterfalls** and **hot springs** can be visited. Backpacking and trekking trips of several days' duration can be arranged in Arequipa with Zárate Expediciones. In Cotahuasi, a local guide who can provide information and arrange mule hire is Marcio Ruíz, who can be contacted at Alojamiento Chávez (see Places to Stay & Eat). One can allegedly hike from Cotahuasi to the coast along the canyon in about two weeks.

## Places to Stay & Eat
The following places in Cotahuasi all charge about US$2.50 to US$4 per person. *Alojamiento Chávez* (☎ 58-1028, Cabildo 125) is a colonial house with a pleasant patio. There are seven rooms sharing two bathrooms. *Hostal Villa* (☎ 58-1018, Independencia 118) has a store and six rooms sharing one bathroom. Opposite, *Hostal Fany Luz* (☎ 58-1002, Independencia 117) has 11 rooms (some with an ancient black-and-white TV) and two bathrooms. They also have a store. *Alojamiento Justo Mota* (Independencia 106) has 10 beds, a restaurant and a bathroom. *Hostal Don Lucho* (Centenario 303) has three rooms, two bathrooms and a restaurant. *Señora Olga Ponce* (Cabildo 104) rents three rooms sharing one bathroom and provides meals. There are a couple of simple restaurants.

In Tomepampa, *Hostal Primavera (in Arequipa* ☎ 28-5089) has four rooms and two bathrooms. In Lucha, *Hostal Wasi Punko (in Arequipa* ☎ 23-7736, 21-4763) is a pleasant rustic building with three rooms, two bathrooms, hot showers and a typical restaurant. In Alca, there's *Hostal Chirino*, with five rooms sharing a bathroom.

## Getting There & Away
From Arequipa, the 385km journey, half of which is on unpaved roads, takes about 12 hours if the going is good. Over three-

AREQUIPA AREA

quarters of the way there, the road summits a 4650m pass between the huge glacier-capped mountains of Coropuna (6425m) and Solimana (6093m) before dropping down to Cotahuasi. Buses return to Arequipa with Transportes Panorama (Avenida Lima 106) at 4:30 pm and Transportes Reyna (Arequipa 201) at 5 pm. Unfortunately, there is no day bus, though daytime transport can be arranged with travel agencies.

## RIVER RUNNING

The river of the Cañón del Colca was first run in 1981, and it is dangerous and difficult. It is not to be undertaken lightly (a friend of mine died in it). A few commercial outfitters do expensive rafting trips through portions of the river. See the January 1993 *National Geographic* for a description of a recent expedition. Easier sections upriver from the canyon can be run. Recently, Mauro Zuñiga (cell 69-6672) started arranging rafting trips on the easier sections from Chivay (ask for him locally).

You can also do easier trips on the **Río Majes** (which the Colca flows into). The *Majes River Lodge* (☎ *47-1221, in Arequipa ☎/fax 25-5819),* in the village of La Central, 190km by road west of Arequipa and 820m above sea level, is the most convenient base. This modern lodge has double rooms with private bath and hot water for about US$20. There is a restaurant, bar and large garden

with outdoor games area and camping (US$2 per person). The lodge is owned by river-runner Julio Zuñiga, and river trips are arranged. A Class III, 8km whitewater run in inflatable rafts costs about US$16, including transport from the lodge. The actual run lasts about an hour and is suitable for beginners. Experienced river runners can take a 25km, Class-IV run lasting three hours for US$29. Costs are per person, with a four-person minimum. Trips may be unavailable during the January-to-March rainy season, when water levels can be dangerously high. (I understand that a landslide recently ruined the rapids on this river, and the lodge may be up for sale – ask locally for current conditions before going there.)

The lodge can also be used as a base to visit Toro Muerto and Valle de los Volcanes (see Toro Muerto Petroglyphs and Valle de los Volcanes later in this chapter) among other places. A guided trip to Toro Muerto is about US$20, and a trip to Valle de los Volcanes is US$200. These prices are per group of 1 to 10 people. The lodge arranges transport from Arequipa, though it is cheaper to take one of the public buses from Arequipa's Terminal Terrestre with Transportes Carpio to Aplao (US$2, 3 hours) and then take a minibus to La Central (or a taxi for US$3.50).

In Arequipa, Expediciones y Aventuras Colca (☎ 28-9179, cell 62-6560, expacolca@

clubinter.org.pe, Jerusalén 407), in the Pizzería Los Leños, does various trips to the Río Majes, including some with overnight camping. They also do a half-day trip on the Río Chili near Arequipa for US$30 per person; there is a three-person minimum. The trip spends 1½ hours on the Class III portion of the river, which is runnable from April to November.

Amazonas Explorer (☎ 21-2813, fax 22-0147, Zela 212, Apartado 333, Arequipa), the local office of a British company (see the Getting There & Away chapter), does an annual trip on the Río Cotahuasi, which includes six days of Class IV and V rapids. This is for folks with some rafting experience. They also do rafting trips on some sections of the Colca.

## MOUNTAIN CLIMBING

There are many high mountains in the Arequipa area that are technically not very difficult. The main problems are extreme weather conditions, altitude and lack of water. Temperatures drop to about -23°C to -29°C at the highest camps, so carry suitable clothing and a tent. Altitudes of over 5000m can easily be reached in a day from Arequipa, and adequate acclimatization is essential. Preferably, spend some time in Cuzco or Puno immediately before a high-altitude expedition from Arequipa. Water may need to be carried; ask locally for current conditions. If you're a beginning climber, remember that people have died in these mountains, though they look like easy climbs. Be aware of the main symptoms of altitude sickness. If in doubt, go back down.

Maps of the area can be obtained from the Instituto Geográfico Nacional and the South American Explorers' clubhouse in Lima.

### Guides

Unless you are sure you know what you are doing, I recommend hiring a reliable guide. Some of the travel agencies in Arequipa claim to have experienced guides, though they aren't always reliable; you should check that they have a little black book that identifies trained and registered guides. I recommend contacting Zárate Expediciones (see Tour Agencies in Arequipa earlier in this chapter). They rent tents, ice axes and crampons; however, climbers should bring their own sleeping bags, climbing boots and warm clothes. I have received reports of other guides pretending that they are Zárates; check identification.

The standard official rate for hiring a mountain guide is US$50 per day, plus the cost of food and transport. One guide can take a group of up to four climbers for this price.

### El Misti

This 5825m-high volcano looms over Arequipa and is the most popular local climb. It is technically one of the easiest ascents of any mountain of this size in the world. Nevertheless, it is hard work, and you normally need an ice ax, and sometimes crampons. The mountain can be climbed year round, but July to November are considered the best months, with October and November being the least cold. January and February are the most difficult, with clouds and snow. At the summit is a 10m-high iron cross, which was erected in 1901. Below the summit is a crater with fumaroles (vents through which volcanic gases escape).

There are several routes, but none of them are clearly marked or easy to find. One route, known as the Apurímac Route, is notorious for robberies. Therefore, it is recommended that you hire a guide. Public transport to the mountain base is hard to find. You can hire a 4WD vehicle for US$50 to take you up to about 3300m and pick you up on your return. Another route, on the back of the mountain, allows you to get up to 4000m by 4WD, but costs US$120 to US$150 for the vehicle.

### Other Mountains

One of the easiest 6000m peaks in the world is **Chachani** (6075m), which is as close to Arequipa as El Misti. You need crampons, an ice ax and good equipment. There are various routes, one of which involves going by 4WD (US$120) to Campamento de Azufrera at 4950m. From here you can reach the summit in about nine hours, if acclimatized, and return in under four. Alternatively, for a two-day trip, there is a good spot to camp at 5200m. Other routes take three days, but are easier to get to by jeep (US$50).

**Sabancaya** (5976m) is part of a massif on the south rim of the Cañón del Colca, which includes **Hualca Hualca** (6025m) and **Ampato** (6380m). Sabancaya is currently the most active of the region's volcanoes and has been erupting in recent years. I am told that the crater can be approached in between eruptions if you have an experienced guide. Sounds like a pretty risky proposition to me. Ampato is a fairly straightforward three-day ascent, and you get views of the active Sabancaya – this seems like a safer option. Ampato has been the site of recent archaeological discoveries (see the boxed text 'Human Sacrifice in the Andes' earlier in this chapter).

Other nearby mountains of interest include **Ubinas** (5675m), a volcano that can be reached from the village of Ubinas, served by a daily 7 am Empresa Municipal Ubinas bus from Arequipa. Their offices are at Espinar 204 and Sepulveda 101. This is a two-day climb, and there is a lot of geothermal activity. **Mismi** (5556m) is a fairly easy three- or four-day climb on the north side of the Cañón del Colca. You can approach it from the villages of Cailloma and, with a guide, find the lake that is reputedly the source of the Amazon. The highest mountain in southern Peru is the more difficult **Coropuna**, which is variously labeled as 6305m or 6425m on maps. The Andes have many remote peaks and altitudes that have not yet been definitively measured.

## LAGUNA DE SALINAS

This lake, east of Arequipa between the mountains of Pichu Pichu and Ubinas, is a salt lake that becomes a white salt flat during the dry months of May to December. Its size and the amount of water in it vary from year to year depending on the weather. During the rainy season, it is a good place to see various flamingo species, as well as other Andean waterbirds. The elevation here is about 4300m.

Buses to Ubinas pass the lake, but catching a bus from the lake back to Arequipa is difficult, because the bus begins at the village of Ubinas and is very full by the time it passes the lake. You can hike around the lake, which can take about two days, then return down the Río Andamayo as far as Chiguata (a long day), from where a daily 4 pm bus returns to Arequipa. There may be other buses – ask at the Terminal Terrestre.

## TORO MUERTO PETROGLYPHS

This is a magnificent and unusual archaeological site in the high desert. It consists of hundreds of carved boulders spread over about 2 sq km of desert. Archaeologists are uncertain of the cultural origins of this site, but it is thought that it was made by the Wari culture about 1200 years ago.

To reach the site by public transport, take a bus to **Corire** (US$2, 3 hours; see Getting There & Away for Arequipa earlier in this chapter) and then walk for about 1½ hours. In Corire there is the basic *Hostal Willy*, which charges about US$3 per night and can provide information on reaching the site. It can get very hot and dry, so bring plenty of extra water and sunblock. If you don't want to sleep in Corire, take an early bus (they start at 5:30 am) from Arequipa and get off at a sign for Toro Muerto 2km before the town of Corire. Here, a dirt track goes up a valley to the petroglyphs; locals will show you the way. Buses return from Corire to Arequipa once an hour, usually leaving at 30 minutes past the hour. There are several simple restaurants along the main street in Corire, some of which serve the local speciality – *camarones* (river shrimp).

The Toro Muerto petroglyphs can also be visited more conveniently but expensively on full-day tours from Arequipa.

## VALLE DE LOS VOLCANES

This unusual valley is covered with scores of small and medium-sized volcanic cones and craters – a veritable moonscape. The 65km-long valley surrounds the village of **Andagua** near the snowcapped mountain of Coropuna. It is a weird and remote area that is seldom visited by travelers. Perhaps that's a good reason to go.

Other sights include the *chullpas* (pre-Columbian funerary towers) at Soporo, a two-hour hike from Andagua. A car can get very close to the site. En route to Soporo is a pre-Columbian city named Antaymarca. Northeast of Andagua, at a place called Izanquillay, the Río Andahua runs through a lava canyon 50m deep but 5m wide. There is a spectacular 40m-high waterfall here.

To get to Valle de los Volcanes, take a bus to Andagua (see Getting There & Away for

Arequipa earlier in this chapter). Return buses leave in the afternoon and arrive in Arequipa in the early hours of the morning, though the driver allows passengers to sleep on the bus until daylight. Adventurers can hike there from Cabanaconde in about six days.

There are a few cheap and basic hostels. One is run by the **Consejo Municipal de Andagua** and is often full. Another is run by **Señor Aguilar**, and it is reportedly better. **Restaurant Sarita**, on the plaza, is cheap and friendly.

# The Lake Titicaca Area

Generations of schoolchildren have been taught that Lake Titicaca – at 3820m above sea level – is the highest navigable lake in the world, and this alone seems to make it a tourist attraction.

In fact, there are many navigable lakes at altitudes of over 4000m, such as Lake Junín in Peru's central Andes, but Lake Titicaca is called the world's highest simply because it has frequent passenger boats and is better known than other higher lakes, which lack passenger craft. If you like trivia, note that Lake Titicaca – at over 170km in length – is South America's largest lake and the largest lake in the world above 2000m. At this altitude, the air is unusually clear, and the deep blue of the lake is lovely. Because various interesting boat trips on the lake can be taken from Puno (Peru's major port on Lake Titicaca), many travelers spend some days in Puno en route to either Cuzco or Bolivia.

There are many other reasons to linger in the area, not the least of which is the incredibly luminescent quality of the sunlight on Peru's high plain, the altiplano. Horizons seem limitless, and the earthy tones of the scenery are as deep as the lake itself. These colors are reflected in the nut-brown faces of the people of the altiplano, as well as in their colonial churches and archaeological monuments, several of which are well worth visiting.

The Department of Puno is also famous for its folk dances, which are the wildest and most colorful in the Peruvian highlands. And, if this isn't enough, there are fascinating Andean animals to be seen – huge herds of domesticated alpaca and llama – and sparkling highland lakes full of waterbirds, such as the giant Andean coot and various species of rosy-colored flamingo.

## Dangers & Annoyances

The 3820m elevation means that travelers run a real risk of getting *soroche* (altitude sickness) if arriving directly from the coast. Rather than flying in from Lima, plan on spending time in Arequipa (2325m) and then Cuzco (3326m) for best acclimatization.

## JULIACA

With a population of about 100,000, Juliaca is the largest town in the Department of Puno and has the department's only commercial airport. It is also an important railway junction, with connections to Arequipa, Puno and Cuzco. The elevation is 3822m, and many of its inhabitants are highland Indians.

The main reasons travelers come here are to make train or plane connections. Some people take the rarely traveled northern route into Bolivia or visit the Monday market, but most people prefer to go on to Puno, where there are better hotels and a view of Lake Titicaca. I have enjoyed wandering around Juliaca and getting away from the gringo trail. A nice day trip (or overnight trip) is to the town of Lampa.

## Information

**Money** Most banks have ATMs and are open weekdays from about 9 am to 1 pm and 4 to 6 pm. There are many casas de cambio and street moneychangers around the intersection of Bolívar and M Nuñez.

**Post & Communications** A post office and two Telefónica del Peru offices are shown on the map.

Internet access is available at Galerías San Martín (a small shopping mall).

**Medical Services** Juliaca's Clínica Americana Adventista (☎ 32-1001, 32-1369, emergency 32-1071, Loreto 315) is the best hospital in the Department of Puno.

**Dangers & Annoyances** If you arrive from the coast, especially by air, take it easy for one or two days – see Altitude Sickness

LAKE TITICACA AREA

in the Health section of the Facts for the Visitor chapter.

The railway station has thieves meeting arriving and departing passengers. Keep your eyes open, your luggage locked and your wits about you. Taxi drivers routinely try to overcharge foreigners.

## Places to Stay

**Budget** The water supply is not reliable in the cheapest hotels. You'll find several cheap, basic cold-water places near the train station and also near the bus stop for Puno (at Piérola and 8 de Noviembre). Some of these are noisy and dirty, but the following are OK. *Hostal San Antonio* (☎ 32-1803, San Martín 347) is basic but clean. Rooms are US$3/5 for singles/doubles without a bathroom, and they have some larger dorm rooms for just US$2 per person. Rooms with a sink and toilet, though not a shower, are US$4/6. Hot showers are an extra US$0.80 for 20 minutes.

They have a sauna for US$3. Hours for the sauna are 10 am to 6 pm; it is open for women on Thursday and Saturday and for everyone on other days. This hotel is building a new wing, which is slated to open in 1999.

*Hotel Don Pedro* (☎ 32-1442, Bracesco 475) charges US$3.25 per person including communal showers and occasional hot water. The small *Hostal Aparicio* (☎ 32-1625, Loreto 270) has some hot water and charges US$3.50 per person. Nearby, *Hostal Loreto* is cheaper. All are basic.

The clean and friendly *Hostal Yarur* (☎ 32-1501, M Nuñez 414) has hot water from 6 to 8 am and 7 to 8 pm. Rooms are US$4.50/5.50 or US$5.50/8 with private bath. *Hostal Sakura* (☎ 32-2072, Unión 133) is OK for US$4/6 with communal hot showers or US$6/9 with private bath and hot water in the morning. *Corona Hotel* (☎ 32-5002, San Martín 259) is clean and has hot water in communal showers from 6 to 9 am, and

## JULIACA

**PLACES TO STAY**
11 Eurobuilding Hotel
12 Hostal Santa María
13 Hostal Yarur
15 Hostal Karlo's-Che-Karlin
17 Corona Hotel
18 Hostal San Antonio
24 La Maison Hotel
26 Hostal Sakura
27 Hotel Royal Inn
28 Hostal Don Carlos
30 Hostal Aparicio
31 Hotel Don Pedro
32 Hostal Peru
34 Hostal Loreto
36 Sámari Hotel
37 Don Carlos Suites Hotel

**PLACES TO EAT**
20 Café Dorado
25 Restaurant Trujillo

**OTHER**
1 Post Office
2 TEPSA
3 Transportes Carhuamayo
4 Cruz del Sur
5 Transportes Huanca, CIVA
  & other companies
6 Ormeño & other bus companies
7 Banco Latino
8 Telefónica del Peru
9 Transportes San Martín & others
  to Moquegua, Tacna
10 Banco Continental

14 Transportes Los Angeles
   buses to Puno
16 CineMark's
19 Telefónica del Peru
21 Interbanc
22 Money Exchange
23 Galerías San Martín, Internet
26 Aero Continente
29 Banco de Crédito
33 Clínica Americana Adventista
35 Minibuses to Puno

To Cuzco, Arequipa

Lambayeque

To Market

To buses for
Huancané, Moho

Ica
Sandia
Salaverry
Ayacucho
Lima
M Núñez
Sandia
Huancané
Moquegua

Huáscar

Plaza
de Armas

† Church

Huayna Capac

Jauregui

2 de Mayo

Piérola

8 de Noviembre

Tumbes

Apurimac

10 ⑤
11 ■

12 ■
15 ▯
Cuzco
16 ●

13 ■

9 ◕
14 ◕

Hill

Staircase

Bolivar

17 ■

18 19
⑤ ☎

San Martin

▼ 20

22 ⑤
23 ●

21 ⑤

J. Chávez

24 ■

25 ▼
Pedestrian
Mall

27 ■

26
■

28 ■

⑤ 29

Manuel Prado

7 de Junio

9 de Diciembre

San Román

M Núñez

31 ■

Plaza
Bolognesi

Train
Station

33 ✚

30 ■

32 ■

Loreto

34
■

35 ◕

Braceseo

Noriega

37 ■

Piura

36 ■

To Puno

0        100        200 m
0        100        200 yards

occasionally for an hour in the evening. Rooms are US$4/7.50 or US$5.25/9 with a sink and toilet but no shower. *Hostal Santa María* (☎ 32-1427, Cuzco 102) has basic but clean rooms with private bath and (they say) hot water all day for US$6/10.

The clean and recommended *Hostal Peru* (☎ 32-1510, Bracesco 409) charges US$5.50/8.50, or US$7/13 with private bath, and has hot water from 5 pm and all night. They have a simple but slightly pricey restaurant. *Euro-building Hotel* (☎ 32-1186, 2 de Mayo 135) is a big hotel with seven floors of dark corridors and reasonably comfortable rooms with cable TV, bath and hot water for US$12/17.

**Mid-Range** The following hotels all have clean rooms with private showers and 24-hour hot water (with occasional lapses), cable TV and telephone. Most of them will give you a discount if you ask for their 'best price.' The recommended *Hotel Royal Inn* (☎ 32-1561, fax 32-1572, San Román 158) charges US$19/25 for slightly worn rooms, but they have one of the best restaurants in town, and room service is available. The small, friendly *Hotel Karlo's – Che-Karlin* (☎ 32-4759, 32-1817, fax 32-4857, Unión 317) charges US$17/26. A decent restaurant is attached. *Sámari Hotel* (☎ 32-1870, 32-1670, fax 32-1852, Noriega 325) is quiet, provides electric room heaters and charges US$18/24. They also have a restaurant. The newest is *La Maison Hotel* (☎ 32-1444, fax 32-1763, 7 de Junio 535), which has the nicest rooms (probably because they are new) and a restaurant open for breakfast. Rates are US$17/27.

*Hostal Don Carlos* (☎ 32-1293, fax 32-2120, 9 de Diciembre 124) has clean, pleasant rooms with heating and minibar for US$32.50/42.50. There is a restaurant. *Don Carlos Suites Hotel* (☎ 32-1571, fax 32-2635, in Lima 224-0275, 476-2468, fax 224-8581, dcarloslim@tci.net.pe, Manuel Prado 335) has old but comfortable rooms for US$64/77 (overpriced) and there is an adequate restaurant.

## Places to Eat

Juliaca's town center seems to have several simple restaurants on every block – they're nothing to write home about, but you certainly won't starve. *Café Dorado* is the best place for coffee and cake. The *Restaurant Trujillo* is quite good, but a little pricey for budget travelers. The restaurant at the *Hotel Royal Inn* is the best I could find.

## Entertainment

There is a definite lack of peñas – you'll find more action in Puno. *CineMark's* sometimes shows films in English. Discos come and go; there are several in the center.

## Shopping

Monday is market day, and Juliaca has some of the cheapest prices for alpaca goods if you bargain. The market is held west of the Plaza de Armas.

## Getting There & Away

**Air** Juliaca airport serves both Juliaca and Puno. Aero Continente (☎ 32-8440), under Hostal Sakura, has two or three flights a day to and from Lima via Arequipa. There are no direct flights to Cuzco. This is subject to change.

**Bus** There are buses to most points in southern Peru, and services are offered by several companies. Buses are available to Arequipa (US$5 and up, 10 to 12 hours) and Cuzco (US$5 and up, eight hours) with Cruz del Sur (☎ 32-2011), Carhuamayo (☎ 32-1511), CIVA (☎ 32-6229), TEPSA, Ormeño and several other companies in the same area. Most buses travel overnight, but a few go during the day. The road to Cuzco is steadily being improved and paved, and journey times are improving. To get to Lima, you need to change in Arequipa or Cuzco.

San Martín (☎ 32-4090) and several other companies at the same intersection have night buses to Moquegua, Tacna (US$6, 10 hours) and Ilo. Day buses are not available. Buses to Huancané (US$1, 1½ hours) leave every hour from Benigno Ballón and Sucre, about four blocks east of Apurímac and 1½ blocks north of Lambayeque (off the map).

For Puno, minibuses (US$0.50) leave when they are full from the southeast corner of Plaza Bolognesi. Colectivo taxis also leave from here. Larger buses (US$0.30) depart from 8 de Noviembre at Piérola.

**Train** Juliaca is the busiest railway crossroad in Peru. The single train station serves Puno to the south, Cuzco to the northwest and Arequipa to the southwest. Although you can get off at intermediate points (notably, the towns of Ayaviri and Sicuani), they are of little interest to most travelers. To continue by train to Machu Picchu, you must change stations in Cuzco.

Tickets are often sold out in advance, so think ahead. Buy the ticket the day before you travel. Ticket-office hours are 7 to 11 am Monday to Saturday, 2 to 6 pm Tuesday to Thursday, and 5 to 7 pm Monday to Friday; but they change often, and lines are invariably long.

See the Puno section later in this chapter for details about trains, times and fares. Fares for northbound trains from Juliaca are a few cents cheaper than from Puno, and trains leave about one to two hours after the Puno departure time.

Passengers arriving in Juliaca on the overnight train from Arequipa and continuing on to Cuzco normally have a couple of hours between trains to wander around. Many salespeople at the station sell alpaca sweaters and ponchos, so if you prefer, you can do your shopping through the carriage window. Bargain hard – prices tend to drop just before the train leaves.

Passengers arriving in Juliaca at night from Cuzco and heading directly on to Puno will find that if they get off the train in Juliaca and continue on one of the minibuses waiting outside the train station they'll get into Puno half an hour ahead of the train. Definitely beware of thieves in the ill-lit Juliaca station, which has a reputation for luggage-snatching and pickpocketing. Read the warnings under Train in Arequipa's Getting There & Away section, and watch your belongings with an eagle eye.

### Getting Around
**To/From the Airport** A bus with an 'Aeropuerto' placard cruises around town before heading to the airport; ask where you

can catch it. The fare is US$0.30. Alternately, bargain for a taxi and expect to pay US$1.25 to US$2. At the airport, you'll find colectivos heading directly to Puno for US$3 a passenger. Touts will try to sell you tours etc, but I don't recommend them.

## LAMPA
This quiet and charming little town is 23km northwest of Juliaca. It's nicknamed 'La Ciudad Rosada' because most of its buildings are painted pink. The attractive church of La Inmaculada can be visited and contains a copy of Michelangelo's famous statue La Pieta, donated by a leading local citizen named Don Enrique Torres Belón, who is buried in the church. A caretaker will show you around. A tiny museum at the back of a shop at Ugarte 462 and Ayacucho contains local pottery. There is a colorful Sunday market.

About 6km west of town over a bridge (ask locals) is Cueva de los Toros, a cave with some animal carvings that look more like llamas than *toros* (bulls). The cave is in some rocks on the right side of the road. En route to the cave, you see some funerary towers similar to the ones at Sillustani (see Around Puno later in this chapter).

### Places to Stay & Eat
Most visitors come on day trips, but you could overnight at the very basic but friendly *Hostal Lima (Lima 135)*, which charges a little over US$1 per person. A *chicken restaurant* on the corner of the plaza opposite the church is one of the better restaurant options.

### Getting There & Away
Buses leave when full from Avenida Huáscar in Juliaca, near the market and a few blocks past where the map stops. Buses charge US$0.75, and there are faster but less comfortable minibuses for a little more. Buses returning from Lampa to Juliaca stop at 2 de Mayo, near the market area.

## NORTHWEST OF JULIACA
Almost 56km northwest of Juliaca, **Pucara** is the first village of any size on the road or rail trip to Cuzco. It is famous as a cerami-

enter and makes the ceramic bulls often een perched on the roofs of houses for ood luck. These are offered for sale at the tation when the train comes through. There re no hotels, but rooms can be rented.

Almost 100km northwest of Juliaca is yaviri, the first sizeable town on the route ɔ Cuzco. The road is paved to here, and aving is continuing. The railway also stops ere. At 3928m above sea level, Ayaviri is a old and not especially attractive market own, although it does boast a colonial hurch. A few kilometers away are the hot orings of Poypoy Kella. There are several imple hotels, of which the best is *Hotel araíso* (☎ *86-3024, 86-3503, L Prado 254*); it as rooms with private bath, hot water and V. Cheaper places include the *Hostal arconi* (☎ *86-3200, J Chávez 735*) and the asic *Hostal Ayaviri* (☎ *86-3142, Grau 180*).

The route continues through the villages f **Chuqibambilla** and **Santa Rosa** – where 1acks and alpaca souvenirs are offered to assengers halting at the railway stations – nd climbs through bleak altiplano to the **bra La Raya**, a pass at 4319m and the ighest point on the trip. This is about 70km eyond Ayaviri, and snowcapped mountains re visible. Near Abra La Raya is an experi- 1ental agricultural station where alpaca and ama herds are kept. The pass also marks the epartmental line between Puno and Cuzco, nd places beyond here are described in outheast of Cuzco in the next chapter.

## ORTHERN ROUTE TO BOLIVIA

his little-traveled, adventurous route into olivia is recommended only for experi- nced off-the-beaten-track travelers who ave little concern for time or comfort. Few ringos use this route, and you should be ɔmfortable communicating in Spanish. ɪrst get an exit stamp from Peruvian igraciónes in Puno. They'll predate the amp by three days to give you time to do ιe trip if you explain which way you are ɔing. Then head to Juliaca.

Decrepit buses full of Andean Indians ravel from Juliaca to **Huancané** many times day (see Getting There & Away in Juliaca). ɔme buses continue to **Moho** en route to

Bolivia. Huancané is a small town of 5000 inhabitants. You can stay at the very basic *Hostal Santa Cruz* (☎ *86-6126, M Castilla 103*), next to where the bus from Juliaca ter- minates. Slightly better hotels are *Hostal Huancané*, on the Plaza de Armas, and *Hostal Grau*, at Grau 108. There are a few cheap restaurants near the plaza.

Several buses leave daily from Huancané on the unpaved road to Moho (US$1.50, two hours). Some buses originate in Juliaca, so you may have to stand. Trucks also do this route. The unsigned and basic *Alojamiento Mojo* just off the main plaza is the only place to stay in Moho at this time – ask around for it. Beds are US$1.50. The town's electricity comes on at night for an hour or two only, so bring spare batteries for your flashlight. Moho is a friendly and clean little place with cobbled streets and about 2000 people. Few foreign visitors are seen.

A truck reportedly runs from Moho to Bolivia most mornings, leaving well before dawn – ask around. If you're not an early riser, you could walk about five hours to **Conima** (which has a basic hostel), on the shores of Lake Titicaca, then follow the shore for another five hours to **Tilali** near the Bolivian border. From here, it's about four more hours to the nearest Bolivian town of **Puerto Acosta**. There are very few vehicles, so don't count on hitchhiking.

Three times a week, a bus goes from Juliaca to Tilali via Huancané, Moho and Conima. These buses leave Juliaca from the 10th block of Lambayeque at the corner with the Colegio Encinas at 6:30 am Tues- day, Friday and Sunday. From Tilali, buses/ trucks head to Puerto Acosta in Bolivia. There is a big weekend market in Tilali, and it becomes easier to find transport to Puerto Acosta, but you might get stuck midweek. There are no hotels, but local families have rooms to stay in. Buses return from Tilali to Juliaca on Wednesday, Saturday, Sunday and the early hours of Monday morning, but I don't know the hours.

At the border is a tiny village with no hotels or restaurants. The police here are reportedly unfriendly, so make sure your documents are in order. The Bolivian migraciones is in Puerto Acosta, where you'll need to get your passport stamped. The office is on the main plaza, and if it's closed, you can often find someone to open it if you ask around; US$1 is charged for this service. There is a basic *alojamiento*, or lodging, on the plaza that charges about US$1 and a couple of cheap restaurants nearby. Transportation out of Puerto Acosta does not leave daily, so take the first vehicle you can, be it truck or bus, heading toward La Paz.

The nearest Bolivian consulate is in Puno. The Puno section of this chapter contains more information about entering Bolivia via normal routes.

## PUNO

Puno was founded on November 4, 1668, near the site of a now-defunct silver mine called Laykakota, but there are few colonial buildings to see. The town has a busy market and offers a good selection of hotels and restaurants. There is plenty to see in the environs.

For many travelers to Peru, Puno (3830m) is the highest place at which they'll spend any amount of time. The weather at this altitude can be extreme. It's very cold at night – particularly during the winter months of June, July and August, when temperatures can drop well below freezing.

If you're cold, buy a thick alpaca sweater from the market – they're cheap. The rainy season is October to May. During the wettest months (December to April), floods and landslides sometimes close the roads briefly. Because the sun is very strong at this altitude, sunburn is a common problem; remember to wear a wide-brimmed hat and use sunblock.

Puno has about 80,000 inhabitants and is the capital of the Department of Puno, mainly because of its important position on the shores of Lake Titicaca. Nearby Juliaca is larger.

## Information

**Tourist Office** Limited tourist information is available in a sweater shop on Lima, northeast of the Plaza de Armas. All the travel agencies and many hotels offer tourist

information. The Policía de Turismo, (☎ 35 7100, Deustua 588) has tourist informatio and provides help in cases of emergency.

**Bolivian Consulate** This is at Arequipa 12 (☎ 35-1251). Visa regulations change fre quently, but citizens of most European cour tries can stay 90 days without a visa; citizer of the USA, Canada, Australia, New Zealand, France and Benelux countries ca stay 30 days without a visa. Many othe nationalities require a visa in advance usually issued for a 30-day stay.

**Immigration** Migraciones (☎ 35-710. Grau 365) will extend Peruvian visas an tourist cards, but they are reportedly slow. may be easier to just go to Bolivia an return.

**Money** Although Bolivian pesos can b exchanged in Puno, travelers to and from Bolivia are advised to buy or sell Bolivia pesos at the border for the best exchang rates.

You'll find most of the banks on Cal Lima. They have ATMs and change trav eler's checks. Moneychangers hang out i front of the banks and may give better rate and faster service, but watch carefully, or yo can be cheated. They normally deal just US cash or Bolivian pesos.

Some hotels may change money fc guests, but at lower rates.

**Post & Communications** The Puno po office, at Moquegua 267, is open from 8 a to 6 pm daily except Sunday, when it close at 1 pm.

There are several phone offices; a cor venient one is on Lima north of Liberta Puno's area code is 054.

Internet service is offered at Arequip 345, office 106, from 9 am to 8 pm Monda to Saturday at US$2 per hour. Dc Gerólamo Restaurant, at Lambayeque 14 has an Internet café that is open daily t 10 pm at US$2.50 per hour.

**Travel Agencies** There are many agenci offering local tours and services. It definite

# PUNO

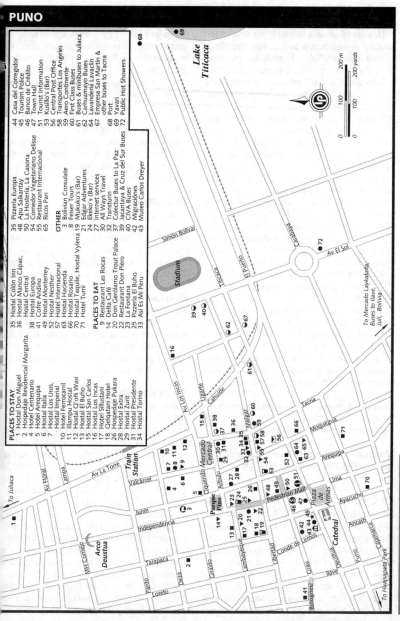

**PLACES TO STAY**
1 Hostal Don Miguel
2 Hospedaje Residencial Margarita
4 Hotel Centenario
5 Hotel Arequipa
6 Hostal Italia
7 Hostal Los Uros,
   Hostal Imperial
10 Hotel Ferrocarril
11 Illampu Hostal
13 Hostal Qoñi Wasi
15 Hostal El Buho
16 Hostal San Carlos
17 Hostal Los Incas
18 Qelqatani Hotel
26 Hospedaje Pukara
28 Hostal Zuirt
29 Hostal Extra
31 Hostal Presidente
34 Hostal Torino
35 Hostal Colón Inn
36 Hostal Manco Cápac,
   Hotel Manco Cápac,
38 Hostal Central
41 Hostal Europa
49 Cofre Andino
52 Hostal Monterrey
57 Hotel Internacional
63 Hostal Hacienda
66 Hostal Rosario
70 Hostal Taquile, Hostal Vylena
71 Hotel Tumi

**PLACES TO EAT**
9 Restaurant Las Rocas
14 Delta Café
20 Don Gerólamo Trout Palace
22 Restaurant Don Piero
23 La Fontana
25 Pizzería El Buho
33 Así Es Mi Peru
35 Pizzería Europa
58 Apu Salkantay
54 La Hostería, La Casona
54 Comedor Vegetariano Delisse
55 Restaurant Internacional
65 Ricos Pan

**OTHER**
3 Bolivian Consulate
8 Mukuku's (Bar)
19 Edgar Adventures
21 Feiser Tours
27 Internet services
30 All Ways Travel
32 Transturin
37 Colectur Buses to La Paz
39 Jacantaya & Cruz del Sur Buses
40 CIVA Buses
42 Migraciónes
43 Museo Carlos Dreyer
44 Casa del Corregidor
45 Tourism Police
46 Banco de Crédito
47 Town Hall
51 Tourist Information
53 Kusillo's (Bar)
56 Central Post Office
58 Transportes Los Angeles
59 Aero Continente
60 First Class Buses
61 Buses & minibuses to Juliaca
62 Carhuamayo Buses
64 Lavandería Lavaclin
67 Empresa San Martin &
   Poder buses to Tacna
68 Yavari
69 Port
72 Public Hot Showers

pays to shop around and talk to other travelers about their experiences.

Beware of street touts hanging around the popular gringo hotels and restaurants. They are not always reliable. Especially beware of the touts on the train from Cuzco; they get on in Juliaca and will sell you hotel rooms, tours, bus/train/plane tickets – anything you want. They claim to offer the cheapest rates, but in fact, they are often more expensive, because they receive commissions for their sales. Never part with your money until you are in a hotel or travel agency – some travelers pay for a service and never see the guide again.

Several agencies have been recommended by readers; the following two were given several warm recommendations. The recommended Edgar Adventures (☎/fax 35-3444, edgaradventures@viaexpresa.com.pe, Lima 328) is run by the enthusiastic and knowledgeable Edgar and Norka, who both speak excellent English and use very good guides. All Ways Travel (☎/fax 35-5552, 35-1085, awtperu@mail.cosapidata.com.pe, Tacna 234) is run by Eliana, who is multilingual. Others that have been recommended include Feiser Tours (☎ 35-3112, Valcárcel 155) and Alina Tours (☎ 35-7139, Lima 343). There are many others. Transturin (☎ 35-2771, Libertad 176) does expensive tours across Lake Titicaca using a catamaran (see Going to Bolivia later in this chapter).

**Laundry** I couldn't find a laundry service by weight – they charge by the piece. Try Lavandería Lavaclin at Deustua 223.

**Medical Services** The best hospital is in Juliaca. The Regional Hospital (☎ 35-2931, Avenida El Sol 1022) is not as good.

### La Catedral

La Catedral, on Plaza de Armas, was completed in 1757. The interior is more spartan than you'd expect after seeing the well-sculpted lower part of the main facade, though there is a silver-plated main altar. Following a 1964 visit by Pope Paul VI, the basilica is allowed to fly the Vatican flag to the right of the main altar. The cathedral is open from 8 am to noon and 3 to 5 pm daily.

### Museo Carlos Dreyer

Just off the plaza at Conde de Lemos 289 the town's main (albeit very small) museum formerly a private collection that wa bequeathed to the city upon the owner death. Hours are 7:30 am to 3:30 pm week days, and admission is US$1. Opening hou change frequently, and it's best to go in th morning.

### Casa del Corregidor

This is one of Puno's oldest houses and is a Deustua 576. It is currently being converte into a cultural center and café, which plar on opening in late 1999.

### Huajsapata Park

This park is atop a little hill about a 1 minute walk southwest of town. Its highe point has a larger-than-life white statue the first Inca, Manco Capac, looking out ov Lake Titicaca, the legendary site of his birt The view of the town and the lake is excellen

### Mercado Central

The central market is always interestin especially in the morning, when the sale people are setting up their stalls. It's full Indian women sitting behind piles of pot toes or peanuts and is also a good place buy woolen clothes.

### Places to Stay

Some of Puno's cheaper hotels have on cold showers, which are painful at this al tude. Others limit their hot water to a fe hours a day or have only tepid electr showers. If you want to economize, you ca stay in a cheap hotel and use the public h showers. The best, on Avenida El So charges about US$1 for a 30-minute h shower and is open between 7 am and 7 p daily, except holidays.

The better hotels fill up quickly when t evening trains arrive, so try to find a room soon as possible. The prices given here ma rise (up to double) during fiestas (especial Candlemas – see the boxed text 'Fiestas Folklore Around Lake Titicaca') and som times in the evening, though hotels are su posed to display the prices of their rooms

## Fiestas & Folklore Around Lake Titicaca

The department of Puno is noted for its wealth of traditional dances – there are as many as 300 varieties. Some dances are rarely seen by tourists, while others are performed in the streets during the various annual fiestas. Many have specific significance, and locals may explain them to you if you make friends with them. Although they often occur during processions celebrating Catholic feast days, the dances usually have their roots in completely different, preconquest celebrations. These pre-Columbian dances are often tied in with the agricultural calendar and may celebrate such events as planting or harvesting. Even if you have difficulty understanding the meaning of the dances, you'll fascinated by the extremely rich, ornate and imaginative costumes that are often worth more than an entire household's ordinary clothes. Included in this show of color and design are grotesque masks, dazzling sequined uniforms and animal outfits, to mention just a few.

The elaborately outfitted dancers are accompanied by musicians playing a host of traditional instruments. Most of the brass and string instruments have obvious Spanish influences, but many of the percussion and wind instruments have changed little since Inca times. These include tinyas (hand drums or tambourines) and wankaras (larger drums), as well as a host of different shakers, rattles and bells. Inca wind instruments include the very typical and well-known panpipes. These come in a variety of lengths and tones, ranging from tiny, high-pitched instruments to huge base panpipes almost as tall as the musician. The pipes, often made from bamboo, are known as antaras, sikus or zampoñas, depending on their size and range. Flautas (flutes) are also seen at most fiestas. The most common are simple bamboo pennywhistles called quenas, while others are large blocks that look as though they've been hollowed out of a plank of wood. The most esoteric of these flutes is the piruru, which is carved from the wing bone of an Andean condor.

Seeing a street fiesta with dancing can be planned, or it can be a matter of luck. Some celebrations are held in one town and not in another; at other times, such as Carnaval, there are fiestas everywhere. Ask at the tourist office about any fiestas in the surrounding area.

Apart from the major Peruvian fiestas listed in the Facts for the Visitor chapter, the following is a selection of fiestas that are particularly important in the Lake Titicaca region. Candlemas is one of the most spectacular and is spread out for several days around the actual date, depending upon which day of the week Candlemas falls. If it falls on a Sunday to Tuesday, things get under way the previous Saturday; if it falls on a Wednesday to Friday, things normally get under way the following Saturday – but this is all subject to change. Puno Week is also a big deal, celebrating the legendary birth of Manco Capac, the first Inca, from Lake Titicaca. There are many colorful and important dances, as well as some wild drinking parties. These fiestas are crowded affairs so watch your pockets.

This list of holidays and fiestas is not exhaustive. Most are celebrated for several days before and after the actual day.

| | |
|---|---|
| January 6 | Epiphany |
| February 2 | Candlemas (or Virgen de la Candelaria) |
| March 7-8 | Saint John |
| May 2-4 | Alacitas (Puno miniature handicrafts fair) |
| | Holy Cross (Huancané, Taquile) |
| July 25 | Saint James (Taquile) |
| September 24 | Our Lady of Mercy |
| November 1-7 | Puno Week |

LAKE TITICACA AREA

a board. The high season (July and August) is expensive; bargain during other months. Many hotels in Puno have triple and quadruple rooms, which work out quite cheaply if you are traveling with friends.

## Places to Stay – Budget

There are cheap, basic hotels near the corner of Libertad and Tacna, most of which are none too clean and have only cold showers. Even if they claim to have hot water, it doesn't always work. *Hostal Extra* (☎ 35-1123, Moquegua 124) charges US$3 per person and has tepid electric communal showers – it's one of the best of the supercheapies. The following charge around US$3 a person and are mentioned here only because they are cheap – they aren't necessarily recommended: *Hostal Torino (Libertad 126)* is one of the cheapest and is OK; *Hotel Centenario (Deza 211)*; *Hostal Rosario (Moquegua 325)* and *Hostal Los Incas (Avenida Los Incas 105)*.

*Hostal Europa (Ugarte 112)* charges US$5/7 for singles/doubles with shared communal showers, and the hotel claims to have hot (or at least warm) water all day. Mixed reports have been received. The similarly priced *Hotel Arequipa (Arequipa 153)* has basic rooms that are just OK, but rates go up to US$6/10 in the high season, which is overpriced. The clean, quiet and decent *Hostal Los Uros* (☎ 35-2141, Valcárcel 135) has hot water in the evenings only and a cafeteria, open for early simple breakfasts. It's often full, which is a good sign. There are only a few single rooms, but plenty of triples and even quads. Rates are US$4.50/7.50/10.50/13.50 for one/two/three/four people with shared bath or US$6/10/13.50/16.50 with private bath.

The friendly and clean *Hostal Central* (☎ 35-2461, Tacna 269) charges US$5 per person in rooms with communal baths and electric showers. *Hostal Manco Capac* (☎ 35-2985, fax 35-6508, hsmancocapac@ punonet.com, Tacna 277) is clean and good and charges US$7/11 with private electric showers. Their business card offers 'Dour Transportation.' *Hospedaje Residencial Margarita* (☎ 35-2820, Tarapaca 130) has

rooms with shared bath for US$7/9 or with private bath for US$9/12. Hot electric showers are available at any time, and they serve breakfast. Their business card invites you to 'taste a warm family.' *Hostal Nesther* (☎ 36-3308, Deustua 268) has hot water from 6 to 8 am and 6 to 8 pm, is clean and isn't a bad choice at US$6/9 for rooms with private baths. Their card advertises 'The Hotel modern Architectural design.'

The clean *Hostal San Carlos* (☎ 35-1862, Ugarte 161) has hot water from 6 to 9 am and 6 to 9 pm. Rooms are US$9/12 with private bath. The central *Hostal Monterrey* (☎ 35-1691, 36-6090, Grau 148) is about this price, although the hot showers have erratic hours. *Hostal Presidente* (☎ 35-1421, Tacna 248) charges US$7/10 in rooms with private bath and cold water, but the communal showers have hot water all day. *Hotel Tumi* (☎ 35-3270, Cajamarca 243) is a reasonable choice for US$7 for small single rooms with private bath and hot water, but their US$17 doubles seem overpriced.

*Hostal Q'oñi Wasi* (☎ 35-3912, Avenida La Torre 119) is small, clean, friendly, has a breakfast cafeteria and is often full. Rates are US$6/8 with shared baths and US$9/12 with private baths and electric showers. Nearby, the similarly priced *Illampu Hostal* (☎ 35-3284, Avenida La Torre 137) is friendly and has hot water. *Hostal Imperial* (☎ 35-2386, Valcárcel 145) is clean and pleasant but has hot water only from 6 to 9 am and 6 to 9 pm. Rates are about US$9/13 with private bath.

## Places to Stay – Mid-Range

The small *Hostal Taquile* (☎ 35-1927, Ayacucho 517) has reasonable rooms with 24-hour hot water and TV for US$11/18. Next door, the smaller, nine-room *Hostal Vylene* (☎ /fax 35-1292) has a cafeteria for breakfast and rooms with private hot bath and TV. Rates are US$10 per person in the high season, but US$10/14/19 for singles/doubles/triples in the low season. *Hostal Zurit* (☎ 35-3665, fax 35-1532, Arbulu 191) has clean rooms with TV, private baths and hot water all the time. They told me they charge US$20/30, but when I asked for the rate in soles, i worked out at US$12/20. Go figure! *Hotel Internacional* (☎ 35-2109, fax 35-5632, Libertad 161) charges US$13/19 and is similar.

The tiny and homey *Cofre Andino* (☎/fax 35-1973, Bolognesi 154) has just six rooms, sleeping a total of nine people for US$25/30. Small groups sometimes rent the whole place. Rooms have TV and hot water from 6 to 8 am and 4:30 to 8 pm. There is a breakfast room. The recommended *Hospedaje Pukara* (☎/fax 36-8448, Libertad 328) has 14 rooms with telephone, cable TV, heating and 24-hour hot water for US$25/40 including American breakfast. They have an eye-catching 4-story-high mural in their public area. The clean and pleasant *Hostal Hacienda* (☎/fax 35-6109, Deustua 297) has 13 rooms around a nice little patio. Rooms have cable TV, telephone and hot showers and run US$35/40 with continental breakfast.

*Hotel Ferrocarril* (☎ 35-2011, ☎/fax 35-752, Avenida La Torre 185), conveniently located across from the train station, was remodeled in 1997 and now has fairly generic mid-range rooms with cable TV, telephone and hot showers for US$33/44 including continental breakfast. The hotel's restaurant is reasonably priced. Others with similar facilities at this price are the friendly and clean *Hostal El Buho* (☎ 35-4214, 35-409, ☎/fax 36-6122, elbuho@inkanet.com.pe, Lambayeque 142), which also has a restaurant; the older but clean *Hostal Italia* (☎ 35-7521, fax 35-2131, hitalia@puno-perured.net, Valcárcel 122) and the just adequate *Hostal Don Miguel* (☎ 35-2873, ☎/fax 36-8228, Avenida La Torre 545).

The very attractive *Hotel Colón Inn* (☎ 35-7090, ☎/fax 35-1432, Colon@mail.cosapidata.com.pe, Tacna 290) is a colonial-style central hotel with modern facilities, a restaurant and room service. Rates are US$40/53. The similarly priced *Hotel Sillustani* (☎ 35-1881, fax 35-2641, htl-sill@map.edu.pe, Lambayeque 195) is clean and adequate, though not as nice. Better is the new and modern *Qelqatani Hotel* (☎ 36-172, fax 35-1052, qelqatani@punonet.com), with 13 rooms and a suite. Rooms are large and have heaters and radio alarms, as well as the usual features. Bathrooms are also good-sized and have a tub and shower. Rates are US$43/56 (the suite is US$85) and a full buffet breakfast is included. There is a good restaurant, and the staff are helpful.

## Places to Stay – Top End

The well-run *Hotel Libertador Isla Esteves* (☎ 36-7780, fax 36-7879, in Lima 442-0166, 442-1995, fax 442-2988, hpuno@libertador.com.pe) is attractively located on an island in the western part of Lake Titicaca. The island is connected to Puno by a 5km road over a causeway, but as there are no buses, access is a pain. Taxis charge about US$2.50 for the trip. About half of the 126 rooms and all the five suites look directly out over the lake, and the beautiful views are the hotel's main attraction. The rooms themselves are clean, comfortable, heated and spacious, but they lack character. There is a good restaurant, bar, lobby and gift shop. Rooms are US$135, suites are US$173, but discounts can be arranged if they aren't busy.

*Posada del Inca Puno* (posada_ventas@el-olivar.com.pe), part of the Posada chain, is building a new hotel 5km from Puno on the shores of Titicaca. The 62 rooms (two are designed for wheelchairs) will all have lake views, cable TV, telephone and heating. A restaurant and bar offer lake-view dining. The hotel is planned to open by December 1999 at US$85/100 including breakfast.

## Places to Eat

The pedestrian street of Calle Lima is lined with popular restaurants. Note that many of these don't advertise their set meals *(el menú)*, which are cheaper than eating à la carte. Ask for the set meal if economizing.

*Apu Salkantay* (☎ 36-3955, Lima 425) is very popular with travelers and serves meals in the US$3 to US$6 range. They have some local dishes, such as trout and alpaca, or try their mixed plate. They also do pizza and have live música folklórica every night. However, the bands tend to move around, so you'll probably hear music almost wherever you eat. Next door, *La Fontana* (Lima 339) has good pizzas. *La Casona* (☎ 35-1108, Lima 517) and *Restaurant Don Piero* (☎ 35-1766, Lima 364) are also good for local food.

LAKE TITICACA AREA

*Pizzería El Buho* (☎ 35-6223, *Lima 347*) is well-recommended for Italian food. *La Hostería* (☎ 35-2553, *Lima 529*) is popular for pizzas (about US$4.50) and has good apple pie and chocolate cake.

*Comedor Vegetariano Delisse* (*Libertad 215*) is cheap and dingy, but it is recommended for early breakfasts and it has vegetarian food. *Delta Café* at the Parque Pino has cake, sandwiches and coffee, though their espresso machine is broken. *Restaurant Las Rocas*, near the Hostal Los Uros on Valcárcel, has good food and is reasonably priced, though it lacks atmosphere. *Ricos Pan* (☎ 35-4179, *Moquegua 330*) is the best bakery in town and serves sandwiches as well.

*Así Es Mi Peru* (☎ 36-7281, *Libertad 172*) serves excellent typical lunches for US$3 to US$6, but isn't open for dinner. *Don Gerólamo Trout Palace* (☎ 35-6840, *Lambayeque 141*) is in an 18th-century house and has an outdoor patio. Apart from trout, they serve alpaca, steak and chicken at reasonable prices. There is an Internet café on the premises. *Restaurant Internacional* (☎ 35-2502, *Moquegua 201*) is one of the best in town and has a wide range of good dishes at medium prices. *Pizzería Europa* (☎ 35-1432, *Tacna 298*) is another decent choice.

## Entertainment

Musicians often do the rounds of the restaurants, usually playing a half-hour set of música folklórica, passing the hat, and then moving on. There are also several pubs that may have recorded or live music and dancing, and are popular both with locals and visitors. Locals especially like *Kusillo's* on Libertad near Arequipa. Tourists go to *Ekeko's* (*Lima 355*), which has a happy hour every night. Also try *Mukuku's* (☎ 35-3319, *Tarapaca 395*).

## Shopping

This is one of the best towns in Peru to get good-quality woolen and alpaca sweaters and other products at fair prices. These items are sold in many places, including Calle Lima, but the open-air market near the railway station may have the best choices if you know how to bargain. Watch for pickpockets here.

## Getting There & Away

**Air** The nearest airport is in Juliaca, abou 44km away. Several travel agents in Pun will sell you tickets and provide shuttl service direct to the airport for abou US$2.50 per person. Aero Continente ha an office at Tacna 305. See the Juliac section for further information about flights

**Bus** The road to Arequipa is in bad shap and is a rough ride. The road to Cuzco i improving and is being paved.

Cruz del Sur (☎ 35-2451, Avenida El So 568) has the best buses to Arequipa (US$7 t US$10, 12 hours), Cuzco (US$6 to US$10, hours) and Lima (US$20, 42 hours, change i Arequipa. All leave between 4 and 5 pm They also have a 6:50 am Arequipa departure Jacantaya (☎ 35-1931, Avenida El Sol 594 Carhuamayo (☎ 35-3522, Melgar 334), CIVA (Melgar at Avenida El Sol) and several other in the area have buses to Cuzco and Arequipa they are usually cheaper than Cruz del Sur.

For Tacna (US$7, 12 hours), try Empres San Martín (☎ 35-2511, Titicaca 210) or on of several others in this block. All have buse leaving at about 5 pm.

Buses to towns on the south side of th lake and the Bolivian border depart fre quently during the day from the Avenida E Ejército side of the Mercado Laykakota.

For buses to Juliaca (US$0.50, about a hour), Transportes Los Angeles leave severa times an hour from the corner of Tacna an Libertad. Buses and minibuses also go fron the corner of Cahuide and Titicaca.

A new company, First Class (☎ 36-403 Melgar 110) has comfortable tour buses t Cuzco every morning. The US$25 far includes beverages and an English-speakin tour guide, who talks about sites that ar briefly visited en route.

**Train** The first few kilometers of the journe out of Puno are along the shores of Lak Titicaca, and the lake views are good. Th Cuzco train leaves at 8 am Monday, Wednes day, Thursday and Saturday, arriving at 6 pr (though it's often hours late). The Arequip train leaves at 7:45 pm on Monday an Friday, arriving at 6 am the following da

View of the volcano El Misti from Arequipa's Plaza de Armas

Monasterio de Santa Catalina, Arequipa

ERIC WHEATER

Indigenous women making a reed mat near Puno

KEN EAKIN

Reed boats made by the Uros people of the Floating Islands, Lake Titicaca

## The Yavari Project

Puno's most fascinating sight is the Yavari, the oldest steamship on Lake Titicaca. In 1862, the Yavari and its sister ship, the Yapura, were built in England of iron parts – a total of 2766 for the two vessels. These were shipped around Cape Horn to Arica, from where they were moved by train to Tacna, then hauled by mule over the Andes to Puno – a process that took six years.

The ships were assembled in Puno, and the Yavari was launched on Christmas Day, 1870, followed by the Yapura 17 months later. (The Yapura was later renamed the BAP Puno and became a Peruvian Navy medical ship; it can still be seen in Puno). Both had coal-powered steam engines, but because of the difficulty of obtaining coal, the engines were powered by dried llama dung (I'm not making this up!). Due to the space requirements needed for the bulky fuel, the Yavari was cut in half, and an extra 12m of length was added to the hull, which is now 50m long and has a 6m beam. In 1914, it was further modified with a Bolinder 4-cylinder diesel engine, which is still there today.

After a long history of service on the lake, the ship was decommissioned by the Peruvian Navy, which sent its antique navigation equipment to a museum in Arequipa for safekeeping. The hull was left on the lakeshore, and because of the dry climate and freshwater, it rusted very little. In 1982, Englishwoman Meriel Larken visited the forgotten boat and decided it was a piece of history that could and should be saved. She formed The Yavari Project in order to buy and restore the vessel, provide local work and attract responsible tourism.

Larken was fortunate in gaining the royal support of Britain's Prince Philip, who had noted the presence of this historic British ship when he visited Lake Titicaca in 1962. She was also fortunate in finding Captain Carlos Saavedra, formerly of the Peruvian Navy, to head the crew aboard the boat. The captain speaks excellent English and is a knowledgeable and enthusiastic leader in this project. He coordinated with the navy in having the original navigation equipment returned from Arequipa, and he is overseeing the process of restoring the vessel to its 1914 appearance.

In 1998, the Yavari was opened to tourism. You can walk down to the dock and be invited aboard by the captain, who'll give you a guided tour. Hours are 8 am to 5 pm Wednesday to Sunday (Monday and Tuesday are maintenance days, but call if you can't visit on other days). Restoration is continuing, and by the early 21st century, the 19th-century vessel should be ready for passage across Lake Titicaca. Ten double cabins are planned, and this will be an opportunity to voyage on one of the world's oldest ships.

The Yavari Project is looking for support both in the way of finance and volunteers. To send donations and receive information, contact The Yavari Project (☎/fax 0181-874-0583, yavari.larken@virgin.net, 61 Mexfield Rd, London, SW15 2RG, UK). In Puno, call Captain Carlos Saavedra (☎ 36-9329, fax 35-2701, yavaricondor@viaexpresa.com.pe).

Check for service changes. Be alert for thieves at the railway station and on the trains, especially the night train to Arequipa (see Arequipa for more information).

The train is often sold out days in advance, and buying tickets in the long lines is a hassle. The ticket office opens at 8 am, and you should get there early. Many travel agents buy up blocks of tickets and sell them at a commission, which saves you time. Be careful of the ticket you buy – there have been complaints of 1st-class tickets being sold for Pullman prices, without the added safety and comfort of that class.

While the Pullman class (also called Ejecutivo, Inka or Buffet class) is safest, 1st class is reasonably safe if you are traveling during the day (to Cuzco) and remain awake and alert. It's also much more interesting – you travel with Peruvians rather than being locked into the tourist car with other foreigners. Some shoestring-budget travelers have taken 2nd class to Cuzco without incident; others have been robbed. On the night train to Arequipa, 2nd class is not recommended. Note that even in the best class, seats are not very comfortable, and the ride is pretty bouncy. Because the road has improved, increasing numbers of travelers are taking the bus to Cuzco, which is faster.

Fares to Cuzco are US$19 or US$23 in the Pullman classes and US$8 in 1st class (also called Económico). Fares to Arequipa are US$13 in Pullman and US$7.50 in 1st class. Meals are served aboard the train, but are not included in the ticket's cost.

**Boat** There are no boats from Puno to Bolivia. The buses with connecting hydrofoil and catamaran services (via Juli or Copacabana, Bolivia – see Going to Bolivia later in this chapter) are very expensive compared to buses from Puno to La Paz.

Boats from the Puno dock leave for various islands in the lake (see Around Puno later in this chapter). Tickets bought directly from the boats at the dock are invariably cheaper than those bought from agencies in town.

In the future, the *Yavari* (see the boxed text 'The Yavari Project') will provide services on the lake.

### Getting Around

A short taxi ride anywhere in town should cost about US$1. Tricycle taxis are a popular way of getting around Puno and are a little cheaper than ordinary taxis.

# Around Puno

There are several excursions to take from Puno. Lake Titicaca trips to the floating islands of Los Uros or to Isla Taquile or Isla Amantaní (inhabited by indigenous Andean people) are all popular. You can also visit the small uninhabited Isla Suasi near the

north shore of the lake or Isla del Sol and Isla de la Luna on the Bolivian part of the lake. Land trips visit the archaeological site of Sillustani. A drive along the southern shores of the lake takes in various small towns famous for their colonial churches and their fiestas. The Bolivian ruins at Tiahuanaco can also be visited.

Most of these excursions can be done cheaply on public transport. Tour companies will arrange guided trips, but they are more expensive and not necessarily worth the extra money unless the guide is knowledgeable and speaks good English. Try to meet the guide beforehand if possible. Edgar Adventures and All Ways Travel are both good and not too expensive.

## SILLUSTANI

The Inca Empire was known as Tahuantinsuyo, or 'the Land of Four Quarters.' The southern quarter was called Collasuyo after the Colla tribe, which, along with the rival Lupaca tribe, dominated the Lake Titicaca area and later became part of the Inca Empire.

Little is known about the Colla people. They were a warlike tribe that spoke Aymara, not Quechua, and they had unusual burial customs for their nobility. Their dead were buried in funerary towers called *chullpas*, which can be seen in various places in the Puno area. The most impressive of these are the chullpas of Sillustani, the tallest of which reaches a height of about 12m; there are several others almost as tall. Standing on a small hilltop in the Lake Umayo peninsula, these towers look very impressive against the bleak landscape. They are either round or square and house the remains of Colla nobility, who were buried in family groups, complete with food and belongings for their journey into the next world. The only opening into the towers was a small hole facing east, just large enough for a person to crawl through. After a burial, the entrance was sealed. Nowadays, nothing remains of the burials. The chullpas, however, are well preserved and worth seeing, both for their architecture and for their impressive location.

The outside walls of the towers are made from massive coursed blocks. These are reminiscent of Inca stonework, but they weren't built by the Incas; archaeologists consider this architecture more complicated. Some of the chullpas of Sillustani are unfinished. Carved but unplaced blocks and a ramp used to raise them to the correct height are among the points of interest at the site. A few of the blocks are decorated – the carving that is most often noticed by visitors is that of a lizard.

Sillustani is partially encircled by Lake Umayo. This interesting Andean lake is home to a variety of plants and waterbirds. Birders should particularly watch for the giant Andean coot, the white-tufted and silvery grebes, the puna ibis, the Andean goose, the black-crowned night-heron, the speckled and puna teals, the yellow-billed pintail, the Andean lapwing, the Andean gull (strange to see a 'sea' gull so far from the ocean) and, if you're very lucky, one of the three species of flamingo found in the Andean highlands.

## Getting There & Away

Tours are offered by a number of agencies and usually leave at 2:30 pm. The cheapest tours are about US$6 and include the entrance fee to the ruins (US$2.50). If the guide is good, this is definitely worthwhile. The round trip takes about 3½ hours and allows you about 1½ hours at the ruins. This schedule is convenient, because the afternoon light is the best for photography, though the site can be pretty crowded in the afternoon. There is a small on-site museum (an extra US$1 for entrance) and gift shop. Dress warmly and bring sunblock.

If you prefer more time at the site, you could hire a taxi for US$15. If you can get a group together, this isn't much more expensive than the tour bus, but you don't get a guide, and you have to pay the entrance fee of US$2.50 per person.

## FLOATING ISLANDS

The Floating Islands (Islas Flotantes) of the Uros people are the Puno area's major tourist attraction and, as a result, have become somewhat overcommercialized. Despite this, the excursion remains popular because there is nothing quite like it anywhere else.

Intermarriage with Aymara-speaking Indians has seen the demise of the pure-blooded Uros, and none exist today. They used to speak their own language but nowadays speak Aymara. Always a small tribe, they began their unusual floating existence centuries ago in an effort to isolate themselves from the Collas and the Incas. Today, several hundred people live on the islands and eke out a living with fishing and tourism.

The lives of the Uros are totally interwoven with the *totora* reeds that grow abundantly in the shallows of Lake Titicaca. These reeds are harvested and are used to make anything from the islands themselves to little model boats to sell to tourists. The islands are constructed from many layers of reeds. The reeds rot away from the bottom and are replaced at the top, so the ground is soft and springy, and you must be careful not to put your foot through a rotted-out section. The biggest of the islands contains several buildings, including a school, post office, basic snack bars and souvenir shops. Solar energy panels have recently been introduced. The inhabitants of some islands have built small huts ('museums') with stuffed birds inside or observation platforms so that you can climb up about 7m or 8m and survey the surroundings from the rickety perch. Small donations are requested. The buildings' walls are still made of totora, but some of the roofs are now tin.

From tightly bundled reeds, the Uros build canoe-shaped boats for transport and fishing. A well-constructed boat can carry a whole family for about six months before beginning to rot. You can usually persuade one of the Uros to give you a ride on a boat, but be prepared to pay and give a tip for taking photographs.

Plenty of women will try to sell you their handicrafts, such as models made from totora and embroidered wall hangings. Be prepared to buy something. There used to be a severe problem with begging children, but this has improved somewhat, as villagers are finding more imaginative and satisfying ways to part you from a few coins. You are asked not to give candy to the kids.

## Getting There & Away

Getting to the Floating Islands is easy: just go down to the docks and hang around – within minutes, you'll be asked to take a trip to the islands. You can hire an expensive private boat or go with the next group. Boats generally leave several times from 7 am until early afternoon if there is enough passenger demand. The standard trip, visiting the main island and perhaps one or two others, takes about four or five hours, and it's best to leave by about 8:30 am. Boats leave as soon as they have 15 or 20 passengers and charge a fixed price – usually around US$3 per person. All the boats are small, rather decrepit motorboats with no life jackets, though I've never heard of an accident.

Many tour agencies in Puno will sell you tickets for an Uros trip and provide a guide for about US$6 per person if there's a big enough group. It's probably worth it to have someone explain what's going on, and often they'll include transport down to the dock as well.

En route to the islands, you may well see the Uros paddling around in their totora boats, fishing or gathering reeds. Various bird species live on and around the lake (see Sillustani earlier in this section), and the ride on the lake can be beautiful in good weather.

## ISLA TAQUILE

This is a real island, not a floating one, and it is less frequently visited than Uros. The long trip is best done with an overnight stay, though day trips from Puno are possible.

Taquile (Taquili on some maps) is a fascinating island. The men wear tightly woven woolen caps and always seem to be walking around the island knitting them. The headgear looks like a floppy nightcap and can only be described as cute. I'm told that men wear red hats if they are married and red-and-white hats if they are single. The women weave the elegant-looking waistcoats, which the men wear with their knitted caps, roughly spun white shirts and thick calf-length black pants, giving them a very raffish air. The women, in their many-layered skirts and delicately embroidered blouses, also look very handsome. These garments, which are among the best-made traditional clothes that I've come across in Peru, can be bought in the island's cooperative store on the main plaza.

The people of Taquile speak Quechua – rather than the Aymara of most Titicaca Indians – and maintain a strong sense of group identity. They rarely marry non-Taquile people, and their lives are untrammeled by such modernities as roads. There are no vehicles, not even bicycles, on the island, and there are almost no dogs. Electricity was introduced in the 1990s, but is not available everywhere.

Although Taquile is very peaceful, the islanders are by no means content to let the world pass them by. When enterprising individuals from Puno began bringing tourists to visit the island, the islanders fought the invasion. It wasn't the tourists they objected to, it was the Puno entrepreneurs. Now the passenger boats to Taquile are owned and operated by the islanders themselves. This control enables them to keep tourism at what they consider to be reasonable levels. Unfortunately, there are rare instances of thieving and begging, so the place obviously isn't perfect. Perhaps tourism is beginning to have negative effects. Try to minimize the impact of your visit.

The island's scenery is beautiful. The soil is a deep, earthy, red color – which, in the strong highland sunlight, contrasts magnificently with the intense blue of the lake. The backdrop of Bolivia's snowcapped Cordillera Real on the far side of the lake completes a splendid picture. The island is 6km to 7km long, with several hills that have Inca terracing on the sides and small ruins on top. Visitors are free to wander around, explore the ruins and enjoy the peaceful scenery. You can't do this on a day trip (well, you can, but you'll miss the returning boat), so you should stay overnight if you can.

San Diego (Saint James Day, July 25) is a big feast day on Taquile. Dancing, music and general carousing go on for several days until the beginning of August, when the Indians traditionally make offerings to Mother Earth, Pachamama. New Year's Day is also festive and rowdy. Many islanders go to Puno for La Virgen de la Candelaria and Puno Week (see Puno earlier in this chapter), and Taquile is liable to be somewhat deserted then.

Recently, a small visiting fee (well under US$1) is charged to independent travelers.

## Places to Stay & Eat

Some people elect to stay overnight on Taquile – a worthwhile decision because, especially in the high season, the island can get very crowded with day-trippers. A steep stairway, from which there are lovely views, leads from the dock to the center of the island. The climb takes about 20 minutes (more if you're not acclimatized), and it is strongly recommended that you don't do it immediately after arriving from the coast – climbing stairs at 4000m is a painful, breathless and potentially dangerous experience if you're not used to it. (One reader claims that she counted over 500 steps, and I'm not going to quibble with that.)

In the center, a group of the inhabitants will greet you, and if you wish, they will arrange accommodations. Individuals and small groups are assigned to island families who will put you up in guest houses sleeping up to 10 people. There is a standard charge of about US$2 per person, and gifts of fresh food are appreciated. Beds are basic (but clean and adequate), and facilities are minimal. You will be given some blankets, but bring a sleeping bag, as it gets very cold at night. Bathing means doing what the locals do: washing in cold water from a bucket, and in a few cases, using the fields as a latrine. If you like a little luxury, overnighting in Taquile is not for you. You can camp if you bring everything. Campers are charged about half of the cost of a bed in someone's house.

If you do decide to stay the night, remember to bring a flashlight, as there is no lighting. It's also a good idea to take in the lay of the land while it's still light. Some friends of mine became completely lost on the island in the dark, couldn't find the house where they were staying, and ended up having to rough it for the night.

Several simple restaurants in the center of the island sell whatever is available; fresh lake trout, boiled potatoes, rice and fried eggs is the normal fare. There is a community-owned restaurant, but increasing numbers of islanders are opening their own small eateries. Some people suggest that supporting a community-owned restaurant is a more equitable way of leaving the tourist dollar, but the entrepreneurial spirit seems to be winning out. Some places act as gathering-and-drinking spots for tourists in the evenings. You can buy bottled drinks, and boiled tea is usually safe to drink, though it's worth bringing a water bottle (and purifying tablets or a filter if you have them). Make sure you have small bills, because change is limited, and there's nowhere to change dollars. Beware of overcharging in restaurants, and settle the price of the meal before you eat it. Bring extra money too; many travelers are unable to resist the high quality of the unique woven and knitted clothes sold in the island's cooperative store.

Although conditions are primitive by Western standards, visiting Taquile is a wonderful experience, and some travelers stay for several days. The people are friendly, and the lifestyle is peaceful and relaxed. I stayed here once at the time of a full moon and watched the sunset and moonrise from a small Inca ruin atop one of the island's hills. It was windless and still, and as the mirror-like lake darkened slowly, I felt that Taquile was its own little world, completely detached from the rest of the earth. When the moon came up over the almost 7000m snowcaps of the Cordillera Real, it seemed twice as bright and much larger than normal in the crystalline air over the lake. An unforgettable evening.

## Getting There & Away

A passenger boat for Taquile leaves the Puno dock every day by 7:30 am, and tour boats leave around 8 am. The 24km trip takes four hours (sometimes including a brief stop at the Islas Uros) and costs about US$8 round trip if you get to the dock early and pay the captain of the passenger boat. You then get about two hours on the island, and the return trip leaves at 2:30 pm, arriving in Puno around nightfall. Tour agencies also offer this trip for about US$10 with a guide. Remember to bring adequate sunblock – the intensity of the tropical sun bouncing off the lake at almost 4000m can cause severe sunburn.

If you want to stay overnight, you can buy a one-way, passenger-boat ride and then come back the next day. Tour agencies offer overnight trips from about US$16 including accommodations and meals, and it's not much cheaper to do it yourself.

## ISLA AMANTANÍ

This island is similar to and a few kilometers north of the smaller Taquile. Because it is farther away from Puno, Amantaní is visited less often than Taquile, and most trips involve an overnight stay. Basic food and accommodations are available (see Taquile for a description of what to expect).

As with Taquile, it's very tranquil, and there are good views, no roads, no vehicles and no dogs. Several hills are topped by ruins, among the highest and best-known of which are Pachamama and Pachatata (Mother Earth and Father Earth), which date to the Tiahuanaco culture. There are several different villages on the island.

Boats to Amantaní leave the Puno dock between 7:30 and 8:30 am most mornings (ask around for the next time of departure), and one-way fares are about US$5 if you pay the captain directly. Boats often stop at the floating islands on the way out, but not on the return trip, which is a few cents cheaper. Several boats and islanders have been recommended, but transport depends on what's in town, and where you stay depends on the islanders. They have a rotating system that gives everybody a fair chance to make some money.

From Puno, it is possible to do an Islas Uros/Amantaní/Taquile/Puno trip. It's more difficult to do the trip in reverse, because few boats go from Taquile to Amantaní. There is a boat from Amantaní to Taquile most days for a fare of US$1.50.

Puno travel agencies charge about US$14 and up for a tour to Amantaní, with one night in Amantaní and quick visits to Taquile and the floating islands. The cheapest tours simply

facilitate buying services that you could buy yourself, but it's not a bad deal. Slightly more expensive tours may add a decent guide, some of which are English-speaking. Meals may be included – check details carefully. Generally, they are a fair value. Three-day, two-night tours are available, with the first night at Amantaní and the second at Taquile. Check the details of a tour carefully, and buy from reputable agents – not street touts.

## ISLA SUASI

This five-acre uninhabited island is near the north shore of Lake Titicaca. In 1998/99, a small hotel was built on it with the objectives of providing tourist access to the lake using local resources, minimizing ecological impact and allowing visitors to learn about the area or simply relax. This looks like a good new project, and I welcome reader feedback.

The hotel runs on solar power and provides modern services (private bathrooms, hot showers, heating) within rustic and harmonious architecture. It can be used as a base to visit other islands or the north-shore towns of Moho and Conima. There are plans to install barbecue areas; rowboats; a sauna; a garden of native plants, herbs and vegetables; and flocks of Camelids on the peaceful island.

Programs of two days, one night; or three days, two nights are offered, with either land or lake transport or a combination of the two. Rates are US$45/70/90 per night for single/double/triple rooms including full breakfast. Other meals are US$12. Reservations can be made at any of the major travel agencies in Puno. Information is available from the friendly owner of the hotel, Martha Giraldo Alayza (☎ 35-1417, cell 62-2772, fax 35-5694, ampjmbm@mail.cosapidata.com.pe).

## ISLA DEL SOL & ISLA DE LA LUNA

The most famous island on Lake Titicaca is Isla del Sol (Island of the Sun), the legendary birthplace of Manco Capac, the first Inca. Both Isla del Sol and Isla de la Luna (Island of the Moon) have Inca ruins. They are in the Bolivian portion of the lake, and you should visit them from the Bolivian port of Copacabana, about 11km beyond the border town of Yunguyo.

## SOUTH-SHORE TOWNS

An interesting bus excursion can be made to the towns of Chimú, Chucuito, Ilave, Juli, Pomata and Zepita on the southern shores of Lake Titicaca, all described later. If you start early enough, you can visit all of them in a day and be back in Puno for the night. Alternatively, you could stay in one of the few hotels in these towns or continue on to Bolivia.

### Getting There & Away

To visit any of the south-shore towns, go to the Avenida El Ejército side of Puno's Mercado Laykakota. Cheap, slow buses and slightly more expensive, faster minibuses leave from here for the south-shore towns and the Bolivian border. Buses to the nearer towns, such as Ilave, are more frequent, but if you're patient, you should be able to leave for the town of your choice within an hour. Fares to the border are under US$2 (or proportionately less expensive to travel to closer towns).

### Chimú

The road east of Puno closely follows the margins of the lake. After about 8km, you reach the village of Chimú – hikers might find this a pleasant lakeshore walk. Chimú is famous for its totora industry, and its inhabitants have close ties with the Uros. Bundles of reeds are piled up to dry, and there are always several reed boats in various stages of construction. Although this is an interesting sight, I found the villagers not particularly friendly to sightseers (though a correspondent tells me that their initial reserve can be overcome).

### Chucuito

The village of Chucuito, about 18km southeast of Puno, was of some importance as a major Lupaca center. Chucuito has two attractive colonial churches – Santo Domingo and La Asunción. Opening hours are erratic.

Near Santo Domingo is a fascinatingly weird archaeological site consisting of dozens of huge, phallic stones. I haven't figured out exactly what they mean – local guides tell various confusing (but entertaining) stories about the carvings. There is a trout hatchery east of the town.

**Places to Stay** The *Hostal Cabañas* (☎ 35-2108; leave a message for Alfredo Sanchez) on the outskirts of Chucuito charges about US$13/20/24 for singles/doubles/triples. Its main attraction is the superb view of the lake, but they also have table tennis and other minor amenities. There is a restaurant.

The new *Taypikala Hotel* (☎ 35-6042, cell 62-3307, fax 35-5887), near the archaeological site, has lake views and rooms with private hot showers for US$40/53. There is a restaurant. The hotel is building meditation rooms and a sauna; the owner is reputedly an Aymara shaman who is into New Age activities.

### Ilave

Near Chucuito, the road turns southeast away from the lake (though the waters can usually be seen in the distance) and soon reaches Platería, a village once famous for its silverware. About 40km from Puno, the road passes through the straggling community of Molleko. This area is noted for the great number of mortarless stone walls that snake eerily across the bleak altiplano.

Ilave is 56km from Puno. It doesn't have the interesting colonial architecture of the other towns, but its position at the crossroads gives it some importance. Ilave also has a Sunday market.

### Juli

The road returns to the lake near the bay of Juli, where flamingos are sometimes seen. Juli is 80km from Puno and is famous for its four colonial churches dating from the 16th and 17th century. They are all in disrepair, but they are slowly being restored as funds become available. San Juan Bautista contains richly framed colonial paintings depicting the lives of Saint John the Baptist and Saint Teresa.

LAKE TITICACA AREA

This church is often open in the mornings for a small fee. The Church of La Asunción offers excellent vistas of Lake Titicaca from its large courtyard. Its belfry was struck by lightning and shows extensive damage. The Church of Santa Cruz has lost half of its roof. The Church of San Pedro, on the main plaza, is in the best condition. It is interesting to see the churches in their unrestored state and get some idea of what the magnificent colonial churches of such popular tourist centers as Cuzco would look like had they not been carefully and extensively restored.

Market days in Juli are Wednesday and Saturday.

**Places to Stay** The very basic *Alojamiento El Rosal (Puno 128)*, just off the main plaza, charges US$2.50 per person. There's also a simple *Hostal Municipal (Ilave 312)* at US$3.50 that has hot water.

## Pomata

Beyond Juli, the road returns to the lakeshore again and continues to Pomata, 106km from Puno. As you arrive in Pomata, you'll see the Dominican church, dramatically located on top of a small hill. It was founded in 1700 and is known for its windows made of translucent alabaster and its Baroque sandstone facade with many carvings, including pumas. Apparently, the name 'Pomata' comes from *puma auta*, which means 'place of the puma' in the Aymara language. As with the other churches in the region, you can never tell exactly when it will be open.

Just out of Pomata, the road forks. The main road continues southeast through Zepita (where there is another colonial church) to the Bolivian border town of Desaguadero; while a side road, leading to the other border crossing at Yunguyo, hugs the shore of Lake Titicaca.

**Places to Stay** The only place seems to be with the *Familia Rosa Pizano*, at house No 30 on the main plaza.

## GOING TO BOLIVIA

For many travelers, Puno and Lake Titicaca are stepping-stones to Bolivia, which borders the lake to the south. For information about Bolivian entrance formalities, see Bolivian Consulate in the Puno section earlier in this chapter. Bolivian time is one hour ahead of Peruvian time.

### Over Lake Titicaca

The Transturin service, which costs about US$145, leaves Puno by bus at 6:30 am and goes to Copacabana, Bolivia, from where a catamaran sails to the Isla del Sol for a quick but interesting visit before continuing to the Bolivian port of Huatajata and on to La Paz by bus, arriving at 5 pm. This service includes hotel transfers, a visit to one or two churches in the south-shore towns, lunch and a guide. They also have longer trips that include an overnight on a catamaran (with comfortable private cabins and meals) for US$235/410 for single/double occupancy. The trips can also be done in reverse. Transturin has an office in Puno, as well as a La Paz (☎ 591-2-320445, 591-2-341787, fax 591-2-391162, transturin@megalink.com, Mariscal Santa Cruz 1295, La Paz).

### Overland

There are two overland routes from Puno to La Paz, Bolivia: via Yunguyo or via Desaguadero. Also, there is a rarely used northern route from Juliaca, described earlier in this chapter.

The Yunguyo route is the more attractive and has the added interest of the boat crossing at the Estrecho de Tiquina. Some travelers like to break the trip in the pleasant Bolivian port of Copacabana, from where the Isla del Sol can easily be visited. The Desaguadero route is more direct but less attractive, and the road is in worse shape for the first 30km on the Bolivian side. This route can be combined with a visit to the Bolivian ruins at Tiahuanaco. The Desaguadero route is slightly faster and cheaper than the Yunguyo route.

**Via Yunguyo** Buses leave from the Avenida El Ejército side of Mercado Laykakota in Puno for the border town of Yunguyo (US$2, 2½ hours). Yunguyo has a couple of basic hotels; the *Hotel Europa* on the Plaza de Armas at US$5 per person has hot water, or try **Hostal Amazonas** half a block from the plaza. But, as there is little of interest in Yunguyo, most people go on to Bolivia. You will find moneychangers in the main plaza and on the street by the border, which is about 2km away. Change just enough to get you to La Paz and count your money carefully. The border is open from 8 am to 6 pm and formalities are fairly straightforward. Exit taxes are sometimes asked for but these are not legal. You can expect the money to go into the official's pocket.

From the border, it's about 10km more to Copacabana. Available transportation ranges from trucks to buses to taxis and is more frequent on Sunday, which is market day in Yunguyo. On weekdays you may have to wait up to an hour. Copacabana is a much more pleasant place than Yunguyo and has several hotels in various price ranges, as well as a port from where inexpensive tours to Isla del Sol are available, so if you want to break your journey, do so here. Keep in mind that Bolivian time is one hour ahead of Peruvian time.

There are several buses a day from Copacabana to La Paz. The trip takes approximately five hours, including a boat crossing of the Estrecho de Tiquina. You have to register with the Bolivian navy to cross – a simple formality but don't miss your bus! The fare is about US$2.50 including the ferry.

If you leave Puno early in the morning, you can reach La Paz in a single day. For about US$7, a Puno to La Paz ticket with a company such as Colectur (☎ 35-2302, Tacna 221) is the most convenient option. They will drive you to Yunguyo, stop at the money exchange, show you exactly where to go for exit and entrance formalities and drive you to Copacabana, where you are met by a Bolivian bus for the trip to La Paz. Although it's not as cheap as buying separate tickets, being guided through the border formalities and provided with a through service is attractive to most travelers and worth the extra couple of dollars.

In La Paz, you can find agents for the through service to Puno in the Residencial Rosario at Ilampu 704, or at Colectur, Sagarnaga 326. Different international exchange rates make the La Paz to Puno trip more expensive than the same journey in the other direction.

See Lonely Planet's *Bolivia* for more details on the Copacabana area.

**Via Desaguadero** Buses leave Puno's Mercado Laykakota market every hour or so for Desaguadero (under US$2, two to three hours), where there are basic hotels that aren't worth using unless you are stuck for the night. **Hotel Montes** charges about US$2.50 per person but is not recommended. A little better is **Hostal Panamericano** (☎ 85-1021, Panamericana 151) near the border, where basic but clean little rooms are US$4/6 with shared cold showers. A better choice is **Hostal San Carlos** (☎ 85-1040, 28 de Julio 322), which charges US$5.50/8 with shared warm shower. A sauna is an extra US$2.50. **Hostal Corona** (☎ 85-1100, 85-1120, Panamericana 248) is the newest and may be better. On the Bolivian side next to the border is **Hotel Bolivia**, with clean double rooms and hot water for about US$9; there is a decent restaurant there.

Border hours are 8 am to 5 pm, though you can cross back and forth outside these hours if you stay within the border area. Bolivia is an hour ahead of Peru, so you can't enter Bolivia after 4 pm Peru time. Moneychangers at the border and a casa de cambio nearby recently had exchange rates as good as La Paz or Puno.

From Desaguadero to La Paz, a bus ride costs under US$2 and takes three or four hours. Buses leave several times during the day. If you leave Puno at dawn, you can be in Bolivia early enough to stop at Tiahuanaco for a quick visit before continuing on to La Paz (the Desaguadero-La Paz bus passes near the ruins).

## BOLIVIA TO PERU

There is rarely any hassle at either border, and you can get 90 days in Peru without difficulty. This is good if your tourist card has almost expired – just go to La Paz for an evening and come back to Peru the next day. See the Visas & Documents section in the Facts for the Visitor chapter for more information.

# The Cuzco Area

This chapter covers the Department of Cuzco, which includes the city of Cuzco, many smaller towns and villages, nearby archaeological sites and the Inca Trail to Machu Picchu. The most direct road link from here to the coast goes via Abancay, the capital of the Department of Apurímac (also in this chapter), then on through the southern part of the Department of Ayacucho to join the Panamericana near Nazca. In the early 1990s, this route was unsafe because of terrorism, but it is now being paved and is safe, though not yet used by many travelers, most of whom arrive overland via Arequipa or by air. Another travel possibility is the very rough road trip from Huancayo through Ayacucho and Abancay to Cuzco.

Although the Department of Cuzco lies in exceptionally beautiful Andean surroundings, its beauty is only a secondary attraction for tourists. Almost every visitor to Peru comes to Cuzco – the heart of the once-mighty Inca Empire – to see the most fascinating and accessible archaeological ruins on the continent.

# Cuzco

☎ 084

Cuzco (Cusco in Spanish, Qosq'o in Quechua) is the hub of the South American travel network and, in this respect, is reminiscent of Kathmandu in Nepal. Both cities attract thousands of travelers, who come not just to visit a unique destination, but also to experience an age-old culture that is very different to their 20th-century way of life.

Cuzco is the archaeological capital of the Americas and the continent's oldest continuously inhabited city. Massive Inca-built stone walls line most of Cuzco's central streets and form the foundations of colonial and modern buildings. The streets are often stepped, narrow and thronged with Quechua-speaking descendants of the Incas.

Cuzco is the capital of its department and has about 300,000 inhabitants. The city is 3326m above sea level, so during your first few days, take care not to overexert yourself if you've flown in from low altitude (see Altitude Sickness in the Facts for the Visitor chapter).

## History

Cuzco is a city steeped in history, tradition and legend. Indeed, it is often difficult to know where fact ends and myth begins. When Columbus arrived in the Americas, Cuzco was the thriving, powerful capital of the Inca Empire. According to legend, the city was founded in the 12th century by the first Inca, Manco Capac, the son of the sun. During his travels, Manco Capac plunged a golden rod into the ground until it disappeared. This point was qosq'o, which means 'the earth's navel' in the Quechua language, and it was here that he founded the city that was to become the center of the western hemisphere's greatest empire.

Parts of this legend are undoubtedly based on fact – the Inca Empire did have its origins around the 12th century, Cuzco did become its capital and Manco Capac was one of the earliest Inca leaders – but the archaeological record shows that the area was occupied by other cultures for several centuries before the rise of the Incas. Little is known about these pre-Incas except that some were involved in the Wari expansion of the 8th and 9th centuries.

The Incas had no written language, and their oral history was passed down through the generations. The empire's main expansion occurred in the hundred years or so prior to the arrival of the conquistadors in 1533. As the oral records of that important period are relatively accurate, our knowledge of Cuzco's history dates back to about the middle of the 15th century. In 1533, the Spanish, led by Francisco Pizarro, reached Cuzco, and from that point on, written

re͟          ͟alled chronicles) were kept.
͟          ͟ounts of Inca history as
re͟          ͟o the Spanish chroni-
cle͟          ͟ these accounts was
*The͟          of the Incas*,
writte͟          ͟a. He was
born in͟          ͟n Inca
princess ͟          ͟d he
lived in Cu͟          ͟en
moved to Sp͟          ͟6.
Although neithe͟          of
the other chronic͟          ͟d
entirely accurate, ͟          ͟od
overview of Inca histor͟

The reigns of the first͟          ͟o
Capac and those who͟          ͟ –
spanned the period fro͟          ͟2th
century to the early 15th͟          ͟all
tribe they governed w͟          ͟al
groups living in the A͟          ͟ds
during the 13th and 14th͟          ͟ese
Incas left few signs of their e͟          ͟ugh
the remains of some of their p͟          ͟still
be seen in Cuzco. In chronol͟          ͟der,
they were:

1. Manco Capac – The Palace of Co͟          ͟a is
   traditionally attributed to Manco C͟          the
   first Inca, but some sources claim that ͟          was
   built by Huascar – the brother of Atahualpa, the
   12th Inca – shortly before the arrival of the
   Spaniards. The massive retaining walls with 11
   niches can be seen next to the Church of San
   Cristóbal, on a hill on Cuzco's northwestern
   outskirts. The walls, at least to my untrained eye,
   seem too well made to be attributable to the
   first Inca, but the story persists.

2. Sinchi Roca – Some of the walls of his Palace of
   Cora Cora can be seen in the courtyards of
   houses to the right of Calle Suecia as you walk
   uphill from the Plaza de Armas.

3. Lloque Yupanqui

4. Mayta Capac

5. Capac Yupanqui

6. Inca Roca – The huge blocks of this Inca's palace
   now form the foundations of the Museo de Arte
   Religioso and include the famous 12-sided stone
   of Hatunrumiyoc.

7. Yahuar Huacac

8. Viracocha Inca – His palace was demolished to
   make way for the present cathedral on the Plaza
   de Armas.

The ninth Inca, Pachacutec, began the empire's great expansion. Until his time, the Incas had dominated only a small area close to Cuzco, frequently skirmishing with, but not conquering, various other highland tribes. One such tribe, the expansionist Chanka, occupied a region about 150km east of Cuzco and, by 1438, was on the verge of conquering Cuzco. Viracocha Inca and his eldest son, Urcon, believed that their small empire was lost, but Viracocha Inca's third son refused to give up the fight. With the help of some of the older generals, he rallied the Inca army and, in a desperate final battle, managed to rout the Chanka. According to legend, the unexpected victory was won because the boulders on the battlefield turned into warriors and fought on the side of the Inca.

The victorious younger son changed his name to Pachacutec and proclaimed himself the new Inca over his father and elder brother. Buoyed by his great victory over the Chanka, he began the first wave of the expansion that eventually created the Inca Empire. During the next 25 years, he conquered most of the central Andes between the two great lakes of Titicaca and Junín.

Historians have frequently compared the mighty military figure of Pachacutec to the likes of Alexander the Great and Genghis Khan. He was also a great urban developer. Pachacutec devised the city's famous puma shape and diverted the Río Sapphi and Río Tullumayo into channels that crossed the city, keeping it clean and providing it with water. He built agricultural terraces and many buildings, including the famous Coricancha temple and his palace on what is now the western corner of the Plaza de Armas.

There was, of course, no Plaza de Armas before the arrival of the Spanish. In its place was an even greater square, divided by the Sapphi Canal. The area covered by today's Plaza de Armas was known as Aucaypata or Huacaypata, and on the other side of the Sapphi, the area now called the Plaza Regocijo was known as the Cusipata. Together, they formed a huge central plaza that was the focus of the city's social life.

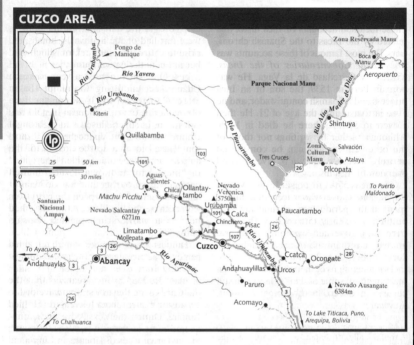

## CUZCO AREA

Pachacutec was fortunate to have a son, Tupac Yupanqui, who was every bit as great a leader as his father. During the 1460s, Tupac Yupanqui helped his father subdue a great area to the north, which included the northern Peruvian and southern Ecuadorian Andes of today, as well as the northern Peruvian coast. After he took over as ruler in 1471, becoming the 10th Inca, the empire continued to expand dramatically. By the time of Tupac Inca's death around 1493, his empire extended from Quito in Ecuador to south of Santiago in Chile.

Huayna Capac, the 11th Inca, was the last to rule over a united empire. When he assumed power after the death of his father, the empire was by far the greatest ever known in the western hemisphere, and there was little left to conquer. Nevertheless, Huayna Capac marched (he would, in fact, have been carried in a litter) to the northernmost limits of his empire, in the region today marked by the Ecuador-Colombia

border. Here, using Quito as his base of operations, the Inca fought a long series of inconclusive campaigns against the tribes of Pasto and Popayán in what is now southern Colombia. He also sired a son, Atahualpa, who was born of a Quitan mother.

By this time, Europeans had discovered the New World and brought with them various Old World diseases. Epidemics, including smallpox and the common cold, swept down from Central America and the Caribbean. Huayna Capac died in such an epidemic around 1525. Shortly before his death, he divided his empire, giving the northern part around Quito to Atahualpa and the southern Cuzco area to another son, Huascar.

Both sons were well suited to the responsible position of ruling an empire – so well suited that neither wished to share power, and a civil war ensued. Huascar was the more popular contender because, having lived in Cuzco for most of his life, he had the people's support. Atahualpa, on the other hand, had lived in outposts of the empire and had few followers around Cuzco. He did, however, have the backing of the army that had been fighting the northern campaigns. In 1532, after several years of warfare, Atahualpa's battle-hardened troops won the major battle of the civil war and captured Huascar outside Cuzco. Atahualpa, the new Inca, retired to Cajamarca to rest.

Meanwhile, Francisco Pizarro landed in northern Ecuador and marched southward in the wake of Atahualpa's conquests. Although Atahualpa was undoubtedly aware of the Spanish presence, he was too busy fighting the civil war to worry about a small band of foreigners. However, by the autumn of 1532, Pizarro was in northern Peru, Atahualpa had defeated Huascar and a fateful meeting was arranged between the Inca and Pizarro.

The meeting, which took place in Cajamarca on November 16, 1532, was to radically change the course of South American history. Atahualpa was ambushed by a few dozen armed conquistadors, who succeeded in capturing him, killing thousands of unarmed Indians and routing tens of thousands more. The conquest of the Incas had begun.

The conquest succeeded for two main reasons. Firstly, Pizarro realized that the emotion of the recent civil war still ran high, and he decided to turn this to his advantage. Accordingly, after holding Atahualpa prisoner for a number of months and then murdering him, he marched into Cuzco and was accepted by the Cuzqueños, because their loyalties lay more with the defeated Huascar than with Atahualpa. Additionally, Pizarro played on the petty intrigues within the Cuzqueño Inca factions.

The second reason for Pizarro's victory was the superior Spanish weaponry. Mounted on horseback, protected by armor and swinging steel swords, the Spanish cavalry was virtually unstoppable. The Spaniards hacked dozens of unprotected Indian warriors to death during a battle. The Indians responded with their customary weapons – clubs, spears, slingshots and arrows – but they were rarely lethal against the mounted, armored conquistadors. Furthermore, in the early battles, the Indians were terrified of the Spaniards' horses and primitive firearms, neither of which had been seen in the Andes before.

It took Pizarro almost a year to reach Cuzco after capturing Atahualpa. In an attempt to regain his freedom, the Inca offered a ransom of a roomful of gold and two rooms of silver. This was to be brought from Cuzco. To speed up the process, Pizarro sent three soldiers to Cuzco early in 1533 to strip Coricancha, or the 'Golden Courtyard,' of its rich ornamentation. Pizarro himself entered Cuzco on November 8, 1533, after winning a series of battles on the road from Cajamarca. By this time, Atahualpa had been killed and Pizarro appointed Manco, a half-brother of Huascar, as a puppet Inca. For almost three years, the empire remained relatively peaceful under the rule of Manco Inca and Pizarro.

In 1536, Manco Inca realized that the Spaniards were there to stay and decided to try to drive them from his empire. He fled from the Spanish and raised a huge army, estimated at well over a hundred thousand. He laid siege to the Spaniards in Cuzco and almost succeeded in defeating them. Only a desperate, last-ditch breakout from Cuzco and a violent battle at Sacsayhuamán saved the Spanish from complete annihilation. Manco Inca retreated to Ollantaytambo and then into the jungle at Vilcabamba.

The Inca Empire was Andean, so situating its capital in the heart of the Andes at Cuzco made a lot of sense. The Spaniards, however, were a seafaring people and needed to maintain links with Spain. Therefore, in 1535, Pizarro founded his capital on the coast at Lima. Although Cuzco remained very important during the first postconquest years, its importance declined once it had been captured, looted and settled. By the end of the 16th century, Cuzco was a quiet colonial town. All the gold and silver was gone, and many of the Inca buildings had been pulled down to make room for churches and colonial houses. Despite this, enough Inca foundations remain today to make a walk around the heart of Cuzco a veritable journey back in time.

Few events of historical significance have occurred in Cuzco since the Spanish conquest, apart from two major earthquakes and one important Indian uprising. The earthquakes, in 1650 and 1950, brought colonial and modern buildings tumbling down, yet most of the Inca walls were undamaged. The only Indian revolt that came close to succeeding was led by Tupac Amaru II in 1780, but he too was defeated by the Spaniards. The battles of Peruvian Independence in the 1820s achieved what the Inca armies had failed to do, but it was the descendants of the conquistadors who wrested power from Spain, and life in Cuzco after independence continued much as before.

The rediscovery of Machu Picchu in 1911 affected Cuzco more than any event since the arrival of the Spanish. With the development of international tourism in the second half of this century, Cuzco has changed from a provincial backwater to Peru's foremost tourist center. Until the 1930s, its main link with the outside world was the railway line to Lake Titicaca and Arequipa. Now, the modern international airport allows daily flights to Lima and other destinations, and roads link Cuzco with the rest of the country. Going to Peru and missing Cuzco is as unthinkable as visiting Egypt and skipping the pyramids.

## Orientation

The heart of the city is the Plaza de Armas, with Avenida Sol being the main business street. Walking just two or three blocks north or east of the plaza will take you to streets little changed for centuries – many are for pedestrians only. The pedestrian street between Plaza del Tricentenario and Huaynapata gives great views over the Plaza de Armas. Recently, the city has had a resurgence of Quechua pride, and the official names of many streets have changed from Spanish to Quechua spellings. Cuzco has become Qosq'o (or Qosco, or variations thereof), Cuichipunco has become K'uychipunko, and so on. Maps usually retain the old spellings, however, and most people still use them.

## Information

**Tourist Office** This is at Mantas 188 (☎ 26-3176). Hours are usually 8 am to 6 pm weekdays and 8 am to 12:30 pm on Saturday.

**South American Explorers** A new SAE clubhouse (☎/fax 22-3102, saec@wayna.rcp .net.pe, Avenida Sol 930) opened in 1999. The postal address in Casilla 500, Cuzco. Hours are 9:30 am to 5 pm weekdays. For more information about the club, see the Lima chapter.

**Boleto Turístico** You can't easily buy individual entrance tickets to many of the major sites in and around Cuzco. Instead, you have to buy a Boleto Turístico (Tourism Ticket), which costs US$10, gives access to 16 different sites and can be purchased from Oficina Ejecutiva del Comité, or OFEC (☎ 22-6919, 22-7037), on Garcilaso at Heladeros. Boletos Turísticos may also be purchased from the tourism office, a travel agent, or at some of the sites. Tickets bought at OFEC are valid for 10 days – check the dates of tickets bought elsewhere. OFEC is open from 7:45 am to 6 pm weekdays and 8:30 am to 1 pm on Saturday.

US$10 represents a good value if you want to visit most of the sites. Within Cuzco, it's valid for La Catedral, the church of San Blas, the Santa Catalina convent, the Museo Histórico Regional, the Museo de Arte Religioso, the Museo Palacio Municipal and the Museo Arqueológico Q'orikancha (but not Q'orikancha itself). All these are described below. The ticket also covers Sacsayhuamán, Qenko, Puca Pucara, Tambo Machay, Pisac, Chinchero, Ollantaytambo, Pikillacta and Tipón – all outside Cuzco. The biggest drawback to the Boleto Turístico is that each site can only be visited once. Other museums, churches and colonial buildings in and around Cuzco can be visited free or for a modest individual admission charge.

**Student Cards** A discount of up to 50% is often available if you present a current international student card with photograph. Recently, the Boleto Turístico was US$5 for bona fide students, who need to show their student card along with the ticket when entering each site. Wherever you go, ask about reductions for students.

**Visas** If your tourist card is about to expire, you can renew it for US$27 per 30 days at the migraciones office on Avenida Sol, next to the post office. It's open from 8 am to 1 pm weekdays. Consider going to Bolivia for a day – you'll get 90 days on your return and save the renewal cost.

**Money** Several banks on Avenida Sol have ATMs that allow Visa or MasterCard cash withdrawals. Casas de cambio give consistently faster service than banks (unless you're using the ATMs), with similar exchange rates and less fuss. There are several on the Plaza de Armas and along Avenida Sol. They are usually in or next to souvenir stores or travel agents and tend to remain open as long as the store is open – often till after dark and on Sunday. Rates are usually within 1% of one another.

Many hotels will accept US dollars, but their exchange rates are not usually as favorable as those offered by the casas de cambio. Street moneychangers can be found outside the banks and casas de cambio, especially at the northwest end of Avenida Sol. Their rates equal what you'll get at the casas de cambio, but check your money carefully before handing over your dollars. Rip-offs are not uncommon, and changing on the street is not recommended unless you know what you are doing and want to change in a hurry.

For traveler's checks, shop around and expect a loss of several percent.

The American Express agent (☎ 22-8431) is Lima Tours (away from the center, take a taxi), which neither exchanges traveler's checks nor refunds lost or stolen traveler's checks – these services are only available in Lima. You can report your lost checks here and buy new ones.

**Post & Communications** The post office (☎ 22-5232, Avenida Sol 800) is open from 7:30 am to 8 pm Monday to Saturday. The post office will hold mail addressed to you

c/o Lista de Correo, Correos Central, Cuzco, Peru.

Telefónica del Peru on Avenida Sol has both national and international telephone and fax services and is open from 7 am to 11 pm.

Internet access is found in several places. The best include the university-run place on Avenida Sol (look for Galeria UNSAAC sign) and Telser (Calle del Medio 117), just off the Plaza de Armas. Telser is open 6:30 am to 1 am daily and has a café.

**Tour Agencies** Tour agencies fall roughly into two groups – those that provide standard tours of Cuzco and the various other ruins in the area, and outfitters that offer adventure tours such as trekking, climbing, river running, kayaking, mountain biking or jungle trips (see Activities later in this chapter, and also the Facts for the Visitor chapter).

There are many tour companies, and I have heard mixed reports about many of them. One letter will say that Top Tours was great, the next will say that they were overpriced with a lousy guide. Another traveler will say that Cheap Tours was great, and the next will say that it was cheap and terribly disorganized. The most common complaints are that the tour did not go according to schedule or as advertised and that a company overcharged.

If you decide to take a tour, ask questions before you pay. First, ask fellow travelers about their experiences, then talk to the tour agency. Is there an English-speaking guide? Will there be many tourists who don't speak English, requiring the guide to repeat everything in two or three languages? (This is a problem when doing a local ruins tour.) How big will the group be? What kind of transport is used? How long will be spent at each place, and how long will be spent eating lunch or traveling or whatever? Can you check the equipment you will be using (for a trek or rafting trip)? Can you meet the guide (particularly for a multiday trip)? Be aware that agencies may merely act as an agent for another company, selling you a trip that is then run by someone else who pays a

# CUZCO

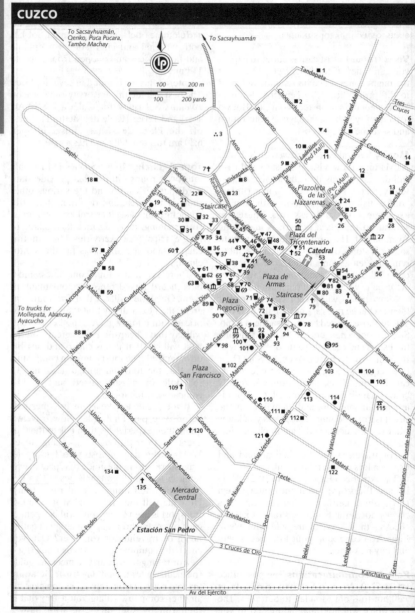

To Sacsayhuamán,
Qenko, Puca Pucara,
Tambo Machay

To Sacsayhuamán

0    100    200 m
0    100    200 yards

Plaza del
Tricentenario

Plaza de
Armas

Catedral

Plazoleta
de las
Nazarenas

Plaza
Regocijo

Plaza
San Francisco

Mercado
Central

Estación San Pedro

To trucks for
Mollepata, Abancay,
Ayacucho

Av del Ejército

# CUZCO

**PLACES TO STAY**
1 Hostal Kuntur Wasi
2 Hostal Choquechaca
5 Hostal El Arcano
6 Hostal Mirador del Inka
8 Albergue Municipal
9 Hostal Huaynapata
10 Hostal El Arqueólogo
11 Hospedaje Rumipunco
12 Hostal Bed & Breakfast
13 Amaru Hostal
14 Hostal Sambleño
18 Hostal Familiar
21 Hotel Carlos V
22 Hostal Corihuasi
23 Hostal Resbalosa
25 Hotel Monasterio del Cusco
28 Hospedaje Acosta
29 Tu Hogar
30 Hostal Suecia II
34 Hostal Royal Qosco
36 Hostal Cáceres
40 Hostal Incawasi
55 Hotel Conquistador
57 Hostal El Balcón
58 Hostal Rikch'arty
59 Hostal Los Niños
62 Picoaga Hotel
63 Hotel Royal Inka II
73 Posada del Inca
75 Hotel Virrey
76 Hostal Plaza de Armas
80 Hostal Loreto
85 Hotel Internacional
   San Agustín
87 Hostal La Casona de
   San Agustín
88 Hostal Qorichaska
89 Hotel Royal Inka I
91 Hotel Cuzco
97 Hotel Libertador
102 Hostal El Solar
104 Hotel Cristina
105 El Dorado Inn
107 Hotel Pascana
111 Gran Hostal Machu Picchu
112 Los Aticos
117 Residencial Madres
    Dominicanas
122 Hotel Los Portales
123 San Agustín Plaza
125 Hotel Don Carlos
134 Hotel Imperio
136 Hostal Centenario
137 Leonard's Lodging

**PLACES TO EAT**
4 Quinta Eulalia
17 Greens
26 Ama Lur
33 Tiziano Trattoria
35 Victor Victoria, Miski Wasi
37 Kusikuy
39 Inka Grill
41 La Estancia Imperial,
   El Mesón de los Portales,
   La Retama
42 Plus Café
43 La Tertulia
44 Chez Maggy
45 Los Cuates, La Ensalada
47 Da Giorgio
49 El Ayllu Café, La Yunta,
   Café Bagdad
51 Acuarium
56 Al Grano
61 José Antonio
66 Café Huaylliy
67 Pucará, El Nevado
68 Govinda Vegetarian
   Restaurant, Café Varayoc
70 El Mesón de los Espaderos
74 Trotamundos
88 Restaurant El Paititi
90 El Truco
94 Trattoria Adriano
98 Auyliyu
100 Kin Taro

**OTHER**
3 Colcampata Ruins
7 Church of San Cristóbal
15 Church of San Blas
16 Plaza San Blas
19 Coin Laundry
20 Tourism Police
24 Church of San Antonio
27 Museo de Arte Religioso
31 Tumi's Video Bar
32 Los Perros Couch Bar
38 Ukukus Bar
43 Amauta Language School
46 Aero Continente
48 Up Town (Disco)
50 Museo Inka
52 Church of Jesús María
53 Church of El Triunfo
54 Paddy O'Flaherty's (Bar)
60 Church of Santa Teresa
64 Municipalidad, Museo Palacio
   Municpal
65 Kamikaze (Bar)
69 Mama Africa Pub
71 Cross Keys Pub
72 Telser Internet
77 Museo de Historia Natural
78 UNSAAC Internet Services
79 Church of La Compañía
80 INDECOPI
81 El Muki (Disco)
84 Convento, Museo
   de Santa Catalina
86 Acupari Language School
92 Tourist Office
93 Church of La Merced
95 Banco de Crédito
96 Craft Market
99 Museo de Historia Regional,
   OFEC Office
101 Farmacia Internacional
103 Banco de la Nación
106 Coricancha Ruins,
    Church of Santa Domingo
108 Transportes Caminos del Inca
109 Church of San Francisco
110 Teatro Municipal
113 Inca Craft Market
114 Centro Comercial Cuzco
115 Telefónica del Perú
116 Museo Arqueológico
    Q'orikancha
118 Transportes Pitusiray,
    Transportes Urubamba
119 First Class Buses to Puno
120 Church of Santa Clara
121 Excel Language Center
124 Milla Turismo
126 Qosqo Center of Native Dance
127 Migraciones (Immigration)
128 Central Post Office
129 Transportes Collasuyo (ticket
    office)
130 Transportes Zela (ticket office)
131 CIVA (ticket office)
132 Expreso Huari (ticket office)
133 Cruz del Sur (ticket office)
135 Church of San Pedro
138 South American Explorers
139 Waterfall Monument

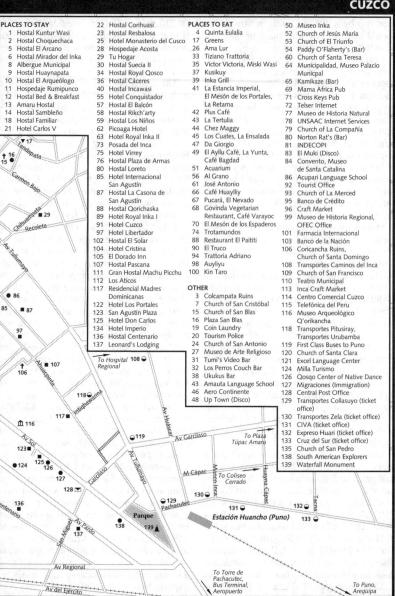

commission. Agents at the airport are notorious for charging a good deal more for a tour run by a cheaper outfit in town. You should deal directly with the tour operator or outfitter running the tour.

Costs vary, so it's worth shopping around. Sometimes there are 'price wars' that can lead to a lot of local bad feeling, as guides are underpaid and vehicles are overcrowded in order to cut corners and offer the cheapest possible trip. This is to everyone's detriment. The cheaper tours are liable to be crowded, multilingual affairs, while the more expensive ones can be tailored to the needs of the individual. The cheapest agencies change names and owners quite often and are less stable than the more expensive outfitters. Budget travelers should ask other travelers for current reports on the cheaper agencies.

Having said all this, I cannot 100% recommend any particular agent, especially the cheaper ones. Those described below are, however, pretty reputable.

The standard tours include a half-day city tour, a half-day tour of the nearby ruins (Sacsayhuamán, Qenko, Puca Pucara and Tambo Machay), a half-day tour of the Sunday markets at either Pisac or Chinchero, a full-day trip to the Urubamba valley (Pisac, Ollantaytambo and, perhaps, Chinchero) and a full-day visit to Machu Picchu. It is worth spending more time, if you can, in the Urubamba valley – staying one or more nights in hotels at Urubamba or Ollantaytambo, for example – to allow more in-depth visits to the sites. The tours can sometimes seem rather rushed, especially with the cheaper agencies.

Dozens of companies offer inexpensive tours, starting around US$6 per person for a half day. The following seem to do a decent job most of the time: Kantu Tours (☎/fax 24-3672, Plaza de Armas), Luzma Tours (☎ 22-2315, 22-2428, Santa Teresa 399), EcoTours (☎ 23-1288, fax 24-4598, Portal Escribanos 189 or Heladeros 150, Plaza Regocijo) and Naty's Travel (☎ 23-9437, 26-1811, Plaza de Armas). There are many others, and their omission does not imply that they don't do a good job.

Lima Tours (☎ 22-8431, fax 22-1266) is the Cuzco office of this major Lima travel agency, and it caters to 1st-class travelers and international tour groups. Milla Turismo (☎ 23-1388, fax 23-1710, Avenida Pardo 675) is geared to providing 1st-class services to international tour groups. It also arranges courses on Andean culture (see Classes later in this chapter).

The basic, one-day Río Urubamba trip with lunch costs US$25 and is offered by many adventure-travel companies. A minimum of four paying passengers is normally required. Luzma Tours (see earlier) is also known among kayakers because English-speaking owner Luz María Anaya is very helpful in sorting out expedition problems. Loreto Tours (☎ 23-6331, Calle del Medio 111) seems to have almost a monopoly on cheap one-day river trips, and Kantu Tours (see earlier) also offers them.

Eric Adventures (☎/fax 22-8475, ericadv@net.cosapidata.com.pe, Plateros 324) offers inexpensive one- and two-day trips on the Urubamba. The two-day trips include food and camping. Eric Arenas of Eric Adventures is a Peruvian kayaking champion who represented Peru in the 1992 Olympics. He also offers kayaking classes on the Apurímac, where he uses a hot spring to comfortably teach the Eskimo roll! A two-day course is US$90. The company also offers other adventure trips, but unfortunately, they lost a river guide a few years ago, so check the experience of whom you go with.

Instinct (☎ 23-8366, ☎/fax 23-3451, instinct@chavin.rcp.net.pe, Procuradores 50) and Mayuc (☎/fax 23-2666, chando@mayuc.com, Portal Confiturias 211, Plaza de Armas) both do three-day rafting trips on the Apurímac for about US$250, including transportation, food and camping. Both companies do other trips as well and have received recommendations from budget travelers; however, cost-cutting can cause problems. It is only fair to say that Mayuc, which is Cuzco's longest-running river operator, had an accident a few years ago, and as a result, a couple of tourists drowned. This is a serious river, so make sure your guides are experts. Mayuc also runs cheap 10-day trips (7 days of rafting) on the Tambopata.

You could make reservations for a Tambopata or Apurímac trip with Amazonas Explorer (☎ 22-5284, fax 23-6826, info@ amazonas-explorer.com). They are very professional, with top-quality equipment and guides. Amazonas Explorer also does other river trips, as well as mountain biking and hiking. See Organized Tours from the UK in the Getting There & Away chapter for more information about their British and Arequipa offices. Another professional outfitter taking advance international bookings for Tambopata trips is Apumayo Expeditions (☎ 24-2030, Garcilaso 265), which has a Lima office (☎ 442-3886, fax 422-5247).

For hiking, Soqllaquasa (Plateros 359) has been recommended for cheap rental gear; check all rental gear carefully. Many companies offer inexpensive guided Inca Trail and other hikes. Budget travelers have recommended the following (though occasional complaints are received; you get what you pay for. See the boxed text 'Inca Trail Tours'). They are arranged in roughly ascending order of cost. Q'ente (☎/fax 23-8245, Plateros 376), SAS (☎ 23-7292, Espaderos 135), United Mice (☎ 22-1139, Plateros 249), Inca Explorers (☎ 23-9669, fax 24-3736, Suecia 339) and Tambo Treks (☎ 23-7718, fax 23-6229, Atocsaycuchi 589, San Blas).

If mountaineering interests you, contact Peruvian Andean Treks (☎ 22-5701, fax 23-8911, postmast@patcusco.com.pe, Pardo 705), which is run by Tom Hendrickson, who has pioneered local climbs. They have some of the best guides and equipment for climbing the local snowpeaks, as well as trekking and jungle trips. They can send you a list of representatives in the USA, Canada, UK, Australia and New Zealand that charge the same rates as in Cuzco; they do a good job. Apu Expeditions (☎/fax 24-6377, apuexpe@ qenqo.rcp.net.pe) is another general allround outfitter catering often to foreign reservations. Southern Cross Adventures (☎ 23-7649, fax 23-9447, Plaza de Armas) includes horse-riding among its activities.

Mountain bikes can be rented, but the quality of the machines tends to be poor, though adequate for an easy ride in the area. Always check them carefully, and make sure that you have a repair kit if you are going a long way. The better bikes are rented only as part of a tour. Try Eco Montaña (☎ 24-2030, Garcilaso 265), which does tours. The best outfitter has been Bicycentro, run by Juan Carlos Salazar – but it was recently closed. Maybe it'll reopen.

Many jungle lodges and outfitters are based in Cuzco and visit the Puerto Maldonado and Manu area; they are listed in appropriate parts of the Amazon Basin chapter.

There are many cheap agencies on Procuradores, Plateros and around the Plaza de Armas. Check them out carefully – some offer a good value, but others are disappointing. Shoestring travelers can visit most places using the cheap public-transport system. Details of this option are given later in this chapter.

**Books & Bookstores** The best source of general information about Cuzco and the surrounding area, including maps of the Inca Trail, Machu Picchu and all the other sites, is the well-recommended book *Exploring Cuzco* by Peter Frost, available locally. Also excellent is John Hemming's *The Conquest of the Incas*.

Several bookstores around the Plaza de Armas sell English-language guidebooks and books about Peru.

**Laundry** Cuzco has good laundry facilities. Places on Suecia, Procuradores, Plateros and Espaderos (just off the Plaza de Armas) advertise that they wash, dry and fold your clothes in a day for about US$2 per kilogram. During busy months, they can get overwhelmed, and their promise of 'in by 10 am, ready by 6 pm' can easily turn into 9 or 10 pm. However, if you are prepared to wait 24 hours, you'll find places up the hill along Suecia and Tecseccocha that will do it for about US$1 per kilogram. The Laundromat on Saphi at Amargura will allow you to wash and dry while you wait, though they don't have many machines.

**Medical Services** For life-threatening injuries and complicated procedures, Cuzco's facilities are limited, and a transfer to Lima is recommended. If you are in a hospital here, you need a reliable, preferably local, person to help you get prescriptions filled etc, as procedures are chaotic. The best clinics are the Clínica Centro Medico Pardo (☎ 24-0387, Avenida de la Cultura 710) and Clínica Paredes (☎ 22-5265, Lechugal 401). The Hospital Regional (☎ 23-1131, emergencies 22-3691) on Avenida de la Cultura is cheaper, but not as good. Dr Oscar Tejada (☎ 23-3836) speaks English and has been recommended by readers. A recommended dentist is Dr Gilbert Espejo H (☎ 22-8074, Centro Comercial Cuzco, Level 2).

**Emergency** The Policía de Turismo (☎ 22-1961) has moved several times in the last few years. Recently, they were on the 1st block of Saphi. They are open 24 hours a day. Some English is spoken, and the police are trained to deal with problems pertaining to tourists. If you have something stolen, they'll help with the official police reports needed for insurance claims and will also tell you how to place a radio announcement offering a reward for the return of your property, particularly if it has little commercial value (such as your exposed camera film, journal or documents).

INDECOPI, the tourist protection office, can help with problems and complaints. English is spoken. They are at the airport (☎ 23-7364) and on the Plaza de Armas (☎ 25-2974, 25-2987).

**Dangers & Annoyances** More tourists are robbed in Cuzco than in any other Peruvian city (but more tourists go to Cuzco than any other Peruvian city). Avoid displays of wealth (expensive jewelry, wristwatches, wallets) and leave most of your money in a hotel safe (carry what you need in inside pockets and/or money belts). Avoid walking alone late at night – revelers returning late from bars and such have been mugged; recently, victims have been choked to unconsciousness and then robbed. It's best to take a taxi at night and go with a friend. Take special care going to and from the Machu Picchu train station and the nearby market – these are prime areas for pickpockets and

bag-slashers. Having said this, I have to point out that in scores of visits to Cuzco between 1982 and 2000, I have never been robbed on the street (though I had a camera taken from my hotel room once – I shouldn't have left it out in plain view).

Also, beware of altitude sickness if you're flying in from sea level. It's worth rereading the Altitude Sickness and Dangers & Annoyances sections of the Facts for the Visitor chapter.

Don't buy drugs. Dealers and police often work together, and Procuradores is only one of several areas in which you can make a drug deal and get busted, all within a couple of minutes.

## Things to See

There are four things to remember when sightseeing: first, buy your Boleto Turístico; second, carry a student card if you have one; third, don't get so excited by what you're seeing that you forget about your pockets and your camera – thieves congregate in the same places as sightseers; and fourth, opening hours are erratic and can change for any reason – from feast days to the caretaker wanting a beer with his friends.

Guided city tours are available from travel agencies. However, most of the sites listed below have local guides available, some of whom speak English. There is not normally a set fee, so you should come to some agreement. The minimum for a small group would be US$1 per person.

**Plaza de Armas** In Inca times, the plaza, called Huacaypata or Aucaypata, was twice as large as it is today. It was the heart of Inca Cuzco and remains the heart of the modern city. Two flags usually fly here – the red-and-white Peruvian flag and the rainbow-colored flag of Tahuantinsuyo (representing the four quarters of the Inca Empire). Colonial arcades surround the plaza. On the northeastern side is the cathedral, fronted by a large flight of stairs and flanked by the churches of Jesús María and El Triunfo. On the southeastern side is the very ornate church of La Compañía. Some Inca walls remain, found in the restaurant on the western corner of the plaza. The quiet pedestrian alleyway of Loreto, both sides of which have Inca walls, is a historic means of access to the plaza.

**Churches** Cuzco's colonial churches are better preserved than those in other cities. Their maintenance directly correlates with the importance of the tourist industry in Cuzco. As there are literally scores of churches, only the most important are described in this section. They are usually open every day, but hours change often. A good time to visit is in the early morning, when the churches are open for services. Officially, they are closed to tourists at this time, but if you go in quietly as one of the congregation, you can see the church as it should be seen – as a place of worship, not just a tourist site.

Religious festivals are a superb time to see the churches. One year, I visited the cathedral at Corpus Christi. The church had been completely cleared of pews, and in their place stood huge pedestals that were supporting larger-than-life statues of various saints in rich vestments. Each saint was being venerated by candlelight, and thousands of candles illuminated the ornate church interior. The place was thronged with people, including several bands of musicians, who wandered around in the smoky atmosphere playing mournful Andean tunes in honor of the saints. As with many highland feast days, it was a fascinating combination of ancient and colorful pagan festivities, somber and prayerful Catholic ritual and modern Latin American mayhem.

Remember, though, that churches are places of worship, and act accordingly – especially if you visit during a service. Photography, particularly flash photography, is normally not allowed – the intensity of repeated flashes seriously damages the pigment of the centuries-old art work inside.

*La Catedral* Started in 1559 and taking almost a hundred years to build, the cathedral is Cuzco's main church and also one of the city's greatest repositories of colonial art. Many of the hundreds of canvases are

from the Cuzco school of painting. This style combines the art of 16th- and 17th-century Europe with the imagination of Andean Indian artists who had only a few Spanish canvases as a guide to what was considered artistically acceptable.

The cathedral has been combined with two other churches. The church of El Triunfo, to the right of the cathedral, is the oldest church in Cuzco and dates from 1536. Left of the cathedral is the church of Jesús María, dating from 1733. El Triunfo is the usual entrance to the three-church complex.

The following description assumes you are entering from El Triunfo. In front of the entrance is a vault containing the remains of the famous Inca historian, Garcilaso de la Vega. Born in Cuzco in 1539, Garcilaso de la Vega left Peru in 1560 for Spain, where he died in 1616. His remains were returned to Cuzco several years ago by the king and queen of Spain.

As you enter the main part of the cathedral, turn right. In the far corner is the entrance to the **sacristy**, which is covered with paintings of Cuzco's bishops, starting with Vicente de Valverde – the friar who accompanied Pizarro during the conquest. Look for Manuel de Mollinedo, Bishop of Cuzco from 1673 to 1699 and one of the most influential supporters of the Cuzco school of art. The crucifixion at the back of the sacristy is attributed to the Flemish painter Van Dyck, though some local guides claim it to be the work of the 17th-century Spaniard Alonso Cano. A similar painting hangs in the Museo de Arte Religioso.

In the corner of the cathedral, next to the sacristy, is a huge painting of the **Last Supper** by Marcos Zapata. This fine example of the Cuzco school depicts a supper consisting of the Inca delicacy *cuy*, or roast guinea pig.

The original wooden **altar** is at the very back of the cathedral, behind the present silver altar, which stands some 10m from the rear wall. Directly opposite the silver altar is the magnificently carved **choir**. It dates from the 17th century and is one of the finest in Peru. (Both the Last Supper and the original altar were closed for restoration in 1998/99, but are projected to reopen in 2000.)

On the far-left outside wall of the main altar, you'll find a large painting of the great **earthquake** of 1650. The city of those days, as shown in the painting, is recognizable as Cuzco even today. The inhabitants are parading around the plaza with a crucifix, praying for an end to the earthquake. Miraculously, the earthquake stopped (don't they all?), and the city was saved. This crucifix, called **El Señor de los Temblores,** or 'The Lord of the Earthquakes,' can be seen in the alcove to the right of the door leading back into El Triunfo. The image has been blackened by the countless votive candles that have been lit beneath it, and the candles are now kept well away from the statue to prevent further smoke damage. The statue is paraded around on Easter Monday.

There are many splendid **side chapels** – some containing the elaborate platforms used to carry the religious statues around during processions, and others with intricate altars. The last side chapel to the left of the altar has a painting of Pope John Paul II during his visit to Sacsayhuamán in 1985.

The cathedral is open to tourists from 10 to 11:30 am Monday to Thursday and Saturday and 2 to 5:30 pm Monday to Saturday. Hours change often. Entrance is with the Boleto Turístico. The huge main doors are open for worship between 6 and 10 am – there is no admission charge during these hours, but tourism is officially prohibited. Discreet, respectful visits normally do not cause a problem.

***La Compañía*** This church on the Plaza de Armas is often lit up at night and can be seen from the train as you come in from Machu Picchu after dark – a splendid sight. Its foundations are built from the palace of Huayna Capac – the last Inca to rule an undivided, unconquered empire.

The church was built by the Jesuits, hence its name: the Church of the Company of Jesús. Work commenced in 1571. The church was destroyed by the 1650 earthquake, but reconstruction began almost immediately. The Jesuits planned to make it the most magnificent of Cuzco's churches. However, the bishop of Cuzco complained that its

splendor should not rival that of the cathedral, and Pope Paul III was called upon to arbitrate. His decision was in favor of the cathedral, but by the time word reached Cuzco, La Compañía was almost complete. It has an incredible baroque facade and is one of Cuzco's most ornate churches.

The interior has the usual array of fine paintings and richly carved altars. Two large canvases near the main door show early marriages in Cuzco and are noteworthy for their wealth of period detail.

Admission is free, but hours are erratic.

***La Merced*** La Merced is considered to be Cuzco's third most important colonial church. It was destroyed in the 1650 earthquake and rebuilt; the present structure, consisting of two sections, dates from 1654.

The church itself is open for worship from 7 to 9 am and 5 to 7:30 pm. To the left of the church, at the back of a small courtyard, is the entrance to the monastery and museum, which are open from 9 am to noon and 2 to 5 pm Monday to Saturday. Entry costs about US$1.50.

The Order of La Merced was founded in Barcelona in 1218 by San Pedro Nolasco. Paintings based on his life hang around the walls of the beautiful colonial cloister. The church on the far side of the cloister contains the tombs of two of the most famous conquistadors, Diego de Almagro and Gonzalo Pizarro. Also on the far side of the cloister is a small religious museum that houses vestments that are said to have belonged to the conquistador/friar Vicente de Valverde. The museum's most famous exhibit is a priceless, solid-gold monstrance, 1.3m high and covered with precious stones, including over 1500 diamonds and 1600 pearls.

***San Francisco*** This church and monastery, dating from the 16th and 17th centuries, is more austere than many of Cuzco's other churches, but it does have a large collection of colonial religious paintings and a well-carved, cedar choir. One of the paintings measures 9m x 12m (supposedly the largest painting in South America) and shows the family tree of St Francis of Assisi, the founder of the order.

His life is celebrated in the paintings hung around the colonial cloister.

Also of interest are the two crypts, which are not totally underground. Inside are plenty of human bones, some of which have been carefully arranged into phrases designed to remind visitors of the transitory nature of life.

The church and religious-art collection is open from 2 to 4 pm Monday to Saturday (subject to change). Admission is US$1.

**Santa Clara** This 16th-century church, part of a strict convent, is difficult to visit. Seeing it became a minor challenge, and I finally found that you can usually get in for mass if you go around 6 or 7 am. It's worth making the effort, because this is one of the more bizarre churches in Cuzco – indeed, in all Peru.

Mirrors cover almost the entire interior; apparently, the early clergy used them to entice local Indians into church for worship. The nuns provide the choir during mass sitting at the very back of the church and separated from both the priest and the rest of the congregation by an ominous grille of heavy metal bars stretching wall to wall and floor to ceiling.

**San Blas** This simple adobe church is comparatively small, but its exquisitely carved pulpit has been called the finest example of colonial wood-carving in the Americas. Legend claims that its creator was an Indian who miraculously recovered from a deadly disease and subsequently dedicated his life to carving this pulpit for the church. Supposedly, his skull is nestled in the topmost part of the carving. In reality, no one is certain of the identity of either the skull or the woodcarver.

Also note the very ornate, baroque, gold-leafed principal altar that was restored recently.

San Blas is open from 2 to 5:30 pm Monday to Saturday. Entry is with the Boleto Turístico.

**Santa Catalina** This convent has a colonial and religious-art museum, with many religious paintings of the Cuzco school, statues,

an ornately friezed side chapel, and the convent's main altar behind steel bars. It's open from 9 am to 5:30 pm Monday to Thursday and Saturday. Friday hours are 9 am to 3 pm; it is closed Sunday. Entry is with the Boleto Turístico; guided tours are available for a tip.

**Santa Teresa** Santa Teresa is a closed convent and difficult to visit. Its church is said to be one of the most beautiful in Cuzco.

**Santo Domingo** The church of Santo Domingo is famous as the site of Coricancha, Cuzco's major Inca temple. The church has twice been destroyed by earthquakes, first in 1650 and again in 1950. It was also damaged in the 1986 earthquake, after which it briefly closed for repairs. Photographs in the entrance show the extent of the 1950 damage – compare the state of the colonial building with that of the Inca walls, which sustained minimal damage in these earthquakes. Also in the entrance is a doorway carved in the Arab style – a reminder of the centuries of Moorish domination in Spain. Remains of the Inca temple are inside the cloister. Colonial paintings around the outside of the courtyard depict the life of Santo Domingo (Saint Dominic). The paintings contain several representations of dogs holding torches in their jaws. These are God's guard dogs, or *dominicanus* in Latin, hence the name of this religious order.

It's open from 8 am to 5 pm Monday to Saturday (may be on Sunday). Admission to both the cloister and the Inca ruins is US$0.75 and guides outside offer tours.

**Inca Ruins in Cuzco** Most Inca ruins are outside the city and are described in Around Cuzco later in this chapter. The main ruin within Cuzco is Coricancha. Other ruins have been converted into colonial or modern buildings, but their walls remain visible.

**Coricancha** This Inca ruin forms the base of the colonial church of Santo Domingo. Today, all that remains of Coricancha (once the Inca empire's richest temple) is the stonework – the precious stones and metals were looted by the conquistadors.

In Inca times, Coricancha (or Q'orikancha – Quechua for 'golden courtyard') was literally covered with gold. The temple walls were lined with some 700 solid-gold sheets, each weighing about 2kg. There were life-size gold and silver replicas of corn that were ceremonially 'planted' in agricultural rituals. Also reported were solid-gold treasures such as altars, llamas and babies, as well as a replica of the sun, which was lost. Within months of the arrival of the first conquistadors, this incredible wealth had all been melted down.

Various religious rites took place in the temple. The mummified bodies of several previous Incas were kept here, brought out into the sunlight each day and offered food and drink, which was then ritually burnt. Coricancha was also an observatory from which priests monitored major celestial activities.

Most of this is left to the imagination of the modern visitor, but much of the stonework does remain and ranks with the finest Inca architecture in Peru. A curved, perfectly fitted, 6m-high wall can be seen from both inside and outside the site. This wall has withstood the violent earthquakes that destroyed most of Cuzco's colonial buildings.

Once inside the site, the visitor enters a courtyard. The octagonal font in the middle was originally covered with 55kg of solid gold. Inca side chambers lie to either side of the courtyard. The largest, to the right, were said to be temples to the moon and stars and were, perhaps, appropriately covered with sheets of solid silver. However, the conquistadors looted the temple riches so fast and so thoroughly that records are hazy. The walls are perfectly tapered upward and, with their niches and doorways, are excellent examples of Inca trapezoidal architecture. The fitting of the individual blocks is so precise that, in some places, you can't tell where one block ends and the next begins as you glide your finger over them.

Opposite these chambers, on the other side of the courtyard, are smaller temples dedicated to thunder and the rainbow. Three holes have been carved through the walls of this section to the street outside. Their purpose is not known but various theories have been advanced. Perhaps they were drains, either for the sacrificial *chicha* drink, for blood or, more mundanely, for rainwater. Alternatively, they may have been speaking tubes connecting the inner temple with the outside. Another noteworthy feature of this side of the complex is the floor in front of the chambers. It dates from Inca times and is carefully cobbled with pebbles.

The buildings described here cover only two sides of the square. There was a larger chamber on each of the other two sides, but only small segments of their foundations remain.

After the conquest, Coricancha was given to Juan Pizarro. He was not able to enjoy it for long, because he died in the battle at Sacsayhuamán in 1536. In his will, he bequeathed Coricancha to the Dominicans, and it has remained in their possession ever since. Today's site is a rather bizarre combination of Inca and colonial architecture, topped with a modern protective roof of glass and metal. See Santo Domingo for business hours and entrance fees.

**Other Inca Walls in Cuzco** The other Inca buildings in Cuzco are not visitor sites in themselves, but can still be admired – most of them from outside.

If you walk southeast away from the Plaza de Armas along the narrow alley of Loreto, there are Inca walls on both sides. The wall on the right-hand side belongs to Amarucancha, or the 'Courtyard of the Serpents.' Perhaps its name derives from the pair of snakes carved on the lintel of the doorway near the end of the enclosure. Amarucancha was the site of the palace of the 11th Inca, Huayna Capac. The church of La Compañía was built here after the conquest, and there is now a school behind the church. Behind the school is a popular tourist market. On the other side of Loreto is the oldest-surviving Inca wall in Cuzco. It's also one of the best. The wall belonged to the Acllahuasi, or the 'House of the Chosen Women.' After the conquest, the building became part of the closed convent of Santa Catalina and so went from housing the Virgins of the Sun to housing pious Catholic nuns.

Heading northeast away from the Plaza de Armas along Calle Triunfo, you soon come to the street of Hatunrumiyoc, named after the well-known, 12-sided stone. The stone is on the right, about halfway along the 2nd city block, and can usually be recognized by the small knot of Indians selling souvenirs next to it. This excellently fitted stone belongs to a wall of the palace of the 6th Inca, Inca Roca. It is technically brilliant but by no means an unusual example of polygonal masonry. In Machu Picchu, there are stones with more than 30 angles (though these are corner stones and are therefore counted in three dimensions) and a block with 44 angles in one plane has been found at Torontoy, a minor ruin roughly halfway between Machu Picchu and Ollantaytambo.

There is a great difference between the wall of Hatunrumiyoc and that of the Acllahuasi. The first is made of polygonal stone blocks in no regular pattern, while the second is made from carefully shaped rectangular blocks that are coursed, or layered, in the manner of modern-day bricks. Both styles are common in Inca architecture. In general, the polygonal masonry was thought to be stronger and was therefore used for retaining walls in terraces. The coursed masonry, which was considered more aesthetically appealing, was used for the walls of Inca temples and palaces.

## Museums & Colonial Buildings

Many museums are in colonial houses, the interiors of which are often as interesting as the exhibits.

**Museo Inka** The museum building, at the corner of Tucumán and Ataud, a steep block northeast of the Plaza de Armas, rests on Inca foundations; it's also known as The Admiral's House, after the first owner, Admiral Francisco Aldrete Maldonado. It was badly damaged in the 1650 earthquake and rebuilt by Pedro Peralta de los Ríos, the Count of Laguna, whose crest is above the porch. Further damage, which occurred during the 1950 earthquake, has now been fully repaired, restoring the building to its position among Cuzco's finest colonial houses.

The architecture has several interesting features, including a massive stairway guarded by sculptures of mythical creatures, as well as a corner window column that from the inside looks like a statue of a bearded man but from the outside appears to be a naked woman. The facade is plateresque – an elaborately ornamented 16th-century Spanish style suggestive of silver plate. The ceilings are ornate, and the views from the windows are good.

The building's restored interior is, filled with a fine collection of metal and gold work, jewelry, pottery, textiles, mummies and more. The museum has 450 *queros* (Inca wooden drinking vessels), which is the largest quero collection in the world; some are in storage. This is the best museum if you are interested in the Incas.

Hours are 8:30 am to 5 pm weekdays and 8:30 am to 1 pm on Saturday. Admission is US$1.70.

**Museo Arqueológico Q'orikancha** This small modern underground museum is in front of the church of Santo Domingo and is entered from Avenida Sol. There are various archaeological displays that interpret both Inca and pre-Inca cultures. Admission is with the Boleto Turístico, and hours are 9:30 am to 6 pm Monday to Saturday.

**Museo de Historia Regional** This museum is in the colonial Casa Garcilaso de la Vega, the house of the Inca historian that is buried in the cathedral. The chronologically arranged collection begins with arrowheads from Preceramic Period and continues with a few pots of the Chavín, Vicus, Mochica, Chimu, Chancay and Inca cultures. There is also a Nazca mummy, a few Inca weavings (some of which show a marked similarity to the older weavings available for sale in the Cuzco area today) and some small gold ornaments excavated from Coricancha between 1972 and 1979, and from the Plaza de Armas in 1996 while the fountain was being renovated. Labels are in Spanish, and there weren't enough of them on my most recent visit. Some pieces from the archaeology museum may be exhibited here during expansion.

Also on display are a few dozen paintings from the Cuzco school, as well as some more recent Mestizo art (mainly with religious themes) and pieces of colonial furniture. There are some changing local art shows. It's open from 8 am to 5:30 pm Monday to Saturday. Entrance is with the Boleto Turístico.

***Museo de Arte Religioso*** This building on Hatunrumiyoc was originally the palace of the Inca Roca but was later used as the foundation for the residence of the Marquis of Buenavista. It later became the archbishop's palace and is sometimes referred to by that name. The church donated the mansion to house a religious-art collection. Many of the paintings are notable for the accuracy of their period detail. There are some impressive stained-glass windows in one part of the museum. The colonial-style tile work of the interior is not original and was replaced in the 1940s.

It's open from 9 to 11:30 am and 3 to 5:30 pm daily except Sunday (when it may be open in the afternoon). Entry is with the Boleto Turístico.

***Museo Palacio Municipal*** The Municipalidad, on the Plaza Regocijo, has a small collection of modern local art on display. Hours are 9:30 am to 5 pm weekdays and sometimes on Saturday. Entry is with the Boleto Turístico.

***Museo de Historia Natural*** This museum is run by the Universidad Nacional, and the entrance is to the right of La Compañía on the Plaza de Armas. It houses a collection of stuffed local animals and birds and a few other items. It's open weekdays from 9 am to noon and 3 to 6 pm; admission is US$0.50.

## Activities

**Photography** The ideal light for photography occurs in the early morning and late afternoon, when the sun is low. The shadows in the middle of the day tend to come out very black in photographs.

Some locals dress in traditional finery and lead their llamas past the most photogenic spots. This is not a coincidence; they expect a tip for posing, and see themselves as working models, not beggars. Some tourists object to paying for these photographs, in which case they shouldn't take them. On the other hand, if you make friends with your potential model, they will help you get shots that are worth paying for.

If you want natural-looking, unposed shots, please be sensitive and discreet. Some travelers seem more concerned with taking a good photograph than with their subject's feelings. Not everyone takes kindly to being constantly photographed doing such mundane things as selling vegetables, breastfeeding their children, or loading their llama.

A wide selection of film is available in Cuzco.

**Trekking & Backpacking** The best time to go trekking is during the May-to-September dry season. At other times, trails turn into muddy slogs, and views are often clouded in. Many people still go off-season, of course, but be prepared for rain and mud.

The Inca Trail is a very popular adventure. You can hire porters, cooks and guides or just rent some equipment and carry it yourself. Tents, sleeping bags, backpacks, stoves – everything you might need for hiking – can be rented in Cuzco, usually for around US$2 per item per day. Check the equipment carefully before you rent it, as some of it is pretty shoddy.

Cheap tours start as low as US$60 per person, but the guides tend to speak little English or not be very informative or environmentally aware, and the food and equipment is often of minimal quality. Don't go on a trip that dumps its garbage on the trail. More expensive outfits provide better food, equipment and services and clean up after themselves, hauling the trash out rather than dumping it in the nearest ruin.

Other popular treks include reaching the Inca Trail from Mollepata, climbing over 4800m-high passes near the peak of Salcantay (6271m, the second-highest peak in the Cuzco area), or the six-day circuit around the area's highest peak, Ausangate (6384m). There are many other options. The hugely popular Inca Trail is described below, but if you want to do other hikes, read *Peru & Bolivia: Backpacking & Trekking* by Hilary Bradt, Jane Letham and John Pilkington.

**River Rafting** The most popular rafting trip is down the Urubamba. Trips typically last half a day (three hours of rafting plus a couple of hours for transportation at either end). Costs start at about US$25. Full-day tours, combining a raft trip with a lunch and a visit to the Pisac or Ollantaytambo ruins, are also offered for a little more money. Two-day trips offer two half days of rafting on different sections of the river, and ruin visits and overnights in the Urubamba valley are possible at extra cost. Many agencies in Cuzco offer these tours, particularly the standard half-day excursion.

The Urubamba is not very wild and offers a great introduction to whitewater rafting, some spectacular scenery and a chance to visit some of the best Inca ruins near Cuzco. Three sections are regularly run. The popular Huambutiyo-to-Pisac section is the easiest and includes three or four hours of fun rafting, as well as a chance to explore the Pisac ruins or market. This section can be run year-round, although during the dry season, it is far from wild. The Ollantaytambo-to-Chilca run is also very popular – it combines the ruins of Ollantaytambo with some exciting rapids and reaches Class III level of difficulty. This run can be combined with the Inca Trail if you want to trek the extra half day along the river from Chilca to the Inca Trail. The most exciting nearby section is the short but action-packed Cañon Huaran, with Class III+ rapids; this is not a frequently offered trip, however. Farther downstream, the river becomes unraftable as it approaches Machu Picchu. The Urubamba beyond Machu Picchu offers more possibilities, but access is limited.

Other rivers that can be run are farther from Cuzco. For these, you definitely need to book with a top-quality outfit with highly experienced guides who know first-aid as well as rafting, because you will be days away

from help in the cases of illness or accident. The Río Apurímac has three- to 10-day options but can only be run from May to November. The rapids are extremely exciting (Classes IV and V), and the river goes through remote and wild scenery with deep gorges. Rafters camp on sandy beaches (where sand flies can be a nuisance), and sightings of deer, otters, condors and even pumas have been recorded. The end of the run enters the recently declared Zona Reservada Apurímac – a huge protected area of rainforest with no tourist services. Three- or four-day trips are most often offered, but this stretch of river has limited camping places, and those that exist are becoming increasingly trashed. Make sure your outfitter removes everything and leaves a clean campsite. Only a few outfitters use appropriate wilderness toilets; others allow groups to shit anywhere, with unsavory results.

An even wilder expedition is the 10- to 12-day possibility on the Tambopata, starting in the area of the Andes north of Lake Titicaca and ending at the Reserva Nacional Tambopata in the Amazon. It takes two days just to drive to the put-in point from Cuzco. The first days on the river are full of technically demanding rapids in wild Andean scenery, and the trip finishes with a couple of gentle floating days in the rainforest. Tapirs, capybara, caiman, giant otters and jaguars have all been seen by keen-eyed boaters. Rapids are Class III and IV, but can be run only from June to October.

**Kayaking** This activity is becoming increasingly popular in the Cuzco area. Some of the river-rafting trips above can be accompanied by experienced kayakers, many of whom bring their own kayaks. A few outfitters have kayaks available (see Tour Agencies earlier in this chapter).

**Mountain Biking** This is another growing industry in the Cuzco area. Currently, the bikes that are available are no more than just adequate, so serious bikers may prefer to bring their own (see Customs in the Facts for the Visitor chapter for details on bringing bicycles into Peru). However, as more bikes are imported, the selection will improve. The cheapest bikes can be rented for about US$8 a day, but they aren't really up to the rigors of unpaved roads on the wilder rides. Better bikes are available for US$15 to US$20 a day, but check them carefully as well. Make sure you get a helmet, puncture-repair kit, pump and tool kit.

There are several excellent one- or two-day biking trips around Cuzco, but they are difficult to describe accurately. It's worth hiring a local guide, or you might get lost.

Longer trips are possible, but a guide and a support vehicle are recommended. From Ollantaytambo, you can go by bike, bus or truck to the Abra de Malaga (4600m) and then downhill to the jungle in three or four days. If heading to Manu, you can break up the long bus journey by biking from Tres Cruces to La Unión – a beautiful, breathtaking downhill ride – or you could go all the way down by bike. (The outfitters of Manu trips can arrange bicycle rental and guides.) The descent to the Río Apurímac would make a great burn as would the journey to the Tambopata, which boasts a descent of 3500m in five hours. Beat that if you can. A few bikers have done the over-500km trip all the way to Puerto Maldonado, which gets hot and sweaty near the end but is a great challenge.

**Birdwatching** Serious birders should definitely get *Birds of the High Andes*, by Jon Fjeldså and Niels Krabbe (see Natural History under Books in the Facts for the Visitor chapter). One of the best birding trips is from Ollantaytambo to Quillabamba, over the Abra de Malaga. This gives a fine cross section of habitats from 4600m down to 950m, but you need to rent a truck or jeep to do it. Barry Walker, owner of Manu Expeditions and the Cross Keys Pub in Cuzco, is the best resident ornithologist and can give serious birders plenty of enthusiastic advice and help setting up a birding expedition.

**Mountaineering & Skiing** Peruvian Andean Treks (see Tour Agencies previously in this chapter) is your best source for information and guides for scaling any of the high peaks in the Cuzco area. There are no skiing areas, but adventurous and expert mountain skiers have been known to carry their skis to a mountain summit and then ski back down.

## Classes

The Excel Language Center (☎ 23-5298, 23-2272, Cruz Verde 336) charges about US$7 an hour for private Spanish lessons and has received several recommendations. They can arrange homestays with local families if you wish. Amauta (☎/fax 24-1422, amautaa@mail.cosapidata.com.pe, Procuradores 50), which is associated with La Tertulia restaurant, provides both Spanish and Quechua classes. Rates are US$215 per week, including 20 hours of classes, family homestay with meals, and other activities. They also have a hostel if you don't want to stay with a family. Classes in Urubamba are also offered. The German-run Acupari (☎ 24-2970, 23-5459, acupari@qenqo.rcp.net.pe, San Agustín 307) also has Spanish and Quechua classes. Rates for 20 hours are US$215 per week for two weeks, then US$120 for additional weeks. Homestays with breakfast and one other meal can be arranged for US$85 a week.

Centro Cultural Andino (☎ 23-1710, fax 23-1388, andinos@wayna.rcp.net.pe, www.andeanstudies.com, Paseo de los Heroes 689), which is associated with Milla Turismo, has a variety of courses. The choices include classes in Spanish, Quechua, and many aspects of Andean culture (such as agriculture, archaeology, architecture, history, geography, folklore, arts and anthropology). Seminars can be combined into tailored programs, and colleges from the USA have sent students to these programs. The Centro Cultural is currently working on providing academic credit for US schools.

## Work

The Excel Language Center has hired English teachers in the past, but you'll need to commit yourself for several weeks. You may find other jobs – bartending, working with a travel agency etc – if you ask around. Many of these jobs are not legal, but work visas can be obtained for some of them.

## Special Events

The area celebrates many fiestas and holidays. Apart from the national holidays, the following dates mark crowded, lively occasions that are especially important in Cuzco:

**Monday before Easter**
The procession of the Lord of the Earthquakes dates from the earthquake of 1650 (see La Catedral under Churches earlier in this chapter).

**May 2-3**
A hilltop Crucifix Vigil is held on all hillsides with crosses atop them.

**First Thursday after Trinity Sunday**
Corpus Cristi is a movable feast that usually occurs in early June and features fantastic religious processions and celebrations in the cathedral.

**June 24**
Cuzco's most important festival is Inti Raymi, or the 'Festival of the Sun.' It attracts tourists from all over the world, and the entire city seems to celebrate in the streets. The festival culminates in a reenactment of the Inca winter-solstice festival at Sacsayhuamán.

**December 24**
This date marks the Santuranticuy, or 'Christmas Eve' shopping festival.

Other festivals are important in particular villages and towns outside Cuzco; they are mentioned in the appropriate sections.

## Places to Stay

Cuzco, the most visited city in Peru, has over 200 hotels of all types, and prices tend to be higher than in less popular parts of the country. It gets rather crowded here during the dry season (June to August), which coincides with the North American and European summer holidays. At this time, accommodations can be tight, especially during the 10 days before Inti Raymi (the major annual winter-solstice festival) on June 24, as well as around July 28, when the national Fiestas Patrias occur. The best hotels are often fully booked for Inti Raymi, and prices for accommodations usually rise substantially during these periods. Nevertheless, you can almost always manage to find somewhere to stay, though not necessarily at the price or comfort level you want.

During the rest of the year, many hotels are sometimes almost empty, and in this buyer's market, it is well worth bargaining for better rates. However, student groups from Lima and other major cities visit Cuzco during the low season, and sometimes they can make budget accommodations hard to find. Late October and November seem to be popular times for student groups, but at any time of the low season, you may find that a sudden influx of tourists has pushed the prices up and made rooms temporarily hard to find. School holidays in January and February are also a busy time.

Many travelers want to spend time visiting nearby villages or hiking the Inca Trail, and most hotels in Cuzco will store excess luggage so that you don't have to lug it around with you. Always securely lock and clearly label all pieces of luggage. It's unlikely that anyone will razor-blade your pack open inside a hotel, but light fingers may occasionally dip into unlocked luggage. Don't leave any valuables in long-term storage, lock and label your luggage and ask for a receipt.

I have stayed in over a dozen hotels in Cuzco, ranging from 1st-class to basic, US$5 per night places. Whatever the price, I usually found the plumbing to be inadequate – even the best hotels occasionally have hot-water problems, most of which are eventually resolved. You may also find that hot showers are available only at specified times of day or at haphazard intervals. The city cuts off the water supply as a matter of course every afternoon, so hotels without their own cisterns have no water during those times.

## Places to Stay – Budget

The best cheap hotels are not always in safe areas, and so what you save by staying there is offset by the fact that you will need to take a taxi after dark or walk back in a large group. These areas are near the two railway stations and in the steep streets to the north of the Plaza de Armas. The hotels themselves are safe enough once you get inside, but people have been mugged or pickpocketed in the streets leading up to them. Nevertheless, it's fine if you go with friends or take a cab. Local police are making an effort to patrol these areas.

Casas de Hospedaje (☎ 24-2710) is an association that provides lodging in small, family-run hostels that are part of a home, and guests are encouraged to hang out with the family. These homes, many of which are in the San Blas area, have an average of about six guest rooms. Some have rooms with private baths, others are shared and breakfast is included in the rates, which range from US$4 to US$9 per person depending on the season and the facilities.

New cheap places mushroom every season; some do a good job, become successful, and raise their prices. Others take their place. Ask other budget travelers for recommendations if you plan on an extended visit.

Many budget travelers recommend **Hostal Resbalosa** (☎ 22-4839, Resbalosa 494), which charges US$4.50 per person for shared rooms, has hot showers, is friendly and helpful and stores luggage safely. Resbalosa is a steep pedestrian-only street, and cabs can only reach within 100m of the hostel. Nearby, **Albergue Municipal** (☎/fax 25-2506, Kiskapata 240) is up a steep hill and has great city views from their balcony. The rooms are clean and have bunk beds for four to eight people, and there is hot water, a large common room, a small café, laundry facilities and safe luggage storage. Rates are US$5 to US$7 per person, depending on the season. The owners are helpful, but you should take a cab to get here at night.

Budget hotels abound in the San Blas neighborhood – a steep climb from the Plaza de Armas. Again, taking a cab at night or returning with friends is recommended. **Hostal El Arcano** (☎/fax 23-2703, Carmen Alto 288) is clean and pleasant and has hot water during the day. Rates are US$4 per person. The friendly **Hostal Kuntur Wasi** (☎ 22-7570, Tandapata 352A) has good views over downtown, charges US$5 to US$8 per person (depending on the season) and has warm showers and kitchen privileges. A couple of rooms have private bath at US$16 for a double. **Hostal Mirador del Inka**

(☎ 26-1384, Tandapata 160) is a basic but clean place that charges US$4 per person with shared showers or US$8 with private showers. Also at US$4, try **Hostal Choquechaca** (☎ 23-7265, Choquechaca 436-B), which has hot water and kitchen privileges. The **Hospedaje Rumipunco** (☎ 22-1101, Choquechaca 339) is an older house with Inca stonework. Two doubles, two triples and a room that sleeps up to seven (all with private hot showers) are about US$5 per person. **Hospedaje Acosta** (☎ 24-1870, Choquechaca 124) is US$9/12 with private bath in the high season. Several readers recommend the friendly **Hostal Sambleño** (☎ 22-1452, fax 26-2979, Carmen Alto 114), which charges US$12/18 for singles/doubles with bath and has 24-hour hot water. Breakfast is available. The quite good **Hostal Huaynapata** (☎/fax 22-8034, Huaynapata 369) charges US$20/25 for clean rooms with bath and breakfast, or about half that price with shared bath or in the low season. They are friendly, and they store luggage and have hot water in the morning.

**Hostal Rikch'arty** (☎ 23-6606, Tambo de Montero 219) has basic rooms and a garden with good views for US$4 per person. Hot showers and tourist information are available. The basic but clean **Hostal Qorichaska** (☎ 22-8974, 23-6364, Nueva Alta 458) is friendly and safe. Rooms are US$5 to US$7 per person with shared bath or US$7 to US$9 with private bath. The prices include breakfast, and there's hot water from 5 am to 11 pm.

The reasonably clean and secure **Hostal Royal Qosco** (☎/fax 22-6221, Tecsecocha 2) is popular with some budget travelers. Basic rooms are US$5/9/12 for singles/doubles/triples with shared bath or US$10 per person with private bath, and there is hot water in the morning. Another option for budget travelers is **Residencial Madres Dominicanas** (☎/fax 22-5484, Ahuacpinta 600), which is run by Dominican nuns on the grounds of Colegio Martín de Porres. It's clean, safe and friendly, and it has hot water. Rates are about US$6 to US$8 per person; some rooms have private baths. **Hostal Cáceres** (☎ 22-8012, Plateros 368) is central, has hot water at times and is reasonably clean, though it is housed in an old and run-down building. Rates are US$5/8 singles/doubles with shared baths or US$12 with private bath.

Hotels near the San Pedro railway station are cheap. Some are a good value, but the area is not a very safe one. **Hotel Imperio** (☎ 22-8981, Chaparro 121), across from the Mercado Central, is clean and friendly and has reliable hot water in the morning and sometimes at other times. It has a hard-core support group of budget travelers who like the staff and the price of US$6 per person for rooms with private bath or a little less without. It's a good value if you don't get mugged outside. On the other side of the Mercado Central is a slew of cheap hotels in an unsafe area – the farther away you are from the market, the better.

Another area to look for rock-bottom prices is around the Huancho (Puno) train station, but it is also rather unsafe at night and is the haunt of pickpockets during the day. There are several hotels here that charge about US$3/5 for basic rooms. They may have hot water in the morning. Look along Tacna, Huayna Cápac, Manco Cápac, Manco Inca, Huáscar, Pachacutec, Tullumayo and Ahuacpinta to find these cheap, basic places.

The clean and friendly **Gran Hostal Machu Picchu** (☎ 23-1111, Quera 282) has OK rooms around two pleasant patios and has hot water most of the time. They charge US$6 per person or US$8.50 with private bath. **Hostal Familiar** (☎ 23-9353, Saphi 661) charges US$15 for a double with bath and has some rooms with shared bath for US$6/10. It has a pleasant courtyard and is clean and often full.

The popular colonial-style **Hostal Suecia II** (☎ 23-9757, Tecsecocha 465) has friendly staff and is often full. There is hot water and a pleasant glassed-in courtyard for snacks and hanging out. However, one traveler reported that there was illegal use of a credit card left in storage. Doubles with bath are about US$20, and there are very few singles, though some rooms sleep up to five. A few cheaper rooms lack bathrooms. Prices drop

a lot in the low season. **Hostal Incawasi** (☎ 22-3992, Portal de Panes 147), on the Plaza de Armas, has a great (if noisy) location and charges about US$12/18 for rooms with shared bath and occasional hot water, though a discount can be arranged in the low season or for long stays. Rooms with private bath are US$18/25. As with many of these hotels, the price is what the market will bear. The staff are friendly enough, but it's the location you're paying for here.

## Places to Stay – Mid-Range
The well-recommended **Hostal Los Niños** (☎ 23-1424, ninos@correo.dnet.com.pe, Meloc 442) is a Dutch-run hotel dedicated to helping local street children. Unfortunately, it's not possible to help every street child in town, but a dozen formerly homeless children live on the premises and are afforded a caring home, education and a chance to earn money in the hotel. The project is expanding, and much of the funding relies on guests' staying at the hotel. Formerly a colonial house, it now has a café with a book exchange, a courtyard surrounded by a traditional-style balcony and large rooms with decent beds. Eight rooms share showers and 12 have private facilities. Rates are US$10 per person with shared hot showers and US$25 for a double with private bath. Several languages are spoken, and laundry, email and information are available.

**Hostal El Arqueólogo** (☎ 23-2569, fax 23-5126, vida@net.cosapidata.com.pe, Ladrillos 425) is clean and has hot water, a nice garden and a cafeteria with a city view. It seems popular with French tourists. Rates are US$30 for a double with private bath (US$24 without) including breakfast. Some rooms will sleep up to five. **Hostal Corihuasi** (☎/fax 23-2233, Suecia 561) is in a colonial-style building, and excellent service has been reported. Rates are US$28/38 for singles/doubles with bath including breakfast. Some rooms have great views. There's a cafeteria and luggage storage, and the hot water is reliable.

Readers have sent in several recommendations for the following places, all of which look OK to me. The pleasant **Hostal Bed & Breakfast** (☎/fax 24-5938, Choquechaca 261) has clean rooms with private hot shower for US$15 per person including breakfast. The similar *Tu Hogar* (☎ 22-1214, fax 25-1460, Chihuampata 548) has TV and English-speaking staff. *Amaru Hostal* (☎/fax 22-5933, Cuesta San Blas 541) is US$18/30 and has some cheaper rooms with shared bath. Ask for discounts in these places if you are staying for several days or in the low season.

An excellent mid-range option is *Los Aticos* (☎ 23-1710, fax 23-1388, andinos@wayna.rcp.net.pe, Quera 253), in a side alley. This place has eight apartments – each with a bedroom and double bed, living room with couch that converts into another double bed, fully equipped kitchenette, hot-water bathroom with hairdryer, writing desk and telephone. It's great for longer stays. Rates for one to four people are US$45 per night, with daily maid service, or US$35 if you book four nights or more, with maid service twice a week. Someone is always on call if you have a problem. There are also double rooms with private bath at US$30 a night.

*Hostal El Solar* (☎ 23-2451, Plaza San Francisco 162) has hot water some of the time and is a clean and comfortable, though older, hotel. They charge US$20/30 including breakfast and less in the low season. *Hotel Virrey* (☎/fax 22-1771, Portal Comercio 165), right on the Plaza de Armas, has two rooms with plaza views. Rates are US$30/40, but you're paying for location rather than value. *Hostal Loreto* (☎ 22-6352, Loreto 115), just off the Plaza de Armas, has Inca walls in some rooms (which makes them rather dark, but how often do you get to sleep next to an Inca wall?). Rates are US$25/40 with bath, towels and hot water in the morning and evening. Some rooms sleep up to five. This place is popular and often full, and has been described as friendly and clean but noisy. Thefts were reported in 1998.

*Hotel Conquistador* (☎ 23-3661, 22-4461, fax 23-6314), just off the Plaza de Armas on Arequipa, looks quite nice and charges about US$30/40 including breakfast. Some rooms are shabby, but they say they have 24-hour hot water. The attractive *Hotel Los Portales* (☎/fax 22-2391, 22-3500, portales@telser.com.pe, Matará 322) is clean and has

reliable hot water. A cafeteria and room service are available. Rates are US$35/45 including continental breakfast and airport pick-up if reserved in advance. A nice touch is the large containers of purified water on each floor. *Hotel Cristina* (☎ 22-7251, fax 22-7233, hcristina@protelsa.com, Avenida Sol 341) is good, clean and friendly. Rates of US$32/45 include continental breakfast. *Hostal Pascana* (☎/fax 22-5771, Ahuacpinta 539) is small, friendly and well run. Rates are US$25/35 including breakfast, and there are good views.

*Leonard's Lodgings* (☎ 23-2831, fax 22-1516, Avenida Pardo 820) has been a reputable, mid-range hostel for many years. Rooms have TV and are US$30/42 in the high season. A café can provide room service, and some staff speak English. The *Hostal Centenario* (☎ 24-4235, fax 23-1681, centenario@mail.interplace.com.pe, Centenario 689) has a restaurant/bar, some English-speaking staff, airport pick-up on request, and nice rooms overlooking a small garden for US$38/48.

The friendly *Hostal El Balcón* (☎ 23-6738, fax 22-5352, balcon@peru.itete.com.pe, Tambo de Montero 222) has great views over Cuzco and is in an attractively renovated building dating from 1630. Rates are US$35/50 including continental breakfast, and a sauna is on the premises. *Hostal La Casona de San Agustín* (☎ 25-2633, fax 22-2908, lcsanagustin@wayna.rcp.net.pe, San Agustín 371) is friendly and well run. Rooms with cable TV, minirefrigerator and telephone are US$30/55 including continental breakfast; a few minisuites are US$65. There is a cafeteria with room service, a Jacuzzi and sauna.

*Hotel Carlos V* (☎ 22-3091, fax 22-8447, Tecsecocha 490) is pleasant and has a cafeteria. Rates are US$40/55 including continental breakfast. *Hostal Plaza de Armas* (☎ 22-2351, fax 22-8948) is on the corner of the Plaza de Armas, but none of the rooms have plaza views. They are, however, renovated and quite good, with cable TV and telephones. Rates are US$58 for singles or doubles including breakfast. The restaurant is reasonable and has excellent espresso.

Reenactment of the Inca festival of the sun (Inti Raymi), Sacsayhuamán

Easter mural made of flower petals, Cuzco

Woman serving fried potatoes at a market in Pisac

Statue of Inca warrior Ollantay in Ollantaytambo

VICTOR ENGLEBERT

Morochuco women racing bareback, Pampa Cangallo, Ayacucho

KEN EAKIN

Cacti in Reserva Nacional Pampas Galeras

KEN EAKIN

Votaries with candles, Semana Santa, Ayacuch

## Places to Stay – Top End

Top-end hotels tend to be full during the high season (often with international tour groups), and advance reservations are recommended. At other times, low-season discounts might be arranged if things are quiet. In the high season, making a reservation through an agency may result in a better price than booking directly yourself. Breakfast is normally included in rates.

*Hotel Cuzco* (☎ 22-4821, fax 22-2832, *Heladeros 150*) is the oldest of Cuzco's 1st-class hotels and has been operating for over half a century. There are many old-fashioned touches, and their ornately paneled bar is one of the most attractive in Cuzco. The hundred or so rooms are large and have a somewhat faded charm, but they are certainly adequate. High-season rates are US$65/75.

*Hotel Royal Inka I* and *Hotel Royal Inka II* (☎ 23-1067, 23-3037, 22-2284, fax 23-4221, *royalinka@mail.cosapidata.com.pe, royalinka@aol.com*) are sister hotels almost next to one another at Plaza Regocijo 299 and Santa Teresa 335, respectively. Both are in interesting buildings dating from the early 19th century, with attractive public areas and rooms that vary somewhat in size and style. As with most hotels in Peru, streetside rooms can be noisy. Both hotels have a restaurant and bar, and rooms have cable TV. The Royal Inka I, with 34 rooms, charges a reasonable US$54/78. The larger Royal Inka II has a sauna, Jacuzzi, massage therapist and beauty salon (all at extra charge). Many of its 65 rooms surround an attractive central atrium, which also contains the restaurant and bar and tends to be noisy with early breakfasters and late revelers. Rates here are US$68/90, but they drop their rates to that of their sister hotel when they aren't full.

The *El Dorado Inn* (☎ 23-3112, 23-1232, fax 24-0993, *doratur@mail.cosapidata .com.pe, Avenida Sol 395)* has a good but pricey restaurant/bar with musicians and dancers in the evening. The 54 rooms are attractive and comfortable with heaters and cable TV; some have balconies with street views. Rooms overlooking the elevator/restaurant area tend to be noisy with early morning departees. Rates are about US$80 single or double.

*San Agustín Plaza* (☎ 23-8121, fax 23-7375, *riviera@telematic.edu.pe, Avenida Sol 594)* is very helpful and friendly and has 26 nice rooms at US$89/109 and a cafeteria with a view of Coricancha. The related *Hotel Internacional San Agustín* (☎ 23-3023, 22-1169, fax 22-1174, Maruri 390) is in an attractive old building with 74 rooms, and it has good service and facilities, including a bar and restaurant. Rates are US$95/110.

*Posada del Inca* (☎ 22-7061, 23-4445, fax 23-3091, *posada_cusco@el-olivar.com.pe, Portal Espinar 142)*, the most central of Cuzco's top-end hotels, lies between the Plaza de Armas and Plaza Regocijo. They have 40 comfortable rooms with TV and bath (two are fully wheelchair accessible) and prices are US$90/100. The staff are friendly and helpful, and all the expected services are available. *Picoaga Hotel* (☎ 25-2330, 25-2331, fax 22-1246, *picoaga@ correo.dnet.com.pe, Santa Teresa 344)* is a 17th-century mansion that was originally owned by the Marqués de Picoaga. There are 70 modern rooms with heating, TV and minirefrigerator for US$100/110, which seems pricey.

The comfortable *Hotel Don Carlos* (☎ 22-6207, 22-4457, fax 24-1375, *dcarlos@ tci.net.pe, Avenida Sol 602)* is an attractive and comfortable new hotel with a 24-hour restaurant and room service. They have almost 50 rooms with cable TV and minirefrigerator for US$116/142 and three minisuites at US$168; breakfast is extra.

*Hotel Monasterio del Cusco* (☎ 24-1777, fax 23-7111, *reserlima@peruhotel.com, Palacio 136)* is arguably Cuzco's most beautiful hotel, with stunning public areas and over 100 rooms surrounding two colonial courtyards in a restored convent. They have good restaurants and 24-hour room service. Rates are US$160/179, and suites range from US$275 to US$320. Unfortunately, their reservation and reception services have been criticized.

The best hotel is *Hotel Libertador* (☎ 23-1961, fax 23-3152, *cusco@libertador.com.pr, Plazoleta Santo Domingo 259)*, which is in a huge old mansion with a fine courtyard. There

### Gringo Alley

The alley leaving the Plaza de Armas on the northwest side – officially named Procuradores (tax-collectors street) – has earned the nickname Gringo Alley because budget travelers have traditionally congregated there.

Gringo Alley has a good selection of cheap bars, pizzerias, restaurants, cafés and souvenir shops that are popular with backpackers and young international travelers. The names and owners of the establishments seem to change periodically, but it's still a good street to explore if you're on a budget.

are a few Inca foundations, and parts of the building date back to the 16th century, when Francisco Pizarro was the occupant at one time. There are over 200 rooms at US$179 (standard) or US$195 (deluxe), and 18 suites for US$350 and up. All have central heating and cable TV. The public rooms are opulently furnished with colonial sofas, iron chandeliers and antique paintings. There's a Jacuzzi, sauna, gift shop and good (though expensive) restaurants. Service is highly professional.

Finally, if you want to stay in the countryside yet be within minutes of Cuzco, go to **Incatambo Hacienda Hotel** (☎ 22-1918, fax 22-2045, hotexsa@mail.cosapidata.com.pe), 2km from the center near Sacsayhuamán. Parts of the hotel used to be Francisco Pizarro's house, and it is surrounded by fields and woodlands. Horse rides can be arranged. The hotel has attractive and comfortable rooms with all modern facilities. Rates are US$90/100, and US$140 to US$160 for suites.

### Places to Eat

As you'd expect in a city with such a cosmopolitan range of visitors, Cuzco has a great variety of restaurants catering to every taste and budget. This section is limited mainly to places I have tried. They can be very popular, especially during the busy season, so make a reservation or be prepared to wait for a table – particularly at the better restaurants.

**Cafés** One of the best choices for breakfast, and a popular meeting place throughout the day, is the simple and reasonably priced **El Ayllu Café** next to the cathedral. They open around 6 am, play classical music and offer a good selection of juices, coffee, tea, yogurt, cakes, sandwiches and other snacks. Next door, **La Yunta** offers a huge variety of juices, as well as cakes, coffee and inexpensive meals. Both of these are very popular and have plaza views. Upstairs is **Café Bagdad**, which has a balcony overlooking the plaza and inexpensive food.

Another excellent and popular breakfast choice is **La Tertulia** on Procuradores. They make yummy homemade bread good strong coffee and have all the usual morning options; they won't allow you to leave hungry with their all-you-can-eat breakfast. They also have a big book exchange and are open throughout the day. Also popular – particularly for cheap breakfasts and lunches – is the **Café Huaylliy** on the 1st block of Plateros. **Café Varayoc** on Espaderos is recommended for a quiet atmosphere conducive to reading, writing or conversing. Their coffee and cakes are good.

New places keep popping up on the Plaza de Armas. Since the last edition, **Plus Café** has become known for good coffees and other snacks, and **Trotamundos** has a bit of everything and is becoming a popular late-night bar/café.

**Vegetarian Food** If you're economizing, the Hare Krishna **Govinda Vegetarian Restaurant** on Espaderos has cheap and adequate food, though the service is very slow. Much better is the attractive **Auyliyu** (☎ 22-2851, Calle Garcilaso 265, 2nd floor). They serve gourmet lactovegetarian food, and it is well prepared, nicely served and recommended (and this comes from me, an unabashed steak and cuy lover). Another good choice is **Acuarium** (Cuesta del Almirante 211).

**Andean Food** A few inexpensive restaurants serve tasty, authentic ethnic Andean

CUZCO AREA

specialities (as opposed to Peruvian food in general). They often have outside patios and are usually open only for lunch or afternoon snacks. Monday seems to be the day off. People with very finicky stomachs might question the hygiene, but if you stick to cooked food, you're unlikely to get sick.

If you want something really Andean, try roast guinea pig, or cuy, an Inca delicacy. Other typical local dishes include *anticucho de corazon* (shish kebab made from beef hearts), *rocoto relleno* (spicy bell peppers stuffed with ground beef and vegetables), *adobo* (spicy pork stew), *chicharrones* (deep-fried chunks of pork ribs, called *chancho*, or of chicken, called *gallina*), *lechón* (suckling pig), *choclo con queso* (corn on the cob with local cheese), *tamales* (boiled corn dumplings filled with cheese or meat and wrapped in a banana leaf), *cancha* (toasted corn) and various *locros* (hearty soups and stews). The meal is often washed down with chicha, which is either a fruit drink or fermented, mildly alcoholic corn beer.

One of the best places and the closest to the central city area is **Quinta Eulalia** (☎ 22-4951, *Choquechaca 384*), which has a colorful courtyard. It's only open for lunch (as are most quintas), and it's rustic. Farther afield, try **Quinta Zárate** on Calle Tortera Paccha, in the eastern outskirts of town. It has a nice garden and good views, but it isn't easy to find, so hire a taxi. These places have limited menus of local food – no hamburgers if you suddenly feel faint of heart. Prices are inexpensive, though not very cheap. You can also get local food in many of the Peruvian and international restaurants listed below.

There are several very funky hole-in-the-wall places along Pampa del Castillo that serve chicharrones hot from the grill, which is often placed in the door. If you like chicharrones, get them *para llevar* ('to go') at lunchtime, when they are fresh and hot.

**Peruvian Food** These restaurants serve Peruvian-style fish, chicken, or meat, perhaps with a small selection of the more traditional Andean dishes and some international food.

Just off the plaza, along the 1st block of Plateros, there are several good restaurants,

most of which have been recommended by one traveler or another, though I occasionally hear gripes from someone. Two stand out and are well recommended; both are slightly pricier than others on the street. **Kusikuy** (☎ 26-2870) has cuy, as well as plenty of other Peruvian and some international choices. The Japanese-run **Pucará** has good food and menus with photographs, so even the linguistically challenged can order a chicken and not get eggdrop soup. Nearby, **El Nevado** has big set meals at low prices. Around the corner on Calle Tigre are the recommended budget restaurants, **Victor Victoria** and **Miski Wasi**. Victor Victoria has an Israeli menu but serves mainly Peruvian food including breakfast. Opposite the expensive Hotel Monasterio del Cusco, **Ama Lur** (☎ 23-6499) serves good moderately priced food. It's closed on Sunday.

There are several good, upscale, somewhat pricey places on the Plaza de Armas. **Restaurant El Paititi** (☎ 22-6992) has genuine Inca walls that were part of the House of the Chosen Women. They often have musicians at no extra charge; bands often wander in and out of the other restaurants as well. The excellent **Inka Grill**

## How to Play Sapo

Some local restaurants that serve Andean specialities are called picanterías (which means 'spicy places') or quintas (which means 'country houses'), but the latter is usually used to refer to inns in the nearby suburbs. Often, they have a sapo (toad), a popular picantería game, rather like darts in an English pub or pool in an American bar. A metal sapo is mounted on a large box, and players toss a metal disk as close to it as possible. Top points are scored when the disk is thrown into the toad's mouth. Other points are scored by landing the disk in various other holes and slots surrounding the sapo. Men will sometimes spend the whole afternoon drinking beer or chicha and competing at this old test of skill.

(☎ 26-2992) is deservedly popular and recommended for both food and service; reservations are a good idea. Nearby is *La Retama* (☎ 22-6372), on the 2nd floor, with innovative versions of some favorite Peruvian dishes and live music at 8:30 pm. *La Estancia Imperial* (☎ 22-4621) is also good, especially for meat dishes. A place for dedicated carnivores is *El Mesón de los Espaderos* (☎ 23-5307), on the corner of the plaza on the 2nd floor of Espaderos 105. They serve *parrilladas* (mixed grills), steaks, cuy or chicken. Get there early or make a reservation to sit in the attractively carved balcony overlooking the Plaza de Armas.

*El Truco* (☎ 23-5295, Plaza Regocijo 262) has a nightly dinner and show (from 8:30 to 10:30 pm) and is a good value. Make reservations in the high season, because it's popular with tour groups. The food is good, as is the show. There is a cover charge, and dinner for two with drinks could run as high as US$50, though you can get by with half that. A newer dinner-and-show restaurant with similar prices is the *José Antonio* (☎ 24-1364, Santa Teresa 356). This is a huge barn of a place.

**Italian Food** The *Chez Maggy* (☎ 23-4861) on Procuradores, another Chez Maggy on Plateros and *Pizzería America*, also on Plateros, are currently the favored places for travelers looking to meet other people and eat good, reasonably priced pizza. Many have live music (a hat is passed for tips) in the evenings. For a wider variety of Italian food, *Tiziano Trattoria* and *Da Giorgio* have both been well recommended. *Trattoria Adriano* has been serving decent Italian food at the northwest end of Avenida Sol for about two decades.

**Asian Food** One of my favorites is *Al Grano* (☎ 22-8032), open from 10 am to 9 pm Monday to Saturday. They have a small and occasionally changing menu of delicious plates from nine Asian countries including Thailand, India, Vietnam and Indonesia. Prices are modest, and it's popular with travelers looking to treat their tastebuds to a change.

Another excellent choice is *Kin Taro* (☎ 22-6181), which serves as authentic a Japanese menu as you'll find anywhere outside of Lima, including trout sushi and saki. Japanese is spoken and written (on the menu).

**Other** *Greens* (☎ 24-3820) is hidden behind the church of San Blas and worth finding. They serve food with a British influence, such as traditional Sunday Roasts (by reservation), as well as curries, steaks and fettuccine. The cook has had international training and experience, and the food shows it. Prices are moderate. Magazines, books, background jazz, chess and backgammon boards, and one room with cable TV make this a place to hang out – they stay open late. They plan on serving breakfast.

Down on Procuradores, keep your eye open for *La Ensalada*, which serves French-influenced food at surprisingly low prices. Also on Procuradores, there's *Los Cuates*, which serves Mexican-style food.

Some of the top hotels have decent restaurants, but prices are high and often charged in dollars rather than soles. The food is somewhat bland and is popular with tourists who have particularly delicate stomachs or want to minimize health risks. Local musicians often play.

Also see Entertainment, immediately following, for more suggestions.

## Entertainment

Several restaurants have live entertainment with dinner every night. If you'd rather listen to music in a slightly looser bar environment, you'll find several places.

**Dancing** The current favorites include *Ukukus Bar* (Plateros 316), which has a variety of both live and recorded music and plenty of dancing. It is a popular gathering spot for travelers. There's a US$1.50 cover charge after 9:30 pm, and a happy hour from 8 to 9:30 pm, so go early. It gets very crowded later on. *Up Town* (Suecia 302) is also a lively dance joint and attracts a wilder crowd – I've been offered drugs here (see Drugs under Dangers and Annoyances in the Facts for the Visitor chapter for the possible consequences of buying drugs). But the music is great. The older **Kamikaze**, up the stairs at the northwestern corner of Plaza Regocijo, has lively taped music and occasional live performers. Across the street is **Mama Africa Pub**, which has live music and is a young budget travelers' hangout, with people sprawled across cushions on the floor. These all have various cover charges, and happy hours; the music tends to be rock and reggae.

Several places offer disco dancing. The fairly expensive **El Muki**, just off the plaza at Santa Catalina 114, is dark, has plenty of alcoves, and has a couples-only rule at the door (though they usually don't count when a mixed group goes in).

Several places have evening folklore dance shows. Usually there are some good dances in traditional costumes, but the music may be recorded and disappointing. Cover charges vary from US$3 to US$6 – shop around. **Qosqo Center of Native Dance** (☎ 22-7901, *Avenida Sol 604*) is the best-known place.

**Bars** The well-known and long-established **Cross Keys Pub** (*Portal Confituría 233*) is easily identifiable from the Plaza de Armas by the huge metal keys hanging outside; it's an English pub run by a British ornithologist, Barry Walker. He knows the area well and is a good contact for the Manu area. There is a dartboard and what may be the most challenging pool tables in town – every shot takes a bananalike trajectory. It's a great meeting place – you can have a conversation here without having to scream over the music – and though not as cheap as some other bars, it does have happy hours from 6 to 7 and 9 to 9:30 pm. Note that these happy hours don't normally include beer. Bar food is available.

**Paddy O'Flaherty's** (*Triunfo 124*) is an Irish pub with balconies overlooking the Plaza de Armas. There's a dartboard, chess and other board games, as well as a TV tuned into sports. Happy hours are 7 to 8 and 10 to 10:30 pm, and food is available. Also on the plaza is **Norton Rat's**, a US-run

bar that can be reached through the entrance of Hostal Loreto. They serve food and have cable TV and pool table.

**Los Perros** (*Tecsecocha 436*) calls itself a 'couch bar,' and most of the seating is in soft, low couches. They have a paperback-book exchange, magazines, Thai snacks, coffees and alcoholic beverages until 1 am.

**Tumi's Video Bar** (*Saphi 478*) shows recently released videos on a 52-inch screen in one room and has a friendly bar next to it. They have pool tables, darts and food, and patrons can choose movies to watch.

Hotel Cuzco is a classic old-fashioned wooden mirrored bar with a bow-tied barman who makes excellent pisco sours. It's frequented by older Cuzco gentlemen and businessmen – women are rarely seen unless accompanied.

## Shopping

The best place to see local artisans making and selling their handicrafts is around Plaza San Blas and the streets leading to it from the Plaza de Armas. The San Blas area has a reputation as Cuzco's artisan quarter and is worth visiting – not only to buy souvenirs and to watch artisans at work, but also to see the interior of some of the buildings. Prices and quality vary greatly, so shop around. The very best pieces may cost 10 times more than what (superficially) appear to be the same items in a store on the Plaza de Armas, but the difference in quality is significant. Bargaining is expected, except in a few of the more expensive stores, where prices are fixed.

Going to the Mercado Central near the San Pedro (Machu Picchu) railway station to buy crafts is not a good idea. This market is a colorful affair, but it is mainly filled with food and household products. If you must go, don't bring much money or a camera, because the thieves are extremely professional and persistent. If you want to look around, you should do so in a group, and look out for one another. This is not the place for crafts.

If you like to shop in a market atmosphere, there's a crafts market on the corner of Quera and San Bernardo and another off Loreto. A nightly crafts market is also held under the arches around the Plaza de Armas and a block over on Espinar. You will often be approached on the street by people trying to sell you all kinds of crafts. This can become a little wearisome when you're not in a buying mood – the only thing to do is say '*No, gracias*' as firmly as possible and show absolutely no interest; the slightest spark of curiosity will inevitably result in five minutes of pestering.

Some of the best places (though not the cheapest) include Taller Olave, to the left of Plaza San Blas, for exceptionally fine and expensive reproductions of colonial sculptures and precolonial ceramics; Santiago Rojas Alvarez at Suytuccato 751, for Paucartambo fiesta masks; Taller Mérida at Carmen Alto 133, for earthenware statues of Indians; the nationally known Mendivil family at the corner of Hatunrumiyoc and Tullumayo, for their hallmark religious figures with elongated necks and other items; and Josefina Olivera at Santa Clara 501, by the San Pedro train station, for old ponchos and weavings. There are many stores along Hatunrumiyoc and Cuesta San Blas and around Plaza San Blas that sell almost any souvenir you can imagine. This is the best shopping area.

There are some warehouses with large selections of sweaters and crafts where you can shop with minimal pressure. A reader recommends La Perez (☎ 23-2186, 22-2137, Mateo Pumachahua 598, Tienda 1, Wanchaq). Serious shoppers can call them, and they'll pick you up from your hotel and bring you back at no charge.

For grocery shopping (Inca Trail food and so on), good selections are found at Mercado El Chinito on Mesón de la Estrella between Quera and Ayacucho, and at another market on the corner of Avenida Sol and Almagro. (These do not compare with the supermarkets found in Lima, however.)

## Getting There & Away

**Air** Cuzco's airport claims international status because of the flights to La Paz, Bolivia. All departures and arrivals are in the morning, because climatic conditions make landing and takeoff difficult in the afternoon. Airport departure tax is US$25 for international flights and US$3 for internal flights.

Flights to Bolivia with Lloyd Aereo Boliviano, or LAB (☎ 22-2990, Pardo 675) go to La Paz. Flights are on Tuesday, Thursday and Saturday, with more services in the high season. The fare is about US$100.

Lima-Cuzco flights are more frequent than from Lima to anywhere else. There are about six (mostly direct) flights a day to and from Lima with Aero Continente during high season. Be aware that many of these get canceled or lumped together with another flight during nonbusy periods. Your best bet is to get the earliest flight available, as the late ones are the most likely to be delayed or canceled. Aero Continente has daily flights to and from Puerto Maldonado and to and from Arequipa. In the past, flights to Ayacucho and Juliaca were available, but with the current dearth of airlines, these are not now offered. There may be flights to Puerto Maldonado with small jungle airlines; ask at the airport or a travel agent in Cuzco.

Same-day connections to Tacna via Arequipa and to most northern cities via Lima can be arranged, but allow for several hours' connecting time, as flights from Cuzco may be late.

Aero Continente (☎ 23-5666, 23-5660, 24-3032, airport 23-5696, Portal de Harinas 181, Plaza de Armas) doesn't normally sell tickets at the crowded airport counters, although it is possible to buy a ticket at the airport on a space-available basis. The military airline Grupo 8 sells tickets at the airport for its flights (usually on Thursday) to Lima and Puerto Maldonado. These flights don't always go, are usually full and normally cannot be booked in advance (though there's no harm in trying). Although fares are somewhat cheaper than those of the commercial airlines, Grupo 8 flights are difficult for tourists to get on. Go to the airport before 6 am on the day of the flight, packed and ready to go, get your name on the waiting list and hope. Grupo 8 also flies via Puerto Maldonado to Iberia or Iñapari near the Brazilian border.

Flights tend to be overbooked, especially during the busy season, so confirm your flight when you arrive in Cuzco, then reconfirm 72 hours in advance and again 24 hours before departure. If you buy your ticket from a reputable travel agent in Cuzco, they'll reconfirm for you.

Check-in procedures at Cuzco airport are often chaotic, and even people with confirmed seats and boarding passes have occasionally been denied boarding because of overbooking errors. (Don't get overly paranoid; this doesn't happen all the time.) Checking in an hour early is recommended (two hours during the busiest holiday periods). During the rainy season, flights can be postponed for 24 hours because of bad weather. Bring valuables and essentials (including medicines and hiking boots if you are doing the Inca Trail) with you on the plane, and securely lock your checked luggage – pilfered or delayed luggage is reported occasionally.

When flying from Cuzco to Lima, check in as early as possible to get a seat on the right-hand side of the plane for the best views of Salcantay's 6271m peak. Some pilots like to fly quite close to the mountain, and the views are sometimes stupendous. (Sit on the left from Lima to Cuzco.) Occasionally, a different route is taken over Machu Picchu, but not often.

**Helicopter** Once upon a time, travelers were able to take a helicopter all the way to Machu Picchu. But in the 1970s, this service was stopped due to the damage that was being inflicted on the ruins by the vibration of the choppers. The new service does not go to the ruins themselves, but to Aguas Calientes, 8km away. Helicusco (☎ 22-7283, in Lima 445-6126, fax 446-7197, dfhr@amauta.rcp.net.pe, Triunfo 379, 2nd floor) has Cuzco-Aguas Calientes flights.

There are good aerial views of Machu Picchu flying in, but not flying out. Views of Ollantaytambo are on the right flying in and left flying out, and a crew member gives a running commentary (English and Spanish) of the scenery you are passing. Unfortunately, the 24-passenger Russian helicopter

that is used has very small portholes, but the ride is still interesting and gets you to Aguas Calientes in just 25 minutes. The helicopter leaves Cuzco daily at 8:30 am and returns at 3:30 pm, but extra flights are offered on demand. The cost is US$80 for a one-way ticket or US$150 for round-trip ticket, and a 50% discount is given to children between the ages of 2 and 12. Milla Turismo and other travel agencies sell tickets and arrange complete packages that include the entrance fee to the ruins, lunch and guided tour.

**Bus – Long Distance** Cuzco has a new long-distance bus terminal in Ttio, on the way to the airport. Buses for towns around Cuzco (see Bus – Sacred Valley, immediately following) and a few other places still leave from elsewhere, but this may change in the future. Buses to most major cities leave from the new terminal, although they still have ticket offices and some departures on Pachacutec, near the Huancho (Puno) train station, so check carefully about departure points when paying for an advance ticket. Agencies on and near the Plaza de Armas also sell tickets.

Cruz del Sur provides bus services to the south of the country, with buses to Sicuani, Juliaca (8 hours) and Puno (9 hours). The road was 80% paved when this book was updated, and locals expect that it will all be paved by about 2000. Other companies, including CIVA, Continental (Ormeño), Expreso Cometa and Transportes Collasuyo, also go to Puno. Prices range from US$6 to US$11, depending on the company and quality of the buses. A new company called First Class (☎ 24-4766, Avenida Garcilaso 210) has comfortable tour buses to Puno that briefly stop at places like Raqchi along the route. Soft drinks, coffee and an English-speaking guide are included. The fare is US$25.

Transportes Zela has through buses to La Paz, Bolivia at 6:30 pm (US$12, 20 hours). Cruz del Sur has day and night buses to Arequipa (12 hours) via Imata; it's a rough journey on a little-traveled road. They'll sell you a ticket to Lima, but you have to change buses in Arequipa. Expreso Huari has buses on a slightly quicker route to Lima via Abancay, Puquio and Nazca. This used to be the most frequently traveled bus route between Cuzco and the capital, but it was closed due to terrorism problems in the late 1980s. It now appears safe.

Trucks for Limatambo, Mollepata and on to Abancay and other destinations leave from various places on Arcopata. Alternatively, take a long-distance bus to Abancay from one of several companies in the new bus terminal. For example, Transportes San Jeronimo goes to Abancay (US$4, 6 hours) and Andahuaylas (US$7, 10 hours) at 11 am and 6 pm; there are several other companies at the terminal. To continue on to Ayacucho, you normally have to change at Andahuaylas, although Expreso Wari goes all the way to Ayacucho. The road to these towns is atrocious and very cold at night. Some companies use cramped, uncomfortable minibuses, rather than full-size buses. Ask before buying a ticket.

There are no buses to the southeastern jungles except for those to Quillabamba (US$5, 8 hours), leaving every night with several companies at the new bus terminal. Carhuamayo has been recommended. Daytime departures are less common, but it's worth the trip, because the scenery while climbing the spectacular 4600m Abra de Malaga pass and then dropping down into the jungle is memorable. (Note that there is no longer a train from Cuzco.) For other jungle destinations, you have to fly, go by truck or go on an expedition. There are daily trucks to Puerto Maldonado during the dry season along a wild and difficult road, and the trip from Cuzco takes two to three days. The trip takes a week or more in the wet, if the road is passable at all. Trucks leave from near Plaza Túpac Amaru, two blocks east of Tacna along Avenida Garcilaso. You could also get a bus to Urcos or Ocongate and wait for a truck there.

Getting to Manu is just as problematic. Transportes Sol Andino has buses to Paucartambo (US$3, 6 hours) on Monday, Wednesday and Friday leaving from the Coliseo Cerrado at 10 am. They are very full, so you should get there by 7 am to get a seat or try to book one with the Andino office on Avenida Huáscar 222. Trucks also do the journey on the same days from the Coliseo Cerrado area – ask around. Continuing from Paucartambo to Manu, there are only passing trucks or expedition buses. From Cuzco, trucks from the Coliseo Cerrado go to Pillcopata (11 hours), Atalaya (16 hours) and Shintuya (20 hours). Most travelers join a tour.

Buses to Oropesa, Urcos, Sicuani and Ocongate leave from near the Coliseo Cerrado on Manco Capac, about five blocks east of Tacna. Buses for Urcos also leave from Avenida Haya de la Torre on the north side of Avenida de la Cultura between the university and Hospital Regional. Take these buses to visit the ruins of Tipón, Pikillacta, Rumicolca and Raqchi.

All the journey times given are approximate and apply only during good conditions. In the wettest months of the rainy season, especially January to April, long delays are possible.

**Bus – Sacred Valley** Buses to Pisac (US$0.50, 1 hour) or Calca and Urubamba (US$0.80, 2 hours) leave frequently with Transportes Pitusiray and Transportes Urubamba from Intiqhawarina, just off Tullumayo, from 5:30 am until dusk. Transportes Caminos del Inca leaves every 20 minutes to Pisac and Urubamba from Avenida Huáscar. These places also have infrequent buses to Chinchero. Buses are always crowded. The Pisac buses will drop you off at the nearby Inca site of Tambo Machay. You can walk back from there to Cuzco and visit the other nearby ruins en route. To get to Ollantaytambo, change at Urubamba.

**Train** Cuzco has two train stations. Estación Huancho (☎ 23-3592, 22-1992), near the end of Avenida Sol, serves Urcos, Sicuani, Juliaca, Puno and Arequipa. It's also referred to as Estación Puno. Estación San Pedro (☎ 22-1291), next to the Mercado Central, serves Ollantaytambo and Machu Picchu. The two stations are not connected. It is therefore impossible to travel directly from Arequipa or Puno to Machu Picchu; you must change lines in Cuzco.

***Estación Huancho (Puno)*** The train for Puno leaves at 8 am Monday, Wednesday, Friday and Saturday and takes about 11 hours (though it is often late). It passes through Juliaca at about 5:30 pm, allowing you to connect with the night train from Juliaca to Arequipa, which leaves later on Monday and Friday.

First-class tickets for the Puno train are often sold out during the high season so, if possible, buy a ticket the day before. The ticket office is open from 9 to noon and 2 to 5 pm weekdays, and 9 to 10 am weekends, though these hours change often. If you have problems getting a ticket, try booking through a travel agent. They may charge a fee; shop around for the best deal.

Fares have varied wildly for several years now, depending on currency fluctuations and railway regulations. See Train under the Puno and Arequipa sections for details of classes and fares.

***Estación San Pedro*** The Machu Picchu train departs several times a day and is the most frequently used train in Peru. This, combined with the station's location near the crowded Mercado Central, makes it a prime target for thieves. In recent years, Peruvian police have increased patrols around the station and on the trains, greatly reducing the risk of rip-offs, but because it's so crowded, you still have to be very vigilant.

Although popularly called the Machu Picchu train, it doesn't go there! The most important stops (for the traveler) are described immediately following.

Ollantaytambo station can be reached by road. This enables travelers to visit the Sacred Valley ruins by bus and then continue from Ollantaytambo to Machu Picchu without returning to Cuzco. All trains stop here.

The halt at Km 88 is where hikers leave the train to begin the Inca Trail. The stop at Km 104 is for the new, shortened version of the Inca Trail. Not all trains stop here.

The last station on the line is at Aguas Calientes, but it's misleadingly called Machu Picchu station. It is 8km from the Machu Picchu ruins, which are reached by bus from the station. The tracks beyond Aguas Calientes used to continue into the jungle at Quillabamba, but catastrophic damage during the 1998 El Niño closed the line, probably permanently.

The train journey begins with a climb out of Cuzco. Because it is too steep for normal railroad curves, this is accomplished in four back-and-forth zigzags. It takes about 30 minutes before you start leaving Cuzco proper. The tracks then drop gently through mainly agricultural countryside to the important station of Ollantaytambo, where all trains stop. From here, you can see Nevado Veronica (5750m) to your right and the Río Urubamba to your left. The train descends down the narrow gorge, affording superb views of the whitewater of the lower Urubamba. On the return to Cuzco, the same process occurs in reverse, except that if it is dark, the view of Cuzco is enhanced by the beautifully floodlit church and cathedral on the Plaza de Armas. Unfortunately, the slow-moving trains on the switchbacks have become the target for rock-throwers, and train crews routinely ask passengers to pull down the window blinds as protection.

There are usually two or three trains a day, with more on demand during the high season. Some are express trains; others are local and stop everywhere. Some services are designated for tourists only and are better guarded and much more expensive, with reserved seating. The cheaper local trains are often late, though the tourist trains are on time surprisingly often. Schedules and services are subject to change, so check with other travelers and at the station, the tourist information office, or a reliable local travel agent to determine current services.

The local train, or *tren local*, is the cheapest and stops everywhere. Watch your backpack carefully; this train has a well-deserved reputation for theft. The train leaves Cuzco daily at 6:45 am, and it takes about five hours to reach Machu Picchu. First-class, one-way fares are about US$5 to Machu Picchu, and 2nd class is about US$4. The train makes very brief stops at some stations – be ready to jump of quickly, particularly at Km 88.

The tourist train, or *tren de turismo*, stops at Ollantaytambo and Machu Picchu, and possibly elsewhere. This is a 1st-class local service leaving Cuzco at 6:25 am, stopping at Ollantaytambo at 8:40 am and arriving at Machu Picchu station at 10:15 am. Round-trip tickets cost US$18 in economy class, or US$34 and US$45 in Pullman and Inka class, respectively. To be honest, I have a hard time in following the frequent changes in what these classes offer – whatever I write will be outdated when you read this, so find out locally. Children 12 and under travel for 50% off in the Pullman and Inka classes.

The electric train, or *autovagón de turismo*, is the train used by most international tour companies and is the most efficient. It leaves Cuzco at 6 am, passing Ollantaytambo at 7:45 am and arriving at Machu Picchu station at 9:10 am. Another train leaves at 9 am if there is demand in the high season. The fare on this train is US$55 round trip (50% off for children). Travel agents sell the trip for about US$90, including the bus from the station to the ruins, entrance to the ruins and a guide. Sometimes, passengers are transferred from Ollantaytambo to Cuzco (or, less often, from Cuzco to Ollantaytambo) by bus to slightly shorten the journey.

The ticket office at the station sells local train tickets at varying hours; call them to ask when tickets are sold. You are advised not to carry valuables when going to buy a ticket, because the market area is prone to theft. Tickets on the more expensive classes can be bought at travel agents or at the Huancho (Puno) station.

## Getting Around

**Bus** Local bus rides cost about US$0.25. There is no easy bus link between the two railway stations.

**Taxi** A taxi ride is about US$1 in town or to the bus terminal, US$2.50 to just outside the airport or US$3.50 to the airport terminal – drivers have to pay an extra fee to enter the airport.

You can hire a taxi for a whole day for about US$40 or US$50 to visit sites around Cuzco. Some drivers speak English. José

Cuba (☎ 22-6179) has received several recommendations.

## AROUND CUZCO
## The Nearby Ruins

'The Nearby Ruins' refers to the four ruins closest to Cuzco: Sacsayhuamán, Qenko, Puca Pucara and Tambo Machay. They are often visited in a day – even less if you're on a guided trip – and entry is with the Boleto Turístico. The cheapest and most convenient way to visit the ruins is to take a bus to Pisac and get off at Tambo Machay, the nearby ruin farthest from Cuzco and, at 3700m, the highest. From there, you can walk the 8km back to Cuzco, visiting all four ruins along the way. Colorfully dressed locals often wait near the sites with their llama herds, hoping to be photographed. Tipping is expected (about US$0.50 is usual), and photographers trying for a free shot will get an unfriendly reception. Travelers wanting a more in-depth description of these and other ruins, as well as details of hikes in the area, are directed to Peter Frost's excellent book *Exploring Cuzco*. This is generally a safe, popular and rewarding walk, but it's advisable to go in a group and to return well before nightfall to avoid potential robbery.

**Tambo Machay** This small ruin, about 300m from the main road, consists of a beautifully wrought ceremonial stone bath and is therefore popularly called El Baño del Inca. Puca Pucara, the next ruin, can be seen from the small signaling tower opposite. There is usually a guard at Tambo Machay who will punch your Boleto Turístico for this site and also for Puca Pucara.

**Puca Pucara** As you return from Tambo Machay, you'll see this small site on the other side of the main road. In some lights, the rock looks very red and the name literally means 'red fort.' It is the least interesting and least visited of the four ruins.

**Qenko** The name of this small but fascinating ruin is variously written 'Qenqo,' 'Qenco,' 'Q'enqo' or 'Qenko' and means 'zigzag.'

Qenko consists of a large limestone rock covered with symbolic carvings, including the zigzagging channels that give the site its name. These are thought to have been used for the ritual sacrifice of chicha or, perhaps, blood. Tunnels are carved below the boulder, and there's a mysterious cave with altars carved into the rock. Qenko is about 4km before Cuzco, on the left-hand side of the road as you descend from Tambo Machay.

**Sacsayhuamán** This huge ruin is the most impressive in the immediate Cuzco area. The name means 'satisfied falcon,' but local guides cannot resist telling visitors that the long Quechua name is most easily remembered by the mnemonic 'sexy woman.'

The most interesting way to reach the site is to climb the steep street of Resbalosa, turn right at the top, go past the Church of San Cristóbal and continue until you come to a hairpin bend in the road. Here, you'll find the old Inca road between Cuzco and Sacsayhuamán. Follow it to the top; the ruins are to the left. The climb is short but steep and takes almost an hour from Cuzco, so make sure you're acclimatized before attempting it. (An acclimatized athlete wrote to me complaining that the walk took barely 20 minutes!) The old road is also a good descent route when returning from visits to the other nearby ruins. The site is open from dawn till dusk, and the guards are very active in demanding to see your Boleto Turístico. Arriving at dawn will give you the site to yourself – tour groups begin arriving in midmorning. However, robberies have been reported early and late in the day, so you should go with friends or a group.

Although Sacsayhuamán seems huge, what today's visitor sees is only about 20% of the original structure. Soon after the conquest, the Spaniards tore down many walls and used the blocks to build their own houses in Cuzco. They left the largest and most impressive of the original rocks, one of which weighs over 300 tons. Most of them form part of the main battlements.

The Incas envisioned Cuzco in the shape of a puma, with Sacsayhuamán as the head.

The site is essentially three different areas, the most obvious being the three-tiered zigzag walls of the main fortifications. The 22 zigzags form the teeth of the puma and are also an effective defensive mechanism – an attacker must expose a flank when attacking any wall. Opposite is the hill called Rodadero, with its retaining walls, curiously polished rocks and a finely carved series of stone benches known as the throne of the Inca. Between the zigzag ramparts and Rodadero Hill lies a large, flat parade ground that is used for the colorful tourist spectacle of Inti Raymi, held every June 24. The site is being actively excavated following the discovery of seven mummies behind the Rodadero Hill.

The magnificent zigzag walls remain the site's major attraction, even though much of this fortification has been destroyed. Three towers once stood above these walls. Only the foundations remain, but the 22m diameter of the largest, Muyuc Marca, gives an indication of how big they must have been. Muyuc Marca, with its perfectly fitted stone conduits, was used as a huge water tank for the garrison. Other buildings within the ramparts provided food and shelter for an estimated 5000 warriors. Most of these structures were torn down by the Spaniards and by later inhabitants of Cuzco, and the resulting lack of evidence makes a precise description of Sacsayhuamán's function difficult. Most authorities agree, however, that the site had important religious and military significance.

The fort was the site of one of the most bitter battles of the Spanish conquest. About 2½ years after Pizarro's entry into Cuzco, the rebellious Manco Inca recaptured the lightly guarded Sacsayhuamán and used it as a base to lay siege to the conquistadors in Cuzco. Manco was very nearly successful in defeating the Spaniards – only a desperate last-ditch attack by 50 Spanish cavalry led by Juan Pizarro finally succeeded in retaking Sacsayhuamán and putting an end to the rebellion. Although Manco Inca survived and retreated to the fortress of Ollantaytambo, most of his forces were killed. The thousands of dead littering the site attracted swarms of carrion-eating Andean condors, hence the inclusion of eight condors in Cuzco's coat of arms.

# The Sacred Valley & Around

The beautiful Vilcanota/Urubamba valley is popularly called *El Valle Sagrado*, or the Sacred Valley, of the Incas. It is about 15km north of Cuzco as the condor flies. The climate is pleasant because of the elevation (600m lower than Cuzco), and there is much to do – visit Inca ruins, bargain in Indian markets, stroll through Andean villages or go river running down the Urubamba. Rafting is one of the Sacred Valley's most pleasant activities, and this option is described under Activities in Cuzco earlier in this chapter.

The most important points of interest in the valley are the ruins of Pisac and Ollantaytambo, both of which require the Boleto Turístico for admission. Other sites can also be visited. Limited accommodations are available in the towns of Pisac, Calca, Yucay, Urubamba and Ollantaytambo. Various tour companies in Cuzco visit the Pisac and Ollantaytambo sites on half- and full-day guided bus tours of the Sacred Valley, but if you have a few days, taking local buses and staying in the valley itself is rewarding.

## PISAC
☎ 084

Pisac is 32km from Cuzco by paved road and is the most convenient starting point for a visit to the Sacred Valley. There are two Pisacs – one is the colonial and modern village lying beside the river, and the other is an Inca fortress on a mountain spur about 600m above. There is a telephone near the bridge into town if you need to make a call.

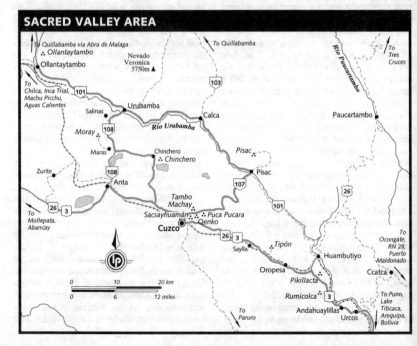

SACRED VALLEY AREA

## Colonial Pisac & Market

For most of the week, colonial Pisac is a quiet, Andean village, and there's little to do except sit and relax in the plaza or visit the clay-oven bakery near the Plaza de Armas for the hot-out-of-the-oven flatbread rolls typical of the area; take a look at their *castillo de cuyes* (a miniature castle inhabited by guinea pigs).

The village comes alive on Sunday, however, when the famous weekly market takes place. This attracts traditionally dressed locals from miles around and garishly dressed tourists from all over the world. Despite being a big tourist attraction, this bustling, colorful market retains at least some of its traditional air. The selling and bartering of produce for locals goes on alongside stalls full of weavings and sweaters for tourists. Many of the stallholders come from Cuzco, and even after hard bargaining, prices in Pisac are not any lower than those in Cuzco. The main square is thronged with people and becomes even more crowded after the mass (given in Quechua), when the congregation leaves the church in a colorful procession, led by the mayor holding his silver staff of office. Things start winding down about lunchtime, and by evening, the village returns to its normal somnolent state.

There's a smaller crafts market on Thursday (fewer tourists, but plenty of handicrafts) and one smaller still on Tuesday, and a few stallholders sell souvenirs every day during the high season, but it's pretty quiet compared to Sunday. Calle Bolognesi has several interesting-looking stores where you can see crafts being made.

## Inca Pisac

The Inca ruins above the village are among my favorites – partly because the walk there is so spectacular, and partly because the site is less visited than others on the tourist circuit, and so, except on Sunday, you don't see too many people. The ruins are reached either by a 10km paved road up the Chongo valley or by a shorter (about 5km) but steep footpath from the plaza. There is little traffic along the road, but it's possible to hire a cab in Pisac to drive you to the ruins for about US$3 (allow time; cabs are few). One reader

reports that a pickup truck drives from Pisac at 7 am to take locals to work. Minibuses occasionally go up this road and drop you off within a kilometer of the ruins, but they don't have a set schedule.

The footpath to the site leaves town from the west side of the church. There are many crisscrossing trails, but as long as you generally head upward toward the terracing, you'll get to the ruins without much difficulty. Allow roughly two hours for the spectacular climb. This is a full-day trip if you take your time and don't rush things. Children and women meet you at the top with soft drinks; after climbing this far with the bottles, the kids deserve to make a few cents!

The ruins are on a hilltop with a gorge on either side. The western gorge (to the left of the hill as you climb up on the footpath) is the Río Kitamayo gorge; to the right, or east, is the Río Chongo valley, where the road ascends. Pisac is famous for its agricultural terracing, which sweeps around the south and east flanks of the mountain in huge, graceful curves, almost unbroken by steps, which would promote erosion, take up valuable cultivation space, require greater maintenance and make walking and working along the terraces more difficult. Instead, different levels of terracing are joined by diagonal flights of stairs made of flagstones set into the terrace walls.

Above the terraces are cliff-hanging footpaths, well defended by massive stone doorways, steep stairs and, at one point, a tunnel carved out of the rock. Walking along these paths is exciting – the views are wonderful, and a pair of caracara hawks often accompanies you. This highly defensible site guards not only the Urubamba valley below, but also a pass into the jungle to the northeast. Pisac's main religious center, near the top of the terraces, features extremely well-built rooms and temples. New excavations occur sporadically. At the back (north end) of the ruins, a series of ceremonial baths was recently reconstructed; in the 1980s, this area was just a grassy hillside. Looking across the Kitamayo Gorge from the back of the ruins, you'll see hundreds of holes honeycombing the cliff wall. These are Inca tombs that, unfortunately, were robbed before being examined by archaeologists. The site is large and warrants several hours of your time.

### Places to Stay & Eat

Pisac is a small village, and accommodations are limited (especially before market day), so get there early or take a day trip from Cuzco. The *Parador de Pisac* (☎ 20-3061) on the Plaza de Armas has five clean rooms with views and shared baths at US$5 per person. One double room has no views, but has a private bath. There's a restaurant, and they are planning on opening a pub. *Residencial Beho* (☎ 20-3001), on the path to the ruins, charges a little less and has cold showers. *Samana Wasi* has rooms for US$3 per person and a cheap restaurant. Some families rent out rooms in their houses; ask around.

*Hostal Pisaq* (☎/fax 20-3062) has a small but pretty flower-filled courtyard and an inter-

esting underground sauna (US$10 shared between four people). Eleven simple rooms with clean beds and shared hot showers are US$10 per person, or a double with private bath is US$26. Breakfast is available for US$3, and there is a restaurant next door.

About 1.5km from the plaza on the road to the ruins is the newly renovated and greatly expanded (in 1998) *Hotel Royal Inka Pisac* (☎/fax 20-3064/5/6), operated by the Royal Inka hotels in Cuzco. The hotel offers a restaurant, bar, sauna, steam room, massage, indoor heated swimming pool, tennis court, games room, horseback rides and local tours. Rates are US$54/78 including breakfast, but discounts for groups, low season or long stays are available.

### Getting There & Away

Minibuses (US$0.50) leave many times a day from Cuzco. When returning to Cuzco or continuing down the Urubamba valley, wait for a bus by the bridge. Many agencies in Cuzco operate tourist buses, especially on market day, or you can hire a cab for about US$20.

### CALCA

About 18km beyond Pisac, Calca is the most important town in the valley, but is of little interest to the traveler. There are some small and unspectacular ruins in the vicinity and a few hotels, such as the dirty *Hostal San Martín*, which has cold water and charges about US$3 per person, or the better *Hostal Pitusiray*, which charges about US$8/12. The clean *Villa María* (☎ 20-2110, Los Santos 388) charges US$3 per person or US$5 per person with bath and hot water, but has only four rooms and occasional water shortages. *El Carmen* (☎ 20-2118, Vilcanota 848) has a tourist restaurant and charges US$10 per person with bath. Few travelers stay in Calca. Good food is served at *Quinta Jacaranda*.

### YUCAY

The pretty little village of Yucay is approximately 18km beyond Calca and has three good hotels surrounding a grassy plaza.

*Hostal Y'llary* (☎ 20-1112, fax 22-6607) has 30 clean, pleasant rooms with private hot showers for US$18/30 singles/doubles including continental breakfast. There is a restaurant, and other meals are available on request. The hostel has a large garden and a camping area with separate hot shower and bathroom; camping is US$6.

*La Posada del Libertador* (☎ 20-1115, fax 20-1116) is a colonial house built in 1810. Its name derives from the liberator Simón Bolívar, who reputedly stayed here in 1825. The hotel has 20 large rooms (all with private hot bath) around a traditional courtyard, and there is a restaurant and bar. Rates are US$40/45 including continental breakfast.

*Posada del Inca* (☎ 20-1107, 20-1346, 20-1347, fax 20-1345, posada_yucay@el-olivar .com.pe) is a well-run hotel that is popular with tour groups. It has a decent restaurant and bar, helpful staff and a small but high-quality gift shop. There is also an interesting little private museum. The entrance is a beautiful 300-year-old building, formerly a monastery and then a hacienda, behind which are attractive flower-filled gardens surrounded by more recent buildings, the restaurant, private chapel, and outdoor eating area. Lunch buffets are available to the public on some days. Most of the 69 spacious rooms are in the buildings surrounding the gardens; a few in the original building are old and rather creaky – one is supposedly haunted. Some rooms are wheelchair accessible. Rates are US$100/115 including buffet breakfast; there are four minisuites at US$135. The hotel can arrange local tours and adventures, including mountain-bike rental (US$10 an hour or US$50 a day, including helmet), river rafting (US$35 a half-day), horseback riding, guided hiking and, most recently, hot-air ballooning.

## URUBAMBA
☎ 084

Urubamba is about 4km beyond Yucay, at the junction of the valley road with the Chinchero road. The town is a pleasant and convenient base from which to explore the Sacred Valley.

### Pottery

Pablo Seminario (☎ 20-1002, 20-1086, fax 20-1177, Berriozabal 405) is a local potter who has become well-known and successful.

Pablo does attractive work with preconquest influence, as well as his own original work, which is different from anything else you'll see in Cuzco. He speaks English and is happy to explain his art to visitors.

His workshop is just off the main highway to Ollantaytambo, at the west end of Urubamba near the Hotel Valle Sagrado de los Inkas.

### Places to Stay & Eat

**Budget** There are a couple of basic cheap hotels in the town center. The best is the friendly *Hotel Urubamba*, on Bolognesi, a couple of blocks from the central plaza and about 10 minutes from the main valley road. Rooms are US$6 for a double. Showers are cold. Another cheap place is *Hostal Vera*, on the main valley road. There is a place that offers showers and camping above the town; ask. You'll find simple restaurants on the plaza and along the road leading from the gas station into the town center. About 100m up this road on the left is the inexpensive *Restaurant Hirano's*, which has been recommended as the best of the cheap places. Also worth trying, especially for lunch, is the *Quinta Los Geranios* (☎ 20-1093) on the main valley road near the gas station. Here, you can get a good three-course lunch for about US$3.

**Mid-Range to Top End** The *Antigua Misión San José de la Recoleta* (☎/fax 20-1004) is a restored mission on Jirón de la Recoleta, on the outskirts of town. They have 26 colonial-style rooms with bathrooms. Doubles are US$45, and continental breakfast is included. A restaurant is on the premises.

Along the main valley road are the following. At the west end of town, *Hotel Valle Sagrado de los Inkas* (☎ 20-1071, 20-1126, 20-1127, vsagrado@correo.dnet.com.pe) has two cold swimming pools (one for kids), an adequate restaurant and 75 comfortable (it soulless) doubles with clean hot showers for an overpriced US$79 double. West of here (just past Km 73) is *Hostal Hammer* (☎/fax 20-1194), where German and English are spoken. It's a quiet place with pleasant gardens – the sign on the wall outside is small. They have eight rooms at US$40/45 singles/doubles with continental breakfast; reservations are suggested.

At Km 75, 3km west of town, is **Willka T'ika** (*☎/fax 20-1181*), which provides attractive rooms with private baths set in tranquil, colorful plant-filled gardens. The guesthouse features yoga, massage and meditation rooms, healing and shamanism workshops and vegetarian meals, as well as arranging various local tours and retreats. Guests need to make advance reservations, and a minimum of 5 and maximum of 26 guests are accommodated in single, double and triple rooms. Rates are US$44 per person including breakfast; optional lunch and dinner is US$6 and US$10. Willka T'ika is operated by Magical Journeys (*☎* in the USA 888-737-8070, fax 415-665-4645, info@travelperu.com, www.travelperu.com), which organizes alternative special-interest tours.

These salt pans date to Inca times, and are still used today to produce salt for cattle licks.

ROB RACHOWIECKI

The most upscale of the hotels is **Hotel San Agustín** (*☎ 22-1025, riviera@telematic.edu.pe*), about a kilometer east of town. Here, the 42 comfortable singles/doubles with heaters and hot water cost US$77/90 including buffet breakfast. New owners have converted the garden into an outdoor buffet-style restaurant, which is full with tour groups eating lunch on weekends and sometimes midweek during the high season. Opposite is **La Casita Restaurant**, which also is popular with tour buses.

**El Maizal** (*☎ 20-1054*) also has excellent buffet-style lunches, as well as sit-down meals. They will prepare traditional Andean food (cuy, quinua, a variety of potatoes, beans, etc) if you ask in advance.

### Getting There & Away
Buses leave Cuzco many times a day from just off Avenida Tullumayo.

Buses back to Cuzco or on to Ollantaytambo stop at the gas station on the main road.

### SALINAS
About 6km farther down the valley from Urubamba is the village of Tarabamba. Cross the Río Urubamba here by footbridge, turn right and follow a footpath along the south bank of the river to a small cemetery, where you turn left and climb roughly southward up a valley to the salt pans of Salinas. It's about a 3km uphill hike.

Hundreds of salt pans have been used for salt extraction since Inca times. A hot spring at the top of the valley discharges a small stream of heavily salt-laden water, which is diverted into salt pans and evaporated to produce a salt that is used for cattle licks. The local salt-extracting cooperative charges about US$1 for entry to this rarely visited and incredible site. However, there is almost never anyone to collect the money if you enter from the path climbing up from the river.

A rough dirt road enters Salinas from above (giving spectacular views), and tour groups visit via this route most days.

## MORAY

The experimental agricultural terraces of Moray are fascinating. Different levels of terraces are carved into a huge bowl, part of which occurred naturally and part of which was further excavated by the Incas. The terraces supposedly have varied microclimates, depending on how deep into the bowl they are, and so they were thought to have been used by the Incas to discover the optimal conditions for their crops. There are two large bowls and one small bowl, each ringed by terraces. Some restoration work began in 1994, and a small on-site museum is planned.

This site is challenging to reach. First, catch a bus or get a ride up the steep road from Urubamba, across the river toward Chincheros. Ask the driver to drop you at the road to Maras. From here, take a trail about 3km to the village of Maras, then follow the trail another 7km to Moray. Ask locals for directions. Taxis and pickups are sometimes available, but not always, so be prepared to walk. The only facilities in Maras are very basic stores, so you should be self-sufficient.

It is possible to drive to Moray. The road is extremely rough and lasts about 13km from the paved Urubamba-Chinchero highway. You need high clearance and a driver who knows the route – not many do. Milla Turismo in Cuzco has organized tours to here and to Salinas for many years.

From Moray you can continue on to Salinas, about 6km away, and on down to Urubamba. This would be a long but satisfying day. There are usually workers in Moray who can point out the trail.

## OLLANTAYTAMBO

This is the end of the road as far as the Sacred Valley is concerned. Like Pisac, Ollantaytambo is a major Inca site at which you use the Boleto Turístico; you can buy a single-entry ticket (US$2) to Ollantaytambo at the ruins. The site, a massive fortress, is one of the few places where the Spanish lost a major battle during the conquest. Below the ruins is the village of Ollantaytambo,

built on traditional Inca foundations and the best surviving example of Inca city planning. The village was divided into blocks called *canchas*, and each cancha had just one entrance, which led into a courtyard. Individual houses were entered from this courtyard, not directly from the street.

The huge, steep terraces guarding the Inca fortress are spectacular and bring gasps of admiration from visitors arriving in the square below. Ollantaytambo is the fortress to which Manco Inca retreated after his defeat at Sacsayhuamán. In 1536, Hernando Pizarro (Francisco Pizarro's younger half-brother) led a force of 70 cavalrymen here, supported by large numbers of native and Spanish foot soldiers, in an attempt to capture the Inca. The steep terracing was highly defensible, and Pizarro's men found themselves continuously showered with arrows, spears, stones and boulders. They were unable to climb the terraces and were further hampered when the Inca, in a brilliant move, flooded the plain below the fortress through previously prepared channels. The Spaniards' horses had difficulty maneuvering in the water, and Pizarro ordered a hasty retreat – which almost became a rout when the conquistadors were followed down the valley by thousands of the victorious Inca's soldiers.

Manco Inca's victory was short lived; soon afterward, the Spanish forces in Cuzco were relieved by the return of a large Chilean expedition, and Ollantaytambo was again attacked – this time with a cavalry force over four times the size of that used in the first attack. Manco Inca retreated to his jungle stronghold in Vilcabamba, and Ollantaytambo became part of the Spanish Empire.

It is probable that the Incas themselves saw Ollantaytambo as a temple rather than as a fortress, but the Spanish called it a fortress, and it has usually been referred to as such ever since. The temple area is at the top of the terracing. Some extremely well-built walls were under construction at the time of the conquest and have never been completed. The stone used for these buildings was

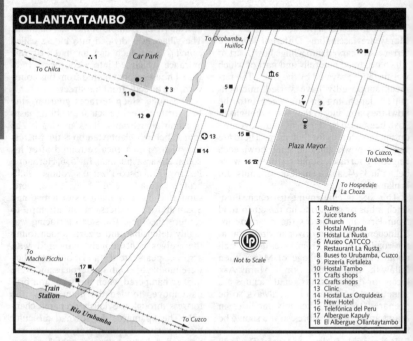

OLLANTAYTAMBO

Not to Scale

1 Ruins
2 Juice stands
3 Church
4 Hostal Miranda
5 Hostal La Ñusta
6 Museo CATCCO
7 Restaurant La Ñusta
8 Buses to Urubamba, Cuzco
9 Pizzería Fortaleza
10 Hostal Tambo
11 Crafts shops
12 Crafts shops
13 Clinic
14 Hostal Las Orquídeas
15 New Hotel
16 Telefónica del Peru
17 Albergue Kapuly
18 El Albergue Ollantaytambo

quarried from the mountainside 6km away, high above the opposite bank of the Río Urubamba. Transporting the huge stone blocks from the quarry to the site was a stupendous feat and involved the effort of thousands of Indian workers. To move the massive blocks across the river, the workers used a mind-boggling technique: they left the blocks by the side of the river, then diverted the entire river channel around the blocks, rather than trying to haul the stones through the river itself.

## Museo CATCCO

Local community history and ethnography are the main focus of this museum, which is open 10 am to 1 pm and 2 to 4 pm Tuesday to Sunday. Admission is US$1.50.

## Places to Stay & Eat

The cheapest accommodations cost about US$3 per person in basic, cold-water places, such as the dark *Hostal Miranda* and the

pleasanter *Hostal Tambo* (☎ 20-4003). A better bet is the *Hostal La Ñusta* (☎ 20-4035), which has a dozen rooms with shared showers at US$7 per person including breakfast at their nearby *Restaurant La Ñusta*, which is a simple but decent place to eat. The hostel has nice balcony views and is planning on rooms with private bath in the future. There's also the *Hospedaje La Choza*, which is inexpensive and reportedly clean. *Hostal Las Orquídeas* (☎ 20-4032) has seven rooms sharing three baths at US$10 per person. Meals are US$2 to US$5. They plan on building a sauna, and it's pleasant enough. You'll find a few basic cafés on the plaza.

On the outskirts of town, about 1km from the center and by the train station, is the recommended *El Albergue Ollantaytambo* (☎/fax 20-4014), run by Wendy Weeks, a North American who has been a local resident for over two decades and knows the area intimately. It is a very clean, pleasant, rustic hostel, with hot showers, lovely garden and sauna (US$5). Rates are US$15 per person, and there is room for a maximum of 16 guests. Breakfast is available for US$4, lunches for US$5 and dinners by advance request for US$10. During the June-to-September season, El Albergue is often full, so don't rely on just showing up. Reservations are accepted.

Almost next door, **Albergue Kapuly** (☎ 20-4017) has about 10 rooms, some with private bath. Rooms surround a quiet garden, and breakfast is available. Rates vary from US$12 double to US$15 per person, depending on room and season.

A new hotel is under construction by the main plaza; it looks mid-range.

## Getting There & Away

You can get to Ollantaytambo from Cuzco either by bus or train, but you must use the train (or walk) if you want to go on to Machu Picchu.

**Bus** Minibuses leave from Urubamba's gas station several times a day, but services peter out in midafternoon. Buses from Cuzco are infrequent, and most people change in Urubamba. Buses return to Cuzco from the plaza.

You can hire a pickup or taxi in Ollantaytambo to go to Chilca for about US$10. Chilca is an alternate start for the Inca Trail.

**Train** Ollantaytambo is an important station, and all trains between Cuzco and Machu Picchu stop at Ollantaytambo 1½ to 2 hours after leaving Cuzco or Machu Picchu, depending on your direction of travel (see Train under Cuzco and Aguas Calientes for details). Schedules change frequently, so check locally for exact details. The tourist trains charge the same expensive fare from Ollantaytambo to Machu Picchu as it does from Cuzco; the local train is much cheaper. However, the tourist trains often include a bus transfer between Ollantaytambo and Cuzco.

## CHINCHERO

This village, unlike those in the relatively low Urubamba valley, is over 3700m above

sea level, or 400m higher than Cuzco, so take it easy if you aren't acclimatized. The site combines Inca ruins with an Andean Indian village, a colonial country church, wonderful mountain views and a colorful Sunday market, so a visit is worthwhile. Access to Chinchero requires a Boleto Turístico.

The Inca ruins, consisting mainly of terracing, are not as spectacular as those at Pisac, but are interesting nevertheless. If you walk away from the village through the terraces on the right-hand side of the valley, you'll find various rocks that have been carved into seats and staircases.

On the opposite side of the valley, a clear trail climbs upward before heading north and down to Urubamba River valley about four hours away. At the river, the trail turns left (downstream) and continues to a bridge at Huayllabamba, where you can cross the river. From here, the Sacred Valley road will take you to Calca (turn right, about 13km) or Urubamba (turn left, about 9km). You can flag down a bus until midafternoon.

The main village square features a massive Inca wall with 10 huge, trapezoidal niches. The colonial church just above the main square is built on Inca foundations. The church is in regular use, but lack of funds has prevented restoration, and it's interesting to compare its interior to those of the highly restored churches of Cuzco.

The Sunday market is marginally less touristy than the Pisac market. There are two markets. One, in front of the old church, sells crafts and sweaters for tourists. Prices in the craft section are similar to those in Pisac or Cuzco, but it's good to see many of the local people still dressed in traditional garb. This is not done just for the tourists – if you come midweek, when there is no market and few tourists, you'll still see the women dressed in traditional clothing.

The other market, held at the bottom of the village (you can't miss it), is the local produce market, which is important to inhabitants of surrounding villages.

Both markets are held to a smaller extent on other days, especially Thursday.

## Places to Stay & Eat

There is reportedly a basic hotel, though most visitors come on day trips.

## Getting There & Away

Buses leave Cuzco from near Avenida Tullumayo a few times each day, some continuing to Urubamba. Buses also go from Urubamba.

# The Inca Trail & Machu Picchu

## THE INCA TRAIL

The Inca Trail is the best-known and most popular hike on the continent and is walked by thousands of people every year; it certainly is an exceptional hike. The views of snow-capped mountains and high cloudforest can be stupendous (weather permitting). Walking from one beautiful ruin to the next is a mystical and unforgettable experience. However, the trail and campsites can get very crowded during the dry season, and if you are an experienced backpacker looking for solitude or remote mountain villages, you may prefer hiking one of the many other available trails.

## Conservation

If you decide that the Inca Trail is not to be missed, please don't defecate in the ruins, don't leave garbage anywhere, don't damage the stonework by building fires against the walls (it blackens and, worse still, cracks the rocks), don't use a wood fire for cooking (the trail has been badly deforested over the past decade) and don't pick the orchids and other plants in this national park.

Since the South American Explorers organized an Inca Trail clean-up in 1980 and collected about 400kg of unburnable garbage, other clean-up campaigns have occurred regularly. Now, the best local outfitters work hard to keep the trail clean and arrange annual clean-ups.

## Preparation

You should take a stove, a sleeping pad, a warm sleeping bag and a tent (or other rain protection). All this equip rented inexpensively in Cuzco, rental gear carefully, as many rent leak badly. Also bring insect repellent, sun block, water-purification tablets and basic first-aid supplies. I know of people who have hiked the Inca Trail with a sheet of plastic and a bag of peanuts. Fine. They can go hungry and freeze if they want to, but such behavior is irresponsible and foolish.

The trek takes three full days (though a leisurely four is more fun), temperatures can drop below freezing at night, and it rains even in the May to September dry season. In the wettest months (January to April), trails can be slippery and campsites muddy. There is almost nowhere to buy food. The ruins are roofless and provide no shelter. Caves marked on some maps are usually wet, dirty overhangs. Although the total distance is only 33km, there are three high passes to be crossed, one of which reaches a height of 4200m. The trail is often steep, so don't be lulled into a false sense of security by the relatively short distance. One reader called it 'the Inca Trial.' Hike prepared.

You can obtain detailed maps and information from the South American Explorers, as well as from trekking agencies and the tourist office in Cuzco. Most maps do not have contours marked on them. The trail is fairly obvious for most of the way, and it's difficult to get lost, especially if you carry a compass. The map in this book is perfectly adequate. There have been occasional reports of robberies on the trail, and you are advised not to travel alone and to never leave gear unattended. The dry season from June to September is the most popular time, as well as the most crowded. For the rest of the year, the trail is fairly empty, but also very wet.

## Trail Fee

It costs about US$17 per person to hike the Inca Trail, which includes a one-day entrance to Machu Picchu (itself a US$10 expense). Students with cards may get a 50% discount. If taking a guided trek, check to see if this fee is included. This fee may increase in the future.

## INCA TRAIL

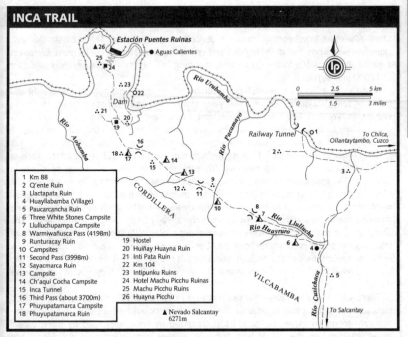

**Estación Puentes Ruinas**
● Aguas Calientes

Río Urubamba

0    2.5    5 km
0    1.5    3 miles

Railway Tunnel ○ 1    To Chilca,
Ollantaytambo, Cuzco

Río Apurimac

Río Pacamayo

CORDILLERA

Río Llullucha
Río Huayruro

VILCABAMBA

Río Cusichaca    To Salcantay

▲ Nevado Salcantay 6271m

1 Km 88
2 Q'ente Ruin
3 Llactapata Ruin
4 Huayllabamba (Village)
5 Paucarcancha Ruin
6 Three White Stones Campsite
7 Llulluchupampa Campsite
8 Warmiwañusca Pass (4198m)
9 Runturacay Ruin
10 Campsites
11 Second Pass (3998m)
12 Sayacmarca Ruin
13 Campsite
14 Ch'aqui Cocha Campsite
15 Inca Tunnel
16 Third Pass (about 3700m)
17 Phuyupatamarca Campsite
18 Phuyupatamarca Ruin

19 Hostel
20 Huiñay Huayna Ruin
21 Inti Pata Ruin
22 Km 104
23 Intipunku Ruins
24 Hotel Machu Picchu Ruinas
25 Machu Picchu Ruins
26 Huayna Picchu

## Warning

The only staffed park station is at the Río Pacamayo campsite. Although the rangers have radios here, they don't always work because of mountain interference. Medical facilities are almost nonexistent. If you have an accident on the trail, it could be days before evacuation can be arranged.

## The Hike

It is interesting to note that various translations of Quechua names are possible, and that those most frequently given are not necessarily the best or most accurate. Anthropologist Cristina Kessler-Noble has provided some interesting variations, some of which are used in this section.

Most people begin the trail from the railway stop at Km 88 (see Getting There & Away later in this section). However, it is also possible to begin at the village of Chilca (or Km 82 – accessible by train, by road from Ollantaytambo, or by river raft),

from where a relatively flat five-hour hike along the south side of the Río Urubamba brings you to the Inca Trail at the ruin of Llactapata. It is also possible to begin at Mollepata, spend three or four days hiking past the magnificent glacier-clad Salcantay, and join the Inca Trail at Huayllabamba. Finally, a new two-day route from Km 104 is also an option (see The Short Hike later in this chapter). Operators in Cuzco can arrange these options, or you can consult Bradt's *Peru & Bolivia: Backpacking & Trekking.* The description below is the standard hike from Km 88. Note that if you begin at Chilca, you can pay the trail fee near where you join the Inca Trail at Llactapata; you don't have to go to Km 88.

After crossing the Río Urubamba at Km 88 (2200m) and taking care of trail fees and registration formalities, you can turn back and then either turn right (west) to see the little-visited site of **Q'ente**, or 'hummingbird,' 1km away, or turn left and begin the Inca

CUZCO AREA

## Inca Trail Tours

Many adventure-travel companies in the USA offer Inca Trail treks. This is by far the most expensive way to go, but all the logistics and 1st-class equipment and guides are organized in advance. A 10-day trip to the Cuzco area, including four nights of trekking, costs well over US$2000 plus airfare.

If you arrive without a previously organized trek, there are several options. If you're fit and have had some backpacking experience, you can hike with what you can carry on your back. Otherwise, you can hire porters, guides and cooks from an adventure-travel agency in Cuzco; some budget travelers hire just one porter to carry a pack, and this is inexpensive.

Guided tours are available from many outfitters in Cuzco from about US$60 and up per person. This includes the local train to the beginning of the trail at Km 88, a tent, food, a porter, a cook and entrance to the ruins. While this may seem like a good deal, consider the following. The lowest costs mean that the porters are asked to carry excessively heavy loads, sometimes weighing as much as they do. Porters might not be provided with camping equipment and food, and so they have to fend for themselves. This leads to their cooking and warming themselves with scarce wood from the already badly damaged woodlands. The cheap guided tours generally have no idea about ecologically sensitive camping, and the result is garbage left everywhere. Some outfitters make no attempt to carry out garbage, bury shit or safeguard the delicate Andean woodlands. It has been 15 years since I first hiked the trail, and the degradation of the route and the ruins is clear. Do whatever you can to preserve this hike.

There are no easy solutions. You can rent gear in Cuzco (or use your own), avoid guided trips, and camp as cleanly as possible. You can even pack out garbage that you encounter. You can go on an expensive guided trip organized by companies used by international adventure-travel companies. At least these folks make some effort to camp cleanly and provide adequate facilities for porters. They also contribute to Inca Trail clean-up campaigns and sometimes will advertise their own clean-up hikes, usually at the beginning or end of the dry season. Or you can use the cheap outfitters and insist on clean camping by setting an example and ensuring that there is enough fuel and tentage for the porters.

Travelers continue to report that they talked to an inexpensive agency and asked to go on a trek with a good guide and a small group. 'No problem!' Unfortunately, once they arrived at the trailhead, they found that several agencies had lumped their 'small groups' together, and they were now a large group of tourists, in addition to porters, cooks and the guide. The guides vary in knowledge, experience and language skills. Whatever an agency says, if you pay low prices, you can't expect high-quality services – though you might get lucky.

Another report suggests that you should make it clear if you don't want to carry anything. Some agencies ask that you carry 'a small day pack,' which ends up being your regular backpack, so clarify this. Find out how many people sleep in tents – two or three? Make your wishes clear, get them in writing and keep reconfirming them at every opportunity.

Some readers reported paying US$70 per person for a trip that included new tents, simple but filling meals, all train/entrance fees and a good guide. So shop around and ask a lot of questions. I have received as many negative as positive reports about cheap Inca Trail treks.

It is normal to tip guides, cooks and porters. Don't forget the porters – they are woefully underpaid and work the hardest of all. Tip them as well as you are able.

Trail as it climbs gently through a eucalyptus grove for about 1km. You will see the minor ruin of **Llactapata**, or 'town on hillside,' to your right and soon cross the Río Cusichaca, or 'joyful bridge,' on a footbridge before heading south along the east bank of the river. Although there are camping possibilities just before Llactapata, most people elect to keep going to beyond the village of **Huayllabamba**, or 'grassy plain,' on the first day. It's about 6km along the river to the village, climbing gently all the way and recrossing the river after about 4km. You can buy bottled drinks in houses near this bridge. Look over your shoulder for views of the snowcapped Veronica, 5750m above sea level.

Huayllabamba, at an elevation of about 2750m, is a village near the fork of the Llullucha (a Quechua word for a type of herb) and Cusichaca rivers. You cross Río Llullucha on a log bridge. It is possible to camp in the plaza in front of the school, but beware of thieves slitting your tent at night. Huayllabamba has a reputation for thievery. Porters can sometimes be hired here to carry your pack. If you want to get away from the crowds, continue south (away from the Inca Trail) along the Cusichaca to the ruins of **Paucarcancha**, about 3km away. You can camp here, though if you do so, you'll need to carry water up from the river and watch your camp – Huayllabamba is not far away.

The Inca Trail itself climbs steeply up along the south bank of the Río Llullucha. After a walk of about an hour, the river forks. Continue up the left fork for a few hundred meters, then cross the river on a log bridge. There are several flat campsites on both sides of the bridge. The area is known as Three White Stones, but these boulders are no longer visible. This site could be your first camp, although there are bugs and local kids to bother you. If you have the energy, push on.

The trail turns right beyond the log bridge and sweeps back to the Llullucha. It is a long, very steep climb to the Warmiwañusca, or 'dead woman's,' Pass. At 4198m above sea level, this pass is the highest point of the trek, but there are campsites before it. Some people prefer to rest for the night at Three White Stones to further acclimatize before making the ascent. The trail passes through humid *Polylepis* woodlands for about 1½ hours before emerging on the high, bare mountain. At some points, the trail and streambed become one, but stone stairs keep hikers above the water. Although the trail climbs steeply, there are a couple of small, flat areas in the forest where you could camp. After emerging from the forest, you reach Llulluchupampa, a flat area above the forest where water is available and camping is good, though it is very cold at night. There are flush toilets at the lower end of Llulluchupampa, and pit toilets at the upper end. This is as far as you can reasonably expect to get on your first day from Km 88. It takes from four to nine hours, depending on your level of fitness, acclimatization and load.

From Llulluchupampa, follow the left-hand side of the valley for the two- to three-hour climb to **Warmiwañusca Pass**. It takes longer than you'd expect because the altitude slows you down.

From Warmiwañusca, you can see the Río Pacamayo, or 'sunrise river,' far below, as well as the ruin of **Runturacay** halfway up the hill, above the river. The trail descends to the river, where there are good campsites. There are flush toilets and even showers here (these are new, and how well they'll work remains to be seen) and an Instituto Nacional de Cultura guard post. The downward climb is long – taking over an hour – and is a strain on the knees. People with knee problems may take longer. At an altitude of about 3600m, the trail crosses the river over a small footbridge – don't venture too far into the vegetation below.

Climb to the right toward Runturacay, or 'basketshaped building,' a round ruin with superb views about an hour's walk above the river. You can also camp here. A few minutes away from the ruin, to your left as you look out into the valley, there is a trickle of water.

Above Runturacay, the trail climbs to a false summit before continuing past two small lakes to the top of the second pass at 3998m, about an hour above Runturacay. If it's clear, there are views of the snowcapped Cordillera Vilcabamba. The clear trail descends past another lake to the ruin of **Sayacmarca**, or 'dominant town,' which is visible from the trail 1km before you reach it. The site, a tightly constructed town on a small mountain spur, is the most impressive of those seen along the trail so far and offers superb views. A long, steep staircase to the left of the trail leads to the site. The trail itself continues downward and crosses an upper tributary of the Río Aobamba, or 'wavy plain,' 3600m above sea level. There are campsites here, at a place called Ch'aqui Cocha, but the ground is boggy after rain, so these are best used in the dry season.

As the trail goes through some beautiful cloudforest on the gentle climb to the third pass, you'll find a causeway across a dried-out lake, and farther on, a tunnel – both Inca constructions. The highest point of the pass, at almost 3700m, is not very obvious. There are great views of the Urubamba valley from here. You soon reach the beautiful ruin of **Phuyupatamarca**, or 'town above the clouds,' about 3650m above sea level and approximately two or three hours beyond Sayacmarca.

Phuyupatamarca has been well restored and contains a beautiful series of ceremonial baths with water running through them (purify it before drinking). Nearby are some pit toilets. A ridge above the baths offers campsites with spectacular views. There are sometimes camp guards here.

From Phuyupatamarca, the Inca Trail makes a dizzying dive into the cloudforest below, following an incredibly well-engineered flight of many hundreds of Inca steps. The trail eventually passes under electric power pylons built down the hill to the dam on the Río Urubamba.

Follow the pylons down to a red-roofed, white hostel that provides youth hostel-type facilities for about US$7 per bed (there are 16), less if you sleep on the floor. Hot showers (US$3), meals and bottled drinks are available, and camping is possible nearby. The hostel is usually full in the high season and can be overflowing during holiday weekends (a reader reports hundreds of people staying here over Fiestas Patrias, with food and drinks running out

and toilets not running at all). Try calling 21-1147 for reservations, or ask in Cuzco travel agencies or the tourist office. A 500m trail behind the hostel leads to the beautiful Inca site of **Huiñay Huayna** (also spelled Wiñay Wayna), which cannot be seen from the hostel. This ruin is about a two- to three-hour descent from Phuyupatamarca.

Huiñay Huayna is normally translated as 'forever young,' but a much more charming translation was explained to me. As 'huiñay' is the Quechua verb 'to plant the earth,' a more accurate translation may be 'to plant the earth young' – perhaps a reference to the young, springtime earth of planting time. From planting comes growing, which yields the connotation 'growing young,' (as opposed to 'growing old'); hence the popular catch-all translation 'forever young.' Peter Frost, meanwhile, writes that the name is Quechua for an orchid that blooms here year-round. There are no doubt several other variations on the translation's theme.

Whatever it means, this exquisite little place warrants the short side-trip and an hour or two of exploration. Climb down to the lowest part of the town, where it tapers off into a tiny and very exposed ledge overlooking the Río Urubamba far below.

About a kilometer above the hostel and Huiñay Huayna is **Inti Pata**, a terraced ruin cleared in 1993.

From Huiñay Huayna, the trail contours around through the cliff-hanging cloudforest and is very narrow in places, so watch your step. It takes about two hours to reach **Intipunku**, or 'gate of the sun' – the penultimate site on the trail. You'll get your first view of Machu Picchu from here. Camping is not permitted because the site is so small.

The descent from Intipunku to Machu Picchu takes almost an hour. Backpacks are not allowed into the ruins, and immediately upon arrival, park guards ask you to check your pack at the lower entrance gate and have your trail permit stamped. It is rather a brusque return to rules and regulations when all you want to do is quietly explore the ruins. The pass is only valid for the day it is stamped, so try to arrive in the morning. For US$5, you can renew the pass for the next day.

After you've explored the ruins, you can stay at the expensive hotel near the site, camp by the river far below (see Places to Stay & Eat in Machu Picchu later in this chapter) or take the 8km road (buses are available) to the village of Aguas Calientes, where there are cheap hotels and restaurants (see Aguas Calientes). You can also take the afternoon train and be in Ollantaytambo or Cuzco by evening.

Doing the hike in reverse, from Machu Picchu to Km 88, is officially not permitted, though people do it occasionally. It's more fun to arrive at Machu Picchu than to depart.

### The Short Hike

Since the last edition of this book, a 'short' version of the Inca Trail has been opened. Leaving from Km 104 (on the railway tracks, where you alight the train), the signed trail crosses the river on a footbridge before climbing steeply to Huiñay Huayna. (A fork in the trail follows down the river past the ruins of Choquesuysuy and then climbs up the right hand of the ravine to Huiñay Huayna, but this is much steeper and not normally used.) Even the 'normal' climb is steeper than most sections of the Inca Trail proper, and takes about three hours. The locally suggested itinerary calls for an overnight at the hostel or camping area near Huiñay Huayna, but this can be extremely crowded. Some hikers have reported reaching Machu Picchu in one day from Km 104 – a long, tiring hike, but certainly doable if you are fit and acclimatized. This trail costs US$12 (as opposed to US$17 on the longer traditional route), but gives a good flavor of what hiking the Inca Trail is like.

### Getting There & Away

**Km 88** Most people take the train from Cuzco to Km 88. The tourist train doesn't normally stop here, and most hikers take the local train. Be aware of thieves working in groups on the train – some will distract you while others snatch your camera, slash your pack or pick your pockets, particularly in 2nd class. It's OK if you are in a group and watch one another's stuff.

Ask where to get off, because although everyone knows the stop, it is very small and badly marked. At Km 88, guards sell US$17 trail permits (US cash or nuevos soles – have the right change) at the footbridge crossing the river. You're ready to hike.

**Km 104** The same story as above, except that you can also hike into the trailhead from Aguas Calientes in a couple of hours.

## MACHU PICCHU
☎ 084

Machu Picchu is South America's best known and most spectacular archaeological site. During the busy dry-season months of June to September, you might see up to a thousand visitors at the Lost City of the Incas, as it's popularly known. Despite the huge tourist influx, the site manages to retain its air of grandeur and mystery (though see the boxed text 'Endangered Machu Picchu' for another point of view) and is considered a must-see for all visitors to Peru.

### History

Machu Picchu is both the best known and the least known of the Inca ruins. It is not mentioned in any of the chronicles of the Spanish conquistadors, and archaeologists today can do no more than speculate on its function. Although Machu Picchu was known to a handful of Quechua peasants who farmed the area, the outside world was unaware of its existence until the American historian Hiram Bingham stumbled upon it almost by accident on July 24, 1911. Bingham's search was for the lost city of Vilcabamba, the last stronghold of the Incas, and he thought he had found it at Machu Picchu. We now know that the remote ruins at Espíritu Pampa, much deeper in the jungle, are the remains of Vilcabamba. Machu Picchu remains a mysterious site, never revealed to the conquering Spaniards and virtually forgotten until the early part of this century.

The site that was discovered in 1911 was very different from the one we see today. All the buildings were thickly overgrown with vegetation, and Bingham's team had to be content with roughly mapping the site. Bingham returned in 1912 and 1915 to carry out the difficult task of clearing the thick

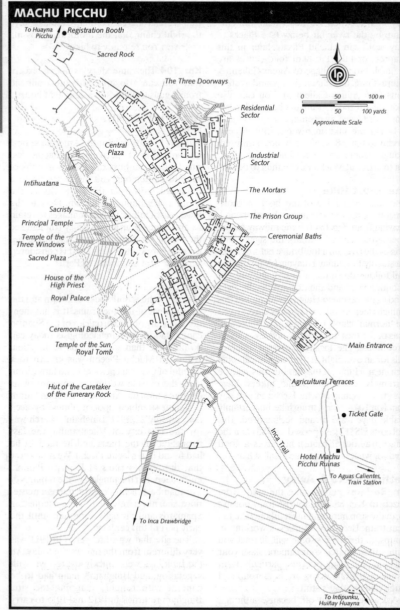

## MACHU PICCHU

To Huayna Picchu • Registration Booth

Sacred Rock

The Three Doorways

Residential Sector

Central Plaza

Industrial Sector

Intihuatana

The Mortars

Sacristy

The Prison Group

Principal Temple

Ceremonial Baths

Temple of the Three Windows

Sacred Plaza

House of the High Priest

Royal Palace

Ceremonial Baths

Temple of the Sun, Royal Tomb

Main Entrance

Hut of the Caretaker of the Funerary Rock

Agricultural Terraces

Ticket Gate

Inca Trail

Hotel Machu Picchu Ruinas

To Aguas Calientes, Train Station

To Inca Drawbridge

To Intipunku, Huiñay Huayna

0    50    100 m
0    50    100 yards
Approximate Scale

forest from the ruins, and he also discovered some of the ruins located on the Inca Trail. Peruvian archaeologist Luis E Valcárcel undertook further studies and clearing in 1934, as did a Peruvian-American expedition under Paul Fejos in 1940-41. Despite these and more recent studies, knowledge about Machu Picchu remains sketchy. Over 50 burial sites, containing more than 100 skeletal remains (about 80% female), were discovered. An early theory that it was a city of chosen women who catered to the Incas' needs has lost support, and it is now thought that Machu Picchu was already an uninhabited, forgotten city at the time of the conquest. This would explain why it wasn't mentioned to the Spaniards. It is obvious from the exceptionally high quality of the stonework and the abundance of ornamental rather than practical sites that Machu Picchu must once have been an important ceremonial center.

Newer finds include some burial sites on Huayna Picchu mountain in the early 1980s and, in late 1986, the exciting discovery of a city larger than Machu Picchu and 5km north of it. Local and US archaeologists have named the city Maranpampa (or Mandorpampa). Neither of the new sites is easily accessible to the general public at this time, though there are plans to eventually open Maranpampa to tourists.

## Admission

The site is open daily from 7 or 7:30 am to 5 pm. They may open earlier; try knocking at the office on the left a short distance before the gate.

Because the site is surrounded by high mountains, it's already broad daylight when the sun comes up over or goes down behind the surrounding mountains. The changes in color and light early and late in the day are very beautiful.

Machu Picchu is Peru's showpiece site, and entrance fees are correspondingly high. Foreigners pay US$10 for a single day's visit but the second day costs only US$5. Students with ID might be charged half price.

Many visitors buy a Machu Picchu combined-ticket book from one of the tourist agencies in Cuzco. This includes round-trip tickets for the tourist train, the bus to and from the ruins, admission to the ruins and lunch at the Machu Picchu Hotel. Make sure your ticket contains all these sections, and shop around. The combined ticket costs about US$110, depending on the agency, most of which provide an English-speaking guide. Cheaper combined tickets are offered using the local train. Check carefully to see what is included. The main drawback is that the combined ticket is valid for just one day, and you only get to spend two or three hours in the ruins before it's time to start returning to the train station. Budget travelers will do best to pay as they go.

You are not allowed to bring large packs or food into the ruins, and packs have to be checked at the gate. You can visit all parts of the ruins, but don't walk on any of the walls, as this will loosen the stonework, as well as prompt an angry cacophony of whistle-blowing from the guards. As the guards check the ruins carefully at closing time and blow their whistles loudly, trying to spend the night is also difficult (and illegal).

You can buy a so-called Boleto Nocturno for another US$10; this will get you into the ruins at night and is particularly popular during full moons. Buy the ticket from the entrance booth during the day – tickets are not sold at night.

The ruins are most heavily visited between about 10 am and 2 pm. Many tours combine visits of Machu Picchu with the Sunday markets at either Pisac or Chinchero, so Sunday is fairly quiet, but Friday, Saturday and Monday are busy. June to August are the busiest months. Try to plan your visit early or late in the day, especially during the dry season (the whole day is best), and you'll have several hours of peace and quiet. An early, wet, midweek morning in the rainy season will virtually guarantee you the ruins to yourself.

## Inside the Ruins

Unless you arrive on the Inca Trail, you'll officially enter the ruins through a guarded ticket gate on the south side of Machu Picchu. About 100m of footpath bring you to the mazelike entrance of Machu Picchu proper, where the ruins lie stretched out before you, roughly divided into two areas separated by a series of plazas. The area to the left of the plazas contains most of the more interesting sites.

About 100m after you see the ruins, a long staircase climbs up to your left to a hut on the southeast spur. This vantage point affords the most complete overview of the site for the classic photograph. The hut, known as the **Hut of the Caretaker of the Funerary Rock**, is one of the few buildings that has been restored with a thatched roof, making it a good shelter in the case of rain. The Inca Trail enters the city just below this hut. The carved rock behind the hut may have been used to mummify the nobility and explains the hut's name.

If you continue straight into the ruins instead of climbing the stairs to the hut, you soon come to a beautiful series of 16 connected **ceremonial baths** that cascade across the ruins, accompanied by a flight of stairs. Just above and to the left of the baths is Machu Picchu's only round building, the **Temple of the Sun**. This curved, tapering tower is said to contain Machu Picchu's finest stonework. Inside is an altar and a curiously drilled trapezoidal window that looks out onto the site. This window is popularly named the **Serpent Window**, but it's unlikely that snakes lived in the holes around it. Probably the holes were used to suspend a ceremonial gold sun disk. The Temple of the Sun is cordoned off, but you can see it from above and below.

Below the towering temple, an almost hidden, natural rock cave has been carefully carved with a steplike altar and sacred niches by the Inca's stonemasons. The mummies discovered at this site inspired its name – the **Royal Tomb**.

Climbing the stairs above the ceremonial baths, you reach a flat area of jumbled rocks, once used as a quarry. Turn right at the top of the stairs and walk across the quarry on a short path leading to the four-sided **Sacred Plaza**. The far side contains a small viewpoint platform with a curved wall, and a view of the snowcapped Cordillera Vilcabamba in the far distance and the Río Urubamba below. The remaining three sides

of the Sacred Plaza are flanked by important buildings. The **Temple of the Three Windows** commands an impressive view of the plaza below through the huge, trapezoidal windows that give the building its name. With this temple behind you, the **Principal Temple** is to your right. Its name derives from the massive solidity and perfection of its construction. The damage to the rear right corner of the temple is the result of the ground settling below this corner rather than any inherent weakness in the masonry itself. Opposite the Principal Temple is the **House of the High Priest**, though archaeologists cannot say with certainty who, if anyone, lived in this building.

Behind and connected to the Principal Temple lies a famous small building called the **Sacristy**. It has many well-carved niches, perhaps used for the storage of ceremonial objects, as well as a carved stone bench. The Sacristy is especially known for the two rocks flanking its entrance; each is said to contain 32 angles, but I come up with a different number whenever I count them.

A staircase behind the Sacristy climbs small hill to the major shrine in Machu Picchu, the **Intihuatana**. This Quechua word loosely translates as the 'hitching post of the sun' and refers to the carved rock pillar often mistakenly called a sun dial, which stands at the top of the Intihuatana hill. This rock was not used in telling the time of day but, rather, the time of year. The Inca astronomers were able to predict the solstices using the angles of the pillar. Thus, the Inca, who was the son of the sun, was able to claim control over the return of the lengthening summer days. Exactly how the pillar was used for these astronomical purposes remains unclear, but its elegant simplicity is remarked upon by many modern observers. It is recorded that there were several of these Intihuatanas in various important Inca sites, but all, with the known exception of this one, were smashed by the Spaniards in an attempt to wipe out what they considered to be the blasphemy of sun worship.

At the back of the Intihuatana is another staircase. It descends to the **Central Plaza** which separates the important sites of the

## Endangered Machu Picchu

Visitors marvel at the stunning beauty of Machu Picchu's natural setting, and Inca Trail hikers spend days walking through a mountain landscape that reveals new wonders at every turn.

But for how much longer?

Recent developments point to a dismal environmental prognosis for the Machu Picchu Historical Sanctuary. Although it is supposedly protected by laws and an act of the Peruvian Congress, this UNESCO World Heritage site is under environmental siege.

The INC, an authority assigned to protect archaeological monuments, has constructed latrines, radio towers and park buildings along the Inca Trail and has added a restaurant to the already disruptive visitor center at the beautiful and well-preserved ruins of Huiñay Hayna. Unfortunately, these developments have been poorly planned. The same agency has granted permission for a consortium to build a cable car spanning the Urubamba gorge at the ruin of Machu Picchu itself, a project that will shatter the aesthetic integrity of Machu Picchu's setting and offload unmanageable numbers of new visitors every day (see www.mpicchu.org).

In the valley below Machu Picchu, the sprawling dormitory town of Aguas Calientes has mushroomed to a population of nearly 1500 permanent inhabitants, with up to 1500 more transients, within the borders of the sanctuary, without planning or control of any kind. Around the sanctuary's borders, farmers steadily encroach upon the protected cloudforest, often setting fires, which in recent years have raged out of control across the mountainsides during the dry months of August and September, wreaking ecological havoc and even threatening the actual ruins of Machu Picchu.

Such is the crisis that in 1998, UNESCO threatened to place Machu Picchu on its list of endangered World Heritage sites if the local authorities failed to adopt a coherent master plan for the development and protection of the park. This they finally did, but it remains to be seen what effect the plan will have; in any case, the cable-car project will go ahead.

The Finnish government has negotiated a $6.5 million debt swap with the Peruvian government for a conservation program at Machu Picchu, but the resistance of entrenched local authorities has obstructed its implementation. Whether listed or not, Machu Picchu is a highly endangered piece of world heritage.

Intihuatana, Sacred Plaza and Temple of the Sun from the more mundane areas opposite. At the lower end of this opposite area is the **Prison Group**, a labyrinthian complex of cells, niches and passageways both under and above the ground. The centerpiece of the group is a carving of the head of a condor, the natural rocks behind it resembling the bird's outstretched wings. Behind the condor is a well-like hole and, at the bottom of this, the door to a tiny underground cell that can only be entered by bending double.

Above the Prison Group is the largest section of the ruins – the **Industrial & Residential Sectors**. These buildings are less well constructed and had more mundane purposes than those across the plaza.

### Walks near Machu Picchu

Several fairly short walks can be taken starting from and returning to the ruins, the most famous of which is the climb up the steep mountain of Huayna Picchu at the back of the ruins. Huayna Picchu is normally translated as 'young peak,' but it is interesting to note that 'picchu,' with the correct glottal pronunciation, refers to the wad in the cheek of a coca-chewing, Quechua-speaking mountain dweller – the wad looks like a little peak in the cheek.

**Huayna Picchu** At first glance, it would appear that Huayna Picchu is a difficult climb, but there is a well-maintained trail. Although the ascent is steep, it's not technically difficult. You begin by walking to the very end of the Central Plaza and turning right between two open-fronted buildings. Just beyond is a registration booth, where you have to sign in; it's only open until about 1 pm. The 1½-hour climb (less if you are athletic and fit) takes you through a short section of Inca tunnel. The view from the top is spectacular, but if you lack either time or energy, I think the view from the Hut of the Caretaker of the Funerary Rock is equally good. (The trail was closed in 1997 and 1998 following a forest fire; it has reopened.)

Another walk begins with a climb part of the way up Huayna Picchu. About 10 minutes from the lowest point of the trail, a thin path plunges down to your left, continuing down the rear of Huayna Picchu to the small **Temple of the Moon**. The trail is easy to follow, but involves steep up-and-down sections, a ladder, and an overhanging cave, where you have to bend over to get by. The descent takes about an hour, and the ascent back to the main Huayna Picchu trail rather longer. The spectacular trail drops and climbs steeply as it hugs the sides of Huayna Picchu before plunging into the cloudforest for a while. Suddenly, you reach a cleared area where the small, very well made ruins are found. Unfortunately, they are marred by graffiti.

From the Temple of the Moon, a newly cleared path leads up behind the ruin and steeply on up the back side of Huaynu Picchu.

**Inca Drawbridge** On the other side of the ruins, a scenic and much less steep walk from the Hut of the Caretaker of the Funerary Rock takes you past the top of the terraces and out along a narrow, cliff-clinging trail to the Inca drawbridge. The trail is marked; there is also a registration booth, at which you're supposed to register before 3 pm, but its opening hours are erratic. The 20-minute walk gives you a good look at the vegetation of the high cloudforest and a different view of Machu Picchu. The drawbridge itself is less interesting than the walk to reach it. You are not allowed to walk right up to the bridge and have to be content with viewing it from behind a barrier about 100m away. Someone crossed both the barrier and the bridge some years ago and fell to their death.

**Intipunku** The Inca Trail ends just below the Hut of the Caretaker of the Funerary Rock after its final descent from the notch in the horizon called Intipunku, or the 'gate of the sun.' Looking at the hill behind you as you enter the ruins, you can see both the trail and Intipunku. This hill, called Machu Picchu, or 'old peak,' gives the site its name. It takes about an hour to reach Intipunku and if you can spare about a full half day for the round trip, it's possible to continue as far as Huiñay Huayna (see the Inca Trail earlier in this chapter).

**Machu Picchu** The ascent of the hill of Machu Picchu is the most difficult and rarely done cleared hike near the ruins. Take the Inca Trail for a few minutes and look for a trail to your right passing through a gap in the walls of the terraces. It's not very obvious, and there's no sign. If you find the trail, it may be overgrown, but you can force your way through the thick vegetation to the top of the peak. Allow well over an hour for the climb and be prepared for disappointment unless the trail has recently been cleared.

## Places to Stay & Eat

*Hotel Machu Picchu Ruinas* (☎ 21-1038, 21-1052, fax 21-1039; in Cuzco c/o the Hotel Monasterio) has 32 rooms with telephones and TV and is the only place to stay at Machu Picchu itself. Rooms without a view cost US$269 single or double, and rooms with mountain views cost US$301. (None have views of the ruins.) Additional beds are US$45. The rates skyrocketed after privatization in 1995 and are expensive for what you get. Despite the expense, it's often full, so reserve as far ahead as possible in the high season. Travel agencies may be able to arrange a discount. You can sometimes get a room on the day you arrive, especially during the low season, but don't rely on it.

During the low season, you can often book a room here in Cuzco with a day or two's notice. Rooms are clean and good-sized, but bland. The best thing about this hotel is the never-ending supply of hot water in the showers in every room. Staying in Aguas Calientes is a better budget option.

The only place to eat at the ruins is in the hotel. The hotel restaurant serves buffet breakfast (US$12.50) and supper (US$20), and a cafeteria on the patio offers overpriced self-service lunches with three courses and a drink for US$16. During the busy season, lunch queues can be very long. There is also a souvenir shop/snack bar where you can buy bottled drinks and candy for about the same price as in the cafeteria. Bring a packed lunch and water bottle if you want to economize. It's illegal to bring food into the ruins themselves, because many tourists litter the site. Don't leave any rubbish whatsoever.

Cheap snacks and drinks can be purchased at the train station in the afternoon.

## Getting There & Away

Most visitors take the train or helicopter to Aguas Calientes, from where buses go directly to the ruins. Alternatively, hike the Inca Trail. There are no other options.

# AGUAS CALIENTES
☎ 084

This village is the closest to Machu Picchu (3km away) and is therefore a frequent destination for travelers wanting to do more than just visit Machu Picchu on the standard one-day train trip from Cuzco. It's a good place to meet other travelers.

## Information

There are coin- and card-operated telephones in the railway station and other places. A medical center and police station (☎ 21-1178) are shown on the map. Small amounts of money can be changed in most hotels and restaurants.

## Hot Springs

Trekkers completing the Inca Trail may want to soak away their aches and pains in the natural thermal springs from which the village of Aguas Calientes derives its name. To get there, follow the path past the Hotel Machu Picchu Inn for about 10 minutes.

Unfortunately, a landslide in April 1995 destroyed the entire hot-springs complex (pools, changing rooms, showers, etc). The rains of 1998 didn't improve things. The hot springs still flow, and you can soak in them, but facilities are still being repaired. Hours are 5 am to 8:30 pm, admission is US$1.50, and bathing suits can be rented. Inquire locally about the current situation.

## Places to Stay

**Budget to Mid-Range** The basic but clean *Hostal Los Caminantes* (☎ 21-1007), next to the railway line, charges US$5/9 for singles/doubles with shared bath or US$11 for a double with bath and warm showers. Some rooms sleep up to five people. Other cheap and basic places include *Alojamiento Sucre* and *Hospedaje Las Bromelias*, both near the plaza. Up the hill, you'll find *Hostal Joe* at US$5 per person or US$10/15 for singles/doubles with bath. Farther up the hill are numerous cheap hotels, including *Hostal La Cabaña* and *Hostal Ima Sumac*, which have been around for a while, have hot water (usually) and are clean. Rooms vary from US$7 per person to US$25 double with bath and breakfast, depending on the season. This is the area to look for new budget hotels.

*Gringo Bill's* (☎ 21-1046, gringobill@yahoo.com) has been a budget travelers' favorite for many years. It attracts a laid-back crowd that enjoys the spacey wall murals and the friendly but slow service in the restaurant. There is 24-hour hot water. High-season rates are US$17/25 with shared bath or US$20/30 with private bath, but low-season and group rates are available.

**Mid-Range to Top End** The *Hostal Presidente* (☎ 21-1034, fax 21-1065, in Cuzco 24-4598), by the railway tracks, is very clean, helpful, friendly and often full. Good-sized rooms with private bath and river views are about US$70/80, or US$60/65 without river views (both including breakfast). They also run the adjoining *Hostal Machu Picchu* (same phones), where smaller rooms are

CUZCO AREA

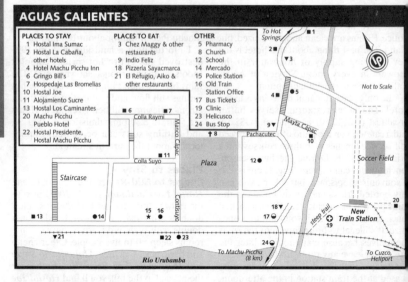

AGUAS CALIENTES

**PLACES TO STAY**
1  Hostal Ima Sumac
2  Hostal La Cabaña,
   other hotels
4  Hotel Machu Picchu Inn
6  Gringo Bill's
7  Hospedaje Las Bromelias
10 Hotel Joe
11 Alojamiento Sucre
13 Hostal Los Caminantes
20 Machu Picchu
   Pueblo Hotel
22 Hostal Presidente,
   Hostal Machu Picchu

**PLACES TO EAT**
3  Chez Maggy & other
   restaurants
9  Indio Feliz
18 Pizzería Sayacmarca
21 El Refugio, Aiko &
   other restaurants

**OTHER**
5  Pharmacy
8  Church
12 School
14 Mercado
15 Police Station
16 Old Train
   Station Office
17 Bus Tickets
19 Clinic
23 Helicusco
24 Bus Stop

about US$22/30 with bath; these may soon be upgraded. *Hotel Machu Picchu Inn*, a partner of Hotel Machu Picchu Ruinas (see Places to Stay & Eat in Machu Picchu), has 75 rooms at US$96 single or double.

*Machu Picchu Pueblo Hotel* (☎ 21-1032, fax 21-1124, in Cuzco 24-5314, fax 24-4669, reservas@inkaterra.com.pe) is about a five-minute walk east of Aguas Calientes. The tourist train stops near the hotel. Large, comfortable bungalows are scattered around an attractive garden, and the 62 spacious rooms are US$173 single or double, though discounts can be arranged. Guests love the flower-filled tropical gardens, though one complains that features like in-room hairdryers, minirefrigerators and cable TV are unavailable in the expensive rooms. There is a good, though pricey, restaurant that is a walk of several minutes from the farthest rooms – not much fun on a dark stormy night! This hotel continues to expand, and a swimming pool is advertised (though it wasn't there when I visited).

Near the hot springs, a new upscale spa/ hotel is planned for 2000.

## Places to Eat

Many cheap restaurants are clustered along the railway tracks, and a few have been criticized for undercooked food or unhygienic conditions. (The tap water is not safe to drink.) Another reasonably good and clean place is *Aiko*. The restaurant by the Hostal Presidente is also quite good. Up along the hill toward the hot springs are numerous restaurants, such as *Chez Maggy*. The *Pizzería Sayacmarca*, by the bus stop for Machu Picchu, is a convenient place for a snack. The better hotels have restaurants, too.

By far, the best restaurant is *Indio Feliz* (☎ 21-1090), which is owned by a French-Peruvian couple. The French cook whips up some delicious meals (I had the trout in mango sauce), and the restaurant itself is very attractive, with friendly staff and tourist information. Prices are higher than at other restaurants, but worth it. They have a popular daily lunch special (soup and salad, with half a dozen main courses to choose from) for US$10, or you can eat á la carte.

There's not much to do in the evening except hang out in one of the restaurants and talk to other travelers over a beer.

## Getting There & Away

**Air** Helicusco has helicopter service between Cuzco and Aguas Calientes. See Cuzco for details. The heliport is a 10-minute walk from town (no roads).

**Bus** Bus rides to Machu Picchu cost US$3 one way and leave from the Río Urubamba bridge for the 8km run up to the ruins. Departures are at 6:30, 7:30, 9, 10:30 and 11:30 am and 12:40, 2:30 and 3:30 pm (subject to change), plus whenever trains arrive. (For people with combined tickets, the return bus ticket to the ruins is included.) There are enough buses to handle the crowds coming off the train.

**Train** Most day visitors take the expensive autovagón de turismo or tren de turismo from Cuzco, arriving at Machu Picchu train station (in Aguas Calientes) about 3½ hours later. Alternatively, you can get a bus to Ollantaytambo and catch the train there, perhaps after overnighting in Urubamba or Ollantaytambo. The cheapest way to travel is on the local train to Aguas Calientes. Spend the night there, a full day at Machu Picchu ruins and another night at Aguas Calientes, then return on the local train. This avoids the tourist train completely and maximizes your time at the ruins (see Cuzco for times).

Aguas Calientes is currently the end of the line from Cuzco. There are two stations; the old one is in the town center and is where the local train terminates; the new one is close to the Machu Picchu Pueblo Hotel and is where the tourist trains terminate. Buy tickets and board trains in the appropriate stations. People who have difficulty walking should note that the path from the new train station to the bus stop for the ruins is short but steep. Currently, the buses don't get to the station, and wheelchairs can't negotiate the steep path; ask in Cuzco about whether this has improved.

The autovagón de turismo leaves at 3 pm daily and is often full with returning daytrippers, so you might not be able to get a one-way ticket. It passes Ollantaytambo at 4:25 pm and arrives in Cuzco at 6:25 pm. During the high season, a second autovagón may leave at 6 pm if there's demand.

The tren de turismo leaves at 4 pm, passing Ollantaytambo at 5:35 pm and arriving in Cuzco at 8:15 pm Monday to Saturday.

The local train leaves at 4:30 pm daily. Hours are subject to change. See Cuzco for fares.

# Southeast of Cuzco

The railway and the road to Puno and Lake Titicaca head southeast from Cuzco. En route are several sites of interest that can be visited from Cuzco in a day.

### SAYLLA

This small village, about 20km from Cuzco, is known for chicharrones. Locals stop by one of several cheap eateries and wash down a plate with a cold beer – yum.

### TIPÓN

This little-known Inca site consists of some excellent terracing at the head of a small valley and is noted for its fine irrigation system. To get there, take an Urcos bus from Cuzco and ask to be let off at the Tipón turnoff, 23km beyond Cuzco and a few kilometers before Oropesa. A steep dirt road from the turnoff climbs the 4km to the ruins.

### PIKILLACTA & RUMICOLCA

Pikillacta is the only major pre-Inca ruin in the Cuzco area, and it can be reached on an Urcos minibus from Cuzco. Pikillacta means 'the place of the flea' and was built around 1100 AD by the Wari culture. Entry is with the Boleto Turístico. The site is just past a lake on the left-hand side of the road, about 32km beyond Cuzco. It is a large city of crumbling, two-story buildings, all with entrances strategically located on the upper floor. A defensive wall surrounds the city. The stonework here is much cruder than that of the Incas. The floors were paved with slabs of white gypsum, and the walls were covered with gypsum as well. You can still see traces of this.

Over the past few years, there has been some new excavation and research, and some human burials were discovered. There are local guides available, particularly on weekdays.

Across the road from Pikillacta and about 1km away is the huge Inca gate of Rumicolca, built on Wari foundations. The cruder Wari stonework contrasts with the Inca blocks.

The area's swampy lakes are also interesting. You can see Indians making roof tiles from the mud that surrounds the lakes.

## ANDAHUAYLILLAS

Andahuaylillas is about 40km beyond Cuzco and 7km before Urcos. (Don't confuse it with Andahuaylas, which is a long way west of Cuzco and is described later in this chapter.) This pretty Andean village is famous for its beautifully decorated church (comparable to the best in Cuzco) and attractive colonial houses.

The Jesuit church dates from the 17th century. It houses many carvings and paintings, of which the best is considered to be a canvas of the Immaculate Conception by Esteban Murillo. There are reportedly many gold and silver treasures locked in the church, and the villagers are all involved in taking turns guarding it 24 hours a day. The church hours are erratic, but you can usually find a caretaker to open it for you (a tip is expected). You can reach Andahuaylillas on the Urcos minibus.

## BEYOND URCOS

The road is paved as far as Urcos, 47km southeast of Cuzco, where there is a basic hostel. From Urcos, one road heads northeast to Puerto Maldonado in the jungle (see From Cuzco to the Jungle), while another continues southeast toward Lake Titicaca. About 60km southeast of Urcos is the village of **Tinta**, which has another fine colonial church and a basic place to stay. About 25km farther is **Sicuani**, a market town of about 40,000 people.

A few kilometers before Sicuani is the little village of San Pedro, and a short walk from here, the ruins of **Raqchi** are visible

both from the road and the railway; they look like a huge aqueduct. These are the remains of the Temple of Viracocha, which once supported the largest known Inca roof. Twenty-two circular columns made of stone blocks helped support the roof; most are now destroyed, but their foundations are clearly seen. This was once one of the holiest shrines of the Inca Empire, but it was destroyed by the Spanish. The remains of many houses and storage buildings are also visible. An entry fee of about US$2 is charged, and there are very few tourists here. In mid-June, Raqchi is the site of a very colorful fiesta with much traditional dancing and other events.

### Getting There & Away

These places can all be reached by bus from Cuzco; it takes less than three hours to reach Sicuani. Alternatively, the railway to Puno parallels this road, and there are stops at the places mentioned. First Class buses between Cuzco and Puno make stops at some of these places, including Raqchi. Accommodations in Sicuani are basic, but if you leave Cuzco early in the morning, you'll have plenty of time to visit Raqchi and return on a day trip.

# From Cuzco to the Jungle

There are three overland routes from Cuzco to the jungle, all by unpaved roads that can be very slow and muddy in the wet months. One road goes to Quillabamba. Another road heads through Paucartambo, Tres Cruces and Shintuya for Parque Nacional Manu; and the other goes through Ocongate and Quince Mil to Puerto Maldonado.

## PAUCARTAMBO

This small village lies on the eastern slopes of the Andes about 115km from Cuzco along a very narrow, though well-maintained, one-way dirt road. There are fine views of the Andes and the high Amazon Basin beyond. On Monday, Wednesday, Friday and possibly

Sunday, the one-way road is used only for travel from Cuzco to Paucartambo; on Tuesday, Thursday and Saturday, it is used only for travel from Paucartambo to Cuzco. Trucks for Paucartambo leave Cuzco early in the morning from near the Urcos bus stop. The journey takes about six hours.

Paucartambo is particularly famous for its very authentic and colorful celebration of the Fiesta de la Virgen del Carmen, held annually on and around July 16, with traditional street dancing, processions and wonderful costumes. Relatively few tourists have seen this fiesta, simply because it's been difficult to reach and because, once you're there, you have to camp, find a room in one of two extremely basic small hotels or hope a local will give you floor space. Tourist agencies in Cuzco, realizing the potential of this fiesta as a tourist attraction, have started running buses specifically for the fiesta. If you go this way, the agency can help arrange a floor or bed to sleep on.

Some Inca ruins are within walking distance of Paucartambo – ask for directions in the village.

## TRES CRUCES

About 45km beyond Paucartambo is the famous jungle view at Tres Cruces, about 15km off the Paucartambo-Shintuya road. The sight of the mountains finally dropping away into the Amazon Basin is gorgeous and is made all the more exciting by the sunrise phenomenon that occurs around the time of the winter solstice on June 21. For some reason, the sunrise here tends to be optically distorted, causing double images, halos and unusual colors, particularly during May, June and July (other months are cloudy). At this time of year, various adventure tour agencies advertise sunrise-watching trips to Tres Cruces. You can also take the thrice-weekly truck service to Paucartambo and ask around for a truck going on to Tres Cruces. Señor Cáceres in Paucartambo will reportedly arrange sunrise-watching trips. Alternately, ask at the police checkpoint. One of the policemen has a truck and can take you for US$45 – split the cost with friends. Make sure you leave in the middle of the night to catch the dawn; there's no point in going otherwise.

## THE ROAD TO PUERTO MALDONADO

This road is almost 500km long and takes about 2½ days to travel in the dry season. A Peruvian road engineer told me that this was undoubtedly Peru's worst road between two major towns. Trucks leave daily from the Coliseo Cerrado or near the Plaza Túpac Amaru in Cuzco. Fares to Puerto Maldonado are about US$15; the cheapest places are in the back, and the more expensive ones are in the cab with the driver. The least comfortable but fastest trucks are the *cisternas* (gasoline trucks) – you have to sit on a narrow ledge on top. Most tourists travel on the daily flight from Cuzco to Puerto Maldonado, but the difficult, tiring trip by road is a good chance to see the scenery of the Andes' eastern slopes.

The road follows the route to Puno until it reaches Urcos, where the dirt road to Puerto Maldonado begins. (You could bus to Urcos and wait there for a truck.) About 125km and seven or eight hours from Cuzco, you come to the highland town of **Ocongate**, which has a couple of basic hotels, such as the *Pensión Josmar* on the plaza. From here, trucks go to the village of **Tinqui**, under an hour's drive beyond Ocongate. It's the starting point for a five- to seven-day hike encircling Ausangate – at 6384m, the highest mountain in southern Peru. There is a basic hotel, and the locals rent mules (about US$7 per day plus US$6 for an *arriero*, or muleteer) to do the trek (see Bradt's *Peru & Bolivia: Backpacking & Trekking*).

Ausangate is the site of the traditional festival of Q'oyoriti, which is held in early June. Thousands of local people converge on the mountain's icy slopes to celebrate the 'star of the snow' with a night trek to the top of a glacier. Tinqui is the gathering point for this. Outfitters in Cuzco have recently begun to arrange guided trips to this relatively little-known (outside of Peru) festival.

After Tinqui, the road begins to drop steadily. The next town of any size is Quince Mil, 240km from Cuzco and the halfway point. The area is a gold-mining center, and the hotel here is often full. You are now less than 1000m above sea level, but still in the Department of Cuzco.

After another 100km, the road into the jungle reaches the flatlands, where it levels out for the last 140km into Puerto Maldonado (see also the Amazon Basin chapter).

## QUILLABAMBA

Quillabamba lies on the Río Urubamba at the end of the Cuzco-Aguas Calientes-Quillabamba railway line, which was damaged by landslides in 1998 and now ends at Aguas Calientes. Access to Quillabamba is now by bus from Cuzco. There are no immediate plans to reopen the railway beyond Aguas Calientes.

At 1050m above sea level, Quillabamba is a hot and humid town of the high jungle. With about 16,000 inhabitants, it is quiet and pleasant (if not particularly interesting) and can be used as a base for trips deeper into the jungle.

The area is an important agricultural one, with cocoa, coffee, achiote (a dye), peppers, peanuts, tropical fruits and coca being grown for the Cuzco market. The coca farmers in this region have strong unions and work to prevent their crops from becoming involved in narco-traffic. Coca, chewed rather than destined for the production of cocaine, plays an important part of the socioeconomic structure of the highland inhabitants. Because the plant can be harvested every three or four months, it is an economically attractive alternative to annual plants.

Banco de Crédito and Banco Continental change money.

### Places to Stay

There are about a dozen hotels from which to choose; none are very expensive and

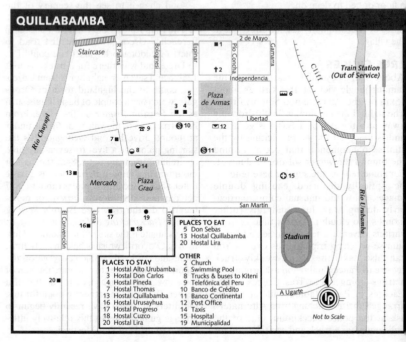

**QUILLABAMBA**

Staircase

Plaza de Armas

Plaza Grau

Mercado

Train Station (Out of Service)

Stadium

Río Chavapi

Río Urubamba

Cliff

A Ugarte

Not to Scale

**PLACES TO EAT**
5 Don Sebas
13 Hostal Quillabamba
20 Hostal Lira

**OTHER**
2 Church
6 Swimming Pool
8 Trucks & buses to Kiteni
9 Telefónica del Peru
10 Banco de Crédito
11 Banco Continental
12 Post Office
14 Taxis
15 Hospital
19 Municipalidad

**PLACES TO STAY**
1 Hostal Alto Urubamba
3 Hostal Don Carlos
4 Hostal Pineda
7 Hostal Thomas
13 Hostal Quillabamba
16 Hostal Ursayhua
17 Hostal Progreso
18 Hostal Cuzco
20 Hostal Lira

some are quite good. Basic places for about US$2.50 per person are the *Hostal Progreso* (no singles), *Hostal Thomas* and *Hostal Urusayhua* (☎ *28-1426, Lima 118*) – all with cold-water communal bathrooms only. *Hostal Pineda* (☎ *28-1447, Libertad 530*) charges US$4.50 per person in rooms with cold private bath.

Clean, cheap and recommended, *Hostal Alto Urubamba* (☎ *28-1131, 2 de Mayo 333*) charges US$6/8 for singles/doubles with shared bath, or US$10/12 with private bath. There are 50 rooms with shared bath, and only 18 with private. The similarly priced and pleasant *Hostal Cuzco* is also clean, but has an erratic water supply. Rooms have private bath and cold water.

*Hostal Quillabamba* (☎ *28-1369, fax 28-2196, Grau 590*) is recommended for clean rooms with private hot showers, a rooftop restaurant, a pool and a pleasant garden. Rates are US$15/22. The slightly cheaper *Hostal Lira* (☎ *28-1324, El Convención 200*) is also good, though its ground-floor restaurant is less attractive. *Hostal Don Carlos* (☎ *28-2564, 28-1371, fax 28-1150, Libertad 556*) is another good choice, at US$19/22 with private bath and hot water.

## Places to Eat
The rooftop restaurant at *Hostal Quillabamba* has good views and offers adequate meals, but the service is slow. *Hostal Lira* has a reasonable restaurant. A few *heladerías* on the Plaza de Armas serve ice-creams and light refreshments. *Don Sebas (Espinar 235)* has good sandwiches, and there are several other cheap places on or near the plaza.

## Getting There & Away
**Bus** Buses for Cuzco leave every day and night. A recommended company is Caruamayo (☎ *28-2497, 28-2324*). Bus stations have moved recently; you'll know where they are when you arrive from Cuzco. It's the only way to get there. The journey takes roughly seven hours and costs about US$5. This rough route – high over the spectacular pass of Abra de Malaga – is a favorite road

for ornithologists, who see many different species of birds as the ecological zones change from subtropical to subglacial. The Abra de Malaga area is also one of Peru's most important tea-producing regions.

Pickup trucks (there is also one bus) leave every morning from the market area for the village of Kiteni, farther into the jungle. The trip is variously reported to last 6 to 12 hours.

A correspondent suggests asking around the plaza for trucks to Huancacalle (a long, bumpy ride), from where you can proceed to Vilcabamba.

**Train** Service has been suspended since the 1998 floods destroyed the tracks.

## VILCABAMBA
Manco Inca and his followers retreated to this jungle site after being defeated by the Spaniards at Ollantaytambo in 1536. The Inca lived here until the Spaniards tracked him down and killed him in 1544. Vilcabamba (also called Espíritu Pampa) slowly fell into disrepair and was forgotten for centuries until it was rediscovered by the American explorer Gene Savoy during expeditions in the mid-1960s. The area, about 70km due west of Quillabamba, was off-limits because of terrorism and other problems in the 1980s, but is now again open to visitation. Although the ruins are of great importance, they have not been properly excavated and are still overgrown.

To get there, you have to walk for several days. The starting point is the village of **Huancacalle**, which can be reached by trucks from Quillabamba. In Huancacalle, there are basic places to stay in people's houses. The ruins of **Vitcos** are about an hour's walk away, and other ruins are nearby. Also in Huancacalle, you can hire mules, arrieros and guides to Vilcabamba. This hike takes several days, and small villages and ruins are passed along the way. It is rough going, with many steep ascents and descents before reaching Vilcabamba at about 1000m above sea level. (More details are found in Frost's *Exploring Cuzco* and Bradt's *Peru & Bolivia: Backpacking & Trekking*.)

While the Huancacalle route is the most direct one, adventurous travelers can find several other routes.

## KITENI & BEYOND

Kiteni is the end of the road as far as this section of the jungle is concerned. This small jungle town has one cheap, basic hotel.

It is possible to continue by river, but as food and accommodations are often nonexistent, you're advised to be self-sufficient. The first major landmark is the **Pongo de Manique**, a steep-walled canyon on the lower Río Urubamba. The canyon is dangerous, and in the rainy season (from December to April), the river runs high, and boat owners are reluctant to go through it (though some reportedly will). Boats as far as the pongo can occasionally be found, on inquiry, in Kiteni – it takes a day.

During the dry season, a few boats continue through the pongo; the river after the canyon is relatively calm, though there are still some rapids. There are few settlements until you reach the oil town of **Sepahua**, two to four days beyond the pongo. There are basic food and accommodations here, and the oil workers are often interested in a new face. From Sepahua, there are flights to Satipo with light aircraft and some flights to Lima for the oil workers. These are not cheap.

InkaNatura (see Organized Tours in the Getting Around chapter) opened a lodge in 1999 between the pongo and Sepahua. It's called the *Machiguenga Cultural Center and Lodge* and is on the lower Urubamba near the Río Timpia. Visits cost US$1175 per person for 4 days/3 nights and US$1325 for 5 days/4 nights, two people minimum, all inclusive, with round-trip charter flights from Cuzco to Timpia. Included is a run through the pongo (river conditions permitting), a visit to the Sabeti clay lick (one of the few licks where all three large macaws can be seen together), visits with local Indians who demonstrate crafts and lifestyle (but not in their homes – Timpia village itself is off-limits, although villagers do own 1/3 of the lodge). Excursions can also be made in season to see military macaws up in the forest hills.

Sometimes, it is possible to continue down the Urubamba to the village of **Atalaya**, two or three days away. A member of the South American Explorers says that the trip to Atalaya is difficult on public transport because there are few boats between the pongo and Sepahua. Instead, you could build (or have someone else build) a balsa raft after passing the pongo (which is too dangerous to raft). En route are the communities of San Iratio (the last place before the pongo), Timpia (where you can have a raft built), Choquorian, Camisea, Liringeti, Miaria, Sepahua, Boteo Pose, Sepal and Puerto Inca. Basic food and accommodations can be obtained from friendly locals in these villages. In return, they often prefer useful gifts to money – flashlights and batteries, fish hooks and lines or basic medicines are good. In Atalaya, there are simple hotels (the *Hostal Dennis* on the main square is about US$7 for a double with a cold but clean shower) and an airstrip with light-aircraft connections to Satipo (see the Amazon Basin chapter). Boats can be found to continue down the river, now the Ucayali, as far as Pucallpa (about one week). The route from Kiteni onward is obviously little traveled and adventurous, especially beyond the Pongo de Manique, but it is possible for experienced and self-sufficient travelers.

The Cabeceras Aid Project – a nonprofit that provides humanitarian aid to the indigenous peoples of the Amazon Basin – knows about this area. You can find out more on their website at www.onr.com/cabeceras.

# West of Cuzco

It is now possible to travel by bus from Cuzco to Lima via Limatambo, Abancay, Chalhuanca, Puquio, Pampas Galeras and Nazca – a remote and spectacular route. From the late 1980s until the late 1990s, guerilla activity and banditry closed this route, but it is now open again, though most buses from Cuzco to Lima still go via Arequipa. This route is slowly being paved; the section just beyond Mollepata is now paved.

Going west through Abancay, Andahuaylas and on to Ayacucho (see the Central Highlands chapter) is a tough ride on a rough road, but is otherwise not dangerous and is often used by independent travelers.

## LIMATAMBO

This infrequently visited village is 80km west of Cuzco by road. Most people just pass through Limatambo on the bus, which is a shame, because it's worth a stop.

The village is named after the small, well-made Inca ruin of Rimactambo, or 'speaker's inn.' The site, better known as Tarahuasi after the hacienda on the grounds, is 2km from Limatambo on the road toward Cuzco. It is better constructed than many other *tambos*, because it was probably used as a ceremonial center, as well as a resting place for the Inca *chasquis*, (runners who carried messages from one part of the empire to another). For those interested in ruins, the exceptional polygonal retaining wall, with its 12 man-sized niches is in itself worth the trip.

There's a basic hostel, as well as a swimming pool that is popular with the locals. The village is in pretty, mountainous countryside at the upper end of the valley of a headwater tributary of the Río Apurímac and is a weekend retreat for Cuzco citizens.

You can reach Limatambo from Cuzco on the Abancay bus or on the truck to Mollepata. If you leave early in the morning, you can visit the ruins here and return to Cuzco on an afternoon bus, making a good day trip.

## MOLLEPATA

The old village of Mollepata is a few kilometers off the main Cuzco-Abancay road and a couple of hours beyond Limatambo. It is the starting point for a longer and more spectacular approach to the Inca Trail, with high passes on the flanks of Salcantay. Directions are given in Bradt's *Peru & Bolivia: Backpacking & Trekking*. Allow about four days to Huayllabamba on the Inca Trail. Mules are not allowed on the Inca Trail, so after Huayllabamba, you'll have to carry your own gear or hire porters (which you can do in Huayllabamba).

Getting to Mollepata is straightforward, if not particularly comfortable. Trucks leave Cuzco from the end of Calle Arcopata early every morning, usually about 7 am. The scenic drive takes three to four hours. Alternatively, take a quicker bus heading to Abancay. Sit on the right if the weather is clear for views of the Salcantay snowcaps. Although you can buy basic supplies in Mollepata, it's best to bring everything from Cuzco. There is no hotel; you can camp if you ask around, but don't leave belongings unattended. If you plan to carry your own gear and dispense with mule drivers and guides, there's no need to stay.

## ABANCAY
☎ 084

This sleepy rural town is the capital of the Andean Department of Apurímac, one of the least-explored departments in the Peruvian Andes. It is a five-hour drive west of Cuzco (in the dry season) and 2377m above sea level. The population is about 95,000, although it doesn't look that big! Despite its status as a departmental capital, Abancay has no scheduled air service, and the place has a forlorn, forgotten air. Travelers use it as a resting place on the long, tiring bus journey between Cuzco and Ayacucho.

The Banco de Crédito changes money.

### Things to See

Abancay is not totally devoid of interest. Its particularly colorful Carnival, held in the week before Lent, is a chance to see Andean festival celebrations uncluttered by the trappings of international tourism and includes a nationally acclaimed folk-dancing competition. Hotels tend to fill early then, so arrive a few days before the carnival gets under way, or make reservations if you can. Another festival is held on November 3, Abancay Day.

Those with an interest in Inca ruins may want to visit the Hacienda of Saihuite, 45km from Abancay on the main road toward Cuzco, near the turnoff to Huanipaca and Cachora. Here, you'll find several large,

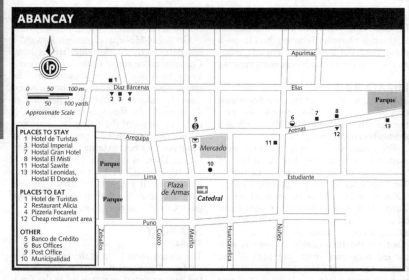

## ABANCAY

*0　50　100 m.*
*0　50　100 yards*
*Approximate Scale*

**PLACES TO STAY**
1　Hotel de Turistas
3　Hostal Imperial
7　Hostal Gran Hotel
8　Hostal El Misti
11　Hostal Sawite
13　Hostal Leonidas,
　　Hostal El Dorado

**PLACES TO EAT**
1　Hotel de Turistas
2　Restaurant Alicia
4　Pizzería Focarela
12　Cheap restaurant area

**OTHER**
5　Banco de Crédito
6　Bus Offices
9　Post Office
10　Municipalidad

*Map labels: Apurimac, Elías, Parque, Díaz Bárcenas, Arenas, Arequipa, Mercado, Lima, Estudiante, Plaza de Armas, Catedral, Puno, Zeballos, Cuzco, Mariño, Huancavelica, Nuñez*

---

carved boulders – the Stones of Saihuite. These intricately decorated stones are similar to the more commonly visited carved rock at Qenko, near Cuzco, but are considered more elaborate.

During the dry season (late May to September), walkers and climbers may want to take advantage of the best weather to head for the sometimes snowcapped peak of Ampay (5228m), about 10km north-northwest of the town. For the rest of the year, the weather tends to be wet, especially during the first four months of the year. The mountain is the center of the 3635 hectare **Santuario Nacional Ampay** – I have read one report that camping and highland birding are good.

### Places to Stay & Eat

Most hotels are poor. The cheapest is the pretty grim *Hostal El Misti*, which charges just over US$2 per person. *Hostal Sawite* (☎ 32-1692, Nuñez 208) charges US$3.50 per person in OK rooms with communal showers and hot water from 6 to 10 am and 1 to 4 pm (subject to change). The noisy *Hostal Gran Hotel* (☎ 32-1144, Arenas 196) charges US$5/6 singles/doubles in rooms with private bath and electric shower.

*Hostal Leonidas* (☎ 32-1199, Arenas 131) is better and has clean rooms with private electric showers for US$7/10 or with shared showers for a little less. Next door, *Hostal El Dorado* (☎ 32-2005) charges about the same and has TV in some rooms.

The new *Hostal Imperial* (☎ 32-1578, Díaz Bárcenas 517) has an unprepossessing entrance but opens up with a parking area and good rooms with 24-hour hot water for about US$13/17 singles/doubles. Opposite, the best hotel in town is *Hotel de Turistas* (☎/fax 32-1017, 32-1628, Díaz Bárcenas 500), in a pleasant, old-fashioned country mansion. Singles/doubles with shared bath cost US$21/33 with bath, cable TV and telephone. There is a restaurant and bar.

The best place to eat may be the restaurant in the Hotel de Turistas. Across the street, there's *Pizzería Focarela* and *Restaurant Alicia* for Peruvian food. Otherwise, you'll find plenty of cheap cafés near the bus stations.

### Getting There & Away

All the bus companies leave from Arenas near Nuñez. Don't ask me why, but all the companies leaving for Cuzco (5 hours) or

Andahuaylas (5 hours) depart at the same times: 6 am and 1 pm in either direction, though an 8 pm bus to Andahuaylas has been added. Fares are about US$4 to either town, and journeys take longer in the wet season. There are no direct buses to Ayacucho, so you change in Andahuaylas. Most companies use small and have rather uncomfortable minibuses. Ask around about minibuses that can drop you in Sahuite.

## ANDAHUAYLAS
☎ 084

Andahuaylas, the second most important town in the Department of Apurímac, is 135km west of Abancay on the way to Ayacucho. It is about halfway between Cuzco and Ayacucho, and is a convenient spot to rest a night if traveling on this very rough but scenic route. When taking buses from Cuzco, don't confuse it with Andahuaylillas, which is in the opposite direction.

There are some 26,000 inhabitants, many of whom speak Quechua as their first language and Spanish as their second. This is a very rural part of Peru and one of the poorest. Only parts of the town center have electricity. The elevation here is 2980m.

### Information
There is no tourism office. The Banco de Crédito changes dollars. The post and telephone offices are shown on the map. Internet services are offered at Bolívar 133 and on R Castillo at JA Trelles.

### Things to See & Do
The colonial **Catedral** on the Plaza de Armas is much more sober than its counterparts in most Peruvian cities.

Andahuaylas' main attraction, the beautiful **Laguna de Pacucha**, is 17km from town and accessible by bus or car. Meals, fishing and rowboat rental are available. A one-hour hike from the lake brings you to the ruins of **Sondor** of the Chanka culture, traditional enemies of the Incas. The site is accessible by car. The ruins are not much restored, but there are good mountain views. Taxis and hotels can arrange transportation.

The annual fiesta is June 28, when there are authentic traditional dances and music performed for the locals. Tourism has not made it to Andahuaylas. In the nearby village of Pacucha (near the lake), the annual fiesta includes lashing a condor to the back of a bull and allowing the two to fight. The condor represents the Indians, and the bull represents the Spanish conquistadors. This event is called the *Fiesta de Yahuar*, or 'blood feast.'

Both Andahuaylas and Pacucha have a Sunday market.

### Places to Stay
**Budget** One of the cheapest places is the adequate *Hostal Cusco* (☎ 72-2148, Casafranca 520), which has occasional hot water during the day, but no water at night. Rates are US$3/5 or US$5/7.50 for singles/doubles with bath. *Hostal Los Libertadores Wari* (☎ 72-1434, JF Ramos 424) is clean and safe and has hot water, but closes its doors at 11 pm. Rates are US$4.50/7 with shared baths and US$6/8 with private baths. The satisfactory *Hostal Las Americas* (☎ 71-1646, JF Ramos 410) charges US$6/8.50 for singles/doubles with bath and hot water in the morning (at other times on request, they say). *Hostal Delicias* (☎ 72-1104, JF Ramos 525) charges the same for clean rooms with private hot baths.

Other budget hotels include *Hotel Los Celajes* (☎ 72-1191, JA Trelles 217) and the basic *Hostal Waliman* (Andahuaylas 266).

**Mid-Range** The *Hotel Turístico Andahuaylas* (☎ 72-1229, 72-1761, Lázaro Carrillo 620) is in an ill-lit neighborhood but provides a parking area. Rates are about US$13/18 in modern, if worn, rooms. The best in town is the modern *El Encanto de Oro Hotel* (☎/fax 72-3066, Casafranca 424), which has rooms with private hot showers, TV and telephone for US$17/24. They have a coffee shop and parking.

### Places to Eat
*Club Social* on the Plaza de Armas serves popular local lunches. *Diego's* (☎ 72-2608, Ramon Castilla 362) serves snacks,

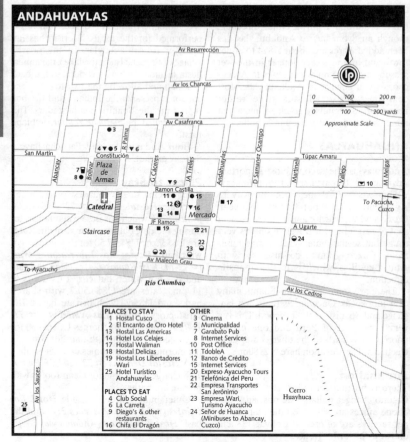

**ANDAHUAYLAS**

Av Resurrección

Av los Chancas

Av Casafranca

San Martín

Constitución

Plaza de Armas

Catedral

Staircase

Ramon Castilla

Mercado

JF Ramos

Av Malecón Grau

Río Chumbao

Av los Cedros

To Ayacucho

To Pacucha, Cuzco

Cerro Huayhuca

Av los Sauces

0    100    200 m
0    100    200 yards
Approximate Scale

**PLACES TO STAY**
1  Hostal Cusco
2  El Encanto de Oro Hotel
13  Hostal Las Americas
14  Hotel Los Celajes
17  Hostal Waliman
18  Hostal Delicias
19  Hostal Los Libertadores Wari
25  Hotel Turístico Andahuaylas

**PLACES TO EAT**
4  Club Social
6  La Carreta
9  Diego's & other restaurants
16  Chifa El Dragón

**OTHER**
3  Cinema
5  Municipalidad
7  Garabato Pub
8  Internet Services
10  Post Office
11  TdobleA
12  Banco de Crédito
15  Internet Services
20  Expreso Ayacucho Tours
21  Telefónica del Peru
22  Empresa Transportes San Jerónimo
23  Empresa Wari, Turismo Ayacucho
24  Señor de Huanca (Minibuses to Abancay, Cuzco)

sandwiches and light meals. There are several other restaurants along this street as well, although none of them are outstanding. *Chifa El Dragón* (☎ 72-1641) is just OK for basic Peruvian-Chinese meals. The 'best' in town is *La Carreta* (☎ 72-2497) on the Plaza de Armas.

A popular place for a drink is *Garabato Pub*. It has a very small sign on the Plaza de Armas, and it is open only in the evening. Some visitors may be disenchanted by the dozens of animal skins (mainly Andean mammals) hanging on the walls.

### Getting There & Away

**Air** The regional airport is about a 20-minute drive south of town and is reached by colectivo buses at US$1 per person (ask at the TdobleA office). Taxis are available for about US$3. TdobleA (☎ 72-1221, Ramon Castilla 429) has Lima flights almost daily.

Flights may be available from Cuzco, sometimes with little-known or upstart airlines. Readers reported in August 1999 that they flew from Cuzco to Andahuaylas for US$15 with Santander Air – an airline that almost every agency in Cuzco had never heard of!

**Bus** Señor de Huanca (☎ 72-1218) has uncomfortable minibuses that go to Abancay (US$4, 5 hours) at 6 am, 1 and 8 pm. The 6 am departure continues onward to Cuzco (US$7, 10 hours). Empresa Transportes San Jeronimo (☎ 72-1400, Andahuaylas 121) has 6 am and 7 pm buses to Cuzco that go through Abancay.

Expreso Ayacucho Tours has minibuses to Ayacucho (US$6, 10 hours) at 6 am and 6 pm. Turismo Ayacucho has a noon bus to Ayacucho that continues to Lima (US$15, 21 hours). The road to Ayacucho goes over very high puna, may be snow-covered and is very cold at night. Make sure to bring adequate clothing or a sleeping bag. Empresa Wari has buses to Lima that go through Nazca.

## CHALHUANCA
Chalhuanca has the basic *Hostal Zegara* and a restaurant, which is often used as a meal stop on the Andahuaylas-Nazca run. It is 120km southwest of Abancay.

## PUQUIO & PAMPAS GALERAS
This village, 189km beyond Chalhuanca, has the basic *Hostal Los Andes* (☎ 45-2103) and simple restaurants. For the last 50km before Puquio, the road traverses an incredibly wild-looking area of desolate, lake-studded countryside that is worth staying awake for.

About 65km beyond Puquio and 90km before Nazca, the road passes through the vicuña sanctuary of Pampas Galeras. Most people visit Reserva Nacional Pampas Galeras from Nazca.

# The Central Highlands

The central Peruvian Andes is one of the least visited and most neglected areas of Peru. The harsh mountain terrain has made ground communications especially difficult, and the region also suffers from a lack of air services. Huancayo, for example, is both the capital of the Department of Junín and Peru's fifth-largest city, yet it lacks a commercial airport. Two of the area's other departmental capitals, Huancavelica and Cerro de Pasco, also lack a commercial airport. The departmental capital of Ayacucho, founded in 1540, received its first permanent public-telephone link with the outside world in 1964, at a time when there were still only a few dozen vehicles servicing the city. These remote cities of the central Andes are surrounded by a rural population that is involved in subsistence agriculture; it is among the poorest in Peru.

It was in this environment of isolation and poverty that the terrorist organization, Sendero Luminoso (Shining Path), emerged in the 1960s and grew in the 1970s. The violent activities of the Sendero escalated dramatically in the 1980s, and headlines all over the world proclaimed Peru's internal unrest. By 1985, however, things had quieted down considerably, and tourists once again returned to these areas, albeit very slowly. Unfortunately, this situation did not last, and in the late 1980s, much of the area was again under Sendero control. Finally, in 1992, Abimael Guzmán, a former professor of philosophy at the university in Ayacucho and the founder/leader of the Sendero, was captured and sentenced to life imprisonment. Soon afterward, several of his top lieutenants were also captured, and the Sendero lost the control it once had over most of central Peru. Places covered in this chapter have been safe to visit since then.

This region has several delightful, friendly colonial towns that are among the least spoiled in the entire Andean chain. The travel itself is exciting too, not only because of the magnificent mountain views, but also because it involves a certain amount of effort. The region still has more communications problems than many other areas of Peru. Traversing the 'bad' roads is a minor challenge, but the rewards of getting off the 'gringo trail' make the hard traveling conditions worthwhile. If you want to travel to a lesser-known part of Peru, read on.

## SAN PEDRO DE CASTA & MARCAHUASI
☎ 064

San Pedro de Casta is a small village at 3180m above sea level and only 40km from Chosica (80km from Lima). About 3km from San Pedro, on foot, is Marcahuasi, a 4-sq-km plateau at 4100m. Marcahuasi is famed for it's weirdly eroded rocks shaped into animals such as camels, turtles and seals. These have a mystical significance for some people, who claim they are signs of a pre-Inca culture or energy vortices. Locals have fiestas here periodically, but usually it's empty.

Because of the altitude, it's not advisable to go there from Lima in one day; acclimatize for at least a night in San Pedro. It takes three hours to hike up to the site. The Trekking and Backpacking Club (see Information in the Lima chapter) has route information and maps and can provide guides if requested. A Centro de Información on the Plaza de Armas in San Pedro also has some information and charges a small fee.

### Places to Stay & Eat
You can camp at Marcahuasi, but carry water, as the water of few lakes there isn't fit to drink. In San Pedro, there are four basic accommodations (with cold-water baths) on or near the plaza. There are a couple of simple restaurants.

### Getting There & Away
Take a bus from Lima to Chosica. Then ask for Transportes Municipal San Pedro, which leaves, usually in the mornings, from Parque Echenique in Chosica.

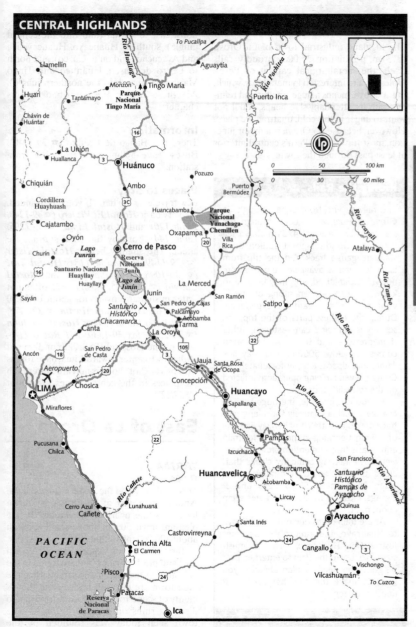

CENTRAL HIGHLANDS

## LA OROYA
☎ 064

The highland industrial town of La Oroya (3731m, population 35,000) proudly calls itself 'the metallurgical capital of Peru.' Unless you're interested in metallurgy, which, in La Oroya, means a huge smelter and refinery with its attendant slag heaps, you'll not want to linger in this cold, unattractive place. However, because La Oroya is a major junction, most travelers to Peru's central interior at least pass through the town.

> ### Riding the Rails
>
> The railway line from Lima through La Oroya to Huancayo passes through the station of La Galera at 4781m above sea level, the world's highest station on a standard-gauge track. On the trip from Lima, oxygen is available, and if you're not yet acclimatized, you may be glad to know it's there – even sitting quietly in your seat is a breathless experience. During the highest parts of the trip, the scenery is stark and bare – striking rather than pretty – and the snow line often comes to below 5000m. You may see llamas and alpacas and, unfortunately, La Oroya's several mining operations inflicted on the splendid landscape.
>
> As you can imagine, the huge vertical change in such a relatively short length of track makes this stretch of railway line one of the most exciting in the world for train enthusiasts (not to mention ordinary travelers). The railway company claims that, along its whole length, the railway traverses 66 tunnels, 58 bridges and 9 zigzags. I lost count, but the figures seem about right.
>
> As the train drops down from La Oroya to Huancayo, the atmosphere becomes festive. Near Huancayo, a band of musicians may board the train to entertain passengers. You need to plan ahead if you want to make this trip, however, as it doesn't run regularly.

From La Oroya, roads lead in all directions: east to Tarma (and into the central jungle); south to Huancayo, Huancavelica and Ayacucho (and on to Cuzco); and north to Cerro de Pasco, Huánuco and Tingo María (and then into the northern jungle). All these towns are described in this chapter.

### Information

There is a Banco de Crédito (☎ 39-1040). Buses leave 500m away from the train station.

### Places to Stay

Few travelers stop here. If you are stranded, the very basic *Hostal El Viajero* (☎ 39-1243, Lima 120) and *Hostal Lima* (☎ 39-1295, Lima 144), both by the train station, are cheap. The slightly better *Hostal Mister* (☎ 39-1149, Arequipa 113), *Hostal Inti* (☎ 39-1098, Arequipa 117) and *Hostal Chavín* (☎ 39-1185, Tarma 281) offer hot water in shared showers for about US$3.50 per person. *Hostal San Martín* (☎ 39-1278, 39-1963, RH Rubio 134) or *Hostal San Juan* (☎ 39-2566, fax 39-1539, RH Rubio 114), both by the Hospital IPSS, 2km or 3km out of the town center toward Lima, have rooms with private hot showers and are better than the places in the center. Rates are about US$7/12.

# East of La Oroya

## TARMA
☎ 064

This small town on the eastern slopes of the Andes, 60km east of La Oroya, is known locally as 'the pearl of the Andes.' It is a pleasant town, 3050m above sea level, with about 120,000 inhabitants.

Tarma has a long history. The overgrown Inca and pre-Inca ruins that are found in the hills and on the mountains surrounding the little town are not well known, and there's plenty of scope for adventurous travelers to discover ruins on the nearby peaks. The town seen today was founded by the

Spanish soon after the conquest (the exact date is uncertain). Nothing remains of the early colonial era but there are quite a number of attractive 19th- and early 20th-century houses that have white walls and red-tiled roofs.

## Information

The tourist office (☎ 32-1010 ext.20, fax 32-1374, mtarma@mail.laserperu.com.pe) is on the Plaza de Armas. Here, Professor Julian Loja Alania and Luis Orihuela are helpful, have leaflets (in Spanish) describing local villages and attractions, and can recommend knowledgeable guides to show you the ruins in the area.

The Banco de Crédito changes money and has an ATM. The post office and telephone company are shown on the map. Internet access is at the Colegio Santa Rosa (Amazonas 892) and is available from 4 to 8 pm daily.

## Things to See & Do

Tarma is high in the mountains, and the clear nights of June, July and August provide some good opportunities for stargazing. There is a small **astronomical observatory** run by the owners of Hostal Central (see Places to Stay later in this chapter). The owners are usually away in Lima, but public use is permitted 8 to 10 pm every Friday. Admission is US$0.30.

The **cathedral** is modern (built in 1965) and is of interest because it contains the remains of Peruvian president Manuel A Odría. He was born in Tarma and organized the construction of the cathedral during his presidency. The clock in the tower dates to 1862.

Several nearby excursions, described later in the Tarma section, include visits to the religious shrine of Señor de Muruhuay in Acobamba (9km from Tarma), the Gruta de Guagapo (33km) (see the boxed text 'The Gruta's Bottomless Depths'), and the weaving village of San Pedro de Cajas (50km).

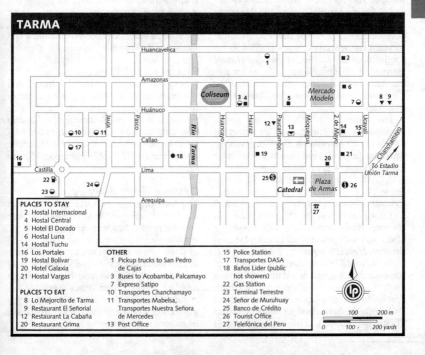

**TARMA**

PLACES TO STAY
2 Hostal Internacional
4 Hostal Central
5 Hotel El Dorado
6 Hostal Luna
14 Hostal Tuchu
16 Los Portales
19 Hostal Bolívar
20 Hotel Galaxia
21 Hostal Vargas

PLACES TO EAT
8 Lo Mejorcito de Tarma
9 Restaurant El Señorial
12 Restaurant La Cabaña
20 Restaurant Grima

OTHER
1 Pickup trucks to San Pedro de Cajas
3 Buses to Acobamba, Palcamayo
7 Expreso Satipo
10 Transportes Chanchamayo
11 Transportes Mabelsa, Transportes Nuestra Señora de Mercedes
13 Post Office
15 Police Station
17 Transportes DASA
18 Baños Lider (public hot showers)
22 Gas Station
23 Terminal Terrestre
24 Señor de Muruhuay
25 Banco de Crédito
26 Tourist Office
27 Telefónica del Peru

0    100    200 m
0    100    200 yards

## Special Events
The big annual attraction is undoubtedly Easter. Many processions are held during Semana Santa (Holy Week), including several by candlelight after dark. They culminate on the morning of Easter Sunday with a marvelous procession to the cathedral along an 11-block route entirely carpeted with flower petals. This attracts thousands of Peruvian visitors, and the hotels are usually full, with prices increasing by up to 50%.

The annual fiesta of El Señor de los Milagros, or 'the Lord of the Miracles,' takes place in late October; the main feast days are 18, 28 and 29. (No, I don't know why there's a 10-day gap.) This is another good opportunity to see processions over beautiful flower-petal carpets.

Other fiestas include Tarma Tourism Week near the end of July.

## Places to Stay
**Budget** The very basic **Hostal Luna** (☎ 32-1589, Amazonas 393), near the Mercado Modelo, has a sign for *agua caliente*, but doesn't have any. Room decor can include recycled car seats. It charges US$3/4.50 for singles/doubles. A better bet is **Hostal Bolívar** (☎ 32-1060, Huaraz 389), which also has shared cold showers but is a bit brighter. There are hot public showers at **Baños Lider** (see map).

The following hotels have hot water, usually in the morning, though they claim all day. **Hotel El Dorado** (☎ 32-1598, Huánuco 488) can be noisy, but is otherwise quite good; rooms with private hot bath are US$5.70/8.40, or a little less with cold shared showers. The old but adequate **Hostal Central** (Huánuco 614) has the observatory mentioned earlier in the Things to See & Do section. Basic rooms are US$4.50/6, or US$7.50/9 with private half-bath and shared showers. **Hostal Vargas** (☎ 32-1460, 32-1721, 2 de Mayo 627) has spacious rooms and some hard beds if you're fed up with sagging mattresses. Rooms with private hot bath cost US$6/10.50, or less with shared bath.

Among the better budget hotels is **Hostal Tuchu** (☎ 32-3483, 2 de Mayo 561), at US$9/10.50 with private bath. The clean **Hotel Galaxia** (☎ 32-1449, Lima 262), on the Plaza de Armas, has only 16 rooms, so it's often full. Rooms are US$10.50/15.50 with private bath. **Hostal Internacional** (☎ 32-1830, 2 de Mayo 307) is also quite good at US$12/16.50 with private bath and a color TV.

**Mid-Range** The town's best accommodations are at **Los Portales** (☎ 32-1411, fax 32-1410, Castilla 512). Set in pleasant gardens at the west end of town, the hotel charges US$44/55 including continental breakfast. The hotel, however, is usually half empty, and if you just show up, you'll get much better rates. Another option is **La Florida** (in Lima ☎ 424-6969, kreida@peru.itt.com.pe), 6k from Tarma. Owned by Peruvian/German couple Pepe and Inga Da'Fieno, this 18th-century hacienda is now a bed and breakfast charging US$18 to US$25 per person in rooms with up to four beds and a private hot bath. Secure camping on the grounds, with bathrooms, is US$3 per person. From here, it's about a one-hour hike to Acobamba and the Señor de Muruhuay sanctuary.

## Places to Eat
Plenty of cheap restaurants line Lima (which becomes Castilla in the west end of town). **Restaurant Grima**, on the Plaza de Armas, is good, and **Restaurant La Cabaña** is acceptable and cheap. **Restaurant Señorial** (☎ 32-3334, Huánuco 138) and **Lo Mejorcito de Tarma** (☎ 32-1766, Huánuco 190) are probably the best in town.

## Getting There & Away
The following are the three areas of town from which transport leaves frequently: near the Mercado Modelo, across from the Estadio Unión Tarma and at the western end of town (see map). On market days (Thursday and Sunday), service is disrupted around the Mercado Modelo, and bus companies near here leave from other streets – ask around. The Terminal Terrestre behind the gas station is new, and more buses may leave from here in the future.

For Chanchamayo (US$2), the area in the central Amazon Basin that includes La Merced and San Ramón (see the Amazon Basin chapter), Empresa de Transportes San Juan (☎ 32-3139), in front of the Estadio Unión Tarma, has buses every hour or two. Some buses continue to Villa Rica or Oxapampa. Transportes Chanchamayo (☎ 32-1882, Callao 1002) has about three buses a day. Comité 20 colectivo taxis leave from the market when they're full and charge US$3.20 per passenger for the precipitous descent to La Merced at about 600m. It's worth doing the trip just for the views.

San Juan and Señor de Muruhuay (☎ 32-0628, Jauja 524) have buses almost hourly to Huancayo (US$2.10). During the rainy season, the route is usually through La Oroya, but in the dry season, they may take a more direct, secondary road through Lomo Largo. This scenic route goes over high puna, where you might glimpse vicuñas.

The bus companies that go to Lima (US$3 to US$6, 6 hours) are listed here in ascending order of price: Transportes DASA (☎ 32-1843, Callao 1012), Expreso Satipo (☎ 32-1065, 32-1005, Ucayali 384), Transportes Mabelsa (☎ 32-3847, Callao 990), Transportes Nuestra Señora de Mercedes (☎ 32-2937, Callao 960) and Transportes Chanchamayo. In Lima, the aforementioned companies have terminals in La Victoria district, which is not the safest area.

Most buses coming or going almost anywhere will stop by the gas station on Castilla. If you want to act like an experienced Peruvian traveler, wait here and hop on the next bus heading to your destination. I hope they have a seat for you!

## Getting Around

Several companies provide service to the nearby towns. Empresa Señor de Muruhuay has frequent buses to Acobamba (US$0.30) and the religious sanctuary there. A bus stop next to Empresa de Transportes San Juan (near the Estadio Unión Tarma) has minibuses going to Acobamba and Palcamayo. Pickup trucks to San Pedro de Cajas leave from Huancavelica near Paucartambo,

usually around noon. Several small companies have buses by the coliseum that go to local villages.

## ACOBAMBA
☎ 064

The village of Acobamba, 10km from Tarma, is famous for the religious sanctuary of **El Señor de Muruhuay**, which is visible on a small hill about 1.5km away.

The sanctuary is built around a rock etching of Christ crucified. Historians claim that it was carved with a sword by a royalist

### The Gruta's Bottomless Depths

About 1500m into the Gruta de Guagapo is an underwater section, first reached in 1972 by an expedition from Imperial College, London. The underwater section was named 'The Siphon,' and a French expedition got through it in 1976. Peruvian teams led by Carlos Morales Bermúdez reached 2000m and 2400m into the cave during two 1988 expeditions. In 1994, Carlos Morales Bermúdez and local Ramiro Castro Barga, accompanied by US and German cavers, reached 2745m into the cave. No one knows how much further it goes.

To get to the cave, ask in Palcamayo. You'll be shown a dirt road winding off into the hills – it's a pleasant 4km walk. The cave is accessed through a large opening in the side of the mountain to the right of the road; Señor Castro's house is on the left. Bottled drinks are available, and prospective expeditions can camp.

The Palcamayo area is also known for the many little-explored Inca and pre-Inca ruins in the surrounding hills. Although they are not very interesting to the casual tourist, an adventurer equipped with camping gear could spend days wandering the hilltops looking for ruins. Luis Orihuela and Julian Loja Alania (see Information for Tarma earlier in this chapter) know many of these places.

CENTRAL HIGHLANDS

officer who was one of the few survivors after losing the Battle of Junín (a major battle of independence fought on August 6, 1824). Despite this, legends relating to the image's miraculous appearance persist. The first building erected around the image was a roughly thatched hut. It was replaced in 1835 by a small chapel. The present sanctuary (the third) was inaugurated on April 30, 1972. It is a very modern building with an electronically controlled bell tower (the bells came from Germany) and is decorated with huge weavings from San Pedro de Cajas.

The colorful feast of El Señor de Muruhuay, held throughout May, has been celebrated annually since 1835. Apart from the religious services and processions, there are ample opportunities to sample local produce and to see people dressed in traditional clothes. There are dances, fireworks and even a few gringos. Stalls sell *chicha* (corn beer) and *cuy* (roast guinea pig), but be wary unless your stomach is used to local food. *Hostal Sumac (☎ 34-1109)* is the only place to stay that has hot water; it charges US$9 per person. Visitors usually stay in nearby Tarma.

## PALCAMAYO
☎ 064

This attractive village is 28km from Tarma and is serviced by several colectivo taxis a day. From Palcamayo, you can visit the Gruta de Guagapo, a huge limestone cave in the hills about 4km away. The cave has been the subject of various expeditions from all over the world. It is one of Peru's largest and best-known caves and is officially protected as a National Speleological Area. Several other, lesser-known caves in the area would also be of interest to speleologists (those who study caves).

A descent into the **Gruta de Guagapo** requires caving equipment and experience (see the boxed text 'The Gruta's Bottomless Depths'). It contains waterfalls, squeezes and underwater sections (scuba equipment required), and although it is possible to enter the cave for a short distance, you soon need technical gear. A local guide, Señor Modesto Castro, has explored the cave on numerous

occasions and can provide you with ropes, lanterns and so on to enter the first sections. He lives in one of the two houses below the mouth of the cave and has a collection of photographs and newspaper clippings describing the exploration of the cave. He doesn't do much caving himself any more, but his son, Ramiro, can be of assistance.

## SAN PEDRO DE CAJAS
☎ 064

The village of San Pedro de Cajas, high in the Andes at an altitude of 4040m, is known throughout Peru for the excellence of its unique and often exported tapestries. Made of stuffed rolls of wool (difficult to visualize until you actually see one), the tapestries can be bought from the weavers for less than you'd pay in Lima. However, as the village is not oriented toward tourists, facilities are very limited, and you'll need some elementary Spanish to communicate.

A bed at the basic hotel run by the *Oscanoa family* will cost under US$3.50. Not surprisingly, there are no hot showers, but the people are friendly. You can eat at the basic restaurant or arrange simple meals at the hotel. Some weavings are available here; ask around if you want to see more. The village has no moneychanging facilities, so change as much money as you'll need before you get there.

### Getting There & Away

Catching a bus from Tarma to Palcamayo is easy enough, but buses continuing on to San Pedro de Cajas are infrequent. You can walk along the 16km dirt road from Palcamayo, past the Gruta de Guagapo, to San Pedro de Cajas. Pickup trucks from Tarma pass by in the early to mid-afternoon, and there are occasional minibuses and other vehicles, so you probably will get a ride along the way. The road climbs most of the way to San Pedro de Cajas, which is about 800m higher than Palcamayo.

Instead of returning to Tarma the way you came, you might walk beyond San Pedro for about 7km or so and come to the main La Oroya-Cerro de Pasco highway. Flag down a bus here.

# South of La Oroya

## JAUJA
☎ 064

The main road to Huancayo heads southeast from La Oroya along the central Andes, passing several towns of note along the way. The first is Jauja, a historic town about 80km southeast of La Oroya, 60km south of Tarma and 40km north of Huancayo.

Before the Incas, this area was the home of an important Huanca Indian community, and **Huanca ruins** can be seen on a hill about 3km southeast of town. An adventurous walk will get you there. Jauja was Pizarro's first capital in Peru, though this honor was short lived. Some finely carved wooden altars in the main church are all that remain of the early colonial days.

About 4km from Jauja is **Laguna de Paca**, a small resort offering a few hotels, restaurants, rowing boats and fishing. A boat ride around the lake will cost about US$8, which can be split between several people. There are ducks and gulls to look at, and you can stop at the **Isla del Amor** – a tiny artificial island not much bigger than the boat you're on.

There is a colorful **market** every Wednesday morning.

### Places to Stay & Eat

Many visitors stay in Huancayo and travel to Jauja on one of the frequent buses. If you choose to stay in Jauja, try the simple *Hotel Ganso de Oro* (☎ 36-2165, R Palma 217), two blocks from the train station. Rooms cost about US$4/6 for singles/doubles with bath, and hot water is sometimes available. *Hotel Santa Rosa* (☎ 36-2225), on the corner of the main plaza, has hot water and charges US$5 per person with shared showers or US$7 per person with bath. The best is reputedly *Cabezon's* (☎ 36-2206, Ayacucho 1025), at US$5 per person with private hot bath.

Out by the lake are several simple hotels such as *El Muelle Azul* (☎ 36-1120). A row of lakeshore restaurants attempt to entice diners with loud music; the lakeside tables

are quieter and pleasanter than the noisy entrances.

Jauja has several cheap, basic restaurants near the Plaza de Armas. *Hotel Ganso de Oro* has a good restaurant. Trout and (during the rainy season) frog are local specialties.

### Getting There & Away

During the day, frequent inexpensive minibuses leave for Jauja from the Plaza Amazonas in Huancayo as soon as they are full.

## CONCEPCIÓN
☎ 064

South of Jauja, the road branches to follow both the west and east sides of the Río Mantara valley to Huancayo. Local bus drivers refer to these as *derecha* (right) and *izquierda* (left). Concepción, a village halfway between Jauja and Huancayo on the east (izquierda) side, is the entry point for the famous convent of **Santa Rosa de Ocopa**.

Set in a pleasant garden, this beautiful building was built by the Franciscans in the early 18th century as a center for missionaries heading into the jungle to convert the Ashashinka and other tribes. During the years of missionary work, the friars built up an impressive collection that is displayed in the convent's museum. Exhibits include stuffed jungle wildlife, Indian artifacts, photographs of early missionary work, old maps, a fantastic library of some 20,000 volumes (many are centuries old), a large collection of colonial religious art (mainly of the Cuzqueño school) and many other objects.

The convent is open daily except Tuesday from 9 am to noon and 3 to 6 pm. Guided admission is US$1.50 (less for students). Frequent colectivos leave from Concepción for Ocopa, about 5km away.

Concepción is easily visited by taking a Huancayo-Jauja 'izquierda' bus. There are a couple of cheap hotels. Try the adequate *Hotel Royal* (☎ 58-1078) on the main plaza; it charges about US$5 per person and has hot water.

## HUANCAYO

☎ 064

Huancayo, a modern city of about 300,000, lies in the flat and fertile Río Mantaro valley, which supports a large rural population. At an altitude of 3260m and about 300km from Lima, Huancayo is the Junín departmental capital. It is the major commercial center and market for people living in the nearby villages.

The town itself is not particularly interesting, but it's an excellent base from which to visit the many interesting villages of the Río Mantaro valley. Huancayo's weekly Sunday market, where both crafts and produce from the Río Mantaro valley are sold, is famous among locals and travelers (see Shopping later in this section).

### Information

**Tourist Office** The tourist office (☎ 23-8480, 23-3251) is in the Casa del Artesano (indoor crafts market) at Real 481. Hours vary, and it's often closed on weekends. The office has information about sightseeing in the Río Mantaro valley, things to do and how to get around on public transport.

Incas del Peru (see Organized Tours & Treks later in this section) is a recommended source for information on just about anything in the area. They have maps of Huancayo and the surrounding areas.

**Money** Banco de Crédito, Interbanc, Banco Continental, Banco Wiese and other banks and casas de cambio are on Real. There are several ATMs where traveler's checks can be changed. Most banks are open on Saturday mornings.

**Post & Communications** The post office is in the Centro Civico. Telephone booths are found all over central Huancayo. Telefónica del Peru will send international faxes.

**Internet** Read your email at Loreto 337, open from 9 am to 8:30 pm daily.

**Laundry** Both self-service (US$3.50 per load, wash and dry, soap included) and drop-off laundry is available at Lavarap (Breña 154). Hours are 8 am to 10 pm Monday to Saturday and 10 am to 6 pm on Sunday.

## HUANCAYO

**PLACES TO STAY**
6  Hotel Plaza
10 La Casa de la Abuela
12 Hostal Tivoli
16 Residencial Baldeón
17 Hostal Pussy Cat
21 Hotel Kiya
22 Hotel Santa Felicita
23 Hotel Olímpico
29 Hotel Rogger
35 Hotel Prince
37 Hotel Centro
38 Hostal Roma
40 Hotel Valle Montaro
43 Hotel Turismo
45 Hotel Torre Torre
47 Hotel El Dorado
48 Hostal y Baños Sauna Las Viñas
50 Casa Alojamiento Bonilla
51 Hostal Palace
52 Hotel Presidente
55 Hostal Villa Rica
59 Hotel Rey
60 Percy's Hotel

**PLACES TO EAT**
7  Chicharronería Cuzco
8  Chez Viena
9  La Cabaña
13 La Pergola
14 Chifa Centro, Koky
18 Antojitos & other budget restaurants
23 Restaurant Olímpico
25 El Viejo Madero

**OTHER**
1  Museo Salesiano
2  Church of La Merced
3  Sauna Blub
4  Turismo Central
5  Cruz del Sur
9  Incas del Peru
11 El Cerezo
15 ETUCSA
19 Lavarap
20 Tourist Office
24 Buses to Jauja

26 Banco de Crédito
27 Wanka Tours
28 Casa de cambio
30 Buses to La Oroya
31 Buses to Jauja
32 Banco Continental
33 Interbanc
34 Internet access
36 Buses to San Jerónimo & Concepción
39 Comité 12 colectivos to Lima
41 Telefónica del Peru
42 Central Post Office
44 Church of La Inmaculada
46 Municipalidad
49 Banco de Crédito
53 Taj Mahal
54 Mariscal Cáceres
56 Empresa Molina
57 TransNacional & many small bus companies
58 Empresa Huáscar

# HUANCAYO

**Dangers & Annoyances** As always, beware of thieves at the bus and train stations and the Sunday market. Readers have reported thefts, so stay alert.

Beware of the altitude if arriving straight from Lima.

## Things to See

The **Museo Salesiano** (☎ 24-7763), which can be entered from the Salesian School, has Amazon fauna, pottery and archaeology exhibits. Hours are 9 am to noon and 3 to 6 pm weekdays; admission is under US$1.

Head northeast on Avenida Giráldez for a good view of the city. About 2km from the town center is **Cerro de la Libertad**, where, apart from the city view, there are snack bars and a playground. About 2km farther (there is a sign and an obvious path), you will come to the eroded geological formations known as **Torre Torre**.

In the city itself, the cathedral and the church of **La Inmaculada** are both modern and not particularly noteworthy. **La Merced**, on the 1st block of Real, is the most interesting church; although there isn't much to see, this is where the Peruvian Constitution was approved in 1839. In the San Antonio suburb, the new **Parque de la Identidad Wanka** is a fanciful park full of stone statues and miniature buildings representing the area's culture.

## Organized Tours & Treks

Incas del Peru (☎ 22-3303, fax 22-2395, incas&lucho@mail.hys.com.pe, Giráldez 6520), in the same building as the restaurant La Cabaña, offers tours arranged by Luis 'Lucho' Hurtado, a local man who speaks English and knows the surrounding area well. He can guide you on adventure treks down the eastern slopes of the Andes and into the high jungle on foot, horseback or public transport. It isn't luxurious, but it's a good chance to experience something of the 'real' rural Peru. Lucho's father has a ranch in the middle of nowhere. You can stay here and meet all kinds of local people. Several people have recommended his trips. If you are unable to get a group together, you may be able to join up with another group. The trips last anywhere from three to eight days

and cost about US$35 per person per day including simple food. Accommodations are rustic, and trips may involve some camping.

Guided day hikes can be arranged for about US$20 per person including lunch. Longer trips beyond the Huancayo area can also be arranged.

The best standard travel agent that has bus tours in the Río Mantaro valley is Wanka Tours (☎ 23-1743, fax 23-1778, Real 565).

## Bicycle Rental

Incas del Peru (see Organized Tours & Treks) rents mountain bikes for US$30 per day including a guide and lunch, or less for a half day or if you want to strike out on your own.

## Language Courses

Incas del Peru also arranges Spanish lessons, which include meals and accommodations with a local family (if you wish) for about US$200 a week. Lessons can be modified or extended to fit your interests, and you can learn to cook local dishes, play the panpipes, or make weavings and other local crafts.

## Special Events

There are hundreds of fiestas in Huancayo and surrounding villages – supposedly almost every day somewhere in the Río Mantaro valley. Ask at a tourist information center. One of the biggest events in Huancayo is Semana Santa (Holy Week), with big religious processions attracting people from all over Peru. Hotels fill up and raise their prices during the festival. Fiestas Patrias (July 28-29) is also very busy.

## Places to Stay

**Budget** Incas del Peru runs the clean and friendly *La Casa de la Abuela (Giráldez 691)*, with a garden, hot water and laundry facilities. It's popular with backpackers. Ten basic rooms sleep two to six people; rates are US$4 per person with shared showers, US$10 for a double with shared showers and US$7 per person with private showers, all including continental breakfast with good coffee. *Residencial Baldeón (☎ 23-1634, Amazonas 543)*, in a friendly family house, charges US$5 per person with shared hot showers, kitchen privileges and breakfast. The *Casa Alojamiento Bonilla* (☎ 23-2103, *Huánuco 332*) is a colonial house run by the friendly, English-speaking artists Aldo and Soledad, who charge US$12 for a double with breakfast and hot-water baths. A few blocks northeast of the map, *Pension Huanca* (☎ 22-3956, *Pasaje San Antonio 113*) charges US$4 with breakfast.

*Hostal Roma* (*Loreto 447*) and *Hostal Tivoli* (*Puno 488*) are very basic hotels with cold-water baths charging about US$4/6. *Hotel Centro* (*Loreto 452*) has similarly priced rooms, as well as rooms with private bath (cold showers) for a couple of dollars more. The basic *Hotel Prince* (☎ 23-2331, *Calixto 578*) charges US$3/5 with shared bath and US$5/6 with private bath and hot water from 7 to 9 am. Hot showers (US$1) and a sauna (US$2) are available at the delightfully named *Sauna Blub* (☎ 22-1692, *Pasaje Veranal 187*), just off Ayacucho.

The simple but clean *Hostal Villa Rica* (☎ 23-2641, *Real 1291*) has hot water from 8 am to 4 pm. Rates are US$4/7 or US$7/10 with bath. *Hotel Torre Torre* (☎ 23-1116, *Real 873*) is basic but clean and has hot water. Rates are US$5.50/7.50, or US$2 more with private bath. *Percy's Hotel* (☎ 23-1208, *Real 1339*) is clean and has hot water during the day with a 30-minute notice. Rates are US$8/11 with private bath and TV, or US$6 for a single with shared bath. There's a restaurant. *Hostal Pussy Cat* (☎ 23-1565, *Giráldez 359*) is also clean and requires a 30-minute notice for hot showers. Rates are US$7/10 or US$8/12 with private bath.

Similar or lower rates are charged at the following, all of which have simple, clean rooms with private baths: *Hotel Rogger* (☎ 23-3488, *Ancash 460*) has TV, *Hostal Palace* (☎ 23-8501, *Ancash 1127*) has hot water during early mornings and early evenings and TV on request, and *Hotel Plaza* (☎ 21-0509, fax 23-6878, *Ancash 171*) has 24-hour hot water and TV in some of the rooms, as does *Hotel Rey* (☎ 21-8109, *Angaraes 327*).

*Hotel El Dorado* (☎ 22-3947, *Piura 425*) charges US$10/12 for decent rooms with hot

showers and TV. The clean *Hostal Valle Mantaro* (☎ 21-2219, *Real 765*) charges US$7/9 with shared bath and US$10/13 with private bath; TV is available for another US$1. *Hostal y Baños Sauna Las Viñas* (☎ 23-1294, *Piura 415*) charges US$12/15 for rooms with private hot bath, cable TV and telephone. Their sauna (US$2) is open 6 am to 9 pm. All three of these seem like a fair value.

**Mid-Range** The *Hotel Santa Felicita* (☎ 23-5476, ☎/fax 23-5285, *Giráldez 145*), on the Plaza de Armas (Constitución), charges US$15/20 for rooms with bath, cable TV and telephone. Next door, *Hotel Kiya* (☎ 21-4955, ☎/fax 21-4957, *Giráldez 107*) charges US$17/21 for clean rooms with telephone, bath, hot water, soap and towel and includes continental breakfast. Note that rooms overlooking Real suffer from street noise. The newer *Hotel Olímpico* (☎ 21-4555, fax 21-5700, *Ancash 408*) has clean but small rooms with cable TV and telephone; rates are US$23/29, and there's a good restaurant.

The two best hotels in the center can both be reserved at hotelhyo@correo.dnet.com.pe. *Hotel Turismo* (☎/fax 23-1072, *Ancash 729*) is a pleasant-looking old building with some wooden balconies and public areas with a certain faded grandeur. Rooms vary in size, amenities and quality. The best hotels (with cable TV, telephone and bath) are about US$33/41. Cheaper rooms with shared bath are overpriced at US$18/23. The hotel also offers a pleasant restaurant and bar. The modern *Hotel Presidente* (☎/fax 23-1275, 23-5419, 23-1736, *Real 1138*) is about the same price for rooms with bath and is the most popular with motorists from Lima. It has a large parking area.

In the El Tambo suburb, about seven blocks north of Río Shulcas, *Hostal América* (☎/fax 24-2005, *Trujillo 358*) has modern rooms with the usual services for US$30/40.

## Places to Eat

Budget travelers will find several cheap restaurants along Arequipa between Puno and Breña. *Antojitos* (☎ 23-7950, *Puno 599*) is the nicest of these. It has lunch specials for US$1.20 and makes pizzas, barbecue,

## Papa à la Huancaina

Visitors to Huancayo should try the local specialty, *papa à la huancaina*, which consists of a boiled white potato topped with a creamy white sauce of fresh cheese, oil, hot pepper, lemon and egg yolk. The whole concoction is served with an olive and sliced boiled egg, and is eaten as a cold potato salad. Despite the hot pepper, its flavor is pleasantly mild.

sandwiches and drinks in the evening, and often has music. They close on Sunday. *La Cabaña* (☎ 22-3303, *Giráldez 652*) has good pizzas, sandwiches, anticuchos and sangría and is a popular hangout for travelers and locals. There's a book exchange, music on weekends and travel information. *Chifa Centro* (☎ 22-4154, *Giráldez 238*) is good for Chinese food. Plenty of chicken places charge about US$1.50 for a quarter-chicken; the best is *El Viejo Madero* (☎ 21-7788, *Breña 125*), which charges US$2 but has juicier and bigger pieces than the other places.

The recommended *Koky* (☎ 23-4707, *Puno 298*) serves good sandwiches, pastries, real espresso and other coffees. *Chez Viena* (☎ 23-4385, *Puno 125*) is a nice coffee/pastry shop with an ornate interior.

*Restaurant Olímpico* (☎ 23-4181, *Giráldez 199*) has been here since about 1940 (though it has been remodeled) and is Huancayo's best-known restaurant. It serves good set menus for about US$2 and Peruvian à la carte plates in the US$5 to US$10 range. Opposite, *La Pergola* (*Puno 444*) is upstairs with a plaza view and courtly atmosphere. Sandwiches, snacks and light meals are inexpensive.

*Chicharronería Cuzco* (*Cuzco 173*) is a hole-in-the-wall run by Doña Juana Curo Ychpas, who makes excellent traditional plates of chicharrones (fried pork ribs) – for dedicated carnivores only – for about US$2. Away from the town center, you'll find several restaurants serving typical food in a slightly rural atmosphere. Northwest of town, Real

becomes Avenida Mariscal Castilla in the El Tambo district. Here, you'll find *La Estancia* (☎ 22-3279, *M Castilla 2815*), which does a great lunchtime *pachamanca* – which contains cuy, pork, lamb, potatoes, beans and tamales, among other possible ingredients, wrapped in leaves and cooked in an underground earth oven (basically, a hole in the ground). Go early and watch them disinter it. A filling lunch is about US$8. Another place to try is *Recreo Huancahuasi* (☎ 24-4826, *M Castilla 2222*), which has a pachamanca for Sunday lunch accompanied by live music.

### Entertainment

Huancayo offers limited nightlife. Travelers frequent the lively *La Cabaña* restaurant, which has quite good folklórica and various forms of rock music on most Thursdays through Sundays. The *Taj Mahal* (*Huancavelica 1052*) is a locally popular club with video karaoke and dancing. *El Cerezo* (*Puno 506*) is a bar with MTV and attracts young locals.

### Shopping

There are two main markets in Huancayo: Mercado Mayorista (daily produce market) and the Feria Dominical (Sunday craft market). The very colorful produce market spills out along the railway tracks from the covered Mercado Mayorista off Ica east of the railway tracks. In the meat section, you can buy various Andean delicacies such as fresh and dried frogs, guinea pigs, rabbits and chickens. Although it's a daily market, the most important day is Sunday, coinciding with the weekly craft market.

The Feria Dominical occupies five or six blocks along Huancavelica to the northwest of Ica. Weavings, sweaters and other textiles; embroidered items; ceramics and wood carvings are sold here, as well as *mates burilados* (carved gourds) – a specialty of the area. These are made in the nearby villages of Cochas Grande and Cochas Chico. The noncraft items range from cassette tapes to frilly underwear. You must bargain hard here to get the best prices; gourds are reputedly the best buy. This is definitely a place to keep an eye on your valuables.

Buyers of handicrafts would do well to familiarize themselves with local crafts by visiting the Casa del Artesano at the tourist information office. The folks at Incas del Peru sell some good-quality stuff and can take you to meet the craftspeople.

## Getting There & Away

**Bus** With no airport and a limited train system, Huancayo depends heavily on bus services, and there are many companies to choose from. Shop around if you're on a tight budget, as fares vary substantially, as do levels of comfort.

Mariscal Cáceres (☎ 21-6633/4, Real 1247) has eight daily buses to Lima (6 to 7 hours). Fares are US$7 to US$9, and their presidential service is recommended, as it is not crowded, makes few stops and has an on-board bathroom. Others recommended for Lima are ETUCSA (☎ 23-2638, Puno 220) and Cruz del Sur (☎ 23-5650, Ayacucho 251), both of which have comfortable nonstop buses with an onboard toilet, and they may serve you a snack en route. ETUCSA has an 11:45 pm departure for US$10.50 and has spacious seats that recline into a semibed. Companies with cheaper and less frequent service to Lima include Empresa Molina (☎ 22-4501, Angaraes 334) and Empresa Roggero (buy tickets at Hotel Rogger), which recently had a US$4 nighttime bus ride. If you're in a hurry, consider taking a colectivo taxi. Comité 12 (☎ 23-3281, Loreto 421) has seven cars to Lima (5 hours) daily and charges US$12 per passenger (three-person minimum, five-person maximum).

Buses to Huancavelica (4 to 4½ hours) charge about US$3 or US$4. Empresa Huáscar, Ancash at Anagaraes, is the best bet, with departures at 7:45 and 9:45 am, noon, and 4 and 10 pm. Several others within a block, such as TransNacional, have buses only at night arriving before dawn, though you can snooze on the bus until daybreak.

Buses to Ayacucho take about 12 hours if the going is good, and they charge about US$7. Empresa Molina has the most departures (7 am and 12:30, 7 and 8 pm; subject to change). This is still a rough road, so expect delays, especially in the rainy season. I couldn't find direct buses to Cuzco – go to Ayacucho first. The journey can be broken at Churcapampa, where there are basic accommodations.

Empresa de Transportes San Juan (☎ 21-4558, Ferrocarril 131) has minibuses almost every hour to Tarma (US$2.50, 4 hours) and can drop you off at Concepción or Jauja. Some continue to La Merced and San Ramón (5 to 7 hours), Satipo (8 hours) and other jungle destinations – their departures change frequently. Turismo Central (☎ 22-3128, Ayacucho 274) has old, long-distance buses north to Cerro de Pasco, Huánuco (US$5, 8 hours), Tingo María and Pucallpa (US$14, 30 hours). They also service Tarma, La Merced/San Ramón and continue to Satipo or Puerto Bermúdez (US$10, 18 hours). Departures are usually once a day, so you don't have much choice.

## Calientes

Calientes, or 'hot ones,' are drinks sold on cold Andean nights. All through the night, you will find people on street corners selling these drinks from little stoves on wheels. Here's a recipe to warm the cockles of your heart.

- half a cup of black tea leaves
- 1 stick of cinnamon
- 1 teaspoon aniseed

Add a generous pinch of each of the following:

- lemongrass
- lemon balm
- chamomile
- fennel
- fig leaves

Put all of the above ingredients into a kettle and boil for 10 minutes. In a cup, put the juice of one lime, 2 teaspoons of sugar or honey and one measure of pisco or rum, then fill the cup with the hot tea mixture. Drink it while it's hot.

**– recipe courtesy of Beverly Stuart**

Local buses to most of the nearby villages leave from the street intersections shown on the Huancayo map. The companies rarely have offices or fixed schedules. You just show up and wait until a bus is ready to leave. Ask other people waiting with you for more details. The tourist office is a good source of local bus information.

**Train** Huancayo has two unlinked train stations in different parts of town. The central station goes to Lima (see the boxed text 'Riding the Rails'). Passenger trains run up from Lima and back from Huancayo on an irregular basis (during the 1999 dry season, the train ran four times a month; see Train in the Getting There & Away section for the Lima chapter).

The Huancavelica train station (☎ 23-2581) is at the south end of town. Train is the best mode of transport to Huancavelica, because the road is not very good.

The train to Huancavelica takes six hours and leaves at 6:30 am (Expreso) and 12:30 pm (Extra) Monday to Saturday and 2 pm Sunday. Tickets are US$2.75/3.25/4 in 2nd/1st/buffet class. The buffet class is slightly more comfortable and has guaranteed seating and the quickest meal service; 2nd is crowded and allows standing; 1st is in between. Try to buy your ticket before you travel, as this service is very popular, and the train is often full. Tickets are sold from noon to 6 pm on the previous day and at 6 am on the day of travel.

On Sunday, there's a faster *autovagón de turismo* (electric train) that takes five hours and leaves at 5 pm. The fare is US$6. There may be a second autovagón on Monday. These details are subject to change, but two trains a day have been leaving fairly reliably for years.

## RÍO MANTARO VALLEY
☎ 064

Two main road systems link Huancayo with the villages of the Río Mantaro valley and are known simply as the left and right of the river. Left *(izquierda)* is the east and right *(derecha)* is the west side of the river, as you head into Huancayo from the north. It is best to confine your sightseeing on any given day to one side or the other because there are few bridges.

Perhaps the most interesting excursion is on the east side of the valley, where you can visit the twin villages of **Cochas Grande** and **Cochas Chico**, about 11km from Huancayo. These villages are the major production centers for the incised gourds that have made the area famous. Oddly enough, the gourds are grown mainly on the coast and are imported into the highlands from the Chiclayo and Ica areas. Once they are transported into the highlands, they are dried and scorched, then decorated using wood working tools.

The gourds can be bought at Huancayo's Feria Dominical, but if you speak Spanish and can hit it off with the locals, you can see

## Market Days Around Huancayo

Each little village and town in the Río Mantaro valley has its own *feria*, or market day. If you enjoy these, you'll find one on every day of the week.

| | |
|---|---|
| Monday | San Agustín de Cajas, Huayucachi |
| Tuesday | Hualhuas, Pucara |
| Wednesday | San Jerónimo, Jauja |
| Thursday | El Tambo, Sapallanga |
| Friday | Cochas |
| Saturday | Matahuasi, Chupaca, Marco |
| Sunday | Huancayo, Jauja, Mito, Comas |

hem being made and buy them at Cochas Grande and Cochas Chico.

Other villages of interest for their handicrafts include **San Agustín de Cajas, Hualhuas** and **San Jerónimo de Tunán.** Cajas is known for the manufacture of broad-brimmed wool hats, though this industry seems to be dying. Hualhuas is a center for the manufacture of wool products – ponchos, weavings, sweaters and other items. San Jerónimo is known for its filigree silverwork and also has a 17th-century church with fine wooden altars. While the villages can easily be visited from Huancayo, most buying and selling is done in Huancayo, and the villages have few facilities for shopping or anything else. The key here is the ability to speak Spanish and make friends with the locals. Going on a tour, guided hike or bike ride (see Information for Huancayo earlier in this chapter) helps as well.

## HUANCAVELICA
☎ 064

Huancavelica, 147km south of Huancayo, is the capital of the department of the same name. High and remote, most of the department lies above 3500m and has a cold climate, though it can get 'T-shirt' hot during the sunny days of the dry season (May to October). The rest of the year tends to be wet, and during the rainiest months (between February and April), the roads are sometimes in such bad shape that Huancavelica can be virtually cut off from the rest of Peru.

This historic city is nearly 3700m above sea level and has a population of well over 40,000 – many have arrived recently to escape from the deadly problems of terrorism in the late '80s and early '90s. Before the arrival of Europeans, Huancavelica was a strategic Inca center, and shortly after the conquest, the Spanish discovered its mineral wealth. By 1564, the Spaniards were sending Indian slaves to Huancavelica to work in the mercury and silver mines. The present town was founded in 1571 under the name of Villa Rica de Oropesa and retains a very pleasant colonial atmosphere and many interesting churches. It's a small but attractive town visited by very few tourists, partly because it's not on the main central-highland road

between Huancayo and Ayacucho. This means that visitors usually must travel from Huancayo and then backtrack.

## Information
**Tourist Office** The Ministerio de Presidencia on Torre Tagle at Raimondi has a tourist information office. The Instituto Nacional de Cultura (INC), on Plaza San Juan de Dios, may have information and displays about the area.

**Money** The Banco de Crédito on V Toledo is your best bet, but I'd bring what I needed with me.

**Post & Communications** The post office and telephone offices are marked on the map.

## Churches
There are seven churches of note. Santa Ana, now in a state of disrepair, was founded in the 16th century and was followed in the 17th century first by the cathedral, then by Santo Domingo, San Francisco, San Cristóbal, La Ascensión and finally San Sebastián. San Francisco is famous for its 11 intricately worked altars. The cathedral has been restored and contains what has been called the best colonial altar in Peru. Santo Domingo and San Sebastián have also recently been restored.

Huancavelican churches are noted for their silver-plated altars, unlike the rest of Peru's colonial churches, which are usually gold-plated.

Visitors find that many of the churches are often closed to tourism. You can go as a member of the congregation when they are open for services, usually early in the morning on weekdays, with longer morning hours on Sunday.

## San Cristóbal Mineral Springs
The San Cristóbal mineral springs (see the Huancavelica map) are fed into two large, slightly murky swimming pools in which you can relax for about US$0.20. For US$0.35, you can have a (semiprivate) shower. The water is lukewarm, but not hot, and supposedly has

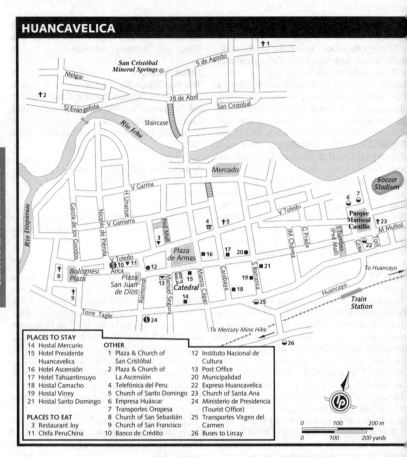

## HUANCAVELICA

**PLACES TO STAY**
14 Hostal Mercurio
15 Hotel Presidente
   Huancavelica
16 Hotel Ascensión
17 Hotel Tahuantinsuyo
18 Hostal Camacho
19 Hostal Virrey
21 Hostal Santo Domingo

**PLACES TO EAT**
3 Restaurant Joy
11 Chifa PeruChina

**OTHER**
1 Plaza & Church of
   San Cristóbal
2 Plaza & Church of
   La Ascensión
4 Telefónica del Peru
5 Church of Santo Domingo
6 Empresa Huáscar
7 Transportes Oropesa
8 Church of San Sebastián
9 Church of San Francisco
10 Banco de Crédito

12 Instituto Nacional de
   Cultura
13 Post Office
20 Municipalidad
22 Expreso Huancavelica
23 Church of Santa Ana
24 Ministerio de Presidencia
   (Tourist Office)
25 Transportes Virgen del
   Carmen
26 Buses to Lircay

curative properties. There is a café, and it's
reasonably pleasant. You can rent a towel,
soap and a bathing suit if you've forgotten
yours (though their selection of bathing
wear is limited and unlovely). The springs
are open from 5:30 am to 4 pm daily except
Friday, when they close at noon to empty
and clean the pools. Ticket sales stop one
hour before closing.

### Market

Market day in Huancavelica is Sunday, and
although there are smaller daily markets,
Sunday is the best day to see the locals in

traditional dress (see Lircay later in the
chapter for a description). The main market
area is near the river.

### Mercury Mine Hike

An interesting hike of about three hours
(round trip) leads to the old mercury mine.
Leave town from near the train station,
heading south. It's a bit difficult to find the
right path at first, but after a few hundred
meters, it becomes an obvious pack-animal
trail. It is a steep ascent, going to over
4000m above sea level, and brings you to
the village of Santa Barbara, with its now

deserted colonial church. Nearby are the abandoned modern mining installations, which were finally closed in 1976. Between the village and the mining installations, you can find the old entrance to the original 16th-century mine, carved into the rock and with a coat of arms beside it. If you have a good flashlight, it's possible to enter it a little ways, but do so at your own risk. A few villagers still extract mercury as a cottage industry, and if you speak Spanish, you might be able to find someone to show you the process. Note that the mine is locally known as *Mina de la Muerte* (death mine), which refers to the deadly effects of mercury.

Apart from the deserted church and mine, the walk is of interest because of the many llama and alpaca herds in the mountain landscape. Huancavelica has many other little-known areas that may be of interest to the adventurous traveler.

## Special Events
Colorful traditional fiestas occur on major Peruvian holidays, such as Carnaval, Semana Santa, Todos Santos and Christmas and others held throughout the year. Huancavelica's Semana Turística (Tourism Week) is held in late September and early October.

## Places to Stay
Most hotels are cheap and have only cold water, but with the natural mineral baths in town, this is not a great hardship. The cheapest places include *Hostal Virrey*, *Hostal Santo Domingo* and a few others on S Barranca.

Better budget places include *Hostal Camacho (Carabaya 481)*, which charges US$3/5 for singles/doubles or US$5/9 in rooms with a half-bath (toilet and sink). They say they have warm showers in the morning and reportedly have good mattresses. Also quite good is the nearby *Hotel Tahuantinsuyo (Carabaya 399)*, which has some well-lit rooms with table and chair for US$3.25/4.75 and others with half-bath for US$4/5.50. Their shared shower is on the cold side of tepid. *Hotel Ascensión*, on the Plaza de Armas, charges US$3.25/5.25, or US$5/6 with a half-bath. They claim to have hot

showers in the morning. *Hostal Mercurio (Torre Tagle 455)* tells me they have warm showers all day and charge US$3.25/5.25, or US$5/10 with a private shower.

The only 'good' place in town is *Hotel Presidente Huancavelica (☎/fax 75-2760)*, which is in a nice old building on the Plaza de Armas. The rooms, however, are very plain (but have a telephone) and cost US$25/32 with bath, or US$16/21 with shared bath and hot showers. Their restaurant serves breakfast only.

## Places to Eat
There are no particularly good restaurants in Huancavelica. The best is *Restaurant Joy (V Toledo 230)*, with good three-course set lunches for US$2 and other meals in the US$3 to US$6 range. Nearby, the *Chifa PeruChina* is also locally recommended. There are many cheaper places.

## Getting There & Away
The train from Huancayo is faster than the buses, but the road goes higher than the train and has better views. I recommend taking the bus one way and the train the other.

**Bus** Almost all major buses depart from Parque Mariscal Castillo, but there are plans to build a new terminal a short way to the east of the stadium. The bus trip to Huancayo takes four to 4½ hours and costs about US$3.50. Empresa Huáscar (☎ 75-1562) has buses at 4, 5, and 10:30 am, and 2 and 9:30 pm (subject to change). Transportes Virgen del Carmen has a 5:30 am bus to Huancayo and a 1 pm bus to Lircay. Other companies go at night. Expreso Huancavelica has a 5 pm bus to Huancayo and a 10 pm bus to Lima via Huancayo. Transportes Oropesa has a 4:30 pm departure to Pisco (US$6, 11 hours) and to Lima via Huancayo (US$7.50) at 5 pm (also subject to change). The bus to Pisco goes through the villages of Santa Inés and Castrovirreyna, reaches an altitude of about 4800m (below freezing at night) and passes many Andean lakes and herds of alpaca, llama and vicuña. I couldn't find a daytime bus. Several buses and minibuses go to Lircay from near the train station.

I couldn't find buses to Ayacucho. The easiest way to get there is to go back to Huancayo.

**Train** The Expreso (☎ 67-1480) leaves Huancavelica for Huancayo at 6:30 am, and the Extra leaves at 12:30 pm Monday to Saturday. The only Sunday train is the Extra at 6:30 am. The autovagón leaves at 5:30 pm Friday and 6:20 am Monday. Buy tickets in advance if possible. See Getting There & Away for Huancayo earlier in this chapter for more information.

## LIRCAY
☎ 064

The small, colonial town of Lircay is almost 80km southeast of Huancavelica. Its main claim to fame is as the center for the department's traditional clothing, which can be seen at Huancavelica's Sunday market. The predominant color is black, but the men wear rainbow-colored pompoms on their hats and at their waists (supposedly love tokens from women), and the women wear multicolored shawls over their otherwise somber clothing. The town has a couple of basic hotels.

## IZCUCHACA
☎ 064

Izcuchaca, the main village between Huancayo and Huancavelica, has a basic hotel, a pottery center, hot springs and archaeological ruins, which are accessible only on foot. There is also a **historic bridge**, which, as legend has it, was built by the Incas and was defended bitterly by Huascar against the advance of Atahualpa's troops during the civil war that was raging in the Inca Empire when the Spaniards arrived.

## AYACUCHO
☎ 064

Founded by the Spanish in 1539, Ayacucho is a small city lying 2731m above sea level. It has a population of 120,000 and is the capital of its department. Despite its remoteness and small size, Ayacucho is arguably Peru's most fascinating Andean city after Cuzco, and is well worth a visit.

Five hundred years before the Inca Empire, the Wari Empire dominated the Peruvian highlands. The Wari's now-ruined capital, 22km northeast of Ayacucho, is easily reached along the paved road that now links it with Ayacucho. Ayacucho played a major part in the battles for independence, and a huge nearby monument marks the site of the important Battle of Ayacucho, fought in 1824.

As mentioned at the beginning of this chapter, the central Andes is one of Peru's least visited areas. Ayacucho is no exception to this. Its first road link with the Peruvian coast was not finished until 1924, and as late as 1960, there were only two buses and a few dozen vehicles in the city. Departmental statistics show that as late as 1981, there were still only 44km of paved roads in the department, only 7% of the population had running water in their houses and only 14% had electricity. Ayacucho has retained its colonial atmosphere more than most Peruvian cities, and many of its old colonial buildings have been preserved.

## Information
**Tourist Office** The Dirección General de Industria y Turismo (☎ 81-2548, 81-3162 Asamblea 481) is a friendly and helpful source of information, maps and leaflets. The Policía de Turismo (☎ 81-2179) is on 2 de Mayo at Arequipa. Local travel agencies are also helpful.

**Orientation** The Plaza de Armas is also called the Plaza Mayor de Huamanga. The street names of the four sides of the plaza clockwise from the east (with the cathedral) are Portal Municipal, Portal Independencia, Portal Constitución and Portal Unión.

**Money** The Banco de Crédito may change traveler's checks. There is also an Interbanc. US cash is readily exchanged.

**Post & Communications** The post office is shown on the map; there are several telephone and fax places on the same block.

**Internet** You can send email from Nivel Técnico (Lima 106).

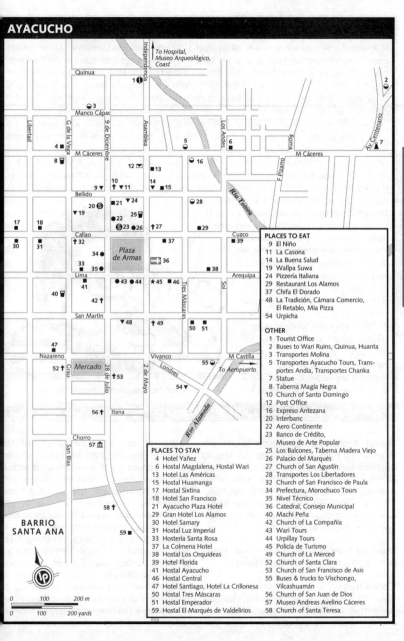

# AYACUCHO

**PLACES TO EAT**
9  El Niño
11  La Casona
14  La Buena Salud
19  Wallpa Suwa
24  Pizzería Italiana
29  Restaurant Los Alamos
37  Chifa El Dorado
48  La Tradición, Cámara Comercio,
   El Retablo, Mia Pizza
54  Urpicha

**OTHER**
1  Tourist Office
2  Buses to Wari Ruins, Quinua, Huanta
3  Transportes Molina
5  Transportes Ayacucho Tours, Transportes Andía, Transportes Chanka
7  Statue
8  Taberna Magía Negra
10  Church of Santo Domingo
12  Post Office
16  Expreso Antezana
20  Interbanc
22  Aero Continente
23  Banco de Crédito,
   Museo de Arte Popular
25  Los Balcones, Taberna Madera Viejo
26  Palacio del Marqués
27  Church of San Agustín
28  Transportes Los Libertadores
32  Church of San Francisco de Paula
34  Prefectura, Morochuco Tours
35  Nivel Técnico
36  Catedral, Consejo Municipal
40  Machi Peña
42  Church of La Compañía
43  Wari Tours
44  Urpillay Tours
45  Policía de Turismo
49  Church of La Merced
52  Church of Santa Clara
53  Church of San Francisco de Asis
55  Buses & trucks to Vischongo,
   Vilcashuamán
56  Church of San Juan de Dios
57  Museo Andreas Avelino Cáceres
58  Church of Santa Teresa

**PLACES TO STAY**
4  Hotel Yañez
6  Hostal Magdalena, Hostal Wari
13  Hotel Las Américas
15  Hostal Huamanga
17  Hostal Sixtina
18  Hotel San Francisco
21  Ayacucho Plaza Hotel
29  Gran Hotel Los Alamos
30  Hotel Samary
31  Hostal Luz Imperial
33  Hostería Santa Rosa
37  La Colmena Hotel
38  Hostal Los Orquídeas
39  Hotel Florida
41  Hostal Ayacucho
46  Hostal Central
47  Hotel Santiago, Hotel La Crillonesa
50  Hostal Tres Máscaras
51  Hostal Emperador
59  Hostal El Marqués de Valdelirios

**CENTRAL HIGHLANDS**

0  100  200 m
0  100  200 yards

## El Sendero Luminoso

It was in the remote environment of Ayacucho that the Sendero Luminoso (Shining Path) guerrilla movement was born. It began in 1962 as the Huamanga Command of the Frente de Liberación Nacional (FLN). But in 1965, it broke away from the FLN, and in the late 1960s, it began to flirt with communism. In the 1970s, when the Sendero was a little-known local organization with headquarters at Ayacucho's University of Huamanga, nonviolent political discussion and dissent within the confines of the campus were its main activities.

The violence with which the world press has frequently identified the Sendero began in the early 1980s and peaked in 1982. The strong military measures taken in 1983, in an attempt to control the organization, were frequently criticized because of the killing of civilians. The spread of the Sendero was halted for a few years in the mid-'80s but, by the end of the decade, a strong Sendero presence was felt not only in Ayacucho, but throughout much of the central Peruvian Andes. The Sendero's objectives appeared to be the overthrow of Peru's present democratic system, the destruction of all bourgeois elements in the country and the return of land to the peasant farmers. The violence employed in the pursuit of these aims contributed to the fact that the Sendero had relatively little popular support in Peru.

In the early 1990s, Ayacucho was considered a dangerous destination, but the situation stabilized in 1993, after the Sendero leaders were captured and imprisoned for life. Since that time, increasing numbers of Peruvian and foreign visitors have visited the area, and it is once again a safe destination.

**Imprisoned Sendero leader Abimael Guzmán**

**Travel Agencies** Morochuco Tours and Wari Tours, both on the Plaza de Armas, organize local excursions and have tourist information. They cater mainly to Peruvian tourists, and their guides speak Spanish. They are the oldest companies; newer agencies are opening. A good one is Urpillay Tours, also on the plaza.

**Medical Services** The hospital is on Independencia, on the north side of town.

## Churches

The 17th-century cathedral on the Plaza de Armas has a religious-art museum that has been closed for years but may reopen. The cathedral and a dozen other colonia churches from the 16th, 17th and 18th cen turies are well worth a visit for their incred ibly ornate facades and interiors, mainl Spanish baroque but often with Andea influences evinced by the plants an animals depicted. Ayacucho claims to hav 33 churches (one for each year of Christ life), but there are in fact several more. Th most important of Ayacucho's churches ar marked on the map. Except for durin Semana Santa (when churches are open fo most of the day), opening hours can b erratic; ask at the tourist office. Recently, US$5 visitor ticket was required to enter a the major churches and colonial houses.

## Colonial Houses

Most of the old mansions are now mainly political offices and can be visited. The offices of the Department of Ayacucho (the *prefectura*) on the Plaza de Armas are a good example. The mansion was constructed between 1740 and 1755 and sold to the state in 1937. On the ground floor is a pretty courtyard where a visitor can see the cell of the local heroine of independence, María Parado de Bellido. Go upstairs to see some excellent tile work.

Also worth a look is the Salon de Actas in the **Consejo Municipal**, next to the cathedral, with its excellent view of the plaza. On the north side of the plaza are several more fine colonial houses, including the **Palacio del Marqués**, at Portal Unión 37, which is the oldest and dates from 1550. There are various others scattered around the town center, many housing professional offices; the tourist office can suggest which ones to visit.

## Museo de Arte Popular

This museum is in the 18th-century Casa Chacón, owned by and adjoining the Banco de Crédito. The popular art covers the *Ayacucheño* spectrum – silverwork, rug and tapestry weaving, stone and wood carvings, ceramics (model churches are especially popular) and the famous **retablos**. These are colorful wooden boxes ranging from the size of a matchbox to a meter or more in height, containing intricate papier-mâché models; Peruvian rural scenes or the nativity are particularly popular, but some interesting ones with political or social commentary can be seen here. Old and new photographs show how Ayacucho has changed during the 20th century. Admission is free.

## Museo Andres Avelino Cáceres

This collection is housed in the Casona Vivanco (28 de Julio 512), a mansion dating from the 16th century. Cáceres was a local man who commanded Peruvian troops during the War of the Pacific (1879-1883) against Chile. Accordingly, the museum houses maps and military paraphernalia

from that period, as well as some colonial art. Admission is US$1, but opening hours are erratic (supposedly 9 am to 6 pm).

## Museo Arqueológico Hipolito Unanue

The museum (also called Museo INC) is in the Centro Cultural Simón Bolívar at the university, a little over a kilometer from the town center along Independencia – you can't miss it. Wari ceramics make up most of the small exhibit.

They are supposedly open 8:30 am to 5 pm Monday to Saturday, but there are few visitors, and the caretakers often take extended lunch breaks. The best time is usually in the morning. Entry is US$1. While there, check the university library for a free exhibit of mummies and a few other things.

## Special Events

Ayacucho's Semana Santa celebration, held the week before Easter, has long been considered Peru's finest religious festival, and it attracts visitors – though relatively few foreigners – from all over the country. Rooms in the better hotels are booked well in advance, and even the cheapest places fill completely. The tourist office has lists of local families who provide accommodations for the overflow.

Each year, the tourist bureau prints a free brochure describing the Semana Santa events with street maps showing the main processions. Visitors are advised to get this detailed information. The celebrations begin on the Friday before Palm Sunday and continue for 10 days until Easter Sunday. The Friday before Palm Sunday is marked by a procession in honor of La Virgen de los Dolores, or 'Our Lady of Sorrows,' during which it is customary to inflict 'sorrows' on bystanders by firing pebbles out of slingshots. Gringos have been recent targets, so be warned.

Each succeeding day is marked with solemn yet colorful processions and religious rites, which reach a fever pitch of Catholic faith and tradition. They culminate on the Saturday before Easter Sunday with a huge all-night party leading up to dawn fireworks to celebrate the resurrection of Christ.

In addition to the religious services, Ayacucho's Semana Santa celebrations include numerous secular activities – art shows, folk-dancing competitions and demonstrations, local music concerts, street events, sporting events (especially equestrian ones), agricultural fairs and the preparation of traditional meals.

The tourist office is a good source of information about the large number of minor fiestas held throughout the department (there seems to be one almost every week).

## Places to Stay

The recent revival of tourism has left Ayacucho a little short on hotel rooms. They tend to fill up, so try to avoid arriving very late in the day for the best choice. Most hotels are quite basic, but new hotels continue to open. Water problems are occasionally encountered.

**Budget** Basic cheapies, which lack hot showers (though this could change), include *Hostal Ayacucho* (☎ 91-2759, Lima 165) at US$3.50/6.50 for singles/doubles. They plan on adding rooms with private baths. *Hostal Sixtina* (☎ 81-2018, Callao 336) charges US$3.50 per person, and *Hostal Central* (☎ 81-2144, Arequipa 188) is US$4/7, or US$6.50/10 with bath.

There are several cheap places near the market and bus-station areas, which tend to be crowded; take the usual precautions with your gear. *Hotel Santiago* (☎ 81-2132, Nazareno 177) is basic and noisy because of the nearby market, but does have some hot water in the morning. Rates are US$3.50/5.50, or US$9 for a double with bath. Next door is the slightly better (but still noisy) *Hotel La Crillonesa* (☎ 81-2350, Nazareno 165), also with hot water in the morning. Rooms are US$4/7.

*Hostal Las Américas* (☎ 81-3903, Asamblea 258) has dingy rooms and cold water for US$3.50 per person, or rooms with private warm showers at US$5.50/8.50. The *Hostal Magdalena* (☎ 81-2910, M Cáceres 816) is clean and has hot water in the morning, but rooms vary in size. Rates are US$4.50/8, or about US$14 for a double with bath. Almost

next door, the basic *Hostal Wari* (☎ 81-3065, M Cáceres 836) is about US$4/7. The basic *Hostal Huamanga* (☎ 81-3527, Bellido 535) has hot water in the morning for US$3.50 per person, or US$7 with private bath.

*Hostal Luz Imperial* (☎ 81-7282, Libertad 591) is OK at US$4/7, or US$10 for a double with bath. Hot water is available in the morning. Both *Hostal Los Orquídeas* (☎ 81-4435, Arequipa 287) and *Hostal Emperador* (☎ 81-4547, San Martín 654) have hot water at times and charge US$4/7.50, or US$12 for a double with bath.

The popular, clean and safe *La Colmena Hotel* (☎ 81-2146, Cuzco 140) is often full by early afternoon. Rates are US$5 per person or US$12/15 with private bath and hot water in the morning and evening. *Hotel Samary* (☎ 81-2442, 81-3562, Callao 329) is simple but clean, has great rooftop views and hot water in the early morning and evening. Rates are US$7/11, or US$11/16 with private bath. Rooms with cable TV are US$2.50 extra. Ask here about a new 1st-class country inn that the owner plans to build on the outskirts of town in 1999.

The friendly *Hostal Tres Máscaras* (☎ 81-2921, 81-4107, Tres Máscaras 194) has a pleasant garden, hot water in the morning and on request, and rooms from US$5 per person, or US$10/15 with private bath and TV. It's a good value, and breakfast is available for US$2. Travelers have recommended the new *Hotel Florida* (☎ 81-2565, Cuzco 310), which also has a nice garden and seems like a good deal at US$11/17 in clean rooms with private bath and TV. Another choice is the *Gran Hotel Los Alamos* (☎ 81-4200, ☎/fax 81-2782, Cuzco 215), at US$9/16 with private bath and US$3 more with cable TV. They have a restaurant.

**Mid-Range** The quiet *Hostería Santa Rosa* (☎/fax 81-2083, Lima 166) has a nice patio with a decent restaurant, but is a little pricey for US$11/18, or US$16/29 with private bath, TV, telephone and (they claim) 24-hour hot water. *Hotel San Francisco* (☎ 81-2959, ☎/fax 81-8349, Callao 290) has a restaurant and bar and will serve meals on a patio. Rooms with cable TV, hot water, telephone as well as minirefrigerator are US$18/25.

*Hotel Yañez* (☎/fax 81-2464, M Cáceres 1210) is in a former clinic and has been described, perhaps tongue-in-cheek, as 'sterile.' Rooms vary – some with shared bathrooms are US$9 per person, but most are with private showers and hot water (sometimes), TV and continental breakfast for US$18/23. The roof has nice views. *Hostal El Marqués de Valdelirios* (☎ 81-3908, fax 81-4014, Bolognesi 720) is a bit far from the center, but is in an attractive colonial building. There is a restaurant, and a bar/disco that supposedly operates on weekends. Rooms all have private baths, but the rooms vary in size and amenities (views, balconies, TV, telephone or number of beds). Rates range from US$13 to US$43.

The *Ayacucho Plaza Hotel* (☎ 81-2202/3/4, fax 81-2314, 9 de Diciembre 184) is considered the best in town. It's a nice-looking colonial building, but the rooms are plain and no more than adequate; the nicest have balconies, some with plaza views. Rates for rooms with bath and TV are US$46/62. The restaurant is just OK.

## Places to Eat

Restaurants within two blocks of the Plaza de Armas tend to be aimed at tourists and are slightly overpriced, though not exorbitant (there are no fancy or expensive restaurants in Ayacucho). *Restaurant Los Alamos* (Cuzco 215) starts serving breakfast at 7 am and continues all day, often with musicians in the evening. Marginally more expensive, *La Casona* (Bellido 463) is popular and recommended by several travelers for its big portions. Opposite, the popular *Pizzería Italiana* (Bellido 490) opens nightly at 5 pm and occasionally has musicians. The wood-burning oven makes this a very cozy place on cold nights; pizzas are US$4 and US$8 for small and large.

The 400 block of San Martín has several decent places, including *Cámara Comercio* and *La Tradición* for cheap set menus, *El Retablo* for chicken and *Mia Pizza. Chifa El Dorado* (Cuzco 144) has been recommended for good set lunches and a variety

of Andean, coastal and Chinese dishes. The simple *La Buena Salud* (Asamblea 204), upstairs, serves vegetarian meals.

*Urpicha* (☎ 81-3905, Londres 272) is a homey place, with tables in a flower-filled patio and a small authentic menu of traditional dishes, including cuy. Most meals are around US$4, and musicians may stop by in the evenings. The neighborhood isn't great, so take a cab after dark.

*Wallpa Suwa* (G de la Vega 240) is a locally popular chicken restaurant. Wallpa Suwa is Quechua for 'chicken thief' – this might lead to some interesting conversations with the locals. *El Niño* (9 de Diciembre 205) is in a colonial mansion with a nice patio. It serves a variety of good Peruvian food and has decent service. A local tip is that seafood arrives from the coast on Saturday, so take advantage of their fish dishes during the weekend.

## Entertainment

Outside of Semana Santa, this is a quiet town, but there is a university, so you'll find a few bars to dance or hang out in, mostly favored by students. The popular *Los Balcones* (Asamblea 187) has occasional live Andean bands (US$1 cover) and a variety of recorded Andean, Latin, reggae and Western rock music to dance to. Their balconies offer a less loud environment for conversation. Nearby, *Taberna Madero Viejo* (Asamblea 131) has recorded rock music. *Taberna Magía Negra* (M Cáceres at G de la Vega) is a bar/gallery with good local art.

There are a few peñas on weekends (as usual, they start late, go until the wee hours and feature Peruvian music). It's best to ask locally about these. *Machi Peña* (Grau 158) reputedly has good music.

## Shopping

Ayacucho is famous as a crafts center, and a visit to the Museo de Arte Popular will give you an idea of local products. The tourist office can recommend local artisans who will welcome you to their workshops. The Santa Ana barrio is particularly well known. The area around the Plazuela Santa Ana has various workshops, including that of the

Sulca family, who has been weaving here for three generations.

## Getting There & Away

**Air** Aero Continente (☎ 81-2816, 81-3326, at the airport 81-6532, 9 de Diciembre 160) has a daily early morning flight to Lima. There used to be flights to Cuzco, but they aren't available at this time.

The airport is 4km from the town center. Taxis charge under US$2.

**Bus** If you travel by the poor, unpaved roads from Abancay or Huancayo, be prepared for long delays, especially during the rainy season (the worst months are February to April). The route from Lima via Pisco to Ayacucho is paved and fast. All routes are spectacular, but unfortunately, many buses travel overnight.

Coming up from the coast near Pisco, the road climbs an incredible series of hairpin bends to Castrovirreyna, a small mountain town with several basic restaurants where buses may stop for meals. Beyond Castrovirreyna, the road reaches an altitude of about 4800m at Abra Apacheta as it passes several blue, green and turquoise Andean lakes. The road flirts with the snowline for over an hour and offers dramatic views of high Andean scenery and snowcaps. Bring warm clothes if traveling at night. Finally, the road begins its descent toward Ayacucho, and the countryside becomes greener as forests of the dwarf *Polylepis* trees appear. Those who suffer from *soroche* (mild altitude sickness) in the high passes will be relieved by the arrival in Ayacucho, a mere 2731m above sea level.

For Lima (US$7, 10 hours), Transportes Molina (☎ 81-2984, 81-1840, Manco Cápac 273); Transportes Los Libertadores (☎ 81-3614, Tres Máscaras 496); Expreso Antezana (☎ 81-1235), on M Cáceres at Tres Máscaras; and Transportes Andía (☎ 81-5376, M Cáceres 896) all have departures, most leaving in the evening. Transportes Molina, Expreso Antezana and Transportes Andía have night buses to Huancayo (US$6, 8 to 10 hours).

Transportes Ayacucho Tours (☎ 81-3532, 81-5405, 81-1017, M Cáceres 880) and Transportes Chanka have daily departures to Cuzco (US$14, 24 to 27 hours) at 6 am. It's a rough trip, and the journey can be broken at Andahuaylas (US$6, about 10 hours), which is serviced by the companies mentioned earlier plus Transportes Andía. Note that these companies change their routes and services frequently. There are other possibilities if you ask around, especially during times of high demand.

A rough road drops about 200km northeast of Ayacucho to San Francisco and Luisiana, in the jungle on the Río Apurímac. This is a good take-out point for rafters after an adventurous descent of the river (see the Cuzco Area chapter). This road is traveled mainly by trucks, though Transportes Ayacucho Tours has buses. There are basic hotels in San Francisco and a better one at Luisiana. Like any highlands-to-jungle road, it's rough, tough and spectacular.

Trucks and buses to Cangallo and Vischongo (US$2.50, 4 hours) leave from the Puente Nuevo area, which is the bridge on Castilla over the Río Alameda. Departures are normally in the morning. Some vehicles may continue on to Vilcashuamán (another hour) if there is enough demand.

## Getting Around

There are four local city buses, one of which goes from the Plaza de Armas to the airport.

Pickup trucks and buses go to many local villages, including Quinua (US$0.75, 1 hour), and to the Wari ruins, departing from the Paradero Magdalena beyond the statue at the east end of Avenida Centenario.

## AROUND AYACUCHO
☎ 064

There are several places of interest that travelers to Ayacucho often visit. The area most frequented is the village and battlefield of Quinua, which is often combined with a visit to the Wari ruins. The Inca ruins of Vilcashuamán can also be visited, and there are other sites of interest nearby.

## Wari Ruins & Quinua

An attractive 37km road climbs about 550m to Quinua, 3300m above sea level. After about 20km, you will pass the extensive Wari ruins sprawling for several kilometers along the roadside. The small site museum (US$0.75) is supposedly open daily (check at the tourist office), though there are more Wari artifacts to be seen in the Ayacucho museum. The five main sectors of the ruins are marked by road signs; the upper sites are in rather bizarre forests of *Opuntia* cacti. If you visit, don't leave the site too late to look for onward or return transport – vehicles can get hopelessly full in the afternoon. Note that you have to pay the full fare to Quinua and remind the driver to drop you off at the ruins.

The ruins have not been restored much, and the most interesting visits are with a guide from Ayacucho. Agencies charge about US$15 per person for a one-day tour combined with Quinua (you need to speak Spanish).

Wari is built on a hill, and as the road from Ayacucho climbs through it, there are reasonable views. The road climbs beyond Wari until it reaches the pretty village of Quinua; buses usually stop at the plaza. Steps from the left-hand side of the plaza, as you arrive from Ayacucho, lead up to the village church. The church is on an old-fashioned cobblestone plaza, and a small museum nearby displays various relics from the major independence battle fought in this area. The museum is open from 8 am to 5 pm daily except Monday and costs about US$0.75 to visit. It is not of much interest, however, unless you are particularly fascinated by the battle fought here. Beside the museum, you can see the room where the Spanish Royalist troops signed their surrender, leading to the end of colonialism in Peru.

To reach the battlefield, turn left behind the church and head out of the village along Jirón Sucre, which, after a walk of about 10 minutes, rejoins the main road. As you walk, notice the red-tiled roofs elaborately decorated with ceramic model churches. Quinua is famous as a handicraft center, and these model churches are especially typical of the area. Local stores sell these and other crafts.

The **white obelisk**, which is intermittently visible for several kilometers as you approach Quinua, now lies a few minutes'

walk in front of you (bus drivers may drive here if there is enough demand). The impressive monument is 40m high and features carvings commemorating the Battle of Ayacucho, fought here on December 9, 1824. The walk and views from Quinua are pleasant. The whole area is protected as the 300-hectare **Santuario Histórico Pampas de Ayacucho.**

There are no accommodations in Quinua, but simple local meals are available at the *Restaurant Sumaq.* There is a small market on Sunday.

## Vilcashuamán & Vischongo

Vilcashuamán, or 'sacred falcon,' was considered the geographical center of the Inca Empire. It was here that the Inca road between Cuzco and the coast crossed the road running the length of the Andes. Little remains of the city's earlier magnificence; Vilcashuamán has fallen prey to looters, and many of its blocks have been used to build more modern buildings. The once-magnificent Temple of the Sun now has a parish church on top of it, which was being restored in 1999. The only structure still in a reasonable state of repair is a five-tiered pyramid, called an *usnu,* topped by a huge double throne carved from stone and used by the Inca.

To get there, take a vehicle from Ayacucho to Vischongo (about 110km by rough but scenic road). The basic *Hostal Titanc* in Vischongo is US$2 per person. From here, it's about 45 minutes by car, or almost two hours uphill on foot, to Vilcashuamán, where there are basic accommodations, such as *Hostal El Pirámide* and *Hostal La Flor de Cantuta,* at about US$2 per person. The best restaurant here is *Pachacutec.*

From Vischongo, you can also walk about an hour to an **Intihuatana ruin** (US$0.75), where there are reportedly **thermal baths.** If coming from Ayacucho, the turnoff to Intihuatana is about 2km before the village, and then another 2km on a trail. You can also walk to a *Puya raimondii* **forest** (see the Huaraz Area chapter for a description of this plant), which is about an hour away by foot.

If you don't want to spend the night, you can do a day tour with an agency from Ayacucho for about US$20 per person. Independent travelers will find buses returning to Ayacucho in the afternoon; ask for times.

# North of La Oroya

The road north of La Oroya passes through the highland towns of Junín, Cerro de Pasco, Huánuco and Tingo María, ending up in the important jungle town of Pucallpa.

## JUNÍN
☎ 064
The village of Junín (no hotels) is 4125m above sea level, 55km due north of La Oroya. An important independence battle was fought at the nearby Pampa de Junín, just south of the village. This is now preserved as the 2500-hectare **Santuario Histórico Chacamarca**, where there is a monument.

About 10km beyond the village is the interesting **Lago de Junín**, which, at about 30km long and 14km wide, is Peru's largest lake after Titicaca. Over 4000m above sea level, it is the highest lake of its size in the Americas. Lago de Junín is known for its birdlife, and some authorities claim that 1 million birds live on the lake or its shores at any one time. It is a little-visited area and a potential destination for anyone interested in seeing a variety of the water and shore birds of the high Andes. The lake and its immediate surroundings are part of the 53,000-hectare **Reserva Nacional Junín**.

The wide, high plain in this area is bleak, windswept and very cold, so be prepared with warm, windproof clothing. There are several small unattractive villages along the road and buses stop quite often. Between these settlements, **herds of llama, alpaca and sheep** are seen.

## CERRO DE PASCO
☎ 064
Cerro de Pasco, at 4333m above sea level and with a population of about 30,000, is the highest city of its size in the world. It's the capital of the Department of Pasco and

rather a miserable place, though the inhabitants are friendly. The altitude makes the town bitterly cold at night, and its main reason for existence is mining.

### Information
Banco de Crédito and Interbanc are on Bolognesi near the Plaza de Armas.

### Southwest of Cerro de Pasco
A poor and infrequently used road goes southwest of Cerro de Pasco to Lima. West of Lago de Junín, the road goes close to the village of Huayllay and nearby the 6815-hectare **Santuario Nacional Huayllay**, known for its strange geological formations. Several hours further southwest is the small town of **Canta**, which has a basic hotel and restaurant and is a few kilometers away from the pre-Columbian ruins of **Cantamarca**, which can be visited on foot.

### Places to Stay & Eat
The friendly *Hotel El Viajero* (☎ 72-2172), on the Plaza de Armas, has clean rooms for about US$3.50 per person. Shared baths have barely tepid water. Nearby, the basic *Hotel Santa Rosa* (☎ 72-2120) charges US$3 per person for rooms with shared, very cold baths. There are also the poor and very basic *Hostal Internacional* and *Hostal Comercio* on Libertad between the plaza and the bus terminal.

The best in the center is *Hostal Arenales* (☎ 72-3088, Arenales 162 at Libertad), near the bus terminal. Clean rooms with hot showers are US$10 double. *Villa Minera* (☎ 72-1113), in the suburbs, has rooms with private baths and hot water for US$9/12. It's a 10-minute cab ride that should cost about US$1.50.

The best restaurant is *Los Angeles*, on Libertad, near the plaza. There are other places on this street.

### Getting There & Away
The bus terminal is five blocks south of the Plaza de Armas. There are buses to Huánuco (US$2, 4 hours), Huancayo (US$4, 6 hours), and Lima (US$6.50, 9 hours) – most going through La Oroya (US$2.50,

3 hours), and a few through Canta. Faster colectivos from the plaza or bus terminal charge US$6 to Huánuco and US$10 to La Oroya.

# HUÁNUCO
☎ 064

Huánuco is 105km north of Cerro de Pasco and, at 1894m above sea level, provides welcome relief for soroche sufferers. It lies on the upper reaches of the Río Huallaga, the major tributary of the Río Marañón before it becomes the Amazon. Huánuco is the capital of its department and the site of one of Peru's oldest Andean archaeological sites – the Temple of Kotosh (also known as the Temple of the Crossed Hands). The town has a museum and a pleasant Plaza de Armas. Although Huánuco dates from 1541, little is left of its colonial buildings.

About 25km south of Huánuco, the road goes through the village of **Ambo**, noted for its *aguardiente* distilleries. This locally popular liquor is made from sugar cane, which can be seen growing nearby. Sometimes the bus stops and passengers can buy a couple of liters.

## Information
The tourist office (☎ 51-2980, General Prado 714) is open 8 am to 1:30 pm and 4 to 6 pm weekdays. The Banco de Crédito (☎ 51-2069), post office and telephone office are shown on the map.

## Museo de Ciencias
This museum at General Prado 495 (☎ 51-8104) is small but well organized, and the exhibits are labeled. They consist mainly of stuffed Peruvian animals, but there are also a few ceramic and archaeological pieces. The museum director, Señor Néstor Armas Wenzel, is dedicated and enthusiastic, and delights in showing visitors around. He particularly likes to talk to foreign visitors and has flags and 'welcome' signs in many languages decorating the entrance lobby. Admission is about US$0.50. Hours are 9 am to noon and 3 to 6 pm weekdays, 10 am to 1 pm on Sunday and closed on holidays.

## The Temple of Kotosh
This archaeological site is also known as the Temple of the Crossed Hands because of the lifesize molding, made of mud, of a pair of crossed hands that was discovered in the ruins by an archaeological team in the early 1960s. The molding is dated to between 4000 and 5000 years old.

Little is known about Kotosh, one of the most ancient of Andean cultures. The temple site is overgrown and difficult to reach, though it lies only 5km from Huánuco, and unless you are very interested in Kotosh, there is little to see. Most people are better off seeing the Crossed Hands in the Museo de la Nación in Lima. If you really want to visit the ruins, ask at the tourist office for directions.

## Places to Stay
Huánuco is the most pleasant town between Lima and Pucallpa, so its hotels, though not very good, tend to fill. You can usually find a bed, but the choices can be limited by late afternoon, so start looking as early as possible.

**Budget** Cheap rooms can be found near the noisy market in *Hotel La Victoria (☎ 51-3152, Huallayco 749)* and other hotels nearby. All have shared cold showers and charge under US$3 per person. *Hotel Imperial (☎ 51-3203, Huánuco 581)* charges US$3.50/5, or US$8/10 with private bath. It's reasonably clean and quiet, but has only cold water. Opposite is the basic *Hotel Marino* with shared baths, or *Hotel Caribe (☎ 51-3645, fax 51-3753, Huánuco 546)*, at US$5 for a double with cold bath. Other pretty basic hotels in this price range are mainly near the market and offer little to recommend them for other than their cheapness. *Hotel Europa (☎ 51-2483, Huallayco 826)* is also cheap and has many rooms, some with private cold shower, so you'll probably get a bed there later in the day. Other basic cheapies include *Hotel Oriente* and *Hostal Viajero*.

*Hostal Las Vegas (☎/fax 51-2315)*, on the plaza, is basic but clean and popular. They have hot water and charge about US$8/13

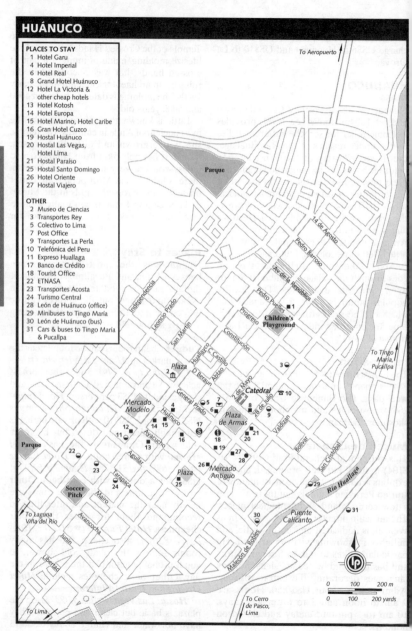

# HUÁNUCO

**PLACES TO STAY**
1  Hotel Garu
4  Hotel Imperial
6  Hotel Real
8  Grand Hotel Huánuco
12  Hotel La Victoria &
     other cheap hotels
13  Hotel Kotosh
14  Hotel Europa
15  Hotel Marino, Hotel Caribe
16  Gran Hotel Cuzco
19  Hostal Huánuco
20  Hostal Las Vegas,
     Hotel Lima
21  Hostal Paraíso
25  Hostal Santo Domingo
26  Hotel Oriente
27  Hostal Viajero

**OTHER**
2  Museo de Ciencias
3  Transportes Rey
5  Colectivo to Lima
7  Post Office
9  Transportes La Perla
10  Telefónica del Peru
11  Expreso Huallaga
17  Banco de Crédito
18  Tourist Office
22  ETNASA
23  Transportes Acosta
24  Turismo Central
28  León de Huánuco (office)
29  Minibuses to Tingo María
30  León de Huánuco (bus)
31  Cars & buses to Tingo María
     & Pucallpa

To Aeropuerto

Parque

14 de Agosto

Pedro Barroso

Av. de la República

Pedro Puelles

Children's
Playground

Progreso

Independencia

Leoncio Prado

San Martín

Constitución

Huallayco

C Castillo

Abtao

D Beraun

2 de Mayo

Plaza

Catedral

28 de Julio

General Prado

Mercado
Modelo

Huánuco

Plaza
de Armas

Valdizán

Ayacucho

Bolívar

San Cristóbal

Aguilar

Mercado
Antiguo

Parque

Tarapacá

Plaza

22

23

24

Soccer
Pitch

Mairo

Río Huallaga

To Laguna
Viña del Río

Avancocha

29

31

Puente
Calicanto

30

Junín

Malecón de Robles

Libertad

To Lima

To Cerro
de Pasco,
Lima

To Tingo
María,
Pucallpa

0       100      200 m
0       100      200 yards

for rooms with bath and TV, and have some cheaper rooms with shared bath. On the same block, the basic *Hotel Lima* (☎ 51-3020) charges US$3 to US$4 per person for rooms with private bath, which may have hot water in the mornings. These hotels have a café. *Hotel Paraíso* (☎ 51-1953) is also OK at US$5/8; some rooms have private bath.

*Hostal Santo Domingo* (☎ 51-2415, 2 de Mayo 814) charges US$6/8 with shared bath and US$7/10 with private cold water bath. *Hotel Kotosh* (☎ 51-7341, Ayacucho 560) charges US$7/10 for rooms with bath and some hot water.

The pleasant and secure *Hostal Huánuco* (☎ 51-2050, Huánuco 777) has a garden, cooking facilities, a good hot-water supply and is often full. They charge US$9/13 in rooms with private bath, and have cheaper rooms with shared bath.

**Mid-Range** *Hotel Garu* (☎ 51-3096, fax 51-3097, Pedro Puelles 459) is decent, well run and a fair value, offering clean rooms with private hot showers and TV for about US$15/25. *Gran Hotel Cuzco* (☎ 51-3263, fax 51-2244, Huánuco 616) is old but isn't bad and has clean, bare but good-sized rooms with private hot showers and cable TV for US$20/30. It has a cafeteria, laundry service and a parking area and is popular with Peruvian businessmen.

*Hotel Real* (☎ 51-2973, 51-3411, fax 51-2765), on the Plaza de Armas, is a fairly comfortable modern hotel with rates starting at US$20. They offer a small pool and sauna, as does the old-fashioned *Grand Hotel Huánuco* (☎ 51-4222, ☎/fax 51-2410), also on the Plaza de Armas. It looks pleasant and has rooms with private bath and TV for US$33/40. It has a restaurant and a parking area.

## Places to Eat

Every hotel on the Plaza de Armas has a restaurant, and there are several chifas or chicken places nearby the plaza. For local lunches, try the restaurants near the Laguna Viña del Río, about 1.5km south of the Plaza de Armas (along Abtao by car, along Leoncio Prado by foot).

## Getting There & Away

**Air** Flight service is irregular and subject to change. TdobleA usually has two flights a week to and from Lima; some flights may continue to Tingo María, Juanjuí and Tarapoto. AeroCóndor and Grupo 8 also have had services in the recent past. The airport is 8km from town.

**Bus** For Lima (US$10, 12 hours), León de Huánuco has 8 am and 8 pm departures. Note that there is an office for tickets near the Plaza de Armas, but the bus leaves from Malecón de Robles. An express colectivo for Lima (US$20, 10 hours) leaves every morning; purchase tickets at General Prado 607 the previous day. Other companies operating buses to Lima are Transportes Rey and the not-so-good ETNASA, which has only night buses.

The route north to Tingo María and then east to Pucallpa goes close to (but not into) the drug-running zone of the Río Huallaga. As long as you travel by day, you should have no problems, but keep your passport handy, as there usually are several police or military checkpoints. Because the trip to Pucallpa usually takes over 12 hours, you should overnight in Tingo María, unless you hear locally that the entire route is completely safe again.

Transportes La Perla (C Castillo 810) has a daily bus to Tingo María and Pucallpa. If you walk along General Prado to the Puente Calicanto and over the Río Huallaga (10 minutes from the town center), you'll find numerous shared taxis or cheaper minibuses all heading to Tingo María (US$2, 4½ hours). You can also flag down passing buses to Tingo María and Pucallpa.

Turismo Central and Expreso Huallaga have several buses a day to Cerro de Pasco and Huancayo (US$5, 8 hours). You can also pick up passing buses at the Puente Calicanto.

To visit the remote towns of La Unión, Tantamayo and other villages, head for the area a couple of blocks southwest of the market. Here you'll find a daily morning Transportes Acosta bus to La Unión (US$6, 8 hours). However, Union Tours (☎ 51-7362,

Tarapaca 383) reportedly has colectivos to La Unión that are faster. For Tantamayo (10 hours to cover 150km), ETNASA has an 8 am bus (US$7). This is also the place to look for transport to other remote villages in the area; there are several small companies on these streets.

## LA UNIÓN
☎ 064

This town is roughly halfway between Huánuco and Huaraz. It is feasible to travel this way to the Cordillera Blanca. La Unión has two or three basic hotels with cold water, of which the best is *Gran Hostal Abilia Alvarado*, at US$5 for a room with one bed. You can find simple meals near the market, though these rudimentary restaurants close early in the evening.

About a three-hour walk (one way) from La Unión are the Inca ruins of **Huánuco Viejo**. Take the path from behind the market heading toward a cross up on a hill. I'm told the walk is worth the effort, but beware of dogs. Vehicles can also be found to take you there. Admission is US$1.50, and the ruins are worth a visit.

A daily bus leaves the plaza early in the day for Lima via Chiquián, from where you can continue on to Huaraz and the Cordillera Blanca; Chiquián itself is also served by a few buses a day. There are also buses and trucks to Huánuco.

## TANTAMAYO
☎ 064

The small, remote village of Tantamayo is in the mountains north of Huánuco. The best of the few hotels can provide information for visiting several ruins within a few hours' walk. Guides can be hired.

## TINGO MARÍA
☎ 064

The 129km road north from Huánuco climbs over a 3000m pass before dropping steadily to the town of Tingo María, which lies in the lush, tropical slopes of the eastern Andes at 649m. The town is on the edge of the Amazon Basin and is hot and humid most of the year. Tingo María could therefore be described correctly as a jungle town, yet it is surrounded by steep Andean foothills.

Tingo María is a thriving market town, though it includes coca (for the production of cocaine) and, to a lesser extent, marijuana among its local products, so the town has a rather unsavory atmosphere and not particularly attractive. It is definitely not a good place to buy drugs. The few foreign visitors mainly stop for one night on their way to Pucallpa.

Nevertheless, the town center is not any more dangerous than any other city. The dangerous area is the Río Huallaga valley north of Tingo María and should be avoided. Remember that growing coca is not necessarily illegal, and coca leaves are legally sold for chewing or making maté in most highland towns. It is the mashing of coca into *pasta básica* for use in cocaine production that is illegal. Local authorities are encouraging the production of other tropical crops, notably cocoa. Bus travel on the Huánuco-Tingo María-Pucallpa route is safe, particularly during the day.

### Information
There is no tourist office. US cash can be changed at Interbanc (☎ 56-1022, Raimondi 263), Banco Continental (☎ 56-2141, A Raimondi 543) and Banco de Crédito (☎ 56-2111, A Raimondi 249), which have a Visa ATM and may change traveler's checks. Cash can also be changed on the west side of the market. The post office is at Alameda Peru 451. The hospital (☎ 56-2017/8/9) is at Ucayali 114.

### Universidad Nacional Agraria de la Selva (UNAS)
The university (☎ 56-2341) runs a **jardín botánico** (botanical garden), which, though rather run-down and overgrown, has labels on some of the plants allowing you to learn something about them. Hours are 8 am to 2 pm weekdays and 8 to 11 am on Saturday; you may need to yell for the gatekeeper. The garden is at the south end of Alameda Peru.

The university itself, 4km south of town, has a small **Museo Zoológico** (Zoological Museum) with a collection of living and mounted animals from around the region.

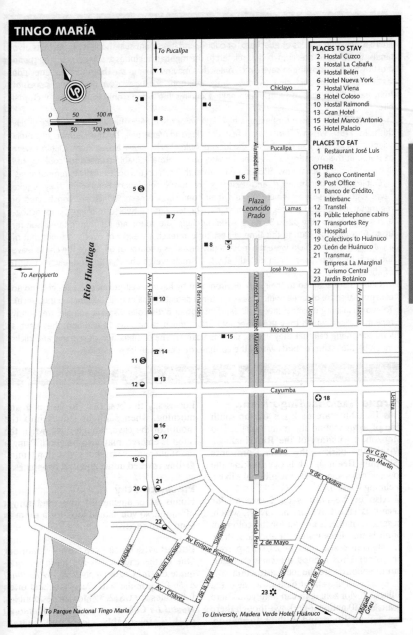

**TINGO MARÍA**

To Pucallpa

Chiclayo

Pucallpa

Plaza
Leoncido
Prado

Lamas

José Prato

Monzón

Cayumba

Callao

Río Huallaga

To Aeropuerto

Av A Raimondi

Av M Benavides

Alameda Perú (Street Market)

Av Ucayali

Av Amazonas

Av G de
San Martín

9 de Octobre

Uchiza

To Parque Nacional Tingo María

Tarapacá

Av Juan Ericson

Av Enrique Pimentel

Surquillo

Alameda Perú

2 de Mayo

Sucre

Av 28 de Julio

Miguel
Grau

Av J Chávez

C de la Vega

To University, Madera Verde Hotel, Huánuco

0    50    100 m
0    50    100 yards

**PLACES TO STAY**
2  Hostal Cuzco
3  Hostal La Cabaña
4  Hostal Belén
6  Hotel Nueva York
7  Hostal Viena
8  Hotel Coloso
10  Hostal Raimondi
13  Gran Hotel
15  Hotel Marco Antonio
16  Hotel Palacio

**PLACES TO EAT**
1  Restaurant José Luis

**OTHER**
5  Banco Continental
9  Post Office
11  Banco de Crédito,
    Interbanc
12  Transtel
14  Public telephone cabins
17  Transportes Rey
18  Hospital
19  Colectivos to Huánuco
20  León de Huánuco
21  Transmar,
    Empresa La Marginal
22  Turismo Central
23  Jardín Botánico

**CENTRAL HIGHLANDS**

## Oilbirds

There is only one species of guacharo, or oilbird, and it is so unusual that it is placed in its own family, the Steatornithidae, which is related to the nightjars. Oilbirds are nocturnal, and spend most of the day roosting in caves in colonies that may number in the thousands. La Cueva de las Lechuzas is one such cave. At dusk, huge numbers of oilbirds leave the cave in search of fruit, particularly that of palm trees, making oilbirds the world's only fruit-eating nocturnal birds.

Palm fruits are known for having a high fat content that gives the oilbirds very fatty or oily flesh. In 1799, when oilbirds were first described in Venezuela by the German explorer/scientist Alexander von Humboldt, the local people already knew about them. Oilbirds were captured in their roosting colonies and boiled down into a valuable oil used for cooking and lighting. This practice is now discouraged, although it still occurs occasionally in remote areas.

Oilbirds feed on the wing, and their feet are poorly developed. For shelter, they require caves with ledges upon which to build their cone-shaped nests, which are constructed of regurgitated fruit and are regularly enlarged. The females lay two to four eggs, and incubation is a relatively long 32 to 35 days. After hatching, the young are fed regurgitated fruit for up to four months. During this time, a nestling can reach a weight of over 1½ times that of an adult. These fat chicks were the most highly prized as a source of oil. Once the chicks leave the nest, they lose their accumulated baby fat. Adults weigh about 400g and reach a length of about 45cm.

Oilbirds are adapted to their dark environment by having well-developed eyesight and an exceptional sense of smell (which may help them detect the palm fruits' distinctive fragrance). To avoid crashing into the cave walls (and into other birds), oilbirds emit audible, frequently repeated clicks, which they use for echolocation, much as bats do. In addition, they have a loud screaming call that they use for communication. The combination of screams and clicks made by thousands of birds within the confines of a cave can be deafening.

## Parque Nacional Tingo María

This 18,000-hectare park lies on the south side of town around the mouth of the Río Monzón, a tributary of the Río Huallaga. Within the park is the **Bella Dormiente** (Sleeping Beauty), a hill overlooking the town. From some angles, the hill looks like a reclining woman.

Also in the park is **La Cueva de las Lechuzas** (the Cave of the Owls), which, despite its name, is known for the colony of oilbirds that lives inside. In addition, there are stalactites and stalagmites, bats, parrots and other birds around the cave entrance, but the oilbirds are the main attraction.

The caves are about 6km away near the village of Monzón; taxis can take you. There is a US$1.50 national-park fee, though there are no facilities and little information.

Locals say the best time to visit is in the morning, when sunlight shines into the mouth of the cave, though dusk, when the oilbirds emerge, may also be good. Bring a flashlight and wear shoes you don't mind getting covered in bat and bird droppings.

## Places to Stay

Hotels are of a generally low standard, yet often full, so you should look for a room as soon as you arrive.

**Budget** Most hotels have only cold showers. One of the cheapest is the basic but adequate *Hostal Cuzco* (☎ 56-2095, A Raimondi 671). It's popular with Peruvians and often full. Rates are US$2.50/4 for singles/doubles. *Hostal La Cabaña* (☎ 56-2178, A Raimondi 644) is reasonably clean and charges

US$4/6. The similarly priced **Hostal Belén** is also OK. The basic **Hostal Raimondi** (☎ 56-2146, A Raimondi 344) seems secure.

**Hostal Viena** (☎ 56-2194, Lamas 254) is clean and a reasonable value. Rooms are US$4/6, or US$5/8 with private bath. **Hotel Coloso** (☎ 56-2027, M Benavides 440) is also US$5/8 with private bath and is clean, but has occasional water failures (which is probably true of all of these places). Also in this price range is **Gran Hotel** (☎ 56-2217, A Raimondi 214). **Hotel Palacio** (☎ 56-2319, A Raimondi 158) looks well run and clean, though the rooms are a bit spartan. Rates are US$4 per person, or US$7/11 with private bath.

The best budget hotel is **Hotel Nueva York** (☎/fax 56-2406, Alameda Peru 553), which charges US$8/12 for rooms with private bath and tepid water, or an extra US$2 for cable TV. Another decent choice at this price is **Hotel Marco Antonio** (☎ 56-2201, Monzón 364).

**Mid-Range** The best is **Madera Verde Hotel** (☎/fax 56-1800), just over 1km south of town. Rates start at US$40, or US$70 for a four-person bungalow, but walk-in rates can be substantially less, and continental breakfast is included. The rooms, which are good sized, have private bath and hot water, TV and minirefrigerator. The hotel is set in pleasant gardens with a pool, playground and simple but adequate restaurant and bar.

## Places to Eat

Hotel Nueva York, Hotel Marco Antonio and Hostal La Cabaña have decent restaurants. **Restaurant José Luis** (☎ 56-1008, A Raimondi 742) is the best of numerous restaurants along Raimondi.

## Getting There & Away

**Air** As with the air service to Huánuco, carriers and schedules change frequently. TdobleA is the only airline flying regularly to Lima at this time. The airport is about 1½km from town on the west side of the Río Huallaga. A cab should cost about US$2.

If you go to the airport and ask around, you can find light aircraft flying to other nearby towns. Cancellations are frequent in the rainy season (January to April), or if there are not enough passengers.

**Bus** The bus schedules change frequently. As a general rule, avoid night travel and avoid the Río Huallaga region due north of Tingo María.

Transtel has an early morning bus to Pucallpa (US$9, about 12 hours). Outside, there are minibuses leaving later in the day. Empresa La Marginal (☎ 56-1254) also goes to Pucallpa, and there are others. The journey from Tingo María to Pucallpa is described in the Pucallpa section of the Amazon Basin chapter.

León de Huánuco (☎ 56-2030), Transmar (☎ 56-3076) and Transportes Rey (☎ 56-2565) have buses to Lima (US$12, 15 hours), though some go only overnight. Also check these companies for Pucallpa departures. Turismo Central (☎ 56-2668) has a night bus to Huancayo (US$8, 12 hours). Colectivo taxis and minibuses leave for Huánuco from Raimondi at Callao. Empresa La Marginal has slow buses to Huánuco.

# The North Coast

This area is part of the great South American coastal desert. On the drive north from Lima, you pass huge, rolling sand dunes, dizzying cliffs, oases of farmland and busy fishing villages, as well as some of Peru's largest and most historic cities. Scattered among these are many important archaeological sites that predate the Incas.

Few travelers appreciate this area of Peru, because most choose to visit the Inca sites and Lake Titicaca to the south. Slowly traveling the north coast, however, allows greater involvement with the local people and often gets you away from the 'gringo scene.' The many archaeological sites here are uncrowded and interesting.

## ANCÓN

The first town north of Lima is Ancón, a seaside resort about 40km from the capital. The beaches are poor and crowded with *Limeños* on day trips during the January-to-March season.

En route from Lima to Ancón on the Panamericana, you'll see many *pueblos jovenes*, or young towns. These shantytowns often have no running water, electricity or other facilities. They are built by peasants migrating to Lima from the highlands in search of jobs and a higher standard of living.

## CHANCAY

Beyond Ancón are the extensive Pasamayo sand dunes. A toll road, appropriately named the *Serpentuario de Pasamayo*, snakes along a narrow ledge and offers good views of the dunes, which stretch on for some 20km to the small village of Chancay. The Chancay subculture existed in this area from about 1100 AD to 1400 AD. The black-on-white ceramic style, for which this coastal culture is noted, is best seen at the excellent Museo Amano in Lima. Chancay itself is a small fishing village of some 10,000 inhabitants and has little to see, apart from a mock

castle, *El Castillo*, visible on the west side of the highway, where there is a restaurant.

At the north end of Chancay, a road goes inland to the village of Huaral, 10km away, and into the Río Chancay valley, where there are a number of little-known ruins.

## THE CHURÍN ROAD

About 20km north of Chancay, a turnoff to the right leads to the small mountain towns of Sayán, Churín and Oyón. This road follows the Río Huaura valley, and a bus from Lima travels this road daily. Buses leave from opposite Lima's Ormeño terminal; ask for Empresa Espadín (☎ 428-5887).

Between Sayán and Churín, the road climbs through strange rock formations and tropical scrub vegetation. Churín, 190km from Lima, is a minor resort known for its good hot springs. It's popular with locals, but very few travelers visit. There are several inexpensive hotels on Avenida Larco Herrera (the main street), the best of which is *Hostal Santa Rosa* (☎ 034-37-3104, 37-3014, Larco Herrera 396). It has mid-priced rooms with private hot showers and TV. Cheaper options include *Hostal San Juan de Churín* (☎ 034-37-3012, Larco Herrera 315) and *Hostal Acuario* (☎ 034-37-3037, Larco Herrera 337). Several inexpensive restaurants serve local food, such as trout and *cuy* (guinea pig).

Beyond Churín, the road continues through the village of Oyón and on to the southern parts of the Cordillera Raura – a remote, snowcapped mountain range. Oyón has four or five basic hostels.

## RESERVA NACIONAL LOMAS DE LACHAY

About 2km north of the turnoff for the Churín road, between Km 105 and Km 106, a marked dirt road heads 4km east of the Panamericana to Lomas de Lachay, a 5070-hectare natural reserve. Lomas de Lachay is a hill that seems to gain most of its moisture from the coastal mists, creating a unique microenvironment of dwarf forest and small animals and birds. There are camping and picnicking areas, latrines and trails. Admission is US$3. There are no buses, so you have to hire a vehicle or walk from the Panamericana.

## HUACHO & HUAURA

The small town of Huacho (population 40,000) is almost 150km north of Lima at the mouth of the Río Huaura. Across the river is the village of Huaura, where San Martín proclaimed Peru's independence. Anyone can show you the building, where there is a very small museum with a Spanish-speaking guide. Entrance to the museum and the balcony from where San Martín spoke is about US$1, or you can see the balcony from outside for free.

There are a dozen hotels in Huacho and Huaura. One of the best is **Gran Hotel La Villa** (☎ 32-1477, 32-3353, FB Cárdenas 196), on the outskirts of Huacho. Rooms have TV, telephones and hot showers, and are around US$40 for a double. Most places are much cheaper and more basic. Very few travelers spend the night, however. You could take a Cruz del Sur bus here, see the balcony, and continue the same day. Buses from Huacho go up the valley, reaching Sayán (see the Churín Road section earlier in this chapter).

## BARRANCA

About 190km north of Lima you reach Barranca. Though small, Barranca is the biggest town in the area. Most buses along the coast stop here on their way to Supe, Pativilca, Paramonga and the turnoff for Huaraz and the Cordillera Blanca, all of which lie within a few kilometers of Barranca. Everything happens within a block or two of the main street, which is also the Panamericana, but there's little to see here.

At the small fishing port of **Supe**, a few kilometers south of Barranca, there are a couple of cheap and basic hotels. The archaeological site of **Aspero** is nearby. Although Aspero is one of the oldest sites in

NORTH COAST

Peru, it has little to offer the untrained eye, and few locals know anything about it.

The village of **Pativilca** is a few kilometers north of Barranca. It has one very basic hotel and a few simple restaurants, but most people stay in Barranca. Simón Bolívar once lived here, and his house is now a small museum. Just north of Pativilca, the road to Huaraz and the Cordillera Blanca branches off to the right. This spectacular road climbs through cactus-laden cliff faces and is worth seeing in daylight. Many people see no more of the north coast than the Panamericana between Lima and the mountain turnoff at Pativilca.

Just 3km or 4km beyond the Huaraz turnoff is the archaeological site of **Paramonga**. This huge adobe temple is attributed to the Chimu civilization, which was the ruling power on the north coast before being conquered by the Incas in the mid-15th century. The massive temple, surrounded by seven defensive walls, is clearly visible on the right-hand side of the Panamericana and is worth a visit. Entry is about US$2.50 and the small on-site museum is open from 8 am to 5 pm. Local buses traveling between Barranca and the port of Paramonga will drop you off 3km from the entrance, or you can take a taxi from Barranca for a few dollars.

### Places to Stay & Eat

You'll find several hotels along the main street. The best of these is *Hotel Chavín* (☎ 235-2358, 235-2253, fax 235-2480, Gálvez 222), which charges about US$18/28 for clean singles/doubles with bath. Nearby, just off the main street, is *Hostal Residencial Continental* (☎ 235-2458, A Ugarte 190), which is clean, secure and a bit cheaper. *Hostal Jefferson* (☎ 235-2184, Lima 946) is clean and friendly at US$12 for a double with bath. There are half a dozen cheaper places, including *Pacífico*, which is reportedly OK. There are plenty of cheap restaurants, the best of which is *Chifa Lung Fung*, on the main street (but beware of being overcharged for 'servicio especial' – check your bill).

## HUARMEY

North of Paramonga, the Panamericana enters a particularly deserted stretch and soon crosses the line dividing the departments of Lima and Ancash. *Hotel de Turismo San Pedro* (☎ 60-0231), in Huarmey, 290km north of Lima, is the best hotel on the 170km stretch of road between Barranca and Casma. A double room with bath costs about US$25. There is also the cheaper *Hostal Mario's* (☎ 60-0266).

There's nothing to do in Huarmey except spend the night in the hotel, though if you have your own transport, you'll find some excellent deserted beaches nearby.

## CASMA & SECHÍN
☎ 044

The small town of Casma is 370km north of Lima. The archaeological site of Sechín is about 5km away and is easily reached from Casma. Once an important colonial port that was sacked by various pirates during the 17th century, Casma's importance has declined greatly, and the town was largely destroyed by the earthquake of May 31, 1970. There's not much to do in either the port (11km from town) or the town itself, and most people only come here to visit the Sechín ruins or to travel to Huaraz via the Punta Callán road – a route offering excellent panoramic views of the Cordillera Blanca.

### Information

There is no tourist office, but Sechín Tours (☎/fax 71-1421, cell 61-9821), in the Centro Comercial Montecarlo, office 7, gives tourist information and travelers' assistance, as well as arranging local tours. The Banco de Crédito (☎ 71-1314, 71-1471) is at Bolívar 111.

### Tours

Sechín Tours takes groups to Sechín for about US$10 per person (four-person minimum) with an English-speaking guide, or for about US$7 with a Spanish-speaking guide. Ask them about other sites. They also rent sand boards (US$2) for sliding down the nearby Manchan dunes (ten minutes by mototaxi).

## Sechín

This site is one of the oldest in Peru (about 1600 BC) and is among the more important and well preserved of the coastal ruins. First excavated in 1937 by the renowned Peruvian archaeologist JC Tello, it has suffered some damage from grave-robbers and natural disasters. The site is 5km southeast of Casma and is easily reached on foot or by taxi; there are good road signs. To get there, head south of Casma on the Panamericana for 3km, then turn left and follow the paved road to Huaraz for an additional 2km to the site. If you're coming from Huaraz, you can visit the ruins en route to Casma if you don't have too much gear.

The site at Sechín, part of which is thought to have been buried by a landslide, is still being excavated, and only some of the area is open to visitors. This consists of three outside walls of the main temple that are completely covered with bas-relief carvings of warriors and captives being eviscerated. The gruesomely realistic carvings are up to 4m high. The warlike people who built this temple remain a mystery and are one of the site's main points of interest. Inside the main temple are earlier mud structures still being excavated; you can't go in, but there is a model in the small on-site museum.

JC Tello, excavator of many pre-Inca sites

There are several other early sites in the Sechín area; most of them have not been excavated because of a lack of funds. From the museum, you can see **Sechín Alto** – a large, flat-topped hill – in the distance. The fortress of **Chanquillo**, consisting of several

NORTH COAST

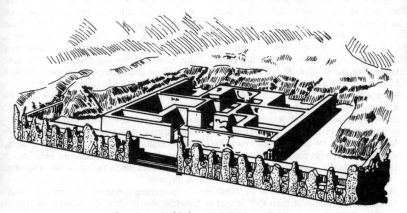

The ruins at Sechín have a mysterious origin.

towers surrounded by concentric walls, can be visited, but is best appreciated from the air. Aerial photographs are on display at the museum. If you wish to explore more than just Sechín, the museum attendant or the people at Sechín Tours can give directions, and there is a detailed area map in the museum.

The Sechín ruins and museum are open 9 am to 5 pm daily and cost US$2 to visit. There is a small shady garden and picnic area – bring your own food. The entry ticket also allows you to visit the Mochica ruins of **Pañamarca**, 10km inland from the Panamericana on the road to Nepeña (the turnoff is about halfway between Casma and Chimbote). The ruins are badly weathered, but some murals can be seen if you ask the guard. The murals are normally covered up for protection.

### Tortugas

This is a small beach resort about 22km northwest of Casma. There's a decent beach with clean water and pleasant swimming in a bay; high season is January to March.

### Places to Stay

Casma has several hotels. The cheapest is the basic, unattractive **Hostal Central**, on the Plaza de Armas, which charges US$4/6 for singles/doubles or US$6/8 with cold-water, private baths. A better budget choice is the clean and friendly **Hostal Gregori** (☎ 71-1073, 71-1173, L Ormeño 579), which charges US$5/7.50 for rooms with shared cold showers or US$8/12 with private baths. **Hostal Indoamericano** (☎ 71-1395, 71-1235, 71-1468, Huarmey 132) is also clean and has some hot water. Rates are US$8/12 or US$10/16. **Hostal Ernestos** (☎ 71-1475) charges US$10/16 for clean rooms with private hot shower and continental breakfast. Some rooms have TV. **Hostal Rebeca** (☎ 71-1143, Huarmey 368) also has rooms with private hot showers for US$12/18, and TV for an extra US$2.

The best place to stay in Casma is the pleasant **Hotel El Farol** (☎/fax 71-1064, in Lima 424-0517, Túpac Amaru 450). It's set in a garden and has a simple cafeteria and bar, and helpful, friendly staff. There's a useful map in the lobby if you plan to explore some of the ruins in the area. Rooms with TV and hot showers are US$16/24 including breakfast. A pool is under construction. The hotel also has similarly priced bungalows with hot showers and an ocean view at the **Tortugas beach resort** (☎ 61-9732).

The best place in the area is the new **Hostal Las Terrazas** (in Lima ☎ 448-0701, 964-9573), which has rooms starting at US$40.

### Places to Eat

There are no fancy restaurants. The inexpensive **Chifa Tío Sam** (☎ 71-1447, Huarmey 138) is one of the better ones. There are several other inexpensive and satisfactory places along the same street, including **Venecia**, on the 2nd block, which has good set lunches (US$1.25). Just off the plaza **Café Lucy** is a friendly place and good for breakfast. **Heladería El Pibe** sells ice cream.

### Getting There & Away

Many companies run buses north and south along the Panamericana, but few have offices in Casma. For Trujillo (US$3, 3 hours) or Lima (US$5, 6 hours), ask where you can flag down a bus as it comes through and hope for a seat. Transportes Vista Alegre has an office next to the Hostal Gregori and sells a limited number of seats on their Trujillo-Lima buses. Turismo Chimbote, on the same block, also has buses to Lima, but only a few seats are available from the Casma office; the majority of the seats are sold in Chimbote. A block away, Turismo Tres Estrellas also has buses to Lima.

Opposite, Transportes Moreno has a 9 pm bus to Huaraz (US$5, 7 hours). I couldn't find a day bus, but there have been day departures in the past, so ask around. The panoramic views of the Cordillera Blanca from the Punta Callán Pass (4225m and 30km from Huaraz) are beautiful and worth a day trip.

There are frequent colectivos and buses to Chimbote (US$1, 1¼ hours), 50km to the north, where there are better connections.

# CHIMBOTE
☎ 044

This is the first major town along the north coast; it is 420km north of Lima. Chimbote is Peru's largest fishing port, and millions of tons of fish were caught here in the 1960s. Since then, the industry has declined because of overfishing. Despite this and the 1970 earthquake (which destroyed much of the city), the population has continued to grow dramatically and is now about 300,000. The town is not a tourist destination, and there's little to do, but Chimbote is a good place to stay overnight if you're heading to Huaraz via the spectacular Cañón del Pato route.

## Information

There is no tourist office. The post office, telephone office and several banks are shown on the map. The local fiesta of San Pedro, patron of fishermen, is June 29, so hotel rooms may be overpriced during the last week in June.

## Places to Stay – Budget

Chimbote offers a good selection of hotels. For those on a tight budget, there are very basic hotels, generally with cold and erratic water supplies. *Hostal Basico Huáscar* (☎ 32-1925), near the bus stations, is US$3.25/5 for singles/doubles. *Hostal Paraíso* (☎ 32-3718, J Pardo 1015) is convenient for the Expreso Continental terminal and clean enough for US$5 for one bed (one or two people) and US$8 for two beds, or US$7/12 for one/two beds with private cold shower. *Hotel El Santa* (☎ 32-1161, Espinar 671) has rooms with baths for US$6/10 and some slightly cheaper rooms with shared baths. Rooms vary in quality here so look at a couple of them. *Hotel Venus* (☎ 32-1339, J Pardo 673) charges US$6/10 for rooms with baths and is friendly, though the rooms are shabby. The

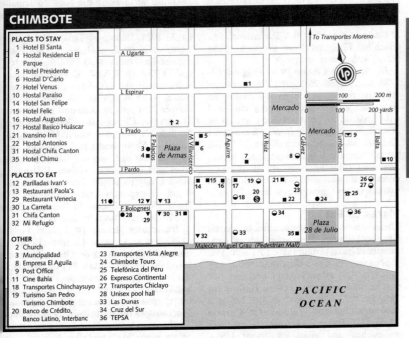

**CHIMBOTE**

**PLACES TO STAY**
1 Hotel El Santa
4 Hostal Residencial El Parque
5 Hotel Presidente
6 Hostal D'Carlo
7 Hotel Venus
10 Hostal Paraíso
14 Hotel San Felipe
15 Hotel Felic
16 Hostal Augusto
17 Hostal Basico Huáscar
21 Ivansino Inn
22 Hostal Antonios
31 Hostal Chifa Canton
35 Hotel Chimu

**PLACES TO EAT**
12 Parilladas Ivan's
13 Restaurant Paola's
29 Restaurant Venecia
30 La Carreta
31 Chifa Canton
32 Mi Refugio

**OTHER**
2 Church
3 Muncipalidad
8 Empresa El Aguila
9 Post Office
11 Cine Bahía
18 Transportes Chinchaysuyo
19 Turismo San Pedro Turismo Chimbote
20 Banco de Crédito, Banco Latino, Interbanc
23 Transportes Vista Alegre
24 Chimbote Tours
25 Telefónica del Peru
26 Expreso Continental
27 Transportes Chiclayo
28 Unisex pool hall
33 Las Dunas
34 Cruz del Sur
36 TEPSA

To Transportes Moreno

A Ugarte

L Espinar

L Prado

Plaza de Armas

L Pardo

F Bolognesi

Mercado

Mercado

Plaza 28 de Julio

Malecón Miguel Grau  (Pedestrian Mall)

PACIFIC OCEAN

0   100   200 m
0   100   200 yards

**NORTH COAST**

reasonably clean *Hostal Augusto* (☎ *32-4431, Aguirre 265)* is clean and charges US$6/8 for rooms with shared baths, or US$8/12 with private baths. *Hotel Felic* (☎ *32-5901, J Pardo 552)* is similar.

## Places to Stay – Mid-Range
The small but clean *Hostal Residencial El Parque* (☎ *32-3963, fax 33-6197, Palacios 309)* charges US$14/21 for rooms with hot showers and TV. *Hotel San Felipe* (☎ *32-3401, 34-3061, J Pardo 514)* is clean and has similar rooms for US$16/24. *Hostal Antonios* (☎ *33-3026, fax 32-5783, Bolognesi 745)* has clean rooms with private hot showers, fans, TV and telephones for US$23/32. It has a café.

*Hotel Presidente* (☎ *32-2411, fax 34-3206, L Prado 536)* is clean and modern. Rates are US$30/44 for good rooms including continental breakfast. Room service is available. The similarly priced *Ivansino Inn* (☎ *33-1395, fax 32-1927, J Pardo 738)* has 12 nice rooms with minirefrigerators, but the front rooms are noisy. Also at this price is *Hostal D'Carlo* (☎/*fax 33-0038, Villavicencio 384)*, which has 17 rooms (some overlooking the plaza) with similar amenities.

*Hostal Chifa Canton* (☎ *34-4388, cell 61-1403, fax 33-6898, Bolognesi 498)* has large attractive rooms for US$35/44 including an American breakfast. It has a good chifa and a pool hall on the premises. The grand dame of Chimbote's hotels is *Hotel Chimu*(☎/*fax 32-1741, Gálvez 109)*, which charges US$35/48 for comfortable if somewhat faded rooms, including continental breakfast. It has a decent restaurant and bar. Both these last two places have minisuites at about US$65.

## Places to Eat
There are no fancy restaurants in central Chimbote, though there are plenty of inexpensive chicken restaurants on J Pardo near the bus stations. *Chifa Canton* (in the eponymous hostel) is very clean and has fast service and moderate prices. *Restaurant Venecia* (☎ *32-5490, Bolognesi 386)* has been recommended for seafood. *La Carreta* (☎ *33-5751, Bolognesi 400)* serves excellent anticuchos and grills for about US$4.

*Restaurant Paola's* (☎ *32-2011, Palacios 202)* makes good sandwiches, ice cream and snacks. *Parilladas Ivan's* (*Bolognesi 387)* is good for steaks. *Mi Refugio* (*Villavicencio 150)* serves various meat and fish dishes and also has disco dancing, which is popular with local couples. The restaurant at *Hotel Chimu* is one of the best in town and serves set lunches for about US$6.

## Getting There & Away
**Air** There are daily flights from Lima with AeroCóndor, some continuing to Cajamarca. Chimbote Tours (☎ *32-5341, fax 32-4792, Bolognesi 801)* sells airline tickets.

**Bus & Colectivo** The most frequent service to Lima (US$7, 6 hours) is with Turismo San Pedro (☎ *34-2016, 32-4453, J Pardo 670)* and Turismo Chimbote, next door. Between these two companies, there are five daily buses to Lima, as well as a night bus to Huaraz.

Going north along the coast to Trujillo, Chiclayo and Piura, as well as south to Lima are the two good companies of Cruz del Sur (☎ *33-1021, Bolognesi 716)* and Expreso Continental (☎ *33-6141, Balta 289)*. There are also Las Dunas (☎ *33-6534, Aguirre 160)* and TEPSA (☎ *32-5261, 32-4941, Bolognesi 940)*, which has kamikaze drivers. Transportes Vista Alegre (☎ *33-1048, 34-3799, Gálvez 225)* goes to Lima and Trujillo only. Transportes Chinchaysuyo has buses going north to Cajamarca as well as Chiclayo, and inland to Moyobamba and Tarapoto. They have an overnight bus to Huaraz. Empresa El Aguila (☎ *32-2416, Gálvez 317)* has 20 buses a day to Trujillo between 6 am and 8 pm. Transportes Chiclayo (☎ *34-2513, Balta 285)* has overnight buses to Piura (US$6) and day buses to Huaraz.

Transportes Moreno (☎ *32-1235, Gálvez 1178)* has services to Huaraz (US$6, 10 hours). Most buses go via Casma, but some travel via the Río Santa valley through Huallanca and the wild Cañón del Pato to Caraz and Huaraz. This route is the most spectacular approach to Huaraz from the coast. Moreno does this route daily, leaving at 7 am. The Moreno terminal is in a poor area that is off the map (take a taxi after dark).

# TRUJILLO
☎ 044

The coastal city of Trujillo, with about 650,000 inhabitants, is Peru's third-largest city, though locals claim it vies with Arequipa for the status of Peru's second-largest city. It is the only important city and capital of the strangely H-shaped Department of La Libertad. Trujillo is about 560km (9 hours) north of Lima and warrants a visit of several days. Founded in 1535 by Pizarro, it is an attractive colonial city and retains much of its colonial flavor.

Nearby is the ancient Chimu capital of Chan Chan, which was conquered by the Incas (local guides say that the Chimu surrendered to the Incas, rather than being conquered). Also in the area are several other Chimu sites and the immense Moche pyramids of the Temples of the Sun and Moon (Huacas del Sol y de la Luna), which date back about 1500 years. If so much ancient culture wears you out, you can relax at the beach village of Huanchaco.

During the 1998 El Niño, central Trujillo was briefly flooded to a depth of a few inches, but suffered less than many other coastal towns.

## Information

**Tourist Offices** The tourism police (Pizarro 402), on the Plaza de Armas, are friendly and can provide a small map of the city and other information. Some will also act as guides, although most have not had any professional guide training. If you ask the tourism police about guides, they usually hook you up with José Soto Ríos, a policeman who speaks some English and has taken an introductory local archaeology course. The office is open daily in the mornings with variable afternoon hours.

The government-run tourist office has closed, but has been replaced by a private office, Caretur, which has changed addresses several times. Recently it was at Independencia 628.

**Visas** The office of migraciónes (☎ 28-2217) is on the 12th block of Larco, about 2km west of the center. Visas and tourist cards can be renewed here for 30 days for the usual US$20 fee plus stamped paperwork (an extra US$1) from the nearby Banco de la Nación. It can be a long process, so it's best to go soon after they open at 9 am. You may be asked for proof of funds or onward tickets.

**Money** Changing money in Trujillo is a distinct pleasure, because some of the banks are housed in colonial buildings. One of my favorites is the Casa de la Emancipación, which houses the Banco Continental (Pizarro 620). This bank gives good rates for cash, but charges a commission on traveler's checks. You can also change traveler's checks with several other banks – shop around for the best rate. Bank lines are long, so go when they open, around 9:30 am. *Casas de cambio* near Gamarra and Bolívar give good rates for cash. There are street moneychangers as well – take the usual precautions. You'll find them on the Plaza de Armas or along Gamarra, near Pizarro and Bolívar. Watch for pickpockets, particularly along Gamarra south of Bolívar.

Money can be withdrawn on Visa cards at Banco de Crédito (Gamarra 562) and on MasterCards at Banco Latino (Gamarra 574).

**Post & Communications** The main post office is at Independencia 286. One of several telephone offices is at Bolívar 637. It is open until 11 pm.

Internet access is available for about US$2/hour at Inter@te, in the Galerias Zarzar shopping center (Bolívar 634) from 9 am to 1:30 pm and 4 to 9 pm Monday to Saturday. There's also Leonardo de Vinci (España 2725), which is open 8 am to 1 pm and 3 to 8 pm weekdays, and 8 am to noon Saturday.

**Travel Agencies** There are dozens of agencies. Chacón Tours (☎ 25-5722, ☎/fax 25-5212, España 106) has been recommended for good flight arrangements. Guía Tours (☎ 24-5170, ☎/fax 24-6353, Independencia 527) organizes daily tours that last 2½ to 4 hours and go to several of the local archaeological sites for US$12 to US$18 per person (two-person minimum). Some agencies have been criticized for supplying guides who speak English but don't know much about the area.

**Guides** It's best to go with a certified official guide who knows the area well and will take you to wherever you want to go, as well as suggest places you may not have thought of. Guiding here is a competitive profession, and you shouldn't believe everything you hear from one guide about the other guides.

Official guides charge about US$6 to US$8 an hour, but will take several people for the same price as one, so get a group together if your budget is tight. Clara Luz Bravo D and her English husband, Michael

White (☎ 24-3347, 25-5043, cell 66-2710, fax 25-5043, in the USA fax 603-462-8596, microbewhite@yahoo.com, Huayna Capac 542) lead tours to all the local sites of interest. They help tourists who want information about staying with local families or getting a massage from a physical therapist. Michael is knowledgeable, educated and recommended. Clara speaks some English and German, has been guiding for three decades, is enthusiastic and knows Trujillo well. They have a decrepit car, which makes you feel like a local. After a tour, they invite you back to their house to talk and buy T-shirts or other souvenirs; bow out firmly if you're not interested.

## TRUJILLO

**PLACES TO STAY**
15 Hotel San Martín
21 Hotel Libertador
32 Hostal Colonial
36 Casino Real Hotel
39 Hotel Pullman
40 Hotel Peregrino
47 Los Conquistadores Hotel
56 Hotel Americano
61 Residencial Los Escudos
63 Hotel Continental,
   Hostal Acapulco
67 Hostal Recreo
68 Hotel Paris
69 Hostal Solari
71 Hotel Sudamericano
72 Hotel Opt Gar
73 Hotel Turismo
75 Hotel Granada
76 Hostal Central, Hostal Lima
77 Hotel Peru
80 Hostal Roma

**PLACES TO EAT**
7 Pizzería Pizzanino
8 El Marisco del Amor
33 Restaurant Vegetariano
   Naturaleza
38 De Marco's Café,
   Café Romano, Asturias
41 Restaurant Big Ben
42 Restaurant Ajos y Mani
45 Parrillada Tori Gallo
57 Las Tradiciones, other
   bars & restaurants
60 La Mochica

73 Chifa Oriental,
   Chifa Ah Chau
74 Restaurant Oasis,
   Restaurant 24 Horas

**OTHER**
1 Clínica Americano-Peruano
2 Museo Cassinelli
3 Buses to Chan Chan,
   Huanchaco, Huaca Arco Iris
4 Hospital Regional
5 Vulkano
6 El Dorado
9 ITTSA
10 Buses to Chan Chan,
   Huanchaco, Huaca Arco Iris
11 Aero Continente
12 Banco de la Nación
13 Cine Primavera
14 Church of Santa Ana
16 Restaurante Turístico Canana
17 Old city wall
18 EMTRAFESA
19 Museo de Zoológia
20 Church of La Compañía
22 Guía Tours
23 Church of San Francisco
24 Ormeño
25 CIVA
26 Cruz del Sur
27 Chacón Tours
28 Post Office
29 Church of San Pedro
30 Church of Santo Domingo
31 Las Tinajas
34 Interbanc

35 Casa Ganoza Chopitea
   (Casa de los Leones)
37 Church of Santa Clara
43 Oltursa
44 Leonardo de Vinci
46 Banco Wiese
48 Tourism Police
49 Banco Central de la Reserva
   del Peru (Casa de Urquiaga)
50 Casona Orbegoso
51 Church of La Merced
52 Banco de Crédito,
   Banco Latino
53 Banco Continental
   (Casa de la Emancipación)
54 Telefónica del Peru
55 Palacio Iturregui
58 Las Dunas
59 Church of Belén
62 Church of San Agustín
64 Inter@te
65 Museo de Arqueológia
   (Casa Risco)
66 Church of El Carmen,
   religious-art museum
70 Cine Star
78 Empresa Agreda
79 Empresa El Aguila,
   Turismo Chimbote
81 TEPSA
82 Cine Chimú
83 Old city wall
84 Chinchaysuyo
85 Local buses to Las Huacas
   del Sol y de la Luna
86 Clara Luz Bravo D

# TRUJILLO

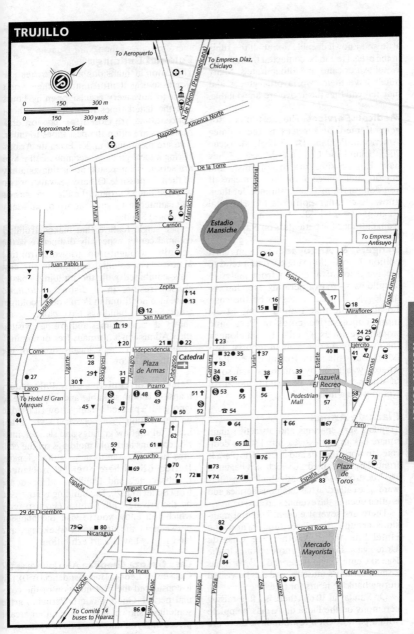

To Aeropuerto

To Empresa Díaz, Chiclayo

N de Piérola (Panamericana)

0    150    300 m
0    150    300 yards
Approximate Scale

America Norte

Napoles

De la Torre

Chavez

Industrial

Salaverry

P Muñiz

Mansiche

Carrion

Estadio Mansiche

To Empresa Antisuyo

España

Juan Pablo II

Comercio

Tupac Amaru

Nazareth

España

Zepita

San Martin

Miraflores

Independencia

Olbegoso

Plaza de Armas

Catedral

Ejército

Corne

Ugarte

Bolognesi

Almagro

Lamarca

Junin

Colón

Estete

Amazonas

Larco

To Hotel El Gran Marques

Pizarro

Plazuela El Recreo

Pedestrian Mall

Bolivar

Perú

Ayacucho

Unión

Plaza de Toros

Miguel Grau

España

29 de Diciembre

Nicaragua

Sinchi Roca

Mercado Mayorista

Los Incas

Moche

Huayna Capac

Atahualpa

Prada

Zela

Suarez

Eguren

César Vallejo

To Comité 14 buses to Huaraz

NORTH COAST

Pedro Puerta is also recommended by travelers. He speaks English and is enthusiastic and knowledgeable about all the ruins in the area. He can be contacted through the Hotel Americano and other hotels. Many hotels have their own favorite guides and may tell you that the above are unavailable.

**Medical Services** The best place for general medical services is the Clínica Americano-Peruano (☎ 23-1261, Mansiche 702), behind the Cassinelli Museum. They have English-speaking receptionists and doctors, and charge according to means. If you don't have medical insurance, let them know. A cheaper option is the Hospital Regional (☎ 23-1581, Mansiche 795); the main entrance for patients is on Napoles.

**Dangers & Annoyances** In my last edition, I wrote that single women tend to receive a lot of attention from males in Trujillo bars – to exasperating, even harassing levels. This continues to be the case. Locals tell me that Trujillo is one of the more conservative cities in Peru, and women are not expected to be out alone in the evenings. As one woman reports, 'This is the only place in Ecuador and Peru where I was hit on by numerous men, some of whom were very persistent and all of whom were a nuisance.'

## Plaza de Armas

Trujillo's very spacious and attractive main square has an impressive central statue dedicated to work, the arts and liberty. The plaza is fronted by the cathedral, which was begun in 1647, destroyed in 1759 and rebuilt soon afterward. The cathedral has a famous basilica and is often open in the evenings around 6 pm.

There are several elegant colonial mansions around the plaza. One is now the Hotel Libertador. Another, the Casa de Urquiaga at Pizarro 446, now belongs to the Banco Central de la Reserva del Peru. It has a small ceramics museum and can be visited during banking hours for free.

On Sunday at 10 am, there is a flag-raising ceremony on the Plaza de Armas, complete with a parade. On a few Sundays, there are also *caballos de paso*, or pacing horses, and *marinera* dances.

## Colonial Buildings

The colonial mansions and churches are worth seeing. Unfortunately, they don't seem to have very regular opening hours and the listed times may change without notice. Some are closed for days on end. Mornings are often the best times to enter. Two are mentioned under Plaza de Armas. Hiring a local guide is recommended if you are seriously interested in visiting as many of them as possible. Otherwise, walk for two or three blocks around the Plaza de Armas and saunter in to any that are open. Many are closed Sunday.

The single feature that makes Trujillo's colonial center especially distinctive is the beautiful wrought-iron grillwork fronting almost every colonial building in the city. This, combined with the buildings' pastel shades, results in a distinct *Trujillano* ambiance not found in Peru's other colonial cities. Several buildings have changing art shows at various times and are best visited then. Admission is normally free or nominal. Hours vary, so check locally. Some of the best-known follow.

**Palacio Iturregui** This early 19th-century mansion is unmistakable and impossible to ignore – it's painted bright yellow (it used to be blue). Built in neoclassical style, it has beautiful window gratings and slender, interior columns and gold moldings on the ceilings. Its main claim to fame is that General Iturregui lived here after he proclaimed Lambayeque's and Trujillo's independence from Spain in 1820. The building is now used by the private Club Central (Pizarro 688) which will allow you to visit the mansion between 11 am and noon weekdays, and later if they have an art exhibition.

**Casa Ganoza Chopitea** Also known as the Casa de los Léones (Independencia 630), this is considered the best mansion of the colonial period. Good, modern Peruvian art is sometimes shown, as are some rather arcane pieces that you may never have a chance to see elsewhere, thus offering relief from the interminable religious and colonial art that is the stock of most museums. Hours vary.

**Casa de la Emancipación** Now the Banco Continental (Pizarro 610), this is where Trujillo's independence from colonial rule was formally declared on December 29, 1820. This is the most reliable place to see changing art and cultural exhibits.

**Other Buildings** The Casona Orbegoso (Orbegoso 553), named after a former president of Peru, is a beautiful 18th-century mansion with a collection of art and furnishings of that period. Also of interest, although not often visited and difficult to find information about, are the Casa Aranda (Bolívar 621) and the Casa de Mayorazgo de Facala (Pizarro 314).

### Churches

Apart from the cathedral, the colonial churches of El Carmen, El Belén, Santo Domingo, San Francisco, La Compañía, San Agustín, Santa Clara and La Merced are worth a look, though getting inside is largely a matter of luck. They often are open for early morning mass, as well as evening masses, but visitors at those times should respect the worshippers and not wander around. The churches are close to one another, and it's easy to stroll from one to the next. San Agustín, with its finely gilded high altar, dates from 1558 and is usually open. La Merced has a dome with noteworthy carvings under a balcony.

The cathedral has a museum of religious and colonial art, as does the Carmelite Museum in El Carmen. El Carmen reputedly has Trujillo's best collection of colonial art. An admission fee of US$2 gains entrance to both exhibits. Hours vary.

### Museo Cassinelli

The Museo Cassinelli is a private archaeological collection at N de Piérola 601, in the basement of a Mobil gas station. One reader points out that collections such as these consist mainly of looted archaeological artifacts. (See the boxed text 'Huaqueros.')

When I visited, I found the gas station without difficulty and spotted several pots and other pieces through the windows. I went inside and asked to see the collection and was told to wait a few minutes. I looked at the haphazardly displayed pots in the garage office and wondered if this was it. After all, what could I expect in an oily garage? After a few minutes, however, I was led through a locked door, down a narrow flight of stairs and through a second locked door – this one heavily armored. On entering the basement, I was astonished to see hundreds of ceramics piled up on shelves that filled the room. The curator showed me dozens of his favorite pieces, letting me hold and examine several as he explained where they came from and what they represented.

Among the most interesting are the whistling pots, which produce clear notes when air is blown into them. I was especially intrigued by a pair of pots representing a male bird and a female bird that appeared to be tinamous (a type of South American bird). Superficially, they were very similar, but when they were blown, each produced a completely different note. These notes corresponded to the distinctive calls of the male and female birds.

Hours are 8:30 to 11:30 am and 3:30 to 5:30 pm Monday to Saturday, and admission is about US$2.

### Museo de Arqueología

This university-run museum at Junín 682 is open 8:30 am to 2 pm Monday to Saturday, and has a small but interesting collection of artifacts from the Huaca de la Luna (see Archaeological Sites Around Trujillo later in this chapter), as well as a reproduction of some of the murals found there. The museum is housed in the 17th-century La Casa Risco, a restored colonial house. The exhibits have signs in Spanish. Michael White (see Guides earlier in this section) can give an explanation in English along with a tour of the Huaca de la Luna. Admission is currently about US$0.70, but there are plans to sell a more expensive, combined ticket that provides entrance to the Huacas del Sol y de la Luna as well. A gift shop has

## Huaqueros

The word *huaquero* is heard frequently on the north coast of Peru and literally means 'robber of huacas.' Huacas are temples, shrines and burial sites of special significance. They are often decorated with sheets of precious metals and other treasures that accompanied a royal burial.

Since the Spanish conquest, huaqueros have worked the ancient graves of Peru. They make their living by finding and opening these graves, then removing the valuables and selling them to anybody prepared to pay for an archaeological artifact. To a certain extent, one can sympathize with a poor *campesino* grubbing around in the desert, hoping to strike it rich; but the huaquero is one of the archaeologist's greatest enemies. The huaqueros' ransacking has been so thorough that an unplundered grave is almost never found by archaeologists. Someone else has always been there first.

Today, visitors to Trujillo and the surrounding sites are sometimes offered a 'genuine' archaeological artifact. These are not always genuine – but if they are, it is illegal to export them from Peru.

VICTOR ENGLEBERT

a small selection of archaeology books, a few of which are in English.

### Museo de Zoología

This museum at San Martín 368 is also run by the university, but the taxidermic collection of Peruvian animals is in poor condition.

### Beaches

The beach at the Trujillo suburb of Buenos Aires is easily reached by local buses, but theft has frequently been reported there. There are several seafood restaurants on the waterfront that are safe enough to eat in. Walking along the beach away from the restaurant area is dangerous, and the 4km walk from Buenos Aires to Chan Chan is especially notorious for muggings. Visit Chan Chan by road instead.

There is a much better and safer beach in the village of Huanchaco, 11km to the north. See Huanchaco later in this chapter.

### Caballos de Paso

Breeding, training and watching the caballos de paso (pacing horses) is a favorite Peruvian activity. The idea is to breed and train horses that pace more elegantly than others. Trujillo and Lima are both centers of this upper-class pastime. *Trujilleños* will tell you that the activity originated in the Department of La Libertad.

## Special Events
Trujillo's major festival is called El Festival Internacional de la Primavera, or International Spring Festival, and has been held annually for well over 40 years. Its attractions include international beauty contests, parades, national dancing competitions (including, of course, the marinera), caballos de paso displays, sports and various other cultural activities. It all happens in the last week in September, and better hotels are fully booked well in advance.

The last week in January is also busy, with the national Fiesta de la Marinera contest. The marinera is a typical coastal Peruvian dance involving much romantic waving of handkerchiefs. Students of folk dance should not miss this one. Again, hotels are booked up.

## Places to Stay – Budget
**Hotels** Many cheap hotels, especially in the poor area east of Gamarra and Bolívar, are used for short stays by young local couples, but aren't dangerous or horribly sleazy. None of these hotels have private showers or hot water, and their standards of cleanliness are not very high. The cheapest is the very basic and shabby-looking *Hostal Peru* (☎ 24-7641, Ayacucho 966), which charges US$2.75 per person in rooms with one bed. Opposite is the divey *Hotel Paris* (☎ 24-2701, Ayacucho 991), at US$3.25/6.25 for singles/doubles. The similarly priced, basic *Hostal Lima* (☎ 24-4751, Ayacucho 718) is quite popular with gringos on shoestring budgets. It looks like a jail but is secure. *Hostal Central* (☎ 24-6236), next door, looks grubby but has some rooms with private cold showers at US$6/8. *Hostal Acapulco* (☎ 24-3524, Gamarra 681) is US$5/6 with private cold bath, but was recently lacking water – this may have been an El Niño-related problem, so check.

The perennially popular *Hotel Americano* (☎ 24-1361, Pizarro 792) is in a rambling and dilapidated old mansion with lots of character. Basic but fairly clean rooms are US$8/11 for cold-water baths, or a bit less without. *Hostal Roma* (☎ 25-9064, Nicaragua 238) is clean and secure, and rooms are US$10.50 for a double with private bath and hot water. The friendly *Hotel Sudamericano* (☎ 24-3751, Miguel Grau 515) is OK for about US$8/12 with private hot showers, which are very cramped. They'll often give you a discount. *Hotel Granada* (☎ 25-6411, Miguel Grau 611) is similar and has some cheaper rooms with shared bath.

Budget travelers often enjoy staying in the nearby village of Huanchaco (see Places to Stay for Huanchaco, later in this chapter).

**Home Stays** Budget travelers can also stay with local families, who charge about US$5 to US$9 per person. Local guide Clara Luz Bravo D and her husband Michael White can help set you up (see Guides earlier in this section).

## Places to Stay – Mid-Range
The line between the best budget and the cheapest mid-range hotels is blurred. Most of these hotels can be pretty noisy if you get street-side rooms, so ask for an interior room for more quiet. *Hostal Colonial* (☎ 23-2993, fax 25-8261, Independencia 618) looks pretty decent for US$10/18 for singles/ doubles with private hot shower. *Hotel San Martín* (☎ 23-4011, fax 25-2311, San Martín 745) has over 100 rooms and therefore is rarely full. It is characterless, but is a fair value at US$15/21 for rooms with private hot showers. You can bargain them down. They have a restaurant and bar. The friendly *Hostel Recreo* (☎ 24-6991, Estete 647) has rooms with telephones, TV and hot-water baths at US$14/18.

*Residencial Los Escudos* (☎ 25-5691, Orbegoso 676) has a pleasant garden and charges US$21/25. *Hotel Turismo* (☎ 24-4181, fax 25-4151, Gamarra 747) has clean, good-sized, but slightly stuffy rooms with telephones, TV and baths with hot water in the mornings and evenings. Rates are about US$17/23.

*Hotel Continental* (☎ 24-1607, fax 24-9881, Gamarra 663) has clean, carpeted singles/doubles with telephones, music, cable TV and baths with hot water for US$21/31. Some of their rooms have quite good city views and are quiet. Their attached restaurant isn't bad. The similarly priced

*Hostal Solari* (☎ 24-3909, fax 25-8959, *Almagro 715*) is also a good choice with similar features. The clean, friendly and well-run *Hotel Opt Gar* (☎ 24-2192, fax 23-5551, *Miguel Grau 595*) has singles/doubles with hot water, TV and telephones at US$25/35 including continental breakfast. Their street-side rooms are very noisy. *Hotel Peregrino* (☎ 20-3988, 20-3990, fax 20-3989, *Independencia 978*) is clean, pleasant and quiet. Rooms have minirefrigerators, cable TV and telephones and cost US$28/45 for singles/doubles. They also have a couple of large suites with Jacuzzis at US$110.

The friendly *Hotel Pullman* (☎ 20-3624, ☎/fax 20-5448, *Pizarro 879*) is on a pedestrian street near the Plazuela El Recreo and therefore doesn't suffer from street noise (though taxis can pull up to within 10m of the hotel entrance). There is a reasonably priced restaurant with room service during the day, a patio and bar. Rooms with minirefrigerators, cable TV, telephones and reliable hot showers are US$35/45 including breakfast.

*Los Conquistadores Hotel* (☎ 24-4505, fax 23-5917, *Almagro 586*) has comfortable carpeted rooms with TV, telephones, minirefrigerators and room service. Rates are about US$42/70 including breakfast. For about the same price, *Casino Real Hotel* (☎ 24-4485, fax 25-7416, *Pizarro 651*) has similar rooms and includes breakfast and airport pick-up in its prices.

## Places to Stay – Top End

The grand dame of the city's hotels, *Hotel Libertador* (☎ 23-2741, 24-4999, fax 23-5641) is in a beautiful old building right on the Plaza de Armas. It is one of two four-star hotels in Trujillo. There is a pool, sauna, good restaurant, pleasant bar, 24-hour coffeeshop and comfortable rooms for about US$73/84. They have a few suites at US$160. Try to avoid street-side rooms unless you want to watch the goings-on, as they are apt to be noisy.

The similarly priced *Hotel El Gran Marques* (☎ 24-9161, 24-9366, ☎/fax 24-9582, *Diaz de Cienfuegos 145*) is a couple of kilometers (about 7 blocks) southwest of the city center. It offers a sauna, exercise room, pool, restaurant and bar and is Trujillo's other top-end choice. Both are good.

## Places to Eat

There are plenty of restaurants near the market, and for the impecunious, the food stalls in the market itself are among the cheapest places to eat in Trujillo. Restaurant prices are also very reasonable, and many places near the center offer set lunches for US$1. A block from the market are several good Chinese restaurants, including *Chifa Oriental* (*Gamarra 735*) and *Chifa Ah Chau* (*Gamarra 769*). The nearby *Restaurant 24 Horas* is inexpensive and always open. *Restaurant Oasis*, next door, is good for local food.

On the 700 block of Pizarro, several cafés and restaurants (popular both with locals and tourists) serve a variety of good food at moderate prices (US$2 for set lunches and US$4 to US$8 for dinners). *Café Romano* has good espresso and cappuccino, as well as breakfast and light meals all day; *De Marco's Café* has Italian dishes and good desserts and ice cream; and *Asturias* has a little bit of everything. Opposite these, there is a *chifa* under the Hotel Americano.

*Las Tradiciones* and other places around the Plazuela El Recreo have inexpensive menus and a variety of meat, chicken and fish dishes. These are hole-in-the-wall places that become drinking dives in the evening. Plazuela El Recreo has the ruined foundations of a building that used to supply drinking water to Trujillo in colonial days.

One of the only vegetarian restaurants in town is *Restaurant Vegetariano Naturaleza* (*Gamarra 459*), which is open for inexpensive lunches. At the other end of the food spectrum, but also open only for lunch, is *Restaurante Ajos y Mani* (☎ 22-3314, *Ejército 168*), which simply serves *cuy* (guinea pig) in five different ways for US$5.

*Restaurant Big Ben* (*España 1317*) is a small place with good ceviches and local seafood in the US$5-to-US$6 range. Cheap ceviches at under US$3 are served at the locally popular lunchspot *El Marisco de Amor* (*Nazareth 510*) and several other places nearby.

*La Mochica (Bolívar 462)* has a variety of mid-priced steaks and seafood, as well as cheaper local dishes. *Parrillada Tori Gallo*, on Bolognesi at Bolívar, has a variety of mid-priced grills, as well as some Mexican dishes, and music on weekends. A good pizza place is *Pizzería Pizzanino (Juan Pablo II 183)*, which is run by the owners of the Café Romano.

## Entertainment

Trujillo's several cinemas often offer the best choices for an evening out. Some of the restaurants above have music on weekends. The *Restaurante Turístico Canana* (☎ 23-2503, San Martín 791) is a disco-pub with reasonably priced meals and live music and dancing on weekends. There is usually a US$2 or US$3 cover charge. *La Luna Rota* (☎ 22-8877, América Sur 2119) has a restaurant, live music and dancing, slot machines – a little bit of everything. On the Plaza de Armas, *Las Tinajas* is a pleasant bar that is very quiet during the week, but attracts a younger, more lively crowd on weekends, when there is live music. The local newspaper *La Industria* is the best source for local entertainment, cultural exhibitions and other events.

## Getting There & Away

Trujillo is Peru's major north-coast city and is serviced by scores of buses making the 24-hour run along the Panamericana between Lima and the Ecuadorian border (and intermediate coastal points). There are also daily flights to and from Lima and other cities.

**Air** The airport is 10km northwest of town. Aero Continente (☎ 24-4042, España 307) has flights to and from Lima and Piura. Aviación Líder flies to Cajamarca in nine-passenger aircraft three times a week and AeroCóndor has daily flights from Cajamarca. Schedules and destinations change often.

**Bus & Colectivo** Many companies operate up and down the coast along the Panamericana Norte. Few go inland. Prices and schedules vary widely from company to company and from month to month. Some companies

have luxury buses with video, bathroom and reclining seats and cost twice as much as regular buses. Shop around for the service/price combination that you want. The details given below are only intended as a rough guide. Bear in mind that buses to Lima tend to leave at night, so if you want to travel by day, book in advance. Most buses leave Trujillo, full and advance booking is recommended for any departure.

For long-distance buses to Lima (US$7 to US$15, 7½ to 10 hours), Piura (US$5 to US$9, 7 to 9 hours) and/or Tumbes (about 15 hours), the corner of Ejército and Amazonas has several major bus companies. These include Ormeño (☎ 25-9782), which has the largest selection of day and night buses to Lima, Cruz del Sur (☎ 26-1801), CIVA (☎ 25-1402) and Oltursa (☎ 26-3055).

If you're heading north, the first major stop is Chiclayo. This journey costs about US$3.50 and takes three to four hours. The locals stand on Avenida Mansiche outside the stadium and catch the next bus heading north. All northbound buses with empty seats will stop here. If you'd rather not bother about watching your luggage while you wait on the side of the road, the most frequent Chiclayo service is with EMTRAFESA (☎ 22-3981, 22-2122, Miraflores 127), with buses leaving on the half-hour during the day and evening; and Vulkano (☎ 23-5847, Carrión 140), with buses leaving on the hour from 6 am to 6 pm. These companies also have buses to Lima and the north coast. Others with coastal service include Las Dunas (☎ 22-1836, España 1445), with comfortable night buses to Lima; ITTSA (☎ 25-1415, Mansiche 171); the nearby El Dorado and TEPSA (☎ 25-5451, Diego de Almagro 849).

There are various bus services inland. Cruz del Sur, Comité 14 (☎ 26-1008, Moche 544), Chinchaysuyo and Turismo Chimbote have buses to Huaraz (10 hours) but all departures are at night. If you want to travel by day, take a bus to Huaraz from Chimbote instead. The route into the highlands is spectacular and daytime travel is recommended for the scenery. Empresa El Aguila (☎ 24-3271, Nicaragua 220) has hourly buses to Chimbote (US$1.75, 2 hours) from 6 am to

8 pm. If you take the 6 am bus, you can connect with the 8 am Moreno bus from Chimbote to Huaraz, especially if you call Moreno to reserve a seat.

Connections from Chiclayo to Cajamarca are better than those from Trujillo, so if you plan to visit both Chiclayo and Cajamarca, it makes sense to visit Chiclayo first. Vulkano and EMTRAFESA both have 10:30 am and 10:30 pm buses to Cajamarca (US$7, 8 hours). Others include El Dorado and Empresa Díaz (☎ 20-1237, N de Piérola 1079) on the Panamericana, about a kilometer northeast of the town center.

If you want to head east from Trujillo to Otuzco, Santiago de Chuco, Huamachuco and Cajabamba, there is a much rougher, longer and older route to Cajamarca serviced by Empresa Antisuyo (☎ 23-4726, Túpac Amaru 760). Several small buses leave in the morning on the interesting side trip to Otuzco (2 to 2½ hours), but may not go farther. For buses to Santiago de Chuco and Huamachuco, try Empresa Sanchez López on Avenida Vallejo, away from the center, or Empresa Agreda (☎ 20-3463, La Unión 149).

For buses to Moyobamba, Tarapoto and Chachapoyas, go from Chiclayo.

## Getting Around

**To/From the Airport** The airport, about 10km northwest of Trujillo, can be reached cheaply on the bus to Huanchaco, though you'll have to walk the last kilometer or so. Ask the driver where the airport turnoff is. A taxi to or from the city center will cost about US$3.50.

**To/From Archaeological Sites** White-yellow-and-orange B colectivos to La Huaca Esmeralda, Chan Chan and Huanchaco pass the corners of España and Industrial, España and Miraflores and other places every few minutes. Minibuses (red-blue-and-white) or buses (green-and-white) for Esperanza go northeast along Mansiche and can drop you off at La Huaca Arco Iris. Minibuses leave every half hour from Suarez for the Huacas del Sol y de la Luna. Fares are roughly US$0.25 on these routes.

Note that these buses are worked by professional thieves looking for cameras and money – keep valuables hidden, and watch your bags carefully.

A taxi or tour group isn't a bad idea, even for budget travelers. The ruins certainly will be more interesting and meaningful with a good guide – some recommended ones are listed earlier in this chapter. They can arrange a taxi or their own vehicle. Alternatively, a taxi to most of these sites will cost US$3 to US$4, then you can hire an on-site guide.

La Huaca Prieta and La Huaca El Brujo, about 60km northwest of Trujillo, near the coast on the north side of the Chicama valley, are harder to reach. Take any bus northbound on the Panamericana for about 40km to the village of Chocope, then ask for microbuses going west on an unpaved road. After 20km, get off at the coastal village of Magdalena de Cao and walk about 5km. It's best to go with a guide.

**Taxi** A taxi ride within the circular Avenida España shouldn't be more than US$1. For sightseeing, taxis charge about US$6 to US$8 per hour, depending on how far you expect them to go.

## ARCHAEOLOGICAL SITES AROUND TRUJILLO

The Moche and Chimu cultures left the greatest marks on the Trujillo area, but are by no means the only ones. In a March 1973 *National Geographic* article, Drs ME Moseley & CJ Mackey claimed knowledge of over 2000 sites in the Río Moche valley. Many of these sites are small and well-nigh forgotten, but included is the largest pre Columbian city in the Americas (Chan Chan), as well as pyramids that required about 140 million adobe bricks to construct.

Five major archaeological sites can be easily reached from Trujillo by local bus or taxi. Two of these sites are Moche, dating from about 500 AD. The other three, from the Chimu culture, date from about 1200 AD to 1300 AD. The recently excavated Moche ruin called El Brujo (60km from Trujillo) can also be visited, but not as conveniently.

## Archaeology & History

**Huaca Prieta** One of the earliest groups in Peru to be studied is the Huaca Prieta people, who lived at the site of that name around 3500 BC to 2300 BC. These hunters and gatherers began to develop simple agriculture. They grew cotton and varieties of bean and pepper – but corn, now a staple, was unheard of. Finds of simple nets and hooks indicate that they primarily ate seafood. They lived in single-room shacks half buried in the ground, and most of what is known about them has been deduced from their middens, or garbage piles. Hence, we know that they were a Pre-ceramic people, didn't use jewelry and had developed netting and weaving. At their most artistic, they decorated dried gourds with simple carvings; similarly decorated gourds are produced today as a Peruvian handicraft. Hot stones may have been dropped into these gourds to cook food.

Huaca Prieta has been one of the most intensively studied early Peruvian sites but, for the nonarchaeologist, it's more interesting to read about than to visit. After all, it's simply a prehistoric pile of garbage. Three nearby huacas at El Brujo are being restored, but are not officially open to the public at this time.

**Chavín** About 850 BC, a major new cultural influence, that of the Chavín, began to leave its mark on the area. This period was named after the site of Chavín de Huántar (on the eastern slopes of the Cordillera Blanca), where a feline-worshipping cult had one of its main centers. The Chavín influence swept over the northern mountains and the northern and central coasts of Peru. At its most simple, the Chavín influence consisted of a highly stylized art form based especially on jaguar motifs. Formerly called the Chavín Horizon (many archaeologists now prefer the term Early Horizon), this was the first major culture in Peru, as well as one of the most artistically developed. The various areas and groups it encompassed were typified by the rapid development of ceramic ware and a common art form. In the Trujillo area, the Chavín influence was represented by the Cupisnique culture. Examples of Cupisnique pottery can be seen in the museums of Lima and Trujillo, though there are no especially noteworthy ruins open to visitors.

In the Trujillo area, archaeologists have identified other geographically smaller and less important cultures that coincided with

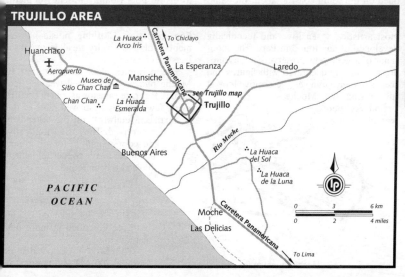

**TRUJILLO AREA**

Huanchaco · La Huaca Arco Iris · To Chiclayo · Aeropuerto · Museo de Sitio Chan Chan · Mansiche · La Esperanza · Laredo · Chan Chan · La Huaca Esmeralda · Carretera Panamericana · see Trujillo map · Trujillo · Buenos Aires · Rio Moche · La Huaca del Sol · La Huaca de la Luna · PACIFIC OCEAN · Moche · Carretera Panamericana · Las Delicias · To Lima

0   3   6 km
0   2   4 miles

the later Cupisnique period. These include the Salinar, Vicus and Gallinazo.

**Moche** With the decline of the Cupisnique period came the beginnings of the fascinating Moche period, which is defined by the Moche culture's impressive archaeological sites and some of the most outstanding pottery to be seen in Peru's museums.

The Moche culture is named after the river that flows into the ocean just south of Trujillo. The word 'Mochica' has been used interchangeably with Moche and refers to a dialect spoken in the Trujillo area at the time of the conquest, though not necessarily spoken by the Moche people. Moche is now the preferred usage.

The Moche culture evolved from the Cupisnique at about the time of Christ. The Moche didn't conquer the Cupisnique; rather, there was a slow transition characterized by a number of developments. Ceramics, textiles and metalwork improved greatly, architectural skills allowed the construction of huge pyramids and other structures, and there was enough leisure time for art and a highly organized religion.

As with the Nazca culture, which developed on the south coast at about the same time, the Moche period is especially known for its ceramics, which are considered the most artistically sensitive and technically developed of any found in Peru. The thousands of Moche pots preserved in museums are realistically decorated with figures and scenes that give us a very descriptive look at life during the Moche period. As there was no

written language, most of what we know about the Moche comes from this wealth of pottery. Pots were modeled into lifelike representations of people, crops, domestic or wild animals, marine life and houses. Other pots were painted with scenes of both ceremonial and everyday life. From these pots archaeologists know that the Moche society was very class conscious. The most important people, especially the priests and warriors, were members of the urban classes and lived closest to the large ceremonial pyramids and other temples. They were surrounded by a middle class of artisans and then, in descending order, farmers and fishermen, servants, slaves and beggars.

Moche ceramics usually depicted priests and warriors being carried in litters wearing particularly fine jewelry or clothing. Further evidence of the authority of priests and warriors is given by pots showing scenes of punishment, including the mutilation and death of those who dared to disobey. Other facets of Moche life illustrated on the pots include surgical procedures, such as amputation and the setting of broken limbs. Sex is realistically shown; one room in Museo Rafael Larco Herrera (in Lima) is entirely devoted to erotic pots (mainly Moche) depicting most sexual practices, some rather imaginative. Museo Cassinelli in Trujillo also has a fine collection. Clothing, musical instruments, tools and jewelry are all frequent subjects for ceramics.

The ceramics also show us that the Moche had well-developed weaving techniques. But rare rainstorms, which occurred every few decades, destroyed most of their textiles. Metalwork, on the other hand, has survived. They used gold, silver and copper mainly for ornament but some heavy copper implements have also been found.

Two Moche sites survived, side by side, a few kilometers south of Trujillo and are easily visited. They are the Huacas del Sol y de la Luna and are described in more detail later in this section.

The Moche period declined around 700 AD, and the next few

Mochica running fox god

contained approximately 10,000 dwellings of varying quality and importance. Buildings were decorated with friezes, the designs molded into the mud walls, and the more important areas were layered with precious metals. There were storage bins for food and other products from throughout the empire, which stretched along the coast from Chancay to the Gulf of Guayaquil (in southern Ecuador). There were huge walk-in wells, canals, workshops and temples. The royal dead were buried in mounds with a wealth of funerary offerings.

The Chimu were conquered by the Incas in 1471, but the city was not looted until the arrival of the Spanish. Heavy rainfall has severely damaged the mud moldings, though a few survived, and others have been restored.

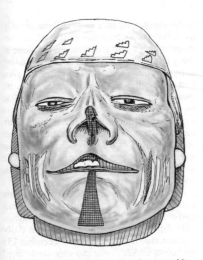

**Pot rendering official with severed nose and lip, Florescent Epoch, Mochica IV**

centuries are somewhat confusing. The Wari culture, based in the Ayacucho area of the central Peruvian Andes, began to expand, and its influence was felt as far north as the Chicama valley.

**Chimu** The next important period in the Trujillo area, the Chimu, lasted from about 1000 AD to 1470 AD. The Chimu built a huge capital at Chan Chan, just north of Trujillo. The Chimu was a highly organized society – it must have been to have built and supported a city such as Chan Chan. Its art work was less exciting than that of the Moche, tending more to functional mass production than artistic achievement. Gone, for the most part, was the technique of painting pots. Instead, they were fired by a simpler method than that used by the Moche, producing the typical blackware seen in many Chimu pottery collections. Despite its poorer quality, this pottery still shows us life in the Chimu kingdom. And while the quality of the ceramics declined, metallurgy developed, and various alloys (including bronze) were worked. The Chimu were also exceptionally fine goldsmiths.

It is as an urban society that the Chimu are best remembered. Their huge capital

**Chimu god**

**NORTH COAST**

## Chan Chan

Most visitors to the north coast want to see Chan Chan, the huge ruined capital of the Chimu Empire. Built by the Chimu around 1300 AD and covering about 28 sq km, it is the largest pre-Columbian city in the Americas and the largest mud city in the world. At the height of the Chimu Empire, it housed an estimated 60,000 inhabitants and contained a vast wealth of gold, silver and ceramics. After Chan Chan's conquest by the Incas, the wealth remained more or less undisturbed. The Incas were interested in expanding their imperial control, not in amassing treasure. As soon as the Spaniards arrived, however, the looting began, and within a few decades, there was little left of the treasures of Chan Chan. The remainder has been pillaged through the centuries by huaqueros, though remnants can be seen in museums. Chan Chan must have been a dazzling sight at one time. Today, only the mud walls and a few molded decorations remain, and the visitor is amazed by the huge expanse of the site as much as anything else.

The damage at Chan Chan has not been caused only by the huaqueros. Devastating floods and heavy rainfall have severely eroded the mud walls of the city. Several decades can go by with almost no rain, but occasionally, the climatic phenomenon of El Niño can cause rainstorms and floods in the coastal desert.

The Chimu capital consisted of nine major subcities, each built by a succeeding ruler – hence the nine areas are often referred to as the Royal Compounds. You could spend hours wandering around these ruins. Each contains a royal burial mound, where the ruler was buried with an appropriately vast quantity of funerary offerings, including dozens of sacrificed young women and chambers full of ceramics, weavings and jewelry. The Tschudi compound, named after a Swiss naturalist who visited Peru in the 19th century and published *Peruvian Antiquities* in Vienna in 1851, is partially restored and open to visitors. Most of the other compounds have also been named after archaeologists and explorers.

Chan Chan is about 5km west of Trujillo (see Getting Around under Trujillo, earlier in this chapter, for information about getting to the ruins). Tschudi lies to the left of the main road; it's a walk of almost 2km along a dusty dirt road. (Sometimes taxis are waiting here, or you can take a taxi from Trujillo.) As you walk, you'll see the crumbling ruins of the other compounds all around you. Stick to the footpath, and do not be tempted to stroll off into the ruins on either side. Not only are these ruins dilapidated, but they are also the haunt of muggers who hope some unsuspecting, camera-toting tourist will enter alone. Stay on the path, and go with a friend or guide if possible.

At the Tschudi complex, you'll find an entrance booth, a snack and souvenir stand and a third booth, where guides are available. Entry is allowed 9 am to 4 pm daily (except January 1, May 1 and December 25) and costs US$2.50; you can stay inside until 5:15 pm. The ticket is also valid for Huaca Esmeralda and Huaca Arco Iris ruins as well as the site museum, but it must be used within two days. You can hire a local guide for about US$5 an hour to make sure you don't miss anything and to be shown the original (not the restored) friezes and decorations. The complex is well marked by arrows, so you can see everything without a guide if you prefer. During the disastrous El Niño rains of 1998, metal roofs were built over the walls to protect them.

**Tschudi Complex** Entry is through a 4m-thick defensive wall. Inside, you turn right and almost immediately enter the huge and largely restored **Ceremonial Courtyard**. All four interior walls are decorated with geometric designs, most of which are new. Just to the right of the massive doorway as you enter, you'll see a few designs at ground level. I'm told those closest to the door, representing three or four nutria (large aquatic rodents), are unrestored. They're slightly rougher looking than the modern work. The design is repeated all the way around the Ceremonial Plaza and is topped by a series of lines representing waves. A ramp at the far side of the plaza accesses the second level (stairways are not a frequent feature of the major Chimu structures). Note also the great restored height of the walls in this plaza. Though all the Chan Chan walls have crumbled with time, the highest of Tschudi's walls once stood over 10m high.

Follow the arrows out of the Ceremonial Courtyard through a door to the right and make a sharp left-hand turn to walk along the **outside wall** of the plaza. This is one of the most highly decorated and best restored of Tschudi's walls. The adobe friezes show waves of fish rippling along the entire length of the wall above a line of seabirds. See if you can tell where the original moldings end and the restored ones begin. As with the nutria designs, the rougher-looking fish are the originals. Despite their time-worn appearance, they retain a fluidity and character somehow lacking in the modern version. Nevertheless, the modern work has been done with care and succeeds in restoring the entire wall.

At the end of this wall, the arrowed path goes through a labyrinthine section known as the **Sanctuaries**. The function of the Sanctuaries is not clear, but their importance is evident in both the quantity and quality of the decorations. Though less restored than the wall, they are the most interesting section of friezes in Tschudi. Their square- and diamond-shaped designs represent, quite simply, fishing nets. Being so close to the ocean, the Chimu based much of their diet on seafood, and the importance of the sea reached venerable proportions. Fish, waves, seabirds and sea mammals are represented throughout the city, and here, in the Sanctuaries, you will find all of them interspersed with the fishing nets. The moon was also very important, and there are several series of full-moon symbols in the Sanctuaries. For the Chimu, the moon and the sea were of religious importance (unlike the Incas, who worshipped the sun and venerated the earth).

From the Sanctuaries, arrows lead into a **second ceremonial plaza**, smaller in size than the main Ceremonial Plaza but similar in shape. It also has a ramp to the second level. From behind this plaza, you can see a huge rectangular depression resembling a drained swimming pool. In fact, it was once a **walk-in well** that supplied the daily water needs of the Tschudi Royal Compound. The water level was reached by a series of ramps from the surface and each compound had its own cistern. The Tschudi cistern is the largest in Chan Chan and measures 130m x 45m.

To the left of the cistern is an area of several dozen small cells that have been called the **military sector**. Perhaps soldiers lived here, or the cells may have been used for storage. These constructions are not very well preserved. A straight path leads you from the military sector almost back to the main entrance, passing a series of storage bins. The final area visited is the **Assembly Room**. This large rectangular room has 24 seats set into niches in the walls, and its acoustic properties are such that speakers sitting in any one of the niches can be clearly heard all over the room.

You are now back by the main entrance, free to wander around again to inspect more thoroughly those areas of particular interest to you.

Chan Chan has eight compounds similar to Tschudi. Unfortunately, as they are in much worse repair and there are no guards, visiting them is not worthwhile nor recommended. It is possible to be robbed in these remote and dusty old ruins, and the path behind Tschudi leading down to and along the beach is particularly notorious for robberies and muggings. If you stay on the dirt road joining the main road with Tschudi, you shouldn't have any problems.

**Site Museum** The site museum contains exhibits explaining Chan Chan and the Chimu culture. It is on the main road to the Chan Chan turnoff, almost a kilometer before the turnoff. Admission is included in the price of the Chan Chan ticket.

## La Huaca Esmeralda

This temple was built by the Chimu at about the same time as Chan Chan. The site is open daily 9 am to 4 pm, and entry is included with the Chan Chan ticket, though it is not sold here, so go to Chan Chan first. Huaca Esmeralda lies at Mansiche, which is halfway between Trujillo and Chan Chan. If you're returning from Chan Chan to Trujillo, the huaca is to the right of the main road, about four blocks behind the Mansiche Church. Thieves reportedly prey on unwary tourists wandering around, so go with friends or a guide, and keep your eyes open.

The site was buried by sand and was accidentally discovered by a local landowner in 1923. He attempted to uncover the ruins, but El Niño of 1925 began the process of erosion, which was exacerbated by the floods and rains of 1983. Little restoration work has been done on the adobe friezes, but it is still possible to make out the characteristic designs of fish, seabirds, waves and fishing nets. The temple consists of two stepped platforms, and an on-site guard will take you around for a tip.

## La Huaca Arco Iris

This is the third Chimu site that can be visited with the same ticket as Chan Chan and Huaca Esmeralda. La Huaca Arco Iris, or the Rainbow Temple, is also known locally as Huaca del Dragón. It is just to the left of the Panamericana in the suburb of La Esperanza, about 4km northwest of Trujillo. (See Getting Around under Trujillo, earlier in this chapter, for bus information.)

La Huaca Arco Iris is one of the best preserved of the Chimu temples simply because it was covered by sand until the 1960s. Its location was known to a handful of archaeologists and huaqueros, but excavation did not begin until 1963. Unfortunately, the 1983 El Niño caused damage to the friezes.

The excavation of the temple took about five years, and the upper parts were rebuilt. It used to be painted, but now, only faint traces of yellow paint can be seen. The temple consists of a defensive wall over 2m thick enclosing an area of about 3000 sq meters. Through the single entrance in this rectangular wall is one large structure, the temple itself. This building covers about 800 sq meters in two levels, with a combined height of about 7.5m. The walls are slightly pyramidal and covered with repeated rainbow designs, most of which have been restored. Some of the decorations are said to show Recuay, Tiahuanaco or Wari influence.

Ramps lead the visitor to the very top of the temple. From here, you can look down into a series of large storage bins. These almost surround the structure and have openings only at the top. There are also good views from the top level of the temple.

There is a tiny on-site museum, and local guides (some speak a little English) are available to show you around the ruin and museum. A tip is expected. You can buy inexpensive, well-made reproductions of Chimu ceramics from the souvenir stand near the entrance.

## Huacas del Sol y de la Luna

The Temples of the Sun and the Moon were not built by the Chimu. They are over 700 years older than Chan Chan and are attributed to the Moche period. They are on the south bank of the Río Moche, about 10km southeast of Trujillo by rough road. (See Getting Around under Trujillo, earlier in this chapter, for bus information.)

Hours are 9 am to 4 pm, but morning visits are recommended as afternoon windstorms start whipping up the dust. Entrance is about US$2 (schoolchildren pay US$0.30.) Because the site is out of the way single travelers, especially women, are advised to go with a friend or hire a guide.

The two huacas, both roughly pyramidal in shape, are usually visited together. The **Huaca del Sol** was the largest single pre-Columbian structure in Peru, although about a third of it has been washed away. Estimates of its size vary, depending on the points of reference used, but recent measurements give a maximum length of 342m, breadth of 159m and height of 45m. The structure was built with an estimated 140 million adobe bricks, many of them marked with symbols. These are not evidence of writing or hieroglyphics; they are merely the hallmarks of the workers who made them. Over 100 symbols have been identified and one theory holds that groups or communities of workers were taxed a certain number of adobe bricks and marked their contributions with distinctive hallmarks to keep track of how many bricks they had provided.

At one time, the pyramid consisted of several different levels connected by steep flights of stairs, huge ramps and walls sloping at 77° to the horizon. Fifteen hundred years have wrought their inevitable damage, and today the pyramid looks like a giant pile of crude bricks partially covered with sand. Despite this, the brickwork remains very impressive from some angles. It appears that there are a few graves or rooms within the structure, and it must have been used primarily as a huge ceremonial site. Certainly, its size alone makes the pyramid an awesome structure, and the views from the top are excellent.

The smaller **Huaca de la Luna** is about 500m away across the open desert. Dozens of pottery shards lie around this open area. Although less impressive in size than the Huaca del Sol, the Huaca de la Luna is more interesting because it is riddled with rooms that contain ceramics, precious metals and some of the beautiful polychrome friezes for which the Moche were famous. The huaca was built around 400 AD, and succeeding generations expanded it. By about 550 AD, six different levels had been built, each one completely covering the previous one. Archaeologists are currently peeling away selected parts of the huaca to discover what lies beneath each layer. At every level, there are friezes of stylized figures, some of which have been well protected by the later levels built around them. Selected areas are being excavated, restored and conserved, and a number of the friezes are now open to the public, with more being stabilized each year. This site has changed a lot since I first visited in 1985, when it looked like an uninteresting pile of rubble. It's worth a visit. Reproductions of some of the murals are displayed in the Museo de Arqueología in Trujillo.

At the entrance of the site is a small snack bar and some souvenir stands. One of the men selling pots here makes them using original molds, so you can buy a modern-day replica of ancient pots for just a few dollars. They are very good, but to take them out of the country, you need to get a permit stating that they are reproductions. Ask the seller for a statement that it is a replica. Getting the official permit is a stupidly long and drawn-out bureaucratic process. It is unlikely that you will be stopped in customs leaving the country, but if you are, the pots may be confiscated. You'll only be out a few dollars, but the hassle of getting the permit is really not worth it.

## Complejo Arqueológico La Huaca El Brujo

This archaeological complex consists of the Huaca Prieta site described earlier and the newly excavated Moche Huaca Cao. It is 60km from Trujillo on the coast and is hard to find without a guide. It is not officially open to tourism, though it is possible to visit – Clara Luz Bravo D and Michael White have both been there many times (see Guides in Trujillo Information earlier in this chapter).

The main section of Huaca Cao is roughly a 27m-truncated pyramid with some of the best friezes in the area. They show multicolored reliefs with stylized life-sized warriors, prisoners, priests and human sacrifices. There are also many burial sites from the Lambayeque culture, which followed the Moche. Many other ruins are in the area, few of which have been properly studied.

## SUGAR ESTATES

Sugarcane is an important crop along the north Peruvian coast. A reader suggests that several sugar estates in the Trujillo area can be visited by those interested in sugar manufacturing and rum production (rum is made from sugarcane). It is best to go in the morning, when guided tours can be arranged. The Casa Grande and Hacienda Cartavio estates in the Chicama valley, some 40km north of Trujillo, can be reached by bus. Departure points change regularly, so ask in Trujillo if you are interested. To visit the Cartavio rum factory, call their public relations office (☎ 43-2313) before noon on weekdays.

## HUANCHACO
☎ 044

The fishing village of Huanchaco, a 12km bus ride northwest of Trujillo, is the best beach resort in the Trujillo area, though you won't find expensive high-rise buildings.

Huanchaco is still very low key and retains its fishing-village ambiance. It's not very good for swimming, except in the late-December to April summer, though surfing is OK year round. Local newspapers have reported fecal contamination.

Of particular interest are the *totora* (reed) boats, which look superficially like those found on Lake Titicaca in the southern highlands. However, unlike the ones on Lake Titicaca, these boats are hollow. Because the fishermen ride on them rather than in them, these high-ended, cigar-shaped boats are called *caballitos*, or 'little horses.' The caballitos are similar to the boats depicted on Moche ceramics 1500 years ago.

The inhabitants of Huanchaco are among the few remaining people on the coast who still remember how to construct and use these precarious-looking craft, and you can always see some stacked up at the north end of the beach.

The reed itself grows at the north end of the village. When the surf is good, the fishermen paddle the boats beyond the breakers to fish and then surf back to the beach with their catch. It's worth seeing. If the surf is too strong, the fishermen might not be able to work for weeks.

Apart from walking on the beach and waiting for the caballitos to go into action, there's not much to do in Huanchaco, and that's one of its attractions. It's a quiet, easy-going place. You can climb up to the massive church at the north end of the village for extensive views of the surrounding area. The church is said to be one of Peru's oldest but is run down, and the area is dangerous at night.

### Dangers & Annoyances

Use the bus to get to Trujillo. There are dangerous slum areas on the beach between Huanchaco and Trujillo, though Huanchaco itself is safe enough.

### Surfing

Surfboards can be rented for about US$5 per day from the Golden Club Hostal or the Restaurant Picollo. La Casa Suiza rents bodyboards.

### Special Events

Huanchaco is host to the Festival del Mar, held every other year (that's even years, though it wasn't held in 1998 because of El Niño) during the first week in May. This festival reenacts the legendary arrival of Takaynamo, founder of Chan Chan. There are various events, such as surfing and dance competitions, cultural conferences, food and music. Carnaval in February is also a big event.

### Places to Stay

Huanchaco is a small town and most people know where the hotels are or where people rent rooms. The recommended *La Casa Suiza* (☎ 46-1825, casasuiza.peru@mailcity .com, Los Pinos 451; no sign) has friendly German- and English-speaking owners. They have a book exchange, TV room, breakfast available, and a rooftop barbecue area. Four rooms with shared showers are US$4 per person, and five rooms with private baths and natural hot showers are US$5 per person. Several readers have recommended *Naylamp* (☎ 46-1022), on the beach at the north end of town. They have a camping area, rooms with private baths and a kitchen. They charge about US$4 per person. Other inexpensive places are *Hostal Solange* (Los Ficus 484), which several shoestring-budget travelers have recommended, and *Hospedaje Huanchaco* (☎ 46-1719, Los Ficus 516) – both are around the corner from Casa Suiza. *Señora Lola* (Manco Cápac 136) is an elderly lady who rents cheap rooms.

The clean *Hostal Huanchaco* (☎ 46-1272, Larco 287) is US$5 per person (communal cold showers) or US$22/25 for singles/ doubles (private hot bath). There is a small pool and pleasant courtyard. *Hostal Esteros* (☎ 46-1300, Larco 616), on the beach, has basic rooms with private hot showers for US$8 per person. Also on the beach, *Golden Club Hostal* (☎ 46-1306, La Rivera 217) has basic run-down rooms with cold water for US$5 per person, or US$10 (private bathroom). Best is the popular, friendly and secure *Hostal Bracamonte* (☎ 46-1162, fax 46-1266, Los Olivos 503). They have a pool, nice gardens, a game room and children's playground. Rooms with private hot showers are US$15/23.

## Places to Eat

Huanchaco has several seafood restaurants, especially near the totora boats stacked at the north end of the beach. None are luxurious, but several are adequate – take your pick. Some places occasionally offer entertainment of sorts, and they usually advertise this in the hotels a few days in advance.

*Restaurant Lucho del Mar* is in a large, white, two-story building on the waterfront. This locally popular restaurant serves large and tasty seafood dishes for about US$5 to US$6. Next door, *La Estrella Marina* has also been recommended as a good typical restaurant. Both have balconies with ocean views. The more elegant *Club Colonial* restaurant on the plaza is very good but a little pricier. On Los Abetos, a couple of blocks from La Casa Suiza, is *Picollo Restaurant*, which serves European-influenced food; and its owners are of French and German descent.

## Getting There & Away

Small buses leave from Industrial at España in Trujillo at frequent intervals from 7 am to 11 pm. The fare is about US$0.30. The bus can drop you off near the hotel of your choice – ask the driver. To return, just wait on the beachfront road for the bus as it returns from the north end, picking up passengers along the way. A taxi from Trujillo is about US$3.30.

## OTUZCO

The small town of Otuzco is, at 2627m above sea level, a two- or three-hour drive inland from Trujillo. There is a large modern church built next to a smaller, older one, which is usually closed. Outside, stairs lead to the shrine of La Virgen de la Puerta, the site of a major pilgrimage every December 15. During this time, the few hotels in Otuzco are usually full, and people sleep in the Plaza de Armas. Otherwise, this is a little-visited but typical town of the western Andean slopes. The drive through coastal sugarcane fields and other subtropical crops (irrigated by the Río Moche) and into the highland agricultural regions (irrigated by the Río Otuzco) is an interesting cross section that only a few travelers experience. It's a rough but scenic drive on unpaved roads.

## Places to Stay & Eat

There are half a dozen basic places to stay. The best is the cheap *Hostal Los Portales* (*Santa Rosa 617*).

A few inexpensive restaurants serve cheap Peruvian food; none seem outstanding.

## Getting There & Away

Empresa Antisuyo has buses from Trujillo. Otuzco is a few kilometers off the Trujillo-Santiago de Chuco road, and it is difficult to find buses on to Santiago de Chuco. You may need to return a few kilometers to the main road. It is reportedly possible to take an early bus from Trujillo, spend a few hours in Otuzco, and return in the afternoon.

## PUERTO CHICAMA

This small port is famous for its surf and has the longest left-handed wave in the world. Not being a surfer, I have no idea what that means but I guess it's pretty important. Surfers tell me that you can get a kilometer-long ride if there's a big swell; otherwise, the waves aren't too good for surfing. May to August are the best months. There is no gear available here – you have to bring it all. The water is cold, and a wet suit is recommended.

## Places to Stay

Puerto Chicama is a surfer's hangout, and there are few other visitors. There are three basic hotels and restaurants, but no electricity at night. *El Hombre* faces the ocean, charges US$6 a double and has good simple meals, but lacks running water. Another hotel has a shower. I've also heard that you can camp.

## Getting There & Away

To get to Puerto Chicama, wait for a bus near the Mansiche Stadium in Trujillo. There are a few direct buses, but it may be easier to take a bus about 40km north along the Panamericana to Paiján and change there for a local bus to Puerto Chicama, another 16km away.

I once met an Australian surfer who was traveling from beach to beach along the Pacific coast. He had his board with him and seemed to have no problems transporting it on the buses.

## PACASMAYO & PACATNAMÚ
☎ 044

The small port of Pacasmayo is 105km north of Trujillo on the Panamericana. The private **Rodriguez Razzetto collection** has museum-quality textiles, pottery and jewelry of the Jequetepeque culture. Visits can be arranged by appointment. Surfers find the long left-breaking waves good from May to August.

The turnoff to Cajamarca is 15km beyond Pacasmayo. A few kilometers farther along the Panamericana, just before the village of Guadalupe, a track leads toward the ocean. The little-visited **ruins** of Pacatnamú lie several kilometers along this track. This large site has been inhabited by various cultures: Gallinazo, Moche and Chimu.

### Places to Stay

There are several cheap, basic but clean hotels in Pacasmayo. These include *El Duke (Ayacucho 44)*, which is run by a Peruvian surfer who charges US$8.50 a double. *Hostal Sol y Mar (Sarmiento 112)* is a cheaper, family-run place with ocean views. There are other cheapies. *Hotel Peru* (☎ 52-1117, Junín 32), on the plaza, has dark rooms with private showers for US$15 for a double. The best hotels are *Hotel Pakatnamú* (☎ 52-2368, fax 52-3255, Malecón Grau 103), on the waterfront, and *Hotel Las Tejas* (☎ 52-3025, fax 52-1484, Pablo Céspedes 112), inland by the cement factory, which dominates the town. Both have singles/doubles with private baths, air-conditioning, minirefrigerators and cable TV for about US$20/30.

In Guadalupe, there's *Hotel El Bosque* (☎ 56-6490), which charges about US$20 a double with private bath.

## CHICLAYO
☎ 074

The next major coastal city north of Trujillo is Chiclayo, just over 200km away on the Panamericana. Founded in the 16th century, Chiclayo remained no more than an outlying district of the older town of Lambayeque through the 19th century. Today, however, Lambayeque is small and almost forgotten, while Chiclayo has become one of Peru's fastest-growing modern cities. Although the city itself has little to see of historical interest, it is vibrant and thriving with good opportunities to meet Peruvians – residents of Chiclayo call the town the Peruvian capital of friendship. It is an important commercial center and is the capital of the coastal desert department of Lambayeque. With a population of over 625,000, it is the fourth-largest city in Peru.

In 1987, a royal Moche tomb at Sipán, about 30km southeast of Chiclayo, was located by researchers. This find proved to be extraordinary, and has been called the most important archaeological discovery in Peru in the last 50 years. Peruvian archaeologists have recovered hundreds of dazzling and priceless artifacts from the site. Excavation continues at the site, and a tourist infrastructure is developing.

Sipán is best visited from Chiclayo. Some of the spectacular finds are displayed in the Bruning Museum in Lambayeque, 11km north of Chiclayo. Other sites worth visiting from Chiclayo are the archaeological ruins at Túcume, as well as a number of coastal villages.

The cathedral was built in the late 19th century, and the Plaza de Armas (Parque Principal) wasn't inaugurated until 1916, which gives an idea of how modern the city is by Peruvian standards. The new Paseo las Musas is Chiclayo's showplace park and has statues of mythological figures in classical style.

### Information

**Tourist Offices** There is no official tourist office here. Detailed tourism information is available through Sipán Tours (☎/fax 22-7022, sipantours@kipu.rednorte.com.pe,

# CHICLAYO

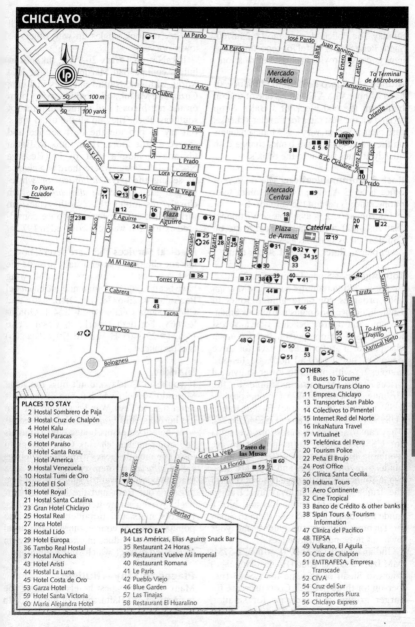

0    50    100 m
0    50    100 yards

To Piura,
Ecuador

To Piura,
Ecuador

To Terminal
de Microbuses

To Lima
Trujillo

**NORTH COAST**

**PLACES TO STAY**
2 Hostal Sombrero de Paja
3 Hostal Cruz de Chalpón
4 Hotel Kalu
5 Hotel Paracas
6 Hotel Paraíso
8 Hotel Santa Rosa,
   Hotel America
9 Hostal Venezuela
10 Hostal Tumi de Oro
12 Hotel El Sol
18 Hotel Royal
21 Hotel Santa Catalina
23 Gran Hotel Chiclayo
25 Hostal Real
27 Inca Hotel
28 Hostal Lido
29 Hotel Europa
36 Tambo Real Hostal
37 Hostal Mochica
43 Hotel Aristi
44 Hostal La Luna
45 Hotel Costa de Oro
53 Garza Hotel
59 Hotel Santa Victoria
60 María Alejandra Hotel

**PLACES TO EAT**
34 Las Américas, Elías Aguirre Snack Bar
35 Restaurant 24 Horas
39 Restaurant Vuelve Mi Imperial
40 Restaurant Romana
41 Le Paris
42 Pueblo Viejo
46 Blue Garden
57 Las Tinajas
58 Restaurant El Huaralino

**OTHER**
1 Buses to Túcume
7 Oltursa/Trans Olano
11 Empresa Chiclayo
13 Transportes San Pablo
14 Colectivos to Pimentel
15 Internet Red del Norte
16 InkaNatura Travel
17 Virtualnet
19 Telefónica del Peru
20 Tourism Police
22 Peña El Brujo
24 Post Office
26 Clínica Santa Cecilia
30 Indiana Tours
31 Aero Continente
32 Cine Tropical
33 Banco de Crédito & other banks
38 Sipán Tours & Tourism
   Information
47 Clínica del Pacífico
48 TEPSA
49 Vulkano, El Aguila
50 Cruz de Chalpón
51 EMTRAFESA, Empresa
   Transcade
52 CIVA
54 Cruz del Sur
55 Transportes Piura
56 Chiclayo Express

MM Izaga 636), which is open 8 am to 8 pm Monday to Saturday, and 8 am to noon Sunday. The Policía de Turismo (☎ 23-6700, Saenz Peña 830) is useful for reporting problems and also provides tourist information.

**Money** The Banco de Crédito (J Balta 630) has a 24-hour Visa ATM and is one of several banks on the 600 block of J Balta. Shop around for the best rates for traveler's checks; cash rates, however, vary less. Moneychangers on the street outside the banks change cash quickly at rates similar to the bank's.

**Post & Communications** The main post office is at E Aguirre 140. The main telephone office is behind the cathedral.

Internet service is available at Virtualnet (San José 462) or Internet Red del Norte, on San José at Angamos, as well as several other places. Rates are US$1.30 per hour.

**Tour Agencies** Sipán Tours (☎/fax 22-7022, sipantours@kipu.rednorte.com.pe, MM Izaga 636) provides complete guided tours in English, French or Spanish. Tours to Sipán, Túcume and nearby beaches typically cost about US$30 for one person, but are much cheaper for a group (US$18 each for three people). They'll try and hook singles and couples up with others to lower individual prices. Tours are also available to the Bruning Museum (US$25 for one person/US$16 each for three people), Batán Grande (US$50/US$29) and Zaña (US$34/US$21). They can arrange shaman sessions (at night) for US$150/US$60. Tours in German are available but cost more. Prices include a guide, a private vehicle, and entrance fees. Sipán Tours will also arrange tours of ruins in the Trujillo and Chachapoyas area. Budget travelers can go by public bus and hire a guide for about US$7 to take them to Sipán or Túcume; you pay the guide's and your own bus fare and entrance fees.

Indiana Tours (☎ 22-2991, ☎/fax 22-5751, MM Izaga 585) has good (English-language) tours to Sipán or Túcume for US$23 (per person for three people). Costs decrease for larger groups and increase for smaller. Other sites can be toured. This is one of the oldest, most experienced and most recommended tour companies in the area. They'll also try to hook singles up with others to lower prices.

InkaNatura (☎/fax 20-9948, inkanort@ lullitec.com.pe, San Martín 120, office 302) works with InkaNatura agencies in Lima, Cuzco and Miami, and provide services both on the north coast and in the rainforest of southeast Peru. They do all the usual tours, but try to provide the best service and charge a little more. Their tours to Batán Grande include a visit to La Reserva Nacional de Poma, where there is a chance of seeing the *pava aliblanca*, or white-winged guan *(Penelope albipennis)*, which closely resembles the North American turkey. This guan species was once considered extinct but was rediscovered in 1977.

**Medical Services** There are several hospitals and clinics; the latter usually provide the best services for travelers. The following have been locally recommended: Clínica del Pacífico (☎ 23-6378, JL Ortiz 420) and Clínica Santa Cecilia (☎ 23-7154, L Gonzales 668). For dental work, Dr César Aristi Ugaz (☎ 23-8405, E Aguirre 374, office 205) is experienced.

## Market

If you're in Chiclayo, don't miss the huge Mercado Modelo, which is one of the most interesting in Peru. Wander around and see the herbalist and *brujo* (witchdoctor) stalls with their dried plants, bones, bits of animals and other healing charms. Other things to look for include heavy woven saddlebags called *alforjas*, an item typical of the area that can be worn over the shoulder with one bag on your front and the other on your back. Woven straw items – such as hats, baskets, mats and ornaments – are also popular. And, of course, there is the usual cacophonous produce market. As always in a crowded market, watch your belongings.

## Places to Stay – Budget

Many of the cheapest hotels are along the main street of J Balta, south of the Mercado Modelo, and on streets east of the mercado.

Most are extremely basic, not especially clean and have little to recommend them aside from their cheap rates. Some are used for short stays. *Hostal Sombrero de Paja*, on Juan Fanning at 7 de Enero, advertises hot water and rooms at US$4/5 for singles/ doubles. *Hostal Cruz de Chalpón* (☎ 23-3004, J Balta 1205) is reasonably clean and charges US$5/6, or US$7/8 with private bath. Showers are cold.

The simple but clean and decent *Hostal Tumi de Oro* (☎ 22-7108, L Prado 1145) charges US$4/5 for one bed and US$6 for a double with two beds and communal showers. They have rooms with private showers for US$7/8 (one bed) and US$11 (two beds). Hot water is available. *Hostal Real* (☎ 23-2868, E Aguirre 673) is basic, but has hot water in private showers. They charge US$7/8 for singles/doubles, but are open to bargaining.

*Hotel Royal* (☎ 23-3421), on the Plaza de Armas, is in an old, run-down building full of character. Some rooms overlook the plaza, which is fun but noisy. Singles/doubles with bath (hot water) cost US$8/11, and rooms with shared showers are US$5.50/9. The friendly *Hostal Lido* (☎ 24-4050, E Aguirre 412) is US$5/8, or US$7/10 with cold bath. They have a nice city view from the top floor. The quiet, clean and secure *Hostal Venezuela* (☎ 23-2665, Lora y Cordero 954) is US$7 for a single and US$9/11 for a double with one/two beds with private bath and hot water. Rooms at the back are quiet. The popular, clean but noisy *Hotel Europa* (☎ 23-7919, fax 22-2066, E Aguirre 466) charges US$11/14/17 for one/two/three people with private bath (electric showers), or less with communal showers.

## Places to Stay – Mid-Range

The new *Hostal Santa Catalina* (☎ 27-2119, Vincente de la Vega 1127) has 10 quiet rooms with electric hot showers for US$10/13 (one bed) or US$17 (two beds). Also small, clean and new is *Hostal Mochica* (☎ 22-1658, Torres Paz 429) at US$12/14 (one bed) and US$17 (two beds). The central *Hostal La Luna* (☎ 20-5945, Torres Paz 688) has clean rooms with TV and good hot showers for

US$10/17. The quiet and pleasant *Hotel Santa Rosa* (☎ 22-4411, fax 23-6242, L Gonzales 927) is also good at US$13/15 for one bed and US$19 for two beds. Rooms have private baths with electric showers, TV and telephones.

Three decent, mid-priced hotels are found on the 1000 block of P Ruiz, and all charge about US$13/17 for singles/doubles with private baths. Rooms have telephones and cable TV and restaurant service is available. They are *Hotel Kalu* (☎ 22-9293, 22-8509, fax 22-8767, P Ruiz 1038), *Hotel Paracas* (☎ 23 6433, P Ruiz 1046) and *Hotel Paraíso* (☎ 22-8161, fax 22-2070, P Ruiz 1064). The Paraíso is about a dollar cheaper than the others.

The clean and comfortable *Hotel El Sol* (☎ 23-2120, ☎/fax 23-1070, E Aguirre 119) charges US$17/22 for singles/doubles with bath and hot water. Rooms have TV and telephones but vary in quality and size, so look around. There is a small pool and parking area. *Hotel Aristi* (☎ 23-1074, 23-3873, fax 22-8673, F Cabrera 102) has a restaurant attached and decent rooms with private hot showers, cable TV, telephones and minirefrigerators for US$17/25. There are a few larger rooms for about US$5 more.

*Hotel Santa Victoria* (☎/fax 22-5074, La Florida 586) overlooks the pleasant Paseo de las Musas and is quiet. Rooms have cable TV, telephones and private baths, and a restaurant with room service is available. Rates are $18/25 including continental breakfast. Similar services are offered at the centrally located *Hotel Costa de Oro* (☎/fax 20-9342, Balta 399) and at *Hotel America* (☎ 22-4476, 22-9305, fax 27-0664, L Gonzales 943). Both are good hotels at about US$20/30. The attractive new and quiet 11-room *Tambo Real Hostal* (☎ 20-5067, 23-3879, L Gonzales 532) charges US$20/25 including continental breakfast.

*Inca Hotel* (☎ 23-5931, 23-7803, fax 22-7651, L Gonzales 622) has rooms with air-conditioning, minirefrigerators, cable TV and telephones. Rates are about US$25/35 including continental breakfast, but there are often discounts if things are slow. The hotel has a restaurant and small casino.

## Places to Stay – Top End

One of Chiclayo's newest place to stay is the pleasant *María Alejandra Hotel (☎ 23-8403, 27-3445, 27-3450, fax 20-8796, Faiques 101)*, in front of the Paseo de las Musas. The rooms are modern and spacious, with cable TV and telephones, and the bathrooms all have bathtubs as well as showers – a rarity in Peru. Some rooms have good views of the plaza, and some rooms are air-conditioned and have minirefrigerators. It is planned to provide air-conditioning in all the rooms. A restaurant is open 7 am to 11 pm, and room service is available 24 hours. There is a karaoke-disco, and tourist information and tours are available. Rates are US$35/45 including continental breakfast, and mini-suites are US$75.

*Garza Hotel (☎ 22-8172, 23-8968, fax 22-8171, Bolognesi 756)* is a good hotel with efficient service, pool, casino, tourist agency, a decent restaurant and bar, and comfortable singles/doubles for US$45/65. All are air-conditioned and have minirefrigerators, cable TV and telephones. Minisuites with Jacuzzis are US$120.

*Gran Hotel Chiclayo (☎ 23-4911, fax 22-4031; granhotel@lima.business.com.pe, F Villareal 115)* is the oldest of Chiclayo's top-end hotels. It has comfortable, air-conditioned rooms with the usual amenities (some with balcony), a pool, casino, gift shop, café, and a restaurant and bar. Some rooms suffer somewhat from street noise, which is the case in almost all of Chiclayo's hotels. Rates are about US$66/80 including continental breakfast and airport transfer. Suites are US$135 to US$155.

## Places to Eat

There are plenty of cheap restaurants on J Balta. Although not the cheapest, the reasonably priced *Restaurant Romana (☎ 22-3598, J Balta 512)* is a good, locally popular place open 7 am to 1 am. They serve a wide variety of food with plenty of local dishes. *Restaurant Vuelve Mi Imperial*, across the street, is cheaper and also good, with friendly service. They serve local food, including cuy.

On the southeast corner of the plaza, the clean and modern *Las Américas* and *Elías Aguirre Snack Bar* have also been recommended for snacks and light meals. Less than a block away, *Restaurant 24 Horas* is simple but OK and really is open 24 hours. For good coffee, *Café Real (☎ 24-5641, L Gonzales 532)*, under Tambo Real Hostal, is open 7:30 am to 11 pm and advertises 38 different kinds of coffee – stick to espresso and cappuccino. They also serve good snacks and meals. *Blue Garden (☎ 23-8855, F Cabrera 638)* is a smart, clean little place serving good ceviches (US$2 to US$4), as well as other plates, including some vegetarian specialities. They are open 10 am to 4 pm daily, though they plan on staying open for the evening as well.

A more expensive restaurant in the city center is *Le Paris (☎ 23-5485, MM Izaga 716)*, which has a decent international menu with meals in the US$4 to US$8 range. They are open 11 am to 4 pm and 7 to 11 pm daily. *Restaurant El Huaralino (☎ 27-0330, Libertad 155)* has good local and international cuisine in the US$5 to US$10 range (expensive by local standards) and some of the cleanest bathrooms in Peru. Unfortunately, visitors are charged more than the price on the menu – a practice that leaves a bad taste in your mouth. The owners, when confronted with this, will unapologetically tell you that you got some kind of special service. A cheaper and more local place for equally tasty and more varied regional food is *Las Tinajas (Mariscal Nieto 348)*. They have been around for years, though their address keeps changing. They open only for lunch.

Two restaurants stand out for excellent typical food at higher prices. *Pueblo Viejo (☎ 20-6701, MM Izaga 900)* serves Chiclayano lunches in an elegantly rustic ambiance; there is an art gallery on the premises. They are open only from noon to 4:30 pm. Perhaps the best in Chiclayo is *Restaurant Típico La Fiesta (☎ 20-1970, Avenida Salaverry 1820)* in the Residencial 3 de Octubre suburb. Salaverry is the western extension of E Aguirre and the restaurant is about 2km west of the Gran Hotel Chiclayo. It's expensive by Peruvian standards, but the food is a delicious variety of local meats and seafood. Hours are 9:30 am to 11 pm daily.

## Entertainment

*Cine Tropical*, on the Plaza de Armas, often has English-language films. For live music, there's *Peña El Brujo* (☎ *23-1224, Vincente de la Vega 1238)*, which has local food and a peña late on Friday and Saturday nights. El Brujo has been around for some years, others come and go. There are several disco-pubs – few last more than a couple of years.

## Getting There & Away

**Air** The airport is 2km southeast of town (US$1 taxi ride). Aero Continente (☎ 20-9916, 20-9917, airport 20-9919, E Aguirre 712) has daily flights to Lima, Tumbes and Trujillo. These services change often. As always, there's a US$3.50 airport departure tax.

Charter and sightseeing flights in small aircraft are available from Aero Servicio Andino (☎ 23-3161, 23-1568, fax 22-4351, airport 22-8953). The company is run by a friendly Swiss-Peruvian couple. They have well-maintained aircraft and are knowledgeable about the area.

**Bus** Many bus companies are near the south end of downtown, which is the best place to look for long-distance buses to Lima or other major north-coast cities. Buses for local destinations leave from other parts of town.

A good number of the bus companies near the corner of Saenz Peña and Bolognesi have one or more buses a day to Lima (US$9 to US$22 depending, on the services desired, 11 to 13 hours). Most have northbound buses as well. Cruz del Sur (☎ 22-5508, 23-7965, Bolognesi 888) has various levels of service to Lima and Tumbes. Oltursa/Trans Olano (☎ 23-7789) have a ticket office at J Balta 598, but buses depart from Vincente de la Vega 101. There is an overnight bus (US$22) – known as *bus cama*, or bus with bed, because the seats fully recline – to Lima, and much cheaper daytime and overnight services. They also have buses to Tumbes. CIVA (☎ 24-4671, Bolognesi 755) has buses to Lima and a 3:30 pm departure for Chachapoyas (US$7, 12 hours). There are several other companies in this area with reliable service to Lima. These buses can drop you off at intermediate towns, including Trujillo. Frequent service to Trujillo is provided by EMTRAFESA (☎ 23-4291, J Balta 110), as well as Vulkano (☎ 23-2951) and El Aguila (☎ 23-3497), which are both at Bolognesi 638. Vulkano also has buses to Cajamarca (US$6 to US$7, 7 hours) at 12:45 and 9:30 pm. El Aguila has buses to Piura (US$3.30, 3 hours) every hour from 6 am to 7 pm and to Chimbote (US$5) at 9:15 am and 4:15 pm.

Empresa Chiclayo (☎ 23-7984, JL Ortiz 010) has frequent, daily service to Piura. Some buses continue to Tumbes. Transportes Piura (☎ 22-4211, Mariscal Nieto 115) has early morning buses to Piura.

Travelers to Cajamarca can also use El Cumbe's (☎ 23-1454, 23-3697, Quiñones 425) day buses. (Quiñones is parallel to and east of M Cápac.) There are other companies, and services change often.

Several companies provide services inland through Jaen and Bagua Grande (US$5), Pedro Ruiz, Rioja, Moyobamba, Tarapoto (US$15, 24 hours) and Yurimaguas (US$25, 36 hours). The road is paved as far as Rioja. For this route, try Paredes Estrella (☎ 20-4879), in the Cruz de Chalpón terminal at J Balta 178. Empresa Transcade (☎ 20-4945, J Balta 110) has morning and night buses to Jaen and Bagua Grande.

TEPSA, on Bolognesi at Colón, has buses up and down the coast. Inside the TEPSA terminal are half a dozen small agencies with buses to small inland towns such as Cajamarca, Chachapoyas, Tarapoto, Huancabamba and others.

## AROUND CHICLAYO

Transportes San Pablo minibuses to Lambayeque leave from the west end of San José every few minutes. They'll drop you off right in front of the Bruning Museum for about US$0.25. A block away, there are frequent buses to Pimentel.

Buses for Sipán, Monsefú and Zaña leave frequently from the Terminal de Microbuses on Nicolás de Píerola at Oriente, northeast of downtown and 600m off the map. Many other small local towns are serviced by this terminal.

Buses to Túcume leave from Angamos near M Pardo – it's hard to find this bus stop, so ask. Bus stops for small local towns change often; keep asking.

## The Coast

Two coastal villages, Pimentel and Santa Rosa, can be conveniently visited from Chiclayo.

**Pimentel** is 14km from Chiclayo and has a good sandy beach that gets very crowded on summer weekends (January to March) but is quiet during the off season. A few kilometers south of Pimentel is **Santa Rosa**, a busy fishing village where a few caballitos may still be seen. There is also a modern fishing fleet. (Pimentel also has caballitos.) You can walk from Pimentel to Santa Rosa in less than an hour or take a local bus. There is an inexpensive hotel in Santa Rosa, and both villages have seafood restaurants, though most are closed in the off season.

Colectivos operate from Santa Rosa to the small port of **Puerto Etén**. Here, you can see a 19th-century train engine in the (disused) train station. There are plans to open a railway museum, but this doesn't look likely to happen in the near future.

From Puerto Etén or Santa Rosa, you can return to Chiclayo via the village of **Monsefú**, 15km away from Chiclayo. Monsefú is known for its handicrafts. Several stores sell basketwork, embroidery and woodwork, and a craft festival called Fexticum is held in the last week of July. The village has a few simple restaurants, of which the simple and rustic **Restaurant Tradiciones** is recommended for good local food.

Colectivos to Pimentel leave from Chiclayo; during summer (January to March), they continue on from Pimentel along the so-called *circuito de playas* (beach circuit) through Santa Rosa, Puerto Etén and Monsefú before returning to Chiclayo the same day. Most beachgoers stay in Chiclayo, because accommodations elsewhere are very limited. Simple rooms, however, can be rented – ask around.

## Lambayeque

Lambayeque, 11km north of Chiclayo, used to be the main town in the area. Today, it has a population of only 20,000 and has been completely overshadowed by Chiclayo. Some colonial architecture can be seen, but the town's Bruning Museum is its best feature. Ask for **La Casa de Logia**, a few blocks away, which locals say has the longest balcony in Peru – you can see it from the street only. Visitors normally stay in Chiclayo. A decent local restaurant with typical food is *El Cantaro* (☎ 28-2196, *2 de Mayo 180*), a few blocks from the museum.

**Bruning Museum** Named after a local collector and businessman, the Bruning Museum (☎ 28-2110, 28-3440) was opened on its present site in the 1960s. The modern building houses a good collection of archaeological artifacts from the Chimu, Moche, Chavín and Vicus cultures, and a new exhibit features finds from the newly discovered site of Sipán. Labels are in Spanish, but even if you don't read Spanish, the museum is worth a visit. The director of the museum is Dr Walter Alva, who was responsible for the discovery, protection and archaeological investigation of Sipán. Museum hours are 8:30 am to 6 pm weekdays and 9 am to 6 pm

**CHICLAYO AREA**

To Piura
Illimo
Batán Grande
Túcume
Batán Grande
Mochumi
To Piura
Panamericana Vieja
Ferreñafe
0   5   10 km
0   3   6 miles
Lambayeque
Río Lambayeque
To Chongoyape
San José
Tumán
Chiclayo
6
Aeropuerto
Río Reque
Pimentel
6
Sipán    Sipán ruins
Reque
Santa Rosa
Monsefú
Puerto Etén
Zaña (ghost town)
108
PACIFIC
OCEAN
To Trujillo, Lima
Mocupe
1

weekends and holidays. The entry fee is US$1, and a guide who speaks English charges US$2.50. There is a small giftshop selling well-made and attractive replicas of the jewelry found at Sipán. Buses from Chiclayo drop you off a block from the museum.

## ARCHAEOLOGICAL SITES AROUND CHICLAYO

Several sites are easily accessible from Chiclayo and are well worth a visit, especially Sipán and Túcume. Chiclayo provides the best (almost only) accommodations in the area.

### Sipán

This site, also known as Huaca Rayada, was discovered by *huaqueros* (graverobbers) from the nearby village of Sipán. When local archaeologist Dr Walter Alva became aware of a huge influx of beautiful objects on the black market in early 1987, he realized that a wonderful burial site was being ransacked in the Chiclayo area. Careful questioning led Dr Alva to the Sipán pyramids, which, to the untrained eye, look like earthen hills with holes excavated in them.

By the time Dr Alva and his colleagues found the site, at least one major tomb had been pillaged by looters. Fast protective action by local archaeologists and police stopped the plundering. Scientists were then fortunate to discover several other, even better, tombs that the graverobbers had missed, including an exceptional royal Moche burial, which became known as The Lord of Sipán. One huaquero was shot and killed by police in the early, tense days of the struggle over the graves. The Sipán locals were obviously unhappy that this treasure trove had been made inaccessible to them and were not friendly to archaeologists. To solve this problem, the locals were invited to train to become excavators, researchers and guards at the site, which now provides steady employment to many of them.

The story, an exciting one of buried treasure, huaqueros, police, archaeologists and at least one killing, is detailed in articles by Dr Alva in the October 1988 and June 1990 issues of *National Geographic* magazine, and

### Maybe You Can Take It with You

The tomb of the Lord of Sipán is the most interesting of the Moche burial sites; indeed, it is considered by some archaeologists to be the most important intact tomb found in Peru. The Lord of Sipán was a divine Mochica leader who was buried in all his finery. His death spelled the doom of several of his subjects, who were buried alive with him. These included a warrior guard whose feet had been amputated (to ensure that he did not run off, perhaps?), three young women, two assistants, a servant, a child, a dog and two llamas. The Lord also took with him a treasure trove of gold, silver, copper and semi-precious stones, as well as hundreds of ceramic pots containing food and drink for the journey beyond.

in the May 1994 issue of *Natural History* magazine. Also interesting is the book *Royal Tombs of Sipán* by Walter Alva and Christopher B Donnan.

Archaeologists continue to work at the site. Some of the tombs have been restored with replicas to show what they looked like just before being closed up over 1500 years ago. The actual artifacts went on a world tour; some returned to the Bruning Museum, where they are now displayed.

**Information** Sipán is open daily 8 am to 6 pm, and admission to the site is US$1. Opposite the entrance is a small on-site museum, which is worth a visit. Nearby are simple snack bars and gift shops. Climb the hill behind the museum for a good view of the entire site and surrounding area.

**Getting There & Away** Public buses to Sipán (US$0.50) leave from the Terminal de Microbuses in Chiclayo several times a day at erratic hours. It is best to go in the morning if traveling by public transport, as buses are infrequent in the afternoon. (There are no hotels at Sipán.) Daily guided tours are available from tour agencies in Chiclayo. Tours take about three hours.

## Túcume

This vast and little known site can be seen from a spectacular cliff-top *mirador* (lookout) about 30km north of Lambayeque on the Panamericana. It's worth the climb to see over 200 hectares of crumbling walls, plazas and no less than 28 pyramids. Túcume was recently studied by a team led by Thor Heyerdahl (an explorer who used a balsa-wood raft, named *Kon Tiki*, to sail from Peru to the Polynesian Islands. The journey was intended to support his theory that South Americans had settled the Pacific Islands rather than the long-held belief that the islands were settled from Asia.). There is a small but attractive and interesting on-site museum. Little excavation has been done, and no spectacular tombs have been found (and perhaps never will be), but it is the sheer size of the site that makes it a memorable visit. More details are found in *Pyramids of Túcume: The Quest for Peru's Forgotten City*, by Thor Heyerdahl, Daniel H Sandweiss and Alfredo Narváez. This book is currently out of print, but is available at most public libraries.

**Information** The site and museum are open 8:30 am to 4:30 pm weekdays and 8:30 am to 6 pm weekends. Admission is US$1. There is a small snack bar.

**Getting There & Away** Although buses go to Túcume from Chiclayo, I recommend that you go to Lambayeque first thing in the morning, visit the Bruning Museum, then continue on to Túcume. Ask anyone at the museum where buses to Túcume leave from; it's just a short walk to the bus stop. At Túcume, you have to walk almost a kilometer from where the bus drops you off. Guided tours are available from Chiclayo, or you can ask at the Bruning Museum and hire a guide there.

## Chongoyape Area

Chongoyape is an old village about 65km east of Chiclayo, in the foothills of the Andes. Buses leave from Terminal de Microbuses in Chiclayo and take about 1½ hours. About halfway to Chongoyape, a few kilometers beyond Tumán, a minor road on your left leads to the ruins of **Batán Grande**, 31km away. This is a major archaeological site where about 50 pyramids have been identified and several burials have been excavated. With the urging of Dr Walter Alva, among others, the site has recently become a National Reserve, but there is no tourist infrastructure. The reserve protects a forest of *algarrobo* (mesquite) trees. As there is almost no public transport, you will have to find a taxi or tour to take you. The 1998 El Niño washed out parts of the road from Chiclayo, and tours were suspended for several months. There are also poor roads to Batán Grande from the villages of Chongoyape and Ferreñafe.

Chongoyape has a cheap and basic hotel. The **Chavín Petroglyphs of Cerro Mulato** are 3km away, and there are a few other minor archaeological sites. The irrigation complex of Tinajones forms a large reservoir just before Chongoyape.

A rough but scenic road climbs east from Chongoyape into the Andes until it reaches Chota (2400m), a 170km journey that takes about eight hours. Two or three buses a day from Chiclayo go through Chongoyape and continue on to Chota, where there are basic hotels. From Chota, a daily bus makes the rough journey via Bambamarca and Hualgayoc to Cajamarca.

## ZAÑA

Also called Saña, this is a ghost town about 50km southeast of Chiclayo. Founded in 1563, this city held a wealth of colonial architecture, with a number of rich churches and monasteries. At one time, it was slated to become the nation's capital. During the 17th century, it survived attacks by pirates and slave uprisings, only to be destroyed by the great flood of 1720. Today, great walls and the arches of four churches poke eerily out of the desert sands. Nearby, the present-day village of Zaña houses about 1000 people. Buses go here from Chiclayo's Terminal de Microbuses, or you can take a tour.

# SECHURA DESERT

The coastal desert between Chiclayo and Piura is the widest in Peru. South of Chiclayo, the Andes almost reach the coast, leaving only a narrow strip of flat coastal desert. North of Chiclayo, this strip becomes over 150km wide in places. This is the Sechura Desert.

Two main roads run between Chiclayo and Piura. The shorter, less interesting one is the Panamericana Nueva (new Panamericana), which goes via Mórrope; while the longer, the Panamericana Vieja (old Panamericana), goes via Motupe. These two roads divide at Lambayeque. In addition, there is a minor unpaved coastal road from Chiclayo via San José and Bayovar to Piura. This last road has very little traffic, but gives access to a few remote fishing settlements and some excellent surfing beaches. Surfers here must be completely self-sufficient, as there are no facilities.

If you want to visit some of the towns between Chiclayo and Piura, find out which route your bus is traveling.

## Panamericana Nueva

On the shorter Panamericana Nueva, Mórrope, about 20km north of Lambayeque, is the only settlement of any size that can be visited from Chiclayo. It is an old colonial town, founded in 1537. The church of San Pedro is the most notable building and has been declared a National Historic Monument. June 29, the feast of San Pedro, is an important holiday, and there are religious processions. Another religious feast day is November 10, in honor of the Cruz de Pañala. Apart from these feast days, which attract hundreds of pilgrims and tourists from Chiclayo and Piura, Mórrope is famous for its ceramics and other local crafts.

Beyond Mórrope, the Panamericana Nueva is a long, straight run through the desert, with no settlements beyond a couple of simple restaurant/service stations. The scenery is flat and bare. It is almost 200km between Lambayeque and Piura. This is the shortest driving route, but I have read reports of strong headwinds from the north and possible muggings, making this a poor choice for those touring the country by bike. The older, inland route is suggested for cyclists.

## Panamericana Vieja

The old Panamericana between Chiclayo and Piura passes the archaeological site of Túcume. Also nearby is the little-visited site of **El Purgatorio**, where there are pyramids from the Chimu period.

**Motupe**, almost 80km north of Chiclayo, is the site of a major religious celebration every August 5. Thousands of pilgrims come from Chiclayo and all over Peru to honor the miraculous **Cruz de Chalpón**, a wooden crucifix kept in a hillside shrine above the town. Accommodations are extremely basic,

---

### Lago La Niña

At 170km in length, Lago La Niña is Peru's second-largest lake after Lake Titicaca. But try as you might, you won't find this lake marked on any Peruvian map. That's because, incredible as it may seem, this huge lake was formed temporarily in the Sechura Desert following the 1998 El Niño floods. The lake forms after any major El Niño event, but the 1998 incarnation was the largest in living memory.

When it occurs, the lake washes out roads (including parts of the Panamericana), floods fields and destroys the livelihood of thousands of campesinos. During the 1998 event, local entrepreneurs brought in small boats and chartered them out for trips on this huge, but only temporary, lake. When you drive through the Sechura Desert, try to imagine a huge body of water stretching as far as the eye can see!

On a more practical note, bear in mind that road conditions on the north coast can be terrible during and after an El Niño event. In early 1998, the road journey (normally a 22-hour bus trip) from Lima to the Ecuadorian border took over four days. By 1999, however, the journey was back to 24 hours.

NORTH COAST

and many pilgrims camp out. The pre-Inca irrigation canals of Apurlec are 12km away from Motupe and can be visited by taxi.

## PIURA
☎ 074

Piura, with a population of over 300,000, is the fifth-largest city in Peru and the capital of its department. Intense irrigation of the desert has made Piura a major agricultural center, with rice and cotton being the main crops. Corn and plantains (bananas) are also cultivated. The department's petroleum industry, based around the coastal oil fields near Talara, is as valuable as its agriculture.

Piura's economic development has been precarious, buffeted by extreme droughts and devastating floods. The department was among the hardest hit by the disastrous El Niño floods of 1983, which destroyed almost 90% of the rice, cotton and plantain crops, as well as causing serious damage to roads, bridges, buildings and oil wells in the area. Piura was declared a disaster area – crops were destroyed, land was flooded, and people had no food, homes or jobs. The El Niño of 1992 washed out roads and bridges north of Piura, and going by bus to Tumbes involved a relay of buses. Passengers frequently had to wade through rivers to meet a successive bus. This was repeated during the 1998 El Niño, when the Bolognesi bridge in central Piura collapsed, killing several people. Bridges on the Panamericana north of Piura have now been repaired, but you are advised to check locally about the latest climatic upheaval.

Piura is referred to as the oldest colonial town in Peru. Its original site, on the north banks of the Río Chira, was called San Miguel de Piura and was founded by Pizarro in 1532, before he headed inland and began the conquest of the Incas. The settlement moved three times before construction at its present location began in 1588. Piura's cathedral dates from that year, and the city center still has a number of colonial buildings, though many were destroyed in the earthquake of 1912. Today, the center of the city is the large, shady and pleasant Plaza de Armas.

The center of the Vicus culture, which existed around the time of Christ, was roughly 30km east of Piura. Although no buildings remain, tombs have yielded a great number of ceramics, which can be seen in the museums of Piura and Lima.

## Information
There is no official tourist-information office. The best place to change cash and traveler's checks and use an ATM is the Banco de Crédito, just off the Plaza de Armas. The Banco Continental is nearby.

Internet access is available at the Rectorado del Universidad Nacional at Apurímac and Tacna from 8:30 am to 10 pm weekdays and 8:30 am to 1 pm Saturday.

Piura Tours (☎ 32-8873, 32-6778, fax 33-4379, piuratours@mail.udep.edu.pe, Ayacucho 585) is an IATA-registered travel agent.

Medical attention can be obtained through Regional Hospital (☎ 34-4682), Hospital de San Juan de Dios (☎ 34-3560) and Clínica San Miguel (☎ 33-5913), which has 24-hour emergency service.

## Museums
The small **Museo Municipal**, on Huánuco at Sullana, has archaeology and art exhibits. Hours are 8 am to 9 pm; entry is free.

On Tacna near Ayacucho is **Casa Grau**, the house where Admiral Miguel Grau was born on July 27, 1834. The house was almost completely destroyed by the 1912 earthquake; it was later restored by the Peruvian navy and is now a naval museum. Admiral Grau was a hero of the War of the Pacific against Chile (1879-80) and captain of the British-built warship *Huáscar*, a model of which can be seen in the museum. Hours change often, and admission is free.

## Churches
The cathedral on the Plaza de Armas is the oldest church in Piura. Although parts of the cathedral date from 1588, the main altar was built in 1960. The side altar of the Virgin of Fatima, built in the early 17th century, was once the main altar and is the oldest. The famed local artist Ignacio Merino painted

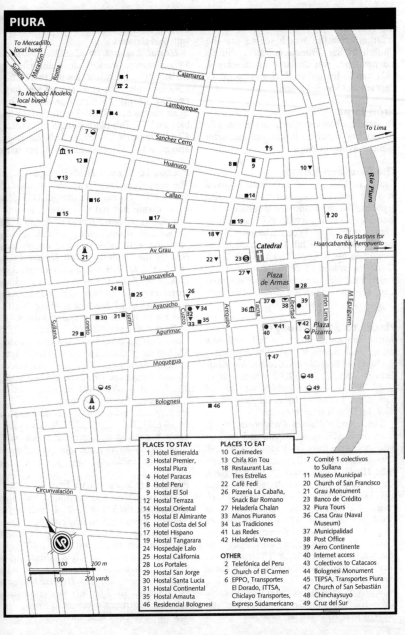

**PIURA**

To Mercadillo,
local buses

To Mercado Modelo,
local buses

To Lima

To Bus stations for
Huancabamba, Aeropuerto

Cajamarca

Lambayeque

Sanchez Cerro

Huánuco

Callao

Ica

Av Grau

Huancavelica

Ayacucho

Apurimac

Moquegua

Bolognesi

Circunvalación

Río Piura

Catedral

Plaza
de Armas

Plaza
Pizarro

Sullana

Matanon

Roma

Loreto

Junin

Sullana

Curco

Arequipa

Tacna

Libertad

Jirón Lima

M. Eguiguren

0    100    200 m
0    100    200 yards

**NORTH COAST**

| PLACES TO STAY | PLACES TO EAT | |
|---|---|---|
| 1 Hotel Esmeralda | 10 Ganimedes | 7 Comité 1 colectivos |
| 3 Hostal Premier, | 13 Chifa Kin Tou | to Sullana |
| Hostal Piura | 18 Restaurant Las | 11 Museo Municipal |
| 4 Hotel Paracas | Tres Estrellas | 20 Church of San Francisco |
| 8 Hotel Peru | 22 Café Fedi | 21 Grau Monument |
| 9 Hostal El Sol | 26 Pizzería La Cabaña, | 23 Banco de Crédito |
| 12 Hostal Terraza | Snack Bar Romano | 32 Piura Tours |
| 14 Hostal Oriental | 27 Heladería Chalan | 36 Casa Grau (Naval |
| 15 Hostal El Almirante | 33 Manos Piuranos | Museum) |
| 16 Hotel Costa del Sol | 34 Las Tradiciones | 37 Municipalidad |
| 17 Hotel Hispano | 41 Las Redes | 38 Post Office |
| 19 Hostal Tangarara | 42 Heladería Venecia | 39 Aero Continente |
| 24 Hospedaje Lalo | | 40 Internet access |
| 25 Hostal California | **OTHER** | 43 Colectivos to Catacaos |
| 28 Los Portales | 2 Telefónica del Peru | 44 Bolognesi Monument |
| 29 Hostal San Jorge | 5 Church of El Carmen | 45 TEPSA, Transportes Piura |
| 30 Hostal Santa Lucia | 6 EPPO, Transportes | 47 Church of San Sebastián |
| 31 Hostal Continental | El Dorado, ITTSA, | 48 Chinchaysuyo |
| 35 Hostal Amauta | Chiclayo Transportes, | 49 Cruz del Sur |
| 46 Residencial Bolognesi | Expreso Sudamericano | |

the canvas of San Martín de Porres in the mid-19th century.

Other churches worth seeing are the Church of San Francisco, where Piura's independence was declared on January 4, 1821, and the colonial churches of El Carmen and San Sebastián.

### Jirón Lima

This street, a block southeast of the Plaza de Armas, has preserved its colonial character as much as any in Piura.

### The Goulden Home

Anita Goulden moved here from England in 1958 and has worked in Piura with orphans, the poor and the disabled since then. Her home is at (☎ 33-4974, lasendita@ lanet.com.pe, Jirón Procer Merino 128), in the Urbanización Club Grau district. The postal address is Apdo 77, Urb Club Grau. Those interested in contributing time or money may like to visit. For more information, see the magazine *South American Explorer*, No 43, Spring 1996.

### Places to Stay – Budget

Water shortages are reported, and few cheap hotels have hot water. The cheapest is the basic but friendly and decent *Hospedaje Lalo* (☎ 32-5798, Junín 838), which charges US$3.50/6 for singles/doubles with shared bathrooms. The musty *Hotel Hispano* (☎ 32-5901, Ica 650) is similarly priced.

The friendly *Hostal California* (☎ 32-8789, Junín 835) is clean, safe and popular with shoestring travelers. Rates are US$4.50/ 8.50 with shared bathrooms. The equally good *Hostal Continental* (☎ 33-4531, Junín 924) charges US$5/7 with shared bathrooms, or US$7/8.50 with private bath. *Hostal Oriental* (☎ 32-8891, Callao 446) is clean at US$4.50/8, or US$6/10.50 with private cold bath. The decent *Hostal Terraza* (☎ 32-5043, Loreto 530) charges US$6/9 with bath, a little less with communal bath. The rooms are small but clean enough. *Hostal Santa Lucia* (☎ 33-4287, Ayacucho 773) charges US$7/12 with private cold shower and will put cable TV in your room for another US$2. The similarly priced *Residencial Bolognesi* (☎ 32-

4072, 30-3828, Bolognesi 427) is a huge, ugly building offering over a 100 acceptable rooms with cold showers.

*Hostal Amauta* (☎ 32-2976, Apurímac 580) is also reasonably clean and charges US$6.50/10 or US$10/12 with bath. They have hot water. The good *Hostal San Jorge* (☎ 32-7514, fax 32-2928, Loreto 960) has clean rooms at US$10/13 with private hot bath and TV. This place is often full. *Hostal El Almirante* (☎ 32-9137, 33-5239, Ica 860) is also good at US$13/16 with private hot bath.

### Places to Stay – Mid-Range

The new, clean *Hotel Paracas* (☎ 33-5412, fax 33-4404, Loreto 339) charges US$13/18 with private hot bath. Opposite, another new place is *Hostal Premier* (☎/fax 30-3704, Loreto 338), which looks good at US$14/21 in rooms with cable TV and telephones. Nearby, the similarly priced *Hostal Piura* (☎ 32-4857, 32-7103, fax 32-7524, Loreto 350) looks OK. Also at this price is the clean *Hotel Peru* (☎ 33-3421, fax 33-1530, Arequipa 476), which has rooms with cable TV and, for a few dollars more, air-conditioning.

*Hostal El Sol* (☎ 32-4461, fax 32-6307, Cerro 455) has decent rooms with hot water, TV and telephones at about US$16/24. They have a small pool. The similarly priced *Hostal Tangarara* (☎ 32-6450, 32-6479, fax 32-8322, Arequipa 691) also has decent rooms with TV, hot water and fans. The clean, modern-looking *Hotel Esmeralda* (☎ 33-1205, 33-1782, fax 32-7109, Loreto 235) has a restaurant and carpeted rooms with cable TV, telephones, hot showers and room service for US$23/30.

### Places to Stay – Top End

In an attractive, old-fashioned building *Hotel Costa del Sol* (☎ 30-2591, 30-2864, fax 33-6469, tucosol@peru.itete.com.pe, Loreto 649) has a bar, restaurant, small pool, casino and well-kept rooms with cable TV, telephones, minibars and air-conditioning at US$55/65. At about this price and with similar services, the new *Hotel El Angolo* (☎ 32-4641, fax 30-1943) has good-sized rooms away from the center of town in the San Eduardo del Chipe suburb.

The best place in the center is the renovated *Los Portales* (☎ 32-1161, 32-2952, fax
32-5920, 32-8795, in Lima 421-7270, fax 442-
9196, Libertad 875) in an attractive building
on the Plaza de Armas. They have a swimming pool, restaurant, room service and air-
conditioned rooms with the usual facilities
for US$65/85 including a buffet breakfast.

## Places to Eat

Some cheap simple restaurants are on the
700 block of Junín near Avenida Grau.

The corner of Ayacucho and Cuzco has
several popular and good restaurants. *Snack
Bar Romano* (☎ 32-3399, Ayacucho 580) is a
local favorite and has been recommended
several times by readers. Meals start at
about US$2.50 and are a good value. They
are open all day. Next door, *Pizzería La
Cabaña* is good but more expensive. Opposite, *Las Tradiciones* (☎ 32-2683, Ayacucho
579) is somewhat pricier than the Romano,
but has good food, is also recommended and
has an art gallery. Around the corner, *Manos
Piuranos* looks good and serves traditional
local food.

At Libertad and Apurímac, the *Heladería
Venecia* offers ice cream and sweet snacks,
and *Las Redes* offers good but pricey Italian
food in a cozy restaurant within a small
shopping mall.

There are a couple of snack bars on the
Plaza de Armas, including the popular
*Heladería Chalan* (☎ 32-5167, Tacna 520),
with a good selection of juices, cakes, ice
creams, sandwiches and other snacks. *Café
Fedi* (Arequipa 780) has snacks such as
tamales, sandwiches and cakes. *Ganimedes*
(Lima 440) is a good vegetarian restaurant.
The best place for Chinese food is the
elegant *Chifa Kin Tou* (☎ 30-5988, Callao
828). *Restaurant Las Tres Estrellas* (☎ 32-
8472) has also been recommended.

## Getting There & Away

**Air** The airport is on the southeast bank of
the Río Piura, about 2km from the city's
center. Aero Continente (☎ 32-5635, airport
34-4503, Libertad 951) has daily flights to
Lima and some other coastal cities. Schedules change often.

**Bus** December to April is the rainy season,
and as described earlier, every decade or so,
roads north and south of Piura may be
closed by floods or washed-out bridges as
the result of an El Niño event. Make local
inquiries about current conditions.

Buses, cars and trucks for various local
destinations leave from the Mercadillo at
the 5th block of Avenida Sullana Norte or
from the Mercado Modelo at the 13th block
of S Cerro (both just off the map).

Several companies have offices on the
1100 block of S Cerro. EPPO (☎ 32-9042, S
Cerro 1141) has buses to Sullana and Talara
every 30 minutes, and buses to Mancora at
2:30 and 4:30 pm. Transportes El Dorado
(☎ 32-5875, 33-6952, S Cerro 1119) has buses
for Tumbes (roughly US$5, 6 hours) seven
times a day. ITTSA (☎ 33-3982, S Cerro
1142) has overnight buses to Trujillo (US$7)
and Chimbote (US$8). Chiclayo Transportes
(S Cerro 1121) has almost hourly buses to
Chiclayo (3 hours). Expreso Sudamericano
(S Cerro 1111) has an overnight bus to Lima
(US$10). Catch buses for Chulucanas oppo-
site EPPO and El Dorado.

The best services to Lima (14 to 18 hours)
are probably with Cruz del Sur (☎ 33-7094),
on Bolognesi at Lima, which has several
afternoon and evening departures for
US$10 and an Imperial Service for US$17.
TEPSA (☎ 32-2761), on Loreto at Bolognesi, has old buses to Tumbes, Trujillo and
Lima, and has a reputation for dangerous
speeding. Nearby, Transportes Piura (☎ 32-
9131) has buses to several coastal destinations.

Chinchaysuyo (Libertad 1147) has
overnight buses to Huaraz (US$16.50), Tru-
jillo (US$6.50) and Chimbote (US$8.50).
CIVA (☎ 32-8093), across the river on Huancavelica (which becomes Castilla on the east
side), has buses to Huancabamba (US$7 to
US$8, 8 to 10 hours) and other small towns
in the Andes east of Piura. Nearby, Divino
Niño Jesús (☎ 34-5248) and Etipthsa (☎ 34-
5174) also have buses for Huancabamba.
Most leave at 8 am and 7 pm.

For Cajamarca and across the northern
Andes, it's best to go to Chiclayo and get a
connection there.

NORTH COAST

The standard route to Ecuador is via Tumbes. The route to Ecuador via La Tina is longer and more difficult, but also more scenic. Take an early morning bus (US$0.50, 1 hour) or a faster Comité 1 colectivo to Sullana, and continue from Sullana to La Tina by colectivo taxis. Sullana has poor, basic hotels; Piura is a better place to stay.

## CATACAOS

The village of Catacaos, 12km southwest of Piura, is famous for its crafts market and for its local restaurants, which are particularly recommended for lunch. You can get there by colectivo from the Plaza Pizarro in Piura.

The crafts market sells a good variety of products, including gold and silver filigree ornaments, wood carvings, leather work and panama hats.

There are a number of little picanterías (local restaurants) serving chicha and dishes typical of the area. Most picanterías are only open two or three days a week, but as there are so many of them, you won't have any difficulty finding several open on the day you visit. They open for lunch rather than dinner, and live music is sometimes played. Typical norteño (northern) dishes include seco de chabelo (a thick plantain and beef stew), seco de cabrito (goat stew), tamales verdes (green corn dumplings), caldo de siete carnes (a thick meat soup with seven types of meat), copus (made from dried goat heads cured in vinegar and then stewed for several hours with vegetables such as turnips, sweet potatoes and plantains), carne aliñada (dried and fried ham slices served with fried plantains) and many other dishes, including the familiar seafood ceviches of the Peruvian coast.

Catacaos is also famous for its elaborate Holy Week processions and celebrations.

## CHULUCANAS

This village is about 55km east of Piura, just before the Sechura Desert starts rising into the Andean slopes. It is locally known for its distinctive ceramics – rounded, glazed, earth-colored pots representing people. These pots are now becoming famous outside of Peru and can be bought in Chulucanas and Piura, as well as in Lima, and even abroad.

The village is reached by taking the Panamericana Vieja due east for 50km, then north on a side road for about 5km more. There are direct buses from Piura. There are a few basic hotels, including *Hostal Chulucanas Soler* (☎ 37-8413, Ica 209), which charges US$6 for a double with bath. There's also *Hostal Junín* (☎ 37-8247, Junín 836) and the cheaper *Hostal Ica*.

## SECHURA

The fishing village of Sechura is on the estuary of the Río Piura, about 54km by road southwest of Piura. It is famous for its 17th-century cathedral and for its nearby beaches, which are crowded with folks from Piura on summer weekends. The most interesting beach is at San Pedro, 11km along a dirt road that branches off the Piura road to the Sechura road to your right about 10km before Sechura. The beach and lagoon here are the haunt of many seabirds, including flamingos.

The beaches have few facilities (San Pedro has none). Sechura has a few simple restaurants and a basic hotel, which is usually full. Camping is possible, but carry plenty of drinking water with you. The best way to visit is on day trips.

## PAITA

The main port of the Department of Piura is the historic town of Paita (population about 50,000), 50km due west by paved road. Paita's secluded location on a natural bay surrounded by cliffs did not protect it from the seafaring conquistadors; Pizarro landed here in 1527 on his second voyage to Peru. Since then, Paita has had an interesting history. It became a Spanish colonial port and was frequently sacked by pirates and buccaneers.

According to local historians:

In 1579, Paita was the victim of the savage aggression of the English filibuster, Francis Drake. Apparently, he heard that the Spanish galleon Sacafuego was in the area, laden with treasure destined for the Spanish crown. With shooting and violence, he attacked the port, reducing its temple, monastery and houses to ashes, and fleeing with his booty.

And to think that I was taught (growing up in England) that Sir Francis was a hero! Drake was not the only one making life miserable for the Spaniards. Numerous privateers arrived during the centuries that followed, with another notable episode occurring in the 18th century, when the Protestant buccaneer George Anson tried to decapitate the wooden statue of Our Lady of Mercy. The statue, complete with slashed neck, can still be seen in the church of La Merced. The feast of La Virgen de la Merced is held annually on September 24.

Paita is also famous as the home of Manuela Sáenz, the influential mistress of Simón Bolívar. She was Ecuadorian, and arrived here upon Bolívar's death in 1850. Forgoing the fame and fortune left to her by her lover, she worked as a seamstress until her death over 20 years later. Her house still stands (people live there), and a plaque commemorates its history. Across the street is La Figura, a wooden figurehead from a pirate ship.

To the north and south of the port are good beaches, which are popular with holidaymakers from Piura during the summer season. A few kilometers to the north is the good beach of Colán. The church there is reputedly the oldest colonial church in Peru. The beach of Yasila, some 12km to the south, is also popular.

### Information

There is a Banco de Crédito, Interbanc and a basic hospital.

### Places to Stay & Eat

Despite the town's historic interest and beaches, Paita has only a few hotels, and most visitors stay in Piura. The best in town is *Hostal Las Brisas* (☎ 61-1023, fax 61-2175, Ayurora 201, at Alfonso Ugarte), which has rooms with telephones, cable TV and private hot baths at US$17 per person. You could also try *Hostal El Farol* (☎ 61-1076, Junín 322), which has rooms with similar facilities. *Hostal Miramar* (☎ 61-1083, Jorge Chávez 418) is in an attractive, though somewhat run-down colonial building with rooms at US$10/13. Cheaper options include *Hostal El Mundo* (☎ 61-1401, Bolívar 402); *Hotel Pacífico* (☎ 61-1013), on the Plaza de Armas; and a few other very basic places.

There are a few basic restaurants on or near the Plaza de Armas. The best place is in *Club Liberal* (☎ 61-1876, Jorge Chávez 162), where the public can eat seafood on the 2nd floor, which has views of the ocean.

The *Playa Colán Lodge*, on the Colán beach, a few kilometers north of Paita, has bungalows sleeping three, five and six people for US$55/65/75. In the low season, there is a US$20 discount. There is a pool, restaurant, bar and beach access. Make reservations at Piura Tours in Piura.

### Getting There & Away

Transportes Dora (☎ 32-6670, S Cerro 1387, Piura) has buses to Paita every 20 minutes.

## SULLANA

Sullana is a modern city 38km north of Piura. It is an important agricultural center and has a surprisingly large population of about 150,000. Despite its size and importance, most travelers find Sullana of little interest and prefer to visit and stay in nearby Piura. There is nothing much to see in Sullana except the hustle and bustle of a Peruvian market town. Watch your belongings – several thefts have been reported.

The main reason to stop here is to catch a colectivo taxi to La Tina on the Ecuadorian border. Where the bus from Piura drops you off, take a taxi (under US$1) to El Mercadillo. At El Mercadillo, colectivo taxis leave for La Tina (about US$3, 2 hours) as long as there are passengers.

### Places to Stay

Sullana has about 10 cheap hotels and plenty of restaurants. Decent budget hotels include the friendly *Hostal San Miguel* (☎ 502-541, 50-1629, Avenida Farfán 204), near the Plaza Grau. They have rooms with shared baths at US$5.50/8 for singles/doubles, or private baths at US$7/9. There are several bus offices nearby. Also quite good is *Hostal Santa Julia* (☎ 50-2714, Grau 1084) at US$7/9 with private baths. *Hostal Wilson* (☎ 50-2050,

*Tarapaca 372)* is one of the cheapest, at US$3.50/5.50 with private baths.

The best is **Hostal La Siesta** (☎ *50-2264, 404 Avenida La Panamericana)*, which is on the outskirts of town. Rooms with private baths, hot water, TV and fans are US$27/32. They also have a swimming pool.

### Getting There & Away

Colectivo taxis from La Tina drop you off on the main street, José de Lama, from where colectivos go to Piura frequently. Cruz del Sur (☎ 50-6733) is at José de Lama 120, and there are several other companies in the first four blocks of José de Lama.

## LA HUACA

This small village is on the Sullana-to-Paita road. About an hour's walk takes you to a hill that contains visible fossil remains of mammoths and evidence of pre-Inca cultures. Local historian Jaime Sarango, has a small museum in his house at the entrance to the village and is knowledgeable about local history and prehistory. Minibuses leave Sullana for La Huaca and Paita from the junction of the Panamericana and José de Lama.

## HUANCABAMBA

The eastern side of the department of Piura is mountainous, has few roads and is infrequently visited by travelers. Huancabamba, 210km east of Piura by rough road, is one of the most important and interesting of the department's highland towns.

The western slopes of the Andes in the Department of Piura are an important fruit- and coffee-growing area. As you travel east from Piura, first on the asphalted Panamericana Vieja and then, after 64km, along the dirt road to Huancabamba, you pass citrus groves, sugarcane fields and coffee plantations. You can break the journey at Canchaque, two-thirds of the way from Piura to Huancabamba, where there are a couple of simple hotels. Beyond Canchaque, the road climbs steeply over a 3000m pass before dropping to Huancabamba at 1957m. This last 70km stretch is very rough, and there may be long delays in the wet season (December to March).

Huancabamba is an attractive country town in a lovely setting – at the head of the long, very narrow Río Huancabamba valley and surrounded by mountains. The Río Huancabamba is the most westerly major tributary of the Amazon. Although only 160km from the Pacific Ocean, the waters of the Huancabamba empty into the Atlantic, some 3500km away as the macaw flies. The banks of the Huancabamba are unstable and constantly eroding. The town itself is subject to frequent subsidence and slippage, and so has earned itself the nickname *la ciudad que camina*, or the town that walks.

Huancabamba has a long history. In Inca times, it was a minor settlement along the Inca Andean Highway between Ecuador and the important town Cajamarca. Although the Inca town is lost, you can still see remnants of Inca paving along the Río Huancabamba.

But Huancabamba is not just geographically, geologically and historically interesting; it is also one of Peru's major centers of *brujería*, which is loosely translated as witchcraft or sorcery. Traditional brujería methods are used both to influence a client's future and to heal and cure. The use of local herbs or potions is combined with ritual ablutions in certain lakes said to possess curative powers. People from all walks of life and from all over Peru (and other Latin American countries) visit the *brujos* (shamans) and *curanderos* (medicine men or healers), paying sizable sums in their attempts to find cures for ailments that have not responded to more modern treatments, or to remedy unrequited love, bad luck or infertility.

Although a few curanderos live in Huancabamba, those with the best reputation are found in the highlands north of the town in a lake region called the Huaringas, almost 4000m above sea level. The main lake is Shumbe, about 35km north of Huancabamba, though the nearby Laguna Negra is the one most frequently used by the curanderos. Trucks go as far as Sapalache, about 20km north of Huancabamba, and you can hire mules from there. There is also a bus that leaves Huancabamba before dawn for the village of Salala, about 45 minutes walk from Sapalache. Many local people (but few gringos) visit the area, so finding information and guides is not difficult. The tradition, however, is taken very seriously, and gawkers or skeptics will get a hostile reception. This is not a trip for the faint of heart.

Also of interest is a dirt road heading roughly west of Sapalache over Cerro Chinguela, which gives access to *páramo* (grasslands) and montane cloudforests – good for serious birders. A hummingbird called the Neblina Metaltail *(Metallura odomae)* was discovered here, and it is the only known Peruvian site for the Red-faced Parrot *(Hapalopsittara pyrrhops)*. Colonists are discovering the area, but ProAvesPeru, a private nongovernment organization, is trying to protect the area.

There are no facilities for credit cards or travelers checks. Bring cash.

## Places to Stay & Eat

There are few places to stay, and those available are very basic – bring a sleeping bag. On the outskirts of town, on the road to Sondor (a village south of Huancabamba), is *Albergue Turístico Municipal*. It charges US$5 per person with private cold bath and is one of the best. Also decent, though basic, is the clean, centrally located *Hostal El Dorado* (☎ 47-3016, Medina 116). It has a restaurant and a helpful owner. Other US$5-per-person hostels include *Danubio (Grau 206)*, on the corner of the plaza, *Minerva (Medina 208)* and *San Pedro (Cenenario 206)*. Restaurants to try include *Casa Blanca*, which serves Peruvian food, and *El Tiburón*, which serves seafood.

## Getting There & Away

The buses to and from Piura take nine hours if the going is good, but in the wet season, the trip can take longer. CIVA (the most reliable), Divino Niño de Jesús and Etipthsa all have buses to Piura (US$7); most leave at 3 am or 7 pm.

## AYABACA

Ayabaca (2715m) is a small highland town in the northeastern part of the Department of Piura, close to the Ecuadorian border. It is possible to cross the border to the Ecuadorian village of Amaluza, but this is an isolated and very rarely visited region. It is of interest primarily to the adventurous traveler. Ayabaca has several colonial buildings.

There is an Inca ruin at Ayapate, several hours away on foot. The site contains walls, flights of stairs, ceremonial baths and a central plaza, but is overgrown. Other Inca sites, such as Olleros, can be found in the region, as well as a variety of pre-Inca ruins; many are unexplored. There are also mysterious caves, lakes and mountains, some of which are said to be bewitched. Those with time could mount an expedition to find unexplored ruins; mules and guides are indispensable. Ornithologists have recently discovered that the area has some excellent birding habitats.

Visit the area in the dry season (late May to early September), when the trails are easily passable; the wet months, especially December to April, are best avoided. You should not attempt to travel through this remote region alone, as it's easy to become lost. Señor Celso Acuña Calle has been recommended as a knowledgeable guide. Other recommendations are for orchid specialist Angel Seminario (Bolognesi 374) and Esteban Aguilera (Ayabaca 113), in the adjoining village of Llacupampa.

The very colorful religious festival of El Señor Cautivo, held from October 12 to 15, is rarely seen by tourists, but locals pack every hotel and sleep in the streets during the fiesta.

Bring cash; credit cards and traveler's checks aren't negotiated. Information is available at the Municipalidad (Cáceres 578), on the Plaza de Armas.

## Places to Stay & Eat

There are a few small, basic hotels. *Hotel Samanaga Municipal (☎/fax 47-1049)*, on the Plaza de Armas, is the best, with a decent restaurant and rooms with TV and hot showers. *Hostel Señor de Cautivo (☎ 47-1084, Cáceres 109)* is also OK. Others are *Hotel Samanaga (☎ 47-1043)*, on Tacna, *Hostal San Martín (Cáceres 192)* and *Hostal Alex (Bolívar 112)*. They are inexpensive.

Ayabaca has a few simple restaurants and shops. If you're planning an expedition, bring what you need with you, as supplies in Ayabaca are limited and basic.

### Getting There & Away

Ask at Piura's Mercado Modelo about daily buses to Ayabaca.

### LA TINA

The small border post of La Tina is too small to qualify as a town. There are no hotels but if you cross the border to the Ecuadorian town of Macará, you'll find adequate facilities. La Tina is reached by colectivo taxis (US$3, 2 hours) leaving Sullana throughout the day. There are slightly cheaper minibuses that stop everywhere and take much longer. The road is paved. There may be customs/passport checks before the border, so have your documents accessible.

This international route continues from Macará to the Ecuadorian mountain town of Loja and is much less frequently traveled but more scenic than the desert route via Tumbes and Huaquillas. If you leave Sullana by 9 am, you can reach Loja the same day.

### Crossing the Border

The Peruvian border post is next to the international bridge over the Río Calvas and is open from 8 am to 6 pm with irregular lunch hours. Formalities are fairly relaxed as long as your documents are in order. There are no banks, though you'll find money-changers at the border or in the Macará market. They'll change cash, but traveler's checks are hard to negotiate.

Travelers entering Ecuador will find vans (US$0.50) and taxis to take them to the small town of Macará (3 km), where the Ecuadorian Immigration building is found on the 2nd floor of the Municipalidad, on the plaza. Normally, only a valid passport is required. You are given a tourist card, which must be surrendered when leaving. Macará has several hotels, the best of which is **Parador Turístico**, on the outskirts of town. There are cheaper hotels in the town center. Also in the town center is Transportes Loja, which has several buses a day to Loja

(US$4.50, 5 hours) and daily buses to Guayaquil (15 hours) and Quito (22 hours) The last daytime departure for Loja is a 3 pm (plus one night bus at 10 pm), so you could make it from Sullana to Loja in one long day. See Lonely Planet's *Ecuador & the Galápagos Islands* for further information.

After crossing the international bridge travelers entering Peru will find migración on the right and the police on the left. Both offices have to be visited. Travelers (especially those who require visas) are occasionally asked for a ticket out of the country. I you don't need a visa, you probably won' be asked. If you are asked, and you don' have an airline ticket, you can usually satisfy the exit-ticket requirement by buying a round-trip ticket to Sullana or Piura. The unused portion is nonrefundable. Mos nationalities, however, require only a touris card, obtainable from the border authori ties, and a valid passport. There is a Peru vian Consulate in Macará. If you arrive a Macará in the afternoon, it is best to stay the night there and continue to Sullana and Piura the following day.

### TALARA
☎ 074

Talara lies on the coast, in the center o Peru's major coastal oil-producing region On the 120km desert drive along the Panamericana from Piura, you'll see the automatic pumps used in oil extraction Although there are some good beaches nea Talara, the town has little to interest the tourist, and its few hotels are often full of o workers and businesspeople. Authorities however, are promoting the beaches in a attempt to attract tourists. One of the bette beaches is at Las Peñitas, 3km to the north

Forty years ago, Talara was a small fishin village. Today, it has a population of 45,00 and is the site of Peru's largest oil refiner producing between 60,000 and 100,00 barrels of petroleum a day. Talara is a deser town, so everything, including water, mus be imported.

Negritos, 11km south of Talara by road, i on Punta Pariñas, the most westerly point o the South American continent. The tar pits c

La Brea, where Pizarro dug tar to caulk his ships, can be seen on the Pariñas Peninsula.

On the north side of Talara are the Pariñas Woods. According to a local tourist-information booklet, the woods 'are perhaps the city's major tourist attraction, where one can encounter magnificent examples of wild rabbits and squirrels, etc, as well as a diversity of little birds that belong to the fauna of the place.' Don't miss them.

## Information

The Banco de Crédito (☎ 38-1269), Interbanc (☎ 38-1823), Banco Continental (☎ 38-890) and Banco Wiese (☎ 38-1150) are all at or near the Centro Cívico. Clínica Santa María (☎ 38-1525) has 24-hour emergency attention.

## Places to Stay

*Hostal Modelo (☎ 38-1934, Sector La Florida)* is one of the cheapest but poorest quality hotels in Talara. They charge US$4/6 with shared and US$5/7 with private bath. *Hostal Talara (☎ 38-2186, Avenida del Ejército 217)* charges US$7/11 with shared bath and US$9/13 with private bath, but has been described as dirty and lacking water (though all hotels can have water problems). A better budget to mid-range choice is *Hostal Grau (☎ 38-2841)*, on Avenida Grau. It charges US$9/13 with shared bath and US$16/20 with private bath and TV.

*Hostal Charito (☎/fax 38-1600, Avenida B 143)* has rooms, some with air-conditioning, for US$35/45. *Hostal César (☎ 38-2364, fax 38-1591, Avenida G 9)* charges US$45/70 and has cable TV in its rooms, which are rather worn. The modern *Gran Hotel Pacífico (☎ 38-2364, fax 38-1719, Barrio Particular)* has air-conditioned rooms with TV and telephones at US$48/64 including breakfast. The hotel features a pool, casino, and small shopping center with cinema. All three hotels have a restaurant. *El Angolo (☎ 38-5421, fax 38-5423, Barrio Particular)* has air-conditioned bungalows with minirefrigerators, cable TV and telephones for US$51/58 and minisuites for US$77. A restaurant and bar with room service and a pool are on the premises.

## Getting There & Away

**Air** Aero Continente (☎ 38-4329, fax 38-4591, airport ☎/fax 38-5843, Centro Cívico) has a daily flight to and from Lima, and a daily flight from Tumbes continuing to Lima. Schedules and destinations change often.

**Bus** Plenty of buses go to Talara from Piura or Tumbes.

## TALARA TO TUMBES

From Talara, the Panamericana heads northeast for 200km to the Ecuadorian border. The road runs parallel to the ocean, with frequent views of the coast. A number of beaches, resorts and small villages are passed on the drive from Talara to Tumbes on the Panamericana. Buses between the two towns (except for direct express services) can drop you off wherever you want.

The ocean is fairly warm, staying at around 18°C all year, though few Peruvians (except for the fishermen) venture into the sea outside the hottest months of January, February and March. Women are advised not to visit the beaches alone.

## Cabo Blanco

About 40km north of Talara is Cabo Blanco, famous for sport fishing. Ernest Hemingway fished here in the early 1950s. The largest fish ever landed here on a rod was a 710kg black marlin, caught in 1953 by Alfred Glassell, Jr. The angling is still good, though it has declined somewhat, and the scenery has not been improved by the oil pumps and related buildings. The fishing club (in Lima ☎ 445-4588) may be able to provide accommodations, though they aren't always open, or you can camp nearby. Also try *Hostal Merlin (☎ 85-6188)*, which has hot showers and a restaurant, but electricity is limited to certain hours. Rates are about US$20/30.

## Máncora

The small fishing village of Máncora, about 30km farther north, has the next well-known beach. This beach has recently become popular with Brazilian surfers. It's been described as 'quite a scene,' and the surf is particularly good from November to March.

NORTH COAST

It's also good for swimming and fishing, but hours of electricity are limited in town. Mud-baths can be visited; a mototaxi will charge US$2 per person for the 30-minute trip.

Bring cash.

**Places to Stay & Eat** The quiet *YHA La Posada* (☎ 85-8328, Panamericana Km 1164), by the bridge at the south end of town, charges US$5 per person and is close to the beach. Also at the south end is *Hostal Sol y Mar* (☎ 85-8106, 85-8088), which is basic, but popular with backpackers and surfers. Rates are US$7 per person, and they have a restaurant. Next door is the more peaceful *Hostal El Ancolo* (☎ 85-8212) at US$8 per person. Nearby, the family-owned *Las Olas* (☎ -85-8109) is popular with surfers and charges US$12 per person. Cheap meals are also available, and the rooms are in nice cabins with attractive ocean views. *Hostal Punta Ballenas* (☎ 68-4538) is also at the south end and charges US$10 to US$20 per person, depending on the room. It has a restaurant and a swimming pool, which was not filled with water when I visited.

In the center of Máncora, on the Panamericana, are *Hospedaje Máncora*, at US$7/10 with private bath, and the clean and quiet *Hostal Sausalito* (☎ 85-8058, in Lima 479-0779), at US$13/18. The latter is close to the beach.

A few kilometers from the center are several pleasant bungalow complexes along what is called La Antigua Panamericana. All are on the beach and have a restaurant. At Playa las Pocitas, there is *Los Corales* (☎ in Lima 907-5863), which charges US$15/35 per person in the low/high season and includes breakfast. Also here is the similarly priced *Casa de Playa* (☎ 85-8005, in Lima 440-6714, fax 440-6782). *Puerto Palos* (☎ 85-8199, fax 85-8198) has a swimming pool and charges US$25/35 per person in low/high season including breakfast.

New in 1999, *Máncora Beach Bungalows* (☎ 85-8125, in Lima 241-6116, fax 241-6115, hantigua@amauta.rcp.net.pe), 3km south of Máncora, has a beachside pool with bar, another pool with a waterslide, a restaurant

serving both north Peruvian and Mexican specialities, and comfortable one- and two-bedroom bungalows with terraces facing the beach. Low-season rates are US$15 per person or US$40 per person including meals. High season (January through March) is US$20 per person, and the rate during holiday seasons (New Year's, Easter, May 1, July 28 and October 8) is US$40 per person. Children get a 25% discount.

### Punta Sal

This beach is about 25km north of Máncora and 70km south of Tumbes, making it a popular spot for *Tumbeños* who enjoy the year-round warm waters. Minibuses run between Máncora and Punta Sal, which is on the beach a couple of kilometers off the Panamericana at Km 1187.

Budget travelers stay at *Los Delfines* which is a family house with vegetarian meals available. They charge US$7 per person. *YHA Punta Sal* (☎ 60-8365) is also family-run and charges US$12 per person. The new *Caballitos de Mar* (☎ 60-8077, in Lima 994-0624, fax 422-8886) charges US$15 to US$20 per person and looks pleasant.

Slightly farther north, off the Panamericana at Km 1190.5, a short road leads to *Blue Marlin Beach Club* (in Lima ☎ 445-8068, fax 447-2072, rescentr@correo.dnet.com.pe), which has good-sized bungalows. They have a beachfront pool, restaurant, bar, and games, and can arrange horseback riding and fishing trips. A fully equipped 32-foot, deep-sea fishing boat with Penn International tackle can be hired for US$650 for 12 hours of fishing. Hotel rates are US$58 per person, double occupancy, including three meals. Rates are higher during the major national holidays. There's also the pleasant *Punta Sal Club Hotel* (☎ 60-8373, in Lima 442-5992, fax 442-2596), off the Panamericana at Km 1192, at about US$70 per person including meals. They have a pool.

### Cancas

About 8km north of Punta Sal is the fishing village of Cancas, which has hundreds of fishing boats and thousands of seabirds wheeling overhead, including pelicans and

Frigate birds

the large, distinctive, black frigate birds with scissorlike tail feathers. There are seafood restaurants here, but I didn't see any hotels.

## Zorritos

About 35km south of Tumbes, Zorritos is the biggest fishing village along this section of coast, and its beaches are frequented by the people of Tumbes. The village is interesting for fishing activities and for the coastal birdlife. You can see frigate birds, pelicans, egrets and many migratory birds.

On the outskirts of town, about 4km north of the town center, is the worn and old *Hostal Zorritos* (☎ 54-4115), which charges US$9 per person. *YHA Hostel Casa Grillo* (☎ 52-5207) is a couple of kilometers south of Zorritos, at Panamericana Km 1236.5. They have a restaurant and information about nearby national parks. Rates are US$7 per person, and camping is US$3 per person. Camping is popular along the beaches (but there are no facilities).

Mid-range choices include *Punta Cocos* (☎ 54-4040, Panamericana Km 1243), which has rooms at US$30 per person; and the quiet, beachfront *Hostal Punta Camerón* (in Lima ☎ 445-6592), which has a pool and charges US$25 per person including meals.

Colectivos to Zorritos (US$1, about 1 hour) leave from the market in Tumbes, as do buses, which are cheaper but slower.

## Caleta Cruz

This popular beach is located about 10km north of Zorritos. There are sandy beaches all the way along the coast from Zorritos, and you'll probably see many surf fishermen catching shrimp larvae in red nylon hand nets. The larvae are then transferred to commercial shrimp farms for rearing. Caleta Cruz also has a picturesque fishing fleet. The road passes banana plantations soon after it leaves the coast on the way to Tumbes. Caleta Cruz has a couple of basic seafood restaurants.

## TUMBES
☎ 074

Tumbes was an Ecuadorian town until Peru's victory in the 1940-41 border war; it is now about 30km away from the border. A garrison town with a strong military presence and a population of about 50,000, it is also the capital of its department, which is Peru's smallest department. Be careful taking photographs in the Tumbes area; it is illegal to photograph anything remotely concerning the military.

## History

Most travelers pass through Tumbes without realizing that the city has a long history. Ceramics found in the area are up to 1500 years old.

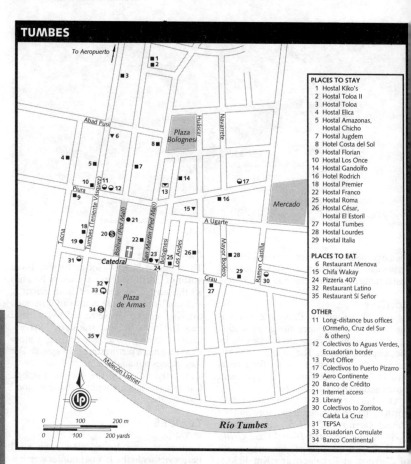

TUMBES

PLACES TO STAY
1   Hostal Kiko's
2   Hostal Toloa II
3   Hostal Toloa
4   Hostal Elica
5   Hostal Amazonas,
    Hostal Chicho
7   Hostal Jugdem
8   Hotel Costa del Sol
9   Hostal Florian
10  Hostal Los Once
14  Hostal Gandolfo
16  Hotel Rodrich
18  Hostal Premier
22  Hostal Franco
25  Hostal Roma
26  Hostal César,
    Hostal El Estoril
27  Hostal Tumbes
28  Hostal Lourdes
29  Hostal Italia

PLACES TO EAT
6   Restaurant Menova
15  Chifa Wakay
24  Pizzería 407
32  Restaurant Latino
35  Restaurant Sí Señor

OTHER
11  Long-distance bus offices
    (Ormeño, Cruz del Sur
    & others)
12  Colectivos to Aguas Verdes,
    Ecuadorian border
13  Post Office
17  Colectivos to Puerto Pizarro
19  Aero Continente
20  Banco de Crédito
21  Internet access
23  Library
30  Colectivos to Zorritos,
    Caleta La Cruz
31  TEPSA
33  Ecuadorian Consulate
34  Banco Continental

At the time of the conquest, Tumbes was an Inca town on the coastal highway. It was first sighted by Pizarro in 1528 during his second voyage of exploration (the first voyage never reached Peru). Pizarro invited an Inca noble to dine aboard his ship and sent two of his men ashore to inspect the Inca city. They reported the presence of an obviously well-organized and fabulously rich civilization. Pizarro returned a few years later and began his conquest of Peru.

Present-day Tumbes is about 5km northeast of the Inca city marked on maps as San Pedro de los Incas. The Panamericana passes through the site, but there is little to see.

## Information

There is no official tourist office. The main street is Tumbes, which is still sometimes called by its old name of Teniente Vásquez. The Ecuadorian Consulate has moved several times. Recently, it was on the west side of the Plaza de Armas and open weekday mornings.

**Money** The Banco de Crédito (☎ 52-5060, Bolívar 261) changes traveler's checks and has an ATM. There's also a Banco Continental (☎ 52-3914, Bolívar 129). After hours, moneychangers in Tumbes hang out on the Plaza de Armas and give fairly good rates for cash if you bargain. Moneychangers will sometimes hope to mislead you into accepting a low rate, thinking you may have just arrived from Ecuador and won't know any better. The same is true of moneychangers at the border. Ask around before changing money. It is best to change excess nuevos soles to dollars in Peru and then dollars to sucres in Ecuador (or vice versa) to get the best rates.

Beware of 'fixed' calculators, shortchanging and other rip-offs. If you don't bargain, especially on the Ecuadorian side of the border, they'll cheerfully give you an exchange rate anywhere from 5% to 50% lower than it really is. Try to find out what the dollar is worth in both Ecuador and Peru from travelers going the other way.

**Post & Communications** The post office ☎ 52-3866) is at San Martín 208. As in all Peruvian towns, long-distance and international phone calls can be made from public phones or one of several Telefónica del Peru offices; try at the corner of Piura and San Martín. Internet access is provided at an office on the 200 block of Bolívar.

**Things to See & Do**
The small, dusty town library, on the Plaza de Armas, displays a few ceramics discovered by workers on the site of the Hotel Costa del Sol. These pottery vessels have been tentatively dated at about 1500 years old. East of the Plaza de Armas, on Grau, there are several old houses dating to the early 19th century. The plaza itself has several outdoor restaurants and is a nice place to relax. The pedestrian streets north of the plaza (especially Bolívar) have several large modern monuments and are favorite hangouts for young and old alike. They are lined with chicken restaurants, icecream shops and hamburger stands, and are full of vibrant Peruvian life. During the day, you can walk along the Malecón for views of the Río Tumbes.

## Beaches
The beaches of Caleta Cruz and Zorritos, southwest of Tumbes, have been described earlier in this chapter.

Another side trip is to **Puerto Pizarro**, about 30 minutes north of Tumbes. Here, the character of the oceanfront changes from the coastal desert, which stretches over 2000km north from central Chile to northern Peru, to the mangrove swamps that dominate much of the Ecuadorian and Colombian coastlines. This change of environment also signals a different variety of birdlife.

Although the water is a bit muddier, it is still pleasant enough for swimming and is less crowded with fishermen than the beach at Zorritos. You can stay at *Motel Pizarro (☎ 54-3045)* on the waterfront for US$10/17 with cold bath. Its restaurant has good meals, though the service is desperately slow. If you have the time, money and inclination, the motel can arrange fishing-boat and water-skiing trips (skis can be rented).

Many people choose to stay in Tumbes and just visit Puerto Pizarro on a day trip.

## Reserva de Biosfera del Noroeste
The Northwestern Biosphere Reserve consists of four protected areas (which are detailed following this section) covering a total of 2344 sq km in the Department of Tumbes and in northern Piura, abutting the Ecuadorian border. Although the four areas are protected by the government, lack of funding means that there is relatively little infrastructure, such as ranger stations or tourist facilities. Much of what is available is funded by private organizations such as the Fundación Peruana para la Conservación de la Naturaleza (FPCN, also called ProNaturaleza), with assistance from international bodies such as the World Wide Fund for Nature and the International Union for the Conservation of Nature.

Information about all four areas is available from the Tumbes FPCN office (☎/fax 52-3412, ptumbes@mail.cosapidata.com.pe, Avenida Tarapaca 4-16, Urbanización Fonavi suburb). It is a short taxi ride from the center of town. They can help set up a visit if you have spare time and money. Insect repellent is strongly advised.

### Parque Nacional Cerros de Amotape

The tropical dry forest ecosystem of Cerros de Amotape is protected by the 913-sq-km national park that was created in 1974. The interesting flora and fauna include crocodiles, jaguars, condors and anteaters. You are unlikely to see much in the way of wildlife without a guide. More common sightings are parrots, deer, squirrels and peccaries. Large-scale logging, illegal hunting and overgrazing are some of the threats facing this habitat, of which there is very little left anywhere.

Guides are available from the village of Rica Playa, just within the park. Two have been recommended: Manuel Porras Sanchez and Roberto Correo. The FPCN suggests the Mellizos Hidalgo family as a good source of local information. There is a national-park control post at Rica Playa.

During the dry season, a morning bus leaves for Rica Playa from the Tumbes market (about 2½ hours), though the road may be impassable during the wet months (January to April). Trucks also make the trip – one is Señor Esteban Hidalgo's truck 'Flecha de Oro.' Señor Hidalgo can be contacted at San Ramon 101 in Tumbes.

Rica Playa is a small, friendly village. Although there are no hotels, you can camp, and local families will sell you meals. It's a good idea to bring some of your own food.

Another way to visit the park is to go to the village of Casitas near Caña Veral, where there's a ranger station. The park chief comes into Tumbes every week and can help you get out there. Buses go to Casitas once a day from the market in Tumbes.

### Bosque Nacional de Tumbes

This 751-sq-km national forest adjoins Cerros de Amotape to the northeast. This forest is similar to the tropical dry forest of Cerros de Amotape, but because it lies more on the easterly side of the hills, it is wetter and has a slightly different flora and fauna, including

monkeys and nutria. Visiting during the we months of January to May is very difficult During the dry months, visits can be arranged, but there is no public transpor and you'll have to hire a truck or jeep Again, the FPCN people can help.

### Coto de Caza El Angolo

This 650-sq-kn extension at the southwest border of Cerros de Amotape is the most remote section o the tropical dry forest.

### Santuario Nacional Los Manglares de Tumbes

This national sanctuary is on the coast and not linked to the other three dry forest areas. Only about 30 sq km in size, i plays an essential role in conserving Peru' only region of mangroves and was estab lished in 1988.

Los Manglares de Tumbes can be visited by going to Puerto Pizarro and taking a dir road northeast for a few kilometers along the coast to the tiny community or E Bendito. There, ask for Agustín Correa Benites, who has a canoe and can show you the mangroves.

### Places to Stay

The large amount of border traffic mean that the hotels tend to be crowded, and during the major annual holidays and occa sional trade fairs, they are often full by earl afternoon. During the rest of the year, it ca be difficult to find single rooms by mid afternoon, though doubles are usually avail able into the evening. Rates can vary considerably from day to day – often it's a seller's market. Most hotels have only cold water, but that's no problem in the heat. Al but the most basic hotels have fans – ask a the front desk. Air-conditioned rooms o fans are recommended during the hottes months (December to March). One reade reported bad mosquitoes in June – a fa helps repel them. There are frequent wate and electricity outages.

**Budget** The cheapest basic hotels start a around US$6 or US$7 for a single and US$ to US$10 for a double, and are locally called

MARY ALTIER

The sleepy beach town of Huanchaco

ROB RACHOWIECKI

The 'Sanctuaries' of Chan Chan's Tschudi Complex

VICTOR ENGLEBERT

Fishermen unloading their catch, Chimbote

Farmer plowing in El Callejón de Huaylas

The *puna* and the peaks, Cordillera Blanca

Lakeside *Polylepis*, Parque Nacional Huascarár

two-star hotels. The following are friendly and reasonably clean hotels and are among the best at this price: ***Hostal El Estoril*** *(☎ 52-4906, Huáscar 361)*, with hot showers; ***Hostal Elica*** *(☎ 52-3870, Tacna 337)*; ***Hostal Tumbes*** *(☎ 52-2203)*; ***Hostal Amazonas*** *(☎ 52-5266, Tumbes 317)*; and ***Hostal Italia*** *(☎ 52-6164, Grau 733)*, with private baths.

***Hostal Franco*** *(☎ 52-5295, San Martín 107)* also seems to be OK. Others with private baths include ***Hostal Los Once*** *(☎ 52-3717, Piura 475)*, which is fairly clean and handy to the buses but is noisy, and the basic but friendly ***Hostal Premier*** *(☎ 52-3077, Tumbes 225)*, which lacks singles. Also in this price range are the poorer-in-quality ***Hostal Kiko's*** *(☎ 52-3777, Bolívar 462)*, ***Hostal Toloa II*** *(☎ 52-4135, Bolívar 458)*, ***Hostal Gandolfo*** *(☎ 52-2868, Bolognesi 420)*, ***Hotel Rodrich*** *(☎ 52-3231, Piura 1002)*, ***Hostal Jugdem*** *(☎ 52-3530, Bolívar 344)* and a few other places in the vicinity of the market.

The better ***Hostal Florian*** *(☎ 52-2464, Piura 414)* charges US$10/14 and has private cold baths. Decent places charging about US$10/14 are ***Hostal Toloa*** *(☎ 52-3771, Tumbes 430)* and ***Hostal César*** *(☎/fax 52-2883, Huáscar 353)*.

**Mid-Range** *Hostal Chicho* *(☎ 52-2282, Tumbes 327)* has private hot shower, TV, telephones and fans for US$12/16. ***Hostal Roma*** *(☎ 52-4137, Bolognesi 425)* is clean and comfortable but is a little more expensive because of its central location. Rooms are about US$14/20 with private cold shower and cable TV. The clean, safe and friendly ***Hostal Lourdes*** *(☎ 52-2126, 52-2966, fax 52-2758, Mayor Bodero 118)* charges US$14/20 in fairly simple rooms with telephones, TV and hot showers. They have a restaurant.

By far, the best hotel in town is ***Hotel Costa del Sol*** *(☎ 52-3991, 52-3992, fax 52-5862, San Martín 275)*. It has a good restaurant, a garden, adult and children's swimming pools, a small casino, exercise equipment and air-conditioned singles/doubles with TV and minirefrigerators for about US$55/65.

## Places to Eat

There are several bars and restaurants on the Plaza de Armas, many with shaded tables and chairs outside – a real boon in hot weather. It's a pleasant place to sit and watch the world go by as you drink a cold beer and wait for your bus.

The best (and priciest) restaurants on the plaza seem to be on the west side. ***Restaurant Latino*** *(☎ 52-3198, Bolívar 163)* is popular and may have live music on weekends. Meals average US$5 to US$8. The nearby ***Restaurant Sí Señor*** is similarly priced. Both serve a variety of tasty dishes, including excellent local seafood. Travelers arriving from Ecuador should try the ceviche – this marinated seafood dish is much spicier than the Ecuadorian version and goes down very well with a cold beer. ***Pizzería 407***, on the north side of the plaza, has decent pizzas. North of the plaza, the pedestrian street of Bolívar has inexpensive chicken restaurants and *heladerías* (ice-cream parlors).

If you're in a hurry to catch a bus or are on a budget, ***Restaurant Menova*** *(☎ 52-3550, Tumbes 362)* is within a block of most bus terminals and sells good, cheap food.

### Paratroopers in the Plaza

One Sunday while having lunch, I noticed a big crowd gathering in the plaza. I asked what was going on and was told that a Peruvian Air Force paratrooper was going to land in the Plaza de Armas. The plaza had several tall trees and, worse still, a couple of very sharp-looking flagpoles in the center. The thought of jumping onto one by accident was so unpleasant that I had to order another beer. An hour later the paratrooper made a dramatic appearance, his descent marked with smoke canisters. Despite the hazards of flagpoles, trees and spectators, he made a perfect landing right in front of the restaurant where I was sitting.

Meals are about US$2. Also inexpensive is *Chifa Wakay* (*Huáscar 417*).

It's unlikely that you will be in Tumbes very long, but if you are, there are plenty of other inexpensive places to choose from in the bus terminal area.

### Getting There & Away

**Air** Aero Continente (☎ 52-1888, 52-2350, fax 52-2678, Tumbes 217) has flights to and from Lima. Some flights stop in Talara. Flights are often full, so reconfirm. Schedules, carriers and routes change frequently. The usual US$3.50 airport departure tax is charged.

**Bus** Most long-distance bus company offices are on Tumbes, especially around the intersection with Piura. You can usually find a bus to Lima within 24 hours of your arrival in Tumbes, but they're sometimes (especially major holidays) sold out a few days in advance. In that case, take a bus south to any major city and try again from there. Carry your passport with you – there are several passport-control stops south of Tumbes.

Buses to Lima take 22 to 24 hours; fares vary from US$14 to US$30, depending on the season and class of bus. Some companies offer limited-stop special service, with airconditioning, bathrooms and video. There are several buses a day; most stop at Piura (6 hours), Chiclayo (12 hours), Trujillo (15 hours) and other intermediate cities. If you arrive in Tumbes early in the morning, there's a reasonable chance you'll get out the same day if you are in a hurry; otherwise, be prepared to spend the night. Most major companies have at least two departures a day. Shop around for the one that suits you. Expreso Sudamericano buses are usually the slowest and cheapest. Cruz del Sur and Ormeño (represented by Expreso Continental) are pretty reliable. TEPSA is fast but has older buses. Olano goes only as far as Chiclayo.

### Getting Around

**To/From the Airport** The airport is north of town, about US$2 to US$4 by taxi depending on bargaining abilities. If you have confirmed flights and are coming from Ecuador, it's faster and cheaper to go direct from the border to the airport and avoid Tumbes altogether.

**Local Transport** If you're heading for Puerto Pizarro, use the colectivos that leave from the east end of Piura (near the market area) and charge US$0.80. Colectivos to the beaches of Zorritos and Caleta Cruz also depart from near the market. The market area is the place to find colectivo taxis, buses and trucks to most local destinations.

**To/From the Border** Colectivos for the border leave from the corner of Bolívar and Piura or from the 300 block of Tumbes (by the main bus terminals), and cost about US$1.50 per person for the 26km journey. If you're in a group, hire a car to take you to the border. A taxi to the border charges about US$5 to US$7.

## TO/FROM ECUADOR

The Peruvian immigration office is in the middle of the desert, about 3km from the border at Aguas Verdes.

Travelers *leaving* Peru must surrender their Peruvian tourist cards and obtain exit stamps from the immigration office. Assuming your documents are in order, exit formalities are usually fairly quick and easy. Immigration is open 8 am to 1 pm and 2 to 6 pm Monday to Saturday, and 8 am to 4 pm Sunday. From the immigration office, mototaxis take you to the border town of Aguas Verdes for US$0.50.

Aguas Verdes is basically a long street full of stalls selling consumer products. It has a bank and a few simple restaurants, but no hotels. The long market street continues into the Ecuadorian border town of Huaquillas via an international bridge across the Río Zarumilla. You may have to show your documents again as you cross the bridge. Huaquillas, on the Ecuadorian side, has similar stalls of consumer products.

The Ecuadorian immigration office is about 4km north of the international bridge. Taxis charge about US$1.30. The office is open 8 am to noon and 2 to 6 pm daily except Sunday, when they close at 5 pm.

Ecuadorian entrance formalities are usually straightforward. Few tourists need a visa, but everyone needs a T3 tourist card, available free at the immigration office. You must surrender your T3 when you leave Ecuador, so don't lose it. Exit tickets out of Ecuador and sufficient funds (US$20 per day) are legally required, but very rarely asked for. Stays of up to 90 days are allowed, but often, only 30 days are given. Extensions can be easily and freely obtained in Guayaquil or Quito. Note that you are allowed only 90 days per year in Ecuador. If you've already been in the country for 90 days and try to return, you will be refused entry. If you have an international flight from Ecuador, you can usually get a 72-hour transit visa to get you to the airport and out of the country.

There are a couple of basic hotels in Huaquillas, but most people make the two-hour bus trip to the city of Machala, where there are much better facilities. See Lonely Planet's *Ecuador & the Galápagos Islands* for further information.

Many people offer their services as porters and guides. Most are very insistent and usually overcharge, so unless you really need help, they're more of a hassle than they're worth. Even if you do need help, bargain hard. Readers have written that not only porters, but border guards, taxi drivers and money-changers all try to rip you off. There are no entry fees into either country, so be polite but insistent with border guards, bargain hard with drivers, and find out exchange rates ahead of time before changing money.

Travelers *arriving* in Peru essentially do the above in reverse. They must surrender their Ecuadorian T3 card at the immigration office north of the border and obtain an Ecuadorian exit stamp in their passports. Take a taxi (or an infrequent bus) to the international bridge, where guards usually inspect but don't stamp your passport. The bridge is crossed on foot, and Peruvian immigration can be reached by continuing for a short distance or by taking a mototaxi.

North Americans, Australians, New Zealanders and most European nationals don't need a visa to visit Peru, but are given a tourist card at the border. Keep this card, as you must surrender it when leaving Peru. Visas are not available at the border, and you have to go back to the Peruvian Consulate in Machala to get one if you need one.

Although an exit ticket out of Peru is officially required, gringo travelers are rarely asked for one unless they look thoroughly disreputable. Latin American travelers are often asked for an exit ticket, so be prepared for this eventuality if you're a non-Peruvian Latin American (or if you are traveling with one). A bus office in Aguas Verdes sells (nonrefundable) tickets out of Peru. The immigration official can tell you where it is.

# The Huaraz Area

Huaraz is the most important climbing, trekking and backpacking center in Peru, perhaps even in all of South America. The city of Huaraz has been demolished several times by massive earthquakes and is therefore not particularly attractive. The surrounding mountains, however, are exceptionally beautiful, and many travelers come to Peru specifically to visit the Huaraz area.

The mountains offer a wide range of attractions, the most evident of which are the many permanently glaciated peaks jutting up to 6000m and above. There are glacial lakes and hot springs. There are Inca and pre-Inca sites, particularly the fascinating 3000-year-old Chavín de Huántar, the most important site in the Americas at that time. There are friendly, interesting people living in remote villages, accessible only by mule or on foot. And there are fascinating flora and fauna, including the 10m-high *Puya raimondii* (the tallest flower spike and largest bromeliad in the world) and the magnificent Andean condor (one of the largest flying birds on earth).

## The Andes around Huaraz

Huaraz is 3091m above sea level and lies in the Río Santa valley, flanked to the west by the Cordillera Negra and to the east by the Cordillera Blanca. The valley between these two mountain ranges is popularly referred to as El Callejón de Huaylas, after the district of Huaylas at the northern end. A paved road runs the valley's length, linking the main towns and providing spectacular views of the mountains. El Callejón de Huaylas is roughly 300km north of Lima, about eight hours by bus.

The Cordillera Negra, though an attractive range in its own right, is snowless and is completely eclipsed by the magnificent snowcapped mountains of the Cordillera Blanca. The lower range is sometimes visited by road from the coast en route to the Cordillera Blanca.

The Cordillera Blanca is about 20km wide and 180km long. In this fairly small area, there are more than 50 peaks of 5700m or higher. In contrast, North America has only three mountains in excess of 5700m (Pico de Orizaba in Mexico, Logan in Canada and Denali in Alaska), and Europe has none. Only in Asia can mountain ranges higher than the Andes be found. Huascarán, at 6768m, is Peru's highest mountain and the highest peak in the tropics anywhere in the world. However, this string of statistics does not do the Cordillera Blanca justice. Its shining glaciers, sparkling streams, awesome vertical walls and lovely lakes must be seen to be appreciated.

South of the Cordillera Blanca is the smaller, more remote, but no less spectacular Cordillera Huayhuash. It contains Peru's second highest peak, the 6634m-high Yerupajá, and is a more rugged and less frequently visited range. The main difference between the two ranges, for the hiker at least, is that you walk *through* the Cordillera Blanca surrounded by magnificent peaks and you walk *around* the smaller Huayhuash, one of the most spectacular mountain circuits in the world. Both ranges are highly recommended for climbers and hikers.

## PARQUE NACIONAL HUASCARÁN

Protecting the beauty of the Cordillera Blanca was first suggested by the well-known Peruvian mountaineer César Morales Arnao in the early 1960s. The idea did not become reality until 1975, when Parque Nacional Huascarán was established. The 3400-sq-km park encompasses not only the highest peak in Peru, but also the entire area of the Cordillera Blanca above 4000m, except Champará in the extreme northern part of the range.

The objectives of the park are the protection and conservation of the Cordillera Blanca's flora, fauna, archaeological sites and scenic beauty, the promotion of scientific

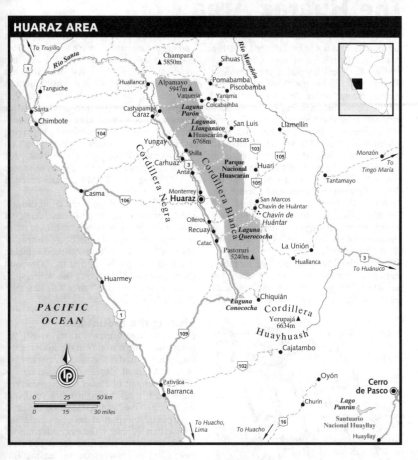

**HUARAZ AREA**

To Trujillo

Río Santa

Tanguche

Santa

Chimbote

Huallanca

Champará ▲ 5850m

Sihuas

Pomabamba

Piscobamba

Alpamayo 5947m ▲

Vaquería

Yanama

Colcabamba

Cashapampa

Laguna Parón

Caraz

Lagunas Llanganuco

▲ Huascarán 6768m

San Luis

Llamellín

Yungay

Shilla

Chacas

Carhuaz

Anta

Parque Nacional Huascarán

Huari

Casma

Monterrey

Huaraz

Olleros

Recuay

Catac

Laguna Querococha

San Marcos

Chavín de Huántar

Chavín de Huántar

Pastoruri 5240m ▲

La Unión

Huallanca

Río Marañón

Monzón

To Tingo María

Tantamayo

To Huánuco

Cordillera Negra

Cordillera Blanca

PACIFIC OCEAN

Huarmey

Laguna Conococha

Chiquián

Cordillera Huayhuash

Yerupajá ▲ 6634m

Cajatambo

Pativilca

Barranca

To Huacho, Lima

To Huacho

Oyón

Churín

Lago Punrún

Santuario Nacional Huayllay

Huayllay

Cerro de Pasco

0    25    50 km
0    15    30 miles

investigation of its natural resources, the publicizing of the park's natural and historic attractions on regional, national and international levels, the stimulation and control of tourism in the park and the raising of living standards for the people living within its boundaries.

Visitors to the park should register at the park office (see Tourist Offices under the Huaraz section) and pay the park fee. This is about US$2 per person for a day visit, or US$22 for a multiday visit if you plan on backpacking or climbing. The US$22 fee is officially valid for 30 days, but it could be accepted for the entire season. You can also register and pay your fee at one of the control stations (not always staffed in the low season) at the Lagunas Llanganuco or Pastoruri glacier (there may be other stations in the future). The money from the fees is used to help maintain trails, pay park rangers (there are a few) and offset the effects of so many visitors in the area. Some oppose regulation; however, the number of visitors to the Cordillera Blanca, while still relatively small by North American or European standards, is increasing fast enough to warrant some sort of governance if the inherent attraction of the mountains is not to be damaged. It seems to me that as foreign visitors are the ones who get the most joy out of the Cordillera Blanca, and are among those causing the greatest change within the area, they should contribute to the financing of the national park with their user fees.

Unfortunately, this hasn't been the case. Alarming numbers of trekkers have changed their routes or arrived at the park gates in the middle of the night just to avoid paying fees. Travelers have to remember that the cheapest option isn't always the correct one. Parque Nacional Huascarán and the Cordillera Blanca are some of the most magical places on the planet; make sure your visit contributes to preserving the longevity of this mountain paradise.

Present park regulations are largely a matter of courtesy and common sense. 'Do not litter' is the most obvious one – obvious, that is, to almost all of us. There are always a

few visitors who leave a trail of yellow film cartons, pink toilet paper, broken bottles and jagged tin cans to mark their path. This is thoughtless, rude and illegal. It's true that locals are among the worst offenders, but 'When in Rome…' is not a sensible reason for imitating the offense. It is also true that people tend to litter more where litter already exists, so each candy wrapper contributes to the overall problem by beginning or continuing this chain reaction. Don't do it. Remember, if you pack it in, you can pack it out. If you can pick up and carry out some extra garbage, you'll start a chain reaction that will benefit everybody.

Other park regulations are: don't disturb, feed or remove the flora or fauna; don't cut down trees or live branches for fires or other use (open fires are illegal); don't destroy or alter park signs; don't use off-road vehicles; don't hunt; don't fish during the off season (September to May); don't fish with explosives or nets and don't take fish less than 25cm in length.

### Visiting the Mountains

Basically, there are two ways to visit the mountains. One is to stay in the towns of the Callejón de Huaylas and take day trips by bus or taxi. A casual glance at the map reveals that the summit of Peru's highest peak is a mere 14km from the main valley road, and spectacular views can certainly be obtained from public transport or day tours. For many people, that is enough. The more adventurous will want to take their backpacks and hike, trek, camp or climb in the mountains. This book gives details of public transport and mentions some of the major hikes, but does not pretend to be a trail guide (see Trail Guidebooks & Maps later in this section).

### When to Go

The best months for hiking, climbing and mountain views are the dry months of June, July and August. May and September are also usually quite good. For the rest of the year, the wet season makes hiking difficult, especially from December to March, because the trails are so boggy, and the weather is frequently overcast and very

rainy. Despite this, you may be lucky and see some spectacular mountain views between the clouds, especially in the days around the full moon. Even during the dry season, however, you should be prepared for occasional rain, hail or snow.

## Mountain Guide Services

Guiding services range from a single *arriero* (mule driver), with a couple of pack animals for your camping gear, to a complete trekking expedition, with arrieros, mules, cooks, guides, food and all equipment provided. You can also hire high-altitude porters and guides for mountaineering expeditions. These are available in Huaraz and, to a much lesser extent, in Caraz. Guides and arrieros with ID cards are recommended.

If your Spanish is up to it and you're not in a great hurry, you can hire arrieros and mules in trailhead villages, particularly Cashapampa, Colcabamba and Vaquería, among others. The going rate for an arriero is about US$10 a day, a mule is US$4 day (cheaper mules are likely to be old and decrepit), but this does not include the cost of the arriero's meals (which you provide). You may need to rent a tent for the arrieros as well. You also have to pay for the days the arriero and mules are walking back, unloaded, to the point of origin. It's difficult to hire a pack animal for yourself; the arrieros will not send out burros without experienced drivers. Horses and mules for riding purposes are also available at about US$10 per day. Bear in mind that it is easier to make arrangements in Huaraz than anywhere else in the area, and that in some towns and villages, arrieros are difficult to find. If you want a guide, the official rates are US$30 to US$50 per day for a trekking guide and US$50 to US$75 for a climbing guide, depending on the route, plus food.

As you enter a valley, you often find a locked gate. The locals will unlock it for you and charge you to go through 'their' valley. The fees have been variously reported as US$2 an animal or US$5 to US$15 per group. Ask the arrieros about these fees. Backpackers without animals can often just climb over the gate.

## Trail Guidebooks & Maps

*Backpacking & Trekking in Peru & Bolivia* by Hilary Bradt is recommended. Several Cordillera Blanca hikes and the Cordillera Huayhuash circuit are included in this book, which also has plenty of background information, including a useful natural-history section. Look for a new 1999 edition.

Jim Bartle's *Trails of the Cordilleras Blanca & Huayhuash of Peru* is now out of print, but a new Spanish-and-English edition is planned for 1999. It is by far the most useful guidebook for hikers.

Meanwhile, the South American Explorers stocks reference and sale copies of maps covering both the Cordillera Blanca and the Cordillera Huayhuash. These detail many of the different hikes in their entirety. This collection, coupled with the SAE's knowledgeable staff, provides a wealth of background information.

Felipe Díaz's *Cordilleras Blanca & Huayhuash* is a useful map that shows the major trails, as well as having town plans; it may not be detailed enough for remote treks. It is updated every few years and is available in Huaraz, Caraz and at South American Explorers' clubhouses.

More detailed IGN topographical maps are hard to find and very expensive in Huaraz; get them in Lima. With 24 hours' notice, Hidrandina (see Huaraz) can provide detailed dye-line maps.

## HUARAZ
☎ 044

The Río Santa valley, in which Huaraz lies, has long been a major Andean thoroughfare, and the Incas' main Andean road passed through here. However, little remains of the valley's archaeological heritage due to a series of devastating natural disasters that have repeatedly destroyed the towns of the Callejón de Huaylas.

The major cause of these natural disasters has been the build-up of water levels in high mountain lakes, causing them to breach and water to cascade down to the valley below. These high lakes are often held back by a relatively thin wall of glacial debris that can burst when the lake levels rise. This can occur

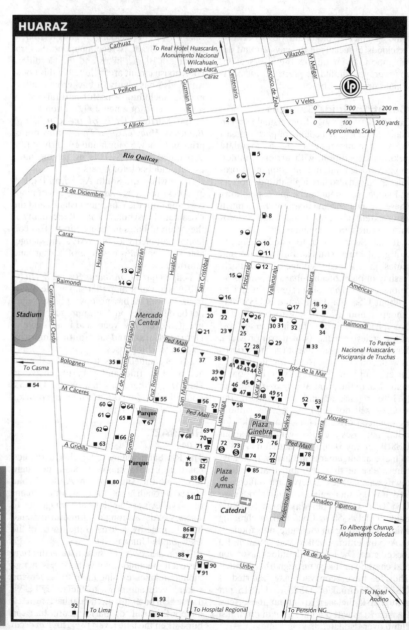

HUARAZ

## HUARAZ

**PLACES TO STAY**
3  Hostal Colomba
5  Hostal Yanett
19  Hostal Los Portales
20  Hotel Barcelona
22  Hostal Cataluña
28  Hostal Eccame
31  Hostal Raimondi
33  Hostal Schatzi
35  Hotel Los Andes
42  Oscar's Hostal
47  Hostal Chong Roca
51  Nilo's Camp
54  Edward's Inn, Señora López
55  Hostal Quintana
56  Hostal Estoico
57  Hostal El Pacífico
59  Casa de Guías
63  Casa de Jaime
65  Pensión Galaxia
66  Hostal Maguina
74  Hostal Landauro
76  Hostal Gyula
78  Grand Hotel Huaraz
79  Hotel Santa Victoria
80  Bed & Breakfast My House
86  Hostal Continental
92  Hostal Piscis, Alojamiento
    El Faralito
93  Hostal Tumi I
94  Hostal Tumi II

**PLACES TO EAT**
4  Recreo La Unión
23  Crêperie Patrick, Chifa Min Hua
24  Campo Base
25  Restaurant Familia
27  Monte Rosa
31  Hostal Raimondi
37  Fuente de Salud
40  Chez Pepe
43  Restaurant Samuels
49  Café Andino,
    El Rinconcito Minero
51  The Bar & More
52  Bistro de los Andes
53  Siam de los Andes
58  Piccolo Café/Pizzería
59  Casa de Guías
67  Cevichería El Ancla
68  Cafe de Paris
69  Montrek,
    Sabor Salud Pizzería
87  Pizza Bruno
88  El Fogón
91  El Café

**OTHER**
1  Hidrandina
2  Universidad Nacional Internet
    Services
6  Buses to Monterrey, Carhuaz,
    Yungay & Caraz
7  Buses to Monterrey, Carhuaz,
    Yungay & Caraz
8  Gas Station
9  Empresa 14
10  Empresa Huandoy
11  Empresa Virgen de Guadalupe
12  Empresa Transvir
13  El Rápido
14  Empresa Huallanca
15  Turismo Chimbote
16  Co-op Trans Ancash
17  Expreso Ancash
18  Empresa El Aguila
21  Transportes TROME
23  New Imantata Bar
26  Móvil Tours
29  Empresa Chinchaysuyo
30  Empresa Chan Chan
32  Transportes Moreno
34  Duchas Raimondi
36  CIVA
38  Chavín Tours
39  Pyramid Adventures, Milla Tours
41  Pablo Tours
44  Bueno y Barato Laundry
45  Mountain Bike Adventures
46  Baloo Tours
48  Cruz del Sur
50  El Tambo Bar
60  Lanzón de Chavín
61  Empresa Trans Sandoval
62  Transportes Rodríguez
64  Chavín Express
69  Montrek
70  La Cueva del Oso Peña
71  Telefónica del Peru
72  Banco de Crédito
73  Interbanc
75  Taberna Amadeus
77  Telefónica del Peru
80  Carlos Ames River Runners
81  Police Station, Tourism Police
82  Post Office
83  Tourist Office
84  Museo Regional de Ancash
85  Banco Wiese, Monttrek Disco
89  Aquelarre
90  Las Kenas Pub

suddenly, as when an avalanche falls from high above the lake, or more slowly, as with rain and snow melt. Earthquakes can also cause the lakes to breach. When this happens, a huge wall of water, often mixed with snow, ice, mud, rocks and other matter, flows down from the lakes, wiping out everything in its path. Such a mixture of avalanche, waterfall and landslide is referred to as an *aluvión*.

Records of aluviónes date back almost 300 years, and three recent ones have caused particularly devastating loss of life. The first of these occurred in 1941, when an avalanche in the Cojup valley, west of Huaraz, caused the Laguna Palcacocha to break its banks and flow down onto Huaraz, killing about 5000 of its inhabitants and flattening the center of the city. Then, in 1962, a huge avalanche from Huascarán roared down its western slopes and destroyed the town of Ranrahirca, killing about 4000 people. The worst disaster occurred on May 31, 1970, when a massive earthquake, measuring 7.7 on the Richter scale, devastated much of central Peru, killing an estimated 70,000 people. About half of the 30,000 inhabitants of Huaraz died, and only 10% of the city was left standing. The town of Yungay was completely buried by an aluvión caused by the quake, and almost its entire population of 18,000 was buried with the city. Evidence of the disaster can still be seen throughout the valley.

HUARAZ AREA

Since these disasters, a government agency has been formed to control the lake levels by building dams and tunnels, thus minimizing the chance of similar catastrophes. The agency concerned is Hidrandina (formerly INGEMMET).

Most of Huaraz has been rebuilt, and it is now a modern, not especially attractive city of about 80,000 and the capital of the Department of Ancash. Its renown as the center for visiting the Cordillera Blanca has led to the development of a thriving tourist industry, with a multitude of hotels and other facilities.

## Information

**Tourist Offices** The Policía de Turismo office, off the Plaza de Armas, is open from 9 am to 1 pm and 4 to 6 pm on weekdays, and 9 am to 1 pm on Saturday. They have general information about the area.

The Parque Nacional Huascarán office (☎ 72-2086) is in the Ministerio de Agricultura building at the east end of Avenida Raimondi. Working hours are 7 am to 2:15 pm weekdays, but it's best to visit in the morning. Staff have limited information about visiting the national park.

Trekkers and climbers will find that the travel agencies and guides mentioned later in this section (see Travel Agencies & Guides) are good sources of information for these activities.

During the May-to-September season, Huaraz is a mecca for climbers and hikers from all over the world. These visitors are a great source of up-to-date information. You'll find them hanging out in the popular bars and restaurants between climbs.

**Money** Banks are on the north side of the Plaza de Armas and on the 6th block of Luzuriaga. The Banco de Crédito (☎ 72-1182, Luzuriaga 669), Interbanc (☎ 72-1502, José Sucre 913) and others have good services. Hours are 9:15 am to 1:15 pm and 4:30 to 6:30 pm weekdays, and possibly Saturday morning as well. Street moneychangers outside the banks also give good rates for US cash with less hassle than the banks (which can have long lines), but check your money carefully before handing over your dollars. Many of the better hotels and tourist agencies will accept US cash at reasonable rates.

**Post & Communications** Both a post office and a Telefónica del Peru are found near the Plaza de Armas, and both are open until 11 pm.

Internet services are provided by the Universidad Nacional, at Centenario 200, from 7 am to 10 pm weekdays, and varying weekend hours. Rates are US$2 per hour. Other places are popping up along Luzuriaga and on Plaza Ginebra.

**Travel Agencies & Guides** Several agencies provide local tours. Pablo Tours (☎ 72-1145, Luzuriaga 501) has received several recommendations for its local bus tours. Other experienced agencies on the same block are Chavín Tours (☎ 72-1578, Luzuriaga 502), which has several minibuses, and Milla Tours (☎ 72-1742, Luzuriaga 528), but these are by no means the only ones. Prices are fixed and include transport (usually in minibuses) and a guide (who may or may not speak English). You should bring a packed lunch, warm clothes, drinking water and sunblock. Any admission fees are extra. There are tours daily during the high season, but at other times, departures depend on whether there are enough passengers. Often, different agencies will pool their passengers.

The four most popular trips around Huaraz each take a full day and cost US$9 to US$10, depending on the tour and number of passengers. One tour visits the ruins at Chavín de Huántar; another passes through Yungay to the beautiful Lagunas Llanganuco, where there are superb views of Huascarán and other mountains; a third takes you through Caraz to Laguna Parón, which is spectacularly surrounded by glaciated peaks; and a fourth goes through Catac to see the giant *Puya raimondii* plant and continues to Nevado Pastoruri, where there are glaciers and mineral springs. These destinations are described in greater detail in the appropriate sections later in the chapter.

Mountaineers and trekkers should check out the hostel Casa de Guías (☎ 72-1811), on the Plaza Ginebra, one block northeast of the Plaza de Armas. They have a list of registered guides and are a good source of hiking and climbing information. Another useful source of information and trekking guides is Tebac (☎ 72-3557, F Sal y Rosas 368) – ask for Miguel Chiri. (F Sal y Rosas runs east-west several blocks south of the Huaraz map.) Make sure your guide is qualified and experienced, particularly if you are hiring a mountain guide. You are putting your life in their hands.

One of the best outfitters, though certainly not the cheapest, is Pyramid Adventures (☎ 72-1864, fax 72-2525, Luzuriaga 530, Casilla 25, Huaraz, Ancash, Peru), which is run by the five Morales brothers (Marcelino, Pablo, Eleazar, Eudes and Néstor). They are knowledgeable, hardworking, honest and friendly, and they provide every level of service at fair prices. The brothers are accomplished mountaineers and have been involved in new ascents and mountain-rescue activities. They specialize in providing full service to trekking and climbing groups, but they can also put you in contact with a couple of arrieros if that's all you want. Eudes Morales speaks English. Baloo Tours (☎ 72-5994, Morales 605) offers guide service and rents good gear. Monttrek (☎ 72-1124, Luzuriaga 646, 2nd floor) is another good source for service and information, and has been recommended.

Some cheaper guide services are available if you shop around, but try to get references from other travelers before contracting with them. The cheapest option is to hire arrieros directly, though this involves speaking Spanish and perhaps some bargaining. Again, get references and check credentials first. The Parque Nacional Huascarán (see Tourist Offices earlier in this section) has a list of certified arrieros.

**Maps** Detailed dye-line maps of the Cordillera Blanca (US$12) and Huayhuash (US$7) can be obtained with 24 hours' advance notice (not always necessary) from Hidrandina, at 27 de Septiembre 773.

Hidrandina is open weekdays 8 am to noon. These maps were made in 1974, so they don't show the latest trails. Tebac (see Travel Agencies & Guides earlier in this section) and other agencies have maps of varying quality.

**Equipment & Rentals** The better guide services can supply everything from tents to ice axes. Rental agencies (there are several along Luzuriaga) rent equipment without your having to hire guides. Recommended rental places are Casa de Guías, Montrek, Baloo Tours and several others along Luzuriaga (see Travel Agencies & Guides earlier in this section, for contact information). The Hostal Quintana also rents equipment. Prices are fairly similar, but the quality and availability of gear varies tremendously – check your gear before heading out.

If you bring your own equipment, remember that *kerex* (kerosene, paraffin) can be purchased from gas stations, and *bencina* (white gas, stove alcohol) is found in hardware stores and pharmacies (a reader recommends Farmacia Huascarán, on Huascarán by the market). Expensive Camping Gaz canisters are usually available in rental places (please carry them out after use). Don't think about using firewood; none is available, and chopping down live trees is illegal. It often freezes at night, so bring an adequately warm sleeping bag. It can rain even in the dry season, so rain gear and a waterproof tent are needed. Wear a brimmed hat and sunglasses, and bring strong sunblock with you, as it is difficult to find in Huaraz. The same applies to effective insect repellent.

Food is no problem. Expensive, lightweight, freeze-dried food is occasionally left over from mountaineering expeditions and can be bought at trekking and rental agencies. You can easily make do with oatmeal, dried soups, fast-cooking noodles and the usual canned goods, all of which are readily available in Huaraz. Ortiz, a store at Luzuriaga at Raimondi, is better than most.

**Laundry** Bueno y Barato (☎ 72-1719, José de la Mar 674) charges US$1.25 per kilogram and does an excellent job. There are other, pricier places.

HUARAZ AREA

**Medical Services** The Hospital Regional (☎ 72-1861, 72-1290), on the 13th block of Luzuriaga, at the south end of town, provides basic medical care, though if you get really sick, go to Lima. There are pharmacies along Luzuriaga.

**Emergency** The police station (☎ 72-1221, 72-1331), just off the Plaza de Armas, has a helpful Policía de Turismo branch. Some officers speak limited English and can help you to report a robbery. For climbing accidents, Casa de Guías can arrange a rescue, but they suggest that all trekkers and climbers carry rescue insurance, which is best purchased before leaving home. Register before heading out on a climb. A helicopter rescue will cost a minimum of several thousand dollars. A guided evacuation by land will cost several hundred dollars per day.

**Dangers & Annoyances** Acclimatization is important. Huaraz's altitude (3091m) will make you feel breathless and may give you a headache during your first few days, so don't overexert yourself. The surrounding mountains will definitely cause altitude sickness if you venture into them without spending a few days acclimatizing in Huaraz. See the Health section in the Facts for the Visitor chapter for more information.

## Things to See
The **Museo Regional de Ancash** (☎ 72-1551), on the Plaza de Armas, is small but quite interesting. There are a few mummies, some trepanned skulls and a garden of stone monoliths from the Recuay culture (400 BC to 600 AD) and the Wari culture (about 600 to 1000 AD). Hours are 9 am to 6 pm on Tuesday to Saturday and 9 am to 2 pm on Sunday and Monday. Admission is US$1.50, and the ticket can also be used at Wilcahuaín (see the next subsection). There is also a **Museo de Miniaturas** on the grounds of the Real Hotel Huascarán. The museum features dolls dressed in traditional costumes, a scale model of Chavín de Huántar and some local pre-Inca carved stones.

The **Piscigranja de Truchas** (Trout Hatchery) enables you to see the stages of the trout-hatching process (have trout for lunch at the nearby Recreo Los Jardínes). You can get there by walking east on Raimondi to Confraternidad Este (just past the Parque Nacional Huascarán office), then turn left and cross the bridge over the Río Quilcay. The hatchery is just beyond. Hours are 9 am to 5 pm daily, and admission is US$0.40. Also east of town is **Jirón José Olaya**, on the right hand side of Raimondi a block beyond Confraternidad. This is the only street that remained intact through the earthquakes and shows what old Huaraz looked like.

For a view of the city, as well as the mountains behind it, you can climb up to the **Mirador de Retaquenua**, about a 45-minute walk southeast of the city. Ask locally for directions, and also ask if it is safe to walk up there.

## Monumento Nacional Wilcahuaín Ruin
This small Wari ruin, about 8km north of Huaraz, is in quite a good state of preservation. It can be reached on foot, or you can hire a taxi for a few dollars. To get there, head north out of town on Avenida Centenario. A few hundred meters past the Real Hotel Huascarán and just before a gas station, a dirt road to your right climbs 6km or 7km (passing through the small communities of Jinua and Paria) to the ruin. (The road continues on for another 20km to **Laguna Llaca**, where there are excellent mountain views. There is no regular transport.) Another way to get to the ruin is along a more attractive footpath, which is harder to find without local help. You could climb up by road and return along the footpath, asking locals the way back to Huaraz.

The site dates to about 1100 AD and is an imitation of the temple at Chavín done in the Tiahuanaco style. Wilcahuaín means 'grandson's house' in Quechua. The three-story temple has a base of about 11m by 16m, and each story has seven rooms, some of which are filled with rubble. Kids in the area will take you inside the ruin with a flashlight and show you around for a tip. The site can be visited daily for a US$1.50 fee, which also includes the Museo Regional in Huaraz.

Instead of returning to Huaraz, you could walk down to the hot springs at Monterrey (see North of Huaraz later in this chapter) along a footpath that takes about 30 minutes. Locals will show you the way or you can hire a kid to walk down with you. From Monterrey, take a bus back to Huaraz.

## Activities

**Hiking & Climbing** Clearly, this is Peru's premier area for hiking and climbing, and there are plenty of outfitters with whom to arrange trips. Of course, many experienced backpackers go camping, hiking and climbing in the mountains without any local help, and you can too. Just remember that carrying a backpack full of gear over a 4800m pass requires a lot more effort than hiking at low altitudes. People hike year round, but the dry season of mid-May to mid-September is the most popular and recommended. December to April is the wettest. Climbers pretty much stick to the dry season for serious mountaineering.

**Mountain Biking** Mountain Bike Adventures (☎ 72-4259, fax 72-4888, olaza@ mail.cosapidata.com, Lúcar y Torre 530, 2nd floor; for faxes, attn: Julio Olaza) is run by Julio Olaza – a lifelong resident of Huaraz who speaks English and has spent time mountain biking in the USA. He understands what is required to run a successful mountain-biking operation. This company has been here since the early '90s and receives repeated visits by mountain bikers because it has decent bikes and knowledgeable, friendly service. Julio knows the region's single-track possibilities better than anyone.

The company offers bike rentals for independent types or guided tours ranging from an easy five-hour cruise to a circuit of the Cordillera Blanca. Rates start at US$20 per day for independent rentals.

**Skiing** There are no ski lifts in the Cordillera Blanca, but there is limited mountain skiing for diehards who want to climb with skis. The glaciers have been receding in recent years, and skiing is difficult. Ask locally for current conditions.

**River Running** The Río Santa can be run year round, though it's pretty low during the dry, high season, and options are limited. It's better in the wettest months of December to April, and April is the best overall.

Outfitters who do river trips include Montrek (☎ 72-1124, Luzuriaga 646), which has been recommended; Carlos Ames River Runners (☎ 72-3375, fax 72-4888, Tarapaca 773), at Bed & Breakfast My House; and JM (☎ 72-8017, Luzuriaga 465), which is a new company.

## Special Events

Holy Week (Semana Santa) is very busy with many Peruvian tourists. Shrove Tuesday (the Tuesday before Easter) is a day of intense water fights – stay inside your hotel if you don't want to get soaked. Ash Wednesday is much more interesting and colorful, with funeral processions for Ño Carnavalon converging on the Plaza de Armas. Here, his 'will' is read, giving opportunity for many jabs at local politicians, police and other dignitaries, before the procession continues to the river where the coffin is thrown in. Participants dress in colorful costumes with papier-mâché heads, some of which are recognizable celebrities.

Huaraz pays homage to its patron, El Señor de la Soledad, beginning May 3. This weeklong festival involves fireworks, music, dancing, elaborately costumed processions and much drinking.

Semana de Andinismo is held annually in June. This attracts mountaineers from several countries, and various competitions and exhibitions are held. The harvest festivals of San Juan are celebrated every year throughout the region in late June, and the smoke from fires lit to burn the harvest chaff fills the valley. Many Peruvians like to spend Fiestas Patrias, July 28-29, in the Huaraz area.

## Places to Stay

Hotel prices can double (even triple) during the local holiday periods, but bargains can be found or made in the remaining October-to-April low season, though October and November are popular months for large groups of students that can take over a hotel. Mining companies sometimes take over a hotel for weeks at a time as well. Travelers wanting to stay a week or more should ask for discounts. Some of the cheaper hotels have only cold water, but you can get a hot shower or sauna at *Duchas Raimondi (Raimondi 904)*. The hot showers are open to the public from 8 am to 8 pm daily and cost about US$2.

The prices given in this section are average dry/high-season rates.

## Places to Stay – Budget

Especially during the high season, citizens meet buses from Lima and offer inexpensive accommodations in their houses. Hostels also employ individuals to meet buses, but beware of incorrect information or over-pricing, and don't pay anybody until you have seen the room.

One of the cheapest places is *Casa de Jaime* (☎ 72-2281, *A Gridilla 267)*, which is basic but friendly and has cooking and laundry facilities and a hot (or tepid) shower. They charge about US$3 per person and can get crowded. I've received both favorable and negative reports about this place.

A very popular budget option is *Albergue Churup* (☎ 72-2584, *churup@hotmail.com, Pedro Campos 735)*, which is run by the friendly family of Juan and Nelly Quirós. They have three locations, all within a block of one another, and offer combinations of dormitory and private rooms, some with private bath for US$3 to US$4. Breakfast, kitchen facilities, a book exchange, laundry, local information and Spanish lessons are available. Another recommended private house is *Pensión NG (Pasaje Valenzuela 837)*, run by Norma Gamarra. The street is parallel to 28 de Julio and a few blocks south along Gamarra. She charges about US$4.50 per person including breakfast and has a hot shower.

I have received recommendations for two other budget places at about US$3 per person. These are *Nilo's Camp* (☎ 75-5974, *Morales 759, 2nd floor; no sign)*, which has laundry and kitchen facilities, and *Hostal La Montañesa* (☎ 72-1217, *Leguía 290)*, at the

intersection of Centenario, a member of the Peruvian Youth Hostel Association.

*Hospedaje La Cabaña* (☎ 72-3428, *José Sucre 1224)* has a patio, information, and rooms with a hot shower for about US$5 per person including continental breakfast, or US$4 without. The friendly, family-run *Alojamiento El Farolito* (☎ 72-5792, *Tarapaca 1466)*, a two-story green house, has rooms, many with private bath and hot showers, for about US$4 per person. They have a TV room, café and laundry service. Nearby is *Hostal Piscis* (☎ 72-2362, *Tarapaca 1452)*, which is clean and helpful and has hot water, breakfast on request, laundry and dorm-beds for US$3 to US$5 per person. Other budget possibilities recommended by readers include *Señora López*, behind Edward's Inn, with doubles for US$5 to US$9 depending on room and season; it is often full in the high season. Also, *Hostal Gyula* (☎ 72-1567, *Plaza Ginebra 632)* has hot showers and beds at US$4 per person.

*Casa de Guías* (☎ 72-1811, *fax 72-2306, Plaza Ginebra 28G)* charges US$5/7.50 per person (low/high season) for beds in dorm rooms and has kitchen and laundry facilities, hot water and a popular restaurant. This is a climbers' meeting place and has bulletin boards of information. They belong to the Peruvian Youth Hostel Association. *Edward's Inn* (☎ 72-2692, *Bolognesi 121)* provides local information, laundry facilities, a café and camping-gear rental. Rates are about US$20 for a double with private bath. Some rooms have dorm beds and cost around US$7. Showers are heated by solar panels, so bathe in the afternoon.

Small, family-run places with hot water include the basic but clean, friendly and popular *Hostal Quintana* (☎ 72-6060, *M Cáceres 411)*, which charges US$3.50/5 per person with shared/private showers; and *Pensión Galaxia* (☎ 72-2230, *fax 72-6535, Romero 638)* charges US$6.50/9 for singles/doubles with private bath. The recently renovated and expanded *Hostal Maguina* (☎ 72-2320, *Tarapaca 643)* has hot water, a café, beautiful terrace views and an owner who speaks several languages. Rates are US$3.50

with shared bath and US$5 with private bath; long-term discounts are easily arranged.

The spartan *Hotel Barcelona (☎ 72-1024, Raimondi 612)* has great mountain views from the balconies, but no hot water and some rooms with rather smelly private bathrooms. Rates are US$3.25/6/7.50 for one/two/three people and communal bath, or US$4/7.50/9 with private bath. The friendly and helpful *Hotel Los Andes (☎ 72-1346, Tarapaca 316)* charges US$3 to US$5 per person. *Hostal Estoico (☎ 72-2371, San Martín 635)* is basic but OK and charges US$4/7 for singles/doubles or US$5/8 with private bath and hot water in the mornings. *Hostal Landauro (☎ 72-1212)*, on the Plaza de Armas, also has occasional hot water and dorm-beds for US$3 or US$7/10 for singles/doubles with private bath. The family-run *Alojamiento Soledad (☎ 72-1196, Amadeo Figueroa 1267)* charges US$6 per person for shared rooms and is recommended by a reader as friendly and safe. It has laundry service.

*Hostal Cataluña (☎ 72-1117, Raimondi 822)* has excellent balcony views, but may close in the off season. Clean rooms with private showers are about US$8/13, and there is hot water from 7 to 9 am and 7 to 9 pm. The pleasant *Hostal Yanett (☎ 72-1466, Centenario 106)* has a small garden and charges US$8/14 for rooms with private bath and hot water; breakfast is available. They close for the low season.

*Oscar's Hostal (☎/fax 72-2720, José de la Mar 624)* charges about US$8/11 and has hot water (24 hours, they say). *Hostal Raimondi (☎ 72-1082, Raimondi 820)* has a small café for 6 and breakfasts and charges US$8/14 with bath. *Hostal Continental (☎ 72-1557, 28 de Julio 586)* is about US$8 per person and is clean, with private bathrooms and hot water. *Hostal El Pacífico (☎ 72-1683, Luzuriaga 630)* charges US$8/10 for rooms with private bath and hot water in the morning. It is popular with Peruvian tourist groups. Some of the interior rooms are windowless and dark. *Hostal Chong Roca (☎ 72-1154, Morales 687)* is quite good for US$7 per person with private bath and hot water. *Hostal Eccame (☎ 72-1933, José de la Mar 671)* has clean, simple rooms with hot water for US$8 per person.

## Places to Stay – Mid-Range

*Hostal Tumi I (☎ 72-1784, San Martín 1121)* is clean, comfortable and quiet, and many of its rooms have great mountain views. There is a good and inexpensive hotel restaurant. Rooms with bath and hot water are officially US$20/33, but discounts are often offered. Almost next door is *Hostal Tumi II (☎ 72-1784 ext 51, San Martín 1089)*, which is also good and costs about US$13/26. Closer to the center is *Hostal Los Portales (Raimondi 903)*, which was being rebuilt in 1999.

The small (9 rooms) *Hostal Schatzi (☎/fax 72-3074, Bolívar 419)* is comfortable and pleasant. Rooms with 24-hour hot water and private bath are US$12/22 including a simple breakfast. The hospitable *Bed & Breakfast My House (☎/fax 72-3375, Tarapaca 773)* has rooms with private hot shower for US$10 to US$12 per person including breakfast. *Hotel Santa Victoria (☎ 72-2422, fax 72-4870, Gamarra 690)* has simple but spacious rooms with private bath, TV and phone for US$12 per person. They have a cozy matrimonial suite for US$55, and there is a restaurant. *Hostal Colomba (☎ 72-7106, fax 72-1501, Francisco de Zela 210)* has bungalows set in a large and pleasant garden full of plants and birdcages. Rates are about US$20/35.

New mid-range to top-end hotels were under construction in 1999. One that should be finished by 2000 is *Grand Hotel Huaraz (☎ 72-2227, fax 72-6536, Larrea y Loredo 721)*, about three blocks northeast of the Plaza de Armas. Rates are expected to start at US$30.

## Places to Stay – Top End

The two best hotels are both about a 15-minute walk from the center. The modern *Real Hotel Huascarán (☎ 72-1640, 72-1709, fax 72-2821)*, on the 10th block of Centenario, has clean, spacious rooms with bath for about US$52/63. There is a restaurant, but it is no more than adequate. It reportedly changed ownership in 1998.

The best is the Swiss-run **Hotel Andino**
(☎ 72-1662, fax 72-2830, Pedro Cochachín
357), which has one of the best restaurants in
Huaraz. It is very popular with international
trekking and climbing groups, and reservations are a good idea for the high season.
Rooms with private bath and oodles of hot
water cost about US$60. Rooms with a
balcony and a great view of the mountains
are about US$80 for a double. Rates are
20% lower in the off season, when reservations are not needed.

## Places to Eat
Budget travelers have plenty of inexpensive
options. **Restaurant Familia** (Luzuriaga 431)
is one of the better cheap restaurants with a
wide choice. For a cheap and typical local
lunch, try the **Recreo La Unión**. It's not fancy,
but it is quite authentic. Local lunches are
also good at nearby Monterrey (see North of
Huaraz). **Restaurant Samuels**, on José de la
Mar, is inexpensive, serves big helpings and is
popular with both locals and gringos.

For breakfasts, **Casa de Guías** is good and
popular with visitors. They offer granola,
yogurt and fruit, as well as the more usual
fare. **Hostal Raimondi** opens around 6 am
for breakfast. The best place for great coffee
(and espressos and lattes), a juice bar and
decent Mexican meals is the popular **Café
Andino** (Morales 753). They have music and
games and also serve alcohol. It's the place
to hang. Also very popular with young
foreign visitors is **Piccolo Café/Pizzería**, a
block away and also on Morales, with
outdoor pavement seating and reasonable
prices. Also worth a look on this street is the
new, Swiss-run **The Bar & More** (Morales
759), which has superb sandwiches, salads
and cocktails in a trendy European setting.
**Bistro de los Andes** (Morales 823) is another
restaurant with a European air, and **El Rin-
concito Minero** (Morales 757) is open all
day and has an outdoor patio.

**Recreo de los Jardines**, a block from the
Trout Hatchery, is a locally popular place
with trout dishes under US$3. For seafood,
the new **Cevichería El Ancla**, near the
Hostal Quintana, has tasty, fresh ceviche but

closes at 3 pm. The agreeable **El Fogón**
(Luzuriaga 928) has a small simple menu of
chicken, trout and great anticuchos; it is
open for dinner only.

A couple of good, economical options for
vegetarians are **Fuente de Salud** (José de la
Mar 562) and **Sabor Salud Pizzería**
(Luzuriaga 674); both have a good lunch
menu or á la carte plates that are served
throughout the day.

The influx of European and North American climbers and hikers has led to the
appearance of several pizzerias and international restaurants that are good, but pricier
than the Peruvian places. Some of them add
a 28% tax and tip to the menu price, so check
if you're on a budget. One of the hottest new
restaurants is **Siam de los Andes**, on the
corner of Gamarra and Morales, serving up
authentic Thai dishes. Check out their street-
side barbecue every other Sunday during the
climbing season. The best pizzerias are **Chez
Pepe** (Luzuriaga 568), which is probably the
most expensive, but also has a good selection
of meat and fish dishes; **Montrek** (Luzuriaga
646), which has a climbing wall on the premises; and the slightly cheaper but also good
**Monte Rosa** (José de la Mar 661). The newer
and very popular **Pizza Bruno**, on Luzuriaga
at 28 de Julio, opens at 5 pm, serves pizza and
has good steaks, salads and seafood. **Campo
Base** (Luzuriaga 407) has Italian and international food, as well as local specialities
such as trout and alpaca. They host live
Andean music on some evenings.

**Café de Paris** (San Martín 687) offers
French pastries, decent burgers, shish kebab
and rotisserie chicken done French style.
The **Crêperie Patrick** (Luzuriaga 422) is recommended for crepes, ice cream and continental dinners. They have a rooftop patio
open in the mornings for enjoying breakfast
under the sun. Next door is the decent **Chifa
Min Hua** for Chinese food. The small **El
Café** (Luzuriaga 975) has European pastries
and good coffees; the owners speak English,
German, Japanese (and Spanish).

The best and priciest restaurant in town is
the Swiss kitchen in the **Hotel Andino**. The
food is delicious, but they open at mealtimes

only, primarily for guests of the hotel, though casual diners will also be served if there's room; a reservation ensures you a seat.

## Entertainment

There are several bars, discos and peñas, and their levels of popularity are everchanging. *Café Andino* (see Places to Eat) is currently very popular. For more of a disco atmosphere, *Las Kenas Pub* (*Uribe 620*) has a happy hour from 8 to 10 pm and live Andean and recorded music starting at 10 pm. *Aquelarre*, upstairs on the corner of Uribe and Luzuriaga, features excellent blues and serves good cocktails. *El Tambo Bar* (*José de la Mar 776*) is popular with gringos and Peruvians, and has good live music in the afternoon and recorded music in the evening. Dancing gets under way at about 10 pm, when it starts to get crowded. Backpackers on a budget could save a night's lodging by dancing here until 4 am and then taking the first bus out of town!

*New Imantata Bar* (*Luzuriaga 424*) is a peculiarly low-roofed drinking and dancing establishment and also gets under way at about 10 pm. *La Cueva del Oso Peña* (*Luzuriaga 674*) also has dancing and a variety of music. *Taberna Amadeus* seems to cater to a local crowd. *Monttrek Disco*, by the Plaza de Armas, has a large dance floor and recorded dance music. There is reportedly a climbing wall inside as well. Bear in mind that there is much less entertainment when it's not the tourist season.

## Shopping

An outdoor crafts market used to be held along Luzuriaga every evening during the tourist season, but the mayor moved it to Raimondi, west of the market. I wouldn't be surprised if it goes back to the more centrally located Luzuriaga. Inexpensive thick woolen sweaters, scarves, hats, socks, gloves, ponchos and blankets are available for travelers needing warm clothes for the mountains. Tooled leather goods are also popular souvenirs. There is a sprinkling of other souvenirs for those who aren't planning on spending time in Cuzco or Lima, where the selection is better.

High-quality, attractive T-shirts with appropriately mountainous designs are made by Andean Expressions (☎ 72-2951). They are sold in several outlets in town, or you can get them from the home-factory where they are made at J Arguedas 1246, near the Iglesia Soledad on the east side of town. Cabdrivers can find it.

## Getting There & Away

**Air** The Huaraz-area airport is at Anta, about 23km north of town. Scheduled air services from Lima and Chimbote are reported occasionally, though I have not found any scheduled flights available on my recent visits to Huaraz. You can charter a flight here.

**Bus** Buses heading north along the length of the Callejón de Huaylas stop near the corner of Fitzcarrald and Raimondi when coming from Lima. Local transport goes as far as Caraz. Buses for Caraz (US$1.25, 1½ hours) leave every few minutes during the day from Centenario on the north side of the river. These will drop you in any of the towns between Huaraz and Caraz.

A plethora of companies have departures for Lima (US$5 to US$10, about 8 hours), so shop around. Most companies depart between 9 and 10 am or 9 and 10 pm. Note, Huaraz is a popular destination for Peruvian tourists, price hikes of 50% and more do occur leading up to and during major national holidays. Some companies begin in Caraz and stop in Huaraz to pick up passengers, but if you have a numbered ticket, there should be no problem getting a seat. Cruz del Sur (☎ 72-5802, Lúcar y Torre 577) has day and evening Imperial nonstop service that includes a cup of coffee and a sandwich along the way – this is comfortable but pricier. Móvil Tours (☎ 72-2555, Raimondi 730) also offers slightly cheaper nightly Imperial service in new buses with more legroom, as well as regular day and night service.

Other companies that service Lima include CIVA (☎ 72-1947, San Martín 408), which has nice day and night buses; Transportes

Rodríguez (☎ 72-1353, Tarapaca 622), which has one day bus and one Imperial night bus; and Expreso Ancash (☎ 72-1102, Raimondi 835), a subsidiary of Ormeño, which has morning, afternoon and night buses. Empresa El Aguila (☎ 72-6666, Raimondi 901) has a night departure in new buses claimed to be Imperial class. Empresa 14 (☎ 72-1282), on Fizcarrald near Caraz, has morning and evening buses, and Co-op Trans Ancash (72-4915, Raimondi 527) has afternoon and evening buses; both are basic and cheap.

Three main bus routes reach Chimbote (US$5 to US$7, 8 hours) on the north coast. One follows the Callejón de Huaylas and passes through the narrow, spectacular Cañón del Pato before descending to the coast at Chimbote. This is a scenic route, but unfortunately, most buses travel it by night. Another daytime route crosses the 4225m-high Punta Callán, 30km west of Huaraz, and provides spectacular views of the Cordillera Blanca. This road comes out at Casma and continues north along the coastal Panamericana to Chimbote. Due in part to severe damage to those two routes during El Niño of 1998, the third route – which takes the road to Pativilca (the same route as Lima-bound buses) and then heads north on the highway – is the one that is now almost always used (check to see if the situation has changed when you arrive).

Most companies with service to Chimbote continue on to Trujillo (US$6 to US$9, 10 hours). Transportes Moreno (☎ 72-1344, Raimondi 892) has day buses on both the Cañón del Pato and Casma routes, and a night bus on the Casma route. Empresa 14, Cruz del Sur and Rodriguez all have night buses to Chimbote that continue on to Trujillo via Pativilca. Turismo Chimbote (☎ 72-1984, Fitzcarrald 286) has late-afternoon and evening service along the same route. Empresa Chan Chan (☎ 72-7315, Raimondi 800) has nonstop service at 9 pm. Empresa Chinchaysuyo (☎ 72-6417, Lúcar y Torre 489) has an 8:30 pm bus to Trujillo and Chiclayo (US$10, 13 hours). Empresa Huandoy (☎ 72-7507, Fitzcarrald 261) has buses to Chimbote (US$5) by way of Casma (US$4)

daily at 8 am, 10 am, and 1 pm, and via the Cañón del Pato every morning, although this service is frequently suspended.

Virgen de Guadalupe (☎ 72-6673, Caraz 605) and Empresa Transvir (☎ 72-7744, Caraz 604) have buses across the Cordillera Blanca via various routes. Buses to Piscobamba (US$6, 7 hours) and Pomabamba (US$7, 8 hours) depart Tuesday, Thursday and Saturday at 6 am; and to Sihuas (US$8, 9 hours) on Tuesday and Saturday at 9 am. Buses along these routes return to Huaraz the following day. Buses via Carhuaz and the spectacular Quebrada Ulta – through a tunnel at the top of the valley, down to the village of Chacas (US$5, 4½ hours) and on to San Luis (US$6, 6 hours) – leave at 7 am daily in both directions. Empresa Huandoy also has occasional service along this route. Chavín Express (☎ 72-4652, M Cáceres 338) offers service via Chavín de Huántar (US$3, 4 hours) to the village of Llamellín (US$4.50, 7 hours) daily at 9 am and to Huari (US$3.50, 6 hours). Buses to Huari depart at 8 am, 10 am, 2 pm and 8 pm (Sunday only). Empresa Trans Sandoval (Tarapaca 621), Lanzón de Chavín (Tarapaca 602) and Empresa Huandoy offer less-frequent departures along these routes.

For Chiquián (and the Cordillera Huayhuash), El Rápido (☎ 72-6237, Huascarán 117) has daily buses (US$2, 3½ hours), and there are others from the same area.

Empresa Virgen de Guadalupe and Empresa Huallanca, on Raimondi at Huascarán, have buses to Huallanca and La Unión (US$4.50, 6 hours) on Tuesday, Thursday, Saturday and Sunday, returning to Huaraz the following day. Connections can be made in La Unión for Huánuco and points farther east and south.

Trucks leave for other villages in the Cordillera Blanca area. Check at the bridge on Fitzcarrald, from where colectivos to Caraz leave, or ask around.

## Getting Around

A taxi ride around Huaraz costs under US$1. A taxi ride to Caraz is about US$20. Other rides can be arranged. Look for taxis at the bridge on Fitzcarrald or along Luzuriaga.

# North of Huaraz

The Callejón de Huaylas road north of Huaraz follows the Río Santa valley and is paved for the 67km to Caraz. This road passes within 14km of Peru's highest peak and links the departmental capital with the other main towns in the area.

## MONTERREY
☎ 044

Just 5km north of Huaraz is the small village of Monterrey, famous for its natural *baños termales* (hot springs). The bus terminates right in front of the springs, so you won't have any difficulty finding them. The hot springs are divided into two sections; the lower pools are cheaper (US$1), in worse condition and more crowded than the upper pools (US$1.30), where there are private rooms (20 minutes for US$1.60 per person). The pools are open from 8 am to 6 pm, and tickets for either level are sold at the lower entrance. The pools are very busy on weekends and are closed Monday for cleaning, so Tuesday is the cleanest day.

### Places to Stay & Eat

The hotels are near the springs – ask anyone for directions. Restaurants are a little further afield, but all are within walking distance.

*Hostal El Nogal* (☎ 72-5929) is the cheapest and has OK double rooms with private bath for about US$20. *Real Hotel Baños Termales Monterrey* (☎/fax 72-1717) is a pleasant older building set in gardens right next to the hot springs. There is a simple restaurant with outdoor dining (overlooking the pool) and reasonably priced meals. Rather spartan rooms with bath are about US$27/36 including breakfast. Bungalows that sleep four are about US$72. You needn't stay at the hotel to use the pool or the restaurant. The nicest is *El Patio* (☎ 72-4965), with rooms and cabins in a pleasant garden or around a patio. Rates are US$40 to US$75 for one to four people, and larger rooms sleeping up to four are US$85 including breakfast. There is a good restaurant open for breakfast, lunch and dinner. Prices are about US$4.50 for an American breakfast and US$8 for dinner entrees.

Apart from the hotel restaurants, there are several good rural places to eat serving local food, especially grills such as cuy, chicharrones, trout and pachamanca. These are along the main Huaraz-Caraz road. *Las Terrazas* is one of the best and has a pleasant riverside location. Prices are US$4 to US$6. *Restaurant Cordillera Blanca* is also good and slightly cheaper, while *El Cortijo* is just a little pricier, but the food is similar.

### Getting There & Away

Monterrey is reached by local buses from Huaraz, which go north along Luzuriaga, west on 28 de Julio, north on 27 de Noviembre, east on Raimondi and north on Fitzcarrald. Try to catch a bus early in the route, as they soon fill up. The fare for the 15-minute ride is US$0.25. A taxi ride to Huaraz is US$3.

## MONTERREY TO CARHUAZ

About 16km north of Huaraz, the road goes through the little village of Taricá, which is famous as a local pottery center. You can stay at the friendly *Hostal Sterling*, which has funky rooms, at US$4 per person or US$6 with bath and hot water. It has a small restaurant and a bar that looks like it hasn't been changed or even dusted since the 1950s.

About 23km north of Huaraz is the tiny Anta airport, and 2km beyond is the small village of Marcará. From here, minibuses and trucks leave regularly for the hot springs of Chancos, 3km to the east, and occasionally continue another 4km to Vicos. It's a 5km walk to the ruins of Joncapampa. Beyond Vicos, the Quebrada Honda trail (for hikers only) continues across the Cordillera Blanca. The rather rustic and dilapidated Chancos hot springs are popular with locals on weekends, when they tend to be crowded. There are steam baths for US$1 per person; better ones in the 'caves' are US$1.60.

Marcará has the basic *Alojamiento Suarez* for about US$6 per person with shared baths.

## CARHUAZ

☎ 044

The small town of Carhuaz is 35km north of Huaraz. It is not a particularly interesting place, but trekkers heading into the Cordillera Blanca via the beautiful Quebrada Ulta may want to stay there. Vehicles from Carhuaz to Shilla leave from near the plaza many times a day; some continue through the Quebrada Ulta and may go over the Punta Olimpica pass. Ask locally. This trekking route is becoming increasingly popular; reportedly, park-entrance fees aren't collected here, but this will probably change.

Carhuaz's annual La Virgen de La Merced fiesta is celebrated September 14-24 with processions, fireworks, dancing, bullfights and plenty of drinking; it's one of the area's best and wildest festivals.

### Places to Stay & Eat

*Hotel La Merced* (☎ 79-4241, *Ucayali 600*), half a block from the Plaza de Armas, has hot water and appears to be the best in the town center. They charge US$6 per person and offer group discounts. *Residencial Carhuaz* (☎ 79-4139, *Progreso 586*), a block from the plaza, has a pleasant courtyard, but is otherwise a basic hotel, though they have hot showers. They charge US$5 to US$10 per person. At the northwest exit of town is *Hostal Delicias*, which claims to have hot water. The basic *Hotel Victoria* (*Comercio 105*) is another option.

Call Felipe Díaz (local cartographer and author) at *Café Heladería El Abuelo* (☎ 79-4149), on the Plaza de Armas, for accommodations in various clean local family lodgings. Most simple rooms are around US$5 per person, though some rooms with modern facilities are US$10 to US$20. At the café, there is a hotel with nice double rooms that have private hot showers for US$35. The café is also a good place to eat (especially ice cream) and get information and is open from 8 am to 9 pm daily. There are a few cheap and basic restaurants. *Los Pinos* (*Amazonas 634*) is the best, and *Las Mercedes* (*Progreso 153*) looks OK.

About 1.5km east of town is the friendly *Casa del Pocha*, a working farm growing organic vegetables and powered by solar panels and wind turbines. They charge US$20 per person including meals and hot showers; a camping area, which is cheaper and has a sauna and horseback riding, is available.

## CARHUAZ TO YUNGAY

Six or eight kilometers north of Carhuaz, the road goes through the little village of **Tingua**, where the *Rancho Chico* restaurant prepares good, typical pachamancas, particularly for Friday, Saturday, Sunday and holiday lunches. A few kilometers beyond is the village of **Mancos**, from where there are excellent views of Huascarán. A road east goes through Musho to the base camp for climbing Huascarán. There is a daily bus or truck from Mancos to Musho, or you can hire arrieros here. In Mancos, *Casa Alojamiento La Plaza* (☎/fax 74-2035, *Plaza de Armas 107*) offers basic dorm accommodations for US$3.50 per person and has hot water and good views of Huascarán.

## YUNGAY

☎ 044

Not far from Mancos is the newly rebuilt village of Ranrahirca (devastated in the 1962 earthquake), followed by the rubble-strewn area of old Yungay, the site of the single worst natural disaster in the Andes. It was near here that the earthquake of May 31, 1970, loosened some 15 million cubic meters of granite and ice from the west wall of Huascarán Norte. The resulting aluvión picked up a speed of about 300km/h as it dropped over three vertical kilometers on its way to Yungay, 14km away. The town and almost all of its 18,000 inhabitants were buried. The earthquake also killed about 50,000 people in other parts of central Peru.

Today, the site, called **Campo Santo**, is marked by a huge white statue of Christ on a knoll overlooking old Yungay. The path of the aluvión can plainly be seen from the road. It costs US$0.50 to enter the site, walking through flower-filled gardens and past occasional gravestones and monuments commemorating the thousands of people who lie buried beneath your feet. At the old Plaza de Armas of Yungay, you can see just the very top of the cathedral tower and a few palm trees, which are all that remain of the devastated village. A replica of the cathedral's facade has been built in honor of the dead.

New Yungay has been rebuilt just beyond the aluvión path, about 59km north of Huaraz. A stark, hastily built town, it offers no attraction in itself, but it is from here that you begin one of the most beautiful and popular excursions in the Cordillera Blanca – the drive to the Lagunas Llanganuco.

The annual festival is October 28.

### Places to Stay & Eat

Although there are several cheap places to stay in Yungay, there's little point in spending more than a night here en route to the mountains. The reasonably clean *Hostal Suizo Peruano* (☎ 79-3003), a block from the Plaza de Armas, charges US$3 per person and has shared hot showers. Next door, the popular *Hostal Gledel* (☎ 79-3048) is about US$7 to US$10, with shared hot showers and meals available.

Other similarly priced hotels include the decent *Hostal Yungay* (☎ 79-3053, 79-3134, 79-3166), which has hot water, and *Hostal Sol de Oro*, which has no hot water; both are on the plaza. Hotels may close in the off season, and private homes often offer accommodations during the high season.

*Complejo Turístico Yungay* (☎ 79-3102), on Prolongación 2 de Mayo on the southern outskirts of town (also called 'Comtury'), has five bungalows with two to eight beds each. The bungalows have TV and hot water, and rates are about US$8 per person. Meals are available.

There are several cheap and simple places to eat in the market next to the plaza. A good one is *Restaurant Turístico Alpamayo*, three blocks north of the plaza, serving cheap local food. *Restaurant La Embajada*, on 28 de Julio a block from the plaza, serves big meals for under US$3 and looks clean and good.

### Getting There & Away

Frequent minibuses run from the Plaza de Armas to Caraz (US$0.50, 15 minutes), and buses en route from Caraz will pick up passengers to Huaraz (US$1.20, about 1 hour) from the southwest side of the plaza.

Buses from Caraz to Lima and buses from Huaraz to Chimbote pick up passengers at the Plaza de Armas.

## LAGUNAS LLANGANUCO
☎ 044

A dirt road goes up the Llanganuco valley to the two lovely lakes of the same name, about 28km east of Yungay. There are great views of the giant mountains of Huascarán (6768m), Chopicalqui (6354m), Chacraraju (6112m), Huandoy (6395m) and others, particularly if you drive a few kilometers beyond the lakes. The road continues over the pass beyond the lakes and down to Yanama on the other side of the Cordillera Blanca; there is often an early-morning truck from Yungay going to Yanama and beyond.

It is also from Yungay that the walker begins the Llanganuco-to-Santa Cruz loop – the most popular and spectacular trek of the Cordillera Blanca. This takes an average of five fairly leisurely days (though it can be done in four days) and is a good hike for everybody, especially beginners, because the trail is relatively well defined. Note that there is a US$2 day-use and US$22 multiday-use fee. See the Bradt book for a hike description, or use the adequate maps available in Huaraz.

The Llanganuco road is also the access route to the Pisco base camp, where the ascent of Nevado Pisco (5752m) begins. This is considered one of the most straightforward high-snow ascents in the range, though it is not to be taken lightly and requires snow and ice-climbing equipment and experience.

To get to the Lagunas Llanganuco, you can go on a tour from Huaraz or take buses or taxis from Yungay. During June, July and August (the height of the dry season), minibuses carrying 10 or more passengers leave from the Yungay Plaza de Armas. The round trip costs about US$5 and allows about two hours in the lake area. A national-park admission fee of around US$2 is also charged. During the rest of the year, minibuses do the trip if there is enough demand, which there often is in April and

May and from September to December. Taxis are also available. Go in the early morning for clear views; it's often cloudy in the afternoon.

## CARAZ
☎ 044

The pleasant little town of Caraz lies 67km north of Huaraz and is the end of the road as far as regular and frequent transport is concerned, although the paved road now continues to Huallanca and is slowly being extended. Caraz is one of the few places in the area that, while suffering some damage, has managed to avoid total destruction by earthquake or alluvion. The town has an attractive Plaza de Armas and several hotels and restaurants, and you can take pleasant walks in the surrounding hills. The population is about 14,000, and the elevation is a relatively low 2270m.

Caraz is both the end point of the popular Llanganuco-to-Santa Cruz trek (which can also be done in reverse starting here) and the point of departure for rugged treks into the remote northern parts of the Cordillera Blanca. The town makes a good base for treks to the north side of Alpamayo (5947m), which one magazine called the most beautiful mountain in the world. Excursions can be made by road to the stunning Laguna Parón and to the Cañón del Pato.

The bright-blue Laguna Parón is 32km east of Caraz and surrounded by spectacular snowcapped peaks, of which Pyramide (5885m), at the end of the lake, looks particularly magnificent. The road to the lake goes through a canyon with 1000m-high granite walls. Although this excursion takes you farther from Huaraz than a visit to the Lagunas Llanganuco and is therefore neither as popular nor as crowded, it is just as attractive as the Llanganuco tour.

The spectacular Cañón del Pato is at the far north end of the Callejón de Huaylas

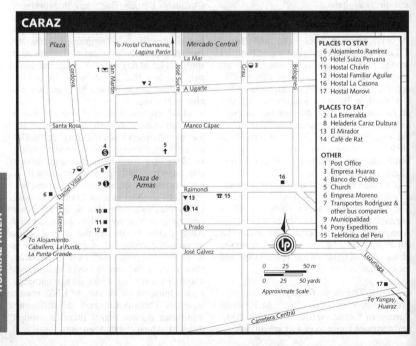

# CARAZ

**PLACES TO STAY**
6  Alojamiento Ramírez
10 Hotel Suiza Peruana
11 Hostal Chavín
12 Hostal Familiar Aguilar
16 Hostal La Casona
17 Hostal Morovi

**PLACES TO EAT**
2  La Esmeralda
8  Heladería Caraz Dulzura
13 El Mirador
14 Café de Rat

**OTHER**
1  Post Office
3  Empresa Huaraz
4  Banco de Crédito
5  Church
6  Empresa Moreno
7  Transportes Rodríguez & other bus companies
9  Municipalidad
14 Pony Expeditions
15 Telefónica del Peru

and is its narrowest point. Buses en route to Chimbote take this road every day, or you can take a pickup truck or taxi from Caraz. There is a cheap, clean hotel in Huallanca at the north end of the Cañón (not to be confused with Huallanca at the southeast end of the Cordillera Blanca).

Although much smaller than Huaraz, Caraz is beginning to develop some infrastructure for tourism.

## Information

Extensive information is provided by Alberto Cafferata, who speaks English, French and Spanish and runs the recommended Pony Expeditions (☎/fax 79-1642, cell 68-2848, ponyexp@pol.com.pe, José Sucre 1266). This is a great source for all local information, and equipment rental, transportation, guides, arrieros, mules, and various excursions can be arranged. Books, maps, fuels and other items are for sale. This is the place to get up-to-date trekking information. Hours are 8 am to 1 pm and 4 to 10 pm daily. Internet access is available.

Limited tourist information is offered in the Municipalidad on the Plaza de Armas.

The Banco de Crédito (Daniel Villar 217) changes cash and traveler's checks. Importaciónes América (José Sucre 721) and Pony Expeditions can change US cash. Post and telephone offices are shown on the map. Internet access is available at Pony Expeditions or at Enter (☎ 79-1642, Santa Cruz 215, 2nd floor).

## Tumshukayko

The pre-Inca ruins of Tumshukayko are about a 30-minute walk on a dirt road north of Caraz.

## Places to Stay

Apart from the independence holidays at the end of July, hotel prices remain quite stable throughout the year, probably because Caraz has not yet been overrun by visitors. Small, family-run lodgings include the simple, clean and friendly *Alojamiento Caballero* (☎ 79-1637, Daniel Villar 485), which has hot showers and charges US$3 per person (inquire at Pony Expeditions).

The basic *Hostal Morovi* (☎ 79-1409), on the 3rd block of Luzuriaga, has rooms with private cold showers for US$6 per person, or US$3 per person with shared hot showers. *Albergue Los Pinos* (☎/fax 79-1130, luisger@hotmail.com, Parque San Martín 103), five blocks southwest of the plaza, is affiliated with the International Youth Hostel Federation and has hot water and cooking facilities. Rates are about US$7 per person, private baths and breakfast are available and there is a camping area for US$2 per person. The noisy, basic but clean *Alojamiento Ramírez*, above the Empresa Moreno bus terminal, is US$3 per person, with communal cold showers. *Hostal La Casona* (☎ 79-1334, Raimondi 319) is one of the best cheap hotels. It's clean, has a patio and hot water and charges US$7/10 for singles/doubles with private bath, less with communal. *Hotel Suiza Peruana* (☎ 79-2166, San Martín 1133) charges a little more but is no better. Next door, *Hostal Chavín* (☎ 79-1171, fax 79-1529, San Martín 1135) is friendly and charges US$8/12 for clean rooms with hot showers. They have a breakfast room and arrange tours. Nearby, *Hostal Familiar Aguilar* (San Martín 1143) has hot water in the morning and charges US$3 per person.

On the outskirts is the German-run *Hostal Chamanna* (cell 68-2802, Nueva Victoria 185), about a 20-minute walk from the center on the road to Cashapampa (ask locals for directions and take a taxi at night). There is a parking area. They have six pleasant cabins set in a pretty garden for about US$15 per double. There are shared hot showers, but private showers are planned. The German owner/chef (highly professional) prepares excellent Alsace (French) regional cuisine and offers cooking lessons. 'Horse-whispering' lessons are also offered.

A few kilometers off the road back to Huaraz is *O'Pal Inn* (☎ 79-1015, in Lima 476-4857), which has spacious bungalows at US$30 for a double (US$38 with breakfast), or US$60 for a double with a kitchenette and living room. All are attractively furnished and have private hot showers.

HUARAZ AREA

## Places to Eat

There are several simple restaurants on or near the Plaza de Armas. *Café de Rat*, above Pony Expeditions, serves breakfasts from 7 to 10 am and snacks, meals and a variety of coffees throughout the day. It also has a book exchange, darts, a bar and music; it's a good place to hang out. They have a fireplace and plaza views. *El Mirador (José Sucre 1202)* also has nice plaza views from the balcony. They serve set lunches and chicken. *Heladería Caraz Dulzura*, next to the Municipalidad, is clean and is the place for ice cream. *La Esmeralda (A Ugarte 404)* is good for *lomo saltado* and set lunches.

*La Punta* (☎ 79-1320, *Daniel Villar 595*), a short walk from the town center, is the place for a typical lunch. They serve cheap highland dishes (including guinea pig), and there is a garden to eat in. If you don't feel like guinea pig, try a hearty bowl of soup. There are two La Puntas, one on each side of the street. *La Punta Grande* has a plant-filled garden with a sapo game, and I like it better.

Also known for typical lunches is the pleasant *Restaurant La Capullana* (☎ 79-1216), about 2km west of town on the road to Cañón del Pato. It offers outdoor dining around a small lake, and prices are very reasonable. Service is spotty however – on some days, you have to yell for the waiter who has to go find a cook. Holidays and weekends are the best times here.

*Recreo Palmira*, on the south side of town just off the main road, has great trout and other local dishes (though the chicharrón de chancho was poor when I tried it). Like other typical restaurants on the outskirts, it's best for lunch. The open-air ambiance is typically rural Peruvian, with a colorful and slightly unkempt garden, rustic furniture, a pond, caged birds and animals, a children's playground and a religious shrine.

Also see Hostal Chamanna, under Places to Stay.

## Getting There & Away

Caraz is often the final destination for buses heading from the coast to the Callejón de Huaylas, and there is frequent transport from here to other points in the area and to the coast.

**Long Distance** Transportes Rodríguez (☎ 79-1184), Expreso Ancash (☎ 79-1023), Móvil Tours (☎ 79-1922) and other companies go to Lima (about US$10, 11 hours). Empresa Huaraz has one or two buses a day to Chimbote, some of which go via the Cañón del Pato and others via Casma. Transportes Rodríguez and the slower Empresa Chichaysuyo go to Trujillo (US$10, 11 hours), but only overnight.

**Caraz Area** Minibuses to Yungay and buses to Huaraz leave from the Plaza de Armas or from the Mercado Central. Taxis and pickups for local excursions also leave from these places. Buses for Cashapampa (US$1.25, 2 hours), for the north end of the Llanganuco-to-Santa Cruz trek, leave six times a day (mainly in the morning) from Grau and Santa Cruz near the market. Also from here are 5 am and 1 pm buses to Pueblo Parón (US$1, 1 hour) for the famous Laguna Parón, which is about 9km farther on foot or by truck if you can find one. Buses return from Pueblo Parón at 6 am and 2 pm. Hours may change on Sunday (I've heard of one 3 am departure).

# South of Huaraz

The road south of Huaraz is the one most travelers to and from Lima use to enter the Callejón de Huaylas, but apart from this, the road is rarely traveled by tourists. Local buses and trucks heading south of Huaraz leave from the bus stop on Avenida Tarapaca, near the Hostal Los Andes (the bus stop is called *el frigorífico* because of its proximity to a cold-storage plant). Scheduled services are described under Huaraz.

The first place of interest south of Huaraz is the Puente Bedoya (a bridge) about 18km away. From here, a dirt road leads 2km east from the highway to the village of **Olleros**, the starting point for the easy three-day trek across the Cordillera Blanca to Chavín.

Recuay is 25km from Huaraz and the only town of any size south of Huaraz. It has a basic hotel and a small museum, but is otherwise of little interest to most travelers, though it is one of the few towns here to have survived the 1970 earthquake largely unscathed.

Catac, 10km south of Recuay, is an even smaller town and the starting point for trips to see the *Puya raimondii*.

## CHIQUIÁN
☎ 044

This small town, 111km from Huaraz, is the center for visiting the small but spectacular Cordillera Huayhuash, the next mountain range south of the Blanca. It has basic hotels and restaurants, but hikers should bring what they will need with them, because few supplies are available.

Chiquián is at 3400m, and there are good views of the Cordillera Huayhuash as you drive to the village. The highest mountain in the range is Yerupajá, which at 6634m is also the second-highest mountain in Peru. Hiking in the Huayhuash usually involves making a circuit of the entire range – this is fairly strenuous and takes almost two weeks. (Bradt's book describes the trail.) Because it is less accessible than the Cordillera Blanca, the Huayhuash has fewer trekking and climbing groups. However, those few who do come have left signs of their passing, and recent visitors have complained of trash-strewn campsites.

Services can be arranged through a couple of small 'agencies.' Going daily rates are US$15 for trekking guides or cooks, US$10 for arrieros and US$5 per burro. It is possible to privately hire an arriero and burros for a little less, but you have to provide them with food and something to sleep in. Trekkers should also be prepared for aggressively territorial dogs; bending down to pick up a rock is usually enough to keep them off.

The annual fiesta is that of Santa Rosa de Lima, in late August, with dances, parades, music and bullfights. There is also a Semana Turística in early July.

### Places to Stay & Eat
The best place to stay in Chiquián is *Los Nogales*, a new hostel two blocks from the plaza. Electric hot showers are available, and clean rooms cost about US$6 per person. *Hostal San Miguel* (☎ 74-7001, Comercio 233), about seven blocks from the plaza, is basic but clean and charges about US$5 to US$8 per person per night; the difference in price appears arbitrary. Hot water is sporadically available, and the place is popular and often crowded. There are a couple of more basic places, such as the *Yerupajá*, on Grau, three blocks from the plaza; it charges about US$4 and occasionally has cold showers. You may be able to find beds in rooms with hot water at about US$6 per person with local families – ask around. A new hotel was under construction in 1999: *Hostal El Rápido*, Figuerado at 28 de Julio, is planning rooms with private hot showers.

The town has a couple of simple restaurants. The best seems to be *El Rincón de Yerupajá* (Tarapaca 351), off the 500 block of Comercio. *El Refugio de Bolognesi* (Tarapaca 471) and *Tío Sam* (28 de Julio 350) are other choices. *Panadería Santa Rosa* (Comercio 900), on the plaza, sells bread and pastries.

### Getting There & Away
If you are interested in Chiquián and the Cordillera Huayhuash, you'll find direct buses from Lima. However, Chiquián is not a particularly exciting town in which to acclimatize, and so you should spend a few days in Huaraz first.

Transfysa (☎ 74-7063, 2 de Mayo 1109) has a 9 am bus to Lima (US$5 to US$6, 8 to 10 hours), or try Turismo Cavassa (☎ 74-7036, Bolognesi 421), which has a 4:30 pm departure, arriving in Lima at the cheery hour of 3 am. However, departure times and companies change frequently, and sometimes, only overnight buses are available. Transportes Virgen del Carmen, on the 8th block of 2 de Mayo; Rápido (Figuerado 216); and Chiquián Tours (2 de Mayo 651) have buses to Huaraz (US$2.50, 3 to 4 hours), mostly leaving in the early morning.

## Puya raimondii

The giant *Puya raimondii* is a strange plant that is frequently confused with others. It is the largest member of the bromeliads, or the pineapple family. Many people think it's an agave, or century plant, and it does have a certain resemblance, but it is not closely related – the century plants belong to the Amaryllis family. Some folks think that *Puya raimondii* is a cactus, but there is no comparison – the two belong to different classes and are about as closely related as a bird and a mammal.

The *Puya raimondii* is a huge, spiky rosette of long, tough, waxy leaves. This rosette can be 2m or more in diameter and takes about 100 years to grow to full size. It then flowers by producing a huge spike, often 10m in height, which is covered by approximately 20,000 flowers – a magnificent sight. This spiky inflorescence is the largest in the world, and the plant remains in flower for about three months, during which time it is pollinated by hummingbirds. After flowering once, the plant dies.

Obviously, with flowering occurring only once every 100 years, most of the plants you'll see won't be flowering. When they do flower, they tend to do so in groups, and this occurs about every three or four years; it is not known why this happens, nor is it clear when the best time for flowering is. Some guides claim the end of the wet season (May) is best. Most say the beginning of the wet season (October and November) is the time to go. You should make local inquiries if you hope to see the *Puya raimondii* in flower, though even when not flowering, it is a fascinating sight. The spiky rosette offers protection to a variety of birds and you may find several nests within the leaves of one plant.

The giant bromeliad is also considered to be one of the most ancient plant species in the world and has been called a living fossil. It is rare and found only in a few isolated areas of the Peruvian and Bolivian Andes. The sites in the Cordillera Blanca are among the best known and receive protection as part of the Parque Nacional Huascarán.

Most people visit the site at the intersection of the Quebrada Raria with the Río Pachacoto, which can be reached by road. Drive 10km south of Catac on the main road and turn left at the Río Pachacoto (there is a national park sign that reads 'Sector Carpa'). Follow the dirt road for about 18km to the Quebrada Raria, where the puyas are to be seen. These areas are also the best place in the Cordillera Blanca to watch for the beautiful vicuña, an infrequently seen wild relative of the alpaca and llama. Camping is possible in both areas.

Tour companies in Huaraz make trips to this site. If traveling by public transport, take any early-morning, Lima-bound bus to the Sector Carpa turnoff and wait for a truck going along the Río Pachacoto road (there are usually several each day). Start heading back by early afternoon if you don't want to spend the night. These trucks act as buses for the locals, and you are expected to pay a bus fare.

The road continues as far as La Unión, where you can find basic hotels and transport on to Huánuco.

Trucks and minibuses leave most mornings north from Chiquián, past the small Cordillera Huallanca to the village of Huallanca. Here there is a basic hotel, and transport continues on to La Unión and Huánuco.

## CAJATAMBO
☎ 044

This is the only other village on the Cordillera Huayhuash trek that is accessible by road. There are some basic hotels in Cajatambo, all with very cold showers. The best is probably the friendly ***Hotel Miranda*** *(Tacna 141)* at US$4 per person. Several simple restaurants provide adequate meals.

Note that if you use Cajatambo to cut short a Cordillera Huayhuash trek from Chiquián, you will have to pay arrieros for their return journey.

At least one old, slow bus runs from Cajatambo to Lima (US$10, 9 hours) every morning at 6 am; there may be others. There is no direct route to Huaraz or Chiquián.

# East of the Cordillera Blanca

The Conchucos valley, as the area east of the Cordillera Blanca is referred to, is much more remote, traditional and lacking in contact with foreigners than the popular western side. Also, transport in this area becomes erratic and difficult during the wettest months. Therefore, travelers need to be prepared for potentially difficult conditions and should remain more open-minded, sensitive and courteous when traveling here.

## CHAVÍN DE HUÁNTAR
☎ 044

This small village (110km from Huaraz) is of little interest in itself, but the ruins of Chavín on the southern edge of the village are well worth a visit.

### The Chavín Culture
The Chavín culture is named after its type site at Chavín de Huántar and is the oldest major culture in Peru. It existed from about 1000 to 300 BC, predating the Incas by about 2000 years. The major period of influence was from about 800 to 400 BC, and the Chavín certainly was an influential culture. Its people didn't conquer by warfare – they simply influenced the artistic and cultural development of all of northern Peru. Archaeologists formerly referred to this cultural expansion as the Chavín Horizon, though Early Horizon is now the preferred usage. Signs of Chavín influence are evident in ruins ranging from the present-day Ecuadorian border to as far south as Ica and Ayacucho. None of these sites are as well preserved or as frequently visited as Chavín de Huántar.

The principal Chavín deity was feline (a jaguar or puma), and lesser condor, snake and human deities also existed. Highly stylized representations of these deities are carved in Chavín sites. The experienced eye can see similarities in the precise yet fluid lines of these carvings, while the nonexpert can tell that any culture capable of such fine work 3000 years ago must indeed have been well advanced.

The artistic work of Chavín is much more stylized and cultist than the naturalistic art of the later Moche and Nazca cultures. Because of this, archaeologists lack an accurate picture of life in Chavín times. However, excavations of middens (garbage dumps) indicate that corn became a staple food, and agriculture improved with the introduction of squash, avocados, yucca and other crops. Better agriculture meant less reliance on hunting, fishing and gathering; more importantly, it allowed leisure time. Thus, art and religion could develop, and so the Chavín Horizon, linking art and religion in its feline-worshipping cults, was able to influence a large part of Peru.

For detailed information, read the excellent *Chavín and the Origins of Peruvian Civilization* by Richard Burger.

### Visiting the Ruins
At first glance, the site at Chavín de Huántar is not particularly prepossessing. There are two reasons for this: most of the site's more interesting parts were built underground, and the area was covered by a huge landslide in 1945. To visit the site properly and to get the most from your visit, you should enter the underground chambers. Although these are electrically lit, the lighting system sometimes doesn't work, and you are advised to bring your own flashlight. It is also worth hiring a guide to show you around.

The site contains a huge central square, slightly sunken below ground level, with an intricate and well-engineered system of channels for drainage. From the square, a broad staircase leads up to the single entrance of the largest and most important building in Chavín de Huántar – the Castillo. With an area of about 75 square meters and height of up to 13m, the Castillo was built on three different levels, each of dry stone masonry. At one time, the walls were embellished with tenons (keystones of large projecting blocks carved to resemble a stylized human head). Only one of these remains in its original place; the others have been moved inside the Castillo in the underground chambers or to museums.

The underground tunnels are an exceptional feat of 3000-year-old engineering; they are so well ventilated that the air is not musty, yet the main entrance is the only external window or doorway. In the heart of the underground complex is an exquisitely carved rock known as the Lanzón de Chavín. It is a thrilling and distinctly mysterious experience to come upon this 4m-high, daggerlike rock stuck into the ground at the intersection of four narrow passageways, deep within the Castillo.

Travelers interested in the Chavín culture are advised to visit the Museo de la Nación in Lima. Two carved rocks, the Raimondi Stela, the Tello Obelisk (smaller but similar to the Lanzón de Chavín) and several of the large, carved keystones that once decorated the Castillo may be examined at the museum.

The site is open daily from 8 am to 4 pm. Entry is about US$2, with an extra fee for photography. If the gate is closed, look around for a guard to open it. Spanish-speaking local guides (Marino Gonzales is quite good) are available to show you around for a small fee, or you can come on one of the frequent guided tours from Huaraz.

## Places to Stay & Eat

Hotels and restaurants in the village of Chavín de Huántar are found on or near the Plaza de Armas – ask anyone. The cheapest are the small *Hostal Inca*, which may manage hot water occasionally, and the basic *Montecarlo* and *Gantu*. These charge US$2.50 to US$5 per person. Better is *La Casona de JB*, which has rooms with private

bath and occasional hot water at about US$5 per person, or the decent *Hostal Chavín*, also with private hot showers, at about US$5.50 per person. The best is the new *Hostal Turístico Rickay* (☎ 75-4068, in Lima 482-0150, cell 999-4647), with a patio, café, and rooms with private hot showers for about US$10 per person.

Camping is reportedly possible at the hot springs about 3km south of town or by the ruins with permission of the guard; try to go in a group, and watch your belongings.

The simple restaurants have a reputation for closing soon after sunset, so eat early. Most are along 17 de Enero, north and south of the plaza. Try *La Portada*, which has set meals around US$1; *Mi Ranchito*, on the plaza, which has local food; *Las Chositas*, which serves trout and has a pleasant courtyard; and *Chavín Turístico*, which is one of the best.

## Getting There & Away

Tour buses make day trips from Huaraz via Catac to Chavín for about US$10 per passenger, not including the ruin entry fee. Chavín Express (☎ 72-4652, M Cáceres 338) offers daily 9 am service from Huaraz to Chavín de Huántar (US$3, 4 hours) en route to the village of Llamellín (US$4.50, 7 hours).

Several buses a week from Lima pass through Chavín on their way to Huari and more remote villages farther north. Several other trucks and minibuses leave Chavín to the north most days. Buses to Lima tend to be full when they come through. A couple of buses a week to Lima originate in Chavín (recently, on Wednesday and Sunday).

The drive across the Cordillera Blanca from Catac is a scenic one. The road passes the Laguna Querococha at 3980m; from here, there are good views of the peaks of Pucaraju (5322m) and Yanamarey (5237m). The road deteriorates somewhat as it continues climbing to the Cahuish tunnel at 4178m above sea level. The tunnel cuts through the Cahuish Pass, which is over 300m higher, before the road descends to Chavín at about 3145m.

Hikers can walk to Chavín from Olleros in about three days (see Bartle's book or Bradt's book).

# NORTH OF CHAVÍN
☎ 044

The road north of Chavín goes through the villages of San Marcos (8km), Huari (40km, 2 hours), San Luis (100km, 5 hours), Piscobamba (160km, 8 hours), Pomabamba and Sihuas. Side roads cross the Cordillera Blanca to the Callejón de Huaylas. The farther north you go, the more difficult transport becomes, and it may stop altogether during the wet season. From Sihuas, it is possible to continue on to Huallanca (at the end of Cañón del Pato) via Tres Cruces and thus return to the Callejón de Huaylas. This round trip is scenic, remote and rarely made by travelers. It shouldn't be too difficult to find transport during the dry season if you really want to get off the beaten track.

## San Marcos

Señor Luis Alfaro, at Progreso 220, by the church, rents rooms with shared hot showers for US$4 or US$5 per person. There is an annual fiesta October 10-12.

## Huari

This small market town has good mountain views, a Banco de la Nación, a hospital and an annual fiesta on the days around October 4. Market day is Sunday. A good hike is to Purhuaycocha, a beautiful lake about 5km away. A two- or three-day backpacking trip continues past the lake emerging at the village of Chacas (see later in this section).

There are half a dozen basic cheap hostels, of which the best appears to be *El Dorado* (☎ 75-3028, Bolívar 353), which has hot showers. Others worth trying are *Hostal Añaños* (☎ 75-3072, Alvarez 437) and *Hostal Paraíso* (☎ 75-3029, Bolívar 263). There are several restaurants; try *Restaurant Turístico El Milagro* (San Martín 589).

Buses for Huaraz and for Lima leave most days from the Plaza Vigil.

## San Luis

This village is reached by infrequent buses from Huaraz via Yungay and Yanama, or by

buses between Huari and Pomabamba (super views coming from Huari). San Luis suffers from water and electricity shortages. There is the very basic *Hostal Rotta*, and the *Restaurant Litta* is an OK place to eat.

## Chacas

This village, southwest of San Luis, is reached by a fairly good road from Carhuaz. Pilar Ames has beds in her house, or ask the Salesian priests at the cathedral for family contacts. The Chacas fiesta is August 15.

## Yanama

A daily morning bus links Yungay with Yanama, passing the famous Lagunas Llanganuco and the village of **Colcabamba** for the Llanganuco-to-Santa Cruz trekking circuit. In Yanama, there is a basic *alojamiento*, or ask the Salesian priests for family contacts. In Colcabamba, stay with the Calonge family, where Elvis offers beds with dinner for US$5. Elvis is well known by everyone, just ask for him.

## Piscobamba

This next village north of San Luis has a couple of basic places to stay and eat.

## Pomabamba

This is the largest village north of Huari and can be the end point for various remote cross-Cordillera treks. There is a small museum by the plaza, a Banco de la Nación, a medical post and natural hot springs on the outskirts of town. The best baths are on Julio Príncipe's property – ask. Julio is also a good contact for hiring arrieros. The poorly preserved ruins of Yaino can be visited on a long day hike.

There are several basic hotels, of which the *Alojamiento Estrada* (☎ 75-1048), by the church, is the best; it charges US$4 per person. Also try the cheaper *Hostal Pomabamba*.

A daily bus for Huaraz (US$9) leaves at the ungodly hour of 2 am. Trucks and buses run irregularly farther north.

# Across the Northern Highlands

The traveler heading farther north into the highlands from the Cordillera Blanca is unable to do so conveniently without returning to the coast and traveling north before returning inland and into the mountains again. The first major city north of Huaraz is Cajamarca, reached by three roads from the coast. The dirt roads from Trujillo and Chiclayo are both rough and difficult, but the road that leaves the Panamericana between these two cities is paved all the way to Cajamarca and is the main access. All three routes are described in this chapter.

From Cajamarca, a very poor road continues northeast across the Andes to Chachapoyas, capital of the Department of Amazonas. A better road to Chachapoyas via Bagua Grande and Pedro Ruíz leaves the Panamericana north of Chiclayo. At Pedro Ruíz, this road forks, and the left road continues down the eastern slopes of the Andes to the jungles of the Department of San Martín. One can safely travel by road through the towns of Moyobamba and Tarapoto as far as the jungle port of Yurimaguas, where the road stops and overland travelers must continue by river (as described in the Amazon Basin chapter). However, the Río Huallaga valley south of Tarapoto toward Tingo María remains Peru's major drug-growing region, and this particular route is not safe for overland travel.

## CAJAMARCA
☎ 044

Cajamarca, 2650m above sea level, is five hours east by paved road from Pacasmayo on the coast. This traditional and tranquil colonial city is the capital of its department and has a friendly population of about 70,000. The surrounding countryside is green and attractive, particularly during the rainy season.

Cajamarca and its environs are steeped in history and prehistory. Once a major Inca city, Cajamarca played a crucial role in the Spanish conquest of the Incas. It was in Cajamarca that Pizarro tricked, captured, imprisoned for ransom and finally assassinated the Inca Atahualpa. The city remains important today as the major city of Peru's northern Andes. It has attractive colonial architecture, excellent Andean food and interesting people and customs. Recently, foreign-operated gold mines in the area have given the city a new air of prosperity. Despite this, it is not a major international tourist center because it lies some distance inland from the 'gringo trail.' Perhaps this makes it even more attractive.

### History
Little is known about the various pre-Inca sites discovered in the Cajamarca area, though they are generally attributed to the Chavín-influenced Cajamarca culture.

About 1460, the Incas conquered the Cajamarca people, and Cajamarca became a major Inca city on the Inca Andean highway, which linked Cuzco with Quito.

After the death of the Inca Huayna Capac in 1525, the Inca Empire, which then stretched from southern Colombia to central Chile, was divided between the half-brothers Atahualpa and Huascar. Atahualpa ruled the north, and Huascar ruled the south. Civil war soon broke out, and Atahualpa, who had the support of the army, gained the upper hand. In 1532, he and his victorious troops marched southward toward Cuzco to take complete control of the Inca Empire. During this march south, Atahualpa and his army stopped at Cajamarca to rest for a few days. The Inca emperor was camped at the natural thermal springs, known today as Los Baños del Inca, when he heard the news that the Spanish were nearby.

By 1532, Atahualpa was certainly aware of the existence of the strange, bearded white men. In 1528, during his second voyage, Francisco Pizarro had invited an Inca noble from Tumbes to dine aboard his ship, and

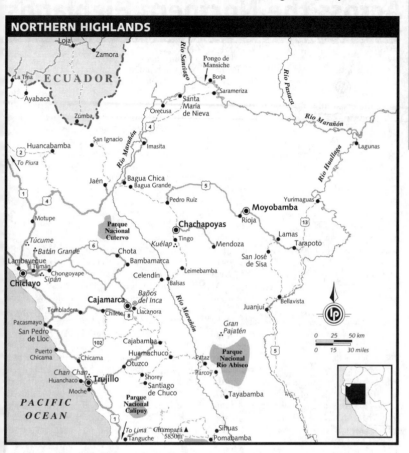

**NORTHERN HIGHLANDS**

word of this would undoubtedly have been passed on to Atahualpa. The Inca, supported by his army and flushed with his victory in the civil war, would not have considered the small, ragged Spanish force a threat.

Pizarro and his force of about 160 Spaniards arrived in Cajamarca on November 15, 1532. They found a temple of the sun, the Inca fortress, some well-made buildings housing the Inca's chosen women, and a central square surrounded by assembly halls called *kallankas*. The city was almost deserted; most of its 2000 inhabitants were

with Atahualpa at his encampment by the hot springs, 6km away. Pizarro sent a force of about 35 cavalry and a native interpreter to Atahualpa's camp to ask the Inca emperor where the Spaniards were to stay. They were told to lodge in the kallankas surrounding the plaza and that the Inca would join them the next day.

The small force of Spaniards spent an anxious night, fully aware that they were severely outnumbered by the Inca troops, estimated at 40,000 to 80,000. The Spaniards plotted throughout the night, deciding to try

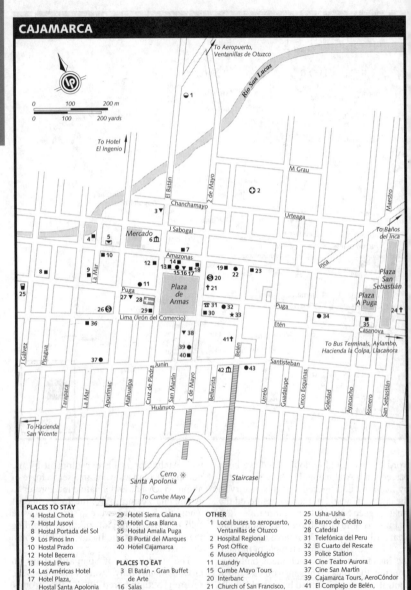

CAJAMARCA

**PLACES TO STAY**
4  Hostal Chota
7  Hostal Jusovi
8  Hostal Portada del Sol
9  Los Pinos Inn
10  Hostal Prado
12  Hotel Becerra
13  Hostal Peru
14  Las Américas Hotel
17  Hotel Plaza,
     Hostal Santa Apolonia
18  Hostal Dos de Mayo
19  Hotel Continental
23  Hotel San Francisco

29  Hotel Sierra Galana
30  Hotel Casa Blanca
35  Hostal Amalia Puga
36  El Portal del Marques
40  Hotel Cajamarca

**PLACES TO EAT**
3  El Batán - Gran Buffet
    de Arte
16  Salas
19  El Cajamarques
27  Cascanuez Café Bar
38  Baca Loca

**OTHER**
1  Local buses to aeropuerto,
    Ventanillas de Otuzco
2  Hospital Regional
5  Post Office
6  Museo Arqueológico
11  Laundry
15  Cumbe Mayo Tours
20  Interbanc
21  Church of San Francisco,
     Museo de Arte Religioso
22  Supermercado San Francisco
24  Recoleta

25  Usha-Usha
26  Banco de Crédito
28  Catedral
31  Telefónica del Peru
32  El Cuarto del Rescate
33  Police Station
34  Cine Teatro Aurora
37  Cine San Martín
39  Cajamarca Tours,
     Tourist Information
41  El Complejo de Belén,
     Tourist Information
42  Museo de Etnografía
43  Aviación Lider

Cerro Santa Apolonia, from where the Inca reviewed his troops, Cajamarca

ROB RACHOWIECKI

The floating shantytown of Belén, also known as the Venice of the Amazon

VICTOR ENGLEBERT

Shipibo woman washing clothes in broken canoe

MARY ALTIER

Eiffel's Iron House, Iquitos

MARY ALTIER

Giant Amazon water lilies (*Victoria regia*)

to entice Atahualpa into the plaza and, at a prearranged signal, capture the Inca should the opportunity present itself. If this did not occur, they were to maintain a 'friendly' relationship and hope for another chance to capture Atahualpa. The next morning, Pizarro stationed his troops in the kallankas, which were perfect for his plan. The kallankas surrounded three sides of the plaza, and each had about 20 doorways, so that many of the Spaniards could emerge and attack at the same time.

Atahualpa kept the Spanish waiting all day, much to their consternation. He didn't break camp until the afternoon and reached Cajamarca early in the evening, accompanied by his vast army. Upon arriving at the outskirts of the city, the Inca ordered the majority of his troops to stay outside while he entered the plaza with a retinue of nobles and about 6000 men armed with slings and hand axes. He was met by the Spanish friar, Vicente de Valverde. The friar, Bible in hand, attempted to explain his position as a man of God and presented the Inca with the Bible. Atahualpa angrily threw the book to the ground and Valverde saw this action as an insult to Christianity. This provided the excuse he needed to absolve the Spaniards in advance for an attack upon the Inca. He rushed back to the kallankas and prevailed upon Pizarro to order the firing of his cannons into the group of Indians. This was the prearranged signal to attack.

The cannons were fired, and the Spanish cavalry attacked with much trumpeting and yelling. The Indians, who had never seen cannons or horses before, were terrified and bewildered by the fearsome onslaught. Their small hand axes and slings were no match for the well-armored Spaniards, who were swinging razor-sharp swords from the advantageous height of horseback. The Indians tried to flee, but the entrance to the plaza was too narrow to allow escape. By sheer weight of numbers, they knocked down a section of wall 2m thick and swarmed out of the plaza in total disarray. Pizarro's horsemen charged after them, hacking down as many Indians as they could. Meanwhile, Pizarro himself led a small contingent that succeeded in capturing Atahualpa. As the sun set over Cajamarca on

**Francisco Pizarro**

the evening of November 16, the course of Latin American history was changed forever. With an estimated 7000 Indians dead and Atahualpa captured, the small band of Spaniards had succeeded beyond their wildest hopes. Now they literally were conquistadors.

Almost immediately after his capture, Atahualpa became aware of one of the weaknesses of the Spaniards – their lust for gold. Accordingly, he offered to fill a large room once with gold and twice with silver in return for his freedom. Astounded by their good fortune, the conquistadors quickly agreed to the offer and led Atahualpa to believe that they would not only release him after the ransom was paid, but would also return him to his northern lands around Quito.

This was a wily move on the part of Pizarro. By promising Atahualpa's return to Quito, he effectively controlled the northern part of the Inca Empire. And by holding Atahualpa captive, Pizarro also maintained control of the southern half of the empire, whose inhabitants, having just been beaten by Atahualpa in a civil war, considered Pizarro a liberator rather than an invader. Playing one Inca faction against the other in this way was Pizarro's strongest weapon. If the Inca Empire had been united when the Spanish arrived, the story of the conquest would have been entirely different.

The gold and silver slowly began to arrive at Cajamarca. Pizarro sent some of his men to Cuzco to ensure the collection of the ransom. Meanwhile, Atahualpa was held as a royal prisoner, with the servants and comfort to which he was accustomed. The Spanish were in no great hurry to collect the ransom; they were also waiting for reinforcements. On April 14, 1533, Diego de Almagro arrived from the coast with 150 soldiers, almost doubling the Spanish force at Cajamarca. Atahualpa began to suspect that the Spaniards were lying to him and that he wouldn't be released and allowed to return to Quito upon payment of the ransom.

Finally, in mid-June of 1533, the ransom was complete, and Pizarro ordered the melting down and distribution of the treasure. Careful records were kept of these procedures, and it is known that about 6000kg of gold and 12,000kg of silver were melted down into gold and silver bullion. At today's prices, this is worth roughly US$57 million, but the artistic value of the ornaments and implements that were melted down is impossible to estimate or recover. The gold and silver was distributed among the conquistadors in strictly controlled quotas.

Atahualpa, still a prisoner, now knew he was not going to be released. He sent desperate messages to his followers in Quito to come to Cajamarca and rescue him. The Spaniards heard of the rescue attempt and became panic-stricken. Although Pizarro was not anxious to kill the Inca emperor, intending instead to further his own aims by continuing to hold Atahualpa hostage and using him as a puppet ruler, the other leading Spaniards insisted on the Inca's death. Despite the lack of a formal trial, Atahualpa was sentenced to death for attempting to arrange his own rescue. On July 26, 1533, Atahualpa was led out to the center of the Cajamarca plaza to be burned at the stake. At the last hour, Atahualpa accepted baptism, and his sentence was changed to a quicker death by strangulation.

Immediately after Atahualpa's death, the Spaniards crowned Tupac Huallpa, a younger brother of Huascar, as the new Inca emperor. With this puppet ruler, the Spaniards were free to march into Cuzco as liberators. During the march, the new Inca died of an unknown illness, and the Spanish arrived in Cuzco on November 15 without an Inca ruler.

Today, little remains of Inca Cajamarca. Most of the great stone buildings were torn down to be used in the construction of Spanish homes and churches. The great plaza where Atahualpa was captured and later killed was in roughly the same location as today's Plaza de Armas, though in Atahualpa's time, it was a much larger plaza. The Ransom Chamber, or *El Cuarto del Rescate*, which Atahualpa purportedly filled once with gold and twice with silver, is the only building still standing.

For a much more detailed description of the momentous events that took place in Cajamarca in 1532 and 1533, see John Hemming's excellent book *Conquest of the Incas*.

## Information

**Tourist Office** A tourist office at El Complejo de Belén is open weekdays 7:30 am to 1:30 pm and 3:30 to 5:30 pm. They plan on opening a tourist-information booth on the Plaza de Armas in the future. Note that most tourist sites are closed Tuesday.

**Money** The Banco de Crédito, on Lima (also known as Jirón del Comercio) at Apurímac, and Interbanc, on the Plaza de Armas, change traveler's checks. US cash can be changed more quickly with moneychangers on the street near the Plaza de Armas; heed the usual precautions.

**Post & Communications** The post office is at Amazonas 443. You can make long-distance telephone calls 8 am to 10 pm at the Telefónica del Peru on the Plaza de Armas.

Internet facilities were available but erratic at time of writing – ask around.

**Tour Agencies** These provide tourist information and inexpensive guided tours of the city and surroundings. They claim to have English-speaking guides, but only one or two guides speak passable English. Cumbe

Mayo Tours (☎ 82-2938, Puga 635) and Cajamarca Tours (☎ 82-2813, 82-5674, 2 de Mayo 323) are the ones most recommended by readers, but there are others. Manuel Portal Cabellos at Cumbe Mayo Tours guides adventurous expeditions into the mountains, rivers and rainforests of northeastern Peru.

**Laundry** The lavandería (☎ 92-3454, Puga 545) charges US$1.30 per kilogram.

**Medical Services** The best services are at Clínica Limatambo (☎ 82-4241, Puno 265), west of town.

## El Cuarto del Rescate

The Ransom Chamber, or El Cuarto del Rescate, is the only Inca building still standing in Cajamarca. Although called the Ransom Chamber, the room shown to visitors is where Atahualpa was imprisoned, not where the ransom was stored. The small room has three trapezoidal doorways and a few trapezoidal niches in the inner walls – a typical sign of Inca construction. Although well constructed, it does not compare with the Inca buildings in the Cuzco area.

In the entrance to the site are a couple of modern paintings depicting Atahualpa's capture and imprisonment. Hours are 9 am to 1 pm and 3 to 5:45 pm daily except Tuesday. Entrance is US$1; the ticket includes El Complejo de Belén and El Museo de Etnografía if they are visited the same day.

## El Complejo de Belén

Construction of the church and hospital of Belén began in the latter part of the 17th century. The hospital was run by nuns. Inside, 31 tiny, cell-like bedrooms line the walls of the T-shaped building. In what used to be the women's hospital, there is a small archaeology museum. The kitchen and dispensary of the hospital now houses an unimpressive art museum.

The church next door has a fine cupola and a well-carved and painted pulpit. There are several interesting wood carvings, including an extremely tired-looking Christ sitting cross-legged on his throne, propping up his chin with a double-jointed wrist and looking

Papers confirming conquest of Peru and depicting Pizarro, Valverde and Atahualpa

as though he could do with a pisco sour after a hard day's miracle working. The outside walls of the church are lavishly decorated.

Opening hours are the same as at El Cuarto del Rescate.

## Museo de Etnografía

This small museum is just a few meters from the Complejo del Belén and has the same opening hours. There are limited exhibits of local costumes and clothing, domestic and agricultural implements, musical instruments and crafts made of wood, bone, leather and stone, as well as other examples of Cajamarca culture.

## Plaza de Armas

The plaza is pleasant and has a well-kept topiary garden. The fine central fountain dates to 1692 and commemorates the bicentennial of Columbus's landing in the Americas. The town's inhabitants congregate in the plaza every evening. Strolling and discussing the day's events are traditionally popular activities, more so in this area of northern Peru than other parts of the country.

Two churches face the Plaza de Armas: the cathedral and the church of San Francisco. Both are often illuminated in the evening, especially on weekends. The cathedral is a squat building, which was begun in the late 17th century and has only recently been finished. Like most of Cajamarca's churches, the cathedral has no belfry. This is because the Spanish crown levied a tax on finished churches and so the belfries were not built, leaving the church unfinished and thereby avoiding taxes. San Francisco's belfries were finished this century – too late for the Spanish crown to collect its tax.

### Church of San Francisco

The church of San Francisco and its small Museo de Arte Religioso and catacombs are open 3 to 6 pm weekdays. Admission is about US$0.50. The intricately sculpted Capilla de la Dolorosa (to the right of the church) is considered one of the finest chapels in the city.

### Museo Arqueológico

This small museum at El Batán 289 (not related to the even smaller one in the Belén Complex) is worth visiting. Its varied ceramics collection includes a few examples of Cajamarca pots and an unusual collection of ceremonial spears, also from the same culture. The Cajamarca culture, which existed in the area before the Inca Empire, is little studied and not very well known. The museum also has black-and-white photographs of various historic and prehistoric sites in the Cajamarca area; its director is knowledgeable and willing to talk about the exhibits.

The museum is run by the Universidad de Cajamarca. Hours are 8 am to 2:30 pm weekdays, but you may have to knock on the door to get in. Admission is free.

### Cerro Santa Apolonia

This hill overlooks the city from the southwest and is a prominent Cajamarca landmark. It is easily reached by climbing the stairs at the end of 2 de Mayo. The pre-Hispanic carved rocks at the summit are mainly Inca, but are thought to originally date back to the Chavín period. One of the rocks, known as the Seat of the Inca, has a shape that suggests a throne. The Inca is said to have reviewed his troops from here. There are pretty gardens around the carved rocks and views of the city. Admission to the hilltop is US$0.50.

### Special Events

Carnaval and Corpus Christi are popular feast days in Cajamarca (see the boxed text 'Feast Days in Cajamarca'). Independence day celebrations at the end of July may include a bullfight. Cajamarca's Tourist Festival is around the second week in August. The various cultural events include art shows, folk-music and dancing competitions, beauty pageants and processions. Hotel and other prices go up during all these events and are usually slightly higher in the dry season (May to September).

### Places to Stay – Budget

Many of the cheapest hotels have only cold water, but you can get a hot bath at Baños del Inca. Cheap hotels that advertise hot water usually have it only a few hours a day.

If you're on a really tight budget, some of the cheapest places include the very basic **Hostal Chota** *(La Mar 637)*, which charges about US$3 or US$4 per person and has communal cold showers. Similar is **Hostal Amalia Puga** *(Puga 1118)*. The reasonably clean **Hotel San Francisco** *(☎ 82-3070, Belén 790)* charges about US$5/9 for singles/doubles in basic rooms with private bath and hot water in the mornings. **Hostal Becerra** *(☎ 82-3496, El Batán 195)* charges US$7/10 in rooms with toilet and basin; showers are communal, and hot water is available. **Hostal Dos de Mayo** *(☎ 82-2527, 2 de Mayo 585)* charges US$5/9 in rooms with sink and toilet; the communal showers have hot water in the evening.

*Hotel Plaza* *(☎ 82-2058, Puga 669)* is in an old and colorful building on the Plaza de Armas. Rooms are creaky and basic, but some are fun, with balconies and/or plaza views. They have hot water in the morning and evening. Rates are US$5/9 with shared bath or US$9/14 with private bath. Also on the plaza is **Hostal Peru** (☎ 82-4030, *Puga 605*), which has hot water all day and charges US$8 per person in basic rooms with private bath – bargain for a lower rate.

The clean **Hostal Jusovi** (☎ 82-2920, *Amazonas 637*) has hot water from 6 to 9 am and no water from 10 pm to 5 am. They charge US$7/12 in rooms with private bath. One of the best cheap hotels is **Hostal Prado** (☎ 82-3288, 82-8313, *La Mar 582*), which is clean and has hot water. Some of the staff speak English. Rates are US$5 per person with shared bath or US$12/20 with private bath. **Hostal Santa Apolonia** (☎ 82-8574, 82-7207, *Puga 649*), on the plaza, is also good and clean, and some rooms have plaza views. Rooms have TV, and hot water is available all day. Rates are US$8.50/13.50 in rooms with shared bath and US$14/17 with private bath.

### Places to Stay – Mid-Range

The last two hotels in the budget section have mid-range rooms as well.

**Hotel Casa Blanca** (☎/fax 82-2141, *2 de Mayo 446*) is a thick-walled, creaky-floored, interesting old building on the Plaza de Armas. It charges about US$16/25 for singles/doubles with reliable hot showers. Rooms are rather dark, but most are good-sized and have TV and telephones. Some have up to five beds; this is a cheaper option if you are traveling with a group. Bargain in the low season. The hotel café isn't bad.

**El Portal del Marques** (☎/fax 82-8464, *in Lima 995-2737, Lima 644*) is a pretty, colonial-style hotel in a renovated mansion. There are 14 rooms overlooking a central courtyard. Rooms have private baths and TV, cost US$16/23 and are a good value. There is a restaurant. Another attractive small hotel with colonial ambiance is **Hostal Portada del Sol** (☎/fax 82-3395, *in Lima ☎ 225-4306, 997-2848, Pisagua 731*). Rooms with TV, telephones and warm electric showers are US$17/27. They also have a pleasant café in a courtyard covered with a stained-glass roof.

**Los Pinos Inn** (☎/fax 82-5992, *pinoshostal@ unc.edu.pe, La Mar 521*) is small and elegantly colonial. There are eight nice rooms, all different but all with TV, telephones and private baths. Rates are US$20/30 including continental breakfast. This is a good hotel that is often full, so call ahead. The clean, pleasant **Hotel Cajamarca** (☎ 82-2532, *fax 82-2813, 2 de Mayo 311*) is also in a colonial house and has a decent restaurant. Rates are US$22/31 with bath and hot water. Under the same ownership is the **Hacienda San Vicente** (☎ 82-2644, *fax 82-2813*), which is a rustic, seven-room hotel on a hill overlooking town. There are pleasant gardens, a picnic area and a colonial chapel, which is sometimes used for weddings and baptisms. Rooms have private bath and cost US$25/45 including continental breakfast and transfers to the Hotel Cajamarca or airport at any time.

## Feast Days in Cajamarca

Like most Peruvian Andean towns, Cajamarca is famous for its Carnaval – this one is a particularly wet affair, and its water fights are worse (or better, depending on your point of view) than usual. Local teenagers don't necessarily limit themselves to soaking one another with water – paint, oil and urine have all been reported! The action begins on the Saturday preceding Lent and continues through Shrove Tuesday. The Corpus Christi processions are also very colorful.

Both of these are Catholic feast days and the dates vary each year, depending on the dates for Easter. Carnaval is the last few days before Lent (which, in turn, is 40 days before Palm Sunday, which is the Sunday before Easter). Corpus Christi is the Thursday after Trinity Sunday, which is the Sunday after Whitsunday (Pentecost), which is the seventh Sunday after Easter. Confused fiesta-goers would do well to buy a Catholic calendar for the year they plan on being in Peru.

*Hotel Sierra Galana* (☎ 82-2470, fax 82-2472, Lima 773), on the Plaza de Armas, used to be the government-run Hotel de Turistas and the only good hotel in town. Now the rooms look jaded and worn, though they are clean and have TV, telephones, and private baths. Rates are US$30/40 or US$60 in mini-suites and include continental breakfast.

The modern *Hotel Continental* (☎ 82-2758, 82-3063, fax 82-3024, Amazonas 760) is over a small shopping mall with shops, a café and a bar. Clean singles/doubles with hot water baths, TV, and direct-dial telephones are US$33/43 for standard rooms and US$42/58 for 'special' rooms, which are a bit bigger. A few executive minisuites are US$73. *Las Americas Hotel* (☎/fax 82-3951, Amazonas 618) is similarly priced.

### Places to Stay – Top End
The best in town is the new, modern but quiet and attractive *Hotel El Ingenio* (☎/fax 82-7121, 82-8733, in Lima ☎/fax 446-9322, vhiko@yahoo.com, Vía de Evitamiento 1611-1709). Rooms are large and comfortable, with TV, direct-dial telephones, minirefrigerators and hot water. Some have patios or balconies, and minisuites have a Jacuzzi. The staff are attentive and helpful, and the grounds are nicely landscaped. There is also a good restaurant and bar. It's a 10-minute walk into town. Rates are US$48/66 or US$70 for a king-sized bed and US$87 for a minisuite.

If you want a quiet country resort, try *Hostal Laguna Seca* (☎ 82-3149, ☎/fax 82-3915, lag.seca@infotex.com.pe), 6km from the Baños del Inca. The hotel has a warm swimming pool, and the hot water in all rooms is fed by the natural thermal springs nearby. Horseback riding, massages and health treatments can be arranged. There is a pleasant garden and an adequate restaurant. Rooms are rustic but comfortable. Rates are US$65/89 for singles/doubles and US$98 to US$114 for suites, though walk-in discounts can be arranged when available.

### Places to Eat
The best restaurant is *El Batán – Gran Buffet de Arte* (☎ 82-6025, kok.bolster@computextos.com.pe, El Batán 369). The food

is varied and international; most plates are in the US$5 to US$8 range. Budget travelers can choose from a set menu (one of eight appetizers, one of eight main courses, and a glass of wine or soft drink) for under US$4. On Friday and Saturday nights, they have live shows of local music – anything from folk songs to traditional Andean music to Afro-Peruvian dance rhythms. There is a full bar. They open for lunch and dinner daily except Monday. Upstairs, there is an art gallery with changing shows every month. Paintings are for sale and the quality is surprisingly high. El Batán is definitely worth a visit.

Another favorite is *Salas* (☎ 82-2867, Puga 637) – a big barn of a place on the Plaza de Armas. It's popular with the locals and serves various local dishes such as cuy, delicious corn tamales and *sesos* (cow brains), which I must admit I've never tried. Prices are very reasonable and the ambiance is local and fun. Also good is *El Cajamarques* (☎ 82-3092), next to the Hotel Continental. This is a lovely upscale restaurant that is perhaps too pricey for local people and so is often empty, but the food is good.

For a coffee and snack (or a meal), *Cascanuez Café Bar* (☎ 82-6089, Puga 554) is a good choice. *Baca Loca*, on San Martín, just off the plaza, is a good pizza place. Several hotels have good restaurants, including Hotel Casa Blanca and Hotel Cajamarca, which may have musicians in the evenings.

### Entertainment
Cajamarca has a couple of cinemas, and there may be a reasonably good English-language film screening at one of them.

A good, small and very local bar is the *Usha-Usha* (Puga 142), run by a local musician who likes to tell stories. Usha-Usha does not serve beer (only very strong mixed drinks or soft drinks) and is closed Sunday.

### Shopping
The market on Amazonas is lively and interesting. Local products to look for include *alforjas* (heavy wool or cotton saddlebags), which can be worn over the shoulder or used on horseback. The local eucalyptus honey sold at the market is worth trying.

For general food shopping, the Supermercado San Francisco (Amazonas 780) has a good selection, despite the fact that the entrance is more like a church than a store.

For local art, see El Batán under Places to Eat.

## Getting There & Away

**Air** Flight schedules to Cajamarca are subject to frequent changes, as well as occasional cancellations and delays. At this time, AeroCóndor has a daily morning flight from Lima to Cajamarca stopping at Chimbote, and from Cajamarca to Lima stopping at Trujillo. The AeroCóndor office is in Cajamarca Tours. Their airplane is small and sometimes overbooked, so reconfirm and arrive at the airport early.

Aviación Lider has a nine-seat aircraft flying to Trujillo three times a week. They have an office at Santisteban and Belén. Other airlines have flown here in the recent past.

Local buses for Otuzco pass the airport (US$0.30), or you can take a taxi (US$1.50).

**Bus** Cajamarca is at an ancient crossroads dating back many centuries before the Incas. Nowadays, daily buses leave Cajamarca on roads heading for all four points of the compass.

Most bus terminals are on or close to the 3rd block of a street called Atahualpa (not to be confused with the Atahualpa in the town center), about 1.5km southeast of the town center on the road to the Baños del Inca. A few companies are on Independencia, off the 1st block of the same Atahualpa. The travel agencies in town often will sell bus tickets.

The most important road is the westbound one, which is paved all the way to the Panamericana near Pacasmayo on the coast. From here, you can head north to Chiclayo or south to Trujillo and Lima. Services to Trujillo (US$6 to US$8, 8 to 9 hours), Chiclayo (US$5.50 to US$7.50, 7 hours) and Lima (US$10 to US$15, 15 to 17 hours) are provided by many companies. Most buses to Lima travel overnight, though a few leave as early as 1 pm, arriving before dawn. CIVA

(☎ 82-1460, Atahualpa 303) and Turismo en Bus (☎ 82-3270, Atahualpa 300) have the most expensive and comfortable night buses. Empresa Atahualpa (☎ 82-3060) has OK buses. Cheaper Lima services are provided by TEPSA (☎ 82-3306, Sucre at Reynafarje), Sudamericano (☎ 82-3270, Atahualpa 300), Nor Peru (☎ 82-4550, Atahualpa 179) and Palacios (☎ 82-5855, Atahualpa 312). For Trujillo, most companies leave in the afternoon and arrive late at night. The earliest bus is often with Vulkano (☎ 82-1090, Atahualpa 315) or Empresa Díaz (☎ 82-7504, Ayacucho 753). The Lima-bound companies also stop in Trujillo. For Chiclayo, El Cumbe (☎ 82-3088, Independencia 242) has three or four buses a day and is the best for daytime travel. Sudamericano and Vulkano also have buses to Chiclayo.

The southbound road is the old route to Trujillo via Cajabamba and Huamachuco. The trip to Trujillo takes two or three times longer on this rough dirt road than it does along the newer paved road via Pacasmayo, although the old route is only 60km longer. The scenery is supposedly prettier on the longer route, but most buses are less comfortable and less frequent beyond Cajabamba. Transportes Atahualpa has a noon bus to Cajabamba (US$5, about 7 hours), but the buses are already half full with passengers from Lima and Trujillo when they reach Cajamarca, and the best seats are usually taken. Palacios also serves Cajabamba. For Huamachuco and on to Trujillo, you have to get another bus at Cajabamba.

The rough northbound road passes through wild and attractive countryside via the towns of Hualgayoc (US$5) and Bambamarca (US$5.50) to Chota (US$6, 9 hours). **Hualgayoc** is a mining village in a beautiful setting. **Bambamarca** has a colorful Sunday morning market. There are basic hotels in Bambamarca (try the *Gran Hotel Bolívar*, a block from the plaza) and more hotels in **Chota**. Buses run from Chota to Chiclayo along a very rough road. Daily Empresa Díaz and Nor Peru buses go from Cajamarca to Chota in the morning.

The eastbound road heads to Celendín, then across the Andes, past Chachapoyas and down into the Amazon lowlands. The road between Celendín and Chachapoyas is very bad and transport is unreliable; if you're going to Chachapoyas, you are advised to travel from Chiclayo via Bagua, unless you have plenty of time and patience. Buses to Celendín (US$5, 5 hours) leave Cajamarca daily with Transportes Atahualpa, Palacios and Empresa Díaz.

## Getting Around

It is easy to find transport to the Baños del Inca. Colectivo taxis and minibuses leave frequently from 2 de Mayo near Amazonas. The fare is US$0.50. Cheaper buses travel along Lima and through the Plaza de Armas to the Baños.

Buses for the Ventanillas de Otuzco leave frequently from about 500m north of the Plaza de Armas and two blocks past the bridge. The fare is US$0.50. The buses go past the airport (US$0.30) and on to Otuzco, leaving you within 500m of the archaeological site.

Bus routes and departure points change occasionally, so ask at the tourist office for the latest details. Other local places are not serviced by public bus, though it is worth checking with the tourist office to see if this has changed. Walk, hitchhike, take a taxi or join a tour.

## AROUND CAJAMARCA

There are several places of interest around Cajamarca. Some can be reached on public transport, while others must be visited on foot, by taxi or with a guided tour. The tour agencies may pool their clients to form a group for any trip, although more expensive individual outings can be arranged.

## Baños del Inca

These natural hot springs are 6km from Cajamarca. The water is channeled into many private cubicles (US$0.50 to US$1.50 per hour), some large enough for up to six people at a time. There is a public pool (US$0.50), which is cleaned on Monday and Friday.

Atahualpa was camped by these hot springs when Pizarro arrived in the area, but

there is nothing to see today except for the springs themselves.

## Aylambo

This village is 3km south of Cajamarca via Avenida Independencia. You can visit the *Escuela Taller de Alfarería* (a pottery trade school) where pottery is sold.

## Cumbe Mayo

Locals claim the name of this site is derived from the Quechua term *kumpi mayo*, or 'well-made water channel.' The site, 23km from Cajamarca by road, has well-engineered pre-Inca channels running for several kilometers across the bleak mountain tops. Nearby are some caves containing petroglyphs. The countryside is high, windswept and slightly eerie. Superstitious stories are told about the area's eroded rock formations, which look like groups of shrouded mountain climbers.

The site can be reached on foot via a sign-posted road from the Cerro Santa Apolonia. The walk takes about four hours if you take the obvious short cuts and ask every passerby for directions. Guided bus tours (US$7) are offered in Cajamarca and last four to five hours. They have been recommended.

## Ventanillas de Otuzco & Combayo

These pre-Inca necropoles consist of hundreds of funerary niches built into the hillside, hence the name *ventanillas*, or 'windows.' The site of Otuzco is in beautiful countryside, 8km northeast of Cajamarca. You can walk here from either Cajamarca or the Baños del Inca. There are also local buses or tours (US$5). The larger and better preserved Ventanillas de Combayo are 30km away and are visited with a US$10 tour.

## Llacanora & Hacienda la Colpa

The picturesque little village of Llacanora is 13km from Cajamarca. Some of the inhabitants still play the traditional 3m-long bamboo trumpet, called the *clarín*. A few kilometers away is the Hacienda la Colpa,

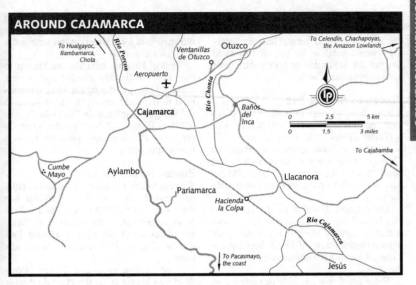

## AROUND CAJAMARCA

To Hualgayoc, Bambamarca, Chota

Río Porcon

Aeropuerto

Ventanillas de Otuzco

Otuzco

To Celendín, Chachapoyas, the Amazon Lowlands

Río Chonta

Cajamarca

Baños del Inca

0    2.5    5 km
0    1.5    3 miles

To Cajabamba

Cumbe Mayo

Aylambo

Pariamarca

Llacanora

Hacienda la Colpa

Río Cajamarca

To Pacasmayo, the coast

Jesús

which is usually visited on a tour combined with Llacanora (about US$5 per person). The hacienda is a working cattle ranch; and in the afternoons, the ranch hands herd the cattle into their stalls by calling out each animal by name. This is a locally famous tourist attraction.

### The Road from the Coast

The highway from the coast to Cajamarca is paved all the way, passing through **Tembladera**, 46km from the Panamericana junction. Interestingly, Tembladera is named not after the tremors of earthquakes, but after the trembling and shivering of malaria victims. The disease was once common in this rice-growing area. Nearby is a new dam and reservoir, which are both visible on the right side.

Another 41km brings you to the mining village of **Chilete** and a basic *hotel*. A partially paved road southwest of Chilete comes out at Chicama on the coast and offers a shorter but much rougher route between Trujillo and Cajamarca.

On a side road 24km north of Chilete is the village of **San Pablo**. It has a basic *hotel* and two or three buses a day to Chilete. An hour's walk from San Pablo is the Chavín site of **Kuntur Wasi** and its stone monoliths. Tours can be arranged to Kuntur Wasi in Cajamarca. You can also walk to San Pablo from Cajamarca via Cumbe Mayo; the walk takes three or four days and is described in *Peru and Bolivia: Backpacking and Trekking* by Hilary Bradt, Jane Letham and John Pilkington.

The drive from the coast goes from desert coastal scenery to green mountains in a matter of a few hours and becomes more attractive the closer one gets to Cajamarca.

### CAJABAMBA

The old route from Cajamarca to Trujillo takes 15 to 22 hours along 360km of dirt road via Cajabamba and Huamachuco. Although this route passes through more interesting scenery and towns than the new road, bus travel is very rough, and some buses travel only at night.

Cajabamba is a very pleasant small town with a 19th-century atmosphere. You'll see more mules than cars in the streets, and the whitewashed houses and red-tiled roofs give the place a colonial air. There is a cinema on the pretty Plaza de Armas. The feast of La

Virgen del Rosario is celebrated around the second week of October with bullfights, processions, dances and general bucolic carousing. Hotels tend to be full at this time. Market day is Sunday, so hotels tend to fill up on weekends as well.

## Places to Stay & Eat

All hotels suffer from periodic water shortages and dim lighting. The best place to stay is *Hostal Flores* (☎ 85-1086, L Prado 137), on the Plaza de Armas, next to the Banco de Crédito. There is a very small sign on the hotel's door. They charge US$3 or US$4 per person. Ask for a room with a balcony onto the plaza.

The cheaper *Hotel Ramal* (Grau 624) and *Hostal Bolívar* (Ugarte 603) are both within a block of the plaza. On the street behind Hostal Flores, at José Sabogal 692, is a cheap basic hotel without a sign (knock on the door).

There are a few passable restaurants on or near the plaza.

## Getting There & Away

Palacios (☎ 85-1348, Lara 551) has a daily bus for Cajamarca and another for Huamachuco. There are also trucks leaving from the market in the morning for Huamachuco. Ask where the Transportes Atahualpa bus for Cajamarca leaves from.

## HUAMACHUCO
☎ 044

The small colonial town of Huamachuco is 53km beyond Cajabamba by very poor road (buses take 3 to 5 hours) and 190km from Trujillo. It has a few places to stay and an impressive Plaza de Armas.

The ruins of the pre-Inca hilltop fort of **Marcahuamachuco** lie within reach of Huamachuco itself, two to three hours away on foot.

During the dry season, there is transport east to **Pataz**, a mining town in the Marañón valley. From Pataz, expeditions can be mounted to the little-explored ruins of various jungle cities, including the recently discovered **Gran Pajatén**. This is an undertaking for explorers and archaeologists only.

The ruins are north of the recently formed Parque Nacional Río Abiseo, which has no infrastructure for travelers at this time and is very hard to get to.

West of Huamachuco, the road heads to the coast at Trujillo, passing the mining village of Shorey after 60 km. Here, a branch road to the south traverses about 40km to the village of **Santiago de Chuco**, birthplace of César Vallejo (1892-1938), who is considered to be Peru's greatest poet. His house is now a museum.

## Places to Stay & Eat

There are three or four cheap hotels in Huamachuco, the best of which is *Hostal San Francisco* (☎ 44-1176, Sánchez Carrión 380). It boasts hot water – the others don't. Rates are about US$4 per person. *Hostal Fernando* (Bolívar 361) is a clean and basic hotel.

Most restaurants are either along Sánchez Carrión or on the Plaza de Armas.

## Getting There & Away

Vuelos Lider, in Trujillo, sometimes flies to Huamachuco.

Palacios (☎ 44-1351, R Castilla 108) is one of two companies going to Trujillo (8 hours).

## CELENDÍN
☎ 044

This pleasant village is 118km away from Cajamarca and at approximately the same altitude. There's not much to do in Celendín, and most travelers just pass through en route to Chachapoyas. There is one cinema that, when I was there in October, was showing an unseasonable film about the resurrection. Market day is Sunday. The annual fiesta, held from July 29 to August 3, coincides with the Fiestas Patrias and features bullfighting with matadors from Mexico and Spain. The fiesta of La Virgen del Carmen is celebrated on July 16.

## Places to Stay & Eat

There are three basic hotels on the 300 block of 2 de Mayo. *Hostal Maxmar* (☎ 85-5414, 2 de Mayo 349) charges US$3 or US$4 per person. Some rooms have private bathrooms, and hot water is available. The manager speaks English and has local information. Other hotels nearby at about this price are the reasonably clean *Hostal Amazonas* and *Hotel José Gálvez*.

The clean *Hostal Celendín* (☎ 85-5041, *Unión 305*), on the Plaza de Armas, charges about US$7 per person in rooms with a toilet and sink. Hot water is sometimes available in the communal shower. Also try *Hostal Loyers* (☎ 85-5210, *J Gálvez 440*). There are a couple of other basic hotels.

The best restaurants (though nothing to get excited about) are *La Reserve* (*J Gálvez 313*) and *Jalisco*, on the Plaza de Armas.

### Getting There & Away

Although both roads into Celendín are terrible, the road from Cajamarca is far better than the one from Chachapoyas.

Empresa Díaz, Transportes Atahualpa and Palacios (☎ 85-5322) are all on or next to the Plaza de Armas (Palacios is at the Hostal Celendín) and have daily departures to Cajamarca (US$5, 5 hours).

### FROM CELENDÍN TO CHACHAPOYAS

Transport from Celendín to Chachapoyas is mostly in trucks, because buses have difficulty negotiating the very demanding but beautiful road, which may be impassable during the wet season. During dry months, there may be one or two minibuses a week (recently on Thursday and Sunday). Pickup trucks don't leave every day, so you can be stuck in Celendín for several days waiting for the next departure, particularly in the wet season. The trip can take from 12 to 24 hours, more if there's a landslide. Road improvements have been planned for years – ask in Cajamarca.

The road to Chachapoyas climbs from Celendín at 2625m over a 3085m pass before dropping steeply to the Río Marañón at **Balsas**, 62km away from and 1600m lower than Celendín. There is a daily truck from Celendín to Balsas (about 5 hours in the dry season). There is a basic hotel here, but onward travel is difficult; most vehicles are coming through from Celendín. The road then climbs again through spectacular rainforests and cloudforests to emerge at the 3678m high point of the drive, the aptly named Abra de Barro Negro, or Black Mud Pass, which gives you an idea of the road conditions during the rainy season. From the pass, the road drops to Leimebamba (immediately following) at the head of the Río Utcubamba valley and follows the river as it descends past Tingo (near the Kuélap ruins) and on to Chachapoyas, about 220km from Celendín. The Balsas-to-Leimebamba section is the worst.

The normal route to Chachapoyas is from the coast at Chiclayo via Bagua; this is a much easier, though less spectacular route.

## LEIMEBAMBA

This remote but attractive little colonial highland town, just over 2000m above sea level, is surrounded by many poorly known archaeological sites. One of the most interesting is on a cliff above Laguna de los Cóndores, where a tomb containing 217 mummies was investigated in 1997. It takes one strenuous eight- to 12-hour day to hike there, or you can hire horses. The mummies are now being studied in the Centro Mallqui in Leimebamba. There is a small museum on the main plaza, and a new, Danish-sponsored museum will open 3km south of town in 1999. A new tomb, three day's walk south from Leimebamba, was discovered in 1999. Local guides (ask at the museums) will take you to visit this and other sites, some of which are easily visited on a day trip, others require several days. Homer Ullilen, the son of the owner of the Hospedaje de la Laguna de los Cóndores, can guide you to sites on their land. Horses cost about US$6 per day, plus another US$6 for the *arriero*, or muleteer.

### Places to Stay & Eat

There are two basic, cheap hostels with an erratic water supply and electricity in the evening. They are on the road between the plaza and the river and charge US$3 per person. *Hospedaje de la Laguna de los Cóndores*, two blocks from the plaza, charges US$5 per person and has hot showers. The owners have land around the archaeological site and provide information. The best of the simple restaurants are *Celis Café, Restaurant Turística* and *El Caribe.*

## Getting There & Away

A 3 am bus leaves daily for Chachapoyas (4 hours) and returns from Chachapoyas at noon Monday to Saturday, and 3 am Sunday. Sign up the night before for a space. There are occasional trucks to Chachapoyas and Celendín.

## FROM CHICLAYO TO CHACHAPOYAS

This route follows the old Panamericana north from Chiclayo for 100km to a turnoff a few kilometers before the small town of Olmos. From the turnoff, a paved road heads east over the Andes via the Porculla Pass, which, at 2145m, is the lowest pass across the Peruvian Andes. The road then drops to the Río Marañón valley. About 190km from the Panamericana turnoff, you reach the town of **Jaén**, which is not always a stop on the bus route because it is a few kilometers off the main road. Although of little touristic interest, Jaén is a place to break the journey. An agricultural center, it has about 10 hotels, including *Hotel Cesar* (☎ 074-73-1277, fax 73-1491, Mesones Muro 168) and *Hotel El Bosque* (☎ 074-73-1492, fax 73-1184, Mesones Muro 632). Both have rooms with private hot showers, telephones and cable TV that cost about US$22 for a double. El Bosque has a pool. Ask around for cheaper places, some of which have rooms with private baths. Several buses a day go to and from Chiclayo (6 hours).

From Jaén, a northbound road heads to San Ignacio near the Ecuadorian border, about 100km away. Since the peace treaty was signed with Ecuador in late 1998, it may soon become possible to cross into Ecuador at this remote outpost.

Continuing east, about 50km beyond the Jaén turnoff on a side road is the village of **Bagua Chica.** It is in the Marañón valley, in the westernmost jungle area in Peru, and offers basic accommodations. Because it is in a low enclosed valley (elevation about 500m), many Peruvians claim that this is the hottest town in the country. From here, a long and difficult trip can be made by road and river to Iquitos (see Sarameriza in the Amazon Basin chapter). The bus usually goes through **Bagua Grande** on the main road about 20km away from Bagua Chica. Bagua Grande has slightly better hotels, including *Hotel Iris* (☎ 074-75-4115), which charges about US$12 for a double with bath; *Hostal Francys* (☎ 074-75-4038); and *Hostal Gran Atlanta* (☎ 074-75-4260), which charges about US$9 for a double. These hotels are close to each other on Avenida Chachapoyas. Minibuses and colectivos run between Jaén and Bagua several times a day. From Bagua Grande, buses, colectivos and pickup trucks make the journey to Moyobamba. This road follows the Río Utcubamba valley for about 70km to the crossroads town of Pedro Ruíz, about 90 minutes from Bagua Grande (see From Pedro Ruíz to Rioja later in this chapter). From here, a bumpy and rough southbound road branches down to Chachapoyas, 54km and another 90 minutes away.

## CHACHAPOYAS
☎ 074

This pleasant little town of 20,000 inhabitants stands on the eastern slopes of the Andes at 2335m.

The Chachapoyan culture was conquered but not completely subdued by the Incas a few decades before the Spaniards arrived. When the Europeans showed up, local chief Curaca Huáman supposedly aided them toward their conquest. Local historians claim that San Juan de la Frontera de las Chachapoyas was the third town founded by the Spaniards in Peru (after Piura and Lima) and, at one time, was the seventh-largest town of Peru.

Chachapoyas is the capital of the Department of Amazonas, which, despite its name, is a mountainous area. The department used to include the lowland regions east to the Brazilian border but, after the 1942 war with Ecuador, these low-lying sections became the new Department of Loreto, and Chachapoyas remained the capital of

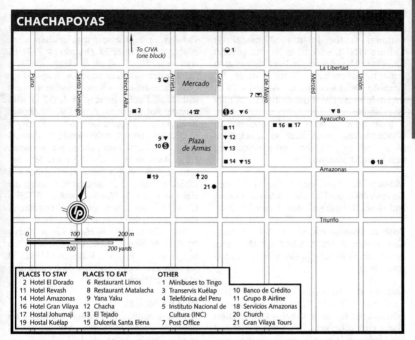

CHACHAPOYAS

| PLACES TO STAY | PLACES TO EAT | OTHER | |
|---|---|---|---|
| 2 Hotel El Dorado | 6 Restaurant Limos | 1 Minibuses to Tingo | 10 Banco de Crédito |
| 11 Hotel Revash | 8 Restaurant Matalacha | 3 Transervis Kuélap | 11 Grupo 8 Airline |
| 14 Hotel Amazonas | 9 Yana Yaku | 4 Telefónica del Perú | 18 Servicios Amazonas |
| 16 Hotel Gran Vilaya | 12 Chacha | 5 Instituto Nacional de | 20 Church |
| 17 Hostal Johumaji | 13 El Tejado | Cultura (INC) | 21 Gran Vilaya Tours |
| 19 Hostal Kuélap | 15 Dulcería Santa Elena | 7 Post Office | |

Amazonas. The department's contact with the Amazon is chiefly through the Río Marañón, one of Peru's two major tributaries of the Amazon and the one that reaches farthest west into the Andes. The Marañón bisects the department and forms most of its western border with the Department of Cajamarca.

The Department of Amazonas has long been difficult to reach, and even today it remains one of the least visited areas of Peru. Along with the neighboring Department of San Martín, it contains vast tracts of the little-explored cloudforest of the Andes' eastern slopes. Within these highland forests are some of Peru's most fascinating and least known archaeological ruins. Although the ravages of weather and time, as well as the more recent attentions of grave robbers and treasure seekers, have caused damage to many of the ruins, some have survived remarkably well and can be visited by the adventurous traveler.

The best known and one of the most accessible is the magnificent site of Kuélap, described later in this chapter. Travelers or archaeologists who want to visit one of the scores of other sites in the area should seek further information in Chachapoyas. Most trips will require at least sleeping bags, and sometimes tents and food as well. One good center for exploration is **Levanto**, a small village about three to four hour's walk south along an Inca road, or 1.5 hours by minibuses in the early morning. Ask the mayor for a place to sleep. Another popular trip is the four- or five-day Gran Vilaya trek from Choctemal to the Marañón canyon through pristine cloudforest and past many ruins.

Chachapoyas is a quiet, friendly town. It provides an excellent base for visiting ruins and has been called 'the archaeological capital of Peru.' The traditional evening pastime of strolling around the Plaza de Armas is a favorite way of relaxing and socializing.

## Information

There is no tourist office. There is a small museum at the Instituto Nacional de Cultura (INC), which has moved several times in the last decade. In 1999, they plan to move to Ayacucho at Grau. Booklets (in Spanish) about local archaeological sites, as well as information about visiting them, may be available here.

Most basic supplies can be obtained in Chachapoyas. Items such as specialized foods, camera gear, film and sunblock are best brought with you.

**Money** The Banco de Crédito will change US cash and traveler's checks. Several stores and Hotel Revash will also change US cash.

**Post & Communications** Post and telephone offices are marked on the map. Access email at Servicios Amazonas (Amazonas 566).

**Guides & Tours** Martín Antonio Olivo Chumbe (☎ 77-7212, Piura 909) can be contacted at the Reina de la Selva radio station above Hotel Revash. He is a recommended local guide and can take you to many nearby ruins, including an expedition to see the enigmatic sarcophagi (coffins in the shape of human beings) high on a cliff wall in the jungle. Trips can last from a day to over a week if you want. He speaks Spanish and doesn't have any gear, so you need to be self-sufficient with equipment.

Gran Vilaya Tours (vilaya@yahoo.com, Grau 624; also contact Hotel Gran Vilaya) has native, English-speaking guides who can arrange day and multiday excursions including archaeology, trekking, climbing, and horseback riding. Englishman Rob Dover is very enthusiastic and knowledgeable about the area. They are planning on opening a Café de Guías information center in Hotel Gran Vilaya in late 1999.

Hostal Revash arranges day tours to Kuélap.

## Places to Stay

*Hostal Johumaji* (☎ 77-0712, Ayacucho 711) has small, carpeted rooms with good lighting and is one of the best cheap hotels. Rates are US$7/11 for singles/doubles with private hot showers, or a little less with cold showers. Also good is *Hotel El Dorado* (☎ 77-7047, Ayacucho 1062), which is clean, safe and friendly and has some rooms with up to four beds. Rates are US$3.50 per person for rooms with shared cold showers, or US$7/11 with private hot showers. Also OK is *Hostal Kuélap* (77-7136, Amazonas 1057); it charges US$3.50 per person with shared cold showers and US$7/12.50 with private hot showers. *Hotel Amazonas* (☎ 77-7199, Grau 565) has some rooms with a plaza view. Rates are US$8/11 with private hot bath. Nearby, the clean and friendly *Hotel Revash* (☎ 77-7391, Grau 517) has a courtyard and restaurant. Rates are US$10/13 with private hot shower.

The best in town is *Hotel Gran Vilaya* (☎ 77-7664, fax 77-8154, vilaya@wayna.rcp .net.pe, Ayacucho 755). Rates are US$25/33 for standard rooms and US$36 for a couple of superior rooms.

## Places to Eat

A locally popular restaurant is *Chacha*, on the plaza. People go there to socialize as well as eat. On the same block, *El Tejado* has large set lunches. Also good for set lunches as well as rice dishes is *Restaurant Limos*, on Ayacucho. *Restaurant Matalacha* (77-8325, Ayacucho 616) has good, large portions of the usual Peruvian fare and good juices. There's a row of juice kiosks at the *mercado*; they claim to use boiled water. *Dulcería Santa Elena* (Amazonas 800) is a recommended bakery.

## Entertainment

The evening promenade around the plaza is the main entertainment. *Yana Yaku* (Arrieta 532) is a pleasant upstairs café and bar with decent cocktails and plaza views. There is also a disco on the plaza.

## Getting There & Away

**Air** Services have been erratic over the years, and there is often only one flight a week to Lima with either Grupo 8 (with a counter inside the Hostal Revash) or TdobleA.

**Bus** The frequently traveled route to Chiclayo (US$7 to US$10) via Bagua normally takes 10 hours in the dry season, or much longer after heavy rain. Transervis Kuélap (☎ 77-8128, Arrieta 412) has a daily bus to Chiclayo at 3 pm, arriving at the TEPSA terminal. CIVA (☎ 77-8048, Arrieta 279) has a daily 4 pm bus to Chiclayo and a 10:30 am bus for Lima (25 hours). Several minibuses go to Tingo (US$1.75, 1½ hours) and may continue on to María (US$3). Taxis charge about US$15 to Tingo and US$25 to María. There are also minibuses to Leimebamba (4 hours).

To continue farther into the Amazon Basin, take a minibus to the crossroads at Pedro Ruíz (US$2, 1½ hours) and wait for an eastbound bus. No direct buses run from Chachapoyas to Moyobamba at this time. A taxi to Pedro Ruíz is US$15, and colectivo taxis are US$3 per person.

Other local destinations are serviced by trucks and minibuses that leave from the Plaza de Armas or market areas. It's a matter of asking around.

## AROUND CHACHAPOYAS

The best place from which to reach the important site of Kuélap used to be the village of Tingo. But a road has now been built, via the villages of Choctemal and María, to within about a kilometer of the site.

In Tingo, there's the basic *Albergue Léon* (US$6 for a double) behind *Restaurant Kuélap*. There's a couple of other restaurants. *Hacienda Chillo*, about 5km south of Tingo, is a nice rustic place to stay, get information about local ruins and arrange mule hire. The owner's name is Oscar Arce – most locals know him. Clean, simple accommodations are about US$30 per person including all meals, but there's no hot water. A German anthropologist, Pieter Lerche, lives nearby and is a good source for archaeological and anthropological information about the area.

Choctemal, closer to Kuélap, has the simple new *Choctemal Lodge* just above the village. It's clean and charges about US$10 per person including meals. Minibuses continue about twice a day to María, from where it's a two-hour walk to Kuélap, unless you have a private vehicle or taxi.

## A Lively Way to Fly

The military airline Grupo 8 has infrequent flights from Lima into various isolated towns in the mountains and jungles. The flights are mainly designed to aid Peruvians living in remote areas. Foreigners can get on these flights if there is space available (which is not very often), and it is always easier to catch a flight in a town other than Lima. Flights are usually delayed, but can be quite an incredible experience.

A friend tells me that Grupo 8 often uses old Russian Antonovs for these flights. Passengers sit on benches along the fuselage walls, and mountains of cargo (including chickens) are piled in between. On one flight, a passenger's two guinea pigs escaped. He ran up and down the plane trying to capture the animals until an air-force crew member appeared, demanding to know what was going on. After hearing the explanation, he replied urgently, 'You'd better catch them fast, because they might chew through the cables, and the controls won't respond.'

## Kuélap

This immense ruined city in the mountains southeast of Chachapoyas is, for most travelers, the main reason to spend time in the region. Kuélap is the best preserved and most accessible of the major ruins in the area. Despite this, the site receives only a few small groups of visitors per day.

In common with the other sites in the area, Kuélap is referred to as a pre-Inca city, though little is known about the people who built it. The Chachapoyas area was the center of a highland people known variously as the Chachapoyans or the Sachupoyans, who were incorporated into the Inca Empire by the Inca Huayna Capac in the late 15th century. They left massive walled cities and fortresses on many of the area's mountaintops. The stonework of these sites is somewhat rougher looking than Inca stonework, but is embellished with patterns and designs missing from the Inca work.

Kuélap is about 3100m above sea level on a ridge high above the left bank of the Río Utcubamba. It is an oval-shaped city about 600m long and entirely surrounded by a massive defensive wall 6m to 12m high. Three entrances pierce this wall. The principal entrance, still used today, leads into an impressive, funnel-shaped, high-walled passageway. This is a highly defensible entrance; it would have been well-nigh impossible for attackers to scale these high walls without being repulsed by projectiles from the defenders perched high above them. Once inside the site, the visitor will find over 400 buildings, most of which are round. One, named *El Tintero* (The Inkpot), is a mysterious underground chamber where, it is locally said, pumas were kept and human sacrifices were thrown in. Another is a lookout tower. The views are excellent.

**Information** The guardians at Kuélap are very friendly and helpful. At least one of them is almost always on hand to show visitors around and answer questions. Don José Gabriel Portocarrero Chávez has been there for years and can show you around the ruins. He is a good source of information on this and other ruins in the area.

The small hostel on the site is run by the guardians. It has a few beds (US$2 each), but if there are more of you, sleeping on the floor is no problem (bring sleeping bags). If you have a tent, camping is also possible. You should carry or purify water, though soft drinks are usually for sale. Basic food is available – but bringing your own is still a good idea. The guardians can arrange simple and inexpensive meals cooked by family members. A small tip or present for the guardians is appreciated – flashlight batteries, a magazine or newspaper, chocolate or canned (or other) food are good gifts.

Entry to the site is US$4.

**Getting There & Away** From Tingo, locals can point out the path to you. You can hire mules to take you or your gear up to the ruins. Hiking up into the mountains to

finally emerge at Kuélap, which is not easy to see until you are almost in front of the ruins, is an exhilarating though strenuous (some say grueling) experience.

The trail climbs from the south end of Tingo at 1900m to the ruins about 1200m above. There are some signposts on the way, and the trail is not very difficult to follow; the main problem is the steepness of the climb. It takes about five to six hours to climb to Kuélap, so it's best to spend the night there. If you leave Chachapoyas in the morning, you can reach the ruins by midafternoon. Remember to bring water, because there is little available at Kuélap and none on the trail. During the rainy season (October to April), especially the latter half, the trail can become very muddy and travel can be difficult.

From Choctemal Lodge, you can hike to Kuélap in about three hours, and from María in about two hours. You can hire a vehicle (best arranged in Chachapoyas) to drive you to within a kilometer of the site.

A good, inexpensive way to go is to take the first minibus in the morning from Chachapoyas to María and continue to Kuélap on foot. Overnight at the site hostel, spend the morning looking around, and walk to the Choctemal Lodge in the afternoon, returning to Chachapoyas the following day.

## FROM PEDRO RUÍZ TO RIOJA

Pedro Ruíz is the small village at the junction of the road to Chachapoyas from the Bagua-to-Moyobamba road. If traveling from Chachapoyas, you can wait here for vehicles to Rioja and Moyobamba. There are a couple of hotels. *Hotel Amazonas*, next to the police station, is clean but has only cold showers. Rates here are US$5/8 with shared and US$7/10 with private bath. The better-looking *Casa Blanca* by the road junction is US$11/16 with private bath.

Crowded minibuses run between Pedro Ruíz and Nuevo Cajamarca (US$7) throughout the day until 8 pm. More comfortable buses pass through Pedro Ruíz from 2 pm until late at night, going to Rioja, Moyobamba (7 hours) or Tarapoto (10 hours).

Ask the locals what time the buses are expected to come through, and be prepared to wait, as they are sometimes full. The road to Tarapoto is paved for the most part.

The journey east from Pedro Ruíz is spectacular – the road climbs over two major passes and drops into fantastic high jungle vegetation in between. It's definitely worth traveling this section in daylight.

One or two hours east of Pedro Ruíz is Laguna Pomacocha. Just before the lake is the village of **Florida**, where there is a basic cheap hotel used by truck drivers. Just beyond the lake is the village of **Balzapata**. Pickup trucks and minibuses provide service between Pedro Ruíz and Balzapata (US$2.50) several times a day during daylight hours. Balzapata is on a ridge overlooking the lake, has a few cheap hotels and restaurants and is a nicer place to spend the night than Pedro Ruíz. You can catch the Moyobamba-bound buses as they come through Balzapata.

A brand-new town built in the 1970s, **Nueva Cajamarca** is inhabited by colonists from the highlands. It has a couple of basic cheap hotels, but it is better to continue in one of the frequent minibuses along the improved road to Rioja (US$1.10, 30 minutes).

## RIOJA
☎ 094
Rioja is a small but busy town with an airport that services both Rioja and nearby Moyobamba, the capital of the Department of San Martín. Both towns were severely damaged by the earthquake on May 29, 1990, and again in a smaller quake in 1991, but they have been rebuilt since then.

There is a Banco de Crédito (Grau 709).

## Places to Stay
There are three or four basic hotels along Avenida Grau. *Residencial Rocio* (☎ 55-8532, Grau 740) is a fair value at US$7/11 with private bath. Cheaper ones are *Hostal San Martín* (☎ 55-8037, Grau 540) and *Hostal Santa Rosa* (☎ 55-8028, Grau 500). The best is *Hostal Vanessa* (☎ 55-8586, fax 55-8013, Faustino Maldonado 505) at

US$18/22. But Moyobamba has a better selection.

## Getting There & Away
**Air** TANS has one or two flights a week to and from Lima. Aero Continente (☎ 55-8622, 55-8438, 2 de Mayo 516) used to have two flights a week, but they are suspended until further notice. Light aircraft may serve other jungle towns. Taxis to the airport leave from the Plaza de Armas.

**Bus** Plenty of minibuses leave from the plaza for Moyobamba (US$1.50, 30 minutes). Buses, minibuses and colectivos go to Tarapoto (US$4 to US$8). Paredes Estrella has buses leaving from next to the Aero Continente office for Tarapoto and for Chiclayo (US$9) daily at noon. Guadalupe (Grau 377) has buses for Lima at 2:30, 6 and 7 pm.

## MOYOBAMBA
☎ 094
A good road links Rioja, at 1400m, with the small town of Moyobamba, at 860m. Moyobamba is the capital of the Department of San Martín and was founded in 1542, soon after the conquest. Moyobamba is a pleasant town and has recovered from the 1990 and 1991 earthquakes.

## Information
There is no tourist office, but you can try asking at the Instituto Nacional de Cultura (INC; ☎ 56-2281) for information. They have a small local museum, open 9 am to 1 pm and 3 to 5:30 pm weekdays.

Money can be changed at the Banco de Crédito (☎ 56-2054, A Alvarado 903). Inforvision (San Martín 425) has Internet access.

## Things to See & Do
The local **hot springs**, or *baños termales*, are about an hour's walk south of town on the Jepelacio road – ask anyone for directions. A mototaxi will cost about US$1, or you can take a Jepelacio bus. There are both hot and cold swimming pools, and the place is very crowded on weekends. Admission is US$3, and they are open until 10 pm.

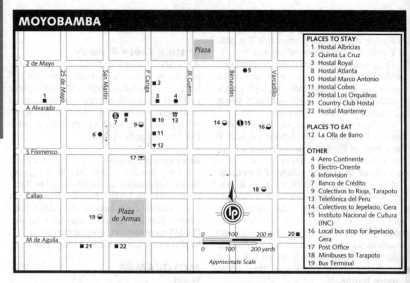

**MOYOBAMBA**

PLACES TO STAY
1 Hostal Albricias
2 Quinta La Cruz
3 Hostal Royal
8 Hostal Atlanta
10 Hostal Marco Antonio
11 Hostal Cobos
20 Hostal Los Orquídeas
21 Country Club Hostal
22 Hostal Monterrey

PLACES TO EAT
12 La Olla de Barro

OTHER
4 Aero Continente
5 Electro-Oriente
6 Inforvision
7 Banco de Crédito
9 Colectivos to Rioja, Tarapoto
13 Teléfonica del Peru
14 Colectivos to Jepelacio, Gera
15 Instituto Nacional de Cultura (INC)
16 Local bus stop for Jepelacio, Gera
17 Post Office
18 Minibuses to Tarapoto
19 Bus Terminal

The **Cataratas del Gera** are quite impressive waterfalls near the Gera hydroelectric project. They can be visited with a free permit, which is available from the offices of Electro-Oriente (☎ 56-2032, 2 de Mayo 589). Take a bus to Jepelacio (US$1.50), and then it's a one- to two-hour walk. Ask anyone in Jepelacio. Go in the morning so as not to get stranded on the way back. A taxi will charge US$18 round trip including waiting time at the falls.

### Places to Stay & Eat

The cheapest is the basic *Quinta La Cruz* (☎ 56-2204), which charges US$3 per person and has shared showers. The basic *Hostal Monterrey* (☎ 56-2145, M de Aguila 584) charges US$4 per person in rooms with private cold showers. Better rooms are available at *Country Club Hostal* (☎/fax 56-2110, M de Aguila 660), which charges US$7/11 and has private baths and a garden. One of the nicest cheap hotels is the clean *Hostal Albricias* (☎ 56-2142, A Alvarado 1066), which also has a garden and charges US$8/11 with private bath. The acceptable *Hostal Cobos* (☎ 56-2153, P Canga 404)

charges US$6/9. *Hostal Royal* (☎ 56-2662, A Alvarado 784) is also OK and charges US$7/12. *Hostal Atlanta* (☎ 56-2063, A Alvarado 865) charges US$8/12 and advertises air-conditioning. *Hostal Los Orquídeas* (☎ 56-2119, M de Aguila 137) is another decent place in this price range.

The best central hotel is *Hostal Marco Antonio* (☎ 56-2045, ☎/fax 56-2319, P Canga 488), which has a restaurant with room service and decent rooms with cable TV, telephones and private hot showers for US$30/42. They arrange local tours. On Jirón Sucre at the northeast end of town, *Hotel Puerto Mirador* (☎/fax 56-2050) has a swimming pool and fine views over the Río Mayo. Rooms with private hot showers are US$30/40, and bungalows are US$60 including breakfast. There is a restaurant and bar.

For local jungle dishes, try *La Olla de Barro* (☎ 56-3110, 56-1034).

### Getting There & Away

**Air** The small Moyobamba airport has no regular services at this time, and Rioja is the main regional airport. Aero Continente (☎ 56-2199, 56-2888) is at A Alvarado 726.

**Bus & Colectivo** Colectivos to Rioja (US$1.50, 30 minutes) and Tarapoto (US$4, 2 to 3 hours) leave about every 30 minutes from the taxi rank on P Canga. Colectivos to Nuevo Cajamarca (US$2.50, 1 hour) also leave frequently from near here. Minibuses to Tarapoto also leave from Callao near Varcadillo. Local buses to Jepelacio and Gera leave from the stop on Varcadillo and colectivos leave from a block over on Benavides.

The bus terminal on the Plaza de Armas has daily departures for Chiclayo at noon, as well as buses to Tarapoto. Buses from Tarapoto to Chiclayo stop here as well.

## TARAPOTO
☎ 094

From Moyobamba, a 116km road drops still farther down the Río Mayo valley to Tarapoto, 356m above sea level, on the edge of the eastern Andean foothills. Tarapoto is the largest and busiest town in the Department of San Martín and the center for the northern lowlands' expanding agricultural colonization. The town has the region's best accommodations and air services, but is also the most expensive. Some of the agricultural expansion has come from the coca-growing in the middle and upper Río Huallaga valley to the south. There have been reports of drug-related problems in that region, particularly from Saposoa south to Tingo María. That route is not recommended for travelers. However, the route from Moyobamba through Tarapoto and on to Yurimaguas is safe at this time. A tourism industry is now developing in the Tarapoto area to take advantage of the whitewater rivers, lakes and forests in the Andean foothills.

## Information
Tour agencies provide local information. Tarapoto has good exchange rates. The Banco de Crédito, for example, changes US cash at rates close to Lima's banks. Traveler's checks can be exchanged. There's also a Banco Continental and Interbanc. Internet access is available at Instituto Blaise Pascal (La Cruz 137 or Maynas 168).

## Things to See & Do
There is not much to do in Tarapoto itself, apart from just hanging out in the Plaza de Armas (which is also called the Plaza Mayor) or visiting the small local museum just off the plaza, but there are several local excursions.

A couple of small travel agencies have recently opened on or near the Plaza de Armas and can provide information and buses to most of the following places. One that has been recommended for standard tourism is Quiquiriqui Tours (☎ 52-4016, Pimentel 314). Another is DEMLA Tours (☎ 52-2131), on the plaza.

Nearby **Lamas** is worth a day trip. This interesting Indian village with a few colonial buildings is well off the normal tourist circuit (though visited by locals) and has an early morning market, a small museum, a reasonable restaurant and two simple hotels. The large indigenous population here has an annual Fiesta de Santa Rosa in the last week of August. The **Laguna de Sauce** is a popular local destination reached by crossing the Río Huallaga on a raft. There is good swimming here, and expensive bungalows are available. Cheaper, and easier to reach by public transport, are **Laguna Venecia** and the nearby **Cataratas de Ahuashiyacu**, about 45 minutes away on the road to Yurimaguas. A small restaurant is nearby, and a 10-minute walk takes you to a locally favored swimming spot.

A **rafting** outfitter with modern equipment is Los Chancas Expeditions (☎ 52-2616, fax 52-5279, chancas@telematic.com.pe, Jirón Rioja 357). They do half-day, full-day and multiday trips on the Río Mayo, 30km from Tarapoto, and on the lower Río Huallaga (not to be confused with the middle and upper Huallaga, where the coca-growing industry is centered). The shorter trips are mainly Class III whitewater, while the longer trips (up to six days, from July to October only) include Class III and Class IV rapids and camping on the river. Costs of a six-day Huallaga trip are US$700 per person including hotel accommodations at either end of the tour and English-speaking

**TARAPOTO**

PLACES TO STAY
2 Hostal Misti
3 Hotel Tarapoto
6 Hotel Nilas
7 Alojamiento Arevalo
10 Hotel Monte Azul
11 Hostal Las Palmeras
15 La Posada Inn
21 Hostal San Antonio
22 Hotel Edinson
25 Hostal San Martín
26 Hostal Miami
27 Hostal Juan Alfonso
29 Hostal Pasquelandia
31 Hostal El Dorado
32 Hostal Meléndez

33 Hostal Lily
34 Hostal Viluz

PLACES TO EAT
1 El Camarón
4 Real Grill
13 Las Terrazas
16 Las Tinajas
20 El Mesón

OTHER
5 Internet access
8 Los Chancas Expeditions
9 Post Office
12 Interbanc
14 Banco Continental

17 Local museum
18 Telefónica del Peru
19 Aero Continente
23 Banco de Crédito
24 Internet access
28 Quiquiriqui Tours,
    SAOSA Airline
30 Transportes Guadalupe
35 Transportes Transamazonica

To Yurimaguas
To El Otro Sitio
To Aeropuerto, Lamas, Moyobamba

0    125    250 m
0    125    250 yards

naturalist guides. Shaman and Ayahuasca ceremonies can also be arranged at extra cost. Inflatable kayaks are available for rent for US$15/25 for a half/full day. They also do tours to the Reserva Nacional Pacaya-Samiria lasting about 10 days at US$550 per person. (See Reserva Nacional Pacaya-Samiria in the Amazon Basin chapter.)

If you're interested in **motorcycling** in the area, motorbikes can be hired at or near the Plaza de Armas for about US$3 per hour (bargain for multihour discounts).

**Fishing** is reportedly excellent from July to September on the Río Huallaga.

## Places to Stay – Budget

Some of the cheapest hotels have water available at certain times of the day. Many hotels have mosquito netting in the windows, but no glass, which would otherwise block out the noise from street traffic.

One of the better budget hotels is the friendly *Hostal Juan Alfonso* (☎ 52-2179, *Urzua 309*), which charges US$4/6 for basic singles/doubles with communal cold showers and US$5/7.50 for rooms with private showers. The basic *Hostal Pasquelandia* (☎ 52-2290, *Pimentel 341*) has rooms with shared bath (US$3/4) or private bath

(US$4/6) and has fans in every room. The basic *Hostal El Dorado* (☎ 52-2643, Urzua 448) charges US$4/6 for rooms with private shower. Other basic places charging about US$3 per person include the *Hostal Meléndez (Urzua 464)* and *Hostal Las Palmeras (M Grau 229)*. Both have communal showers only. The clean *Hostal Viluz* (☎ 52-6837, Levau 340) charges US$4.50/7.50 with private bath. *Hostal Misti* (☎ 52-2439, L Prado 341) has a shower and fan in every room and charges US$5.50/9.50. The similarly priced *Hostal Miami* (☎/fax 52-2038, Urzua 257) has TV in the rooms.

The recommended *Hostal San Antonio* (☎ 52-5563, Pimentel 126) has clean rooms with private hot showers, fans and cable TV (with some US channels) for US$10/13. The *Hostal San Martín* (☎ 52-2108, M de Compagnon 273) is OK at US$10/15. *Hotel Tarapoto* (☎ 52-2150, ☎/fax 52-4942, M Grau 236) charges US$13/20, is also quite good and offers TV. Several nice new places have opened in response to the recent increase in tourism. One is the quiet *Alojamiento Arevalo* (☎ 52-5265, Moyobamba 223), which charge US$10/15 in rooms with cable TV and private cold shower.

## Places to Stay – Mid-Range

A recommended hotel near the town center is *Hotel Monte Azul* (☎ 52-2443, 52-3145, fax 52-3636, C Morey 156), which has a restaurant and comfortable air-conditioned rooms with minirefrigerators, cable TV and telephones for US$24/32 including breakfast. The decent *Hotel Edinson* (☎ 52-2723, 52-2293, fax 52-2498, Pimentel 117) has a restaurant, bar, room service and a disco. Rooms, which have cable TV, fans and hot showers, are US$14/21, or US$28 with air-conditioning. Breakfast is included.

The charming *La Posada Inn* (☎ 52-5557, ☎/fax 52-2234, San Martín 146) has a restaurant and rooms with cable TV, telephones and minirefrigerators in the US$25 to US$45 range, depending on room size and whether you want air-conditioning. The pleasant, modern *Hostal Lily* (☎ 52-3154, 52-3341, fax 52-2394, in Lima 438-2690, Pimentel 405) has a swimming pool, restaurant/bar, air-

conditioning and rooms with cable TV and telephones for US$40/55 including breakfast. The new *Hotel Nilas* (☎ 52-7331, fax 52-7332, Moyobamba 173) has air-conditioned rooms with minirefrigerator, cable TV and telephone. Rates start at US$50. The hotel features a swimming pool, exercise equipment and a restaurant/bar.

*Hotel Río Shilcayo* (☎ 52-2225, fax 52-4236, in Lima 438-2690, hotelrsh@telematic .com.pe) is almost 2km out of town. It is quiet and cool and has a swimming pool and sauna, which is free for hotel residents and open to others for a small fee. There is a restaurant, bar, and rooms with the usual modern amenities for US$44/60 including breakfast and airport transfer. They also have bungalows for US$68.

*Puerto Palmeras* (☎ 52-3978, fax 52-9980, in Lima 242-5550, ctareps@protelsa.com.pe) is a resort 3km south of town on the road to Juanjuí. It claims to be the most luxurious in the department and charges about US$65/94. The same company operates the similarly priced *Puerto Patos Sauce Lodge* at the Laguna de Sauce.

## Places to Eat

*El Mesón* and *Las Terrazas*, both on the Plaza de Armas, have decent set lunches and are among the cheaper good places in this pricey town. Nearby, *Las Tinajas* has good set lunches and reasonably priced Peruvian dishes. *El Otro Sitio*, on the 13th block of Leguía, northwest of the center, has outdoor tables and good sandwiches and other food. For local cuisine, try *La Patarashca* (☎ 52-3899, Lamas 267), off Manco Cápac and a block north of Rioja. If you are economizing, head to the market area for the cheapest restaurants. The best and priciest restaurants are *El Camarón* (☎ 52-3960, La Cruz 237) and *Real Grill* (☎ 52-2183, Moyobamba 131). Both prepare the local giant river shrimp in various ways.

## Entertainment

*Las Rocas* (old) and *Papillón* (new) are locally popular night clubs in the Morales district. A mototaxi can take you there at night for under US$2.

## Getting There & Away

**Air** Aero Continente (☎ 52-4332, 52-7212, fax 52-3704, airport ☎ 52-4110, San Martín 127) has two daily nonstop flights to and from Lima. TANS has about four flights a week from Lima. SAOSA Airline (☎ 52-1975, Pimentel 316) has daily flights in small aircraft to Pucallpa, Contamana and Orellana. AeroTaxi Iberico (☎ 52-2073, 52-2123) has an office at the airport and flies light aircraft to various jungle towns. Just show up in the morning and see what is available. Planes fill up fast. You can also charter a flight to most jungle destinations – you have to pay for all five passenger seats, but that's no problem if you can get a group together.

**Bus** Tarapoto is an important junction. From here, roads head west to Moyobamba and beyond, north to Yurimaguas and the Amazon Basin, and south to Juanjuí and Tingo María, in descending order of road quality.

Several companies head west via Moyobamba, Chiclayo and Trujillo to Lima (about US$25, 30 to 36 hours). Most leave between 10 am and 3 pm. These include Transportes Transamazonica (☎ 52-2732, Tahuantinsuyo 152), Transportes Guadalupe (☎ 52-3992, Raimondi at Levau) and Paredes Estrella (☎ 52-3681, Prospero 1212). If you're going to Moyobamba, ask about frequent faster minibuses and colectivos.

Minibuses, pickup trucks and other vehicles for Yurimaguas leave from the mercado in the southeast suburb of Banda de Shilcayo and take four to six hours in the dry season, possibly a lot more in the wet. (There are plans to pave it in 2000.) Costs are US$3.50 to US$7, depending on the vehicle. Though vehicles leave several times a day, I'd leave early in the morning to enjoy the scenery and avoid the hottest hours. Transportes Transamazonica also has buses to Yurimaguas. The 130km road climbs over the final foothills of the Andes, and emerges on the Amazonian plains before continuing on to Yurimaguas. It is one of the most beautiful drives in the area. For more information about Yurimaguas and river travel into the jungle, see the Amazon Basin chapter.

The southbound journey via Bellavista to Juanjuí (145 km) and on to Tocache and Tingo María (485 km) is dangerous and not recommended because of drug-running and problems with bandits. This is where much of Peru's clandestine coca and marijuana crops are produced. If you must go, definitely avoid traveling at night, and see if any flights are available. Bellavista, Juanjuí and Tocache all have basic hotels. Tingo María, which is safe enough, is described in the Central Highlands chapter.

# The Amazon Basin

About half of Peru is in the Amazon Basin, yet it merits only one chapter in this book. Why is this? The answer is inaccessibility. Few roads penetrate the rainforest of the Amazon Basin, and therefore, few towns of any size have been built. Those that exist started as river ports and were connected with towns farther downstream, usually in Brazil or Bolivia. Only a few decades ago, the traveler from Peru's major jungle port of Iquitos had to travel thousands of kilometers down the Río Amazonas to the Atlantic and then go either south around Cape Horn or north through the Panama Canal to reach Lima – a journey of several months. With the advent of roads and airports, these jungle areas have slowly become a more important part of Peru. Nevertheless, this area contains only about 5% of the nation's population.

Five main jungle areas are accessible to the traveler. Starting in the southeast, near the Bolivian border, the first of these is Puerto Maldonado, a port at the junction of the Tambopata and Madre de Dios rivers. Puerto Maldonado is most easily reached by air (there are daily flights from Cuzco) or by an atrociously bad dirt road (an uncomfortable two- or three-day journey by truck). West of Puerto Maldonado and more accessible from Cuzco is Parque Nacional Manu, which is one of the best areas of protected rainforest in the Amazon. Southeast of Puerto Maldonado are numerous lodges and campsites in the Zona Reservada Tambopata-Candamo and in the Parque Nacional Bahuaja-Sonene.

In central Peru, almost due east of Lima, is the area known as Chanchamayo. It consists of the two small towns of San Ramón and La Merced, both easily accessible by road from Lima, and several nearby villages.

A new but very rough jungle road has been built from La Merced north to the important port of Pucallpa, the capital of the Department of Ucayali and the third region described in this section. Most travelers to Pucallpa, however, take better roads from Lima via Huánuco and Tingo María, or fly.

Farther north is the small port of Yurimaguas, reached from the North Coast by road (the long journey is described in Across the Northern Highlands) or by air from Lima.

Finally, travelers can reach Peru's major jungle port, Iquitos, by river boat from Pucallpa and Yurimaguas or by air from Lima and other cities. It is impossible to reach Iquitos by road.

## PUERTO MALDONADO
☎ 084

Founded a century ago, Puerto Maldonado has been important as a rubber boom town, a logging center, and more recently as a center for gold and oil prospectors. It is also important for jungle crops such as Brazil nuts and coffee. There is also some ranching. Because of the logging industry, the jungle around Puerto Maldonado has been mostly cleared.

The various commercial enterprises centered on Puerto Maldonado have made it the most important port and capital of the Department of Madre de Dios. It is an unpleasant, fast-growing town with a busy frontier feel and a population of about 37,000. It is interesting to experience this boom-town atmosphere, but otherwise, there isn't much to see. Puerto Maldonado can be used as a starting point for trips into the jungle. The best of these are at the nearby jungle lodges. It is also possible to continue into the Brazilian or Bolivian jungle or to Parque Nacional Manu, but these trips are not straightforward.

### Information
**Tourist Offices** The Ministerio de Industria y Turismo (☎ 57-1413, 57-1164, 57-1421, Fitzcarrald 411) has tourism information, and a desk at the airport can provide limited information.

AMAZON BASIN

**AMAZON BASIN**

**Immigration** To leave Peru via the rarely used posts of Iñapari (for Brazil) or Puerto Heath (for Bolivia), check first with immigration officials in Puerto Maldonado. Before 1998, you had to get exit stamps in Puerto Maldonado, but recently, exit stamps were available at the border – this could change again. In Puerto Maldonado, the immigration office (☎/fax 57-1069, cell 61-2068) is on the 2nd block of 26 de Diciembre (but it has had at least three addresses since the last edition). Foreign visitors can extend their visas or tourist cards here for the standard

US$28 fee. If you're flying from Cuzco to Iñapari, check with immigration in Cuzco.

**Money** The Banco de Crédito on the Plaza de Armas will change US cash or traveler's checks and has a Visa ATM. You can also try the nearby Banco de la Nación, or a casa de cambio on the corner of Puno and G Prada. Brazilian cruzeiros and Bolivian pesos are hard to negotiate.

**Post & Communications** The offices are shown on the map. Internet access is available at Compunet (Velarde 814). A new Internet place on Velarde is Data System.

**Laundry** There is one at Velarde 898, and another one is almost next door.

**Hospital** The Hospital Santa Rosa (☎ 57-1019, 57-1046) is at Cajamarca 171.

**Tour Guides** Many visitors arrive with pre-arranged tours and stay at one of the jungle lodges described later in this chapter. If you're not one of these visitors, you can arrange a tour when you arrive. Beware that there are crooked operators out there – shop around, don't prepay for any tour and if you are giving an advance deposit, insist on a signed receipt. If you agree to a boat driver's price, make sure it includes the return trip. When not working, guides hang out in restaurants in town; La Casa Nostra has recently been a popular gathering spot.

One recommended guide is Hernán Llavé (☎ 57-2243), who speaks some English. If he's not on a tour, you'll find him in the baggage reception area of the airport waiting for incoming flights. You can reach him by calling the airport (☎ 57-1531) any day before 8:30 am. Another honest freelance guide is Willy Wither (☎ 57-2014, compured@compured.limaperu.net), who speaks some English and German and is very enthusiastic. Nadir Gnan (☎ 57-1900) speaks English and Italian, and has firsthand expertise on mining activities. The *motorista* (boat driver) Victor Yarikawa, and guide Arturo Balarezo (ask at the Hotel Wilson) are other possibilities.

## Jardín Zoológico

You could have a quick look in the zoo, where several species of monkeys (spider, capuchin, howler and tamarin) have become domesticated to the point that they like visitors to hold them. But beware of the white-faced capuchin, who is a pickpocket. Unfortunately, some animals are kept in very small cages.

The zoo is 2km out of town on the airport road. Admission is US$1. A motorcycle taxi will charge about US$2 to take you, wait for a quick visit and bring you back.

## Madre de Dios Ferry

A cheap way (US$0.15) of seeing a little of this major Peruvian jungle river is to cross it. It takes about five minutes, and *peki-pekis* (motorized canoes) leave from the dock several times an hour. The Río Madre de Dios is about 500m wide at this point; on the other side you can continue by truck, minibus, motorcycle, or on foot.

## Places to Stay

**Budget** Puerto Maldonado has about 15 hotels, but they tend to start filling up by late morning, and foreigners may be overcharged. Several inexpensive hotels provide basic four walls, a bed and a cold communal shower for about US$2.50 or US$3 per person. *Hostal Chávez* is the cheapest in town at US$2.50 per person, and it looks it. Other very basic cheapies are *Hostal Español* (☎ 57-2381), which is recommended only for cheapness, and *Hostal Moderno* (☎ 57-1063), which is somewhat cleaner.

Slightly better places include the clean but rather noisy *Hotel Tambo de Oro* (☎ 57-2057), which charges US$3 per person. *Hotel Kross* (☎ 57-2331) and *Hotel El Astro* (☎ 57-2128) have rooms with shared baths for US$3.50 per person or with private baths for US$5/8 for singles/doubles.

*Hotel Wilson* (☎ 57-1086, G Prada 355) has long had a reputation for being a good value, though the cheaper rooms are getting run down. It has a simple café and rooms with communal showers for US$5/8, or better rooms with private cold shower and fan for US$8/12. *Hostal Royal Inn* (☎ 57-1048) has large, clean rooms with private bath for US$8/12 and is a better choice. *Hotel Rey Port* (☎ 57-1177) is similarly priced and is just adequate. Others in this price range are *Hostal Gamboa* (☎ 57-4122) and *Hotel del Solar* (☎ 57-1571).

Away from the center, by the airport, is the pleasant and friendly *Iñapari Lodge* (☎ 57-2575, fax 57-2155), which charges US$5.50 per person for rooms with communal showers. They have a camping area, restaurant and bar. Inexpensive horseback, bicycle and other tours can be arranged.

AMAZON BASIN

**PUERTO MALDONADO**

*Río Madre de Dios*

Staircase

Billinghurst

0    100    200 m
0    100    200 yards

Loreto

*Plaza de Armas*

D Carrion

Cuzco

2 de Mayo

G Prada

J Troncoso

Tacna

Ica

*Mercado Modelo*

Fitzcarrald

To Aeropuerto, Laberinto

To Hospital, Hotel Don Carlos

*Río Tambopata*

**PLACES TO STAY**
2   Hostal Moderno
3   Wasai Lodge
10  Hostal Cabaña Quinta
11  Hostal Chávez
12  Hotel Rey Port
14  Hostal Español
16  Hostal Royal Inn
20  Hotel Tambo de Oro
21  Hotel del Solar
24  Hotel Wilson
26  Hotel El Astro
29  Hostal Gamboa
30  Hotel Kross

**PLACES TO EAT**
6   El Califa
7   Pizzería El Hornito/
    Chez Maggy
15  Chifa Wa-Seng
18  La Casa Nostra
19  La Cusqueñita,
    Marisquería Libertad
28  El Tigre

**OTHER**
1   Ferry crossing dock,
    river-boat hire
4   Capitanía
5   Migraciones
8   Banco de la Nación
9   Banco de Crédito
13  AeroCóndor
17  Aero Continente
22  Telefónica del Peru
23  Casa de cambio
25  Motorcycle hire
    (several places)
27  Post Office
31  Trucks to Cuzco, buses
    to Laberinto
32  Compunet
33  Laundry
34  Ministerio de
    Industria y Turismo

**Mid-Range** About a kilometer southwest of the center, above the banks of the Río Tambopata, is *Hotel Don Carlos* (☎ 57-1029, fax 57-1323, in Lima 224-0275, fax 224-8581, dcarloslim@tci.net.pe, León Velarde 1271). They charge US$29/35 for adequate singles/doubles with cold shower, fan, TV and air-conditioning. There is a small restaurant that opens on demand.

*Hostal Cabaña Quinta* (☎ 57-1045, 57-1864, fax 57-1890, Cuzco 535) is the best in the town center and has a decent restaurant and friendly staff. A few rooms with fans and shared bathrooms are US$11/17 (these are being phased out). Rooms with fans, TV and private cold showers are US$15/23. A few rooms with air-conditioning, warm water and minirefrigerators are US$30.

*Wasai Lodge* (☎ 57-2290, fax 57-1355 wasai@telematic.edu.pe), on the Madre de Dios waterfront, has 18 rooms with bath, hot water, telephones, TV and fans; four of them also have air-conditioning. Rates are US$30/40 and an extra US$10 for air-conditioning. There is a restaurant and bar. The lodge arranges one-day and overnight trips into the area for about the same prices as lodges advertise in Cuzco.

Outside Puerto Maldonado are some jungle lodges, described later in this section.

## Places to Eat

There are no fancy restaurants in Puerto Maldonado, and most are fairly basic. *Pizzería El Hornito/Chez Maggy* (☎ 57-2082), on the Plaza de Armas, is a popular hangout that serves pasta and wood-oven, thin-crust pizza. *La Cusqueñita* is clean and has a good set lunch for only US$1.20, as well as a variety of other dishes. *Marisquería Libertad*, next door, is similarly priced. The more expensive *Chifa Wa-Seng* is also quite good. The simple *El Califa* (☎ 57-1119, Piura 266) is open only for lunch and serves good regional specialties in a rustic setting, though it's slightly pricey. *El Tigre* is recommended for its *ceviche* (marinated seafood dish). The best café is *La Casa Nostra*, with great juices, snacks and coffee. The restaurant in the *Wasai Lodge* is also satisfactory.

The best restaurant is *Brombu's* (☎ 57-3230), on the way to the airport. In a peaceful setting that combines adobe walls and thatched roofs, Fernando Rosemberg and his wife serve local delicacies and international dishes. They plan to offer lodging in the future. (A recent report is that it's closed temporarily – call ahead.)

In the Mercado Modelo, look for freshly squeezed fruit juices and other jungle staples, such as *fariña*, a muesli-like yucca concoction eaten fried or mixed in lemonade. Also in the market, look out for children selling hot, fresh *pan de arroz* in the early morning (7 to 8 am). This bread is made from rice flour, yucca and butter and takes three days to prepare.

Regional specialties include *juanes* (rice steamed with fish or chicken in a banana leaf), *chilcano* (a broth of fish chunks flavored with the native cilantro herb) and *parrillada de la selva* (a barbecue of marinated meat in a Brazil-nut sauce). A *plátano* (plantain) is served boiled or fried as a side dish to many meals.

## Getting There & Away

Most people fly from Cuzco. The road or river trips are only for adventurous travelers prepared to put up with discomfort and delay.

**Air** The airport is about 7km out of town. There are daily scheduled flights every morning to and from Lima via Cuzco with Aero Continente (☎ 57-3701/2, airport 57-2357, Velarde 508). But these may be canceled because of rain (the wet season is December to April, but cancellations are possible at other times), so allow some flexibility in your schedule. A new airline, AeroCóndor (☎ 57-3120) has flights to Cuzco from Monday to Saturday, some continuing to Arequipa. They fly old Fokkers or Russian planes and may be gone by the time you read this; these small airlines change often. Their office is shown on the map. Grupo 8 has two flights a month from Cuzco to Puerto Maldonado and on to Iberia, and occasionally flies to Iñapari. (It is a 7km walk from the Iñapari airstrip to the village.) Flights are subject to delay, cancellation or overbooking, and the departure day changes. Grupo 8 can be contacted at the Cuzco and Puerto Maldonado airports, and on the 12th block of 2 de Mayo in Puerto Maldonado. If you want to fly, get to the airport early on the day of the flight, and be persistent.

Light aircraft to anywhere can be chartered as long as you pay for five seats and the return trip. Ask at the airport.

**Truck** Ha! You noticed – the heading doesn't read 'Bus.' During the highland dry season, trucks to Cuzco leave from the Mercado Modelo on E Rivero, or from outside the swimming pool, which is two blocks south of the mercado on the same street. Although it's only about 500km, the road is so rough that the trip takes three days or more, depending on weather conditions. (See the Road to Puerto Maldonado in the Cuzco chapter.)

There are also trucks and some vans or minibuses leaving from Puerto Maldonado to the nearby town of Laberinto (US$2, 1½ hours), and to Iberia en route to the Brazilian

AMAZON BASIN

border. Buses to Laberinto leave several times during the morning from the corner of Ica and E Rivero, supposedly at fixed times but usually not until they are full. Faster colectivo pickups also leave from here.

**River Boat** You can hire boats at the Río Madre de Dios ferry dock for local excursions or to take you downriver to the Bolivian border. It is difficult to find boats up the Madre de Dios (against the current) to Manu, and though it is possible to fly to Boca Manu on chartered light aircraft, this is normally done from Cuzco. Cuzco is a better place than Puerto Maldonado from which to reach Manu.

Occasionally, people reach Puerto Maldonado by boat from Manu (with the current) or from the Bolivian border (against the current), but transportation is infrequent. Be prepared for long waits of several days or even weeks.

## Getting Around
*Motocarros* (motorcycle rickshaw taxis) can take two or three passengers (and light luggage) to the airport for about US$2.50. Short rides around town are under US$1.

There are also TaxiMotos. These are Honda 90s that will take one passenger around town for about US$0.25, but don't expect a motorcycle helmet.

**Motorcycle Rental** You can rent motorcycles if you want to see some of the surrounding countryside; go in pairs in case of breakdowns. There are two or three motorcycle rental places on G Prada. They charge about US$1.25 per hour and have mainly small, 100cc bikes. Bargain for all-day discounts.

## AROUND PUERTO MALDONADO
A bus trip to the nearby gold-rush town of **Laberinto** is the only land journey that you can take to see the countryside around Puerto Maldonado. You can leave in the morning and return in the afternoon, but don't miss the last bus, as the one hotel in Laberinto is a real dive and usually full of drunk miners. Laberinto itself is just a

shantytown. However, you can take trips up and down the Río Madre de Dios to various nearby communities, some of which are involved in gold panning. The miners come into Laberinto to sell their gold at the Banco de Minero. You may see buyers blow-torching the gold to melt and purify it. If the bank runs out of money, the miners may barter their gold in exchange for gas, food and other supplies.

## Down the Río Madre de Dios
This river flows past Puerto Maldonado eastbound, heading into Bolivia and, eventually, Brazil and the Amazon proper.

An attractive jungle lake, **Lago Sandoval** is about two hours away down the Madre de Dios. Half the trip is done by boat and the other half on foot (about a 3km hike). Bring your own food and water. For about US$25 to US$30 (you have to bargain, but several people can travel for this price), a boat will drop you at the beginning of the trail and pick you up later. The boat driver will also guide you to the lake if you wish. With luck you might see caiman, turtles, exotic birds, monkeys and maybe the rare endangered giant river otters that live in the lake. There are two lodges on the lake (see Places to Stay – Jungle Lodges, later in this section) and the best way to see wildlife is to stay overnight and take a boat ride on the lake, though day trips are offered.

Various other overnight trips can be undertaken. One is to **Lago Valencia**, just off the Madre de Dios about 60km away, near the Bolivian border. At least two days are needed, though three or four days are suggested. This lake reportedly offers the region's best fishing, as well as good bird watching and nature observation (bring binoculars). There are trails into the jungle around the lake.

South of the Río Madre de Dios and along the **Río Heath** (the latter forming the border between Peru and Bolivia), the **Parque Nacional Bahuaja-Sonene** (encompassing the former Santuario Nacional Pampas del Heath and some adjoining areas) has been established. This has some of the best wildlife in Peru's Amazon region though much of it is hard to see. Infrastructure in the park is limited, and wildlife-watching trips are only just beginning. There is a lodge that arranges tours to a nearby *colpa* (clay lick), a popular attraction for macaws and parrots.

Apart from fishing and nature trips, visits to beaches, Indian communities, salt licks and gold-panning areas can be made in the Lago Valencia/Río Heath area. Some excursions involve camping or staying in simple thatched shelters, so bring a sleeping bag and hammock. Be prepared for muddy trails – two pairs of shoes are recommended, a dry pair for camp use and a pair that can get thoroughly wet and covered with mud. Insect repellent, sunblock and a means of purifying water are essential.

## Up the Río Tambopata

This river is a major tributary of the Río Madre de Dios, joining the latter river at Puerto Maldonado. Boats go up the river past several good lodges and into the huge **Zona Reservada Tambopata-Candamo**, one of the largest protected areas in the country. Visiting the reserve is quite easy if you book a guided stay at one of the lodges within the reserve. One of the highlights of the reserve is the Colpa de Guacamayos (macaw clay lick), one of the largest natural clay licks in the country. It attracts hundreds of birds and is a spectacular sight (see the January 1994 *National Geographic* for a photographic story). Note that a US$2 reserve entrance fee is charged to people staying at a lodge, and there is a US$20 camping fee (though few people camp, and facilities are almost nonexistent). Recently, a US$20 fee was reported for visiting the colpa as well.

## Places to Stay – Jungle Lodges

The area's jungle lodges can only be reached by boat. Reservations should be made in Cuzco or Lima, as it can be difficult to contact the offices in Puerto Maldonado. Although it may be possible to get rates a few dollars cheaper by booking in Puerto Maldonado, it's not really worth it. These lodges do deal with international tour groups and can be full at any time, but are often fairly empty.

### Friajes

Although the Puerto Maldonado region is hot and humid year round, with temperatures averaging 27°C and often climbing above 32°C, there are occasional cold winds from the Andes. Known as *friajes*, these winds can make temperatures plunge to 9°C or even lower. It's worth having a light jacket or sweater in case this happens. The friaje's effect on the wildlife contributes to the high species diversity and endemism of the region.

Although two-day/one-night packages are available, a minimum stay of three days/two nights is recommended, because the first and last day are usually consumed by air travel to and from Cuzco. This means that the last day usually involves departing the lodge after a pre-dawn breakfast to catch the late-morning flight to Cuzco. All prices should include round-trip transportation from Puerto Maldonado airport to the river and the lodge, as well as meals, accommodations and some local guided tours. The guides come and go, and the quality and depth of their knowledge is highly variable. Airfare to Puerto Maldonado is extra. Discounts can normally be arranged if it's the low season (December to April) and you are traveling as a group (usually five or more) or planning a long stay. All the lodges will happily arrange longer stays.

Accommodations are rustic but comfortable enough. Unless indicated otherwise, lodges normally lack electricity, except for perhaps a generator to run a refrigerator in the kitchen. Lighting is by kerosene lantern, and you should definitely pack a flashlight. Showers are cold, which is normally very refreshing at the end of a sweaty day, and beds usually have mosquito netting. Visitors will see a large variety of tropical plants, insects and birds, but remember that mammals are elusive and hard to see in the rainforest. Don't go with high expectations of seeing jaguars and tapirs. Monkeys and bats are the most frequently sighted mammals.

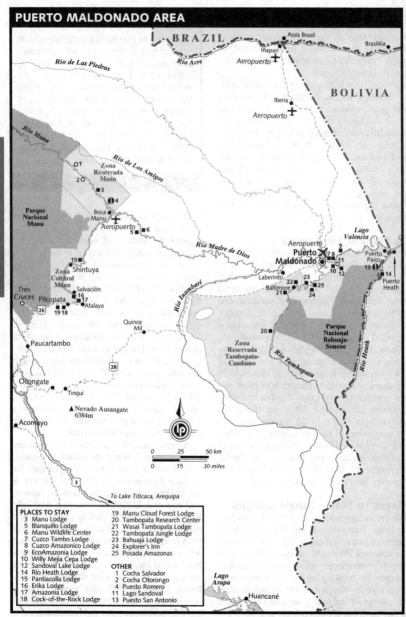

**PUERTO MALDONADO AREA**

PLACES TO STAY
3  Manu Lodge
5  Blanquillo Lodge
6  Manu Wildlife Center
7  Cuzco Tambo Lodge
8  Cuzco Amazonico Lodge
9  EcoAmazonia Lodge
10  Willy Mejía Cepa Lodge
12  Sandoval Lake Lodge
14  Río Heath Lodge
15  Pantiacolla Lodge
16  Erika Lodge
17  Amazonia Lodge
18  Cock-of-the-Rock Lodge

19  Manu Cloud Forest Lodge
20  Tambopata Research Center
21  Wasai Tambopata Lodge
22  Tambopata Jungle Lodge
23  Bahuaja Lodge
24  Explorer's Inn
25  Posada Amazonas

OTHER
1  Cocha Salvador
2  Cocha Otorongo
4  Puesto Romero
11  Lago Sandoval
13  Puesto San Antonio

0    25    50 km
0    15    30 miles

To Lake Titicaca, Arequipa

If you ask around on the riverfront or the Ministerio de Industria y Turismo in Puerto Maldonado, you'll hear about inexpensive *casas de hospedaje*, which are often run by local farmers and their families. These places are small, very rustic, reached by boat, offer the cheapest places to stay (meals are available) and are geared toward travelers on a very tight budget. I don't necessarily recommend these, because guides are rarely provided and the rainforest nearby is usually secondary growth and sometimes degraded, but it may be suitable for some folks. At least it puts some money into the economy at a grassroots level.

**Along the Madre de Dios** The closest lodge to Puerto Maldonado is the rundown *Cuzco Tambo Lodge*, 10km downstream. In late 1998, it was under new ownership, and remodeling is planned. They do local tours to Lago Sandoval and to gold-panning areas. Reservations can be made at Aero Continente in Puerto Maldonado.

Farther down the Madre de Dios, about 15km away from Puerto Maldonado, the more comfortable *Cuzco Amazonico Lodge* also offers local tours and perhaps a better look at the jungle. The 45 rustic rooms have private bathrooms and porches with hammocks. They charge US$153 per person (double occupancy) for three days/two nights or US$213 for four days/three nights. There are 18km of trails in a private reserve around the lodge. Reservations for the Cuzco Amazonico Lodge can be made in Lima (☎ 422-6574, fax 422-4701) and in Cuzco (☎ 24-5314, fax 24-4669, Julio C Tello C-13, Urbanización Santa Mónica).

Roughly 30km from Puerto Maldonado is *EcoAmazonia Lodge*, with 41 rustic bungalows, each with private bath and a screened sitting room. There are several trails of varying length from this lodge, including a three-hour hike to a canopy platform. Boat tours to local lakes and along the rivers are also offered. Rates are US$150 or US$200 per person (double occupancy) for three days/two nights or four days/three nights, including all services from Puerto Maldonado airport. Reservations are made in Cuzco

Macaws

(☎ 23-6159, fax 22-5068, ecolodge@chaski .unsaac.edu.pe, Portal de Panes 109, Plaza de Armas).

**Lago Sandoval** Between the last two lodges, but on the opposite (south) side of the river, is a 3km trail leading to Lago Sandoval. The flat trail has boardwalks and gravel and is easily passable year round. From the end of this trail, you can continue 2km on a narrower, less-maintained trail to an inexpensive lodge, or take a boat ride across the lake to the best lodge in this area.

The inexpensive lodge is the family-run *Willy Mejía Cepa Lodge*. Willy's father, Don César Mejía Zaballos, homesteaded the lake 50 years ago and has been offering basic accommodations to budget travelers for 14 years. They have room for 13 people, but are expanding to be able to accommodate over 20. Showers and bathrooms are shared and are separate from the sleeping areas. For a group of four people, they'll charge US$30 per day including transportation from Puerto Maldonado, simple family meals, a bed and excursions (in Spanish). If you can get there yourself, they'll charge about US$12 a person per day for a bed and food. You can get information in Puerto Maldonado at Velarde 487.

The best lodge is **Sandoval Lake Lodge**, which is on the other side of the lake. Getting there is half the fun. After hiking the 3km to the lake (bicycle rickshaws are available for luggage and for people with walking difficulties), you board paddled canoes to negotiate narrow canals through a flooded palm-tree forest inhabited by hundreds of nesting red-bellied macaws. Emerging from the flooded forest, you are silently paddled across the beautiful lake to the lodge, which is owned and operated by InkaNatura (see Tours, later in this chapter). Conservation organizations funded by InkaNatura are studying and protecting the endangered giant river otter, of which several pairs live in the lake and can sometimes be seen during early morning boating excursions. Various monkey species and a host of birds can also be spotted, as well as caiman, frogs and lizards. Hikes into the forest are also offered, and guides are multilingual and knowledgeable.

The spacious lodge is built on a hilltop about 30m above the lake and is surrounded by primary forest. The hilltop was a former farm, and the lodge was built from salvaged driftwood, so the owners pride themselves on the fact that no primary forest was cut during construction. (This is also true of some other lodges, though not always mentioned.) The rooms (with heated and tiled showers and ceiling fans) are the best in the area, and the restaurant/bar area is huge, airy and conducive to relaxing and chatting. Rates are a good value at US$180 per person (double occupancy) for three days/two nights, and US$250 for four days/three nights. Extra nights are US$70.

The caiman, cousin of the crocodile

**Along the Río Heath** InkaNatura has also built the simpler, eight-room **Río Heath Lodge**, about two hours south of the Río Madre de Dios on the Río Heath, which forms the border between Peru and Bolivia. Technically, the lodge is on Bolivian land and has Bolivian staff, though it is Peruvian owned. From the lodge, there is access to a clay lick (on the Peruvian side), where various parrot and macaw species can be seen (binoculars recommended). Trails into the new Parque Nacional Bahuaja-Sonene are being laid out, and field biologists have assessed this area as one of the most biodiverse in southeastern Peru. The lodge, which was built in 1998, is remote and rustic, with clean but communal warm showers. Reports on how it's doing are welcomed. Rates for a four-day/three-night trip (with the third night at Sandoval because of the distances involved) are US$695 per person (double occupancy) from Puerto Maldonado. Extra nights are US$75.

**Along the Tambopata** The new **Posada Amazonas** is about two hours from Puerto Maldonado along the Río Tambopata, followed by a 10-minute walk. Unique among the area's lodges, the Posada is on the land of the Ese'eja Native Community, and tribal members, as well as local mestizos, are among the guides. (Several other lodges use 'native' guides, but these are often mestizos rather than tribal members.) Harpy eagles have often been seen nesting around the community (see the July/August 1998 edition of *International Wildlife* magazine for the story of Ese'eje involvement in protecting this endangered bird), and many visitors are lucky enough to see a Harpy – the largest eagle in the Americas. There are excellent chances of seeing macaws and parrots on a small salt lick nearby, and giant river otters are often found swimming in lakes close to the lodge. Guides at the lodge are mainly English-speaking Peruvian naturalists with varying interests. One day you might go on a hike with a bird-watcher and the next with a botanist. Ese'eja villagers, accompanied by translators, guide ethnobotanical walks with explanations of how the products of the rainforest are used by Indian communities. The lodge has 24 large double rooms with private hot showers and windows overlooking the rainforest. Mosquito nets are provided. Reservations are made with Rainforest Expeditions (in Lima ☎ 421-8347, 221-4182, fax 421-8183, rainfore@ amauta.rcp.net.pe, Galeón 120, Lima 41), who also operate the Tambopata Research Center (see later in this section).

*Explorer's Inn* is 58km from Puerto Maldonado on the Río Tambopata. It takes three to four hours of river travel to reach the lodge, which is located in the former 5500-hectare Zona Preservada Tambopata (itself now surrounded by the much larger Zona Reservada Tambopata-Candamo). Almost 600 species of birds have been recorded in this preserved zone, which is a world record for bird species sighted in one area. There are similar records for other kinds of wildlife, including over 1200 butterflies. Despite these records (which are scientifically documented), the average tourist won't see much more here than anywhere else during the standard two-night visit. The 38km of trails around the lodge can be explored independently or with naturalist guides. The latter are usually British or American university students who may or may not know much about the area, depending on how long they have worked here. Most of them are enthusiastic guides and try hard, though a few find guiding to be an imposition on their studies. The area is more pristine than the lodges on the Madre de Dios. Rates are about US$180 for three days/two nights. Tours to the salt lick cost extra. Reservations can be made at Peruvian Safaris (in Cuzco ☎ 23-5342, Plateros 365, in Lima ☎ 433-9213, 433-7963, fax 332-6676, safaris@amauta.rcp.net.pe, Garcilaso de la Vega 1334).

Some 10km beyond Explorer's Inn is a low-key, ecolodge/research station called *Bahuaja Lodge*. Rustic accommodations cost US$165 for four days/three nights and US$35 for additional days, including three meals, bedding, mosquito net and guided walks on 25km of trails, as well as gold-panning, fishing and other diversions. Trips to the macaw licks

and local lakes with giant-otter populations can be arranged. In 1998, the first full year of operation, several scientists were engaged in long-term research projects and provided interesting background to the locally guided activities. Information is available in Puerto Maldonado (☎/fax 57-3348, bahuaja-lodge@ mail.studlima.com.pe, Fitzcarrald 334) or ask in La Casa Nostra café for Tina Smith, who speaks English and Spanish and can help with anything locally.

About 45 minutes farther up the Río Tambopata from the Explorer's Inn is *Tambopata Jungle Lodge*, with bungalows set in secondary jungle. Although there are several farms in the area, the lodge is within the Zona Reservada Tambopata-Candamo, and a short boat ride will get you out into primary forest. Tours to nearby lakes and to the salt lick are offered, and naturalist guides are available. There are 30km of well-marked trails, which you can wander at will without a guide. Rates are about US$160 for three days/two nights or US$190 for four days/three nights, but the salt-lick overnight trip adds several hundred dollars to the cost. Reservations can be made in Cuzco at Peruvian Andean Treks (☎ 22-5701, fax 23-8911, postmast@patcusco.com.pe, Pardo 705). They can send you a list of representatives in the USA, Canada, the UK, Australia and New Zealand that charge the same rates.

A little farther up the Tambopata, near the community of Baltimore, are several small casas de hospedaje; inquire in Puerto Maldonado about these.

Shortly past Baltimore, the small *Wasai Tambopata Lodge* is operated by Puerto Maldonado's Wasai Lodge. Like all the other lodges, it can be reached by river, or you can take a truck for about an hour and hike in for another three or four hours (guides are provided). A macaw lick is an hour away by boat; there is a nearby jungle waterfall and numerous jungle trails. Rates are US$268 for four days/three nights.

About seven hours from Puerto Maldonado, Rainforest Expeditions runs the *Tambopata Research Center*, locally called the Colpa Lodge after the famous Colpa salt lick nearby. (They also operate Posada Amazonas, mentioned earlier in this section.) Research here included breeding and reintroducing macaws into the wild. The project was a success and is currently being monitored for long-term results. The lodge is fairly simple, with 13 double rooms sharing four showers and four toilets, but because of the distances involved, rates are higher than the other places. If you're interested in seeing more macaws than you ever thought possible, it's worth the expense, although the owners point out that occasionally, due to poor weather or other factors, the macaws aren't found at the lick. Still, about 75% of visitors get good looks at macaw, though you shouldn't expect to get the kinds of photos in the *National Geographic* article (unless you are a professional with lots of time). Travel time to the lodge varies, depending on river levels and the size of your boat motor. It might be an all-day trip from Puerto Maldonado, and a stopover is usually made at Posada Amazonas, two hours from Puerto Maldonado. Reservations can be made with Rainforest Expeditions or International Expeditions (☎ 800-633-4734, 1 Environs Park, Helena, AL 35080, USA). International Expeditions will arrange a complete package including air travel from the USA.

## GOING TO BOLIVIA
You can hire a boat at Puerto Maldonado's Madre de Dios dock to take you to the Peru/Bolivia border at Puerto Pardo (Puerto Heath is on the Bolivian side, a few minutes away from Puerto Pardo by boat). The trip takes half a day and costs about US$80 – the boat will carry several people. With time and luck, you may also be able to find a cargo boat that's going there anyway and will take passengers more cheaply.

It's possible to continue down the river on the Bolivian side, but this can take several days (even weeks) to arrange and is not cheap. It's best to travel in a group to share costs, and you should avoid the dry months of July to September (when the river is too low). From Puerto Heath, continue down the Río Madre de Dios as far as Riberalta (at the confluence of the Madre de Dios and

Beni, far into northern Bolivia), where road and air connections can be made. Basic food and shelter (bring a hammock or sleeping pad) can be found en route. When the water is high enough, boatman Freddy Lobetano (nicknamed 'Pan Dulce') takes cargo and passengers from Puerto Maldonado to Riberalta and back about twice a month, but this trip is rarely done by foreigners.

The Peruvian and Bolivian border guards can stamp you out of and in to their respective countries if your passport is in order. Visas are not available, however, so get one ahead of time if you need it. Formalities are slow and relaxed – they don't see many travelers, so be prepared to sit around for an hour, chatting about your trip, and maybe bring some fruit or cigarettes to share with the guards.

## GOING TO BRAZIL
An unpaved road goes from Puerto Maldonado to Iberia and on to Iñapari, on the Brazilian border. It's in good shape during the dry months, but can be very slow in the wettest months. The road leaves from the north side of the Madre de Dios, which is crossed by frequent passenger ferries. Pickup trucks and minibuses leave several times a day from the other side of the river and reach Iberia in about five to six hours in good conditions. They charge US$15. Along the road, there are a few small settlements of people involved in the Brazil-nut industry and some cattle ranching and logging. These settlements have only a few hundred inhabitants, a couple of stores, a place to eat and possibly a basic place to stay. After some 170km, you reach Iberia, where there are a couple of very basic hotels. This is the largest town on the road; it has about 4000 inhabitants and twice-monthly air service from Cuzco with Grupo 8.

The village of Iñapari is another 70km beyond Iberia. Iñapari is occasionally serviced by Grupo 8 (the airport is 7km from town), but most people arrive by road. This section of road is in worse shape than the Puerto Maldonado-Iberia section. It takes about four to five hours and costs about US$9. On some days, there are vehicles

## Ants

Of the hundreds of ant species in the Amazon rainforests, the leaf-cutter ants live in colonies numbering in the hundreds of thousands. Their homes are huge nests dug deep into the ground. Foraging ants search the vegetation for particular types of leaves, cut out small sections and, holding the leaf segments above their heads like a small umbrella, bring them back to the nest. The ants can be quite experimental, bringing back a variety of leaves, and even pieces of discarded nylon clothing or plastic wrappers that they may discover on forays into the forest.

Workers within the nest sort out the leaves that will easily decompose into a type of compost; unsuitable material is ejected from the nest after a few days. The composted leaves form a mulch, on which a fungus grows. The ants tend these fungal gardens, for they provide the main diet for both the adult ants and for the young that are being raised inside the nest.

When a particularly good source of leaves has been located, ants lay down a trail of chemical markers, or pheromones, linking the nest with the leaf source, often 100 yards or more away. People frequently come across one of these trails in the jungle, with hundreds of ants scurrying along carrying leaf sections back to the nest, or returning empty-handed for another load.

Army ants and other species may want to prey upon this ready and constant supply of foragers. To combat this, the leaf-cutter ants are morphologically separated by size and jaw structure into different castes. Some specialize in tending the fungal gardens, others have jaws designed for cutting the leaf segments, and yet others are soldier ants, which, armed with their huge mandibles, accompany the foragers and protect them from attackers. Close observation of the foragers will sometimes reveal yet another caste – a tiny ant that is so small that it rides along on the leaf segments without disturbing the foragers. The function of these riders is still unclear, but biologists suggest that they may act as protection against parasitizing wasps that try to lay their eggs on the foragers when they are occupied with carrying leaves.

A colony of leaf-cutter ants can last for a decade or more. New colonies are founded by the emergence of a number of potential queens, who mate and then fly off to found another nest. They carry some of the fungus used for food with them. This is essential to 'seed' the new nest. The rest of the new queen's life is spent laying tens of thousands of eggs, destined to become gardeners, foragers, soldiers, riders, or perhaps even new queens.

going all the way from Puerto Maldonado, but most travelers change in Iberia.

Peruvian border formalities can be carried out in Iñapari if your passport is in order. Stores around the main plaza will accept and change both Peruvian and Brazilian currency; if leaving Peru, it's best to get rid of your soles here. Small denominations of US cash are often negotiable. A block north of the plaza, **Hostal Margarita** has basic but reasonably clean rooms for US$3 per person.

From Iñapari, it is about a kilometer on foot to Assis Brasil in Brazil, but the Río Acre must be waded (travelers Joeri Apontoweil and Bianca Dijkstra report knee-deep water when crossing in July). It's hard to change Peruvian currency in Assis, which has better hotels; rates start at US$7 per person. There is no Brazilian immigration in Assis, and you need to travel to Brasiléia (a small town on the Brazilian border with Bolivia) to get passport stamps. Neither Iñapari nor Brasiléia is set up to issue visas. (See Iquitos later in this chapter for more information on Brazilian visa and entry requirements. If you need a visa for Brazil, get one in Lima or in your home country.) Brasiléia is about three hours from Assis by bus (US$9), which leaves at 6 am and 1 pm. A taxi will cost about US$36 and can be shared. Travel along the Río Acre to Brasiléia is reportedly possible when the water is high.

Charter flights can be arranged in Puerto Maldonado to Iberia, Iñapari or Río Branco in Brazil.

## MANU AREA

The Manu Biosphere Reserve covers almost 20,000 sq km (about the size of Wales), is the biggest protected rainforest area in Peru and is one of the best places in South America to see a wide variety of tropical wildlife. The reserve consists of Parque Nacional Manu, which covers almost ¾ of the area but can be entered only by a few researchers with specialized permits; the zona reservada, which has a lodge, camping areas, and can be visited with guided groups; and the zona cultural, which contains a few villages and road

access and can be entered by anyone. There isn't much difference between the rainforest in the accessible zona reservada and that of the parque nacional, and tour operators often refer to the former as the latter, even though the park itself is not entered. In addition, the areas around the reserve provide good wildlife-watching opportunities, especially near the Manu Wildlife Center, which is outside the reserve.

Manu has a greater biodiversity than any other reserve because it starts in the eastern slopes of the Andes and plunges down into the lowlands, thus covering a wide range of cloudforest and rainforest habitats. Several Indian groups continue to live here as they have for generations; some of these have had almost no contact with outsiders and do not appear to want contact anyway. Fortunately, this wish is respected. The most progressive aspect of the reserve is the fact that so much of it is so carefully protected – a rarity anywhere in the world.

The area was first protected in 1973. UNESCO declared it a Biosphere Reserve in 1977 and a World Natural Heritage Site in 1987. One reason the reserve is so successful in preserving such a large tract of virgin jungle is that it is remote and relatively inaccessible, and therefore has not been exploited by rubber tappers, loggers, oil companies or hunters, so wildlife is less threatened here than in much of Peru's rainforest.

Visiting Manu on your own requires a great deal of time, self-sufficiency and money, as well as an ability to travel in difficult conditions. It is now illegal to enter the reserve without a guide. It is easier and more worthwhile to go with an organized group, which almost every visitor now does. This can be arranged in Cuzco or with international tour operators. It is an expensive trip, but if you want to minimize expenses, you should arrange your trip in Cuzco and be very flexible with your travel plans. Travelers often report returning from Manu three or four days late. Don't plan an international airline connection the day after a Manu trip.

The best time to go is during the dry season from June to October; the reserve may be inaccessible or closed during the rainy months (January to April), except to visitors staying at the two lodges within the park boundaries (see Into the Reserve, later in this chapter). Permits, which are necessary to enter the park, are arranged by tour agencies. Transportation, accommodations, food and guides are also part of tour packages. Most visits to the park are for a week, although three-night stays at the lodge can be arranged.

## From Cuzco to Manu

If arriving overland, the first stage of the journey involves taking a truck from Cuzco via Paucartambo and Pilcopata to **Shintuya**. Trucks along the one-way road leave Monday, Wednesday, Friday and possibly Sunday from the Coliseo Cerrado in Cuzco. In the dry season, it takes about 20 hours to get to Shintuya. Breakdowns, flat tires, extreme overcrowding and delays are frequent, and during the rainy season (and even during the dry season), vehicles slide off the road. It is safer, more comfortable and more reliable to take the costlier tourist buses (which are basically heavy-duty trucks modified with seats) offered by the Cuzco tour operators.

There are two lodges between Paucartambo and Pilcopata. *Cock-of-the-Rock Lodge* is owned by Selva Sur, a local conservation group, and is operated by InkaNatura. Opened in 1997 and a few minutes' walk from a lek (mating ground) for cocks-of-the-rock (brightly colored rainforest birds that live on rock cliffs and outcrops; they conduct elaborate communal mating 'dances'), this lodge offers exceptional cloudforest birding at a pleasant 1600m elevation. The owners claim you can get photos of male cocks-of-the-rock displaying about 7m from your camera. The lodge has a restaurant and eight double rooms with shared hot showers. Normally, visitors overnight here en route to

Manu, but the lodge can be used as a destination in itself for cloudforest birding. Rates, including meals and round-trip transportation from Cuzco, are US$800 per person, double occupancy, for three days/two nights; discounts are available for longer stays and larger groups. In 1999, Manu Nature Tours opened (and is expanding) *Manu Cloud Forest Lodge*, near the same stretch of road. The lodge provides a few rooms with private hot showers, a restaurant, and birding opportunities in the high cloudforest.

The truck trip is often broken at **Pilcopata**, which is the biggest village along the road. There are a couple of basic hotels and a few stores. A bed costs about US$5, or floor/hammock space is US$2.50.

About 40km before Shintuya is the village of **Atalaya** on the Río Alto Madre de Dios. Across the river is the very pleasant *Amazonia Lodge* (☎/fax in Cuzco 23-1370, amazonia@correo.dnet.com.pe), in an old hacienda in the foothills of the Andes. The lodge offers clean, comfortable beds and communal cool showers for US$60 per person; simple but satisfactory meals are also included. There is no electricity, but that is more than compensated for by the low number of mosquitoes. There are trails into the forest, and the birding is excellent. Birders could profitably spend a few days here in relative comfort. The lodge can make transportation arrangements on request, or the tour agencies in Cuzco can make reservations. From Atalaya, boats leave for *Erika Lodge*, on a private reserve on the banks of the Alto Madre de Dios. Information is available from Ernesto Yallico (☎ 22-7765, Casilla 560, Cuzco). The lodge provides simple accommodations and meals, and camping is allowed. Rates are about US$35 per person, including meals.

The village of **Salvación**, about 10km closer to Shintuya, has a national-park office and a couple of basic hotels. Ask here for boats into the

Kinkajou

zona reservada – the park personnel may know of any trips planned for the near future, and if you're lucky, you might be able to join them.

Shintuya is the end of the road at this time and is the closest village to the park, but it has only a few places to stay. You may be able to camp at the mission station by talking to the priest. The Ecuadorian/Dutch Moscoso family lives 30 minutes downriver from Shintuya and operates *Pantiacolla Lodge*, which can be booked through Pantiacolla Tours in Cuzco. The rate is about US$55 per person including food. The lodge is on the margin of the parque nacional, and good wildlife sightings have been reported. There are 11 double rooms.

Boats can travel from Pilcopata, Atalaya, Salvación or Shintuya toward Manu. People on tours often start river travel from Atalaya after a night in a lodge. The few visitors who attempt to travel independently hire a boat in Shintuya, usually for at least several days. Expect to pay several hundred dollars for a week, plus US$100 to US$200 for gas. You might have to wait several days for a boat to become available unless you've made advance arrangements through the operators in Cuzco; they can arrange a boat and driver even if you don't take a full tour.

The boat journey down the Alto Madre de Dios to the Río Manu takes almost a day, depending on how fast a boat you have. At the junction is the village of **Boca Manu**, with simple stores and bars. This village is known for building the best river boats in the area, and it is interesting to see them in various stages of construction. A few minutes from the village is the Boca Manu airstrip, often the starting point for commercial trips into the park. Trans Andes (in the Cuzco airport ☎ 22-4638) flies small aircraft here most days for US$105. Most seats are taken up with tour groups, who can also charter the aircraft if necessary. A US$10 airport fee is charged, payable in Cuzco before you leave.

## Into the Reserve

The virgin jungle of the zona reservada lies up the Río Manu northwest of Boca Manu. At the Romero guardpost, about an hour from Boca Manu, you pay a park entrance fee of US$15 per person. Continuing beyond is only possible with a guide and permit, both arranged through Cuzco operators. Near Romero are a few trails. (During a recent stop at this guardpost, I saw a Muscovy duck, green ibis, rufescent tiger-heron and white-winged swallow all at the same time in a single binocular field.)

Another six hours upstream is **Cocha Salvador**, one of the park's largest and most beautiful lakes, where there are camping and hiking possibilities. Other areas in the park also have trails and camping. If you're patient, wildlife can be seen in most areas. This is not wide-open habitat like the African plains. The thick vegetation will obscure many animals, and a skilled guide is very useful in helping you to see them.

During a one-week trip, you can reasonably expect to see scores of different bird species, several species of monkey, and possibly a few other mammals. Jaguars, tapirs, giant anteaters, tamanduas (a kind of anteater), capybaras, peccaries and giant river otters are among the common large mammals of Manu. But they are elusive, and you can consider a trip very successful if you see two or three large mammals during a week's visit. Smaller mammals you might see include kinkajous, pacas, agoutis, squirrels, brocket deer, ocelots and armadillos. Other animals include river turtles and caiman (which are frequently seen), snakes (which are less often spotted) and a variety of other reptiles and amphibians. Colorful butterflies and less pleasing insects also abound.

There are two lodges within the park. *Manu Lodge* is operated by Manu Nature Tours and is normally used by their tour groups. Twelve double rooms are screened and have comfortable beds; there are cold showers. The lodge is on Cocha Juarez, a 2km-long oxbow lake, and is about a kilometer from the Río Manu. For an extra fee, a climb up to a canopy platform can be arranged. There is a 20km network of trails from the lodge around the lake and beyond. Beyond Manu Lodge is the rustic *Matsiguenka Albergue*, which was built in traditional style by Matsiguenka Indians in 1998.

Ask at the conservation agencies in Cuzco for information.

Camping, usually on the sandy beaches of the Río Manu, Cocha Salvador, Cocha Otorongo or a few other lakes, is another possibility. Tour operators can provide all necessary equipment. During the rainy season (January to April), these beaches are flooded and the park is closed to camping. Campers should be prepared with plenty of insect repellent during the rest of the year.

## Manu Wildlife Center & Area

A two-hour boat ride southeast (right) of Boca Manu on the Río Madre de Dios takes you to *Manu Wildlife Center*. The center is a jungle lodge jointly owned by Manu Expeditions, Selva Sur and InkaNatura, all of which accept reservations. Although the lodge is not in Manu Biosphere Reserve, it is recommended for its exceptional wildlife-watching and birding opportunities. There are about 16 double cabins, some with private bath (private facilities are planned for all cabins), hot showers, a dining room and a bar/hammock room. The lodge is set in tropical gardens.

There are 48km of trails around the Manu Wildlife Center, where 10 species of monkeys, as well as other wildlife, can be seen. Two canopy platforms are a short walk away, and one is always available for guests wishing to view the top of the rainforest and look for birds that frequent the canopy.

A 3km walk through the forest brings you to a natural salt lick, where there is a raised platform with mosquito nets for viewing the nightly activities of the tapirs. This hike is for visitors who can negotiate forest trails by flashlight. Visitors may wait for hours to see the animals. Nothing is guaranteed, but the chances are excellent if you have the patience. (I was lucky enough to see a mother and nursing young on my second visit after a hot, silent, three-hour wait. I also saw a red brocket deer and an armadillo on these nocturnal excursions.) Other visitors have reported good sightings within a few minutes of their arrival. Note that there isn't much happening at the lick during the day.

A short boat ride on the Madre de Dios brings visitors to a well-known salt lick that attracts various species of parrots and macaws. Most mornings, you can see flocks in the hundreds. The largest flocks are seen from late July to September. As the rainy season kicks in, the numbers diminish, though I was impressed by the display when I visited in November. Numbers continue to fall in the early months of the year, and June is the worst month – when birds don't visit the salt lick at all. May and early July aren't reliable either, though ornithologists report the presence of the birds in other nearby areas during these months, and birders will usually see them.

The macaw lick is visited on a floating catamaran blind, providing a concealed enclosure from which 20 people can view wildlife. The catamaran is stable enough to be able to use a tripod and scope or telephoto lens, and gets about halfway across the river. The boat drivers are experienced and won't bring the blind too close to disturb the birds.

In addition to the trails and salt licks, there are a couple of nearby lakes where paddled catamarans provide transportation and giant otters may be seen (as well as various birds and other animals). Visitors wishing to see the macaw and tapir lick, lakes and canopy, and to hike the trails in search of wildlife should plan on a three-night stay at the Manu Wildlife Center, though shorter and longer stays are workable.

Apart from staying at the Manu Wildlife Center, there is also *Blanquillo Lodge*, which provides basic facilities and a camping area nearby. Some companies in Cuzco arrange this cheaper option.

If you continue down the fairly busy Madre de Dios, past gold-panning areas to Puerto Maldonado, you won't see much wildlife. This takes 14 hours to two days and may cost as little as US$10 if you can find a boat heading that way. But transportation to Puerto Maldonado is infrequent, and almost all visitors return to Cuzco.

## Tours

However you do it, an expedition to Manu will not be cheap, and unless you go on a guided tour, the park is not easy to reach. It is, however, the best area in Peru to see jungle habitat and wildlife. Allow at least one week for the trip.

Many tour operators in Cuzco offer trips to Manu. It is important to check whether the company is permitted to operate within the zona reservada, as very few are. The companies listed in this section were recently all authorized to operate within Manu by the national-park service and maintain some level of conservation and low-impact practices. (Check with the national-park service or ask the tour company for documents that verify their authorization.) The number of permits to operate tours is limited, and other agencies that may offer 'Manu' are either operating outside the zona reservada or are acting as intermediaries for an authorized operator.

The costs of tours depend partly on whether you camp or stay in a lodge, and whether you arrive/depart overland or by air. The more expensive companies also offer more reliable and trained multilingual guides, better-maintained equipment, a wider variety of food and intangibles such as local experience, suitable insurance and emergency procedures. All agencies provide transportation, food, purified drinking water, guides, permits and camping equipment or screens in lodge rooms. Personal items such as a sleeping bag (unless staying in a lodge), insect repellent, sunblock, flashlight with spare batteries, suitable clothing and bottled drinks are the client's responsibility. Binoculars are highly recommended – rent some in Cuzco if you don't have any.

The cheapest tours start at almost US$500 and last eight days and seven nights, including bus and boat arrival and departure on the first two and last two days. Shorter tours, with flights, can be arranged but are more expensive. The cheapest authorized agency is Expediciones Vilca (☎/fax 25-1872, manuvilca@ protelsa.com.pe, Amargura 101); they do camping tours, but I haven't had any feedback about them, though the guide I spoke to seemed pleasant and knowledgeable. Pantiacolla Tours (☎ 23-8323, fax 25-2696, pantiac@ mail.cosapidata.com.pe, www.pantiacolla .com, Plateros 360) continues to be recom-

mended by budget travelers. Pantiacolla Tours' owners were raised in the area and are knowledgeable. Their cheapest trips (US$700 per person, nine-day/eight-night trip including overland transportation) usually combine staying at their own lodge and camping. These tours can include camping near the macaw lick by the Blanquillo Lodge.

Manu Expeditions (☎ 22-6671, 23-9974, fax 23-6706, adventure@manuexpeditions.com, www.manuexpeditions.com, Pardo 895) is highly recommended for camping trips. They have some fine guides, but if you are lucky enough to go with the owner, British ornithologist and longtime Cuzco resident Barry Walker, you will really be in excellent hands, particularly if birding is your main interest. (Barry was featured in Michael Palin's *Full Circle* travel series on BBC.) All guides are experienced and knowledgeable about the flora, fauna and ecology of the rainforest. Costs include food and all camping gear (thick mattress pads, roomy two-person tents and large screened dining tents with folding camp stools and table). Cooks prepare three-course dinners, and alcoholic beverages are available. A camp crew takes care of putting up tents, and the camping trips are as comfortable as conditions permit.

As co-owners of the Manu Wildlife Center, Manu Expeditions' trips often include three nights at this lodge. Their most popular trip leaves every Sunday except in February and March and lasts nine days/ eight nights, including overland transportation to Manu with an overnight at Amazonia Lodge, four nights of camping in the zona reservada, three nights at Manu Wildlife Center and a flight back to Cuzco. This costs US$1595. The overland section can include a mountain-biking descent if arranged in advance. A six-day trip, excluding the Manu Wildlife Center, is US$1200. A four-day/ three-night trip to the Manu Wildlife Center and a round-trip flight is US$1095. Extended trips, with stays at Cock-of-the-Rock Lodge and more nights at Amazonia Lodge, can be arranged.

Manu Nature Tours (☎ 25-2721, fax 23-4793, mnt@amauta.rcp.net.pe, www.manu peru.com, Pardo 1046) operates the respected

Manu Lodge, which is open year round, even when the zona reservada is closed to camping. The lodge has 12 double rooms (private baths are planned) and a dining room/bar next to a lake, which is home to a breeding family of giant otters. A 20km trail network provides ample opportunities for spotting monkeys and birds, and guided visits to lakes and observation towers are also provided. An eight-day/seven-night tour, with five nights at Manu Lodge, going in by road and out by air, will cost roughly US$2100 per person, double occupancy during fixed departures (on Friday twice a month). This includes a bilingual naturalist guide and all meals; for an extra fee, mountain-biking or whitewater rafting can be incorporated into the road descent. Alternatively, you can fly in to and out of Boca Manu, which is a few dollars cheaper. Shorter trips with round-trip air transportation are US$1450 for three nights, or US$1625 for four nights.

InkaNatura (☎ 24-3408, 62-3666, ☎/fax 22-6392, inkanatura@chavin.rcp.net.pe, www .inkanatura.com, Avenida Sol 821, 2nd floor, Cuzco; see Organized Tours in the Getting Around chapter for more information), a co-owner of Manu Wildlife Center, can also arrange stays at that lodge and combine this with visits to other parts of the southeastern Peruvian rainforest. Most companies offer discounts during the low season (November through April) and for groups.

## CHANCHAMAYO
☎ 064

The most accessible jungle region east of Lima is known as Chanchamayo and comprises the neighboring towns of **La Merced** and **San Ramón**. These towns are entry points for farther excursions into the jungle. San Ramón is about 300km east of Lima and La Merced another 11 km. Chanchamayo and the surrounding jungle regions are popularly called La Selva Central, or Central Jungle. The area is noted for coffee and fruit production.

All buses to the region terminate in La Merced, the center for ground transportation in the region and the more important of the two towns. It has a population of over 10,000 and is a major coffee-marketing center. La Merced has a greater choice of hotels and restaurants, though the quieter San Ramón boasts the regional airstrip nearby. The two towns (locals consider them to be one) are linked by frequent colectivos.

La Merced is the center for vehicles heading north to Oxapampa and Pozuzo, northeast to Puerto Bermúdez and southeast to Satipo.

### Information
Both towns have a Banco de Crédito, and La Merced also has an Interbanc. There is a post office in La Merced and telephone offices in both towns. La Merced has a small hospital (☎ 53-1002).

### Things to See & Do
There is a colorful daily market in La Merced. A weekend market at San Luis de Shuaro, 22km beyond La Merced, is also interesting – local Indians visit it. You'll find a basic hotel here. Campa Indians occasionally come into La Merced to sell handicrafts.

Avenida 2 de Mayo is good for views of La Merced; the stairs at the north end afford a good view of the town, and from the balcony at the south end, there is a photogenic river view.

An interesting botanical garden is on the grounds of El Refugio Hotel in San Ramón.

### Places to Stay
**La Merced** The cheapest hotels are not particularly clean and have an erratic water supply, though you can bathe in the river as the locals do. *Hostal Romero* (☎ 53-1106, Palca 419) is a decent cheapie at US$4.50/7 for singles/doubles. They have a few slightly more expensive rooms with private bath, though water supply is for only a few hours a day. The most basic places are *Hostal Chuncho* (☎ 53-1161, Lima 220) and *Hostal Iquitos* (Callao 210), which charge US$3/5. Slightly better digs are found at *Hostal Roca* (Ayacucho 256) and *Hostal Santa Rosa* (☎ 53-1012, 2 de Mayo 447), which charge US$4/6.

*Hostal Residencial San Felipe* (☎ 53-1046, 2 de Mayo 426) is friendly and charges

AMAZON BASIN

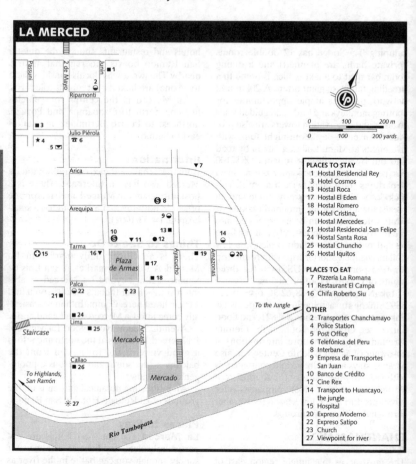

**LA MERCED**

| 0 | 100 | 200 m |
| 0 | 100 | 200 yards |

**PLACES TO STAY**
1  Hostal Residencial Rey
3  Hotel Cosmos
13  Hostal Roca
17  Hostal El Eden
18  Hostal Romero
19  Hotel Cristina,
   Hostal Mercedes
21  Hostal Residencial San Felipe
24  Hostal Santa Rosa
25  Hostal Chuncho
26  Hostal Iquitos

**PLACES TO EAT**
7  Pizzería La Romana
11  Restaurant El Campa
16  Chifa Roberto Siu

**OTHER**
2  Transportes Chanchamayo
4  Police Station
5  Post Office
6  Telefónica del Peru
8  Interbanc
9  Empresa de Transportes
   San Juan
10  Banco de Crédito
12  Cine Rex
14  Transport to Huancayo,
   the jungle
15  Hospital
20  Expreso Moderno
22  Expreso Satipo
23  Church
27  Viewpoint for river

US$5/8. Also good is the popular *Hotel Cosmos* (☎ 53-1051), on Julio Piérola at Passuni. It has clean rooms with private bath at US$8/10. *Hotel Cristina* (☎ 53-1276, Tarma 582) charges US$8/12 for rooms with private bath. Next door, *Hostal Mercedes* (☎/fax 53-1304, Tarma 576) has rooms with TV and hot water for US$10/13.

*Hostal Residencial Rey* (☎ 53-1185, Junín 103) provides towels, soap, toilet paper and sometimes hot water. There are telephones in the rooms, and a cafeteria on the top floor serves good breakfasts. Climb onto the roof for a view of the town. Rooms are US$14/18.

*Hostal El Eden* (☎ 53-1183, 53-2340, Ancash 347), on the plaza, has OK rooms with TV, telephones, fans and private baths with cold water for US$14/18.

**San Ramón**  Most of San Ramón's hotels are clustered within a block of the intersection of Avenida Paucartambo and the main street, Avenida Progreso. The cheapest includes *Hotel Colón* (☎ 33-1120, Progreso 266) at US$4.50/7. *Hotel Chanchamayo* (☎ 22-1008, Progreso 291) is quite good at US$4.50/7.50 or US$7/10 with private bath. *Hotel Conquistador* (☎/fax 33-1157,

*Progreso 298)* is a good hotel that charges US$15/21 but raises rates in the high season.

My favorite hotel in the Chanchamayo region is *El Refugio Hotel* (☎/fax 33-1082, *Ejército 490)*, which is about a 10-minute walk from the town center. The hotel grounds are also a small but well-designed botanical garden. The various exotic plants are labeled and tend to attract butterflies and birds. Comfortable bungalows with hot showers cost about US$20/25. Cheaper rooms with cold showers are available.

## Places to Eat

**La Merced** There are many more restaurants here than in San Ramón. *Restaurant El Campa*, on the plaza, has very good Chinese and Peruvian dishes that are not very expensive. There is an outdoor area, where you can dine under thatched roofs. *Chifa Roberto Siu* (☎ 53-1207, *Junín 310)*, on the plaza, is decent, and *Pizzería La Romana* (*Arica 309)* is your best pizza choice.

**San Ramón** The *Chifa Felipe Siu* (☎ 33-1078, *Progreso 440)* is good, and the chifa in the *Hotel Conquistador* is also OK. The restaurant in *El Refugio Hotel* is just as good.

## Getting There & Away

**Air** The Chanchamayo airstrip is about a 30-minute walk from San Ramón. Colectivos and taxis go there.

The main airlines do not fly into this airstrip, and service is provided by local companies with light aircraft. There are daily flights to Puerto Bermúdez.

For other destinations, your best bet is to turn up at the airport early (before 9 am) and wait for a flight. Planes carry between five and nine passengers and leave as soon as they are full. Other frequent destinations are Atalaya, Satipo, Puerto Inca and Pucallpa. If you are traveling in a group, you can charter your own plane to almost anywhere in the region (you can charter a plane by yourself too, but you have to pay for the empty seats). One company is Amsa (☎ 33-1254).

There is a simple airport cafeteria serving snacks and cold drinks, including beer.

**Bus** There are direct buses from Lima to Chanchamayo, though some travelers find it convenient to break the journey at Tarma. It is worth trying to travel the 70km stretch from Tarma to San Ramón in daylight for the views (at 850m, San Ramón is a 2200m descent from Tarma).

Most buses leave from La Merced and pick up passengers in San Ramón, so there is a better seat selection in La Merced. Companies that make the eight- to 10-hour journey to Lima are Transportes Chanchamayo (☎ 53-1259), Expreso Moderno (☎ 53-1977) and Expreso Satipo. Fares are US$6 to US$7.

Empresa de Transportes San Juan (☎ 53-1522) charges about US$4 for the six-hour journey to Huancayo (with stops at Tarma and Jauja). Colectivos to Huancayo from Avenida Tarma at Amazonas are faster and charge a bit more. San Juan also has buses to Oxapampa and Villarica.

If you are looking for transportation into the jungle, go to the east end of Avenida Tarma, where you'll find all kinds of trucks, cars, minibuses and jeeps. Minibuses will take you to Satipo (US$4.50, 6 hours), Oxapampa (US$3.50, 4 hours) and Puerto Bermúdez (US$6.50, 7 to 9 hours), as well as to intermediate towns such as San Luis de Shuaro (en route to Oxapampa). Colectivo taxis are more expensive. Schedules are haphazard – go down there as early as you can and ask around. Sometimes you can buy tickets the night before, but as things are generally disorganized, you may have to rely on luck and persuasiveness.

## Getting Around

Minibuses cruise around La Merced, picking up passengers that are going to San Ramón (US$0.30). In San Ramón, buses head northeast on Progreso and then along Pardo en route to La Merced.

## SATIPO
☎ 064

This small jungle town is the center of a minor fruit-producing region and lies about 130km by road southeast of La Merced. Satipo is also linked by road to the highlands of Huancayo. There is a Banco de Crédito.

## Places to Stay

For such an isolated little town, Satipo has a surprising number of hotels. Among the best is *Hotel Majestic (Plaza Principal 408)*, which charges US$18 for a double room with warm showers; they have electricity from 6 pm to midnight only. The fairly basic *Hostal Palermo (☎ 54-5020, Manuel Prado 229)* charges US$10 for a double with a grubby bath. Other possibilities include *Hostal San José (☎ 54-5105, 54-5990, AB Leguía 670)* and *Hostal Residencial Colonos (☎ 54-5155, Colonos Fundadores 572)*. There are several other cheap and more basic hotels.

## Getting There & Away

**Air** There is an airport where light aircraft can be chartered. Flights to Pucallpa, San Ramón and other jungle towns leave irregularly, when there are enough passengers.

**Bus** Minibuses leave many times a day for La Merced. A few slower but more spacious buses leave every morning and evening for La Merced, some continuing to Lima. Ask around – it's a small town. Empresa de Transportes La Selva has several buses a week leaving at 7 am to Huancayo (US$9, 12 hours) via the spectacular but difficult direct road through Comas.

## OXAPAMPA & POZUZO

About 75km north of La Merced is the ranching and coffee center of Oxapampa. It used to be important for logging, but most of the trees have now been cut down. Look around at your fellow passengers on the bus north from La Merced – occasional blonde heads and blue eyes attest to the several hundred German settlers who arrived in the mid-19th century. Their descendants live in Oxapampa or in Pozuzo (about 4 to 6 hours north of Oxapampa by daily minibus; longer in the wet season) and have preserved many Germanic customs: buildings have a Tyrolean look to them, Austrian-German food is prepared and an old-fashioned form of German is still spoken by some families. Although the area has been settled for over 100 years, it is remote and rarely visited. The people are friendly and interested in talking with tourists.

East of the Oxapampa-Pozuzo road is the 122,000-hectare **Parque Nacional Yanachaga-Chemillén**, which is largely inaccessible and has no tourist services.

Oxapampa has a Banco de Crédito and several simple and cheap hotels. The hostels *Arias, Liz* and *Mama Lily* have been recommended as clean and charge about US$3 per person. Pozuzo also has several hotels, of which *El Tirol* is the best. It charges about US$10 per person including meals. *Hostal Prusia* is also OK.

## PUERTO BERMÚDEZ
☎ 064

Puerto Bermúdez is a sleepy port on the Río Pachitea, reachable from La Merced by bus. Looking at the huddle of dugout canoes tied up to the mud bank of the small river flowing past the town, it is difficult to imagine that one can embark here on a river journey that would eventually lead down the Amazon to the Atlantic.

The area southeast of Puerto Bermúdez is the home of the Ashaninka Indians. This is the largest Amazon Indian group in Peru. In the late 1980s and early '90s, attempts were made to indoctrinate the Ashaninka by the Sendero Luminoso guerrillas. When the guerrillas were unable to get the Indians' total support, they tried intimidation by massacring dozens. Thankfully, Sendero activity has been reduced since the capture of the guerrilla leaders. People interested in learning more about the Ashaninka can contact the *jefe* (leader) of the official local native organization, ANAP, based in Puerto Bermúdez. Permission to visit villages with a local guide can be obtained.

## Places to Stay & Eat

The best place to stay is the friendly and helpful *Albergue Humboldt (☎ 76-0210)*, near the river. They offer simple rooms with shared showers for US$3 per person. There's electricity from 6 to 11:30 pm, and you can sleep in a hammock or camp. Three meals, plus drinking water, tea and coffee, are offered for about US$5 a day.

Another basic hotel right by the river is *Hostal Tania*, which charges US$3 per person for a bed, four walls and a river view. The river view is pretty, especially at dawn and dusk. The town's one main street has simple eateries.

## Getting There & Away
Minibuses to and from La Merced are frequent. Continuing north, the road deteriorates, and erratic transportation to **Ciudad Constitución**, **Zungaro**, **Puerto Inca** and Pucallpa is often by truck. This trip is very rough and can take two to three days; the communities passed have extremely basic hotels and other facilities. Boats go north to Ciudad Constitución and Puerto Inca, but do not have particular schedules. During the dry season, the river may be too low for passage, and the road is the better bet. During the wet months, the road can be barely passable, and boats are better. You can also fly from the airstrip. The folks at Albergue Humboldt know what's going on.

There have been problems reported with drug-running and nighttime assaults. Travel during the day for safety.

## PUCALLPA
☎ 064

With an approximate population of 200,000, Pucallpa is Peru's fastest-growing jungle town and the biggest to be linked directly with Lima by road. It is the capital of the Department of Ucayali but is not a particularly attractive city. Apart from a few modern banks and hotels, many of its buildings have been hastily constructed in concrete with tin roofs. Its roads are slowly being paved, but many of those away from the town center are still red mud quagmires in the wet season and choking red dust in the dry. The huge flocks of vultures circling lazily over the markets, plazas and docks are one of Pucallpa's most startling sights. The roofs of the buildings around the food market are often crowded with scores of the huge black birds silently waiting for scraps to be thrown out. The town is dirty and noisy, and few travelers enjoy it, though locals take pride in the town's progress and growth. The visitor, having felt the pulse of

the city in the languid flapping of the vultures' wings, isn't left with much to do.

When you are ready to move on, go down to the Pucallpa docks to find a river boat heading to Iquitos; while you're looking, you can experience firsthand the rough-and-tumble atmosphere of a busy, hard-working river port.

One hint: Just as you've become used to remembering that 'll' is always pronounced 'y' in Spanish, you have come to one of the very few exceptions to this rule; Pucallpa is pronounced 'pu-**kal**-pa.'

## Information
The Dirección Regional de Industria y Turismo (☎ 57-1303, 2 de Mayo 111) has limited tourist information.

Several banks change money and traveler's checks and have ATMs. Street money-changers hang around the Hotel Mercedes. Western Union is at Viajes Laser (☎ 57-1120, fax 57-3776, Raimondi 470), which is one of the better travel agencies in Pucallpa, but for jungle guides, go to Yarinacocha. Email services were lacking in 1998.

The Clínica Santa Rosa (☎ 57-5218, Inmaculada 529) has 24-hour medical attention and is quite good for stool, urine or blood tests if you get sick.

## Things to See & Do
The best thing to do is take the short bus trip to nearby Yarinacocha, a lovely oxbow lake where you can go canoeing, observe wildlife, visit Indian communities and purchase their handicrafts. Yarinacocha is the tourist area of Pucallpa, yet it is far from touristy – simple hotel, restaurant and boat services are provided in a casual atmosphere. It's worth spending a couple of days here. (See Yarinacocha, later in this chapter.)

About 4km from the center, off the road to the airport, is **Parque Natural**. Here, you'll find an Amazon zoo, a museum displaying Shipibo pottery and a few other objects, a small children's playground and a snack bar. Admission is US$0.70, and hours are 8:30 am to 5:30 pm daily. A motocarro will charge about US$5 to take you there, wait for an hour, and take you back.

AMAZON BASIN

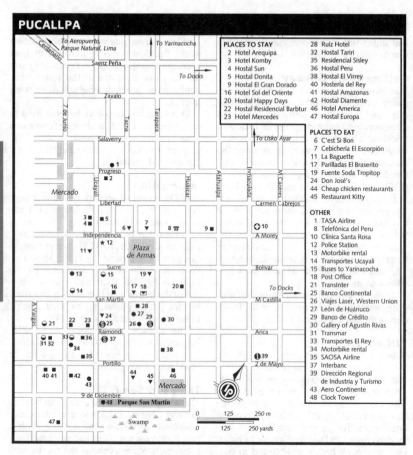

## PUCALLPA

To Aeropuerto,
Parque Natural, Lima
Centenario
Saenz Peña
To Yarinacocha
Zavalo
To Docks
7 de Junio
Tacna
Tarapaca
Salaverry
Ucayali
Progreso
■1
■2
Mercado
Huascar
Atahualpa
Inmaculada
M Cáceres
To Usko Ayar
Libertad
Carmen Cabrejos
3■
4■
■5
6▼
7
▼
8☎
9■
✛10
A Morey
Independencia
★12
11▼
Plaza
de Armas
Sucre
●13
●15
19▼
Bolivar
●14
16
17 18
▼ ✉
20■
To Docks
San Martín
M Castilla
A Vargas
●21
22
■
23
■
▼24
●27 29
26● ⑤
●30
Arica
Raimondi
■28
33●
31 32
■36
●34
⑤37
■35
●39
2 de Mayo
40 41
■42
●43
44
▼
45
▼
■46
Mercado
Portillo
9 de Diciembre
●48  Parque San Martín
47■
Swamp

0    125    250 m
0    125    250 yards

### PLACES TO STAY
2  Hotel Arequipa
3  Hotel Komby
4  Hostal Sun
5  Hostal Donita
9  Hostal El Gran Dorado
16 Hotel Sol del Oriente
20 Hostal Happy Days
22 Hostal Residencial Barbtur
23 Hotel Mercedes
28 Ruíz Hotel
32 Hostal Tariri
35 Residencial Sisley
36 Hostal Peru
38 Hostal El Virrey
40 Hostería del Rey
41 Hostal Amazonas
42 Hostal Diamente
46 Hotel America
47 Hostal Europa

### PLACES TO EAT
6  C'est Si Bon
7  Cebichería El Escorpión
11 La Baguette
17 Parilladas El Braserito
19 Fuente Soda Tropitop
24 Don José's
44 Cheap chicken restaurants
45 Restaurant Kitty

### OTHER
1  TASA Airline
8  Telefónica del Peru
10 Clínica Santa Rosa
12 Police Station
13 Motorbike rental
14 Transportes Ucayali
15 Buses to Yarinacocha
18 Post Office
21 TransInter
25 Banco Continental
26 Viajes Laser, Western Union
27 León de Huánuco
29 Banco de Crédito
30 Gallery of Agustín Rivas
31 Transmar
33 Transportes El Rey
34 Motorbike rental
35 SAOSA Airline
37 Interbanc
39 Dirección Regional
   de Industria y Turismo
43 Aero Continente
48 Clock Tower

Usko Ayar (☎ 57-3088, Sánchez Cerro 465) is the gallery of the visionary local artist Pablo Amaringo, who has used *ayahuasca* for artistic inspiration (ayahuasca is a hallucinogenic drink made from a vine). There is also a small school for Amazon artists. Hours are 10 am to 5 pm daily. Tell drivers it's near the Iglesia Fray Marcos.

Agustín Rivas is a famed local wood-carver whose work graces the lobbies of some of Pucallpa's best hotels and businesses. The 2nd floor of his house (☎ 57-1834, Tarapaca 861) serves as his gallery. Ring the bell to enter.

## Places to Stay

**Budget** One of the cheapest hotels in town is *Hostal Europa*, on the 1100 block of 7 de Junio. It's dirty and rundown, though probably the best of the three dives on the same block. I wouldn't recommend any of them for single female travelers. Rates are under US$4 per person and rooms vary in quality, so look at several if you are determined to economize. The better *Hostal Diamante* (☎ 57-3772, 7 de Junio 1021) has basic rooms with bath and fan for US$5/8.50 for singles/doubles. *Hostal Sun* (☎ 57-4260, Ucayali 380) isn't bad and charges US$4.50/7.50 for fairly clean singles/doubles with shared cold showers. *Hostal Amazonas (☎ 57-1080, Portillo 729)* has basic and dingy rooms with private bath and fan for US$7/8. Almost next door, *Hostería del Rey (☎ 57-5815, Portillo 747)* is similarly priced but looks a bit nicer.

The clean, friendly and recommended *Residencial Sisley (☎ 57-5137, Portillo 658)* charges US$8.50/12 for rooms with private cold showers, fans and TV. The small, friendly, reasonably clean and popular *Hostal Residencial Barbtur (☎ 57-2532, Raimondi 670)* is similar and has a few cheaper rooms with shared bath. The bigger *Hostal Peru (☎ 57-5128, Raimondi 639)* is US$8.50/13.50 with bath and fan, and has some rooms with shared bath at US$6/9.

*Hostal Tariri (☎ 57-5147, Raimondi 733)* is OK at US$6/9. *Hostal Donita (☎ 57-1480, Ucayali 369)* is adequate at US$6/9 or US$8.50/14 with private bath.

**Mid-Range** All the following have rooms with private baths, fans and TV. *Hotel Komby (☎ 57-1184, Ucayali 360)* seems like a good deal at US$12/16 for clean rooms. There is a swimming pool, restaurant and bar. The similarly priced *Hostal El Virrey (☎ 57-5580, ☎/fax 59-0579, Tarapaca 945)* has a restaurant and is a good value; their rooms have telephones. The new *Hostal El Gran Dorado (☎ 57-3330, ☎/fax 57-3338, Independencia 204)* charges US$14/17 and plans on adding more expensive air-conditioned rooms.

One of the best mid-range hotels is the clean *Hotel Arequipa (☎ 57-1348, 57-3112, fax 57-3171, Progreso 573)*. They charge US$15/20 for rooms with fans, or US$24/28 with air-conditioning, hot showers and minirefrigerators. Rooms have telephones and cable TV, and there is a restaurant. *Hostal Happy Days (☎ 57-2067, fax 57-1940, Huáscar 440)* has small but clean rooms on a quiet street for US$15/20.

*Hotel America (☎/fax 57-1378, 57-5989, Portillo 357)* has small, simple rooms with minirefrigerators, telephones and air-conditioning for US$31/42 or US$18/22 with fans. There is a small restaurant, and continental breakfast is included. *Ruíz Hotel (☎ 57-1280, fax 57-1028, San Martín 475)* charges US$35/48 including breakfast. Rooms are spartan, but bigger than average, and have cable TV, telephones, warm showers, minibars and air-conditioning. The central *Hotel Mercedes (☎ 57-5120, ☎/fax 57-1191, Raimondi 610)* was Pucallpa's first good hotel and has a certain dated charm and character. It has a pool, restaurant and bar. Rates are US$42/53 for rooms with telephones, minirefrigerators and air-conditioning or US$23/30 with fan. Suites are US$65.

**Top End** The modern and central *Hotel Sol del Oriente (☎ 57-5154, fax 57-5510, San Martín 552)* has a swimming pool, bar, restaurant and air-conditioned rooms with telephones and hot water. Rooms are overpriced at US$50/75 including continental breakfast. Suites start at US$105.

## Places to Eat

The town abounds with cheap or mid-range restaurants, though few are especially noteworthy. The heat in the middle of the day means that restaurants tend to open early (by 7 am) for breakfast. Many are closed Sunday.

As Pucallpa is usually hot, places to drink are as important as places to eat. For a variety of cold, freshly squeezed fruit juices, *Don José's (Ucayali 661)* is good. In addition to juices, they serve reasonably priced meals and sandwiches.

*La Baguette (Ucayali 490)* is clean and sells bread, cakes and pastries. For ceviches and other meals in the US$3-to-US$6 range, a good place is *Cebichería El Escorpión*, on the northwest side of the Plaza de Armas. It is clean and has sidewalk tables for viewing the plaza. Ice-cream and snack places on the plaza include *C'est Si Bon* and *Fuente Soda Tropitop*.

Of the many inexpensive local places, *Restaurant Kitty (Tarapaca 1062)* is clean and popular. A couple of decent, cheap and popular chicken restaurants are on Tacna near Parque San Martín. A quarter chicken with an order of fries is about US$2.25. There's also a chicken place by the Plaza de Armas. For good grills (steak, fish and venison), *Parrilladas El Braserito (San*

AMAZON BASIN

*Martín 498)* is a good choice. Most meals are US$5 to US$8. The better hotels have decent restaurants.

The local beer, San Juan, has the distinction of being the only beer brewed in the Amazon – whether that is the entire Amazon or just the Peruvian Amazon is open to discussion.

If you want to splash out a little, go to *El Establo* steak house. It's out of town, on the road to the airport (take a taxi), and serves the best steaks and grills in town. Meals are in the US$6-to-US$15 range. This is Pucallpa's best restaurant, and it is open noon to 3 pm and 6 to 11 pm Monday to Saturday.

## Shopping
The local Shipibo Indians wander the streets with souvenirs. More of their work is seen near Yarinacocha.

## Getting There & Away
**Air** Pucallpa's airport is small but busy. Most airlines have offices in the city center and at the airport, about 5km northwest of town. Aero Continente (☎ 57-1903, Ucayali 850) has daily direct flights to and from Lima and Iquitos. TANS has recently begun operating these routes as well.

Services to other towns (such as Ciudad Constitución, San Francisco, Tarapoto, Juanjuí, Atalaya, Sepahua, Contamaná, Bellavista, Tingo María, Tocache and Uchiza) are provided by small local airlines using light aircraft. Servicios Aereos del Oriente, or SAOSA (☎/fax 57- 1138, airport 57-8667, 57-2637, Portillo 654), flies most days to Tarapoto (US$50) and other destinations. Transportes Aereos, or TASA (☎ 57-5221, airport 57-5227, Progreso 547), has flights to Cruzeiro do Sul in Brazil. TASA also sometimes uses floatplanes from Yarinacocha to towns down the Río Ucayali. These and several other small airlines also provide charter services. It is often best to just go to the airport in the morning and ask around if you plan on flying to a jungle town. Often, a small plane will go as soon as it has filled its seats. Note that luggage is limited to 10kg per passenger.

**Bus** A direct bus to and from Lima takes about 24 hours in the dry season, but you can break the journey in Huánuco and Tingo María. The journey can take two days or more during the rainy season (especially January to April) if the road has been closed by mud slides.

León de Huánuco (☎ 57-2411, Tacna 655) and Transportes El Rey, on Raimondi at 7 de Junio, both have daily 10 am buses to Lima (US$13). Transmar (☎ 57-4900, Raimondi 793) has buses to Lima for US$12 at 7:30 and 10:30 am. Opposite, TransInter has daily buses to Tingo María.

Transportes Ucayali, on San Martín at 7 de Junio, has cars to Aguaytía and Tingo María (US$10, 6 hours) leaving about every hour starting at 4 am. At the same corner and along 7 de Junio, there are small bus companies that have minibuses to Aguaytía and Tingo María. Also ask around here for minibuses and trucks heading south to Zungaro, Ciudad Constitución and Puerto Bermúdez.

**River Boat** Pucallpa's port, called La Hoyada, is about 2.5km northeast of the town center, along unpaved roads. During the drier months (June to October/November), boats cannot reach the port and, instead, leave from El Mangual, 3km away along a very dusty road. Minibuses from the center charge about US$0.50 for the ride. Locals tell me that during the rainy season (February to April), boats go to the Plaza San Martín in Pucallpa.

Anyway, wherever the port is, you can get river boats along the Río Ucayali from Pucallpa to Iquitos (US$15 to US$25 including basic meals, 3 to 5 days). Boats announce their departure dates and destinations on chalkboards near the docks. It's easier to get a passage when the river is high. In the dry season, the river is too low for many of the boats, and passages are slower. This is not a trip for everyone; some people enjoy the experience, though one reader writes that the boat to Iquitos was 'jam-packed, stinky, dirty, awful, so we flew.' Another writes that he brought canned food and found the

## From Lima to the Amazon by Bus

A journey from coastal Lima climbs the steep western slopes of the Andes to a breathless 4843m above sea level, continues along the Andes at an average of over 4000m for several hours, then begins the dizzying descent down the cloudforested slopes of the eastern Andes to Pucallpa, at a mere 154m. This incredible change of scenery and altitude gives the traveler an exceptional look at Peru in cross section, and is one of the continent's most exciting and demanding intercity bus journeys.

From Tingo María (in the Central Highlands), the unpaved road climbs over the final pass in the eastern Andes before descending to Pucallpa in the Amazon Basin proper. There is an interesting story connected with building the road over this pass.

Until the 1930s, the road reached only as far as Huánuco, and engineers were carrying out surveys to find the easiest route to extend the road to Pucallpa. They were unable to find an obvious pass over the last range of the Andes and were preparing for an expensive road-building project. One of the engineers had been studying historical documents and maps of the region, some of which had been made as long ago as the 18th century by Franciscan missionaries exploring the area. One document, recounting a 1757 expedition by Padre Abad, led to the rediscovery of an extremely narrow, steep-walled gorge through the final mountain barrier. The road was built through this pass, saving much time and money, and reached Pucallpa in 1941. The pass is now named El Boquerón del Padre Abad.

Driving through the pass is spectacular and should be done in daylight. Exotic vegetation clings to waterfall-covered vertical walls, and there are several natural pools where it is possible to swim. The birdlife is prolific, and the careful observer may see troops of monkeys scurrying along the cliffs' ledges.

Unfortunately, public transportation only takes you through the pass; it's not a destination. Ideally, you could take a Tingo María-Pucallpa bus and get off at the pass, walk about 4km along the road (through the pass) and flag down a later bus. Otherwise, you'll have to be content with tantalizing glimpses through the bus windows. If you can't find a bus on to Pucallpa, you could stop at the village of Aguaytía. Between Aguaytía and Pucallpa, there are several police checkpoints; these take up a lot of time but are not a problem if your papers are in order. The checkpoints are to control drug-trafficking, and this section should be done in the daytime for safety.

three-day, high-water trip interesting, but would have found a longer trip tedious. Almost no English is spoken, but people are friendly.

Because airfares are not much more expensive than river-boat fares, there are fewer passenger boats than there used to be. Food is provided, but it is very basic and travelers often get sick – bring some of your own food and don't eat anything that isn't hot. Hammocks, toilet paper and mosquito repellent are essential but not provided. The

market in Pucallpa sells hammocks, but the mosquito repellent is of poor quality. Bottled drinks are sold on board, but it's worth bringing some large bottles of water or juice. If heading to Brazil, it's more convenient to fly to Iquitos and begin your river journey from there.

Jungle 'guides' approaching you on the Pucallpa waterfront are usually unreliable and sometimes dishonest. There isn't much to do in the way of jungle trips from the dock anyway. If you want to make an excursion

## A Road to Brazil?

Some maps show roads continuing east of Pucallpa to Cruzeiro do Sul in Brazil. This is wishful thinking in the extreme, because there is not even a jeep track part of the way there – absolutely nothing.

Japanese lumber importers, however, are making an effort to get this road built so they can import Amazon timber from Brazil more cheaply. Environmentalists are concerned that this will exacerbate the already uncontrolled felling of the Amazon rainforest.

into the jungle, you should look for a reliable service in Yarinacocha. For a river-boat passage, ask at any likely looking boat, but don't pay until you and your luggage are aboard the boat of your choice. Then pay the captain (*capitán*) and no one else.

Don't wander around the docks with your luggage looking for a boat; arrange a trip, then return with your luggage. Boats are sometimes delayed for some days before the cargo is loaded, but captains will often let you sling your hammock and stay aboard at no extra cost while you wait for departure. Be aware of the danger of theft in La Hoyada dock area and keep in mind that drug-running boats leave from here too. Police vigilance, however, has considerably decreased the number of drug-running boats in recent years.

Finding a boat to the ports of Contamaná and Requena is not difficult. Ask around for speedboats to Contamaná (US$22, about 5 hours). The return trip (US$27, 6 to 7 hours) goes against the current. They leave daily about noon in each direction. You will probably want to return to Pucallpa, because onward travel from Contamaná to Iquitos is not easy.

Contamaná has a colorful waterfront market, a frontier-town atmosphere and, like most river towns, is settled mainly by mestizo colonists. Accommodations are limited in Contamaná. There are reportedly two dirty, noisy hotels that charge about US$2.50 per person, and the better *Hotel Mechita* (☎ 094-85-1025, 85-1055, 85-1063, 85-1001). At Hotel Mechita, rooms with private bath and TV cost about US$10 per person. The village of **Roroboya**, a little over halfway between Pucallpa and Contamaná, is a Shipibo Indian community.

The next major port is **Orellana**, where *Hostal Laurita*, by the waterfront, charges about US$2.50 per person and has nine rooms that share two showers. There are other basic places to stay.

In the town of **Requena** (2 to 4 days from Iquitos), *Hotel Municipal* is basic, clean and charges US$5 per person. For about US$9 per person, stay at *Hotel Plaza Requena*, which has eight rooms with private cold baths and a plunge pool; or the six-room *Hotel Río Seco*, which has a restaurant and dance hall. From Requena, boats to Iquitos leave on most days, taking about 12 to 15 hours. Big boats with cabins and hammock space leave at 3 pm Sunday and Wednesday for US$4 (hammock) or US$7 (cabin). Locals in the small villages along the river are often helpful and friendly. The bigger ports have public telephones, which the locals use to let their families know how the trip is going.

### Getting Around

Motocarros will take you to the airport or Yarinacocha for under US$2, but you may have to bargain. Taxis are not much more expensive, except for the usual airport markup. Buses to Yarinacocha (US$0.25) leave from the corner of Ucayali and other places. Colectivo taxis charge US$0.30 and leave from the same corner.

Motorcycles can be rented for about US$3 per hour or US$22 for 12 hours (6 am to 6 pm). There are plenty of places in the town center; some are shown on the map.

### YARINACOCHA

Yarinacocha lies about 10km northeast of downtown Pucallpa. This attractive oxbow lake, once part of the Río Ucayali, is now entirely landlocked, though a small canal links the two bodies of water during the rainy season. The road from Pucallpa goes to the small port of Puerto Callao, which is the population center of the lake. Here, there are a few places to stay, several bars and restaurants, and boats for trips around the lake. You can visit Shipibo Indian villages and buy handicrafts or watch for wildlife in and around the lake. My wife and I have seen freshwater dolphins in the lake, a sloth and a meter-long green iguana in the trees, as well as plenty of exotic birds such as the curiously long-toed wattled jacana (which walks on lily pads) and the metallic-green Amazon kingfisher.

## Tours & Guides

Whether your interest lies in birdwatching, photography, visiting Indian villages, fishing, botany or just relaxing on a boat, you'll find plenty of peki-peki boat owners ready to oblige. Take your time in choosing; there's no point in going with the first offer unless you are sure you like your boat driver. Ask around, and be aware that some boat drivers are dishonest and may be involved in drug-trafficking. Guides are also available for walking trips into the surrounding forest including some overnight trips. If you are interested in fishing, the dry season is said to be the best.

A recommended guide is Gilber Reategui Sangama, who owns the boat *La Normita* on Yarinacocha. He has expedition supplies (sleeping pads, mosquito nets, purified drinking water) and is both knowledgeable and environmentally aware of the wildlife and people. As with all the local guides, he speaks little English, though he has an assistant who does. He is safe and reliable, and will cook most of your meals for you. He charges about US$35 per person per day, with a minimum of two people, for an average of three to five days. You can leave a message for him at his sister-in-law's (☎ 57-9018), or at La Cabaña Lodge (see Lakeside Lodges under Places to Stay & Eat later in this section). If he is not available, he recommends his uncle, Nemecio Sangama, who owns the boat *El Rayito*.

The boats of Pablito Tours do similarly priced overnight trips; one reader recommends them. When I stopped by the dock looking for Gilber Reategui recently, a boat driver on a Pablito Tours boat told me that Gilber's boat had sunk (which it certainly hadn't), so I have a hard time trusting him. Mauricio (nicknamed 'Boa') is a good guide but has no equipment. Others who have been recommended for local day tours include the friendly Miguel 'Pituco' Tans (☎ 59-7494) and his boat *Pituco*, Marly Alemán Arévalo and his boat *Julito* and Roy Riaño and Jorge Morales.

A good boat trip is up the northeast arm of the lake (to your right as you look at the lake from Puerto Callao) to view wildlife or visit the Shipibo village of San Francisco. Ask the boat driver to float slowly along, so that you can look for birdlife at the water's edge or sloths *(perezosos)* in the trees. Sunset is a good time to be on the lake. There is also a botanical garden that can be reached by a 45-minute boat ride followed by a 30-minute walk. Admission is US$0.70, and they are open daily 8 am to 4 pm. Go early in the morning to watch birds on the walk there. For short trips, boat drivers charge about US$5 an hour for the boat. It is always worth bargaining over the price, but the best way to do it is to set a price for the boat and then ask the boat driver if you can bring a couple of friends. As long as there are only a few of you, they don't normally complain, and you can split the cost.

## The Mission

There is a large, modern American missionary base on the outskirts of Puerto Callao that is affiliated to the SIL (Summer Institute of Linguistics). The missionaries have made contact with various Amazon tribes and work to translate the Indian languages into English and Spanish. By making a funcitonal alphabet for these previously unwritten languages, the missionaries hope to translate the New Testament into the area's many different Indian languages. There are opponents to the mission who feel the Indians will lose their tribal and cultural identities by becoming Christianized.

AMAZON BASIN

AMAZON BASIN

## Shipibo Indians & Their Handicrafts

The Shipibo Indians live along the Río Ucayali and its tributaries in small villages of simple, thatched platform houses. They are a matriarchal society. San Francisco, at the northwest end of the lake, is one village that is often visited.

The Shipibo women make fine ceramics and textiles decorated with highly distinctive, geometric designs. Some of the women come into Pucallpa to sell their pottery and material. It is also possible to buy directly from their villages, but the selection is not very good, and the villagers are distrustful of outsiders, particularly because of problems with guerrillas and drugrunners in the early 1990s.

The Shipibo also run a very fine cooperative craft store that collects work from about 40 villages. The store, called Maroti Shobo, is on the main plaza of Puerto Callao. There are many ceramics to choose from, and because each piece is handmade, it can be considered unique. Lengths of decorated cloth and other handicrafts are also available, but it is the ceramics that make the place really worthwhile. The pieces range from small pots and animal figurines to huge urns. The friendly staff (who speak primarily Spanish) will arrange international shipping if you buy a large piece. Prices are fixed (no bargaining) but are very fair. I bought my favorite South American handicraft here and every time I look at my sensitively molded, two-headed, ceremonial drinking pot, I am reminded of Peru.

## Places to Stay & Eat

**Puerto Callao** There are three small hotels in Puerto Callao near the waterfront; anyone can point them out to you. *Hotel El Pescador* is the cheapest place to stay. Its main attraction is its waterfront location; otherwise it's a pretty basic hotel with an erratic water supply. Rooms are about US$4/6. The new *Hotel El Campesino* is similar.

A short dirt road to the left along the waterfront leads to the best hotel in Puerto Callao – the 34-room *Hostal Los Delfines* (☎ 59-6423, fax 57-1129). For US$6, you can get an old, wooden cabin with a basic private

bath. Newer rooms are large and clean with fans, TV and private baths for US$9/13 (a little less for rooms without TV).

Several inexpensive restaurants and lively bars line the Puerto Callao waterfront.

**Lakeside Lodges** There are three jungle lodges around the lake. The Swiss-owned but American-managed *La Cabaña* (☎ 61 6679, 59-6786, Apartado 62, Pucallpa) is a 10 minute peki-peki ride across the lake from Puerto Callao (about US$2). The manager are an older couple, Ruth and Leroy Hert zler. Ruth was born and raised in the area and knows it well. The lodge became rundown due to lack of tourism during the terrorism years of the early 1990s, but is now recovering. They have a good *Rainforest Restaurant*, which you can visit even if you aren't staying there. The managers provide information and arrange local tours including overnight trips (US$35 to US$50 per person). The lodge is quiet, pleasant and has 15 simple bungalows with private baths and electricity. Rates are US$35 per person including all meals. You can hike to the botanical gardens in about an hour.

A few minutes beyond is *La Perla* (☎/fax 61-6004, Casilla 288, Pucallpa), which is run by Thomas and Rosaura, a younger German/Peruvian couple. Thomas speaks English and French. They have three double rooms, which share one bath, and charge US$25 per person including all meals, or US$30 per person if you book ahead and they meet you at the airport. They also arrange tours, and you can walk to the botanical gardens in about an hour.

About 30 minutes from Puerto Callao in a different direction is the Peruvian-owned *Pandisha Albergue* (☎ 61-6744, 57-5041). There are eight rooms with private bath and electricity from 6 am to 10 pm. Small rooms with one double bed are US$10, and larger rooms with two beds are US$15 (single or double). Rates include breakfast; other meals are available on request and cost about US$4. Their bar is popular with locals on weekends when there is music, but during the week, it is quiet.

## AGUAYTÍA
A little over halfway from Pucallpa to Tingo María is the small and fairly pleasant jungle town of Aguaytía, a possible base for visiting the nearby Boquerón del Padre Abad, on the main Pucallpa-Tingo María route. Aguaytía is on a river of the same name, which is spanned by an impressive suspension bridge.

### Places to Stay & Eat
There are a few cheap and basic hotels. The most pleasant seems to be an unnamed place above a store opposite the main bus

offices. It's clean and friendly, and it charges about US$5/7.50 in rooms with shared bath.

Most of the restaurants are along Sargento Suarez and charge US$1 for a simple set lunch.

### Getting There & Away
The main road, just above the town, has a police control point. Minibuses to Tingo María (US$4, 4 hours) leave from here every hour or so during daylight. Nearby are bus offices with daily departures for Pucallpa and Lima.

Dugout canoes with outboards leave in the mornings for various small settlements on the Río Aguaytía.

## YURIMAGUAS
☎ 094
Locals call Yurimaguas 'the pearl of the Huallaga.' It is the major port on the Río Huallaga, and boats to Iquitos can be found here. Reaching Yurimaguas can involve a long road trip (see the Across the Northern Highlands chapter) or a flight from Lima. With an approximate population of 26,000, Yurimaguas is a quiet, pleasant little town that hasn't changed much in the last decade – quite different from the bustling boom-town atmosphere of Pucallpa. There are signs of the rubber days, such as the expensive imported tiles that decorate the walls of the buildings at the end of Avenida Arica, but generally it is a sleepy port where you may have to wait a couple of days for a river boat to Iquitos. Bring a couple of good books.

### Information
There is no tourist office, but the Consejo Regional, on the Plaza de Armas, can give information. Banco de Crédito or Banco Continental will change US cash or traveler's checks. Paraíso Azul, on Huallaga at M Castilla, has a public pool.

### Places to Stay
None of the hotels have hot water at this time, though most have private bathrooms. *Quinta Ruthcita* has shared baths and charges US$2.75/4 for singles/doubles. The following hotels all charge about US$3.25/5

**YURIMAGUAS**

PLACES TO STAY
1 Hostal El Cisne
5 Hostal Residencial Estrella
6 Hostal Florindez
8 Hostal Baneo
11 Quinta Ruthcita
15 Hostal Cajamarca
18 Hostal Jáuregui
19 Hostal César Gustavo
20 Hostal de Paz
21 Hotel Luis Antonio
23 Quinta Lucy
25 Hostal El Naranjo
26 Leo's Palace

PLACES TO EAT
7 Copacabana
12 Chifa Kung Wa
13 Pollería La Posada
16 La Prosperidad

OTHER
2 Minibuses to Tarapoto
3 Minibuses to Tarapoto
4 Paraíso Azul (swimming pool)
9 Telefónica del Peru
10 Aero Continente
14 Hammock shops
17 Church
22 Pickup trucks to Tarapoto
24 Banco de Crédito
27 Banco Continental
28 Post Office

---

for singles/doubles. **Hostal Baneo** (☎ 35-2406, M Castilla 304) has both shared and private baths and fans. **Hostal Jáuregui** has dark and dingy rooms with bath but no fan. **Quinta Lucy** (☎ 35-1575, Jáuregui 305) has private baths, as do **Hostal El Cisne** and **Hostal Residencial Estrella** (☎ 35-2218, López 314), but these lack overhead fans. A table fan can be requested. The best of the basic places is the clean and quiet **Hostal César Gustavo** (☎ 35-1585, Atahualpa 102), which has rooms with private bath and fan for US$5/7.

**Hostal Florindez** (☎ 35-2102, López 305) has basic rooms with private bath for US$5/7, and air-conditioned doubles for US$8. **Hostal de Paz** (☎/fax 35-2123, Jáuregui 429) is a good value and charges US$7/9.50 for clean rooms with bath, fan and TV. Also good is the quiet **Hostal Cajamarca** (☎ 35-2380, Manco Cápac 114), which charges the same for similar rooms. They serve breakfast (at an extra cost). **Hostal El Naranjo** (☎ 35-2650, fax 35-1504, Arica 318) is clean, quiet and recommended. Rooms with bath, fan and TV are US$10/13, and the place has a restaurant. **Leo's Palace** (☎/fax 35-2213, Lores 108) is the oldest of the better hotels and is now a bit run down. It has a few simple but spacious rooms

with bath, fan and a balcony overlooking the Plaza de Armas, though some rooms are smaller or lack balconies. Rates are about US$7/10, or US$17 for an air-conditioned double. They have cable TV (for an extra US$2) and a restaurant.

The best is **Hostal Luis Antonio** (☎/fax 35-2061, Jáuregui 407), which charges US$13/17 for rooms with baths, TV and fans, and another US$7 for air-conditioning. They have a restaurant and swimming pool.

## Places to Eat

The hotel restaurants are among the best, but they aren't anything special. Also OK is **Copacabana** for standard food, **Pollería La Posada** for chicken, **Chifa Kung Wa** for Chinese food and **La Prosperidad** for tropical juices and sandwiches.

## Shopping

Stores selling hammocks for river journeys are on the north side of the market.

## Getting There & Away

**Air** TANS (☎ 35-2387) flies from Lima via Tarapoto on Thursday, Saturday and Sunday. Aero Continente (☎ 35-2592, Libertad 139) has also serviced this route in the past, though it doesn't at this time. Carriers, schedules and routes change frequently. Charter and local companies fly light aircraft to various nearby towns – ask at the airport.

**Bus** The only route out of Yurimaguas is the rough road to Tarapoto, which has improved considerably. Two bus companies, Paredes Estrella and Transportes Guadalupe, usually leave at 7 am from their offices on the outskirts of town on the road to Tarapoto. The trip takes four hours and costs US$4.

Minibuses (US$6) leave from Tacna and pickup trucks leave from J Riera several times a day from 4 am to 6 pm. Leave in the morning to enjoy the great scenery and to avoid the slight chance of being assaulted on the road at night (reports of nighttime holdups are now diminishing). The trip takes four to six hours, depending on the weather, and costs US$7 in the cabin or US$5 in the back (beware of sunburn). The trip may take longer in the wet season.

**River Boat** Cargo boats from Yurimaguas follow the Huallaga to the Río Marañón and on to Iquitos. The trip usually takes about three days (captains insist they can do it in 36 hours, but there are numerous stops for loading and unloading cargo). There are several departures a week, usually at about lunchtime (though captains may claim earlier). Passages should cost about US$15 on deck, or a little more in a cabin. Boat information is available from the Bodega Davila store (☎ 35-2477), by the dock.

As with other river trips, bring a hammock, mosquito repellent, purified water or tablets and a supply of food – unless you are prepared to eat the very basic and monotonous food that is available on board. Bring extra Peruvian cash in case there are delays. Because Yurimaguas has fewer air and road services than Pucallpa, the river link is more important, and the cargo boats are accustomed to taking passengers. The journey can be broken at Lagunas, just before the Río Huallaga meets the Marañón.

## Getting Around
Mototaxis charge about US$0.60 to the port, or you can walk 13 blocks north.

## LAGUNAS
This village is the best point from which to begin a trip to the Reserva Nacional Pacaya-Samiria, described later in this chapter. Lagunas is small and remote, so you should bring most supplies with you. There are no moneychanging facilities, and food is limited and expensive.

### Guides
Guides are available here to visit Pacaya-Samiria, and they charge less than guides in Iquitos. They speak only Spanish. Some guides will hunt and fish, but this is to be discouraged because you are, after all, visiting a reserve. If you tell the guides not to hunt, they'll abide by your request. Fishing for the pot is OK. The going rate is about US$8 per passenger per day for guide and boat; food is extra.

Very good guides are Job Gongora and his nephews, who can be contacted at the Hostal La Sombra. They are reliable and knowledgeable and will cook and paddle for hours in the park. Paddling is better than motorboat if you want to approach animals quietly. A reader who is an ornithologist highly recommends a guide by the name of Gamaniel Valles (☎ 40-1005, Fitzcarrald 520), who charges a bit more than others but is very knowledgeable about the wildlife and is a decent cook. He also can be contacted through the Hostal La Sombra. Other guides who have been recommended are Edinson Saldaña Gutiérrez and Juan Huaycama; both are well known locally.

### Places to Stay & Eat
The hotels are very basic, but you don't have much choice. The best is *Hostal Miraflores* (*Miraflores 249*), which has clean rooms with shared showers for about US$3 per person. *Hostal La Sombra* (☎ 40-1063), also known as Hostal Piñedo, has hot, stuffy little rooms at US$2 per person. The owners are friendly and the place is safe. Shared showers and food are available. The smaller *Hotel*

*Montalbán* is another OK possibility. You can stay in a *hostel* above the Farmacía, but they don't have showers (buckets of water are provided). *Alojamiento Guerrero* is near the dock and has beds for about US$1; the bathrooms are described as 'ghastly.' *Doña Dina*, in a blue-fronted building just off the plaza, serves good cheap meals.

### Getting There & Away

Boats from Yurimaguas take about 12 hours and leave most days around noon, which means a midnight arrival. If continuing on to Iquitos, ask when boats are expected, and be at the dock at midnight. The boat usually docks for about 20 minutes to load passengers.

## RESERVA NACIONAL PACAYA-SAMIRIA

At 20,800 sq km, this reserve is the largest of all of Peru's protected areas. In common with many reserves in South America, Pacaya-Samiria both provides local people with food and a home and protects ecologically important habitats. In this case, an estimated 30,000 people live on and around the reserve. Juggling the needs of the human inhabitants and the protection of wildlife is the responsibility of 25 rangers, whose training and salaries are paid for by contributions from the US government and private organizations in partnership with the Fundación Peruana para la Conservación de la Naturaleza (FPCN). The staff also teaches inhabitants how to best harvest the natural renewable resources in order to benefit the local people and to maintain thriving populations of plants and animals. Despite this, three rangers were murdered by poachers in late 1998.

The reserve is the home of aquatic animals such as the Amazon manatee, pink and gray river dolphins, two species of caiman, the giant South American river turtle and many others. Monkeys and birds are quite abundant.

The best way to visit the reserve is to go by dugout canoe with a guide from Lagunas and spend several days camping and exploring. The area close to Lagunas has suffered from depletion by hunting, so you need

several days to get deep into the least disturbed areas. The new ranger stations will charge a nominal fee to enter the reserve (about US$3) and you can then stay as long as you want. Officially, you need a permit from INRENA in Lima, but this is rarely enforced. Information is available at the reserve office in Iquitos.

The best time to go is during the dry season, when you are more likely to see animals along the riverbanks. Although the rains ease off in late May, it takes a month or so for the water levels to drop, making July and August the best months to visit. September to November aren't too bad, and December and January often have fairly low water. The heaviest rains begin in January and the months of February to May are the worst times to go. February to June tend to be the hottest months.

Travelers should bring plenty of insect repellent and plastic bags (to cover luggage) and be prepared to camp out.

## SARAMERIZA

Sarameriza is a tiny port on the upper Marañón and the westernmost point from which to start a river journey down the Amazon, though this trip is very rarely done. Expect passport checks on this route. This is a developing region and roads may improve compared to my description below.

To get to Sarameriza (or Puerto Delfus, a few kilometers away), you must first go to Bagua, on the Chiclayo-to-Chachapoyas route in the northern Andes. From Bagua, minibuses leave a few times daily to Imasita (where there is a basic hotel), about five hours from Bagua. The road from Imasita to Sarameriza is in very bad shape and may be impassable. Ask in Imasita how best to continue. Alternatively, you can get a boat from Imasita along the Marañón to Santa María de Nieve (about 8 hours, departures every few days). The river is relatively narrow and the scenery is good. The village is at the confluence of the Marañón and Nieve rivers and has basic accommodations and restaurants. From Santa María, the boat trip to Sarameriza takes another 12 hours, though the trip can be broken at the hotel in the mestizo village of Borja, about two hours before Saramariza. Just before Borja, the rapids of the Pongo de Mansiche have to be navigated; these may be a barrier in high water.

This area is the home of some 50,000 Aguaruna Indians who are descended from Jivaro headshrinkers. There is much pressure on them from Peruvian settlers and, recently, oil companies. The latter have minimized impact on the Indians by using helicopters to bring in supplies, and thus avoided building roads for truck shipments. Mestizo settlers in the villages of Imazita and Santa María de Nieve routinely travel between the two places, but they consider it dangerous to stop en route at any of the Aguaruna settlements. Adventurers have tried to float down this section of the Marañón on rafts. In 1989, three French citizens and a Peruvian were shot to death while floating downriver. In 1995, two Americans were shot and one was killed on the same stretch (see the US magazine *Outside*, November 1995, for a report). However James Sleeman, a British geologist working in this area with the Aguaruna in 1997, reports that he found the area safe as long as you speak Spanish and ask for local advice at every opportunity. The major dangers are health related; medical facilities and communications are very limited, so don't get sick or a snakebite. A good suggestion is to wear long pants and boots to protect yourself from snakes.

Saramariza has accommodations and an air-conditioned oil camp. Cargo boats leave Saramariza for Iquitos every 10 or 15 days, so be prepared to wait. The river journey takes about five days. Obviously, this is a trip for the self-sufficient traveler with a spirit of adventure, plenty of common sense and a lot of spare time. Good luck!

## IQUITOS
☎ 064

With a population approaching 400,000, Iquitos is Peru's largest jungle city and the capital of the huge Department of Loreto, the largest of Peru's 24 departments. Iquitos is linked with the outside world by air and the Río Amazonas; this may be the largest city in the world that can't be reached by road. There are cars to get you around, but motorcycles seem to be the preferred mode of transportation (as in many jungle towns) and this makes Iquitos a very noisy city.

Iquitos has a varied and interesting history. It was founded in the 1750s as a Jesuit mission, fending off attacks from Indian tribes who didn't want to be converted. The tiny settlement survived and grew very slowly until, by the 1870s, it had some 1500 inhabitants. Then came the great rubber boom, and the population increased about 16-fold by the 1880s. For the next 30 years, Iquitos was at once the scene of ostentatious wealth and abject poverty. The rubber barons became fabulously rich, and the rubber tappers (mainly local Indians and poor mestizos) suffered virtual enslavement and sometimes death from disease or harsh treatment. Signs of the opulence of those days can still be seen in some of the mansions and tiled walls of Iquitos.

The bottom fell out of the rubber boom as suddenly as it had begun. A British entrepreneur smuggled some rubber-tree seeds out of Brazil, and plantations were seeded in the Malay Peninsula. It was much cheaper and easier to collect the rubber from the orderly rows of rubber trees in the plantations than from the wild trees scattered in the Amazon Basin, and by WWI, Peru's rubber industry was at an end.

Iquitos suffered a period of severe economic decline during the ensuing decades, supporting itself as best it could by a combination of logging, agriculture (Brazil nuts, tobacco, bananas and *barbasco* – a poisonous vine used by the Indians to hunt fish and now exported for use in insecticides) and the export of wild animals to zoos. Then, in the 1960s, a second boom revitalized the area. This time, the resource was oil, and its discovery made Iquitos a prosperous modern town. In recent years, tourism has also played an important part in the economy of the area.

Although most travelers use Iquitos as a base for excursions into the jungle or as a place to wait for river boats along the Amazon, there are several interesting places to see in and around the city itself.

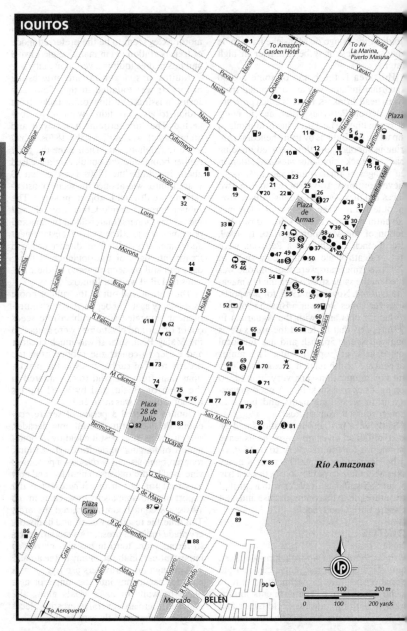

# IQUITOS

**PLACES TO STAY**
3 Hostal Baltasar
5 Hostal Ambassador
10 Roland's Amazon
   River Lodge
16 Hostal La Pascana
18 Hostal Jhuliana
19 Hostal Karina
22 Hostal Amazonas
23 Hotel El Dorado
25 Hotel Plaza
26 Amazon Suites
29 Hostal Safari
33 Hotel Acosta I
43 Real Hotel Iquitos
44 Hotel Morona
53 Hostal Libertad,
   Hostal Excelsior
54 Hostal Perú
55 Hostal Fortaleza
61 Hostal Tacna
65 Hostal Europa
66 Hostal Maflo
67 Hostal Isabel
68 Hotel Victoria Regia
70 Hostal Lima
73 Hostal Dos Mundos
77 Hostal Monterrico
78 Hostal María Antonia
79 Hostal San Antonio
83 Hotel Río Grande
84 Hostal Anita,
   Hostal Lozano
86 Hostal Económico
88 Hotel Sol Naciente
89 Hostal Alfert

**PLACES TO EAT**
20 Chifa Chong,
   Chifa Can Chau
30 Nuevo Mesón
31 La Casa de Jaime
32 La Olla de Oro
38 Regal Bar & Restaurant
39 Ari's Burger
51 Gran Maloka
63 Cebichería Paulina
74 Chifa Wai Ming
76 Several chifas & restaurants
85 La Pascana

**OTHER**
1 Coin Laundry
2 Coin Laundry
4 Cybernet Café
6 Amazonas Sinchicuy Lodge
   (office)
7 Anaconda Lara Lodge (office)
8 Expreso Loreto (boat office)
9 Dreams Discotheque
11 Reserva Nacional Pacaya-
   Samiria Office
12 Dr Rafael Urrunaga (dentist)
13 Noa Noa Nightclub
14 Café-Teatro Amauta
15 Jungle Xports (International
   Expeditions' office)
17 Tourism Police
21 Western Union
24 Dr Victor Antonioli
26 Air Amazonas
27 Municipalidad, Tourist Office
28 Photo shop

34 Church of San Juan Bautista
35 Colombian Consulate
36 Banco de Crédito
37 Grupo 8 Airline,
   Iquitos Travel
38 Iron House, British Consulate
40 Cumaceba Lodge (office)
41 Coin Laundry
42 Loving Light Amazon Lodge
   (office)
45 Brazilian Consulate
46 International telephone booths
47 Servicios Aéreos Amazónicos
48 Banco Wiese
49 Aero Continente
50 Manugare Internet
52 Post Office
56 Banco Continental
57 Yacumama Lodge (office)
58 TANS Airline
59 Escandolo Discoteca
60 Biblioteca Amazónica,
   Museo Etnográfico
62 Motorcycle rental
64 Moisés Torres Viena (tour guide)
69 Interbanc
71 Turismo Pacífico
72 Migraciones, Police Station
75 Cine Bolognesi
80 Motorcycle rental
81 Dirección Regional de Turismo
82 Local buses to Laguna
   Quistacocha & airport
87 Colectivos to Laguna
   Moronacocha
90 Boats for hire to Belén area

## Information

**Tourist Offices** The tourist office is on the north side of the Plaza de Armas. They are open 7:30 am to 2:45 pm on weekdays and can give you maps of the area, as well as up-to-date information. They are planning on expanding hours and services. You can also try the Dirección Regional de Turismo (☎ 23-4170, R Hurtado 645).

Various commercial jungle guides and jungle lodges give tourist information. This is obviously biased toward selling their services, which is fine if you are looking for guides, tours or jungle lodges.

INRENA's Reserva Nacional Pacaya-Samiria office (☎ 23-2980) is located at Pevas 363.

**Consulates & Documents** The Brazilian consulate (☎ 23-2081) is at Lores 363; the Colombian consulate (☎ 23-1461) is at Putumayo 247, on the south side of the Plaza de Armas; and the British consulate is in the Iron House, on the Plaza de Armas.

There are different entry requirements for travelers of different nationalities when crossing into Brazil or Colombia; regulations change often, so it is worth checking with the Brazilian or Colombian embassy at home or in Lima or Iquitos before you go.

**Immigration** Migraciones (☎ 23-5371) is next to the police station at Brasil 147 (but has moved frequently in recent years). You can extend your tourist card or visa there. If you are arriving/leaving from Brazil or Colombia, you will get your entry/exit stamp at the border.

**Money** There are several banks (they are shown on the map) where you can change traveler's checks, get advances on a credit card or use an ATM. They have competitive rates. For changing US cash quickly, you'll find street moneychangers on Lores at Próspero. They are generally OK, though a few might have 'fixed' calculators. Use your own. The ones at Morona and Próspero have been cheating tourists recently. Western Union money transfers can be arranged at Western Union (☎ 23-5182, Napo 359). Changing Brazilian or Colombian currency is best done at the border.

**Post & Communications** The post office (☎ 23-4091, Arica 403) is open 8 am to 6 pm weekdays, and until 4:30 pm Saturday. The international telephone booths at Lores 321 are open from 7 am to 11 pm daily.

Internet facilities are available at the Cybernet Café (Fitzcarrald 335), which serves drinks, plays recorded music and is open daily 9 am to 11:30 pm. There's also Manugare Internet (Próspero 273).

**Travel Agencies** There are many agencies that sell airline tickets and other services. Iquitos Travel (☎ 23-1104, Próspero 213) and Turismo Pacífico (☎ 23-1627, R Palma 180) are both recommended, but most others will do the job as well. If they sell you an air ticket, ask them for a free ride to the airport.

Jungle-lodge operators have offices in Iquitos. Their addresses are given with the description of the lodges (see Jungle Lodges under Exploring the Jungle later in this chapter).

**Laundry** Wash your stinking jungle clothes in one of several convenient coin-operated laundries, such as the one at Putumayo 150, which is open 7 am to 10 pm. A couple of others are marked on the map.

**Medical Services** There are about five hospitals, but you'll probably get better care at a private clinic such as Clínica Ana Stah (☎ 25-2535, Avenida La Marina 285), which has 24-hour emergency service. English-speaking, private doctors include Dr Victo Antonioli (☎ 23-2684, Fitzcarrald 156) an the dentist Dr Rafael Urrunaga (☎ 23-5016 Fitzcarrald 201).

**Emergency** The tourism police (☎ 24-2081 are at Lores 834. The national police have a office on the 1st block of Brasil.

## The Iron House

Every guidebook tells of the 'majestic' Iro House designed by Eiffel (of Tower fame).  was made in Paris in 1860 and was importe piece by piece into Iquitos around 1890 during the opulent days of the rubber boon to beautify the city. Three different iro houses were imported at this time, but onl one, at the southeast corner of the Plaza d Armas, survives. It looks like a bunch c scrap-metal sheets bolted together and wa once a store and the Iquitos Club. Nov there is a café downstairs and, upstairs houses the British consul and the Regal Ba & Restaurant.

## Azulejos

Some other remnants of those rubber-boom days remain. Among these are the *azulejo* handmade tiles imported from Portugal t decorate the mansions of the rubber baron Many buildings along Raimondi and Malecó Tarapaca are lavishly decorated with azulejo Some of the best are various governmer buildings along or near the malecón.

## Library & Museum

On the malecón, at the corner with Moron. is an old building housing the Bibliotec Amazónica and a small Museo Etnográfic Both are open on weekdays. The museu includes life-size wood carvings of membe of various Amazon tribes.

## Belén

A walk down Raimondi (which turns int Próspero) and back along the malecón interesting, not only to see some of the til faced buildings, but also to visit the Belé market area at the southeast end of town. Belén itself is a floating shantytown with a certain charm to it (the locals call it the Venice of the Amazon, but others would call it a slum). It consists of scores of huts built on rafts, which rise and fall with the river. During the low-water months, these rafts sit on the river mud and are dirty and unhealthy but, for most of the year, they float on the river – a colorful and exotic sight. Several thousand people live here, and canoes float from hut to hut selling and trading jungle produce. If you speak a few words of Spanish, you can find someone to paddle you around for a fee. Ask at the end of 9 de Diciembre. The area seems reasonably safe in daylight.

The market, within the city blocks in front of Belén, is a raucous, crowded affair common to most Peruvian towns. All kinds of strange and exotic products are sold among the mundane bags of rice, sugar, flour and cheap plastic and metal household goods. Look for the bark of the Chuchuhuasi tree that is soaked in rum for weeks and used as a tonic (served in many of the local bars). Chuchuhuasi and other Amazon plants are common ingredients in herbal pain-reducing and arthritis formulas manufactured in Europe and the USA. All kinds of other medicinal and culinary offerings are on sale: piles of dried frogs and fish, armadillo shells, piranha teeth and a great variety of tropical fruits. Pasaje Paquito is the block where they sell medicinal plants. It makes for exciting shopping or sightseeing, but remember to watch your wallet.

Nicole Maxwell's *Witch-Doctor's Apprentice: Hunting for Medicinal Plants in the Amazon* has been recommended for good background on medicinal plants in the Iquitos area.

## Laguna Moronacocha

This lake forms the western boundary of the town. To get there, take the colectivo that departs from 2 de Mayo and leaves the city center along Ejército. The ride takes about 15 minutes. There really isn't much to see but there are a couple of very basic bars with views of the lake. It's a good place to relax with a cold beer and watch the sun set.

## Nearby Villages & Lakes

About 16km from town, past the airport, **Santo Tomás** has a few bars overlooking Mapacocha, a lake formed by an arm of the Río Nanay. You can rent boats (paddles or motors) by asking around. A motorboat with driver is US$5 to US$10 an hour, or you can paddle your own canoe for less. **Santa Clara** is about 15km away, on the banks of the Río Nanay. Boats can also be rented, and locals swim off the beaches formed during low water levels. Both villages can be reached by motocarros (about US$3) and taxis.

**Corrientillo** is a lake near the Río Nanay. There are a few bars around the lake, which is locally popular for swimming on weekends. It's about 15km from town; a motocarro will charge about US$3.

## Laguna Quistacocha

This lake lies roughly 15km south of Iquitos and makes a pleasant day trip. A motocarro will charge about US$3, but cheaper minibuses leave several times an hour from Plaza 28 de Julio. There is a small zoo of local fauna and a taxidermy display. The zoo has been improved recently under an Australian director who sometimes is available to show you around.

An adjoining fish hatchery has 2m-long paiche (a river fish), which tastes excellent but its popularity and loss of habitat has apparently caused a severe decline in its numbers (see the boxed text 'Fruit-Eating Fish'). An attempt to rectify the situation is being made with the breeding program at the fish hatchery. There is a pedestrian walk around the lake (in which people swim, though it looks murky), and paddleboats are for hire. It's fairly crowded with locals on the weekend but not midweek. Admission is US$1.

## Sachamama

These are botanical gardens, 27km from town on the paved road that ends at Nauta (take a taxi). The place is locally recommended for an introduction to plants; I haven't been here, but readers report that shaman ceremonies using ayahuasca can be arranged.

## Fruit-Eating Fish

Fruits are borne on plants growing on land, while fish spend their lives in the water. This simple and self-evident statement leads to the assumption that fish don't eat fruit, and it was not until recently that exactly the opposite became generally known.

In fact, dozens of Amazon fish species rely on fruit as the mainstay of their diet. Every year, the river bursts its banks and floods up to 100,000 sq km of riverside forest. Thus fish can swim into the forest and eat floating or sunken fruit – there are even vegetarian piranhas. Some fish have developed extremely strong jaws that work like nutcrackers to enable them to eat the hardest seeds. One of the largest Amazon (and one of the world's largest freshwater) fish, the paiche (also called the pirarucu), which can grow to well over 2m in length and weigh in at almost 90kg, is a fruit-eater.

During the rainy months, frugivorous fish glut themselves and fatten up for the lean times ahead. As the floodwaters recede during the drier months, the fish lose their main source of food and simply stop eating until the next flood gets them back to the fruit. Fish biologist Michael Goulding reports that of 167 frugivorous fish caught during a dry-season fishing trip, none had had a recent meal.

Fish play an extraordinarily important part in the economy of the Amazon. Even the poorest families can fish for food, and this is the main source of protein for Amazon dwellers. From 1970 to 1975, the fish catch in the Amazon Basin declined by 25% – a serious threat. Studies showed that logging along the riverbanks caused a loss of habitat for frugivorous fish. Apart from losing their main source of food, these fish also lost their breeding grounds. Many species of carnivorous fish that rely upon the frugivores for food were adversely affected. Goulding estimates that as much as 75% of the fish sold in the major Amazon fish market of Manaus, Brazil, rely ultimately on the flooded forest. These are among the most compelling reasons against logging and clearing the riverside forest.

## Places to Stay

Some of the budget places have an erratic water supply. Check the water supply before paying. Mosquitoes are rarely a serious problem, and mosquito netting is not provided.

The best hotels tend to be booked up on Friday and Saturday. The busiest season is from May to September, when prices may rise slightly.

**Budget** All these hotels have private baths and fans unless otherwise indicated. The hotels in the next two paragraphs are among the best in their price ranges. The clean and friendly *Hostal Alfert* (☎ 23-4105, G Saenz 001) is popular with travelers on a tight budget. Rooms are US$7 for one or two people and the hotel is quiet, with a view of the Amazon. *Hostal Tacna* (☎ 23-1645, Tacna 516) is basic and noisy, but clean and

one of the cheapest at US$4.50/6.50 fo singles/doubles. Also one of the cheapest i *Hostal Monterrico* (☎/fax 23-5395, Aric 633), which is basic but OK for US$6/7 i rooms with bath and fan.

The simple *Hostal La Pascana* (☎ 23 1418, fax 23-2974, Pevas 133) has a sma garden and is good, safe, friendly, popula with travelers and often full. Call ahead i possible. Rooms are US$9/12. The quiet an clean *Hostal Lima* (☎ 23-5152, Próspero 549 has fair rooms (their business card describe them as 'soberly decorated') for US$9/12.

Those on a budget can also try the ver basic and noisy *Hostal San Antonio* (☎ 23 5221, Próspero 661), which is the cheapest i town at US$3.50/4 and lacks fans. One reade describes it as 'dire' while another calls i 'friendly and a good value.' The similarl priced but even more basic *Hostal Anit* (R Hurtado 742) is friendly but has wate roblems. Next door, the slightly better *Hostal Lozano* (☎ 23-2486, R Hurtado 772) charges US$6/9 in rooms with basic shower nd fan. The friendly and clean *Hostal Karina* (☎ 23-5367, Putumayo 467) has hot vater and charges US$5/7. *Hostal Perú* ☎ 23-4961, Próspero 318), *Hotel Morona* ☎ 22-1055, Morona 420) and *Hostal Fortaleza* (Próspero 311) are basic and noisy but re reasonably clean for US$7/9 with private ath and fan. *Hostal Sol Naciente* (☎/fax 23-952, Próspero 1073) charges US$7/10 in lean rooms with hot water, TV and fan. *Hostal Económico* (Moore 1164) is clean, heap and away from the center.

*Roland's Amazon River Lodge* (☎ 23-979, Nauta 307) has dark rooms with TV, ans and private baths for US$10. *Hostal Libertad* (☎ 23-5763, Arica 361) has TV in ome rooms, which have bathrooms, but are therwise fairly simple. Rates are US$8.50/13 vith a US$3.50 surcharge for rooms with air-onditioning. *Hostal Baltasar* (☎ 23-2240, Condamine 265) is clean and good with oubles at US$12 with fan and US$17 with ir-conditioning – all have private bath. *Hostal Dos Mundos* (☎ 23-2635, Tacna 631) as clean rooms with TV for about US$15 louble. *Hostal Excelsior* (☎ 22-4064, Arica 79) charges US$7/10 in rooms with fans and JS$14/17 with air-conditioning. *Hostal Maflo* (☎ 24-1257, Morona 177) has clean ooms with fans and TV for US$9/14 including continental breakfast. Also in this price ange is *Hostal Isabel* (☎ 23-4901, Brasil 64), which has varied rooms ranging from oor to quite good.

**Mid-Range** All of the hotels in this section ave rooms with air-conditioning and rivate bath, though they might lack hot vater (not a major problem in the heat of quitos). A few may have some cheaper ooms with a fan. *Hostal María Antonia* ☎ 23-4761, 24-3643, fax 22-1996, Próspero 16) is adequate for US$30/40 in rooms with able TV and telephones. Breakfast is included. *Hostal Safari* (☎ 23-5593, 23-3828, Napo 118) has adequate rooms with TV and elephones for US$27/35. *Hostal Ambasador* (☎/fax 23-3110, 23-1618, Pevas 260)

charges US$30/40 in rooms with cable TV, refrigerators, telephones and hot water. A restaurant offers room service.

The friendly *Hostal Europa* (☎ 23-1123, 23-4744, fax 23-5483, heuropa@telematic .edu.pe, Próspero 494) has rooms with hot water, telephones, refrigerators and cable TV for US$35/50. They have a restaurant. *Hostal Jhuliana* (☎/fax 23-3154, Putumayo 521) boasts a swimming pool, cafeteria and bar and carpeted rooms with hot water, refrigerators, cable TV and telephones for US$35/45. *Hotel Acosta 1* (☎ 23-5974, fax 23-1761, chasa@telematic.edu.pe), on Huallaga at Araujo, lacks the pool but is otherwise similar and charges US$30/38 including continental breakfast.

*Real Hotel Iquitos* (☎ 23-1322, 23-6222, 23-1011, fax 23-2262, in Lima 425-1670), on Malecón Tarapaca, is the grand dame of Iquitos' hotels. Its rooms are a bit shabby, though clean enough, and the view over the Amazon compensates for the deteriorated decor. New owners in 1998 may improve the place. Rooms are US$45/55 including continental breakfast.

Also around the same price range, the modern *Hostal Amazonas* (☎/fax 24-2431, amazonas@tvs.com.pe, Arica 108) has a prime location on the Plaza de Armas and is popular with Peruvian businesspeople. Carpeted rooms have hot water, refrigerators, cable TV and telephones, and a restaurant is on the premises.

Ten blocks from the center, *Amazon Garden Hotel* (☎ 23-6140, Cabo Pantoja 417), at Yavari, has 13 rooms with cable TV, telephone, minirefrigerators and hot shower. The hotel is in a garden setting with a large pool, dining room and bar. Rates are US$45/50.

**Top End** The attractive *Amazon Suites* (☎ 22-4311, Napo 274) is centrally located on the Plaza de Armas and has spacious rooms at US$55/60 and minisuites for US$98/120/140 for doubles/triples/quads. All have large hot showers, minirefrigerators, cable TV and plenty of storage space. A pleasant patio bar next to a Jacuzzi pool offers cocktails, breakfasts and light meals.

*Hotel Río Grande* (☎ 24-3530, 24-3532, riogrande@tvs.com.pe, Aguirre 793) is a modern hotel on the Plaza 28 de Julio. Their restaurant is above average.

*Hotel Victoria Regia* (☎ 23-1983, 23-2904, fax 23-2499, Ricardo Palma 252) has a restaurant, bar, swimming pool and good rooms with the usual amenities for US$66/80. *Hotel El Dorado* (☎ 23-7326, 23-1742, fax 23-2203, dorado@tvs.com.pe, Napo 362) is good and has all the facilities described above plus a Jacuzzi. Rooms are US$66/80, with some deluxe rooms at US$90. Note that these top-end hotels are generally quite small, with only a few dozen rooms, and they are often full, so reservations aren't a bad idea.

The new *Hotel Plaza* (☎ 22-2555, fax 22-4304, Napo 266) opened in late 1999 and is the town's best, with 64 spacious rooms (some with plaza views) starting at US$150.

## Places to Eat

Those wishing to economize can eat at small restaurants and stalls in the market area, but this is not recommended if your stomach is unaccustomed to Peruvian food. There are several inexpensive chifas and other restaurants near the Plaza 28 de Julio, the best of which is *Chifa Wai Ming* (☎ 23-4391, San Martín 464), which is a little more expensive than the others but is worth it. Cheaper restaurants are found on Tacna and Huallaga in the blocks north of Plaza 28 de Julio. Two good chifas almost next to each other are *Chifa Chong* (Huallaga 165), which has set meals for US$2.50, and *Chifa Can Chau* (Huallaga 173), which has sweet-and-sour chicken prepared with fresh pineapple.

Slightly pricier but good eateries include the following. *La Pascana* (☎ 22-3548, R Hurtado 735), on the waterfront, is a simple place with good ceviches and fine Amazon river views; they are locally popular for lunch but closed otherwise. *Restaurant Cebichería Paulina* (☎ 23-1298, Tacna 591) is also good for ceviches, local food and good set lunches at about US$2. *La Olla de Oro* (☎ 23-4350, Araujo 579) has a good selection of local and Peruvian food at reasonable prices. *Ari's Burger* (☎ 23-1470), on

the corner of the Plaza de Armas, is a brightly lit and clean joint known locally a 'gringolandia.' They are open almost always serve American-style food as well as som local plates and ice creams, change U dollars and are generally helpful an popular with foreign travelers. On anothe plaza corner is *Regal Bar & Restauran* (☎ 22-2732), on the 2nd floor of the famou Iron House. The British consul, Mr Phi Duffy, owns the Regal and conducts con sular business on the premises. The plaza view balcony is a great place for a beer an a snack or meal, and you can examine par of the restored Iron House.

*Nuevo Mesón* (☎ 23-1857), on th malecón at Napo, is a little pricey and serve local specialties (including jungle animals the local turtles are protected and shoul not be served, but deer and peccary are fa game). On the same block, *La Casa d Jaime* (☎ 24-4377) has good local and Peru vian dishes, including steaks, fish and vege tarian plates. It is friendly, helpful an recommended – I liked the food here th best. *Gran Maloka* (☎ 23-3126, Lores 17( has quite good local and Peruvian food in a elegant upscale (by Iquitos standards setting. It's one of the few air-conditione restaurants.

## Entertainment

*Cine Bolognesi*, on the Plaza 28 de Juli shows films, sometimes in English.

There are several places to meet for cold beer or other drinks and hear musi both recorded and live. Several places ar found along the pedestrian blocks of th malecón north of Napo. *Café-Teatr Amauta* (☎ 23-3109, Nauta 250) has liv Peruvian music on most nights and has a ba as well as a café. *Regal Bar*, on the Plaza d Armas, is good for a quiet drink and cha There are other places nearby.

For dancing, the most locally popular plac is *Agricobank*, on Condamine, a couple blocks north of the map. It's a huge, outdoo place where hundreds of locals gather fe drinking, dancing and socializing; a US$1.7 cover is charged. The more upscale *Noa No Nightclub* (☎ 23-2902, Pevas 292) charges

US$6 cover and is a very trendy disco. Other dance clubs include *Escandalo Discoteca*, on the malecón, *Dreams Discotheque*, on Tacna near Napo, and *Latin Limits*, on the road to the airport.

## Shopping

There are a few shops on the 1st block of Napo selling jungle crafts, some of high quality and price. The first block of Nauta has a street market of cheaper souvenirs. Shipibo Indians also hang out on the streets here, on the Plaza de Armas and on the malecón selling their wares. A good place for crafts is Mercado de Artesanía San Juan on the road to the airport – bus and taxi drivers know it.

Although items made from animal bones and skins are available, I discourage their purchase. Most visitors come to the jungle to see some wildlife, not to help destroy it by purchasing animal products. It is illegal to import many of them into North America and Europe.

Camu-Camu Amazonia Art Gallery (☎ 25-3120, Trujillo 498) exhibits works by Francisco Grippa (see the boxed text 'Francisco Grippa – Amazon Artist' later in this chapter). The gallery is about 1km north of the map.

Film and camera batteries are sold at the Photo Shop (Raimondi 142) just off the Plaza de Armas.

## Getting There & Away

Plane or boat are your only choices – all roads into the jungle stop within 20km or so.

**Air** Iquitos has a small international airport with flights to Miami and Colombia, as well as local flights. There have been flights to Brazil in the past, but none at this writing. Direct Miami-Iquitos flights were suspended in March 1999 with the closing of AeroPeru; this important route may be offered again with another airline in the future.

Aero Continente, (☎ 24-3489, 24-2995, airport 26-0874, Próspero 232) and TANS (☎ 23-4632, Lores 127) have offices in town. There are five flights a day to Lima, one stopping in Tarapoto and another in Pucallpa. Fares, schedules and airlines change frequently. Grupo 8, next to Iquitos Travel at Próspero near Putumayo, also may have flights. TANS has Saturday flights to remote jungle towns like Caballococha, near the Colombian border. (Caballacocha has one basic and one better hotel on the plaza, and you can get boats from there to Leticia, Colombia every day.) Twice a month, TANS flies to Río Ucayali villages such as El Estrecho, Angamos, Requena, Orellana, Punta Hermosa, Contamaná and possibly on to Pucallpa. Air Amazonas (☎ 22-4201, 22-4220, Napo 272) has twin-engined planes to Leticia, Colombia, three times a week, connecting with flights to Bogotá. They are planning services to Yurimaguas and Tarapoto. Servicios Aéreos Amazónicos (Arica 273) flies to Caballococha and Leticia on three other days a week. Flights are often full and subject to cancellation or postponement. Schedules, destinations and fares change frequently, so check locally.

Charter companies at the airport have five-passenger planes to almost anywhere in the Amazon. Rates are around US$300 an hour.

Airport departure tax is US$25 for international flights and US$3.50 for domestic flights.

**Boat** Iquitos is Peru's largest and best-organized river port, and is quite capable of accepting oceangoing vessels as it did in the rubber-boom days. Most boats today, however, ply only Peruvian waters, and voyagers must change boats at the border. (See also the River Boat section in the Getting Around chapter.)

Boats normally leave from Puerto Masusa, on Avenida La Marina about 2km or 3km north of the center (maybe closer if the water is very high in May to July). Boats have a chalkboard to tell you which boats are leaving when, for where, and whether they are accepting passengers. Although there are agencies in town, it's usually best to go to the dock and look around.

Upriver passages to Pucallpa (4 to 8 days) or Yurimaguas (4 to 6 days) cost about US$20 to US$30 per person. It takes longer when the river is high or the boat is going against the current. Boats leave about three times a week to Pucallpa, more often to Yurimaguas, and there are more frequent departures for the closer intermediate ports.

Downriver boats to the Peruvian border from Brazil and Colombia leave about twice a week and take two days. Fares are US$15 to US$20 per person, but gringos have to bargain hard. If you are on a tight budget, you can often sleep aboard the boat while waiting for departure; this enables you to get the best hammock space (away from the engine, and not under a light that attracts insects and keeps you awake). Boats often leave many hours or a few days late.

If you're in a hurry, Expreso Loreto (☎ 23-4086, 24-3661), on Loreto at Raymondi, has fast motor launches to the border at 6 am every two days. The fare is US$50 for the 12-hour trip including lunch.

Amazon Tours & Cruises (see Cruises later in this chapter) has weekly cruises on comfortable ships that go from Iquitos to Leticia, Colombia leaving on Sunday. Most passengers are foreigners on a one-week, round-trip tour, but one-way passages are sold on a space-available basis.

Beginning January 18, 2000, Amazon Tour & Cruises have scheduled departures from Iquitos to Manaus on the *M/F Marcelita*, leaving every four weeks on Tuesday. They arrive in Manaus on Thursday (10 days later) with a half-day stop in Leticia (where you can also join the boat). Returns from Manaus are on Tuesday, two weeks after the departure from Iquitos. The *Marcelita* is a four-deck Amazon river vessel with 24 cabins and two suites; all have private baths and air-conditioning. Guided shore excursions to local villages and onboard lectures are part of the cruise. Rates are US$2195/2390 for single/double cabins (get a partner to save money) including shore excursions and meals.

## Getting Around

**Taxis & Buses** The distinctive motocarros cost less than a taxi and are fun to ride, though they don't provide much protection in an accident.

Taxis tend to be more expensive than in other Peruvian cities, and a taxi ride to the airport costs about US$5, less in a motocarro.

Buses and trucks for several nearby destinations, including the airport, leave from the Plaza 28 de Julio.

**Motorcycle** You can find someone to rent you a motorcycle if you are persistent enough – two places are shown on the map. Make sure you get a *Tarjeta de Propieded de la Motocicleta* (registration) and a *Documento Libre de Multas* (which will help if you are stopped by a bribe-hungry policeman). A 24-hour day costs US$35 to US$70, depending on the machine. Hourly rates (US$3 to US$5) are available.

## EXPLORING THE JUNGLE

Basically, excursions into the jungle can be divided into three types: visits to jungle lodges (which is what most visitors do), a cruise on a river boat outfitted for tourism (an increasingly popular option) and the more demanding camping and walking trips.

### Jungle Lodges

There are quite a wide range of options at varying prices. Most can be booked from abroad or in Lima, but if you show up in Iquitos without a reservation, you can certainly book a lodge or tour and it'll cost you less. Bargaining is not out of the question if you are on a tight budget, even though operators show you fixed price lists. If the lodge has space and you have the cash, they'll nearly always give you a discount, sometimes a substantial one. If planning on booking after you arrive, avoid the major Peruvian holidays, when many places are filled with Peruvian holidaymakers. June to September (the dry months and the summer holiday for North American and European visitors) are also quite busy, though bargains can be found if you're flexible with time. It's worth shopping around.

The lodges are some distance from Iquitos, so river transport is included in the price. Most of the area within 50km of the city is not virgin jungle, and the chance of seeing big game is remote. Any Indians will be acculturated and performing for tourism. Nevertheless, much can be seen of the jungle way of life, and birds, insects and small mammals can be observed. The more remote lodges have more wildlife.

A representative two-day trip involves a river journey of two or three hours to a jungle lodge with reasonable comforts and meals, a 'typical' jungle lunch, a guided visit to an Indian village to buy crafts and perhaps see dances (though tourists often outnumber Indians), an evening meal at the lodge, maybe an after-dark canoe trip to look for caiman by searchlight, and a walk in the jungle the following day to see jungle vegetation (and if you are lucky, monkeys or other wildlife). A trip like this will set you back about US$60 to US$150, depending on the operator, the distance traveled and the comfort of the lodge. On longer trips, you'll get farther away from Iquitos, see more of the jungle, and the cost per night drops.

**Places to Stay** All prices quoted here are approximate; bargaining is often acceptable; and meals, guided tours and transportation from Iquitos should be included.

The well-established and recommended *Explorama Lodges* (☎ 25-2526, fax 25-2533, amazon@explorama.com, Avenida La Marina 340) owns and operates four lodges and is an involved supporter of ACEER, or Amazon Center for Environmental Education and Research (see the boxed text 'ACEER's Canopy Walkway,' later in this chapter). You could arrange a trip to visit one or more lodges (each of which is very different) combined with ACEER.

*Explorama Inn* is 40km northeast of Iquitos on the Amazon and is their most modern lodge. It has 24 rustic thatched cottages, which all have screened windows, fans, lighting, private bath and porch. Good food, short guided walks and boat rides are available for a taste of the jungle; there is some primary forest nearby. One highlight is the *Victoria regia*, or giant Amazon water lily, which has leaves almost 2m across – large enough for a child to lie down on without sinking. This lodge is a good option for people who really don't want to rough it. Rates are

US$195 per person, double occupancy, for a two-day/one-night package, extra nights are US$80, and discounts for groups and families are available (as for all the lodges).

*Explorama Lodge* is 80km away on the Amazon near its junction with the Río Napo. Built in 1964, this was one of the first lodges constructed in the Iquitos area and remains attractively rustic. The lodge has several large palm-thatched buildings containing a total of 72 rooms with shared coldwater bathrooms; covered walkways join the buildings, and lighting is by kerosene lantern. Guides accompany visitors on several trails that go farther into the forest than do those at the Explorama Inn. Rates here are US$275 for three days/two nights, and extra nights are US$80.

*Explornapo Camp* is 160km from Iquitos on the Río Napo and has 20 rooms with shared shower facilities. The highlights are guided trail hikes in remote primary forest, birdwatching, an ethnobotanical garden of useful plants (curated by a local shaman) and a visit to the canopy walkway at the nearby ACEER. Because of the distance involved, on five-day/four-night packages, you spend the first and last night at the Explorama Lodge. Costs are US$855 per person, double occupancy (less in groups), and extra nights are US$95.

From the Explornapo Camp, a two-hour walk takes you to *ExplorTambos*, which is the most rustic. Guests (16 maximum) sleep on mattresses on open-sided sleeping platforms and covered with a mosquito net; don't plan a passionate honeymoon here! Basic latrines and washing facilities are provided, and wildlife-watching opportunities here are better than at the lodges. Rates are US$120 per person per night, including guided hikes on remote trails.

You can either visit ACEER from the Explornapo Camp (half-hour walk) or you can stay at the center, which has 20 rooms in buildings similar to those at Explorama Lodge (described earlier in this section). This should be booked ahead, because accommodations are often used by researchers, workshop groups, or international tours. Rates are US$140 a night if

## ACEER's Canopy Walkway

Until the 1970s, biologists working in the rainforest made their observations and collected specimens from the forest floor and along the rivers, unaware that many plant and animal species spent their entire lives in the canopy. When scientists began to venture into the treetops, they discovered so many new species that the canopy became known as the new frontier of tropical biology. Until recently, it was difficult to visit the canopy unless you were a researcher, but it is now possible for travelers to climb to the top of the rainforest at the Amazon Center for Environmental Education and Research (ACEER).

The highlight at ACEER is an awesome hanging walkway that stretches almost half a kilometer through the rainforest canopy, reaching a height of 35m above the ground. It is about a 10-minute walk from ACEER. The canopy is reached by stairs and is accessible to any able-bodied visitor. The views are excellent, and birders spend hours up there. A couple of warnings, however. It can get hot on top of the trees, so bring sun protection and a water bottle. Also, go with realistic expectations. Binoculars will enable you to see scores of tropical bird species, but you are not likely to spot many mammals in the canopy.

ACEER is unique in the Amazon, and many people come to Peru solely to visit it. ACEER is a nonprofit foundation created in 1991 by Conservación de la Naturaleza Amazónica del Peru AC (CONAPAC) in conjunction with and supported by various individuals and private companies, including Explorama and International Expeditions. The main goal is to preserve rainforest habitats through sustainable natural-resource development, including ecologically responsible tourism and local and global education. ACEER is located on the 1000 sq km Amazon Biosphere Reserve. For more information, contact ACEER Foundation, 10 Environs Park, Helena, AL 35080, USA.

added to the Explornapo five-day/four-night trip, or you can exchange nights at the Explornapo Camp for nights at ACEER by adding US$45 a night. All visitors contribute US$25 per night (included in the cost) toward the ACEER Foundation.

International Expeditions (see Cruises, later in this chapter) organizes regular guided trips from the USA to ACEER,

including all flights and other arrangements. They also present a recommended annual International Rainforest Workshop, usually held at ACEER.

Admittedly, visiting the ACEER walkway is not for everyone. It's not cheap, involves a lot of travel, is quite rustic and may terrify you if you are afraid of heights. There are many other good lodges in the Iquitos area that are easier and cheaper to reach and will give you a rewarding look at the rainforest. One of the better establishments is *Yacumama Lodge* (☎/fax 24-1022, 23-5510, Lores 149), which is run by Eco Expeditions (☎ 305-774-0067, 800-854-0023, fax 305-774-0064, ecoexpd@aol.com, 1172 S Dixie Hwy, Suite 487, Coral Gables, FL 33146-2918 USA). The lodge is almost 200km south of Iquitos on the Río Yarapa, a small tributary of the Río Ucayali. There are about 20 cabins, all carefully screened. A cheaper dormitory-style building is planned for students and budget travelers.

The lodge has been built with some thought to reducing impact on the rainforest. Although bathrooms are shared (separate facilities for men and women) in an effort to consolidate waste in environmentally acceptable septic tanks, hot showers are available through solar panels. Treated water is provided for brushing teeth. Meals and jungle excursions have been recommended. A one-week package from Miami, including airfare, five nights at the lodge with a night at Iquitos at either end, all meals and guided excursions, is about US$1800 from Eco Expeditions. Ask at the reservations office for local rates.

*Amazon Jungle Camp* is run by Amazon Tours & Cruises (see Cruises, below) and is near the mouth of the Río Momón, an Amazon tributary just north of Iquitos. It provides first/last nights in Iquitos for passengers on one of the many river cruises offered by this company and can also be used by individual travelers who want to experience a jungle lodge close to Iquitos. Note that you can't get there from Iquitos by car; a river taxi is required and will be provided at the beginning and end of your stay. The lodge has about two dozen rooms with private toilets and is lit by kerosene lanterns. Cold showers are in a separate building. Rates are about US$145/220 for singles/doubles for one night, including river taxi, meals and short excursions with a discount for passengers taking a cruise or tour. Extra nights are US$100/140. This company also operates several small, remote and very rustic expedition camps and can provide a variety of cruise/lodge options.

*Loving Light Amazon Lodge* (☎ 24-3180, Putumayo 128) has a US office (☎ 425-836-9431, info@junglelodge.com, 7016 248th Ave NE, Redmond, WA 98053). This lodge is about 100km from Iquitos on the Río Yanayacu, a minor tributary of the Amazon. A circular thatched dining room/reception lodge is connected by walkways to ten bungalows with private showers and screens. Each sleeps up to four people, and lighting is with kerosene lanterns. The usual jungle tours are available, and there are opportunities to listen to musicians in the evenings, or learn about ayahuasca and other spiritual ceremonies conducted by a local shaman. For a quick look, a two-day/one-night trip is US$150, or a five-day/four-night trip is US$400 to US$600. Discounts are offered for groups of three or more. The lodge can arrange camping expeditions for US$125 per person per night.

One of the oldest and best-established lodges is *Amazonas Sinchicuy Lodge* (office at Paseos Amazonicos, ☎/fax 23-3110, Pevas 246). The lodge is on a small tributary of the Amazon, only 25km northeast of Iquitos, and offers fairly standard but well-run tours ranging from US$80 for a one-day trip to US$210 for a three-day/two-night trip – these are advertised costs for a single passenger, but substantial reductions for groups and walk-in discounts can be easily arranged. They also do longer trips that visit other parts of the jungle. Rooms are screened, and showers are shared.

*Anaconda Lara Lodge* (☎ 23-9147, fax 23-2978, Pevas 210) is on the Río Momón about 40km from Iquitos. It is used both for day trips to get a taste of the jungle and for overnights. A day trip may include a one-hour, fast boat ride to the lodge, a two-hour hike to a village, lunch and drinks, and a stop on the return at a Boras Indian village with a dance and craft sales. This costs about US$50, less if you bargain or if there's a big group. An overnight stay is about US$90 including meals and a nighttime river excursion.

*Cumaceba Lodge* (☎/fax 23-2229, cell 61-0656, cumaceba.lodge@mailcity.com, Putumayo 184) is 35km from Iquitos on the Amazon River. They have 15 screened rooms with private showers and can arrange more adventurous trips, where you would stay in simple, open-sided shelters. The lodge itself can be the destination for a day-trip from Iquitos (about US$30 to US$50 per person depending on season and group size) or overnight trips with the usual jungle excursions (4 days/3 nights for US$140 to US$200).

In the last edition of this book, I mentioned **Amazon River Lodge**, which is run by Andres A Peña Guerra. I have since been informed (by the local tourism office and by people on a boat that were held up at gunpoint) that this is an unlicensed operation and the owner has a criminal record for robbing tourists. This lodge claims to be recommended by Lonely Planet and other guidebooks and, although some clients have been satisfied, Amazon River Lodge is **not recommended**. Other places open and close – check with the tourist office to make sure that they are legitimate.

## Cruises

Amazon Tours & Cruises (☎ 23-3931, 23-1611, fax 23-1265, amazon@amazoncruises .com.pe, Requena 336), off Avenida La Marina, has been operating comfortable cruises for over two decades. They can be reached in the USA (☎ 305-227-2266, 800-423-2791, fax 305-227-1880, amazoncruz@ aol.com, 8700 W Flagler St, Suite 190, Miami, FL 33174).

The 44-passenger M/V *Río Amazonas* is their largest ship (length 146 feet) and has 21 air-conditioned cabins with private showers and two or three beds. The 29-passenger M/V *Arca* has 10 air-conditioned cabins with upper/lower bunks and three cabins with three beds. All cabins have private showers. The 20-passenger M/V *Delfin* has 10 cabins with upper/lower bunks, fans and four shared showers/toilets. The 16-passenger M/V *Amazon Explorer* has eight air-conditioned cabins with upper/lower bunks and private showers. All these are typical three- or four-decked Amazon river boats with a lot of romantic charm, and they are comfortable but not luxurious. All have dining areas and

bars and plenty of deck space for watching the river go by. Each is accompanied by a full crew including an experienced bilingual local naturalist guide. Small launches are carried for side trips. Smaller boats are also available for tours or charter.

M/V *Río Amazonas* or M/V *Arca* leave Iquitos on Sunday, usually with a complement of passengers who arrived from Miami on the previous Saturday flight. They spend three days sailing downriver to Leticia/ Tabatinga and three days returning to Iquitos. Stops are made at jungle towns, Indian villages (for dancing and crafts sales), and almost a day is spent looking around the colorful Colombian port of Leticia and neighboring Tabatinga in Brazil. Short side trips are made to lagoons and up tributaries, and hikes in the jungle last from one to a few hours. This trip is on a well-traveled and long-settled part of the Amazon and gives a good look at the river and its inhabitants today. Wildlife enthusiasts will see dozens of bird species, pink dolphins, beautiful butterflies and other insects, but you aren't guaranteed to see monkeys or other mammals.

The US tour agency Explorations (☎ 941-992-9660, 800-446-9600, fax 941-992-7666, goxploring@aol.com, 27655 Kent Rd, Bonita Springs, FL 34135) sells complete one-week packages from Miami-(Lima)-Iquitos-Leticia and return on either the M/V *Arca* or M/V *Amazonas*. Packages cost US$2050 to US$2250 and include airfare from Miami, an American biologist guide who accompanies you from Miami and throughout the trip (in addition to the onboard local naturalist guide), predeparture information, all meals and hotel nights at either end. If you book with Amazon Tours & Cruises, you'll get the tour for about half the price (without airfare from Miami, hotels, or US guide) but some dates are unavailable, if they have been blocked out by US tour groups. If you just show up in Iquitos, you can get an even cheaper rate on a space-available basis, but with boats leaving once a week, you might have to wait for a week or two for space to become available. One-way passages for travelers wanting to continue into or arrive from

Brazil or Colombia are also sold on a space-available basis – these are open to bargaining.

The smaller M/V *Delfin* has departures for trips south to the Nauta area of the Río Marañón and to other areas. The smaller boats have a variety of destinations to various other rivers. All of these are available for charter from Amazon Tours & Cruises.

International Expeditions (☎ 205-428-1700, 800-633-4734, fax 205-428-1714, nature@ietravel.com, 1 Environs Park, Helena, AL 35080, USA) has a fleet of boats (all named after gems) and can arrange weeklong cruises upriver from Iquitos. These are the most elegant and modern boats on the Peruvian Amazon – all have three decks, air-conditioned double cabins with private showers, good dining and viewing facilities, and experienced guides. They visit the Río Tapiche (a minor tributary of the Ucayali) and the Pacaya-Samiria area, where there are much greater opportunities to see more wildlife (particularly various monkey species) than there are on the Amazon. Pink dolphin sightings occur several times a day, and there are plenty of birds for the birdwatcher. The boats are the 16-passenger *La Esmeralda*, 26-passenger *La Turmalina*, 28-passenger *La Amatista* and the eight-passenger *La Malaquita*. I have received enthusiastic recommendations about these boats, which have weekly departures. Rates for all-inclusive nine-day/eight-night (six nights aboard boat) packages departing from Miami are US$2800 (US$2900 on *La Malaquita*. A three-day extension to the ACEER lodge before the voyage can be added for US$900. International Expeditions is represented in Iquitos by Jungle Xports (☎ 23-1870, Pevas 199), but they don't sell trips there.

## Roughing It

Various jungle guides can be found in Iquitos. They'll approach you at the airport, in restaurants or on the street. Their quality and reliability varies considerably, so get references for any guide, and proceed with caution. Some guides have criminal records – some for robbing tourists. All guides should have a permit or license; if they don't, check with the tourist office. The better jungle-lodge companies can provide reputable guides. Amazon Tours & Cruises arranges trips using thatch-roofed, open-sided expedition boats in which you sling a hammock or camp on shore. These trips are complete with guide, crew and cook and last from one to six nights. Rates depend on how many people are in a group, and the longer tours are much more economical. A six-night tour with seven passengers is US$380 per person; with two passengers it is US$700 per person.

Moisés Torres Viena, on Brasil near Próspero, has been organizing trips for many years and is probably reliable, though not cheap. His jungle expeditions include camping, overnights in Indian villages, long walks in the jungle and catching your own food. Some river travel is involved. Moisés doesn't speak English. Tours reportedly last from a couple of days to over a month.

A reader reports that you can stay with a family in La Tipishaca, a day's boat journey from Iquitos. Accommodations are in simple shelters, and you eat what the family does for a realistic jungle experience. Costs are US$20 per day, including guided walks. The Iquitos contact is Sr Rios Torres (☎ 23-9156, 23-6024, Próspero 520, 2nd floor).

Another reader recommends Orlando Cueva Flores (☎ 22-4327, fax 23-5037, 23-1111, orlando.guide@mailcity.com, Soledad 718), who is an ex-commando and organizes good customized jungle expeditions for small groups (3 to 6 people). These include primitive camps, survival skills, travel by canoe and/or motorboat to native areas. He speaks Spanish and some regional dialects. Be specific with what you want; he hunts for the pot, so ask him to bring food if you don't want to hunt the wildlife you are observing. Trips last from four to 30 days and cost US$60 to US$80 per person per day.

## PEVAS

About 145km downriver from Iquitos, Pevas is Peru's oldest town on the Amazon. Founded by missionaries in 1735, Pevas now has about 2500 inhabitants but no cars, post office or banks; the first telephone was installed in 1998. Most of the residents are mestizos, with a sprinkling of Indians from four tribes. The people are friendly and easygoing. Pevas is the most interesting town between Iquitos and the border and is visited regularly (if briefly) by the cruise boats traveling to Leticia.

## Places to Stay

*Casa de la Loma* (the house on the hill) is another reason to visit Pevas. This rustic but attractive lodge is on the outskirts of Pevas and offers Amazon views and interesting activities. With its hilltop breezes and views, it is the best place to stay between Iquitos and Leticia. North Americans Judy Balser and Scott Humfeld own and manage the lodge. They are cousins by relation and nurses by profession. After a 1992 Pevas visit, they decided to provide this friendly yet isolated community with medical care, including mental health. Casa de la Loma was established in 1994 as a simple but clean and comfortable lodge to help Judy and Scott finance their medical work. They are very connected with the community and can help visitors with activities ranging from playing in a soccer game to fishing for piranha. Guided jungle excursions and discussions and demonstrations about local social, medical and political issues can be arranged. This is a place to spend a few days and get to know the town and the inhabitants, join in a fiesta or shop at the market.

Casa de la Loma has five screened rooms, which share three clean showers. A small aviary houses parrots and other birds in a rescue and rehabilitation project. A restaurant and bar provide tasty meals based on local produce and fish, and Saturday night often sees a dance that is frequented by locals.

Casa de la Loma can be contacted by fax in

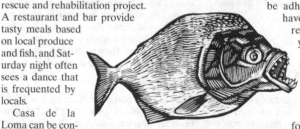

**The notorious piranha**

Iquitos at 22-1184; make sure that Casa de la Loma is clearly addressed and allow a few days for a reply. Their mailing address is PO Box 555, Iquitos. Reservations can also be made through Amazon Tours & Cruises in Iquitos. They can arrange complete packages with transportation from Iquitos, guided tours and meals for one to seven nights; the average cost is US$395 per person (two minimum) for four days/three nights. For information and reservations in the USA, contact Greentracks (☎ 970-884-6107, 800-966-6539, fax 970-247-8378, www.greentracks.com, 10 Town Plaza, Durango CO 81301). Greentracks can make lodge reservations for US$75 per person per night including meals.

Judy and Scott encourage drop-in visitors. There is nearly always space available and you can negotiate rates to about US$65 per person per night including all meals and activities.

There is also the basic *Hospedaje Rodríguez*, near the Pevas Plaza, which offers beds and food for a few dollars. Artists have been known to stay at Francisco Grippa's house.

## Getting There & Away

If you haven't arranged transportation with one of the agencies, just go down to the Iquitos docks and get on a boat to Leticia – stops are made at Pevas. (The same applies if you are coming from Leticia.)

## THE TRI-BORDER

Even though you are in the middle of the Amazon jungle, border formalities must still be adhered to, and officials have little to do other than refuse you passage if your documents are not in order. With a valid passport and visa or tourist card, border crossing is not a problem.

When leaving Peru for Brazil or Colombia, you'll get an exit stamp at a

## Francisco Grippa – Amazon Artist

Apart from visiting with the locals, there are two places that make Pevas worth a trip. One is La Casa del Arte, a huge thatched-roof structure dominating the town. This is the home, studio, gallery and muse of Peruvian artist Francisco Grippa, who has come a long way from his home town of Tumbes on Peru's northern desert coast. As a young man, he went to Los Angeles, USA, where he worked in a restaurant, learned English and saved enough money to attend art school. He returned home, interested in exploring the Peruvian Amazon and experiencing the area as an artist. The result is La Casa del Arte, where Grippa's explosively colorful paintings fill the walls.

Grippa handmakes his canvas from local bark, similar to that formerly used by local Indians for cloth – a unique feature of his art. His paintings have mainly Amazon themes, though political satire and mysticism crop up occasionally. Although Grippa regularly returns to Los Angeles, where his work is exhibited and sold, he spends most of his time in Pevas. You can also buy his canvases in Iquitos and right here in his gallery, where the effervescent and friendly artist will welcome you with a banana and cold beer while you browse – the Amazon equivalent of a wine and cheese party.

Francisco Grippa can be contacted in Iquitos through Amazon Tours and Cruises, or the Camu-Camu Gallery. In Pevas, just visit La Casa del Arte. Also, check out www.art-and-soul.com/grippa.

Peruvian guardpost just before the border (boats stop there long enough for this, though make sure the captain knows before you leave Iquitos).

There are several ports at the three-way border that are several kilometers apart and connected by public ferries. They are reached by air or boat, but not road. The biggest town, Leticia in Colombia, boasts by far the best hotels, restaurants and a hospital. You can fly from Leticia to Bogotá on almost daily commercial flights. Otherwise, infrequent boats go to Puerto Asis on the Río Putumayo; the trip takes up to 12 days. From Puerto Asis, buses go farther into Colombia.

The two small ports in Brazil are Tabatinga and Benjamin Constant, both have basic hotels. Tabatinga has an airport with flights to Manaus. Tabatinga is a continuation of Leticia, and you can walk or take a taxi between the two with no immigration hassles, unless you are planning on traveling farther into Brazil or Colombia. Boats leave from Tabatinga downriver, usually stopping

in Benjamin Constant for a night, then continuing on to Manaus, Brazil, a week away. Brazilian entry formalities are in Tabatinga. It takes about an hour to reach Benjamin Constant by public ferry.

Peru is on the south side of the river and currents here create a constantly shifting bank. The old ports of Ramón Castilla and Islandia are now disused. Most boats from Iquitos will drop you at Santa Rosa, where there are Peruvian immigration facilities and from where a motor canoe can take you to Leticia in about 15 minutes. If you are heading for Colombia or Brazil, Lonely Planet has guidebooks for both countries.

If you are arriving from Colombia or Brazil, you'll find boats in Tabatinga and Leticia for Iquitos. Expect a charge of US$20 or less for the three-day trip on a cargo river boat, US$50 for an Expreso (12 to 14 hours), which leaves daily. The cruise ships leave Wednesday and arrive in Iquitos on Saturday morning. Ask in Leticia about flights to Iquitos.

With three borders and four ports to choose from, the best place to base yourself is in Leticia. Remember that however disorganized things may appear, you can always get meals, beds, money changed, boats and other services simply by asking around. The locals are used to the different way of doing things on the river, so ask them. As my Polish mother used to tell me, 'Koniec języka za przewodnika' – which, perhaps, is an appropriate way to finish this book. Roughly translated, it means 'Use your tongue as your guide.'

# Language

## Latin American Spanish

### Pronunciation

Spanish is a largely phonetic language – there is a clear and consistent relationship between pronunciation and spelling. In addition, most Spanish sounds have English equivalents, so English-speakers should not have much trouble being understood if the following rules are adhered to.

Peruvian Spanish is considered to be one of the language's 'cleanest' dialects – enunciation is relatively clear, pronunciation is very similar to Castilian Spanish (the official language of Spain), and slang is infrequently used.

### Vowels

Spanish vowels have simple English equivalents, and their pronunciation is basically consistent.

**a**  as in 'father'
**e**  as in 'met'
**i**  as in 'feet'
**o**  as in 'for'
**u**  as in 'rule' It is silent after *q* and in the groups *gue* and *gui*, unless it is marked by a diaeresis ('*argüir*,' '*antigüedad*'), in which case it is pronounced as the English *w*.
**y**  As a vowel (ie, when at the end of a word or when standing alone), it is pronounced as the Spanish *i* ('*ley*'). As a semiconsonant or consonant, it's somewhere between the *y* in '**y**onder' and the *g* in 'bei**g**e,' depending on the region ('*apoyo*').

### Consonants

Spanish consonants resemble their English equivalents, with some major exceptions. The pronunciations of the letters *f, k, l, m, n, p, q* and *s* are virtually identical to English.

The consonants *ch, ll* and *ñ* are generally considered distinct letters. But recently, many dictionaries have ceased to treat *ch* and *ll* as separate letters, so words beginning with those letters are often found in the respective *c* and *l* sections of dictionaries. However, *ñ* continues to be consistently treated as a separate letter.

**b**  resembles its English equivalent; referred to as 'b larga,' (see **v**)
**c**  as the *s* in '**s**ee' before *e* and *i*; otherwise as the English *k*
**ch**  as in '**ch**urch'
**d**  as in '**d**og,' but between vowels and after *l* or *n*, the sound is closer to *th*
**g**  as the *ch* in the Scottish 'lo**ch**' before *e* and *i*, otherwise as the *g* in '**g**o'
**h**  invariably silent. If your name begins with this letter, listen carefully when immigration officials summon you to collect your passport.
**j**  as the *ch* in the Scottish 'lo**ch**'
**ll**  as the *y* in '**y**ellow'
**ñ**  as the *ni* in 'o**ni**on'
**r**  is a short *r* except at the beginning of a word, and after *l, n* or *s*, when it is often rolled
**rr**  very strongly rolled
**t**  as in '**t**ame,' but without aspiration
**v**  indistinguishable from *b*, and referred to as 'b corta,' (see **b**)
**x**  as in 'ta**x**i,' except for a very few words, when it is pronounced as *j*
**z**  as the *s* in '**s**un'

### Stress

Stress is very important, since it can change the meaning of words. In general, words ending in vowels or the letters *n* or *s* have stress on the next-to-last syllable, while those with other endings have stress on the last syllable.

Thus *vaca* ('cow') and *caballos* ('horses') are both stressed on the next-to-last syllable, while *ciudad* ('city') and *infeliz* ('unhappy') both have stress on the last syllable.

Written accents will almost always appear in words that do not follow the rules above, such as *sótano* ('basement'), *América* and *porción* ('portion'). When counting syllables, be sure to remember that diphthongs constitute only one. When a word with a written accent appears in capital letters, the accent is often not written, but is still pronounced.

## Gender & Plurals

In Spanish, nouns are either masculine or feminine, and there are rules to help determine a noun's gender (there are of course some exceptions). Feminine nouns generally end with *-a* or with the groups *-ción, -sión* or *-dad*. Other endings typically signify a masculine noun. Adjectives also have masculine (ending in *-o*) or feminine (ending in *-a*) forms.

If a noun ends in a vowel, the plural is formed by adding *s* to the end. If a noun ends in a consonant, the plural is formed by adding *es* to the end.

## Articles & Agreement

In English, there is a definite article ('the') and indefinite articles ('a' or 'some'). Spanish also uses both definite and indefinite articles, but each has feminine and masculine forms, as well as singular and plural forms.

### Feminine
| | |
|---|---|
| the house | *la casa* |
| the houses | *las casas* |
| a house | *una casa* |
| some houses | *unas casas* |

### Masculine
| | |
|---|---|
| the book | *el libro* |
| the books | *los libros* |
| a book | *un libro* |
| some books | *unos libros* |

Articles and adjectives must agree in gender and in number with the nouns they describe.

| | |
|---|---|
| a funny boy | *un chico chistoso* |
| the funny girls | *las chicas chistosas* |
| the pretty house | *la casa bonita* |
| some pretty rooms | *unos cuartos bonitos* |

## Greetings & Civilities

In their public behavior, South Americans are very conscious of civilities, sometimes to the point of ceremoniousness. Never approach a stranger for information without extending a greeting, and avoid using the familiar form of speech with anyone that you do not know well.

| | |
|---|---|
| Hello. | *Hola.* |
| Good morning. | *Buenos días.* |
| Good afternoon. | *Buenas tardes.* |
| Good evening/night. | *Buenas noches.* |
| Goodbye. | *Adiós.* |
| Mr/Sir | *Señor* |
| Mrs/Madam | *Señora* |
| unmarried woman | *Señorita* |
| male/female friend | *amigo/a* |
| Bye/See you soon. | *Hasta luego.* |
| Yes. | *Sí.* |
| No. | *No.* |
| Please. | *Por favor.* |
| Thank you. | *Gracias.* |
| Many thanks. | *Muchas gracias.* |
| You're welcome. | *De nada.* |
| Pardon me. | *Perdón.* |
| Excuse me. | *Permiso.* |
| (used when asking permission) | |
| Forgive me. | *Disculpe.* |
| (used when apologizing) | |
| Good luck! | *¡Buena suerte!* |
| May it go well for you. | *Que le vaya bien.* |
| (used when parting) | |

## Small Talk

How are you?
  *¿Cómo está?* (formal)
  *¿Cómo estás?* (familiar)
How are things going?
  *¿Qué tal?*
Fine, thanks.
  *Bien, gracias.*
Very well/badly.
  *Muy bien/mal.*
What is your name?
  *¿Cómo se llama?* (formal)
  *¿Cómo te llamas?* (familiar)
My name is…
  *Me llamo…*
It's a pleasure to meet you.
  *Mucho gusto.*

The pleasure is mine.
    *El gusto es mío.*
Where are you from?
    *¿De dónde es?* (formal)
    *¿De dónde eres?* (familiar)
I am from…
    *Soy de…*
Where are you staying?
    *¿Dónde está alojado?* (formal)
    *¿Dónde estás alojado?* (familiar)
How old are you?
    *¿Cuántos años tiene?* (formal)
    *¿Cuántos años tienes?* (familiar)
I'm 29.    *Tengo veintinueve años.*
Are you married?
    *¿Es casado/a?* (formal)
    *¿Eres casado/a?* (familiar)
I am single.
    *Soy soltero/a.*
I am married.
    *Soy casado/a.*
May I take a photo?
    *¿Puedo sacar una foto?*
Of course.
    *Por supuesto.*
Why not? *Cómo no?*
Sure.    *Claro.*
It's hot/cold.
    *Hace calor/frío.*

Curious South Americans, from officials to casual acquaintances, will often want to know what travelers do for a living. If it's something that seems unusual (many would find it difficult to believe, for example, that a gardener could earn enough money to travel the world), it may be easiest to claim to be a student or teacher.

What do you do?
    *¿En qué trabaja?* (formal)
    *¿En qué trabajas?* (familiar)
What's your profession?
    *¿Cuál es su profesión?*
I am a…    *Soy…*

| | |
|---|---|
| student | *estudiante* |
| teacher | *profesor/a* |
| nurse | *enfermero/a* |
| lawyer | *abogado/a* |
| engineer | *ingeniero/a* |
| mechanic | *mecánico/a* |

## Language Difficulties

I don't speak much Spanish.
    *Hablo poco castellano.*
I (don't) understand.
    *Yo (no) entiendo.*
Do you understand me?
    *¿Me entiende?* (formal)
    *¿Me entiendes?* (familiar)
Do you speak English/Spanish?
    *¿Habla inglés/castellano?* (formal)
    *¿Hablas inglés/castellano?* (familiar)
Could you repeat that?
    *¿Puede repetirlo?* (formal)
    *¿Puedes repetirlo?* (familiar)
Could you speak slowly please?
    *¿Puede hablar despacio por favor?*
    (formal)
    *¿Puedes hablar despacio por favor?*
    (familiar)
How do you say…?
    *¿Cómo se dice…?*
What does…mean?
    *¿Qué quiere decir…?*

## Toilets

The most common word for 'toilet' is *baño*, but *servicios sanitarios* is a frequent alternative. Men's toilets will usually be labeled *Hombres*, *Caballeros* or *Varones*. Women's toilets will usually be marked *Señoras* or *Damas*.

## Getting Around

| | |
|---|---|
| Where is…? | *¿Dónde está…?* |
| the airport | *el aeropuerto* |
| the train station | *la estación de ferrocarril* |
| the bus station | *la estación de autobuses* |
| the bus stop | *la parada de autobuses* |
| the ticket office | *la boletería* |
| What time does…? | *¿A qué hora…* |
| the airplane | *el avión* |
| the train | *el tren* |
| the bus | *autobus* |
| the ship | *el barco/buque* |
| leave/arrive? | *sale/llega?* |

I'd like a ticket to…
    *Quiero un boleto a…*
What's the fare to…?
    *¿Cuánto cuesta hasta…?*

Is there a student discount?
    *¿Hay descuento estudiantil?*

| 1st class | *primera clase* |
| 2nd class | *segunda clase* |
| single/one-way | *ida* |
| return/round trip | *ida y vuelta* |
| car | *auto/carro/coche* |
| pickup (truck) | *camioneta* |
| taxi | *taxi* |
| truck | *camión* |
| hitchhike | *hacer dedo* |
| luggage checkroom | *guardería/equipaje* |

## Directions

How do I get to…?
    *¿Cómo puedo llegar a…?*
Is it far?
    *¿Está lejos?*
Go straight ahead.
    *Siga/Vaya derecho.*
Turn left
    *Voltée a la izquierda.*
Turn right.
    *Voltée a la derecha.*
I'm lost.
    *Estoy perdido/a.*
Where are we on this map?
    *¿Dónde estamos aquí en el mapa?*

| north | *norte* |
| south | *sur* |
| east | *este/oriente* |
| west | *oeste/occidente* |
| there | *allí* |
| around there | *por allá* |
| here | *aquí* |
| around here | *por aquí* |
| downhill | *por abajo* |
| uphill | *por arriba* |
| avenue | *avenida/jirón/paseo* |
| block | *cuadra* |
| street | *calle/paseo* |

## Accommodations

| Where is there …? | *¿Dónde hay…?* |
| a hotel | *un hotel* |
| a boarding house | *una pensión/ residencial, un hospedaje* |
| a youth hostel | *un albergue juvenil* |

What does it cost per night?
    *¿Cuánto cuesta por noche?*
Does it include breakfast?
    *¿Incluye el desayuno?*
May I see the room?
    *¿Puedo ver la habitación?*
I don't like it.
    *No me gusta.*

| double room | *habitación doble* |
| single room | *habitación para una persona* |
| full board | *pensión completa* |
| private bath | *baño privado* |
| shared bath | *baño compartido* |
| too expensive | *demasiado caro* |
| cheaper | *más económico* |
| discount | *descuento* |

## Around Town

| I'm looking for… | *Estoy buscando…* |
| the ATM | *el cajero automático* |
| the bank | *el banco* |
| the embassy | *la embajada* |
| my hotel | *mi hotel* |
| the market | *el mercado* |
| the post office | *el correo* |
| the tourist office | *la oficina de turismo* |

What time does it open/close?
    *¿A qué hora abre/cierra?*
I want to change some money/traveler's checks.
    *Quiero cambiar dinero/cheques de viajero.*
What is the exchange rate?
    *¿Cuál es el tipo de cambio?*
I want to call (Canada).
    *Quiero llamar a (Canadá).*

| airmail | *correo aéreo* |
| black market | *mercado negro, mercado paralelo* |
| credit card | *tarjeta de crédito* |
| exchange house | *casa de cambio* |
| letter | *carta* |
| registered mail | *certificado* |
| stamps | *estampillas* |

## Food

I would like…
    *Quisiera…*

I would like the set lunch, please.
*Quisiera el menú por favor.*
Is service included in the bill?
*¿El servicio está incluido en la cuenta?*
I'm a vegetarian.
*Soy vegetariano/a.*
The bill, please.
*La cuenta, por favor.*
Thank you, that was delicious.
*Muchas gracias, estaba buenísimo.*

| | |
|---|---|
| breakfast | *desayuno* |
| lunch | *almuerzo* |
| dinner | *cena* |
| (cheap) restaurant | *restaurante (barato)* |

The following is a list of foods, drinks and other menu vocabulary and their English translations.

| | |
|---|---|
| *agua con gas* | carbonated water |
| *agua mineral* | mineral water |
| *agua potable* | drinking water |
| *agua sin gas* | noncarbonated water |
| *aguardiente, pisco* | strong liquor |
| *anticucho* | shish kebab |
| *arroz* | rice |
| *azúcar* | sugar |
| *cabro, cabrito* | goat |
| *calamares* | squid |
| *camarones* | shrimp |
| *cangrejo* | crab |
| *carne* | meat |
| *cerdo, chancho* | pork |
| *cerveza* | beer |
| *ceviche* | raw seafood marinated in lime or lemon juice, often with other seasonings |
| *chaufa, chaulafan* | fried rice (Chinese style) |
| *chicharrones* | fried pork skins |
| *choclo* | corn on the cob |
| *cordero* | mutton |
| *cuy* | guinea pig |
| *el menú* | set menu |
| *empanadas* | meat and/or cheese pastries |
| *ensalada* | salad |
| *estofado* | stew |
| *frutas* | fruit |
| *helado* | ice cream |
| *huevos fritos* | fried eggs |

| | |
|---|---|
| *huevos revueltos* | scrambled eggs |
| *jamón* | ham |
| *jugo* | juice |
| *langosta* | lobster |
| *leche* | milk |
| *lechón* | suckling pig |
| *locro* | meat and vegetable stew |
| *lomo* | beef |
| *mantequilla* | butter |
| *maracuya* | passionfruit |
| *mariscos* | seafood |
| *mora* | blackberry |
| *naranja* | orange |
| *naranjilla* | local fruit (tastes like bitter orange) |
| *palta* | avocado |
| *pan* | bread |
| *papas fritas* | french-fried potatoes |
| *parrillada* | grilled meats |
| *pescado* | fish |
| *piña* | pineapple |
| *pollo* | chicken |
| *postre* | dessert |
| *queso* | cheese |
| *sandía* | watermelon |
| *sopa, chupe* | soup |
| *toronja* | grapefruit |
| *torta* | cake |
| *tortilla* | omelet |
| *trucha* | trout |
| *verduras* | vegetables |

## Shopping
Can I look at it?
*¿Puedo mirarlo/a?*
How much is it?
*¿Cuánto cuesta?*
That's too expensive for me.
*Es demasiado caro para mí.*
Could you lower the price?
*¿Podría bajar un poco el precio?*
I'll take it.
*Lo llevo.*

| | |
|---|---|
| bookstore | *la librería* |
| general store/shop | *la tienda* |
| laundry | *la lavandería* |
| market | *el mercado* |
| pharmacy, chemist | *la farmacia/ la droguería* |

| | |
|---|---|
| supermarket | *el supermercado* |
| cheaper | *más barato* |
| too expensive | *demasiado caro* |
| less | *menos* |
| more | *más* |
| large | *grande* |
| small | *pequeña/o* |

## Health

I need a doctor.
    *Necesito un médico.*
Where is the hospital?
    *¿Dónde está el hospital?*
I'm allergic to antibiotics/penicillin.
    *Soy alérgico/a a los antibióticos/*
    *la penicilina.*
I'm pregnant.
    *Estoy embarazada.*
I have been vaccinated.
    *Estoy vacunado/a.*
I am sick.
    *Estoy enfermo/a.*
I have… *Tengo…*

| | |
|---|---|
| altitude sickness | *soroche* |
| diarrhea | *diarrea* |
| nausea | *náusea* |
| a headache | *un dolor de cabeza* |
| a cough | *tos* |

## Emergencies

| | |
|---|---|
| Danger! | *¡Peligro!* |
| Be careful! | *¡Cuidado!* |
| Help! | *¡Socorro!* |
| Fire! | *¡Incendio!* |
| Thief! | *¡Ladrón!* |
| I've been robbed. | *Me robaron.* |
| Don't bother me! | *¡No me moleste!* |
| Go away! | *¡Déjeme!* |
| Go away! (stronger) | *¡Que se vaya!* |
| Get lost! | *¡Váyase!* |

## Time & Dates

| | |
|---|---|
| What time is it? | *¿Qué hora es?* |
| It's one o'clock. | *Es la una.* |
| It's seven o'clock. | *Son las siete.* |
| | |
| midnight | *medianoche* |
| noon | *mediodía* |
| half past two | *dos y media* |
| quarter past two | *dos y cuarto* |

| | |
|---|---|
| two ten | *dos con diez minutos* |
| twenty to two | *veinte para las dos* |
| today | *hoy* |
| this morning | *esta mañana* |
| this afternoon | *esta tarde* |
| tonight | *esta noche* |
| tomorrow | *mañana* |
| yesterday | *ayer* |
| week/month/year | *semana/mes/año* |
| last week | *la semana pasada* |
| next month | *el mes que viene* |
| always | *siempre* |
| before/after | *antes/después* |
| now | *ahora* |
| rainy season (winter) | *el invierno* |
| dry season (summer) | *el verano* |

## Days of the Week

| | |
|---|---|
| Monday | *lunes* |
| Tuesday | *martes* |
| Wednesday | *miércoles* |
| Thursday | *jueves* |
| Friday | *viernes* |
| Saturday | *sábado* |
| Sunday | *domingo* |

## Numbers

| | |
|---|---|
| 1 | *uno/una* |
| 2 | *dos* |
| 3 | *tres* |
| 4 | *cuatro* |
| 5 | *cinco* |
| 6 | *seis* |
| 7 | *siete* |
| 8 | *ocho* |
| 9 | *nueve* |
| 10 | *diez* |
| 11 | *once* |
| 12 | *doce* |
| 13 | *trece* |
| 14 | *catorce* |
| 15 | *quince* |
| 16 | *dieciséis* |
| 17 | *diecisiete* |
| 18 | *dieciocho* |
| 19 | *diecinueve* |
| 20 | *veinte* |
| 21 | *veintiuno* |
| 30 | *treinta* |
| 31 | *treinta y uno* |

| | | | |
|---|---|---|---|
| 40 | *cuarenta* | 200 | *doscientos* |
| 50 | *cincuenta* | 1000 | *mil* |
| 60 | *sesenta* | 5000 | *cinco mil* |
| 70 | *setenta* | 10,000 | *diez mil* |
| 80 | *ochenta* | 50,000 | *cincuenta mil* |
| 90 | *noventa* | 100,000 | *cien mil* |
| 100 | *cien* | one million | *un millón* |
| 101 | *ciento uno* | one billion | *un billón* |

# Aymara & Quechua

The following list of words and phrases is obviously minimal, but it should be useful in areas where these languages are spoken. Pronounce them as you would a Spanish word. An apostrophe represents a glottal stop (the 'sound' in the middle of 'uh-oh!').

## Basics

| English | Aymara | Quechua |
|---|---|---|
| Hello. | *Kamisaraki.* | *Napaykullayki.* |
| Please. | *Mirá.* | *Allichu.* |
| Thank you. | *Yuspagara.* | *Yusulipayki.* |
| How do you say…? | *Cun sañasauca'ha…?* | *Imainata nincha chaita…?* |
| It is called… | *Ucan sutipa'h…* | *Chaipa'g sutin'ha…* |
| Please repeat. | *Uastata sita.* | *Ua'manta niway.* |
| How much? | *K'gauka?* | *Maik'ata'g?* |

## Some Useful Words

| English | Aymara | Quechua |
|---|---|---|
| condor | *malku* | *condor* |
| father | *auqui* | *tayta* |
| food | *manka* | *mikíuy* |
| friend | *kgochu* | *kgochu* |
| house | *uta* | *huasi* |
| llama | *yama-karhua* | *karhua* |
| lodging | *korpa* | *pascana* |
| man | *chacha* | *k'gari* |
| moon | *pha'gsi* | *kiya* |
| mother | *taica* | *mama* |
| no | *janiwa* | *mana* |
| river | *jawira* | *mayu* |
| ruins | *champir* | *champir* |
| snowy peak | *kollu* | *riti-orko* |
| sun | *yinti* | *inti* |
| thirst | *phara* | *chchaqui* |
| trail | *tapu* | *chakiñan* |
| water | *uma* | *yacu* |
| woman | *warmi* | *warmi* |
| yes | *jisa* | *ari* |
| young | *wuayna* | *huayna* |

LANGUAGE

## Numbers

| English | Aymara | Quechua |
|---------|--------|---------|
| 1 | *maya* | *u'* |
| 2 | *paya* | *iskai* |
| 3 | *quimsa* | *quinsa* |
| 4 | *pusi* | *tahua* |
| 5 | *pesca* | *phiska* |
| 6 | *zo'hta* | *so'gta* |
| 7 | *pakalko* | *khanchis* |
| 8 | *quimsakalko* | *pusa'g* |
| 9 | *yatunca* | *iskon* |
| 10 | *tunca* | *chunca* |

# Acknowledgments

## THANKS

Many thanks to the following readers (apologies if we misspelled your name) who took the time to write to us about their experiences in Peru:

A Bernstein, Aase Popper, Aäron Mozsowski, Abigail Reponen, Adam Baird, Adam Livett, Adam Wilson, Adele Drexler, Adriano Rossi, Aernout Nieuwkerk, Alan Brooke, Alan Firth, Alan Dean Foster, Alberto Cafferata, Aler Grubbs, Alex Halbach, Alex Thorne, Alex & Tamar Krupnik, Alexander Uff, Alexander Wuerfel, Alexandre Pouget, Alfred Beyer, Alice Gilbey, Alina van Maggelen, Alison Alessi, Alison Barber & John Murphy, Alison & Simon Porges, Alistair Bool, Allison Wright & Alan Michell, Alois Neumier, Amitabh Chand, Amy Denman, Andre Poulis, Andrea Graner, Andrea Tavazza, Andreas Hitzcar, Andreas Rehberg & Laura Bassotti, Andreas Tanberg, Andree Thomas, Andres Velole & Bertha Elzinga, Andrew Dick, Andrew Harrington, Andrew Haynes, Andrew Holmes, Andrew Manning, Andrew Marcus, Andrew & Karen Cockburn, Andrzaj Nowak, Andy Bolas, Andy Hammann, Andy Walters, Andy Whittaker, Andy Sweet & Nancy Rainwater, Angelika Teuschl & Kurt Plöckinger, Anibal Bejar Torres, Anilu Cigéas, Anja West & Morten Bjerg, Ann Jones, Ann Venegas, Ann & Bill Stoughton, Anna Carin Gustafson, Anna-Maree Van Der Steen, Annabel Falk, Anne Hammersbad & Adam Roberts, Anne Wilshin, Anne Lise Opsahl & Kristin Bolenc & Nina Kyelby, Anneliese Lehmann, Annie Pageau, Anony Verbaeys, Anthony V Yuro, Arash Bakhtari, Armin Dipping, Arnold Parzer, Arnon & Gil Nashilevich, Arnoud Troost & Fenna den Hartog, Arthur GH Bing, Arun Mucherjee, Audrey Rudofski, B Muldrow, B Nominisat, Barbara Ashum, Barbara Vogeltanz, Bark Diak, Barry R Masters, Bart VanOvermeire, Bart & Patricia Winr, Becky Mills, Ben Anderson, Ben Whiting, Bente K Fremmerlid, Bernd Becker, Beth Fridinme, Bethua Frederick, Bettina Fredrich & Werner Dettli, Bettina Schondorf, Betty Sheets, Bill Kemball, Bill & Victory Henderson, BL Underwood, Bo Maslanka, Bob Kemp, Bob Redlinger, Bogdan J Wnuk, Bonnie Cameron, Bonnie Y Yoshida, Brad Chisholm, Branko Fajdiga, Brendon Douglas, Brent Matsuda, Brent Sorensen, Brian Ambrosio, Brian Bentley, Brian Harness, Brian Smith, Brian & Lorna Lewis, Brigitte Knoetig, Bruce Friedman, Bruce Hartnett, Bruno Fontaine, Burt Richmond, Byron Heppner, C Romero, Cameron Hutchison, Carie Small, Carlos Muniz, Carmel Castellan & Alexandra Taylor, Carol Oshana, Carolina Miranda, Caroline Fric, Casper Vogel & Lianne van der Linden, Catherine Stewart & Lee Hallam, Catherine Tomkees, Cathy Sarjeant, Cathy Biggar, CB Denning, Cecilia Rossel, Cees & Arlinde Vletter, Ceinwen West, Ceri Bacon, Chantal Melser, Charles Mays, Charlotte Blixt & Dirk Schwensen, Cheyenne Valenzuela, Chris De Cat, Chris Keavney, Chris Korsten, Chris Seifert, Chris H Bumann, Christian Bufnoir, Christian Haug, Christian Kunow, Christian Weidner, Christiane Hess, Christina Maile, Christine Markham, Christine Strasser, Christine Zoller & Bernhard Schmidt, Christoph Glauser, Christophe Philippe, Christopher Billich, Cindy Swain, Clara Ugarte, Clare Becker, Clare Conner, Clare Willey, Claude Deladoeuille, Claude-AJ Visinand, Claus Rasmussen, Cliff Matheson, Clive Henman, Clive Ponsonby, Clive Walker, Colin Emmott, Colin Lewis, Colin & Miki Maclean, Conner Gorry, Connie Schuler, Coraleigh Listen, Corey & Amanda Carpenter, Corina Bakker, Cornelia Hurek, Corthout Andre, Curtis Alan Clark, D Dubbin, Dagmar Lais, Dairne Fitzpatrick & Cherie Anderson, Dale & Adrienne de Kretser, Dale & Kevin Coghlan, Dalma Whang, Damita & Adam Price, Dan Morris, Daniel Boag, Daniel Christen, Daniel Curtis, Daniel Levitt, Daniel Brenig & Lynn Boatwright, Danielle Deutscher, dArrol Bryant, Dave Kramer, Dave Tamblyn, David Anthes, David Balfour, David Dolan, David Morris, David Roth, David Clapham & Alison Hoad, David L Huntzinger, David P Grill, Davis Lee, Dawn & Kevin Hopkins, Dean Simonsen, Debbie Dolar, Deborah Lowe, Deborah Sinay, Deivy Centeiro, Denise & Malcolm McDonaugh, Dennis Chambers, Dennis Shilobod, Derek Brill, Desiree Palmen, Diana Kirk, Diane O'Connor, Diederik Lugtigheid, Diego Navarro, Dikrán P Lutufyan, DN Griffiths, Dom Barry, Donald Povey, Donna Florio, Dorianne Agius, Doug & Francesca

Nurock, E MacDonnell, Ed Bardos, Ed Bekovich, Ed Hudson, Ed Palao, Edith Föllinger, Edna Lee, Eduardo Angel, Edward Ball, Edward Barlow, Edward Canapary, Egan Arnold, Eileen Cameron, Eli Merritt, Eliose Liles, Elise Richards, Ellen-Karine Levesen, Emile Schenk, Emma Burke, Emma Dean, Emma Friers, Emmanuel Pierson, Enrique Olivares L, Erik Goodbody, Erika Spencer, Erin O'Rourke, Erith French, Ernestein Idenburg, Esther Mietes, Esther Sutton, Esther & Marieke Gieteling, Etain OCarroll, Etienne Waterval, EW Street, F & AH Workman, Faeze T Woodville, Ferdinand Höng, Filippo Dibari, Fiona Steggles, Florence & Peter Shaw, Fortini Scarlatou, Frances Reid & Lili Pâquet, Francoise Pohu, Frank Buechler, Frank Harmsen, Frank Murillo, Frank Rheindt, Frank Campbell, Friedhelm Grosch, G Mommers, Gareth Brahams, Gary Palmer, Gary Smith, Gavin Tanguay, George Frangakis, George Karutz, Gergo Sved, Gerry Friebe, Gert van Lancker & Sandra van Henste, Gil Salomon, Gilbert Verbeken & Marita Blighman, Gisela Janson, GJ Davies, GM Hosty, Gour Sen, Graham Charles, Graham Prentice, Greg Carter, Grenville Hopkinson, Guenther Kalkofen, Guido Steinberg, Guy Foux, Guy Vanackeren, H Cardiff, Hal & Pat Amens, Hannah Morley, Harold Burns, Hartmut Köhler, Haruo Miyata, Hasso Hohmann, Heather Brown, Heidi Stacher, Hek Kleinberg, Helen Trott, Helena Cerin & Miso Kanlic, Helene Budzinski, Henrik Schinzel, Herbert Stirmlinger, Ian Macmillan, Ian Samways, Ian & Lynn Grout, Iggy Ferruelo, Ilan Tesler, Indranil Sen, Ingvild W Andersen, Ir Moshe, Irene Ivarsson, Iris & Stefan Niederberger, Dr Irmgard Bauer – an experienced South America traveler, Isabel Armendariz, J Carlucci, J Stavenuiter, J Arthur Freed, Jacek & Anna Czarnoccy, Jack & Lisa Bowers, Jacky Upson & Martin Scott, Jacob Henriksen, Jacob Waiman, James Gibson, James Hardy, James Pan, James Sleeman, James F Clements, Jamie Monk, Jan Janousek, Jan Vermande, Jane Golding & Rachel Clemons, Jane Kelly, Janet Hobbs, Jaroslav Lébl, Jarrod & Cathy Kelly, Jason Richard, Jason Verschoor, Jasper F Buxton, Jay Howarth, Jean-Luc Krieger, Jean-Marc Delarte, Jeanine Buschor, Jeff Holt, Jeff Levy, Jeff Taylor, Jeffrey Kok, Jennifer Haefeli, Jennifer McGowan, Jennifer Williams, Jenny Paley, Jens Haubold, Jens Udsen & Signe Steninge, Jeremy Flanagan, Jeremy Glass, Jeremy Thompson, Jeroen Vahrmeijer, Jerry Azevedo, Jesper Nissen & Mettine Due, Jessica Parker, Jessica Lowe & Nathan Kesteven, Jesus Lopez de Dicastillo, Jim Wold, Jim & Miki Strong, Jo Hobbs, Joan Plested, Joanna Gardner & Peter Symons, Joanna Luplin, Joanne & Greg Hampson, Joe Collins, Joe Mcspedon, Joeri Apontoweil & Bianca Dijkstra, Johanna Zevenboom, John Bennett, John Beswetherick, John Randall III, John Straube, John Taylor, John C Perry, John D Wilkinson, John E Jacobson, Joke Collewijn, Jonathan Smith, Jose & Alejandra Cuba, Josep Panella, José Ignacio Pichardo Galán, Josie Cali & Emmanuel Espino, Joyce Zinbarg, Jozef Varnagy, JP Beaufils, JP Hart Hansen, Juan Galvan D, Judith Hytrek & Barbara Vogeltanz, Judith Rhodes, Judy R Williams, Julia Epstein, Julia Hinde, Julia Knowles, Julia Lehmann, Julia Richards, Julia C Crislip, Julian & Jacquie Hart, Juliane Thiessen, Julianne Power, Julie Tilghman, Julie Wichman, Julie Winans, K Parain, Kaare Rysgaard Moller, Karen Czulik, Karen Mojorovich, Karen Marie Møller, Karen Marie Winterhalter, Karin Offer, Kate & Mathew Heal, Kath Jones, Katherine Pike, Kathryn Martys, Kathy Arteaga, Kathy Kiefer, Katie Nicholls, Katrina Schneider, Katy Foster, Kay Buikstra, Kay Knightley Day, Kees Meerman, Kees van Zon, Kelly Beairsto, Ken MacLennan, Kenneth Dreyfuss, Kerry Mullen, Kerstin Brandes, Kerstin Mechlem, Kevin Golde, Kevin & Clare Langford, Khamer Done, Kiki Bours, Kim Baron, Kit Cooper, Kit Herring, Kristen Holtz-Garcia, Kurt Holle, Kurt Plockinger, Lachlan Mackenzie, Lars Roennov, Lars C Brunner, Lenden Webb, Leon van de Kerkhof, Les Melrose, Liam Schubel, Lidy van der Ploeg, Linda Broschofsky, Linda Layfield, Lisa Clarke, Lisa Karolius, Lisel Sjögren, Liz Manship, Lorenzo Gennaro, Lorenzo Gordon, Lorén Korún, Lori Willocks, Louie Hechanova & Peter Hertrampf, Louise Sullivan, Louise Van de dKop, Luc Schouten, Lucas Kellet, Luce Lamy, Lucy Harper, Lucy Stockbridge, Lucy C Porter, Lucy W de Alió, Luigi Romagnoli, Luke Skinner, Lynda Seal, Lynn H & Michele G Patterson, M Daeleman, M Drews, M & R Huguet, MA Midson, Magisteele Magisteele, Maitu Mac Gabhann, Mandy Kells & Sarah Jerebine, Maneola Lope, Manoela Lopez, Manola Azzariti, Manuel Barrenechea Solis, Marc Bohn Marcelo F Neira, Marco Silvi, Marcus Lee, Margaret Cantrell, Margaret Quinlan Sharma, Margaret Vernon, Mari Tomine Lunden, Maria Gardner, Marianne Lipshutz, Marijke Keet, Marile Bohm & Marc Ditschke, Marilyn Flax, Mario Mathieu, Marise Traverzo, María Isabel Espinal, Mark Gertzberg,

Mark Miller, Mark Siaon & Maribeth Long, Mark Wenban, Martijn Regelink, Martin Schroeder, Mary Bell, Mary Marsella, Mary Teahan, Mathew Gore, Matt Anderson, Matt Cleary, Matt Oliver, Matt Robshaw, Matthew Burtch, Matthias Heimberg, MC Kerby, MC Whirter, Melanie Ringel, Melody Hall & James West, Mélanie Walsh, Michael Gacquin, Michael Giacometti, Michael Goldfarb, Michael Hahne, Michael White & Clara Bravo, Michaela Young-Mitchell, Michelle Hecht, Miga Rossetti, Miguel Pro, Mike Clulow, Mike Clyne, Mike Tolan, Mike & Pauline Truman, Mikkel Levelt, Miranda Hoogendoorn, Miriam Gayoso, Miriam Torres, Mollie Dobson, Monica Bargigli, Monica Middleton, Monique Reeves, Morten Jacobsen, Myles Jelf, Nagy Szilvia, Natalia Gonzolez M, Natalie Vial, Natasha Holt, Neal Firth, Nick Lansdowne, Nicky Heyward, Nikki Kroan, Niko Wolswijk, Nina Hillesund, Nina Newhouser, Nina Wanendeya, Noreen A Fordyce, Oda Karen Kvaal, Olav Østrem, Oli Hein & Peter Eshelby, Ollie Clayton, Omer Brombery, Ondrej Frye, Oscar Brian, Owen Duxbury, Owen Jensen, P Van Rompaey, Pablo Pwoa Dallvorso, Paisley Drab, Pam Davis, Pam Wadsworth, Paolo Paron, Pascal Sommacal, Pat Gilmartin, Patricia Edmisten, Patricia Grau, Patrick Goosen, Patrick & Jayne Taylor, Paul Bannister, Paul Bouwman, Paul Cooke, Paul Steng, Paul Tonkin, Paul & Betina Bojsen, Paul & Sarah Fretz, Paul J Barrett, Paula Hanna, Paula Saunders, Penny Creswell, Penny Sturgess, Per-Gunnar Ling, Perry Beebe, Peter Ditlevsen, Peter Foster, Peter Irvine, Peter Lewis, Peter Walsh, Peter & Angela Holden, Peter V Lindsay, Petra de Boer, Petra Mueller, Petra Zellmer, Phil McKenzie, Philip Goldberg, Philippe Aubé, Phillip Andrus, Phiona Stanley, Pier Nado, Pieter Nuiten, Piotr Golec, Preb Stritter, R Costigan, R Murray, R Sleeman, R Lightbulb Winders, Ralf Bergmann, Ralph E Stone, Ray Dunn, Ray VarnBuhler, Raynald Losier, Rebecca Lush & Tim Allman, Reinhard Skinner, Reinhard Urban, Remmert DeVroome, Reto Westermann & Maria-José Blass, Rich Lloyd, Richard de Witts, Richard Ward, Richard & Alison Pett, Richard & Dalinda Guerrero, Rick Thompson, Rick DeMasi, Riet Raats, Ripton Johnson, Rob Dover, Rob & Lee Williams, Robert Barth, Robert A Pierce, Robie Loomer, Robyn Christie & Mark Dellar, Robyn Glaser & Georg Holthausen, Rod Ballantyne, Ron Vermaas, Ronald Schop, Rosaleen O'Shea, Rose Lee, Ross Hamilton, Roy & Becey Rogers, Russ Essex, Russell Willis, Ruth & Charlie Gilmore, RW Visser, Sabrina & Frank Van Dierendonck, Sacha Quadrelli, Sally Smith, Salvatore Casari, Sam Loose, Samantha Bianchi, Samuel Larsson, Sandy Rosas, Sanna-Leena Rautanen, Sara Tizard & Pat Coleman, Sarah Gardner, Sarah Mclean, Sarah & Rupert Mclean & John Mayhead, Saskia van Doorn, Schona Jolly, Scott Harris, Scott T York, Serena Hadi, Sergei Guschin, Sergio Lupio, Setha Lingam, Sébastien Grammond, Shannon Orton, Sharon Frazzini, Shaun AB Giles, Shawn Snowden, Sheelin Coates, Sheldon C Belinkoff, Shona Taner, Silvia Decet, Simie Takashima, Simon Brown, Simone Ludwig, Simone Yurasek & Salvador Guerra, SR Gage, Stan Zalewski, Stefan Ott, Stefan Westmeier, Stefania & Carlo Caminito, Stephen Lawrence, Stephen Portnoy, Stephen Scott, Stephen T & Kathryn T Nicol, Steve Harris & Claire Bonnet, Steven Kusters, Steven Mincin, Steven Suranie, Stuart Buxton, Sue Oakes, Suheil Dahdal, Susan Kealey, Susan Regebro, Susan Vaughan, Susie Krott, Suzanne Brown, Suzanne DuRard, Sylvie Micolon, Tamar Adelaar & Robin Bollweg, Tamir Horesh, Tarun Devraj, Teresa Mendez de Vera, Terry Culver, Tessa Katesmark, Thea Wirds, Theon Pearce, Thomas Bryson, Thomas Burkle, Thorun Werswick, Tiffany M Doan, Tim Helbo, Tim Phipps, Tim Renders, Tom A Plange, Tomasz Stafiej, Toni Farrugia, Tony & Irena Grogan, Toop Felber, Tracy Ferrell, Tricia Burnett, Trine Hovset, Twan van Enckevort, Ursula & Holger Theobald, Ute Balwaceda, V Line, V Love, Verhofstadt Lieven, Vic & Lora Fasolino, Vicki Irvine, Viktor Håokansson, Vincent WJ Eijt, Walt Shaw, Wandy van Beek & María van Daal, Wendy Hamas, Werner Detti, Werner Ginzky, Werner Richter, Werner Bull, Wigolf & Lele Huss, Will Askew, Will Markle, Will Race, William Smalley, Willy Minkes, Wim Vos, Xavier Verdaguer, Xavier Cordero Lopez, Yoav Yanir & Tamar Bar-El, Yossi Tnaumi, Yvonne Bell, Yvonne Markestein, Yvonne Post, Zbynek Dubsky.

# Index

## Boxed Text

## MAP LEGEND

### BOUNDARIES

| | |
|---|---|
| ·· ■— ·■— ·■— | International |
| ···■— ·■— ·■— | Departmental |

### HYDROGRAPHY

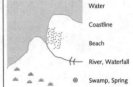

| | |
|---|---|
| | Water |
| | Coastline |
| | Beach |
| ⤙⤙ | River, Waterfall |
| ⊚ | Swamp, Spring |

### ROUTES & TRANSPORT

| | |
|---|---|
| | Freeway |
| | Toll Freeway |
| | Primary Road |
| | Secondary Road |
| | Tertiary Road |
| | Unpaved Road |
| | Pedestrian Mall |
| | Trail |
| ············· | Walking Tour |
| | Ferry Route |
| ┼┼┼┼ | Railway, Train Station |
| ═══Ⓜ═══ | Mass Transit Line & Station |

### ROUTE SHIELDS

| | |
|---|---|
| 24 | National Highway System of Peru |
| 113 | Departmental Highway System of Peru |
| BR 364 | Brazilian Highway |

### AREA FEATURES

| | |
|---|---|
| | Building |
| | Cemetery |
| | Ecological Reserve |
| ⌐ | Golf Course |
| | Park |
| | Plaza |

### MAP SYMBOLS

| | | | | | |
|---|---|---|---|---|---|
| ✪ | NATIONAL CAPITAL | ✚ | Airport (domestic) | ⚲ | Mosque |
| ◉ | Departmental Capital | ✈ | Airport (international) | ▲ | Mountain |
| ● | LARGE CITY | ∴ | Archaeological Site, Ruins | 🏛 | Museum |
| ● | Medium City | ❸ | Bank, Money Exchange | ⌂ | Observatory |
| ● | Small City | ✕ | Battlefield | ← | One-Way Street |
| ● | Town, Village | ⴱ | Beach | ♠ | Park |
| ○ | Point of Interest | ⚡ | Border Crossing | ℗ | Parking |
| | | ⛪ | Cathedral | )( | Pass, Tunnel |
| | | ⌂ | Cave | ⊓ | Picnic Area |
| ■ | Place to Stay | ✝ | Church | ★ | Police Station |
| ▲ | Campground | ⬟ | Dive Site | 🏊 | Pool |
| ⛁ | RV Park | ◎ | Embassy | ✉ | Post Office |
| ⌂ | Refugio | ⛴ | Fish Hatchery | ☎ | Public Telephone |
| | | ⤬ | Footbridge | ⚓ | Shipwreck |
| ▼ | Place to Eat | ⚜ | Garden | ❖ | Shopping Mall |
| ▮ | Bar (Place to Drink) | ⛽ | Gas Station | ✡ | Synagogue |
| ☕ | Café | ⊕ | Hospital, Clinic | 🜊 | Trailhead |
| | | ❶ | Information | ◓ | Transportation |
| | | 🗼 | Lighthouse | ⛰ | Volcano |
| | | ✳ | Lookout | 🍷 | Winery |
| | | ⛫ | Monument | 🦁 | Zoo |

*Note: Not all symbols displayed above appear in this book.*

---

## LONELY PLANET OFFICES

**Australia**
PO Box 617, Hawthorn 3122, Victoria
☎ 03 9819 1877  fax 03 9819 6459
email talk2us@lonelyplanet.com.au

**USA**
150 Linden Street, Oakland, California 94607
☎ 510 893 8555, TOLL FREE 800 275 8555
fax 510 893 8572
email info@lonelyplanet.com

**UK**
10A Spring Place, London NW5 3BH
☎ 020 7428 4800 fax 020 7428 4828
email go@lonelyplanet.co.uk

**France**
1 rue du Dahomey, 75011 Paris
☎ 01 55 25 33 00 fax 01 55 25 33 01
www.lonelyplanet.fr

World Wide Web: www.lonelyplanet.com *or* AOL keyword: lp
Lonely Planet Images: lpi@lonelyplanet.com.au